Medieval Warfare

Other Volumes of Delbrück's *History of the Art of War*
Available in Bison Book Editions

Warfare in Antiquity, Volume I

The Barbarian Invasions, Volume II

The Dawn of Modern Warfare, Volume IV

Medieval Warfare

HISTORY OF THE ART OF WAR
VOLUME III

By Hans Delbrück

Translated from the German by Walter J. Renfroe, Jr.

University of Nebraska Press
Lincoln and London

First Bison Book printing: 1990
Most recent printing indicated by the last digit below:
10   9   8   7   6   5   4   3

Library of Congress Cataloging-in-Publication Data
(Revised for volumes 3–4)
Delbrück, Hans, 1848–1929.
History of the art of war.
Translation of: Geschichte der Kriegskunst im Rahmen der politischen Geschichte.
Reprint • Originally published: History of the art of war within the framework of
political history.
Westport, Conn.: Greenwood Press, c1975–c1985.
Contents: v. 1. Warfare in antiquity—[etc.]—v. 3. Medieval warfare—v. 4. The
dawn of modern warfare.
1. Military art and science—History. 2. Naval art and science—History. 3. War—
History. I. Title.
U27.D34213 1990   355'.009   89-24980
ISBN 0-8032-6584-0 (set) ISBN 0-8032-6585-9 (Vol. III)

Reprinted by arrangement with Greenwood Press, Inc.

Originally titled HISTORY OF THE ART OF WAR WITHIN THE FRAMEWORK
OF POLITICAL HISTORY, by Hans Delbrück, Volume III, THE MIDDLE AGES.
Translated from the German by Walter J. Renfroe, Jr., and published as part of the
Greenwood Press Series, Contributions in Military History, in Westport, CT, 1982.
Copyright © 1982 by Walter J. Renfroe, Jr. Maps drawn by Edward J. Krasnobor-
ski. Originally published in German under the title GESCHICHTE DER KRIEGS-
KUNST IM RAHMEN DER POLITISCEN GESCHICHTE. All rights reserved.

Table of Contents

BOOK IV
The Late Middle Ages

BOOK V
The Swiss

List of Illustrations

Translator's Foreword

This translation of Delbrück's third volume of *Geschichte der Kriegskunst im Rahmen der politischen Geschichte* is based on the second edition of that volume, which was published in Berlin in 1923. As in the two preceding volumes, I have adhered as closely as possible to the original, both in spirit and style, without adding notes or comments.

As in Volume II, the Latin and Greek quotations have been translated into English by Dr. Everett L. Wheeler, to whom I am most grateful for this important contribution. The Latin texts, as given in Delbrück's work, have been retained, with the shorter passages included in the body of the work and the longer ones in the appendixes. Of the relatively few Greek quotations, some have simply been translated into English, with an asterisk following the quotation to indicate that the original was in Greek, while the translations of a few of the more important words and expressions are accompanied by a transliteration of the Greek. In cases where a quoted passage lends itself to varying interpretations, Dr. Wheeler has given the interpretation that supports Delbrück's argument.

The figures for distances in German miles, often used by Delbrück, have been converted into English miles.

Page references to Volumes I and II are based on the pagination of the Greenwood translations of those volumes.

I am happy to have this opportunity to express my gratitude to my wife Ruth, who spent hundreds of hours patiently writing out the initial version of this translation as I dictated the text.

BOOK I

Charlemagne and His Successors

Chapter I

Charlemagne

Previously, the Germans had moved into the provinces of the Roman World Empire as a warrior class. Then, accompanied by terrible destruction and suffering, they had finally extended like a thin layer over those provinces, a new skin so to speak, and had thereby founded new Romanic-Germanic political systems.

In the Frankish Kingdom, the form for maintaining the warrior class continuously available for use had been found in the feudal system, the organization of vassals obligated by the granting of fiefs. With this warrior element, the Carolingian dynasty had saved the state from the Moslems and had then built it up anew in a process lasting for generations.

These warriors were predominantly mounted men and had to bring their own supplies with them. Consequently, the equipping of even one such warrior was a very heavy burden. In one of the Old Frankish people's laws, the value of weapons and animals is given to us in detail.[1] If we combine these numbers and then express the value of a warrior's equipment in numbers of cows, we arrive at the following list:[2]

Helmet	6 cows
Coat of mail	12 cows
Sword and scabbard	7 cows
Leg greaves	6 cows
Lance and shield	2 cows
Battle steed	12 cows

The equipment of a single warrior therefore had the value of 45 cows, or, since 3 cows were considered the equivalent of a mare, 15 mares, or the large domestic animals of a whole village.

In addition, there was the supply of rations, the cart with its draft animal or a pack animal to carry the provisions, and the serving man to take care of the animal.

The Frankish warrior who moved into the field from the Loire region against the Saxons, or from the Main to the Pyrenees, was therefore completely different from the warrior of the earliest Germanic period, who regarded it not as a burden but as a benefit to provide himself with weapons, and who waged war only in his neighboring area. And the settled warrior, who intends to return home again, is also different from the warrior of the *Völkerwanderung,* who no longer looked backward but only forward. The Carolingian warriorhood was a class that was composed of a small—in fact, a very small—fraction of the entire population, and it was only in the form of vassalage and the possession of fiefs that this class was able to exist and maintain itself.[3]

The transition from the system of the ancient levy of his people by the king as the leader of the people to the levy of vassals by the king as the supreme lord of the feudal system took place very slowly and probably not simultaneously in all regions and parts of the kingdom. The beginnings of the vassalage system are already apparent in the first century of the Merovingian dynasty, but the general levy of the people was still legally and formally existent under Charlemagne. It did not die out completely and give way to exclusive dependence on the vassal system until the time of Charlemagne's grandsons. It was only in the militia, the mobilization for defense against an enemy invasion, that the ancient general obligation for military service continued to survive.

In the Romanic areas of the Frankish Kingdom, this division into social strata must have taken place more easily and more clearly than in the Germanic areas. In the Romanic, the great mass of the population continued to be composed of the tenant farmers, the peasant serfs, as was the case previously in the Roman Empire. Neither was the urban population, the *plebs urbana,* considered to be completely free, and the artisans and shopkeepers were no more warriors than were the farmers.[4]

Only the warriors, predominantly of Germanic origin, were the freemen, *liberi, ingenui,* often also called *nobiles.* They were extremely small in number,[5] not more than a few hundred in a district of 2,200 square miles, partly living on small properties, partly on large estates, partly on their own land, partly on fiefs, and partly as vassals in the service and at the court of a lord, without property of their own.

The concepts of the period were so completely dominated by the fact that the freeman was the warrior and the warrior the freeman, that, as early as the fifth and sixth centuries, authors simply used the word *miles* for laymen whose class they wished to contrast with that of the cleric.[6] When, late in the Middle Ages, we still hear that in the legal terminology of the County of Anjou the word *franchir* (to cross, surmount) means *anoblir* (to ennoble), and not, for example, *affranchir* (to free), that sounds to us like a petrified expression that still sheds light on a period long gone.[7]

Before the incorporation of the Saxons, the Frankish Kingdom contained few purely Germanic areas. On the Rhine, as in Swabia and Bavaria, considerable remnants of the Romanic inhabitants remained in place under the Germanic conquerors and in the same social relationship to them as in the Romanic area. But there developed similar relationships among the Germans in these mixed regions, especially among the Germans in the purely Germanic areas at the mouth of the Rhine, on the Scheldt, in Hesse, and on the Main: a large part of the population more or less gave up its full freedom and moved out of the warrior class. We do not have direct proof for this, nor can we see when, how strongly, and how fast this development took place. But we can conclude with certainty that it did happen, first of all from the unity in the character of the military system of the entire kingdom. From the regulations concerning the army mobilization which have come to us in the sources, we see that the warriors of each region always had to bring their complete equipment and rations with them. It is also evident that specific contingents were not required from each area according to its population and its ability to provide such units, for example, but that, on the contrary, either all or a certain part of the men qualified for military service were required. The assumption, therefore, was that the freemen obligated for military service were spread rather evenly throughout the country. Otherwise, of course, very serious injustices would have arisen, if, for example, a district in Hesse had had to mobilize and equip almost all of its adult men while a district in the interior of Gaul, where there were only a few freemen above the tenant farmers and inhabitants of the towns, needed to provide only these few. Now, inasmuch as there were only a few freemen in the individual districts in the interior of Gaul, because of the small number of Germans who settled there, then the social organization in the eastern parts of the kingdom must already at that time have been quite similar to the organization in the west.

We can support this point by a second indirect piece of evidence. We see that this same development had taken place even among the Saxons, who were still pagans. The sources reveal that a class of men who were less than fully free played an important role among them, and under Louis the Pious we hear that these partially free men (*frilingi et lazzi:* freemen and half-free) formed a huge group.[8] In 842, they formed a conspiracy, the *Stellingabund,* in order to demand the rights they had had in the pagan period. That could be so understood as showing that it was the hegemony of the Franks that had taken their full liberty from them, and we may well assume that the Franks actually pushed freemen down into the lower class. But the people's demand did not call for the restoration of their freedom but for the providing of their ancient class rights, which had presumably been decreased. Consequently, there can be no doubt that a large class of such partially free men also already existed in the pagan period; we shall come back to this point in our study of the Saxon wars.

The smaller the number of freemen was throughout all the districts of the kingdom, the more easily was it possible for the two procedures—the older one, where the king called up the freemen for war through his counts, and the newer one, where the king called up the seniors with their vassals for war—to exist side by side and to conflict with each other. The final and logical solution was that those members of the old class of freemen who continued to be warriors entered into vassalage, while those who became farmers sank to a status of partial freedom, with the result that there no longer existed warriors who were not vassals. A positive regulation that each freeman was to have a senior appears first in the sources under Charles the Bald in 847. But in the year 864 we again find regulations,[9] and even as late as the year 884 a source indicates that a freeman (as such, not as a vassal) was to move into the field with the others.[10] The reality of life was already so far removed from such requirements that authors simply used the expression *vasallisch* (in the manner of a vassal) for the word *kriegerisch* (in the manner of a warrior).[11]

In Charlemagne's time, the two diametrically opposed military systems still existed side by side. Whereas the texts of a series of documents seem to leave no doubt that the mass of freemen, even if not all at the same time, did perform military service in alternation, other sources prove that already at that time only vassals took to the field.

Even the same freemen who had become vassals were called up by the count under the powers of punishment of the royal summons, and the sources do not give us any direct clarification as to how the two procedures were reconciled in a practical way. Since the system of vassalage assumed the dominant role so very soon after the great emperor's death, we must assume that the struggle whose beginnings we must recognize already under the first successors of Clovis was already essentially decided under Charlemagne in favor of the vassal system. The levy of the total body of freemen continued to exist only as a theoretical form, applied for practical purposes only in individual cases and under rather large landowners. But it was not only the tenacity of the inherited legal forms that kept the general levy formally alive so long, but also a positive and very strong motive. This was retained for so long because the levy was the only way in which a free German could be forced into service to the state, especially into payment of taxes (except for juridical service). If the levy had been dropped while a part of the subordinate warriors had still not become vassals and had not been forced down into a status of partial freedom, these subjects would have been completely eliminated from public service. For this reason Charlemagne, and probably also his predecessors, issued edicts for the freemen who did not move into the field to form groups according to their possessions and to equip one of their members. Until now these regulations have been interpreted to mean that, if, for example, three men each of whom owned one hide of land were supposed to equip one of their number, this applied to his complete supplies, including rations and means of transportation. In arriving at this concept, however, the point was overlooked that such a requirement was much too great to be met from three hides of farmland. This actual furnishing of rations for the army naturally had to be the task of the huge number of partially free men and serfs, who were obliged to do this either by their lords or by the counts. Those freemen whose property did not exceed one or two hides of normal farmland and who were supposed to support one of their comrades either provided a money payment only or gave a piece of equipment or clothing to outfit him personally. Even this they probably did grudgingly enough. For under their very low economic conditions, every weapon, every piece of leather material or cloth, every ham or cheese that was demanded from them was an important item. But, since we must, of course, picture the actual warriors as mounted men, the most important and expensive item of their entire equipage was the horse. They marched out to war almost year after year, and often enough the returning warrior probably had to give up his faithful steed during the long march and did not bring it back with him. War is always much more costly in horses than in men. But a peasant is not in a position to provide a useful war-horse every few years. Most peasants owned no horses at all, least of all suitable war-horses, but did their work with oxen or cows.

Consequently, the regulations of the Carolingian kings concerning the forming of freemen into groups, each of which was to send one of its members off to war, is to be considered essentially as a disguised tax levy. In most cases, it was not a real call-up but a legal right for the king to demand contributions from these freemen and at the same time a limitation of this right against completely arbitrary misuse by the officials. If, for example, the said three owners of a hide of land had outfitted one of their number in the usual way, or, as they probably normally preferred, had provided the necessary equipment, which the count then gave to one of his vassals, or a corresponding compensation for this obligation, they had done their duty, and the count could not demand anything further from them.

We find royal edicts on this subject that seem to be very precise. In the year 807 it was prescribed on one occasion for the region west of the Seine that whoever owned five or four hides of land was to take the field himself, three men who possessed one hide each were to group themselves, or one with two hides and one with one hide; two with one hide each were to form a group with one man owning less; and those owning half-hides were to provide for one man for every six. Among those not owning land, six men possessing 5 pounds were to outfit one man and give him 5 *solidi*. As specific as these regulations are, we should not be deceived into thinking that everything was done according to such edicts. First of all, from the top, with respect to the higher officials, these edicts meant practically nothing. Let us imagine an administration whose leaders are all ignorant of the written language, who are dependent on their scribes as translators for every bit of information, every list, every report, every account. It was absolutely impossible for the central government to obtain a reliable idea of how many men were available in each district with how much property. When, in the reign of King Edward III, the English parliament once decided to draw up a tax under a new method, it assumed in its calculation of the amount to be received that the kingdom had 40,000 parishes; later, it turned out that there were not even 9,000.[12] The number of knightly fiefs was estimated as 60,000 by some and as 32,000 by others, including the royal ministers; in reality, there were not even 5,000. And this, as we shall see later, while England had a real central administration; the Frankish Kingdom did not have a central administration, so that it has not even provided us with estimates that might serve as an example. In the course of this work, we shall encounter many more similar indications, like those we have taken from English history, that medieval administrations had absolutely no grasp of the higher numerical relationships of their political system.

Under Louis the Pious, there seems to have been an attempt in 829 to draw up a kind of central listing showing the property ownership for the kingdom. We have four different versions of this law, but characteristically these four editions do not have the same details. In one of them, the case where two men should group themselves is missing, in another the provision for a group of six is excluded, in the third only the group of three men is mentioned, and in the fourth nothing at all is prescribed concerning the formation of groups.

The probable explanation is that in the process of estimating property and dividing men into groups there was so much leeway for discretionary estimates and arbitrariness that even such specific differences in the regulation made no difference. On all sides, certain patterns and estimates were probably turned in, which then became fixed. Even if the prescription was actually carried out—and this is doubtful—they probably did not get very far with it, for even if such a gigantic task was accomplished with a certain degree of reliability, it was still suitable only for the moment. In just a few years everything was changed again as a result of deaths and inheritances. But even in the first year it was of very little use because for the move into the field personal situations also played a very important role, especially the case of sickness, and they could not be checked from above. Finally, however, it could not have been the intention of the law and of the ruler that the basic concept "every freeman marches" or "every prescribed group of freemen sends one man" was to be carried out literally. For the prerequisite for this would have been the really equal distribution of freemen throughout all the districts according to their capabilities. Even a small inequality in this distribution would, under the conditions of constant renewal of the campaigns and the demands of war, have resulted in a very heavy burden for those districts that happened to be inhabited by more freemen, especially those with preponderantly Germanic populations. In the Roman Empire, the central authority, the senate, had constantly reapportioned the military burden on the basis of carefully maintained census lists in the wards. The empire of Charlemagne had no such administrative procedure. There, in the final analysis, despite certain regulatory edicts from above and inspection by government legates (*missi*), the important business had to be left to the discretionary judgment of the counts. Whenever the army assembled, the emperor or his field commander inspected the individual contingents and, with their small numbers, easily recognized who had a well-equipped body of men of normal strength behind him and who had somewhat fewer or poorer appearing followers. Regulations concerning the providing of a specific number of warriors are only very seldom found, even in the entire later medieval period.[13] And that is quite natural, since it was precisely the quality of the unit, which can neither be counted nor measured, that was primary in this warriorhood. The form in which the monarch presses for full-strength contingents is always that in which he requires that all those who are obligated are supposed to come. I believe I can also conclude from this that basically the freemen who, according to the literal text, were being levied, hardly came into consideration, for despite everything that we have discussed above, there must indeed have remained great inequalities in the distribution of freemen throughout the land. On the other hand, it can be assumed that the vassals were actually present in the various districts to a degree corresponding quite closely to their ability to contribute to the levy. Only then did the edict that all men of the warrior class should also move out have a reasonable, practicable meaning.

In accordance with the literal text of the capitularies cited above, we would have to assume that all those subject to military service were regarded as of equal value militarily and went on campaign in a certain sequence of alternation. That was perhaps still possible under the first Merovingians, when the mass of the Franks were just undergoing the transition from their original warrior condition to the peasant life and the peasant character. At that time, such edicts concerning a campaign may at first have been issued and have corresponded to the real situation. In the period, however, from which the edicts have come down to us, when the Franks on the one side had already become actual peasants and on the other side the vassals had become a separate warrior class, the mobilization of peasants in alternation was a complete impossibility. In a burgher-peasant society, the inclination, opportunity, and capability for the warrior life are very uneven, and a competent warrior with basic natural warlike instincts is very rare. The prescribed contingent (we may disregard the differences in the individual documents) is considerably smaller than is apparent at first glance from the numbers we find there. The great mass, of course, is not to be found among the owners of a number of hides of land but those possessing a single hide or half-hide. On the one hide or half-hide, however, often more than one man of military age is to be found. All of them are subject to military service, but the burden is apportioned according to property ownership. If, for example, the levy was made in strict conformance with the decrees of 807, hardly more than 10 percent of the adult freemen and youths would be mobilized. But the count who would have reported to the army with alternating tenths, or even sixths or fourths, of his peasants would undoubtedly have made a very strange impression on his imperial lord and his official colleagues. There is no reason to assume that the military usefulness would have proved any more effective than when later, in the Thirty Years War, it was ordered in Brandenburg that each village or several villages together would provide one man and send him to the place of assembly with rations, weapons, and munitions. In the ninth century, just as little could be accomplished with such a levy as was later possible in the seventeenth century.[14]

Throughout the entire Middle Ages, we shall find time after time and in various forms the expedient of using an edict literally calling all citizens for military service but actually intended as a means for the levy of taxes.

In the preceding volume we proved that, as early as the end of the sixth century at the latest, and from that time on, it was not the general levies but the vassals who brought about the decision in the wars of the Merovingians. Even the last traces of the ancient general levy disappeared under Charlemagne's grandsons. And so it is certain that the military system was not again based on the peasantry, which had long since become unwarlike.

We must therefore interpret Charlemagne's capitularies as meaning that the owners of land or the groups of landowners, if there was not by chance among them a man inclined to go to war, provided the vassal of a count with the equipment that they were obliged to give, the *adjutorium*, and he took over the wartime service for them. That was a very satisfactory interpretation of the imperial edict for both sides: the peasants, who preferred to stay at home, and the count, who wanted not just an armed man but a competent, willing, and obedient warrior. All of the statements that seemed to require so specifically that one of the obligated men himself was to take to the field are to be regarded as pure administrative flourishes, which were retained for generations, perhaps even for centuries. In reality, in the capitularies concerning levies we are dealing with the imposition of war taxes, which were measured differently in the different years and for different regions. It was, of course, quite natural for the Saxons to be more heavily levied for a war against the Sorbs or even the Bohemians than for a war in Spain.

The conclusion that the capitularies which speak of the vassals give a better reflection of Carolingian reality than do those that appear to prove the existence of the general levy is completely supported by determination of the army strengths. The smaller the armies were, the more certain it is that they were composed of professional warriors. A count who led out, let us say, only 100 warriors from a district having perhaps 50,000 inhabitants did not take 100 different men each year but had his fixed unit, of which he knew that they would do him credit.

The most important document of the Carolingian military system from the objective viewpoint and especially for our study is the regulation that the individual contingents were to bring along with them from home the necessary supplies and materials for an entire campaign. In the ancient Roman armies, as in modern ones, the state provided for these needs; for this purpose, the commander sets up depots at suitable places, prescribes deliveries, buys supplies, and transports them to the depots with his supply columns. Whatever is used up is replaced by continuing, systematic resupply. The Carolingian warrior, on the other hand, was to carry with him from home everything he needed for the entire campaign, including the march out and back. The estimate we made in the previous volume (p. 436) concerning the size of this requirement amounts to more than the entire burden of a pack animal, the full burden of one draft animal for every single common soldier. Even that, however, is sufficient only if we imagine that the contingent from each county also brought along a herd of live animals for slaughter. If we understand that these warriors considered themselves as a favored class, that in many areas they were already directly referred to as the "nobles," and that they were the successors of conquerors and not restrained by strict discipline as the legionaries had previously been by their centurions, we shall have to picture these units as also being demanding in their needs. They were not satisfied with simple expedient measures, and, even if they were camped outdoors in wind and weather, they still expected to be provided, even if not richly, with camp necessities of every type as well as with a good supply of beverages. In a personal edict (811), Charlemagne forbade mutual toasting ("ut in hoste nemo parem suum vel quemlibet alterum hominem bibere roget": "That no one in the army should ask his comrade or any other man to drink"), and anyone in the army who was found drunk was required to drink only water until he controlled himself better ("quosque male fecisse cognoscat": "he should acknowledge that he did wrong"). There must therefore have been no small number of wine and beer kegs following along behind the Carolingian warriors. Whether they themselves brought them along or whether merchants accompanied the army, the train columns that followed this type of army must have extended out of sight. The number of supporting men and animals was several times larger than the number of combatants, and with their carts and pack animals they occupied much more space on the march route than the combat troops. The fact that the Carolingian armies brought with them from home and transported themselves all their supplies for the entire duration of the campaign, attested to in the sources, is convincing proof that the armies were very small.[15] Large armies with columns of that kind would have been able neither to move nor to feed their horses and draft animals. We may assume that Charlemagne seldom had more than 5,000 or 6,000 warriors assembled in one place, since that number, together with their baggage train, would have covered the length of a full day's march of 14 miles. We can probably accept 10,000 combatants as the absolute maximum strength of a Carolingian army. In doing so, however, we must realize that the concept of "combatant" is not a sharply defined one. We must consider those

5,000 to 6,000 men as predominantly mounted men; but the mass of personal servants accompanying the leaders, the counts, bishops, and great vassals, as well as the train orderlies who led the mules and drove the wagons, were armed and more or less militarily inclined,[16] useful at least for combat support missions, foraging and laying waste enemy land. We have also, of course, pictured the older Greek and Roman lightly armed troops as being somewhere in the middle between combatants and serving men.

The sparseness of the sources on the Carolingian period, which always give only a broad treatment of the sequence of events, deceives us all too easily concerning the importance and influence of individual phenomena and individual facts, as well as concerning the burden that the annual levies imposed on the country. But we may, for example, carry our picture over to a Frankish county under Charlemagne when we hear how Emperor Frederick II in 1240 required that his juridical official in Ferre Idronti mobilize the vassals of his district according to their capabilities but that the official had the greatest difficulties doing so: eighteen vassals (*feudatorii*) were said to be in service already, but the others were said to be so reduced in their means that they could not be equipped so soon ("adeo imminuta erat, quod tam cito non poterat praepari"). Finally, eighteen (no more than eighteen!), by being given subsidies, were equipped from a district so large that the emperor maintained direct correspondence with its leader.

The realization that we have to imagine the Carolingian armies as very small, quality armies, and not as massive peasant armies, as has been the custom until now, is confirmed by a series of individual reports on their composition. That is, it is evident that an army was formed by contingents from the most distant areas.

In 763 Bavarians were used in Aquitania. In 778 the Bavarians, Alamanni, and East Franks participated in the campaign in Spain; in 791 the Saxons, Thuringians, Friesians, and Ripuarians in the campaign against the Avars; in 793 the Aquitanians in lower Italy; in 806 the Burgundians in the campaign to Bohemia; and in 818 the Alamanni, Saxons, and Thuringians against Brittany. On several occasions the Aquitanians moved out to Saxony; in 815 King Bernhard came with the Lombard army ("cum exercitu") to the imperial diet in Paderborn; in 832 Lothair came to Orléans with the Lombards and Louis with the Bavarians.[17] Even if we imagine each one of these contingents as a very limited people's levy, this would still have meant the assembling of gigantic armies. Under the conditions of provisioning the army as we have learned them, that was completely impossible. On the other hand, in

order to assemble armies of moderate size, it would not have been necessary to have the Bavarians march to Spain, the Ripuarians to the Theiss,
the Burgundians to Bohemia, the Aquitanians to Saxony, and the Saxons
to Brittany if there had existed among the population something even
only approximating a general military obligation. For in every single one
of these regions, there were 100,000 men and more with healthy bodies.
The combining of such varied contingents, the movements back and
forth, the extremely long marches with their toll of strength and materials are understandable only if the commander sought to surround himself with professional warriors rather than units of burghers and peasants.

This concept is also confirmed by the reports on the individual military
actions.

In 778, while Charles was in Spain, the Saxons rebelled and, murder-
ing and burning, advanced as far as the Rhine. Charles received this news
when he was already on the march back, in Auxerre, and he immediately
dispatched against the Saxons the East Franks and Alamanni that he had
with him ("Cujus rei nuntium, cum rex apud Antesiodorum civitatem
accepisset, extemplo Francos orientales atque Alemannos ad propulsan-
dum hostem festinare jussit. Ipse ceteris copiis dimissis etc." *Ann.
Lauresh.*: "When the king had received a report of this matter at the city
Auxerre, he immediately ordered the Eastern Franks and the Alamanni
to hasten to repulse the enemy. After the other troops had been sent
away, he . . . etc." *Annals of Lorch*). Although the rampaging Saxons cannot possibly have been so very numerous, and although the East Frank
contingent that Charles led across the Pyrenees can only have been
rather small, the Rhine areas were already so drained of useful warriors
that they could not defend themselves against the Saxons. It was only
when the army returned from Spain that the strength of the Franks
became great enough to permit them to oppose the invaders.

THE *SCARA* AND THE CASTLES IN THE ROYAL DOMAINS

A military system based on a situation where the warrior class lives on
its properties spread across the entire breadth of the country and for
every campaign must first be levied, equipped, and assembled by
marches lasting for weeks is a very cumbersome system and is useless for
small-scale military missions, border defense, and quarrels with
neighbors. Even if the warrior class that was settled in the border areas
was more numerous than in the interior of the country and if warriorhood, military skill, the will to fight, and armament extended in these

areas to considerably larger groups, a levy simply from a border area and its neighboring regions was still always very small and of little use, especially for offensive purposes, since these men did not wish to leave their own properties unprotected. We find, therefore, that under Charlemagne the levy of vassals was supplemented by a body of troops that was named the *scara* (unit). We could perhaps best translate it with the word "*Wache*" (guard). It was a small unit of men, a standing organization, so to speak, that was not settled on the land but was maintained at the court or in a camp, a life-guard of the emperor that was strong enough to undertake smaller military expeditions independently, without reinforcement and support by the national levy. Since these were mostly young men, they were also called "*tirones*" (recruits) and "*juvenes*" (youths).[18] The corresponding German expression is *Haistalden* or *Austalden,* from which our modern word *Hagestolz* ("old bachelor") is derived, since they could not have a family. They were also used for the permanent garrisoning of strongholds in conquered territory, since the enfeoffed vassals could be called away from their land for only a certain time.

These constantly ready units were employed not only for military purposes outside the country but also in the interior against robbers and for police service; from this there arose the words *Scharwache* (guard unit) and *Scherge* (constable). They were also used—or, more accurately, specially trained and suitable men among them were used—for all kinds of technical purposes, for example, to survey the borders, which was a very important task at that time. We later find under King Knut of Denmark-England the *Hauskerle* (fellows of the household) as similar organizations; *milites aulici, palatini* (soldiers of the court), whom we meet in later centuries,[19] are the same thing insofar as their purpose is concerned.

These units or life-guards, as direct subordinates of the king and the court, were also provided for by the court and in the manner of the court. The Frankish kings, like the Germans, had no real residence but were constantly moving about through their broad kingdom in order to exercise personally their royal responsibilities in keeping with the nature of the state.[20] This moving about would have been unbearably difficult if it had always been necessary to take along all the provisions for the entire administration and the royal household. Not only did this not happen, but, on the contrary, it was even a special reason for the mobility of the monarchy that it found its provisions everywhere, that the royal domains, instead of sending their produce to distant central points, only needed to keep it ready in place for the provisioning of the royal court. The pro-

visions were not sent to the court, but the court moved from one provisioning point to another. Konrad Plath has proven that the Merovingian kings had already built themselves countless castles (*Pfalzen*) in their
day, often only one day's journey apart, apparently for the purpose of
serving as places of shelter for the traveling court. It was more eco-
nomical to erect these many large structures than to transport the produce of the domains to distant places year after year, and many of these
products—meat, game, fish, eggs—simply could not be transported very
far. No doubt it cannot be said in so many words that the traveling
monarchy was a product of the barter economy—it was based more
deeply in the nature of the Germanic monarchy—but in any case it was
closely related to the barter economy, and it was because of this relationship that it became so customary and lasted so long.

Very recently, Carl Rübel has proven that during the Carolingian
period imperial castles were built step by step along the routes associated
with the Saxon wars, large domain courts that formed points of concentration for the produce of the surrounding farms.[21] Consequently, these
imperial castles were capable of providing not only for the court but also
for the *scara* accompanying it or engaged on an independent march for
one or several days, and they gave these units a mobility that could never
be attained by an actual national army. For the latter, the custom of
bringing along its own rations was retained, since, of course, the supplies
of the imperial castles were not sufficient for several thousand men. A
few military highway zones and border regions could not bear the military burden for the entire empire; therefore, the actual army had to
provide and transport its own supplies.

THE OATH OF LOYALTY

We are given an accurate reflection of the history of Germanic warriorhood by the history of the Germanic oath of loyalty, which we can
still trace with sufficient certainty, even though it is not proven by the
sources for every period.[22] The ancient Germans had no general oath of
loyalty but knew only the oath that the retainers swore to their lord.
Under the immediate successors of Clovis, we find the general oath of
loyalty to the king. His subjects swore "*fidelitas et leudesamio*" ("loyalty
and submission") to him. This formula reveals that the oath was copied
from the ancient retainer oath: the entire population subjected itself to a
military commander. It is quite possible that the first occasion where the
entire mass of warriors was called on to swear an oath to their leader

occurred in the Roman service, in which, of course, not simply individual units but the entire population as such participated. We find the subjects' oath that the Germans took to their king not only among the Franks but also among the East and West Goths and the Lombards. With the Anglo-Saxons, however, who were not in the Roman service, we do not find it until much later, in the tenth century, based on the Frankish pattern.

This general Frankish subordinates' oath became obsolete under the later Merovingians. Even the first Carolingians, including Pepin the king, did not require any general oath of loyalty. It was absorbed by the vassal's oath that had developed in the meantime. Indeed, even the subject's oath under the Merovingians was not taken by all the inhabitants but only by the actual, true people in the sense of the period, the warriors, and these warriors became vassals.[23] So now only the king's direct vassals took the oath to him, and their subordinate vassals were obligated to him only through the intermediary of their suzerains. Charlemagne recognized the danger of this arrangement when, on the occasion of an uprising, probably that of the Thuringian Hardrad in 786, the rebels based their defense on the fact that they had not, after all, taken any oath to the king. As a result of this case, as is expressly stated in the introduction to the proclamation that has been preserved for us, the king now ordered that all subjects over twelve years of age take an oath directly to him, an oath that he then had them repeat several times, particularly when he took the title of emperor and when he proclaimed the order of his succession.[24] The subjects who were to swear this oath were individually enumerated: it was to be taken by the bishops and abbots, the counts, the royal vassals, the *vicedomini,* archdeacons, canons, clerics (except those monks who were under vows), the bailiffs, *hunni,* and the entire people, all over twelve years of age and through the age where they were still strong enough to be able to participate in the court sessions and carry out the orders of their suzerains, even in those cases where they were not direct subjects of the king but who, as subjects or servants of counts or bishops or abbots, possessed fiefs from them and were equipped with horse and weapons, shield, lance, sword, and dagger.

This listing may serve as a new piece of evidence that the military system at that time was already a completely feudal one. It is true that those scholars who accept the general military obligation of all freemen as still existing under Charlemagne have continued to hold that, in accordance with the form of this oath, the entire population ("cuncta generalitas populi": "the whole mass of the people") had to take the oath. But if it were really intended to apply to all the subjects, the detailed special listing of all the various categories of those to be obligated would have been superfluous. What is actually intended is the totality of the warrior class and with it the clergy. Whoever is not a warrior is not a free man in the full, true sense of the term and is not counted among the population in the political sense, whereas on the other hand even unfree men who have entered the warrior class are called upon to take the oath. Only through this interpretation do the expressions of the chronicles become understandable when they report that all the Aquitanians,[25] or all the Lombards,[26] had come to the king, subjected themselves to him, and sworn loyalty to him. The word "all" in these expressions does not refer to the millions of burghers and peasants but to those to whom this really applied, namely, the warriors, who could actually almost be assembled in a single place and whom Charlemagne wanted to have obligated to him directly, not simply via an intermediary. The form of the oath that was established after the imperial coronation states that the man taking the oath promises to be as loyal as a man was expected to be to his lord in accordance with the law ("sicut per directum debet esse homo domino suo": "just as by right a man ought to be to his own master"). Nothing could be more characteristic of the spirit of the times than this formula: the original concept, as the man understood it, a concept supported by the law of the land, was not loyalty to the king but the opposite; what seemed natural and understandable to the common man was the loyalty that the vassal owed to his suzerain. And now the emperor also demanded this loyalty from them, so that the suzerain, supported by the loyalty of his men, could not turn against the emperor.

In the following period, however, this superimposing of the subject's oath on the vassal's oath was quickly abandoned again, and with it the unity, solidarity, and authority of the monarchy.

At the time of the renewed oath-taking in 802 to the new emperor, Charles had special instructions published concerning the obligations arising from this oath. It was particularly emphasized that the oath was binding not only for the lifetime of the emperor. Here, too, we recognize once again that the vassal's oath was the dominant concept, from which the subject's oath was newly created. For the vassal's oath was regarded as purely personal, creating no tie to the heirs or the family; rather, a new mutual act from both sides was required. But the subject's oath now applied to both the monarch and his dynasty, and that point had to be made specifically clear.

Those same instructions also introduced the special duty not to convert imperial fiefs into private property, a point once again indicating the characteristics of the vassal of those taking the oath.

Finally, it should also be noted that the equipment of an unfree man who was to be sworn included the horse as well as his weapons. This cannot possibly mean that dismounted warriors did not need to take the oath; furthermore, they can hardly have been simply overlooked, but we can assume, rather, that the warrior was a mounted warrior. There simply were not others, or they did not come into consideration.

ARMAMENT AND TACTICS

Concerning the arms of the Frankish warriors under Charles, our sources are so contradictory that they form an excellent example of how little credence can be given to that type of detail. In the letter of summons to Abbot Fulrad (Vol. II, p. 449), it was prescribed that each mounted man (*caballarius*) was to be equipped with shield, lance, sword, short sword (dagger), bow and arrows. Helmet and armor are not mentioned, so that we would have to imagine the Carolingian mounted men as lightly equipped mounted archers, but the combination of the shield with the bow is unusual. A shield interferes with the handling of the bow and provides only a very insufficient protection during the drawing and shooting; a coat of mail or a firm buff-coat is a much more logical protective arm for an archer.

In the capitularies, too, there is quite often other reference to the bow as part of the equipment.[27] In the sources recounting actions, however, the bow is mentioned only seldom.[28]

The warriors of both the Carolingian and later periods, like the older Germans, appear as close-combat fighters with sword and lance, and they also use the lance as a projectile. While it is true that only the shield is normally mentioned as a protective arm,[29] nevertheless, when Einhard refers on one occasion to the heaviness of the Frankish arms and the Monk of Saint Gall seems to describe it as completely of iron in his famous description of Charlemagne and his army, we must no doubt conclude that they wore coats of mail. At one point, the capitularies require a coat of mail only on the part of owners of more than twelve hides of land,[30] but on another occasion without any specific basis.[31]

Perhaps we can reconcile these apparently contradictory reports by understanding that shield, lance, and sword were the traditional weapons required from ancient times, which were repeated as a matter of form. The requirement for bows and arrows was added specifically because these weapons were not really native to the Germans, but the army command believed it important that they be on hand. Helmet and coat of mail, on the other hand, were not mentioned, since everybody who was

in a position to provide himself with these costly items gladly did so. If
the coat of mail was specifically mentioned on one occasion, as in the
wording of the capitulary of 805, the requirement was limited to the
more well-to-do but was made particularly strict for them by the special
warning that anyone who had a coat of mail but did not bring it with him
would forfeit his entire fief along with the coat of mail.

We cannot assume that bows and arrows were supposed to be brought
into general use by means of these proclamations. While a bow is easily
made, preparation of a really good one is difficult. Furthermore, a good
archer, especially a mounted one, can be developed only by strenuous
training.

Regardless of how the individual sources are to be explained, this
much is certain, that we can picture the majority of Charlemagne's warriors as clad in a moderately heavy coat of mail and a conical helmet
without visor, with a shield on the left arm, fighting with sword and
lance. Bows and arrows were used only as auxiliary weapons.[32]

In the sources we have no reports on the tactics of the Carolingian
period, that is, concerning the distribution and cooperation of the
arms—mounted men, archers, lancers—and only from later reports and
events could we draw any conclusions. There was no training, and actual
battles were so rare that it was no doubt impossible to establish fixed and
traditional forms for a battle formation and a real art of fighting. Charles's
biographer, Einhard (Chap. 8), points out that in the war with the Saxons,
which lasted thirty-three years, there were still only two real open battles, at Detmold and on the Hase, both within five weeks, in 783.
Neither Desiderius, king of the Lombards, nor Tassilo, duke of Bavaria,
was willing to risk a battle. Consequently, a study of the tactics at this
point and for this period is neither called for nor directly feasible.

EXCURSUS

THE CAROLINGIAN CAPITULARIES ON THE MILITARY OBLIGATION

Our study has led us to the conclusion that, from the *Völkerwanderung* on, those con-
stituting the military force in the Frankish Kingdom were numerically a very limited warrior class. *This conclusion eliminates all ideas that still in his time Charlemagne took the field
with a "peasant army,"*[33] *whether the military obligation was presumably based on the ownership of land or on a general military obligation.* Charlemagne's much studied reform of the
military system, which is supposed to have formed the transition from people's army to
vassal army, not only did not take place, as Boretius has already shown, but the gradual
transformation of the ancient Germanic people's army into a vassal army was already
completed in Charles's time, except for certain final touches. This thesis that we have
elaborated in the foregoing chapter we must now test against the wording of the original

sources. In the appendix to his *Contributions to the Critique of the Capitularies (Beiträge zur Capitularienkritik)*, Boretius has assembled all the capitularies on the military system. Let us repeat here the passages that are important for us, but arranged by topic rather than in chronological order. The text is taken from the second edition of the capitularies in the *Monumenta Germaniae, Capitula regum Francorum denuo ediderunt Alfred Boretius et Victor Krause*.

* * *

(See Appendix 3 for the Latin text of each passage from the capitularies and other documents quoted in the remainder of this chapter.)

EXTRACT FROM THE GENERAL *CAPITULARE MISSORUM* (CAPITULARY OF LEGATES) OF 802. *M. G.*, 1. 93.

> 7. That no one should venture to ignore the call to arms of our lord the emperor, and no count should be so presumptuous as to dare that any of these who have been obligated from his district to do military service either forego any defense of their area or attention to this duty.

Today it is generally recognized that "hi qui hostem facere debiti sunt" ("these who have been obligated to do military service") applies in theory to all freemen. According to the text of the capitulary under consideration, the count is to leave none of these men at home.

It is clear that we have here only an administrative formula without any real content. For in reality it was always only a fraction, and from a predominantly Germanic county even only a small fraction, of the freemen who could actually take the field.

* * *

Those capitularies that arrange the obligated men in groups seem to offer a possibility for practical implementation.

EXTRACT FROM A CAPITULARY FOR THE REGIONS WEST OF THE SEINE. 807. *M. G.*, 1. 134.

> A memorandum, just as we have ordered on account of the famine, that all from beyond the Seine should do military service.
> First, all who appear to have benefices should enter the army.
> Whatever freeman seems to have five holdings in his property similarly should do military service, and whoever has four holdings likewise should do it, as well as whoever has three. And wherever two will have been found, of which each appears to have two holdings, the one should equip the other and whoever will have been the more capable should do military service. Where two will have been found, of which the one has two holdings and the other has one, similarly they should combine and the one should equip the other, and whoever will have been the more capable should enter the army. But wherever three will have been found, of which each has one holding, two should equip the third; whoever of these is more capable should enter the army. Indeed those who have a half holding—five should have the sixth equipped. And whoever will have been found so poor, who has neither dependents nor his own landed property, nevertheless, at a cost of [? 5 pounds?] five should

equip a sixth. [And where there are two who seem to have slight landed property, they should equip a third.][34] Five *solidi* are collected from the above-mentioned poor who appear to have no landed property for the one who does military service. In regard to this measure no one should ignore his lord.

This capitulary at first presents a puzzle through its introduction: "propter famis inopiam" ("on account of famine"), all men beyond (west of) the Seine are to take to the field! Boretius (*Beiträge*, p. 118) chose to interpret that as meaning that in a time of general famine the regions west of the Seine were the least affected and therefore had to bear the year's military burden. But this seems to me completely impossible, especially since the specific regulations follow immediately, according to which definitely not *all* but only certain numbers are to move out. I would like to assume that in the copying it was simply a matter of the omission of the word *"non"* before *"omnes."*

All the possessors of fiefs were supposed to take the field, as well as all freemen who had private property of more than five, or four, or three hides of land. Two men each possessing two hides were to outfit one man, and one man owning two hides could also be paired with another having one hide. Of three owners of one hide, two were always expected to equip the third, and of six owners of half a hide, five were to outfit the sixth. In like manner, groups of six men not owning land were to band together and equip one of their number. The monetary measure that served as a basis for this is not specifically reported, probably 5 pounds or 100 *solidi;* the man who was mobilized was to be given 5 *solidi* to take with him.

CAPITULARE MISSORUM (CAPITULARY OF LEGATES) OF 808. M. G., 1. 137.

1. That every freeman who possesses four holdings of his own or by a benefice of someone should equip himself and should enter the army of his own accord, either with his lord if his lord will have gone or with his count. With whoever indeed will have had three holdings of his own should be associated whoever has one holding, and he should render aid to the former so that the former may be able to serve for both. And with whoever has only two holdings of his own should be joined another who likewise has two, and one of them should enter the army with the support of the other. Also, with whoever has only one holding of his own should be associated three who similarly have one, and they should render him support and only he should enter the army. The three in fact who rendered aid should remain at home.

While this capitulary is similar to the previous one, it differs from it noticeably in all its details. In the previous one there is a basic unit of three hides, and in this one, four; in the first one there is also a provision for nonowners of land, but not in this one; in the previous one *all* enfeoffed men are to take the field, but in this one the call is based on the amount of property.

CAPITULARY OF UNCERTAIN DATE, PROBABLY 807 OR 808. *M.G.*, 1. 136.

2. If it will have been necessary to bring relief to part of Spain or Avaria, then five-sixths of the Saxons should prepare themselves. And if it will have been necessary to bring relief to part of Bohemia, two-thirds should prepare. If, in fact, there will have been the necessity to defend our country around Sorbenland, then all should come en masse.

3. Concerning the Friesians we decree that the counts and our vassals who are seen to have benefices, and the horsemen, all should come en masse well equipped to our assembly. The rest indeed are the poorer; six-sevenths should prepare themselves, and thus they should come to the announced assembly well equipped for military service.

FOUR VERSIONS OF THE REGULATIONS FOR THE BASIC ROSTERS OF 829. *M.G.*, II: P. 7, CHAP. 7: P. 10, CHAP. 5; P. 19, CHAP. 7.

We decree and we order that our legates should diligently inquire how many freemen reside in each county who are able to do military service at their own expense, and how many of these there are of which the one aids another, also how many of these there are who as a third is aided and equipped by two others, also how many of these who as a fourth is aided and equipped by three, and how many of these who as a fifth is aided and equipped by four, and how many of them are able to make the same military campaign. They should also report the sum of these on our list.

*   *   *

We decree and we order that our legates should inquire how many freemen reside in each county who are able to make a military campaign at their own expense, and how many of these there are who as a third aided and equipped by two, a fourth by three, a fifth or a sixth by four are able to make a military campaign. They should bring a brief summary of these to us.

*   *   *

We decree and we order that our legates should diligently inquire how many freemen reside in each county. Hence, truly with this attentiveness this list should also be examined through each *centena*, so that they may know accurately and may write down who are able to go on a military expedition. Then, obviously according to our command concerning whoever cannot go on a military campaign, two should furnish aid to a third. And they should have those promise loyalty to us with an oath whoever have not yet promised loyalty to us.

*   *   *

We decree and we order that our legates diligently inquire how many freemen reside in each county who are able to make a military expedition, and they should bring to us a short summary of them. And they should have those promise loyalty to us with an oath who have not yet promised loyalty.[35]

Since Boretius, the foregoing capitularies have been interpreted as meaning that it was first of all a question of temporarily applicable edicts that were proclaimed in the same way year after year and were carried out about as promulgated until in the "basic roster" of 829 it was sought to establish a general arrangement, which, of course, did not succeed, since the direct levy of freemen soon disappeared completely. But in 864 (*Capitulare Pistense, M. G.*, 2. 321) Charles the Bald repeated the regulations concerning the basic roster (in accordance with the first version).

With respect to the regulations promulgated for the Saxons and Friesians, we cannot determine under what circumstances they were issued, whether it was a one-time regulation or whether a continuing condition was intended.

There is no doubt that the other capitularies are to be understood not as laws but as temporarily applicable regulations, but the idea that they were actually carried out according to their literal wording is contradicted by other capitularies.

We have already found in the extract from the capitulary of 808, shown above (p. 32), that it was taken for granted that a man who took to the field had a senior. This point also appears in the capitulary of Boulogne of 811, Chapter 9 (*M. G.,* 1. 167): "quicumque liber homo inventus fuerit anno praesente cum seniore in hoste non fuisse, plenum heribanum persolvere cogatur." ("Whatever freeman will have been found in the current year not to have been in the army with his lord should be compelled to pay the full army tax.") According to this, there was no free warrior who did not have his senior, and was therefore a vassal. When the capitulary continues: "Et si senior vel comis illius eum domi dimiserit, ipse pro eo bannum persolvat" ("And if his lord or count will have sent him home, he should pay the tax for that man"), that obviously does not mean that the man was placed either under his senior or under the count, but only that the former as well as the latter can have been in collusion with him. The same point is to be understood from the capitulary of 819, paragraph 27, *M. G.,* 1. 291, on p. 41 below (shown by Boretius in *Beiträge* as the capitulary of 817), where it is not at all a question of failure to report by freemen but only of the penalties for vassals, and at the assembly in Meersen in 847 Charles the Bald proclaimed: "Volumus etiam, ut unus quisque liber homo in nostro regno seniorem, qualem voluerit in nobis et in nostris fidelibus accipiat." ("We also decree that each freeman in our kingdom should accept a lord, whomever among us and our vassals he wanted.")

"Mandamus etiam, ut nullus homo seniorem suum sine justa ratione dimittat nec aliquis eum recipiat nisi sicut tempore antecessorum nostrorum consuetudo fuit." ("We also command that no one forsake his lord without just cause, nor should anyone accept him except just as it was the custom in the time of our predecessors.")

Consequently, the text of our sources shows on the one hand peasant levies with alternating personnel and on the other hand a levy composed exclusively of vassals. These arrangements are mutually exclusive. We could possibly imagine a vassal army supplemented by a peasant levy. But an army in which it is a prerequisite that every warrior have a senior and the warriors are still called freemen, contains no peasants at all, for the peasant who has a senior is no longer free; whoever has a senior and is at the same time free is a warrior. How then are we to solve this contradiction?

Most apparent is the contradiction between the edicts of the sources in the proclamations of Charles the Bald. And it is for this reason that we also find the solution here. It is clear that, when the *Edictum Pistense* of 864 repeats an old regulation concerning the formation of groups, that is simply a carryover from the past. The same king who announced this edict had, of course, already ordered at Meersen long before that every freeman was to have his senior, and the same *Edictum Pistense* that requires in one of its chapters the formation of groups prescribes in another one (Chapter 26) that all Franks who have a horse or can procure one are to move out into the field with their counts. The one regulation is so very much like the others a mere repetition of words and only serves as an illustrative example of how uncertain the application of laws is to actual circumstances. I remind the reader of the equally meaningless military laws of the West Goths cited in the previous volume and call attention to the Assize of Arms of the Plantagenets in Book II, Chapter 5 of the present volume.

Now what seems to be a fact in the reign of Charles the Bald, namely, that capitularies sometimes present only ancient military formulas that stand in full contradiction to the reality of life, can, and in fact must, also be assumed for Charlemagne's period. Already during his regime and in any case even before him, the personal levies must actually have existed only on paper. Even the *"famis inopia"* ("famine") that is referred to in the capitulary of 807 is perhaps nothing more than a petrified administrative form.

At this point I cite the wording of a report in the *Annal. Bertiniani* of the year 869, where once again the attempt is made to draw up a statistical picture of the country, so to speak, but this time already on a feudal base.[36]

> And before he went to Conde, he sent a letter throughout his whole kingdom that the bishops, abbots, and abbesses should see to it that on the first of May they make a list of their offices—how many holdings each had; the vassals of the lord, however, should list the benefices of the counts and the counts the benefices of their vassals, and they should bring to the aforementioned assembly a list of the churches there. And he ordered to be sent to Pistres one hagastald per hundred holdings, one wagon with two oxen per thousand holdings according to the above-mentioned decree, along with other essentials which much burden his kingdom, in order that the hagastalds might inhabit and garrison the castle which he ordered to be built of wood and stone there.

The difference between the concept proposed here and the generally accepted one lies in the earlier dating and the reasons. Brunner, in *German Legal History* (*Deutsche Rechtsgeschichte*), 2: 206, says: "Of the general military service there finally remained no vestige except a war tax on those who could not give personal military service." I see the reason for the change not only in the economic "not-able-to-serve" but just as much in the military qualities. Brunner goes on to say: "The sequence of actual developments led to the situation where the count provided a competent man and equipped him by means of the taxes that he laid on those remaining at home. In doing so he was certainly not prevented from taking this warrior from his own group of subordinates." That is certainly correct, but the reasons for the change were already at work from Clovis on, and they were already as good as completed in Charlemagne's reign, when only an antiquated form still clung laboriously to life.

> *The result of this establishing of other dates and reasons for the genesis of the knightly military system is the creation of the relationship between the medieval military system and the Völkerwanderung and the conquest of the Romans by the Germans, a relationship that was obscured by the insertion of a peasant militia army and general military obligation during the Merovingian period.*

We shall have occasion later to return once again to the evolution of the military obligation into a tax obligation. That it had already been effected for all practical purposes in the reign of Charlemagne, while the ancient forms calling for the personal levy still continued in use, is proven by the formulas used at the same time that cause us to see the army as one consisting purely of vassals. We cannot determine with certainty how far back this divergency between the wording of the proclamations and actual practice goes.

As an example of how little can be concluded directly from the wording of a proclamation, we may consider a letter in which in the year 817 the archbishop of Trier, acting as an imperial legate, ordered the bishop of Toul to mobilize his men for a campaign to Italy against the rebellious King Bernhard (cited in Waitz, *Constitutional History* [*Verfassungsgeschichte*], 4: 465, and in Prenzel, *Contributions to the History of Military Organizations*

under the Carolingians [Beiträge zur Geschichte der Kriegsverfassung unter den Karolingern],
Leipzig, 1887, p. 23, from Bouquet, 6: 395). It orders, by command of the emperor:

> Insofar as all prepared themselves in such a way that they can set out for war in
> Italy . . . that by ingenious shrewdness you should be diligent to announce with the
> greatest haste to all abbots, abbesses, counts, vassals of the lord, and all the people of
> your diocese, for whom it is proper to render military service to the royal power,
> that, insofar as they were equipped, if it will have been announced to them in the
> evening, in the morning they should start for Italy, and if in the morning, in the
> evening without delay.

There can be no question but that for a campaign across the Alps to Italy each district
provided only a quite small number of warriors. According to the *Annal. Laurish. (Annals
of Lorch),* the army was assembled "ex tota Gallia atque Germania" ("from all Gaul and
Germany"). Nevertheless, the letter speaks pompously of "cuncto populo, quibus convenit
militiam regiae potestati exhibere" ("to all the people for whom it is proper to render
military service to the royal power").

*   *   *

MEMORIAL OF 811. *M. G.*, 1. 165.

> 3. They also say that in cases where someone refuses to grant his own man to a
> bishop, abbot, count, judge, or centenarius, they seek pretexts against that poor man
> whereby they are able to find fault with him and always make him enter the army,
> until the poor man willingly or unwillingly should hand over his own man or sell
> him. Indeed others who handed over their man remain at home without the distur-
> bance of anyone.

> 5. Others also say that they should arrest those poorer men and should make
> them enter the army, and they let go those who maintain that they are able to give a
> man according to their property.

The military organization based on the vassal system and fiefs naturally had to lead to a
degrading of those freemen who left the warrior class. The counts, by using their discretionary
powers, sought to hasten this process and to bring these men of lowered status into
their personal dependency. In the *Life of Louis the Pious (Das Leben Ludwigs des Frommen),*[37]
by Thegan, Chap. 13, it is recounted that the emperor sent commissars throughout the
empire immediately after his accession to the throne to help restore to their rights those
degraded persons who had been deprived of their patrimony or their freedom. Heusler, in
his *Constitutional History (Verfassungsgeschichte),* in keeping with the commonly accepted
concept, relates that to peasants. Consequently, I wish to point out expressly that in
Thegan's text it is not a question of peasants but of degraded men in a very general way.

We recognize how this process of development occurred from an Italian capitulary of
898 (*M. G., Capitularia Regum Francorum [Capitularies of the Kings of the Franks],* 2: 109),
which prescribes: "ut nullus comitum arimannos in beneficia suis hominibus tribuat" ("that
none of the counts should grant warriors to their men in benefices"). The former free
warriors were gradually pushed down so far into the class of tax-obligated men that the
counts could risk treating them completely as tenant farmers and giving them away with

their farms as fiefs. The prohibition that the king placed on this procedure probably had but little effect.

*   *   *

REGULATIONS CONCERNING PUNISHMENTS

CAPITULARY OF 802. *M. G.*. 1. 96.

29. Concerning the poor to whom our lord the emperor grants in his mercy that they ought to exempt according to his decree, (he orders) that judges, counts, and our legates should not have them arrested in light of this grant.

34. That all are fully and well equipped whenever our order or proclamation arrives. [Similarly stated in a special capitulary of the year 802, *M. G.*; 1. 100]. If anyone, however, then should have said that he was unprepared and should have ignored the order, he would be brought to the palace, and not only that man but also all who venture to transgress our edict and our order.

CAPITULARY OF 805. *M. G.*, 1. 125.

19. We decree concerning the army tax that our legates in this year should exact it faithfully and without the favor of any person, flattery, or alarm according to our order. That is that they should take the regular tax, that is, 3 pounds, from a man having 6 pounds in gold, silver, mail tunics, brass, unimpaired clothes, horses, oxen, cows, and other property (and wives and children should not be despoiled of their clothes in this matter). Whoever indeed will not have had more than 3 pounds in the aforementioned rate, he should pay 30 *solidi* (that is, a pound and a half). But whoever will have had no more than 2 pounds, he should pay 10 *solidi*. If indeed he should have had 1 pound, 5 *solidi* would be paid, so that he may be able to equip himself for the service of God and our use. And let our legates be on guard and diligently seek lest through some inborn evil they subvert our justice by handing over or entrusting their charge to another.

CAPITULARY OF 808. *M. G.*, 1. 137.

2. We decree and we order that our legates should likewise diligently inquire who in the past year when the army was summoned remained at home against that command which we ordered to be made concerning free and poorer men in the manner recounted further above; and whoever will have been found who neither aided his comrade in joining his host according to our order nor went himself should be fully liable for our army tax and he should make a pledge for paying it according to the law.

3. But if by chance such a man should have been found who says that by order of his count, vicarius, or centenarius he had given this by which he ought to equip himself to the same count, vicarius, centenarius, or some of their men, and for this reason he had neglected that campaign and our legates should have been able to discover that this was indeed thus, the one by whose order that man remained at

home would be liable and would pay the army tax, whether he be a count, vicarius, or the representative of a bishop and abbot.

CAPITULARY OF 810. *M. G.*, 1. 153.

12. That legates should diligently inquire about the army tax. Whoever could join the army and did not should pay the army tax, if he has the means by which he may be able to pay. And if he will not have had the means by which to be able to pay, let him become liable and be listed and let nothing be exacted for this until it comes to the notice of our lord the emperor.

CAPITULARY OF BOULOGNE. 811. *M. G.*, 1. 166.

1. Whatever freeman will have been summoned to the army and will have refused to come, he should pay the full army tax, that is, 60 *solidi,* or if he will not have had the means from which to pay that sum, he should surrender himself into the servitude of the prince as a pledge of liability until, as decreed by the prince, he should be through time paid up for his liberty. And if that man who surrendered himself to servitude because of the army tax should have died in that servitude, his heirs would not lose his inheritance which belongs to them, nor their freedom, and they would not become liable for the army tax.

2. That a count should not dare to exact the army tax by any reason of guard duty, military service, garrison duty, encamping, or in regard to another decree, unless our legate in advance should refer the levy to us and should grant to him his own approval as a third party subsequently through our order. Indeed, the army tax should be exacted neither in land nor in dependents, but in gold and silver, clothes, arms, animals, or other goods that are useful.

MEMORIAL OF 811. *M. G.*, 1. 165.

6. The counts themselves say that some of their peasants do not obey them, nor do they want to discharge the decree of our lord the emperor, saying that in regard to the army tax they ought to render account to the legates of our lord the emperor and not in fact to a count. Even if he should have sent his own house into the emperor's service, he would get no respect from this unless he should let him into his house and should do whatever pleased him.

When we look over these provisions for punishment, we recognize that the old levy system on the occasion of mobilizing the army existed legally, it is true, but it functioned only very poorly or not at all. Sometimes at one place and sometimes at another it was sought to bring the machine into motion, to reform it, to replace the individual parts with others, according to the complaints that were received.

The law in the sources states that when the army was levied, the count required 60 *solidi* for the army. It is not easy to imagine what a sum of 60 *solidi* meant in the economic life of the day.[38] The theme is ancient, but the value of the money may have changed very much from Clovis to the time of Charlemagne's successors, and the *solidus* itself did not remain unchanged; in Charlemagne's reign a fiscal reform took place. The original *solidus* was a gold coin about equal in value to 12 present-day marks. The Ripuarian law (36. 11) gives the value of a good healthy cow as 1 *solidus,* of an ox as 2, a mare as 3, a stallion as 12, and a sword with scabbard as 7 *solidi.* In a supplement to the Salic law, a serving man is valued at 25 to 35 *solidi,* a maid at 15 to 25, and in another passage the value of a common slave is estimated at 12 *solidi.* In keeping with this scale, a fine of 60 *solidi* for a common peasant would have been absolutely exorbitant. A peasant would not just be ruined if he had to pay the value of 60 cows or 30 oxen or 20 mares—he was simply unable to do it. The threat of a fine of 60 *solidi,* even if it could ever actually be collected in some other way, could not at all have been conceived for the simple owner of one hide of land. We get a somewhat different picture when we consider that in one levy capitulary a half-hide of land is equated to possession of 100 *solidi.*[39]

Since the actual land was hardly appraised, the sum of 200 *solidi* is to be considered equivalent to the house, the farm equipment, the weapons, and other mobile property of the independent peasant. A fine of almost one-third of this value would always have been exorbitant, to be sure, but not physically impossible. For the Chamavian Franks the fine for being absent from the mobilization was originally only 4 *solidi,* and among the Lombards 20 *solidi,* but under the Carolingians the standard amount of 60 was introduced everywhere.[40] If the fine of 60 *solidi* was exorbitant for a peasant, it amounted to much less for a rich man than participation in a campaign of several months cost him. He was therefore in a position to buy himself out of service with a moderate payment of money. Arbitrary increase of the fine by the legates or even by the counts was out of the question. That was no doubt the basis for the capitulary of 802, paragraph 34, where it is ordered that the person failing to report for service should be brought before the court. The call to service is not mentioned at all. If this regulation had been intended to apply to the general levy of all freemen, it would have brought entire *"Völkerwanderungen"* to the emperor's current seat of government.

On the other hand, the fine of 60 *solidi* for the little man was absolutely prohibitive. At times there was no other remedy but for the emperor to lower it (capitulary of 802, paragraph 29), a move which, of course, then undermined the future effectiveness of the punishment; or the emperor had to reserve for himself the decision in individual cases (capitulary of 810), which amounted to the same thing for the little man. Then it was tried with a graduated scale based on the individual's financial condition. This method also failed, since the determination of the value of a person's holdings is very difficult and subject to all kinds of arbitrary judgment. An attempt was therefore made by means of a temporary reduction to a menial status, a regulation that presumably contributed much toward hastening the process that was already under way whereby the small common freeman gave up his freedom and in some way or other became dependent on another man. For even if the children of those who were reduced to dependency by the capitulary of 811 were supposed to be guaranteed their freedom, they themselves supposedly renounced it. For one in such a menial position, working off a debt of 60 *solidi* was such a task that he probably had to work at it most of his life. During this time any possible military inclination and tradition in the family had disappeared, and the next generation, faced with the choice of again being levied for war or being able to remain at home as a tenant farmer, subject only to certain duties and burdens, under the control but also the protection of a lord, probably often preferred the latter alternative.

As strong as the regulation concerning the fine for not reporting for military service seems to have been, it takes on a completely different aspect when we realize that it was not the count but only the legate who was authorized to collect it. The legates were very prominent lords who traveled through a number of counties as royal commissars and inspectors. It is impossible that in every county they looked into more than a very few cases of neglect of military service, assessed the individual's fortune and the fine to be levied, and collected the amount judged in the form of cattle, weapons, cloth, etc.

From time to time there appear as tax collectors individual officials, especially titled as inspectors for the failure to report for service. But as early as 802, when Charlemagne once ordered that only rich men were to be appointed as legates because poor men misused their office for the oppression of the people, it is clear that subordinate tax collectors with their arbitrary assessments must have been full-fledged blood suckers.

It appears, therefore, that the right to collect the fine was occasionally granted also to the counts, a point that the subordinates refused to recognize as legitimate—quite naturally so, for they were, of course, thereby completely placed at the mercy of the counts' whims.

The count used his levy authority (memorial of 811) to badger and ruin the people so that they would be ready to turn over their possessions to him and become his serfs. Against this, the central administration had nothing but prohibitions and pious wishes. For once again a real check and control as to whether the individual was overburdened or favored in the levy procedure, and whether the produce, cattle, clothing, and weapons turned in by him were correctly assessed was impossible.

Only once (capitulary of 808) do we find in all the threats of punishment a reference to the fact that by far the majority of militarily obligated men were indeed not really called up at all but were only required to make a contribution. The count in any case forced the direct delivery of these payments. From the very start, therefore, the fines for failure to serve were directed principally at the wealthier men, a point that is, of course, also indicated in most of the regulations. Even in those regulations, however, it can be seen that the punishment as such and the avoidance of military duty were in no way the only considerations, but the fiscal aspect was just as important. In the Carolingian Empire there were enough brave and willing fighting men; a systematic arrangement for collecting taxes was of much more value to the emperor than a landowner obeying the call to duty only half willingly or against his will. Therefore, it was not just a possible matter of indulgence but to assure that the emperor received his share that the fine was to be collected not directly by the counts but through the legates. Finally, this fine simply became a tax. When the *Annales Bertiniani* for the year 866 report "heribanni de omnibus Francis accipiuntur" ("Army taxes are received from all the Franks"), it is here no longer a fine for failure to report but a tax that is being collected. Since all the Franks were required to pay it, this tax can no longer have had anything to do with the old concept of 60 *solidi* equaling 60 cows. Later we find the tax substituting for military service set at from 2 to 3 *solidi*.[41]

The regulation in the capitulary of 808, paragraph 3, that the official who takes in a payment and in return allows the payer to remain at home shall himself forfeit 60 *solidi* can naturally not be understood as meaning that this procedure was absolutely forbidden but only that any official was to be punished who collected the payment but embezzled it and did not equip anybody with it. The fact that the latter point is not mentioned at all could be considered as another proof that it was taken for granted.

*   *   *

CAPITULARY OF BOULOGNE. 811 *M. G.*, 1. 166.

3. Whatever man holding our fiefs will have been summoned to the army and will not have come to the assigned assembly should abstain from meat and wine as many days as he was proven to have come after the assigned assembly.

There is a certain inherent contradiction between the strictness of the royal fine for a man who avoids military service and this fine for a man who comes too late. The latter has no other punishment than having to abstain from meat and wine for as many days as he was late in arriving—a regulation that was all the less to be feared in that its execution could in the final analysis not be checked on. If we actually had in these laws and regulations an expression and echo of reality, we would have to say: nothing was more convenient for a Frank on the occasion of a campaign than to delay his reporting until the principal action was already over. Then nothing more could happen to him than to be ordered to follow a vegetarian regime for a few weeks or months, and nobody checked on how he made out with this merciful punishment except his own conscience.

* * *

DISPENSATIONS

CAPITULARY OF 808. *M. G.*, 1. 137.

4. Of the counts' men who are bound to land, the following ought to be exempted and should not be ordered to be liable for the levy: two who are detached with the count's wife and two others who are ordered to remain to guard his district and to do our service. For this reason we now order that as many districts as each count has he should detach at his house a pair of men for guarding these in addition to those two who are with his wife. All the others indeed he should have with him at full strength, and, if he should have remained at home, he should send them with that man who goes to the army in his stead. Indeed, a bishop or abbot should detach at his house only two land-bound laymen.

CAPITULARY OF BOULOGNE. 811. *M. G.*, 1. 167.

9. Whatever freeman will have been found in the current year not to have been in the army with his lord should be compelled to pay the full army tax. And if his lord or count should have left him home, the lord or count would pay the same tax in his behalf and he would pay as many taxes as he left men at home. And because in the current year we granted to each lord a pair of men whom he might leave at home, we order that they should point out those men to our legates, because we yield the army tax only to these men.

CAPITULARY OF LEGATES OF 819.[42] *M. G.*, 1. 291, CHAP. 27.

That our vassals and the vassals of bishops, abbots, abbesses, and counts who in the current year were not in the army should be liable for the army tax, with the exception of these who for the compelling reasons established by our lord and father Charles were left at home, that is, (any man) who was left at home by his count to keep the peace and to guard his wife and house, and similarly by a bishop, abbot, or abbess to keep the peace, to gather the harvest, to manage the household, and to receive legates.

If we compare the dispensations that are enumerated in these capitularies, it appears as if they were different in different years: on one occasion the count is allowed to leave behind only two men, but another time four men. Whether that was actually intended is unimportant in comparison with the question as to which category these two or four men belonged to. All the militarily obligated men fit for service? Whereas at other times several hides of land together provided only one man, in this year were all men supposed to have been levied as a special situation? Boretius (pp. 118, 123) is not entirely clear on this point. It seems obvious to me that the regulations make sense only if they apply to a very small group, where two or four men fewer actually matter; in other words, that here, too, it was not the general levy but only the vassals or fief-holders that were being considered.

In a capitulary of the years 801–813 (M. G., 1. 170, Chap. 8), it is decreed that each *vicarius* (*hunno*) was to keep two wolf hunters, who were excused from military service.

THE LEVY

According to the capitulary of Aachen of 801–813 (M. G., 1. 171, Chap. 9): "de hoste pergendi, ut comiti in suo comitatu per bannum unumquemque hominem per sexaginta solidos in hostem pergere bannire studeat" ("On the departure of the army. That it should be the business of a count to proclaim in his county by decree that each man in lieu of 60 solidi enter the army"), the count summoned all warriors, including the vassals of other seniors.

According to the letter from Archbishop Hatti to the bishop of Toul (see p. 35, above), the levy was carried out in such a way that the legate wrote to the bishop and the latter announced the levy, "omnibus abbatibus, abbatissis, comitibus, vassis dominicis vel cuncto populo parrochiae tuae, quibus convenit militiam regiae potestati exhibere" ("to all abbots, abbesses, counts, vassals of our lord, and all people of your diocese, for whom it is appropriate to perform military service for the royal power").

On the other hand, Abbot Fulrad received his summons directly from the emperor. (See the letter in Vol. II, p. 449.)

These are obviously contradictions that led Waitz (1st ed., 4: 513, note) to doubt how far one could stretch the concept of *unumquemque hominem* (each man) in the first-named capitulary.

I have no doubt that this meant *all* warriors, even the vassals of other warriors. The contradiction is the same, and it is no greater than the one that runs throughout the entire military system in Charlemagne's regime. It was not yet so completely forgotten that the freeman, even as the vassal of another, was a subject of the king, and that is why the count summoned him legally on the occasion of a royal levy. From a practical viewpoint, of course, he appeared only in the retinue of a suzerain, and for that reason direct summons went out to the great suzerains.

The sending of the summons through the intermediary of the legate to a bishop and by him to the counts and the great suzerains of his diocese has no more significance for the levy itself than a direct summons.

EQUIPMENT

CAPITULARY OF ESTATES OF 800 OR EARLIER. M. G., 1. 82.

64. That the *basternae,* our wagons, have been well made, and their coverings have been well overlaid with hides, and they have been so put together that, if the need for floating will have occurred, they can cross rivers with the provisions which were within and that water in no way can get in, and our material, just as we said, can cross quite safely. We also make this command that flour should be sent in each

wagon for our use, that is twelve bushels, and they should send twelve bushels according to our standard in which they bring wine. They should also have a shield, lance, quiver, and bow in each wagon.

CAPITULARY OF AIX-LA-CHAPELLE. 801–813. *M. G.*, 1. 170.

10. That the provisions of the king as well as of the bishops, counts, abbots, and magnates of the king should be carried in a wagon: flour, wine, salted pork, and food in abundance, mills, mattocks, axes, drills, slings, and those men who know how to throw well with them. The marshals of the king should bring stones for them in loads of twenty if necessary. And let everyone have been prepared for military service, and they should have all tools in sufficient supply. Each count should hold two-thirds of the grass in his county for the need of that army, and he should have good bridges and good boats.

CAPITULARY OF LEGATES FOR THE REGIONS WEST OF THE SEINE. 807. *M. G.*, 1. 134.

3. And so all our loyal captains with their men and with a wagon and gift, as much as they were better able to supply, should come to the arranged assembly. Each of our legates throughout the individual districts should make an inspection of one of our vassals and he should order according to our word that a wagon from each county should come with that smaller band of men, and he should bring them to us peacefully in such a manner that nothing remains there and in the middle of August they are at the Rhine.

The *basternae* are a particular kind of cart, drawn by two animals. They were to be provided with watertight leather tarpaulins. Twelve *modii* of flour or 12 *modii* of wine were to be loaded on each cart. The *modius* is supposed to have been about 52 liters; a liter of flour weighs only about 600 grams, a liter of wine 1,000 grams. By this calculation a flour wagon was loaded with not much more than 800 pounds, and a wine wagon with between 1,300 and 1,400 pounds. We can see how such regulations were taken only in a very general way. A net load of more than 1,300 pounds for a two-animal team was very high for the conditions of that day (see Vol. II, p. 444). If they did not regard such regulations in general simply as approximate norms but as actual requirements, they probably reckoned with the fact that the 1,300-plus pounds formed, of course, only the starting load, which became less from day to day. On the other hand, that would also apply to the flour wagons, and it should not be forgotten that placing together in one train similar vehicles that are so unevenly loaded would be an impracticable organization.

THE ITALIAN CAPITULARIES

The capitularies concerning the military system that have come down to us from the Lombard Kingdom (likewise collected in Boretius, *Contributions to the Critique of the Capitularies* [*Beiträge zur Capitularienkritik*]) differ considerably in details from the Frankish ones, but they agree in their basic points and therefore happily confirm our interpretation.[43]

From them we see much more clearly than in the Frankish Kingdom how among the Lombards a warrior class lived in the middle of an unwarlike population from the days of the *Völkerwanderung* and propagated itself. To the present time we have not been able to imagine such a warrior class that was not a closely knit people, formed no large retinue, and was not even based on fiefs. So it came about that in the standard work for medieval Italian legal history, *History of the Municipal Organization of Italy* (*Geschichte der Städteverfassung von Italien*), by Carl Hegel, the truth of the matter actually stands literally before us, because the sources are completely clear, but then it is pushed aside by false changes because it seemed to the author so impossible from a practical viewpoint.

The testimony refers both to the Lombard areas and to those that were not subjugated by the Lombards.

Gregory I (590-604) once wrote to the inhabitants of Ravenna, enumerating all the individual classes, including the "warriors" (*milites*). The same thing appears in another letter to the inhabitants of Zara or Jadera.[44]

Toward the middle of the seventh century, when the Greek emperor wanted to have Pope Martin taken prisoner, he recommended to his governor that he first feel out the attitude of the Roman "army" and, if it should be opposed, that he take no action.[45]

If we could still imagine that it was in this case only a question of a band of mercenaries that happened by chance to be there, we shall no longer have to consider this interpretation as necessary when we see that the class of warriors (*milites*) and the *Optimates militiae* (nobles of military service) are constantly referred to in the sources of the following century. Even in the elections of the popes they (*primates exercitus:* nobles of the army) have their right, and they are called upon to subscribe to the final election decree. Hegel himself says (1: 253) this army can have been neither an army of mercenaries nor an entire people's army. He therefore claims that it was composed of a "respected warrior class from the nucleus of the citizenry." "The Romans were again militarily inclined, and the people had become an army" (p. 250). These were the members of the Roman community who were fully qualified by landownership and competence in the use of weapons, primarily the former large estate owners (p. 254).

But how then are the owners of houses in Rome and Ravenna supposed to have become militarily competent again, whereas the remainder, the "*cives honesti*" ("honorable citizens"), as the modest burghers were called in contrast to the house owners, were not militarily inclined? They not only suddenly became competent in arms, but they even had a military organization of honorable age, the "*scholas militiae*" ("elite units of military service"), as they were formerly called by Constantine the Great and which Pope Hadrian sent out against the Frankish King Carol (Hegel, p. 259). In Ravenna they were of such a savage nature that on Sundays they carried out bloody contests of arms before the gates of the city, contests in which the various quarters of the city fought against each other (Hegel, p. 263).

For the descendants of the burghers whose service in battle Belisarius had once declined with thanks, while readily acknowledging their good will, this seems, after all, a much too remarkable change, especially under the protection of Greek governors or clerical regents. There must be a completely different factor in play here, and it is not difficult to find.

This new warrior class was not a class of house owners who had suddenly become militarily inclined. On the contrary, these were the barbarian warriors who had gradually become Romanized and assimilated as citizens and perhaps may even have become owners of houses and other property but in this process had still retained their warrior-like character for generations and had maintained it through practice. Indeed, they were constantly needed, and without them the country would have been utterly defenseless.

When Otto the Great held his famous synod in Saint Peter's in 963, there were still present "omnis Romanorum militia" ("the whole army of the Romans").[46]

In contrast to the Goths, the Lombards had never been a single, closely knit people but rather a military alliance in which the race forming the core had been joined by Gepids, Saxons, Pannonians, Noricans, and even Bulgars. Immediately after their conquest of the country, they broke up into small domains under thirty-five dukes and even later still had a weak elective monarchy. We must imagine that in the period of the duchies in each of the larger cities the leader of a band (clan patriarch, *hunno*) settled, seized power, took what he wanted, and assigned to his men whatever it pleased him to grant and command. The source reports that many prominent Romans at that time were killed or driven out because of the greed of the invaders are probably correct.[47] There may have been very few Roman owners of large estates left. The Roman population in general moved into the status of only partial freedom; the Romans became *aldien* (or *liti*), while the Lombards formed the only fully free class, the warriors, or *arimanni*. And it was, of course, also like this among the Franks, but with the difference that with them, thanks to the strong monarchy, it was possible from the start for prominent Roman families to gain protection for their lives and property and through admission to the royal service and into the warrior class themselves to become members of the ruling, fully free class (see Vol. II, p. 392), something that can hardly have been the case among the Lombards.

Hartmann's assumption, in *History of Italy in the Middle Ages* (*Geschichte Italiens im Mittelalter*), 2: 1: 42 and 2: 2: 50, that every Lombard became a landowner and such an important one that he could move into the field as a mounted man, is certainly incorrect. For the most part, the new landowers were the king, the dukes, and a number of retainers and officials. The common Lombard warriors were, for the reasons developed in Vol. II, p. 323, either not settled on land at all, but lived in the retinue of the king, the dukes, and the bailiffs, or they probably lived on a tenant farm but not from its produce, having there only a living place and a minimum of provisions while they depended principally on the compensation for their service, from fighting, and from booty. In the work cited above, 2: 1: 52, Hartmann draws up a rather large number of Italian place names that are formed with "*fara*" (clan). This leads to the conclusion that rather large groups of Lombards settled together here—that is, not as large-estate owners but as small landowners. But a small landowner cannot go to war with a horse provided from his own means.

The following expression, used by Hartmann, 2: 2: 52, is erroneous: "The warlike Lombard race had moved out in order to enjoy income without work, its spread throughout Italy was the winning of labor-free income." This sentence is closer to the truth than that other one, to the effect that the Germans had come into the Roman Empire in order to have land assigned to them on which they could live as peasants. Nevertheless, Hartmann's statement omits the principal point, namely, that the conquerors did not simply take income from the land, but they dominated it and took over the service of the warrior class. The invaders came at first as pure robbers and plunderers, as the Vikings did later; but when they had settled on a continuing basis and had seized power, they then also offered their services in return. We can effectively oppose Hartmann's rhetorical exaggeration, which is not drawn from history but from a modern doctrine carried over into history, with the fact that the knightly language designated war itself by the word "work."

In the description that Hartmann, 2: 1: 132, gives of the changes in the military system in the part of Italy that remained Roman in the sixth and seventh centuries, we read: "It could be said that, as a result of the localization of the military system, the military economy was changed from a money economy to one based on barter." The substance of this sentence is correct, but the cause-and-effect relationship must be turned about: because the money economy had gone over to a barter economy (ever since the third century), the military system had to "become localized"—that is, instead of pay, the troops had to depend on provisions in kind and finally on landownership.

*   *   *

EDICT OF LIUTPRAND OF THE YEAR 726. *M. G. LEG.*, 4. 140.

> Chap. 83. Concerning all the judges, when there will have been need to make a
> military campaign, let them leave behind no other men except only those who have
> one horse, this is six men, and they should raise six horses in addition to their own
> pack animals; and of the poorest men, who have neither houses nor their own lands,
> they should leave behind ten men and these men should perform for the judge three
> services per week until the judge returns from the army. A village mayor indeed
> should leave behind three men who have a horse, and they should raise three horses
> in addition to their own pack animals; and of the lesser men they should leave five
> men at home, who may perform services for the mayor until he returned—three
> services per week, just as we will instruct for a judge. Certainly a manorial bailiff
> should raise one horse, and he should raise one from the lesser men who may
> perform services for him, and he should thus perform the services, just as it is said
> above. And if a judge, village mayor, or manorial bailiff should have dared to leave
> behind more men without the permission or order of the king who obliged him to
> go on a military campaign, he would pay his own wergeld to the sacred purse.

Just as did the Frankish regulation, this one, too, was derived from the ancient German
concept that basically, whenever there was a mobilization for war, all the men moved out.
Not directly expressed but implicit in this is the point that it was a question only of the
warriors, the Lombards and those Romanics or half-Romanics who had perhaps been
admitted to the military community. But this basic principle could no longer be completely
carried out. In order to arrive at a selection process, the Franks established the group
system; the Lombards applied a different technique: the judges were authorized to excuse
from service and leave at home in their district six men owning a horse and ten who did not;
in like manner, the town mayors were allowed to excuse three horse owners and five
without horses; and finally the *saltarii* (*decani*, manorial bailiffs) were each allowed one
horse owner. The men who were thus excused were obliged in return to work three days a
week for their superiors, with their horses if needed, as long as the campaign lasted. If we
imagine that they could avoid this work by some kind of contribution, we then have a result
very similar to that of the Frankish group process.

It is significant that the Lombard regulation stems from the year 726 and is therefore
much older than the Frankish capitularies that have survived. This point may serve us as
evidence that the need to limit and control the general levy by means of dispensations
among the Franks as well also went much farther back than is directly proved by those
capitularies that happen to have been passed down to us.

Hegel, in his *Geschichte der Städteverfassung von Italien*, 1: 430, has claimed that this edict
shows that at that time in the Lombard Kingdom it was no longer a question of the national
race, for the edict applied to *all* freemen, even the Romans. But Hegel himself has already
justifiably supported the opinion that originally all the Romans were reduced to *aldien*.
Consequently, there were not any free Romans, and those who existed in the eighth
century were men who had been freed and their offspring or immigrants. There cannot
have been so very many of them. But of their number many may actually have entered the
warrior class.

*   *   *

CAPITULARY OF AISTULF OF 750. *M. G. LEG.*, 4. 196.

Chap. 2. Of those men who are able to have a breastplate or at least have the means, and lesser men who are able to have a horse, shield, and lance or at least have the means, and those men who are not able to have them and do not have the means by which to acquire them, they should have a shield and a quiver. And it was established that a man who has seven estates with tenants should have his own breastplate along with the rest of his armament, and he should have horses. If in addition he will have had more than that number, he should have horses and the rest of his armament. Likewise it was decreed that those men who do not have estates with tenants and have forty measures of land should have a horse, shield, and lance; the prince likewise decreed for lesser men that if they are able to have a shield, they should have a quiver with arrows and a bow,[48] and likewise for men who are traders and do not have money. The richer and powerful should have breastplate, horses, shield, and lance; men of lesser rank should have horses, shield, and lance; and the poorer should have quivers with arrows and bows.

Chap. 7. Concerning judges, village mayors, and agents who let powerful men go home or away from the army. They who do this should pay just as the edict, our document, maintains.

The capitulary has the form simply of a suggestive record of decisions made in oral negotiations and oral proclamations. The king requires that certain men must have a complete set of equipment with armor, others are to have horse, shield, and lance, and the poorest simply shield and quivers, that is, bows and arrows. It is not stated whether those who report for duty incorrectly equipped are threatened with punishment, or what kind of punishment they might receive; this point seems simply to have been omitted by the scribe. Anybody owning seven hides is to report on horseback, fully armored, and those owning more land are to provide a man thus equipped for every seven hides. A man owning only forty yokes of land is to report on horseback with shield and lance; and the poorer men where possible with a shield and in any case with quivers, bows, and arrows;[49] the same requirement applies to those in business—*negotiantes* (merchants, traders, artisans) who own no land. But the more important and more well-to-do among them are to report fully armored, those of moderate means on horseback with shield and lance.

There is no question here of dispensations. Either the king this time actually intended to lead the entire army levy into the field—it was a question of wresting Ravenna back from the Greeks—or, realizing that the regulations on this subject were of no practical value, he placed the execution of the plan squarely in the hands of the officials. And the few regulations, too, that actually were promulgated, were, of course, very incomplete; it is especially difficult to see how those men owning between forty yokes and seven hides of land were to be equipped. There is also the question of what kind of men were to be provided, fully armored, by the large-estate owners for every seven hides.

The most interesting point is the inclusion of the *negotiantes*. From this point we can realize to what extent the old warrior class had not only tended to become farmers but had also moved toward assimilation with the burgher class. We have already found among the Burgundians (Vol. II, p. 330) an indication that far from all of those immigrating into the country settled on the land, and it is, of course, obvious that the counts who lived in cities must have kept a quite significant unit of men close to them and housed them in the city. Hegel has already pointed out that the Lombards in their conquests settled predominantly not in the country but right in the cities.[50] *Arimanni* are continuously mentioned as the influential inhabitants of cities.[51] In the periods of peace between wars, they began to turn to some civilian occupation, but without immediately completely giving up their warrior qualities, and the same development took place among the landowners in the country. We may cite as an analogy from a later period a privilege that Archbishop Gebhard of Bremen announced to the burghers in 1233;[52] he promised that he would not levy the *mercatores* (merchants) for war against their will "exceptis illis mercatoribus, qui vel tamquam minis-teriales, vel tamquam homines ecclesiae ab ecclesia sunt feodati" ("with the exception of those merchants who either as officials or as men of the church have been enfeoffed by the church"). We see therefore that in Bremen the warrior class included enfeoffed people who were at the same time *mercatores*.

*   *   *

EXTRACT FROM AN ITALIAN CAPITULARY OF LEGATES OF CHARLEMAGNE. *M. G.*, 1. 206.

7. Concerning the capability of freemen: that they should do military service according to the size of their property.

13. That counts should not venture to accept or to seek a levy or any contribution for the army from freemen except if a legate from our residence or a legate of our son should come to request that levy.

*   *   *

LOTHAIR'S LEVY FOR A CAMPAIGN AGAINST CORSICA. FEBRUARY 825. *M. G.*, 1. 324.

We decree that all the counts should maintain this bond among those who go to Corsica with them and who are obliged to remain there.

1. We decree that vassals of our house who are *hagastalds* and frequently serve in our palace should remain; their men whom they had before and who recommended themselves to them for this undertaking should remain with their lords. We wish to know who they are who remain on their property and we still wish to consider who goes and who remains. We in fact desire that those who hold our benefices and continue in public life should go.

2. We decree that truly men of bishops or abbots who abide in public life should go with their counts, except for two whom he chose; and we wish that their free *hagastalds* should all be compelled to go except four.

3. Indeed, with regard to the other freemen whom they call *bharigildi*, we decree that all the counts should keep this rule: namely, that they should go who have so great a means of wealth that they are able to go at their own expense and for whom in addition health and strength proved useful; those indeed who have the wealth and, nevertheless, are not able to go should aid the healthy and the poorer. In truth, to freemen of the second rank, who because of their own poverty are not able to go at their own expense but can contribute a share, two, three, or four (in fact, others if it will have been necessary) should be joined who in the view of the count may supply the assistance by which one of them can go. In this way let that order be observed down to others who by their own excessive poverty neither are fit to go nor are able to offer assistance to another. Counts should grant deferments accord-ing to the ancient custom of our vassals to be observed by their counts.

* * *

EXTRACT FROM LOTHAIR'S CAPITULARY OF MAY 825. *M. G.,* 1. 319.

1. We decree that freemen who have so much property from which they are well able to do military service and, being ordered, refuse to serve should on their first offense be subject to the penalty established according to their law. If indeed he will have been negligent a second time, he should pay our army tax, that is 60 *solidi;* if indeed anyone will have been involved a third time in the same misdemeanor, he should know that he will lose all his property or must be sent into exile. Certainly, concerning poor freemen who are not able to do military service at their own expense, we entrust to the loyalty of the counts that among two, three, four, or more if it will have been necessary they should offer assistance to the one who seems better to do our service. Also, as regards these who because of excessive poverty are able neither to do military service at their own expense nor to offer assistance, let them be kept in reserve until they are able to recover.

The fact that the Lombards were overcome by the Franks without even waging a battle may be due less to the larger size of the Frankish Kingdom—for, after all, the Carolingians can only have led moderate-sized armies across the Alps—than to the civilianization of the Lombards, which was not counterbalanced by any feudal system. Now we can see from the preceding capitularies that Charlemagne carried the Frankish military organization over into his Lombard Kingdom. There was a definite emphasis on the point that, when groups were formed to provide a man for the levy, a procedure that was left entirely to the discretion of the counts, the most capable man from a physical viewpoint was to be selected. This suggests the idea that this measure was actually carried out for a time until the pure vassal warrior class also came into existence in this area.

* * *

According to the following capitulary of Louis II of the year 866 (*M. G.,* 2. 94), there was, of course, an attempt even at that time to continue and transform the old system. It reads:

1. Whoever is able to possess his own wergeld from movable property should go in the army. Two who indeed have a moderate wergeld should, joined together, equip the more capable man so that he may be well able to go. Certainly poor men should do guard duty of the coast or of their neighborhood. So it is evident that those who have more than 10 *solidi* of movable property should do the same guard duty. Indeed, let nothing be required of those who do not have more than 10 *solidi* of movable property. Also, if a father will have had a son and the son is more capable than the father, the son should go equipped by his father. If indeed he will have had two sons, whichever of them will have been the more capable should go; the other, however, should remain with his father. But if he will have had more sons, all the more capable should go, and only one, who will have been less capable, should remain. Concerning brothers not separated, we decree according to the capitulary of our lord and father that if there will have been two, both should go; if there will have been three, the one who appeared less capable should remain and the others should go; also, if more will have appeared rather capable, they should go and the less capable one should remain. We decree that there should be no deferment from this

stipulation by order, warrant, or any reason, and neither a count nor a *gastaldus* nor their agents should grant a deferment, except that a count should leave behind one man in each county to guard the same place and two men with his wife. Therefore bishops should not leave behind a layman.

2. In fact, whoever will have dared to remain at home contrary to this law, we ordered his property to be seized forthwith for our use by our legates whom we have at our command and to throw him out; for we want it to be known to all that according to this law property already was confiscated by our predecessors, but by pity they earned the right to claim it. Now, however, know henceforth most certainly that of whomever the property will have been confiscated he will with difficulty earn its recovery.

3. (Here are listed a number of names and regions.) We decree that these should evict the populace, should see to their surveillance, and should have them reside in castles even in peacetime. Now if any legates will have dared to pass them by, he should not confiscate the property of all who will have remained at home nor should he evict them, and if the legate himself will have been found, he should lose his own property. If a count will have left anyone behind with a deferment or his own vassal, except for what we said further above, he should lose his office; similarly, their agents should lose their property and their position, if they will have let anyone go.

4. But if a count or our vassals, although not detained by some illness, will have remained at home or if the abbots and abbesses will not have sent their men in the fullest number, they should lose their offices and their vassals should lose both their property and their benefice. Of the bishops, however, whose vassal will have remained at home without an obvious illness, for such negligence he should pay the following penalty—to reside in the border area until the army should go there another time, insofar as the lord will have deigned to grant this.

5. You should most definitely know that we desire to discharge this campaign with as many men as possible and we establish that if a bishop, count, or our vassal will have been detained by a doubtful illness, the bishop certainly through his legate (whom he considers the better), a count indeed and our vassals in person should affirm by oath that he had remained at home for no reason except that he had been unable to perform this duty because of a most definite illness.

6. In fact, we decree that all should bring with them all their military equipment so that when we have inspected this and have had a list made they may not appear negligent, but also may deserve to have our favor. Moreover, they should have clothing for a year and indeed provisions to last until the country will be able to produce a new harvest.

According to this capitulary, those men are to belong to the field army who own their wergeld in personal property, that is 150 *solidi* for the common freeman, and of those who own half the wergeld in personal property, one man of every two is to be sent. Relief is granted in a few cases, when father and son or several brothers together occupy an undivided parcel of inherited land.

We cannot measure the real effectiveness of this regulation, since we have no measure as to how many men were estimated as having their full wergeld or even only half of it in personal property. In any case, there must have been very many who owned less and the fact that these men were completely excluded from the field army and were mustered only for guard duty or, if they owned less than 10 *solidi,* did not serve at all, necessarily inclines us to approach this whole regulation very cautiously. Even among the men of lesser means, there must have been some who were militarily quite useful and among the well-to-do many who were quite useless. In an army in which the weaknesses of the individual are not compensated for by closely knit and well-disciplined tactical units, a levy based simply on property ownership is not an appropriate means of obtaining troops eager for battle. Consequently, we can hardly avoid the suspicion that in this case, as in that of the edict of Charles the Bald in 864, we are dealing with a pure theory, the concept of an eager advisor at the court that has hardly any connection with the reality of life. The strictness with which the implementation was required and the dispensations were to be limited to a minimum is in any case no proof that the edict actually was carried out in that way.

SCARA

In my explanation of the *scara,* I went back to older concepts espoused by Eichhorn, Stenzel, Lorentz, Barthold, and Peucker, concepts that were then disputed particularly by Waitz (*German Constitutional History* [*Deutsche Verfassungsgeschichte*], 4: 514) and Nitzsch and that have since been generally abandoned, although energetically championed again by Baldamus. Waitz says: "The concept that there existed entire armies of men in the imperial service, as has been said, and that many campaigns were carried out simply by such armies is an assumption that cannot be justified." On the contrary, I think that it is not an assumption but a fact that can be proven with certainty both objectively and literally.

There can be no doubt at all that there always existed warriors in considerable numbers at the courts, and this point is proven in the sources. In Adalhard's court regulations of 826, which are preserved for us in an extract by Hinkmar,[53] it is explained how the body of men who are always present at the court are to be fed. The warriors who have no duties are provided for in alternation by their captains; the serving men (squires) and the vassals of the great lords at the court are provided for by their lords, so that they can live without robbing and stealing.

* * *

27. So that that multitude which always ought to be at the palace might be able to be there continually, it was kept in these three classifications. In the one it is evident that they are battle-ready soldiers without official duties, since the kindness and concern of the lords was put before them and food, clothing, gold, silver, horses, and other decorations were more often offered to them, sometimes individually, some-times as occasion, budget, and rank yielded a very worthy opportunity. Neverthe-less, they always used to have continuing support and a spirit inflamed more and more ardently for obedience to the king, because their officers (called captains) eagerly from one day to another used to call them in individual groups to their estates and hastened to pay them not so much with gluttony as with desire of true friendship and charity, so far as each was capable. Thus it happened that a man rarely remained after a week who was not summoned by some business of this sort.

28. The second classification by its individual duties is similar to students, who clinging to their individual master, both honored and were honored in their indi-vidual posts as the opportunity occurred, so that they might be supported by a lord seeing them and speaking to them. Likewise, the third classification was of older as well as younger boys and vassals, which everyone eagerly made provision to have so far as he was able to govern and support without sin, i.e., robbery or theft. Obvi-ously, among these classifications that have been named, apart from these who

always going and returning frequented the palace, it was desirable that they should meanwhile always be sufficient for a crisis if the enemy suddenly attacked. Always, however, as it was said, the majority of them should be resolute with enjoyment, cheerfulness, and a quick mind on account of the kindnesses recorded further above.

The warriors living at the court also appear in Emperor Lothair's levy against Corsica of the year 825.[54] In this proclamation, a distinction is made between the "dominici vasalli qui austaldi sunt et in nostro palatio frequenter serviunt" ("vassals of the lord who are *hagataslds* and often serve in the palace") and the others "qui in eorum proprietate manent" ("who remain on their property").

For those warriors provided for at the court (not living on their own fief), the names *scara, scarii, scariti* are frequently used in the sources. Whenever the Frankish king stationed his *scara* (units) in garrisons in cities and strongholds that he wanted to secure, those could not have been levies of enfeoffed vassals, since such vassals wanted to return home at the end of a specific period. ("Francos misit Aquitaniam continendo, similiter et in Bituricas Francorum scaram conlocavit": "He sent the Franks to control Aquitania, and similarly he stationed a *scara* of Franks in Bourges"; and "perfecta supradicta castella et disposita per Francos scaras resedentes et ipsa custodientes": "the above-mentioned castles were built and laid out by Frankish *scarae* inhabiting and guarding them").[55]

In the struggle between Pepin and Waifar of Aquitania, Fredegar's successor distinguishes "rex Pippinus in quatuor partes comites suos, scaritos et leudibus suis ad persequendum Waiofarium transmissit" ("King Pepin sent his counts in four divisions, the men of his *scarae* and his entourage (*leudes*) to pursue Waifar"). No matter how this passage is interpreted, it is clear that there is a distinction between the *scariti* and the *leudes* (vassals).[56]

And it can have been no more of a question of vassal levies in 803, when Charlemagne sent his *scariti* into the surrounding area where it seemed expedient, without waging actual warfare ("sine hoste fecit eodem anno, excepto quod scaras suas transmisit in circuitu, ubi necesse fuit"; "In the same year he acted without an army except that he sent his own *scarae* into the neighborhood where it was necessary").[57]

When Charlemagne transplanted the Saxons in 804 from the Wigmodia district into another region, he had them conducted by his *scarae* ("misit scaras suas . . . ut illam gentem foris patriam transduceret": "he sent his own *scarae* . . . to transfer that nation outside the country").[58]

In a source concerning the division of the Duchy of Benevento of the year 851,[59] each of the contracting parties was authorized to move through his area with his army and his *scara* ("vos vestrumque populum liceat per terram meam transire contra illos hostiliter et cum scara, ad vindicandum absque homicidio vel incendio et depraedatione seu zala de populo et terra mea et oppressione castellorum portionis meae, excepta erba et ligna et aqua, quos vobis non negabimus": "Let it be permitted that you and your people go through my territory against them with your army and your *scara* to punish them without the murder, burning, looting or pillage of people, my land, and seizure of the castles of my territory, with the exception of grass, wood, and water, which we will not deny you").

When Emperor Arnulf besieged Bergamo in 894, the annals of Fulda mention that the *milites palatini* had fought with particular zeal under the eyes of their lord.[60]

On one occasion a bishop had a man arrested by an "ostinarius vel scario"[61] ("member of the army or member of a *scara*"), who later in the account is called "vasallus."

In 869 Charles the Bald had a conflict with Bishop Hinkmar of Laon, who refused to obey a summons from the king. The king thereupon dispatched a *scara* to bring the bishop in by force ("scaram ex quamplurimis comitibus regni sui confectam Laudanum misit, ut ipsum episcopum ad eum violenter perducerent": "He sent to Laon a *scara* from as many counts of his realm as possible to bring back the bishop to him by force").[62]

In one instance, in 877, the *scariti* appear specifically as the entourage, the retinue of a count palatine, not simply as common soldiers. It is prescribed that, in case the count palatine should be unable to do so, "unus eorum, qui cum eo scariti sunt" ("one of them who are members of the *scara* with him") should conduct the court hearings in his place.[63]

Even if we should believe that one or another of these passages would permit some other interpretation, there are still enough of them to prove that in the Carolingian period there were armed men at the courts who were used for both military and police purposes and were referred to, among other designations, by the word *scara* and its derivatives.

This point is not negated by the fact that the word *scara* and its derivatives also appear with other meanings, such as simply "army unit" and "army,"[64] and then again as "service" or "performance" that is required of certain farms or families.[65] On the contrary, it is specifically this branching of the meaning of the word that gives new proof of its root.

Waitz was satisfied with the conclusion that on the one hand the word *scara* generally "meant army units, small or large, including also entire armies, without regard to their composition or organization," and on the other hand that it had "a completely different meaning," that is, the "performance of duties by dependent men for their lords," especially courier and escort services.[66] How did it happen that the same word could take on such a different meaning? Our interpretation gives the answer to this question: the original concept is that of the service of the military man (*Kriegsknecht*), the strong armed hand constantly available in the house of his lord. From this starting point, we come on the one hand to the "military unit" (*Kriegsschar*) and finally to the completely general concept of "army;" for, since these armed men were maintained not only at the royal court but also every individual count, bishop, or abbot had a certain number of them, together they formed a significant part of the overall army,[67] and it was possible that smaller expeditions were carried out by them alone, without calling up enfeoffed vassals.

In many other passages where the men of the *scara* appear in a military undertaking, it is therefore not immediately apparent whether it is a question of the call-up of vassals or of the household warriors whom we envisage (or, to use the Danish expression, "house fellows" [*Hauskerle*]). But since these warriors of the household also performed duties as armed escorts, sentries, couriers, gate guards, and police, the designation was broadened to cover all these services, even when they were not carried out by such permanently assigned serving men but were imposed as continuing requirements on men living on the property and families or farms. If one considers the original meaning of the word as the services performed, messenger service, or something of the sort, then it is difficult to see how the word is supposed to have come to mean "army." If the meaning "army" is considered to be the original sense, then it is difficult to see how, for example, the obligation to travel twice a year by boat to Saint Goar or Duisburg, a requirement placed on a peasant of the Prüm Monastery, can be referred to as "*scara*."[68]

Baldamus comes closest to the correct concept in *The Military Organization under the Later Carolingians* (*Das Heerwesen unter den späteren Karolingern*), pp. 69 ff., where he also assembles the convincing citations. I would like to disagree with him only on the point that he considers security and police service as the basic significance of the *scara*, speaks of an "amalgamation" of the police and military systems, and finds in it the transition to the condition where the police were considered as a part of the army. It is not a question of the melding of two separate functions: the police function is not the original one, to which the

military one was later added, but there is at the base of all this an original, completely
unitary concept, that of the armed might that has to overcome both internal and external
enemies. The retinue that the ancient Germanic prince had around him, "in bello prae-
sidium, in pace decus" ("in war his guard, in peace his honor"), naturally served him also
in peacetime, not simply theoretically for the enhancement of his prestige but also practically for the establishment and maintaining of his authority. The *scara* was the same thing,
only in a much lower social status; the retainers were the dining companions of their lord,
whereas the men of the *scara* were a much larger number of common fighting men, naturally
in large part unfree men, the successors of the *pueri* ("boys") of the Merovingian period
and the predecessors of the *ministeriales* of the following centuries. Of course, we should
not regard the latter as identical, for, at least according to the generally accepted assumption, the status of the unfree man is the significant trait of the *ministeriales,* a point that can
neither be proven nor assumed concerning the men of the *scara.* The process that we
observe in the later period, where on the one hand the lack of freedom of the *ministeriales*
becomes looser and looser and more and more meaningless, and on the other hand freemen voluntarily give up their freedom and enter this condition, probably had already begun
much earlier than we can directly establish from the sources. Consequently, when Baldamus
directly questions the development of the *ministeriales* from the men of the *scara,* he
certainly is correct to the extent that the men of the *scara* were not unfree men, abstractly
speaking. But the factor of freedom and lack of freedom is not the only one in these institutions, and not the deciding one. This decisive factor is the work of the warrior in the
direct service of a lord. Basically, Baldamus is saying essentially the same thing; the difference that perhaps still remains between us lies only in the formulation and expression
of the concept.

(Added in the second edition). A certain analogy in the reverse direction is offered by the
fact that, as is now proven in the fourth volume of this work, the word *Landsknecht*
originally meant a policeman and was then extended to refer to soldiers.

NOTES FOR CHAPTER I

1. *Lex Ripuaria* (Ripuarian Law), 36. 11. *M. G. LL.,* 5. 231.

2. A cow is equated to 1 *solidus.* The expression "3 *solidi,*" which we
find in one of the manuscripts, is obviously false, since an ox is counted
as 2 *solidi* and a mare as 3. In a capitulary of Louis the Pious of the year
829, a cow is indicated in one place as the equivalent of 2 *solidi.*

3. (Note to the second edition). The economic base of the Carolingian military organization is, as shown in Vol. II, a barter economy.
Alfons Dopsch, in his *Economic Development of the Carolingian Period*
(*Wirtschaftsentwicklung der Karolingerzeit*), especially Vol. II, para. 12, has
recently claimed to prove that the generally accepted concept of this
barter economy is incorrect and that there existed along with it a very
considerable money economy. Consequently, he claims, the contrast
between antiquity and the Middle Ages in this respect and in general is
very overemphasized. I cannot agree with him. I find, on the contrary, the
conclusions of my studies on the changes in military organization to be a

new confirmation of the accepted concept. The transition from the Roman legionary to the medieval knight is not conceivable without the shift of the ancient money economy into a barter economy. See my review of Dopsch in the *Deutsche Politik*, 26 (1921): 620. "Römertum und Germanentum."

4. The *plebs urbana* (urban dwellers) were not considered as com-, pletely free in the Merovingian period. Brunner, *German Legal History* (*Deutsche Rechtsgeschichte*), 1: 253, says: "We cannot determine with certainty how the decrease in freedom was expressed in a legal sense." There can be no doubt that it is a question of the difference between the warrior and the nonwarrior. That point is not clear in Brunner because he believes, like Roth, in a general military obligation. According to the capitulary *M. G. Capitularia Reg. Franc.*, ed. Boretius, 1: 145, the tenant farmers were counted among the unfree men.

5. God. Kurth, in "The Nationalities in Auvergne" ("Les Nationalités en Auvergne"), *Bulletin de la Classe des Lettres de l'Académie Belgique*, 11 (1899): 769 and 4 (1900): 224, proves with respect to Auvergne that no Franks at all settled there. In that region, even the great families holding the position of count were Romanics. Of almost all of the few Germans who appear in Auvergne, it can be proven that they did not settle there, except perhaps for a very few West Goths.

6. Numerous references in Guilhiermoz, *Essai sur l'origine de la noblesse française,* p. 490.

7. *Ancien Coutumier d'Anjou.* Cited by Guilhiermoz, p. 366.

8. Nithard IV, Chap. 2.

9. Already explained by Boretius, *Contributions to the Critique of the Capitularies (Beiträge zur Capitularienkritik)*, p. 128, as a simple repetition from previous documents.

10. Cited by Baldamus in *The Military Organization under the Later Carolingians (Das Heerwesen unter den späteren Karolingern)*, p. 12.

11. Hinkmar of Reims writes in the document against his nephew, the bishop of Laon (870): "De hoc quippe vitio superbiae descendit quod multi te apud plurimos dicunt de fortitudine et agilitate tui corporis gloriari et de praeliis, atque, ut nostratum lingua dicitur, de vassaticis frequenter ac libenter sermonem habere, et qualiter ageres si laicus fuisses irreverenter referre." ("Certainly it comes from this sin of pride that many among the masses tell you to boast of your body's strength and agility and of battles, and, as it is said in our language, to speak willingly and often with vassals and to reply disrespectfully, just as you would act if you had been a layman.") I take this interesting extract of the document from Guilhiermoz, *Essai sur l'origine de la noblesse française,* p. 438, where other examples of that special usage are also given.

12. Maitland, *Domesday Book and Beyond,* 1891, p. 511.

13. When it is reported in the *Annales Bertin.* for the year 869 that for the garrison of a newly erected fort Charles the Bald called up one *gastaldus* (*scaramannus:* warrior without a fief) from every 100 hides of land and a wagon with two oxen from every 1,000 hides, this does not give us any specific number, since it was not known at the court how many hides there were in each county. Consequently, this is only a very approximate reference, like the levy by groups.

14. In his *German and French Constitutional History* (*Deutsche und französische Verfassungsgeschichte*), Ernst Mayer has no doubt recognized the contradiction in the source material, but the solution that he gives in Vol. I, p. 123, is impossible. He claims that on the Rhine, in Bavaria, and in Gothic Southern France only the Germans took the field, whereas between the Seine and the Loire the general military obligation applied also to the Romans. One can imagine how such a Roman militia would have shown up between the Franks and the Goths!

15. That also applies when, as we later find prescribed in the Weissenburg service law and elsewhere, the *ministeriale* was supposed to be provisioned by the *curia* after the crossing of the Alps. Baltzer, pp. 69, 73. Waitz 8: 162.

16. A manuscript of the Theodon Capitulary of 805, Chap. 5, contains the sentence: "et ut servi lanceas non portent, et qui inventus fuerit post bannum hasta frangatur in dorso ejus" ("and that the unfree should not carry lances, and a spear should be broken on the back of whoever was found doing so after the order"). Waitz, *Verfassungsgeschichte,* 1st ed., 4: 454, interprets that to mean that the common soldiers who followed their lords to war were absolutely forbidden to carry the lance as their individual weapon. This interpretation is not acceptable. That chapter has to do with the bearing of weapons in peacetime ("*in patria*": "in one's own country") and with the suppression of feuds. Freemen were forbidden to carry arms (shield, lance, and armor) in peacetime, but no specific punishment was provided. In the case of serving men, this prohibition was backed by a threat of punishment.

17. The source passages are to be found in Prenzel, *Contributions to the History of Military Organization under the Carolingians* (*Beiträge zur Geschichte des Kriegswesens unter den Karolingern*), Leipzig dissertation, 1887, p. 34, and in Waitz, *Deutsche Verfassungsgeschichte,* 4: 455.

18. Multiple references are to be found in Guilhiermoz, p. 245.

19. *Annales Fuldenses* (*Annals of Fulda*) for the year 894; *Annales Altahenses* (*Annals of Niederalteich*) for the year 1044; Thietmar, 6: 16.

20. Peez, in "The Travels of Charlemagne" ("Die Reisen Karls des Grossen"), *Schmollers Jahrbücher für Gesetzgebung,* 2 (1891): 16, assem-

bles all of Charlemagne's travels and estimates that on the average he covered 1,100 miles each year of his reign. In the year 776 his travels amounted to almost 1,900 miles, and in 800 he covered almost 2,000 miles.

21. *Imperial Courts in the Lippe, Ruhr, and Diemel Areas (Reichshöfe im Lippe-, Ruhr-, und Diemelgebiet)*, 1901. *The Franks: Their System of Conquest and Settlement in the German Regions (Die Franken, ihr Eroberungs- und Siedlungssystem im deutschen Volkslande)*, 1904.

22. Brunner, *Deutsche Rechtsgeschichte*, 2: 57 ff., where all the source passages are also cited.

23. Daniels, in *Manual of German Imperial and National Legal History (Handbuch der deutschen Reichs- und Staatenrechtsgeschichte)*, 1: 424, 463, has already correctly observed that under the Merovingians the entire population cannot possibly have taken the oath. But his basis from the sources, on the other hand, has been correctly rejected by Waitz, *Deutsche Verfassungsgeschichte,* 2d ed., 3: 296. The entire argument, however, arose from the erroneous interpretation of the basic concept, that is, of the Frankish people. Daniels was entirely right in believing that only the warriors took the oath, but he was in error in believing that this warrior class was already a class of vassals at that time. Waitz was right in his belief that the entire people (*Volk*) took the oath but incorrect in identifying this "people" with the population. As a result of our determination that the sources of the period are referring to the warriors (*Kriegsvolk*) when they say "people" (*Volk*), the entire dispute has become baseless. From the formal, juridical, and source-based viewpoints, Waitz is right; but objectively, in that the warrior class of the Merovingian period was the precursor of the vassal class of Carolingian times, Daniels is right.

24. The oath in the *Capitulare missorum* (Capitulary of legates), *M. G.,* 1. 66 reads as follows in the corrected text (see Appendix 2 for Latin text):

How that oath ought to have been sworn by bishops and abbots, or counts and vassal princes, also deputies, archdeacons and clerks.

3. Clerics, who do not seem to live completely like monks; and where they keep the rules of Saint Benedict according to his order, they should promise in word as much as in truth, and some of these the abbots especially should bring to our lord.

4. Then advocates, deputies, or whoever will have been elected as elders, and the whole mass of the people, twelve-year-old boys as well as old men, whoever had come to the assembly and are able to

fulfill and observe the order of their lords, whether peasants or men of bishops, abbesses, and counts or men of others, royal sub-tenants, tenants, clerics, and serfs, whoever as honored men hold benefices and services or were honored in vassalage since they are able to have the horses of their lord, arms, shield, lance, sword, and short sword, all should swear. And they should carry with them the names and number of these in a list, the counts likewise divided by single *centenae* [subdivisions of a county], just as those who were born within a district and will have been peasants and those from elsewhere who have been committed in vassalage.

Finally, warnings to those who want to escape the oath.

25. *Contin. Fred.*, Chap. 135 (*Chronicarum quae dicuntur Fredegarii scholastici libri IV cum Continuationibus:* Four books of Chronicles which are said to be by Fredegarius Scholasticus with continuations).

26. *Annales Lauresh.* (*Annals of Lorch*) for the year 773. The duke of Benevento and all the Beneventans were also summoned to do their duty by messengers. Waitz 3: 255.

27. Waitz 4: 437.

28. Baltzer, p. 48, believes that the bow was not mentioned as a weapon of war in Germany before the twelfth century. But that is not correct. The opposing pieces of evidence are assembled in Waitz, *Verfas-sungsgeschichte* 8: 123. Widukind 3: 28 tells of two outstanding warriors who were cut down by arrows in 953. In 3: 54, Otto has the Slavs fired on with arrows. Bruno, Chap. 61, mentions *"sagittarii"* ("archers"). *Con-tinuatio Reginonis* (*Continuation of the Annals of Regino*) for 962 has the Germans using marksmen (*"sagittarii et fundibularii":* "archers and sling-ers") in the siege of an Italian stronghold. Richard Richer has a similar account at the siege of Verdun in 984.

29. As cited in Waitz 4: 458.

30. *Capitulary of Diedenhofen* of the year 805. *M. G.*, 1. 123. "De armatura in exercitu sicut iam antea in alio capitulare commendavimus, ita servetur, et insuper omnis homo de duodecim mansis bruneam habeat; qui vero bruniam habens et eam secum non tullerit, omne be-neficium cum brunia pariter perdat." ("Concerning armament in the army let it thus be observed, just as we have already commanded before in another capitulary. In addition, every man with twelve holdings should have a mail tunic; indeed, whoever possesses a mail tunic and will not have brought it with him should lose his whole benefice together with his mail tunic.")

31. *Capitulary of Aachen. M. G.*, 1. 171, Chap. 9.

De hoste pergendi, ut comiti in suo comitatu per bannum unumquemque hominem per sexaginta solidos in hostem pergere bannire studeat, ut ad placitum denuntiatum ad illum locum ubi iubetur veniant. Et ipse comis praevideat quomodo sint parati, id est lanceam, scutum et arcum cum duas cordas, sagittas duodecim. De his uterque habeant. Et episcopi, comites, abbates hos homines habeant qui hoc bene praevideant et ad diem denuntiati placiti veniant et ibi ostendant quomodo sint parati. Habeant loricas vel galeas et temporalem hostem, id est aestivo tempore.

Chap. 17. Quod nullus in hoste baculum habeat, sed arcum.

(When the army is on the march, [we order] that it should be the business of a count to proclaim by edict in his county that each man in lieu of 60 *solidi* should do military service, and that they should come to the assembly announced at that place where it is commanded. The count himself should have an eye to how they have been equipped, that is, lance, shield, a bow with two strings, and twelve arrows. Each of them should have these. Bishops, counts, and abbots should have these men who see to this well, and they should come on the day of the announced assembly and there they should show how they have been equipped. They should have breastplates, helmets, and an army for the season, that is in the summer time.

Chap. 17. That no one in the army should have a staff, but a bow.)

32. Gessler, *The Cutting and Thrusting Weapons of the Carolingian Period* (*Die Trutzwaffen der Karolingerzeit*), Basel, 1908. See also in this connection *Zeitschrift für historische Waffenkunde*, Vol. V, 2: 63. According to Lindenschmidt, p. 151, almost all the bows found in Merovingian graves are 7 feet long. Köhler, 3: 113, states 5 feet.

33. Roth, *Feudalism and the Unit of Dependents* (*Feudalität und Untertanenverband*), p. 33. Baltzer, *On the History of the German Military System* (*Zur Geschichte des deutschen Kriegswesens*), p. 2. Boretius, *Contributions to the Critique of the Capitularies* (*Beiträge zur Capitularienkritik*), p. 123.

34. The words in brackets are found in the manuscripts in a later passage, where they make no sense. Boretius placed them here, where they are reasonably acceptable but at least superfluous. In any event, the handwritten version of the capitulary has little reliability.

35. This fourth version is repeated in the edition of the *Monumenta* as a simple variant of the second version, probably not entirely correctly.

36. *SS.* I, p. 481.

37. *SS.* II, p. 593.

38. Soetbeer, *Studies on German History* (*Forschungen zur deutschen Geschichte*), Vols. I and II. Peschel, "On the Variations of the Relative Currency Value, etc." ("Ueber die Schwankungen der Werthrelation usw."), *Deutsche Vierteljahresschrift,* 4 (1853): 1 ff.

39. Capitulary of 807. See pp. 31 and 32, above. Waitz 4: 473.

40. Boretius, *Beiträge,* p. 145.

41. In *Polyptychon Irminonis* 2: 274 (**XXV**. 20), two men together pay 2 *solidi* as substitute levy tax (*Heerbann*): "Solvunt de airbanno sol. II. Polypt. de St. Maur des Fossés, Chap. 6." ("They pay 2 *solidi* for the army tax. *Polyptychon* of Saint Maur des Fossés, Chapter 6.") (Guérard, *Polyptychon of Irminon,* 2: 284). "Solvunt vestiti mansi hairbannum pro homine redimendo de hoste sol 3." ("Invested estates pay 3 *solidi* to hire men for the army.") Compare Waitz 4: 485, Note 5 (1st ed.) and Flach, *Les origines de l'ancienne France,* 1: 321. See also Waitz 8: 147, Note 5, and p. 148, Note 1. Waitz believes that in the sources quoted there it is a question of "the old legal fine," "that clergical establishments were excused from or had it turned over to them." It seems to me that under Otto III, Henry II, and Henry V there can no longer be a question of the *Heerbann* in the sense of "the old legal fine" but that it was simply a matter of tax. Kötzschke, "Army Taxes in the Carolingian Period" ("Heeressteuern in karolingischer Zeit"), *Historische Vierteljahresschrift,* 10 (1899): 231 gives evidence of the relationship between a later Saxon tax and the *adjutorium* introduced in the Carolingian period.

42. Still indicated in Boretius, *Beiträge,* as the Capitulary of 817.

43. The punishment for absence from the levy is similar to the Frankish *Heerbann,* but differently provided for in its details. A distinction is made between the first, second, and third instances. Brunner, *Deutsche Rechtsgeschichte,* 2: 213.

44. "Mariniano Episcopo Ravennati cum ceteris fratribus et coepis copis sacerdotibus, levitis, clero, nobilibus, populo, militibus Ravenna consistentibus. Ep. VI, 31. Nobilibus, militibus ac populo Jaderae. Ep. VI, 27." ("To Marinianus, bishop of Ravenna, with his other brothers, fellow bishops, priests, deacons, clerics, nobles, people, and soldiers at Ravenna. Epistle VI, 31. To the nobles, soldiers, and people of Jadera. Epistle VI, 27.") Cited by Hegel, *History of Municipal Organization in Italy* (*Geschichte der Städteverfassungen von Italien*), 1: 196.

45. "Si inveneritis contrarium in tali causa exercitum, tacitum habitote." ("If you will have found the army hostile to such a thing, keep quiet henceforth.") Hegel, *Städteverfassungen von Italien,* 1: 239.

46. Liudprand, *Historia Ottonis* (*The History of Otto*), Chap. 9.

47. Paulus, II, Chap. 32.

48. In the *Monumenta* and Boretius, the second chapter ends here, with the word *acrum* (bow), the third chapter begins with *Item,* and between *habent* and *qui* there is a colon instead of a period. The sense of the third chapter would therefore be: "With respect to those merchants who have no money, we ordain: the '*majores et potentes*' (richer and powerful) shall have armor, a horse, etc." That is obviously impossible, and Boretius, *Beiträge,* p. 132, has therefore interpreted *pecunias* as real property. But *pecunias* does not mean land ownings. For the interpretation of this passage, I turned to my colleague Heinrich Brunner, and with his advice I have undertaken the changes of the arrangement and punctuation through which all the difficulties seem to be eliminated in the most felicitous way.

49. I believe I may be allowed to interpret the text in this way. The conjecture "ut si non possunt habere scutum" ("that if they are not able to have a shield") has been justifiably rejected by Boretius, p. 133. The sentence must be read in this way: "ut si possunt habere scutum, habeant [scutum] cocorra cum sagittas et arcum; [si non possunt habere scutum, habeant cocorra cum sagittas et arcum]." ("that if they are able to have a shield, they should have [a shield], quiver with arrows and bow; [if they are not able to have a shield, they should have a quiver with arrows and bow]"). I do not mean that the words in brackets should be inserted in the text; rather, it is more in keeping with the abrupt, incomplete style of the whole document that they should not be included; but we must have something like them in mind as we read the passage.

50. 1: 345, 368.

51. Hegel 2:27.

52. *Book of Original Bremen Documents* (*Bremer Urkundenbuch*), ed. Ehmk and Bippen, Vol. I, No. 172.

53. M. G., *Capitulare reg. Francorum,* 2: 517.

54. M. G., *Capitulare,* 1: 352.

55. *Annales regni Francorum,* ed. Kurze, pp. 24, 48. In the revision, the words shown above are replaced by "dispositoque ibi necnon et in Biturica civitate Francorum praesidio" ("after a garrison of Franks had been stationed there and at Bourges") and in the second passage "in utroque (castello) non modico praesidio relicto" ("after a large garrison had been left in each [castle]").

56. M. G. SS. Rer. Meroving., 2. 192, Chap. 135 (52). The most logical interpretation would seem to me to be that the author is listing the counts with their levies, the king's own men whom he settled in the

country, and the soldiers of the court (*Hauskerle*), the standing military escort and life-guard.

57. *Annales Lauresham., SS.* 1. 39. Similarly, *Annales Guelferbytani* for the year 793. *SS.* 1. 45.

58. *Chronik von Moissac. SS.* 2. 257.

59. *LL.* 4. 221.

60. *SS.* 1. 409.

61. Monach Sangall. *Gesta Caroli,* SS. 2. 738.

62. *Annales Bertin., SS.* 1. 480.

63. *Capitulare Caracense* (*Capitulary of Carcassonne*), Chap. 17. *Capitularia Regum Francorum,* 2. 359. The fragment of a capitulary in Vol. I, 213, may not be interpreted in any other way: "Ut missi nostri una cum sociis qui in eorum scara commanere videntur" etc. ("That our legates together with their comrades who are seen to remain in their *scara* ...").

64. *Annales regni Francorum,* ed. Kurze, p. 40: "mittens quatuor scaras in Saxoniam" ("sending four *scarae* into Saxony") (774); in the revision (and similarly quite often): "tripertitum misit exercitum" ("he sent an army in three divisions"). Hinkmar speaks of a "scara de Nortmannis" ("*scara* of Normans") *SS.* 1. 515. Erchambert *hist. Lang.,* Chap. 35: "super Saracenorum scaram irruit" ("he attacked a *scara* of Saracens"). *SS.* 3. 252. Other passages are to be found in Waitz, *Deutsche Verfassungsgeschichte* 4: 611 (2d ed.). The opinion to the effect that the evidence that under some circumstances *scara* simply means "army" or "army unit," as, for example, in Charles' letter to his wife Fastrada (*M. G. Form. Merov. et Karol.,* p. 510), was sufficient to contradict the other interpretation has been abandoned by Waitz himself in his second edition (4: 514; 2d ed., p. 610).

65. These passages are so frequent that special citations are not necessary. Cäsarius von Heisterbach says: "Scaram facere est domino abbati quando ipse jusserit, servire et nuncium ejus seu litteras ad locum sibi determinatum deferre." ("To do a *scara* is to serve the lord abbot when he ordered and to take his message or letter to the place determined by him.")

Lothair assigns five freemen to the Murbach Monastery on the condition that they should now provide for the monastery the same service they have previously given the state. In this document the "*iter exercitale,*" consequently the levy for the war, is distinguished from "*scaras.*" The source reads: "de itinere exercitali seu scaras vel quamcumque quis ire praesumat aut mansionaticos aut mallum custodire, aut navigia facere vel alias functiones vel freda exactare: et quidquid ad partem comitum ac juniorum eorum seu successorum exigere poterat." ("to guard with the levy, whether *scarae* or whatever anyone ventures to turn out, either the way-stations or the assembly place or to make voyages or to discharge other duties or penalties: whatever he could exact in behalf of the counts, their subordinates or successors.") Bouquet 8: 366, No. 2, cited by Baldamus, p. 71.

66. *Deutsche Verfassungsgeschichte* 4: 23 (2d ed., p. 26).

67. "servientes . . . quos scaremannos vocamus . . . cum ceteris nostrae familiae militibus servire debent" ("men in service . . . whom we call *scaremanni* . . . ought to serve with the other soldiers of our household"). *Mittelrheinische Urkundenbücher* 382. Vol. I, p. 439.

68. Baldamus, p. 76.

Chapter II

The Subjugation of the Saxons

Now that we have become convinced of how small Charlemagne's armies were, there arises with renewed persistence this question: How could he succeed in subjugating those Germanic peoples against whom the Romans, with their so much larger, economically so much stronger empire, and their perhaps tenfold stronger, disciplined armies had previously failed? For it is not only physically, on the same soil, but also to some extent spiritually the same struggle that once took place between Germanicus and Arminius that was now taking place between Charles and Wittekind. Charles not only assumed the title Augustus but he also intended, being Germanic by descent, to renew the concept of the Roman Empire and to extend the Roman system, as it survived in the form of the Church, over those peoples on the banks of the Weser who defended themselves from this yoke 750 years earlier. Although undoubtedly very strong dislocations, extirpations, and migrations had taken place, the tribes to the west and east of the Weser, who had now become known as Saxons (how this came about is not known; Tacitus did not yet know this name), were basically the same ones or very close relatives of those who fought the battle of the Teutoburger Forest, stood up to Germanicus at Idistaviso and the dike of the Angrivarii, and maintained their freedom and their individual way of life so long, only now to have to surrender both.

The first great difference between the times of Emperor Augustus and those of King and later Emperor Charles is that the pagan Germanic area that was still free in the second period was much smaller than in the first. The immediate right bank of the Rhine, Hesse, and Thuringia already belonged to the Frankish Kingdom. When the Romans, advancing on the Lippe route, pushed up to the Weser, they found themselves deep in enemy territory, threatened on all sides, with only a single link to their rear. The border of the kingdom that Charles took over extended a few miles south of the Lippe and up to the Saale, so that the Frankish army was able to move into Saxony both from the south and the west and could withdraw in either direction.

It is probably also important for us to realize that the area of the Saxons extended no farther to the east than the Saale and the Elbe. Even to the west of the Elbe there were already hostilely inclined Slavic tribes. Even if the Germans to the east of the Elbe did not in earlier days intervene directly in the struggle with the Romans, it may well have influenced the decisions of the leaders on both sides to know that behind the Cherusci there were still more Germanic tribes that were capable of entering the war.

If then the task of the Frankish-Roman emperor was from the start a much smaller one, nevertheless he lacked the most important supporting factor which had enabled the Romans to wage their wars—the fleet that had brought them their provisions across the North Sea and up the Ems, the Weser, or the Elbe. Charles would have found it just as impossible as Germanicus to feed armies of 60,000 to 70,000 men in the interior of Saxony without the use of the sea route and the support of a large fleet. The fact that he carried out his operations with much smaller armies enabled him to dispense with the fleet.

Our question, then, boils down more specifically to this: How did it come about that Charles, with a much smaller army, finally reached the goal that eluded the Romans? In the final analysis, the answer must be sought less on the side of the attackers than on that of the defenders. If the Saxons had been the same kind of men that the Cherusci, Bructeri, Marsi, and Angrivarii had once been, armies of a few thousand mounted men would not have been able to do much against them. But time had left its mark even on these sons of nature; the transition from the prehistoric natural condition into human, historical development had been initiated and carried through to fruition. The strength of the early Germanic tribes was based on absolute barbarism, in which the man is only a warrior and only the warrior is a man. This condition had already disappeared by the eighth century. We learn from the sources that in Saxony unfree men and men possessing only partial freedom were very numerous.[1] It is not unlikely that that was the result of a subjugation of Germans by Germans and that the spread of the Saxon name was related to those events. Unfree men and men of limited freedom are no longer warriors in the full sense, the sense of Arminius's contemporaries and compatriots. The Saxons had not yet progressed to the point of building cities and developing urban life. With that exception, however, we may imagine their condition as similar to that in which Caesar portrays the Gauls. The separation of the population into a warrior class or knightly class on the one hand and peasants and burghers with little warlike inclination on the other hand, as Caesar once found the situation in Gaul and as it had developed anew in the Frankish Kingdom—this separation must already have been strongly pronounced among the Saxons. Otherwise, they would not have so quickly and easily adapted themselves to the social conditions of the Franks after their conquest. But if this was the case, Charlemagne found himself facing a completely different task from the one that Tiberius and Germanicus had once faced. The Roman commanders could advance into Germany only with very large armies and could send out only very strong detachments, because without a great superiority they would have been exposed to destruction at any moment. The Saxons, despite all the individual courage they may have had, were no longer so dangerous. In the following chapters, we shall be shown again and again what a difference in military strength is caused by an interval of a few stages of civilization. The pagan Saxons had become a few stages—perhaps not yet many stages—more economic-minded, more civilianized, and softer than the Cherusci. That is the ultimate reason why much smaller armies than that of Varus could risk moving through their country.

But with this basic difference not only are the numbers changed but also the other strategic conditions of waging war.

The large size of the Roman armies resulted in the immeasurable difficulty of feeding the troops, a situation that bound the Romans almost entirely to the water routes. The smaller Carolingian armies were able to take along their provisions by land.

The cultivation of the land had also no doubt progressed considerably, another factor that facilitated the feeding of men and horses, draft oxen, and meat animals for the invading enemy.

Nevertheless, the Franks' task was still difficult enough. There could be no thought of a strategy like that which Caesar once used in Gaul, namely, that large armies remained concentrated, established themselves in the middle of the country, and immediately overwhelmed any rising opposition. Charles, of course, did not have such armies at his disposal. Let us see how the Frankish king went about his mission.

In the year 772 Charles pushed out from Hesse via Obermarsberg on the Diemel, where the Eresburg was situated and was now captured, into Saxony. He moved as far as the Weser and there made a treaty with the Saxons (or only with the Angrians). Although no real opposition was offered, the Franks did not move more than some 45 miles beyond the border.

After the Saxons in 774 made an incursion into Frankish territory, moving as far as Fritzlar, the Franks began in the following year, after the king had returned from subjugating the Lombards in Italy, the systematic attack that was to lead to the complete subjection of the Saxons. First of all, the Frankish army, without significant opposition, captured the two Saxon border forts, Sigiburg (Hohensyburg) on the Ruhr and Eresburg, moved on to the Weser, where a Saxon army tried in vain to prevent their crossing, and proceeded up to the Ocker, north of the Harz Mountains. One corps, which was moving on the left bank of the Weser via the Teutoburger Forest and the Wiehen range, allowed itself to be surprised by the Saxons at Lübbecke and seems to have surrendered on the condition of being allowed to withdraw freely.[2] In the meantime, however, the Eastphalians and the Angrians had already negotiated with Charles on the Ocker and had subjected themselves, and when the Frankish army, returning across the Weser, now appeared in the area of the Westphalians, they too gave in and sent hostages.

These events allow no other conclusion than that there existed among the Saxon leaders a strong faction that was not unhappy to see their country enter into the Frankish imperial union and that indeed perhaps definitely desired this. Already in a much earlier day, of course, perhaps the majority of the Cherusci princes had favored the Romans; we recall, even if it is poetic fiction, that famous conversation between Arminius and his brother Flavus. Despite the preceding struggles, and although the Franks had destroyed the sacred Irmen column in 772, the Saxons now submitted to them without a decisive battle and without the Franks' having taken a very important part of their country. It may be some 95 miles from the Frankish border to the Ocker. It might perhaps not be impossible that the Saxons only made a pretense of submitting and hoped to deceive the Franks with friendly words and that Charles was willing to settle on a treaty because his teams and his rations were not sufficient for a campaign farther into their country. But the following events show that he really was counting on a half-voluntary annexation of the Saxons and was justified in this anticipation. He not only refrained from moving forward to the lower Weser or the Elbe, but he also occupied as bases for his domination only the two border forts of Sigiburg and Eresburg. When in the next year the freedom-loving Saxons rebelled again, captured Eresburg, and vainly blockaded Sigiburg, Charles needed simply to appear on the scene in order to bring about at once another shift of power and give the upper hand to the Frankish faction.[3] While he was still at the sources of the Lippe and had therefore just crossed the border, crowds of Saxons came to meet him in order to plead for his mercy and to submit to him once again. Even now he did nothing more to

Fig. 1   GERMANY FROM THE RHINE TO THE ELBE

strengthen his hegemony than to restore the Eresburg and to build on the Lippe, and therefore still very close to the border, the Karlsburg, a fort whose exact location is not known. The next year (777), in the area where the Saxons had subjected themselves, near the sources of the Lippe in Paderborn, Charles held a general diet and a synod at which the leaders of the Saxons appeared, with the exception of the Westphalian Wittekind, who had fled to the Danes.

When in the following year (778) Charles was on the far side of the

Pyrenees, Wittekind once again called his compatriots to arms. They thrust across the border, pushed up to the Rhine at Deutz, moved a certain distance up the Rhine, and withdrew through the Lahn valley. But they had taken only one of the three Frankish forts on Saxon soil, Karlsburg. On their retreat they were overtaken on the Eder by Frankish warriors returning from Spain and suffered losses, and when the king himself appeared in the following year with a significant army, there was once again no question of serious opposition. A stronghold that the Saxons had erected on the Westphalian-Frankish border, north of the Lippe at Bocholt, was taken by the Franks. Charles marched up to the Weser, and all the people submitted to him. (The route he followed and the place "Medofulli," where he reached the Weser and set up his camp, cannot be determined.) The next year (780), without encountering any opposition, he moved for the first time as far as the Elbe, which he reached north of Magdeburg, at the mouth of the Ohre.

In 782 there took place at Paderborn, the place at which all the Saxons could most easily assemble with the Franks, a new diet, which proclaimed the complete incorporation of Saxony into the Frankish-Christian King-dom. The Saxon nobles, who had stood at the head of the people in the manner of the ancient princes (*principes* of Tacitus), were changed into counts, officials of the king, and on pain of death pagan worship was forbidden, and baptism was ordered. Priests were to be installed in all areas and provided with land and servants, and the tithe was to be paid to the churches.

That was too much for the Saxons.[4] Wittekind returned from Den-mark and at Süntel Mountain inflicted a serious defeat on a detached Frankish corps that moved out against him without proper security (782). The reports concerning the place and details of this engagement are so conflicting that we cannot say anything specific about it. But in spite of this victory, the uprising did not become general. When the king himself appeared with an army, Wittekind did not risk opposing him but fled to the Danes, and the other leaders appeared before Charles and placed all the blame on Wittekind alone. As we observe the sequence of events, it is clear that Charles cannot possibly have had such a very large army with him. In the spring, but not until there was enough fodder available, Charles had moved to Paderborn and had held his diet there. When he returned across the Rhine—that is, around the end of June—he received the report that the Sorbs had invaded Thuringia, and he sent troops out against them. While under way, this corps received information of the Saxon uprising, joined other troops, Ripuarians whom a certain Count Theoderich led up on his own initiative, and suffered the defeat at Süntel

Mountain, which therefore can hardly have taken place before August or September. Even if Charles, as can be freely assumed, proclaimed a levy of troops immediately on hearing the first report of the Saxon rebellion, nevertheless the mobilization, the dispatching of the levy summons, the assembling of the vassals from their courts, the equipping and the gathering of provisions from the peasants—these actions always required a certain length of time,[5] so that contingents from the more distant areas cannot possibly have been on the Weser that same fall. The straight-line distance from Paris to the Westphalian Gate is 600 kilometers, which we may estimate as the equivalent of 900 kilometers of marching distance, or two months of marching time. Charles celebrated Christmas again back in Diedenhofen.

The mere appearance of the king with a small Frankish army, therefore, had sufficed to disarm the Saxons.

Charles marched into the heart of Saxony, to the lower Weser, and at Verden he had executed a large number of guilty persons, presumably including those who were adjudged guilty because they had not actively opposed the rebellion (autumn 782).

In this case, as so often, severity failed to achieve its purpose. Now for the first time, inflamed with a savage thirst for revenge, the Saxons arose en masse, and in the following year (783) they opposed the Franks in open battle.

The first encounter took place in the Teutoburger Forest near Detmold, near the Dören ravine, where the Germans had once defended and saved their freedom. Now the Saxons were defeated, but despite his victory, Charles withdrew to Paderborn to await reinforcements. From a purely military viewpoint, this move cannot be explained. A withdrawal following a victory eliminates the morale gain, the most important part of the successful action. If the Franks had really been victorious, they would necessarily have been strong enough in any event to await their reinforcements here, two to three days' march in advance of Paderborn, whereas the withdrawal could not help but give the appearance of a defeat or at least make the victory appear doubtful and give new confidence to all the wavering spirits in Saxony, leading them into Wittekind's camp. Since in any case an engagement did take place at Detmold and the Franks no doubt cannot have been beaten, since that would have had more drastic results, the circumstances can probably be clarified in this way: Charles had at first advanced with a very small corps, because he assumed that once again the majority of the Saxons would promptly subject themselves to him and might in fact ally themselves with him. The engagement at Detmold was probably not particularly significant, but it showed the king that this time the Saxons would stand up to him. He realized that his advance with a small force was a mistake and that, despite his victory, he was in a very precarious situation north of the mountain range. Consequently, he was willing to accept the morale-related disadvantages of the withdrawal because he had no alternative, in order first of all to await the arrival of the approaching troop units in a secure place. Only a short time later he was able to move forward again, and this time, only a little more than four weeks after Detmold, he won the decisive victory on the Hase, perhaps near Osnabrück, although the exact location is not known. This victory was followed up with the greatest energy; laying waste the countryside, the Frankish army crossed the Weser and advanced to the Elbe. While it is true that they withdrew again in the autumn—on 9 October Charles was in Worms, and he celebrated Christmas and Easter in Heristal on the Meuse—nevertheless, he moved out again in the spring of 784, crossed the Rhine at the mouth of the Lippe, and reached the Weser at Huculbi (Petershagen), downstream from Minden. There Charles split his army, since there was apparently no longer any determined opposition to be expected from the Saxons. A corps under his eldest son, Charles, turned back toward Westphalia and later had a fight on the Lippe. The king himself swung first toward the south, to Thuringia, and from there he pushed northward again into Eastphalia. In the imperial records, heavy flooding is shown as the reason for his not moving farther northward from Huculbi or directly toward the east. We may also surmise that the question of rations also played a role in this; by first going into the old province of Thuringia, the king was able to replenish his provisions there.

Although the Eastphalians now seem to have subjected themselves to him, the war still had to be carried on, and Charles decided not to give his opponents another chance to recover during the winter. Moving in from the south (the king celebrated Christmas at Lügde on the Emmer, some 16 miles east of Detmold, not far from the left bank of the Weser), the Franks advanced to the Westphalian Gate (Rehme). They did not risk moving farther forward, however, but withdrew 45 miles to the border fort of Eresburg (Obermarsberg), where Charles himself spent the entire winter and kept the border districts (a term that the Frankish chronicler extended with strong exaggeration to almost all the districts) continuously stirred up. As the chronicler specifically observes, he had to have his provisions moved up from Frankish territory. But in the spring he had such extensive preparations made that he could then advance into the Barden district on the lower Elbe. When he was so far forward, he was statesman enough, as conqueror, to engage in negotiations with

Wittekind, who had fled across the Elbe, and to offer him peace and friendship. Wittekind recognized the hopelessness of his cause, subjected himself, went to Charles' court, and had himself baptized. The struggle that had begun with the rebellion in the summer of 782 was thereby ended in 785, after three years.

The later movements and conflicts that took place from 793 to 804, although not insignificant, offer nothing more of interest from the viewpoint of military history. The war consisted entirely of wasting sweeps. Only the East Elban Saxons in Holstein once again offered opposition in the open field; against them Charles made much use of the help of the Slavs, the Abodrites, and the Wilzians. The decisive means that the emperor used in this decade to pacify the land was a massive movement of the Saxons in order to settle them on Frankish soil. When Charles once again concentrated on Saxony in the winter of 797–798, he did not establish his camp again at Eresburg, but farther eastward, at the confluence of the Diemel in the Weser, near Heristal (Herstelle). The Romans, when they had moved forward from Aliso, had swung half-northward to the Westphalian Gate because of their link with their second base, the sea, but Charles, even now, remained as close as possible to his home territory.

This difference leads us once again to a comparison of the aspects of this conduct of war with that of the Romans in the same regions. The Romans based their conduct of war on the waterways, especially the Lippe and the large supply depot on the upper Lippe, Aliso. This place on the upper Lippe, now called Paderborn, also played an important role in the Carolingian campaigns, but this was only an almost chance coincidence. The reasons that led into the same area both times are completely different. Charles, too, no doubt used the Lippe route on a few occasions, but his main line of attack led up from the south, from Hesse, to the Weser.[6] The fact that Hesse and Thuringia already belonged to his kingdom provided for him from the start a completely different situation from that of the Romans; coming from that area, each time he was quickly on the Weser and in the middle of the country. But we are not told whether he perhaps used the Fulda as a supply line. He no doubt knew how important the water route was for moving up provisions, and for that reason he did, of course, undertake to link the Main and the Danube with a canal, but that played no part in the Saxon campaigns. No large depots were established; the various contingents, small as they were, had to bring along their own provisions. The first campaigns, in 772 and 774, took place in autumn, when the Lippe was completely unnavigable.

It is obvious, however, that concern for provisions was also a decisive point in the Carolingian conduct of war. On numerous occasions advances were broken off, cases where energetic conduct of operations would obviously have required a continuation and where no obstacle was offered by enemy resistance. The reason can no doubt be sought only in the area of provisions. We must credit the Frankish king with a very great accomplishment in that he finally succeeded in pushing to the lower Weser and the lower Elbe without the help of a fleet coming to join him from the North Sea, for the terrain itself offered the invading enemy only very scant resources.

In the spring of the year 16, when the main body of the Roman army was encamped at Aliso, awaiting the arrival of the fleet on the Weser, the commander used the time to have roads built to the Rhine (see Vol. II, pp. 113 and 128). When Charles was encamped at Eresburg in the winter of 784-785 and was pressing the Saxons, the royal records report the same action on his part.[7] It is now interesting for us to examine how it came about that the Romans, while laying out roads in this region and for the purpose of supporting their military operations, chose as their central point a site on the upper Lippe, and that Charles did exactly the same thing but chose a place on the upper Diemel, some 23 miles south of the Romans' location.

The Romans used an advanced base as far forward in the enemy territory as possible, with communication by water, in order to establish a large supply depot. This water route was provided by the Lippe. Even if it dried up in midsummer (the month of September had the lowest water level; see Vol. II, p. 132), in springtime it offered in the highest degree the opportunity to move up all of the army's needs almost to its source with little effort. The strong standing army was capable and always ready to hold the advanced post, or, in case of necessity, to relieve it.

Charles, with his army of vassals, could not hold a post that was very far advanced in enemy territory, nor with his rather small army and the system of self-supply for the contingents did he need a large supply depot and communications by water. In return, however, he was in a position to attack the Saxons not only from the Rhine but also from Hesse. Consequently, his main base in the first period of the struggle was necessarily situated at the point where the two lines of operation, from the Rhine and the Main, intersected. That was on the upper Diemel, at Eresburg. If Charles had perhaps chosen the Fulda as his line of advance and established himself directly on the Weser, the direct route toward the west, to the Rhine, would have become too long. If he had established himself at once on the upper Lippe, that would already have been too deep in enemy territory. If he had established his base in the Ruhr region, for example in the area of Brilon or Rüthen (on the Möhne), he would have had too poor a link with Hesse.

At Eresburg, however, all the routes that were important for him came together: from the south via the Eder valley and the Itter valley, from the west the routes along the Ruhr and the Möhne. Toward the east, the route extended down the Diemel to the Weser, and northwards over the Sintfeld to the upper Lippe, to Paderborn and the passes through the Teutoburger Forest.

The question arises as to why Charles did not establish Paderborn directly at the confluence of the Alme and the Lippe, but a good 2½ miles from that point, on the small tributary Pader. The question of the *Hellweg,* that famous road that does not follow one of the tributaries of the Rhine but extends parallel to and between the Ruhr and the Lippe from Paderborn through Soest, Unna, and Dortmund to Duisburg, is related to the point concerning the location of Paderborn.

This problem has recently, and in my opinion definitively, been solved by Carl Rübel in his frequently cited books. The *Hellweg* is an installation of Charlemagne, precisely from the period of the Saxon wars. It linked a series of newly established royal courts in a particularly fertile area and, consequently, formed a military road along which a unit that was not too large could find provisions from point to point. The name is to be explained as "*Hallweg,*" the route along which the alarm was given from post to post in case of an enemy incursion. This road served the Frankish ruler in the same way the water route of the Lippe had served the Romans. For Charles, the water route, unusable for several months in the summer and autumn, had no real importance. He therefore established the city that served in the plain as terminal point of the *Hellweg,* from which roads led into the mountains in various directions, at a place where plentiful springs with very good water provided a resting place and power for the operation of mills.

The roads dotted with royal courts in the manner of the *Hellweg* extended through the Saxon-Frankish border area along the Ruhr, the Lippe, and Diemel, both in the direction of these rivers and also perpendicular to them as links between one river valley and the other. Certainly, Charlemagne later established such relay roads dotted with royal courts throughout all of Saxony. Schuchhardt has recently pointed out the likelihood that Hanover, for example, at the point where the Leine begins to be navigable, was one such Carolingian installation.[8]

Finally, one more question presents itself: if the area of Paderborn was such an important strategic point both for the Romans and for Charlemagne, how does it happen that this place never played any special role afterwards and Paderborn did not even develop into an important city? The answer is that there is nothing absolute about the strategic importance of a place, but, in addition to the continuing geographical conditions, such importance depends on the given historical conditions for each period. Today Bibracte and Alesia are villages, whereas in Caesar's time Paris did not yet play any role. It was a chance coincidence that both Drusus and Charlemagne established a base in the vicinity of the confluence of the Alme and the Lippe; their reasons were not the same. Later, even the natural conditions changed to some extent. In the Middle Ages two strong interests fought for every stream, navigation and mills. After the principal traffic had once shifted from the Lippe to the *Hellweg*, the mills won the upper hand on the river, which, after all, was navigable hardly two-thirds of the year, and they pushed navigation completely into the background. The attempt by the city of Soest in 1486 to gain control of the Lippe water route is very important for us, to be sure, as evidence that they no doubt recognized the importance and usefulness of the river, but it failed, as was to be expected under the disrupted political conditions of Westphalia in that period.

Without a water route, therefore, Paderborn, too, was not able to develop significantly.

NOTES FOR CHAPTER II

1. Nithard 4: 2. *Annales Bertin.* for the year 841.

2. Rübel, *The Franks: Their System of Conquest and Settlement (Die Franken, ihr Eroberungs- und Siedelungssystem)*, p. 400, in accordance with the precedent set by Oppermann, *Atlas of Low German Fortifications (Atlas niederdeutscher Befestigungen)*, believes that the large fort, Babilonie, the ruins of which have been preserved, is connected with the battle of Lübbecke in 775. The installation, like all Frankish relay courts, is divided into a smaller, better preserved part, the *palatium* (palace), and a larger one, the *heribergum* (army camp), the bivouac for the army. The *heribergum* of Babilonie has an area of 7½ hectares. On the occasion of excavations in the autumn of 1905, however, scholars believe they have determined, on the basis of potsherds, that the stronghold was not a Frankish installation but a Saxon one.

3. At the northwest end of the Deister can be seen the remains of a Carolingian watchtower, the *"Heisterburg,"* the construction of which has also been connected with the campaign of 775. Nevertheless, it was not

built until later. In the accounts of the rebellion by the Saxons in 776, the chronicles speak only of the conquest of Eresburg and the siege of Sigiburg. See Rübel, *Die Franken,* p. 24, Note.

4. Rübel supposes that the method of the Franks, which called for marking off specific borders for the communities and thus drawing the wilderness areas which had formerly constituted the borders into the royal domains, also aroused the anger of the Saxon people.

5. The later German law books governing the vassalge system contain the regulation that the lord is to summon the vassal as much as six weeks before the beginning of the campaign.

6. Rübel, *Royal Courts, (Reichshöfe)*, p. 97, goes too far when he says: "In general, Charles customarily followed the courses of the streams in his campaigns and had his provisions moved up on the waterways." We have direct evidence of this only for the campaign against the Avars in 791; for the diet at Paderborn in June 785, the provisions may have been moved up on the Lippe in advance. In 790, according to Einhard's account, Charles moved by ship from Worms to Saltz on the Frankish Saale, where he had a palace, and followed the same route back, thus covering both times a large distance upstream. But many campaigns that we can trace were completely separate from the water routes.

7. "et dum ibi resideret multotiens scaras misit, et per semet ipsum iter peregit; Saxones, qui rebelles fuerunt, depraedavit et castra coepit et loca eorum munita intervenit et vias mundavit." ("and while he was residing there, he often sent out his *scarae* and made a campaign on his own; he plundered the Saxons who were rebels, captured their camp, disrupted their fortified positions, and cleared the roads.") The *"vias mundavit"* has previously—and also very recently, by Mühlbacher, *German History under the Carolingians (Deutsche Geschichte unter den Karolingern)*, p. 134—been translated as "cleared the routes," which would therefore be understood as meaning cleared off guerrilla bands or robbers. But this interpretation hardly seems acceptable, since such bands were normally not on the routes but hidden in the countryside. Consequently, I have no doubt at all that Rübel in *Royal Courts (Reichshöfe)*, p. 95, is correct when he translates it as "constructed passable routes."

8. "On the Origin of the City of Hanover" ("Ueber den Ursprung der Stadt Hannover"), *Zeitschrift des historischen Vereins für Niedersachsen*, 1903.

Chapter III

The Carolingian Empire, The Normans, and the Hungarians

Charlemagne's empire had no inner unity; it was the creation of the dynasty, the Arnulf family. According to the Germanic law of inheritance, all the sons had an equal claim on family property. An attempt in 817 to reconcile the unity of the empire with this right of inheritance by means of a law of succession led only to family feuds, and the internal discord in the dynasty now helped the new political principle, the feudal law, to come fully into its own. It finally eliminated completely the old principle, the subjects' bond, which, at least theoretically, had still obtained under Charlemagne. The sons of Louis the Pious, who fought with their father and among themselves, had to try to win supporters. In doing so, they sacrificed what until then had been the firmly held concept of the governmental offices. When the king now appointed counts, they were no longer officials with revocable appointments, but the appointment was regarded as the granting of a fief. The king could no longer revoke the appointment as he saw fit, and when a count died, if he left a son, the son claimed the right to assume the position of the father and be granted the county. Natural factors necessarily led to the development of this situation. For, inasmuch as a real verification of the count's administration by the central government was next to impossible, only a close tie between the county and the personal and family interests of the count could offer a certain guarantee of helpful action and restraint from the grossest abuses. It was particularly impossible for a military organization based on vassalage and fiefs to function in the hands of frequently changing officials.

But as the counties now gradually became fiefs, the royal authority evaporated. The situation once again was like that under the later Merovingians. King Pepin and Charlemagne had been able to restore and maintain the royal authority by ruling the far-flung kingdom as a unit. Any count who did not promptly obey their commands would have had to fear their displeasure. The counts of Louis the German and Charles the Bald, and especially those of their successors, heeded a royal summons only to the extent they wished to do so. The kings could not even exercise severity against an individual. He would be protected by the sense of class solidarity of his colleagues, on whose assistance the king had to depend in the dynastic discord.

The very feudal organization that had provided the Carolingian nation with an effective warriorhood was now responsible for the nation's dissolution.

At this moment, a new and frightful enemy appeared in the Occident, the last remnant of the Teutonic race still immersed in crude barbarism, the heathen Normans.

Scholars have suggested the most varied reasons why the Franks, so militarily powerful up to that point, were not capable of defending their land against the Normans. It has even been a question of decreased population as a result of Charlemagne's many wars. Actually, we may assume that the freedom from civil wars for several generations and the period of almost complete peace under Louis the Pious until 830 had been very beneficial for the economic prosperity of the country and also an increased population. But it was precisely the modest demands that Charles had made for military forces on the individual districts and the peaceful period under Louis that had limited military skill and experience to a very restricted circle. Nevertheless, as long as a central administration with unchallenged authority existed, armies of considerable size could still be assembled. But after this central authority had disappeared and the king was forced to rely on the good will of the counts, bishops, and vassals, levies could no longer be called up from the more distant regions.

We now see a repetition of the conditions that developed in the Roman Empire after the *limes* was penetrated. The Norman armies were certainly no stronger, were in fact probably weaker, than those of the Germans that had plundered the Roman provinces in the fourth and fifth centuries. All these Vikings came from Denmark and Norway, countries so small or unfertile that they could not possibly support large populations. At times, Swedes may also have participated in the Norman incursions, but at that time they were looking principally in the opposite direction. As Varangians they subjugated Russia and in Constantinople came together with their ethnic relatives, who had sailed through the straits of Gibraltar and the Mediterranean. These Norsemen cannot have terrified Europe through their numbers but only because, in them, there appeared once again those ancient Germanic warlike qualities that had caused ancient Rome to shudder when the Cimbri and Teutones approached, characteristics which a half millennium later shattered the empire into pieces.

We can follow the sequence of these developments most clearly among the Anglo-Saxons. The blending of the Anglo-Saxon lands in the British Isles into a unified kingdom by King Egbert in 827 had just occurred when the Viking attacks began. One would think that the large Germanic kingdom would necessarily have been able to defend itself against the pirate hordes. But the warlike strength with which the forebears of the Anglo-Saxons had conquered the island and subjected the Celts 400 years earlier had completely disappeared. We shall consider the sequence of these developments in still more detail below: how the ancient Germanic conquerors finally fell under the domination of the Danes and then of the Gallicized Normans.

These developments were not quite so bad for the kingdoms of the Frankish Empire, where the feudal system had still maintained somewhat more of a warrior class, than they were for the Anglo-Saxons, but even the Frankish feudal forces could not stand up to the Vikings. Most important of all, even Charlemagne himself had, according to Ranke's expression, lacked a half of total power, a sea force. He had been aware of this weakness and had had ships built (in 800), but there cannot have been much accomplished in this area, for when the Normans appeared again, in 810, with 200 ships, they were able to destroy Friesland without opposition. Nothing was done under Louis the Pious, who would have had plenty of time and resources to create a naval force, and in the civil wars that broke out afterward it was no longer possible to make the great effort that the construction of a fleet required. Through their possession of a fleet and their skill of navigation, the Normans were able to appear unexpectedly now here, now there on the coast, and even if they were only a few thousand men, what a long time passed before a few thousand vassals were assembled and moved up! Before they arrived, the enemy could be long gone with his booty, and the temptation was always there for the more distant counts not to plunge into the large expense of a campaign but to remain at home and conserve the strength of their counties.

Once even the peasants were apparently called up to ward off the terrible enemies, but the chronicler tells us that, although a huge mass was assembled for battle, the Normans destroyed this common mass, which was ignorant of warfare even though well armed, and slaughtered them like cattle.[1] The peasants, Ripuarian Franks, must therefore have turned tail at the first encounter.

And so it was possible for the Normans to burn Cologne and Aachen, to move up to Coblenz and even to Trier, and finally, while Emperor Charles III was staying in Italy, to besiege Paris. At the same time, the coasts of the Mediterranean, especially of Italy, were exposed to the attacks of Saracen pirates, who plundered Naples and Saint Peter's in Rome.

Up to this point, we may not have particular trouble understanding these events if we remember how helpless the Roman Empire had been in the face of the invasions of the Germanic hordes, which, as we now know, were also so small in numbers of warriors. But it requires a certain effort to understand that, even when the forces of the entire empire were once again assembled and the Normans, instead of withdrawing to their ships, met the attack head on, they still could not be defeated.

The Norsemen's earlier attacks and wasting expeditions had been favored either by their superiority at sea, which enabled them to make surprise attacks everywhere, or by the divisions within the dynasty and the struggles of the Franks among themselves. Finally, the empire was once again united under Charles III, son of Louis the German. Now we might expect to see such large armies assembled as to overpower the Normans wherever they met them. But this did not happen.

Once before, Charles, as king of the East Frankish Kingdom, Lorraine, and Italy, had assembled a large army and led it against the Normans, who had established a secure camp at Aschloo (Elsloo) on the Meuse. Since even the Italians had provided reinforcements, we may assume that the Frankish army was not insignificant. Instead of attacking the Normans, Charles made a treaty with them, in accordance with the terms of which their leader, Gottfried, was baptized, married a Carolingian princess, and was allocated part of Friesland as a residence for himself and his men. In addition, 2,412 pounds of gold and silver had to be paid (882). According to the testimony of contemporaries, the army was dissatisfied with this agreement and would have preferred to fight. Nevertheless, it can be assumed that the emperor and his advisors believed they would gain more by receiving the Normans peacefully in the empire than by risking a questionable victory.

But even this political solution failed in the face of the events at Paris. Charles appeared with the entire imperial army on the north bank of the Seine and occupied Montmartre. The Normans moved back to the south bank, but there they stood fast. This would have been the moment for a great decisive action. Charles did not risk it but instead made a new treaty in which he promised the Normans 700 pounds of silver as ransom for Paris and assigned them winter quarters in Burgundy which, under a certain Count Boso as king, wanted to break free from the empire.

His contemporaries all placed the blame for this shameful treaty on the completely incompetent and cowardly king and denounced his confidants as traitors. The opposition was so strong that Charles III was deposed a short time later. But from the military history viewpoint, the affair was not yet finished. There is no doubt that this Charles had absolutely nothing heroic about him, but if there had existed in the army and its leaders an unlimited belief in victory, there would certainly have been among the Frankish leaders men who would have made their voices heard and could have prevailed upon the emperor to appoint a commander to lead them into battle.

We must also take pains to determine the factors that made the decision of the emperor (which, after all, was not made without being considered in a council of war) appear understandable from an objective viewpoint.

No doubt Frankish kings sometimes succeeded in conquering the Normans, particularly King Louis the Stammerer (a few years earlier, in 881, at Saucourt) and King Arnulf, successor to Charles III, at Louvain, five years later (891). These victories, however, cannot have been very significant, including even the second, well-known battle, for even if the report of a writer that the Franks had lost only a single man may be seen as a very distorted boast, in any event the battle had only minor direct results. Only a few weeks later, the Normans again took position in precisely the same place where they had suffered the defeat and set out from there on a plundering expedition to Bonn and thence into the Ardennes.

We may, however, also make a comparison with the conduct of King Henry I of Germany a generation later against the other barbarian enemy, the Hungarians, who at that time were sorely pressing the occidental world. Even Henry, who left behind the reputation of being a strong king, considered it advisable to pay the Hungarians a regular tribute for nine consecutive years and with this tribute did not even buy the security of his entire kingdom, but only that of his own duchy of Saxony. We cannot assume that there was a significant difference between the military skill of the Germans in 924 and that of the Franks in 886. Consequently, what we must clearly realize and what must become and remain a basic point for our historical understanding from start to finish is the fact that the assembled forces of the huge Carolingian Empire and of its still gigantic subordinate kingdoms were just sufficient to strike an approximate balance with an invading barbarian people of small size, so that the question of who held the upper hand in any single situation depended on the particular circumstances, especially the leaders. The Hungarians were finally defeated in open battle by Otto the Great, who with a strong hand took control of the forces of all of Germany. The Normans were never actually defeated. A part of them settled permanently in Britain, while another part, under Duke Rollo, was settled at the mouth of the Seine by treaty in 911, in the manner envisaged by Charles III in the Treaty of Elsloo (to say nothing of a still earlier attempt). When Denmark and Norway also accepted Christianity in the course of the tenth century, the remainder of these peoples entered the sphere of the occidental civilization and gradually lost their dangerous, purely warlike character.

The Viking voyages of the North Germans, therefore, were quite similar to the movements of the Germans in the *Völkerwanderung,* not only in their origin and their nature, but also in their ending and their results. A part of the wanderers finally settled in the areas they had originally plundered and deliberately destroyed. There was a difference, however, in that the Frankish Empire was not as completely defenseless as the Roman Empire had been.

After the firm nuclei of the disciplined legions had disappeared, the Romans hardly produced any kind of useful warriorhood from their own race. They could not defend themselves in any way other than by playing off one group of barbarians against another and taking them into their military service. When Gaiseric attacked Carthage, the city was defended by Goths ("cum Gothorum foederatorum manu": "with a band of Goth *foederati*"). Narses conquered the Goths with the help of Herulians, Lombards, and Huns. The Frankish and Anglo-Saxon kingdoms, and later the Germans, fought with the Normans and Hungarians, and, whether defeated or victorious, they at least fought with their own forces and native inhabitants. If, as was earlier believed, the Frankish army under Charlemagne had been a peasant army, or in other words, if the great mass of the population had still been militarily skilled and usable in war, it would be completely incomprehensible that, one generation after the demise of the emperor, this people of many millions could not hold off the savage invaders. But the military skill of even the Germanic peoples in the Carolingian Empire had already been limited for a long time to a very thin layer of the population. Even Charlemagne's armies had been very small, as we have been able to determine from other circumstances. Consequently, even his great-grandsons could not assemble masses of competent soldiers, but only more or less numerous units of knights.

Let us now return to the situation of Charles III and his relief of the siege of Paris. For almost a year, since November 885, the Normans had been in position before this city, had assaulted it heavily, and at times had so tightly enclosed it that communications with the outside were possible only by stealth or force. Paris was already a large city.

Even if the chroniclers' reports that the Normans numbered 30,000 or even 40,000 men are worthless, their army must have been of considerable strength. When Charles now approached with the relief army, the Normans did not take position for battle in the open field but withdrew into a well-fortified camp on the south bank of the Seine. The Franks were faced with the task of either storming this camp or surrounding it and starving the defenders into submission. The chances of success in an assault appear very questionable. If we imagine Caesar in a similar strategic situation, he would unquestionably have surrounded the enemy army with ditches and palisades and would finally have starved it into submission. Essential to this action was the necessity for the besieging army to be able to feed itself for a long enough period. One would think that the Frankish emperor could have brought up the necessary provisions on the favorable route provided by the Seine and its tributaries. But the administrative prerequisites for such action were missing. A Carolingian army depended on the fact that each contingent would bring along its own rations. Charles was already in the immediate vicinity of Paris in August 886, but the treaty was not effected until November. Presumably, the contingents were not assembled before that month. When the last ones arrived, the earlier arrivals had already consumed their three months' supply of provisions. There were no experienced and resourceful suppliers who, with sufficient cash, could have ferreted out even small hidden supplies of food and organized their transport from distant places. Nothing was to be obtained by requisitioning produce in the surrounding area, which the Normans had completely stripped, and at a greater distance from the scene of operations the royal authority was not strong enough to take by force and move up whatever supplies were available.

If we look back to Charlemagne's time, the conditions were essentially the same, but we may not conclude that the same thing could have happened under such a mighty ruler. While the changes which had taken place between his time and that of his great-grandson were very small from the technical military viewpoint, they were all the greater politically, and this political factor also controlled the individual military actions. Under Charlemagne, there would not have been a siege of Paris and a buying off of the enemy, because a different kind of opposition would have been offered from the start. The Normans' military successes were the result not simply of their own savage courage but principally of the differences of the Franks among themselves, the dissolution of the empire, and the civil war. The first victories and successes which these conditions made possible for the Normans gave them self-confidence and a sense of superiority that continuously increased and developed. The opposite held true for the Franks, not only because they were filled with an awesome respect for their savage opponents but primarily because the royal authority was continuously paralyzed, even after the empire was reunited. As we found in Caesar's war in Gaul, a very important factor in Roman victories was their administrative superiority; perhaps the final and decisive reason for the miserable agreement Emperor Charles III made with the Normans before Paris was nothing more than the administrative inability of the Frankish Kingdom, restricted as it was by the feudal system, to feed throughout the winter the army it had finally assembled with so much effort and difficulty. Charlemagne would undoubtedly have had so much power over his counts as to hold the army assembled and force the provision of the necessary rations.

During the siege, a part of the siege army under the sea king Siegfried had been persuaded to withdraw in return for a gift of 60 pounds of silver. Immediately after Charles had come to agreement with the besiegers and had withdrawn, we hear that King Siegfried appeared again and sailed up the Oise behind the emperor. The Fulda annals report that the approach of this relief army influenced Charles's decision to come to an agreement. This conclusion is not necessarily supported by the actual situation, and we must pass over the question as to whether the chronicler was accurately informed. For we could also argue just the opposite point, that the approach of a new army would have offered the opportunity to move against it and first of all fight a battle in the open field against a smaller enemy army. If the Franks had won, the victory would have given them a sense of superiority and would also have influenced a possible decision to attack the fortified camp of the Normans at Paris.

But there is no point in speculating on such possibilities, since we do not known enough about the actual events. The fact remains that the ruler of united France did not risk attacking, overcoming, and punishing a simple pirate people in the middle of his own territory. Consequently, the military power of the Frankish Kingdom was unbelievably small.

EXCURSUS

THE SIEGE OF PARIS

In addition to the short reports of the chronicles and annals, we are given more detailed information on this siege in a long epic poem by the monk Abbo, who was present at the siege.[2] His hexameters are so contrived, embellished, and pompous that the real sense is often hardly understandable. Unfortunately, the miracles of Saint Germanus play a larger role in the account than do the actual military actions, so that in the area of military history we learn hardly more than the point that both sides made extensive use of bow and arrow.

As best I can see, all scholars to date, both German and French,[3] have assumed that the Franks had sacrificed the outlying areas of the city on both banks of the Seine from the start and had defended only the *cité* on the island. But that seems to me impossible.

The island is so small that it could not shelter for a year the population of a large city, such as Paris was described, and numerous details of the siege cannot be reconciled with that assumption. But the apparently contradictory passages can also be interpreted differently. The whole matter depends on the question of the bridges. At first, the Normans attacked a tower that covered the exit of a bridge on the north bank. When they were unable to overcome the brave defenders, they sent three burning rafts against the bridge, guiding them with ropes from the bank and taking advantage of an easterly wind (Abbo, 1. 375 ff.). This makes it appear as if the besiegers completely controlled the north bank. This attack also failed to achieve its purpose, for the rafts were driven against the stone pillars of the bridge, where they were extinguished by the Franks. A few days later, on 6 February 886, however, the besiegers had the good luck of having the bridge broken by the river. Now no aid could be brought to the defenders. The Normans attacked simultaneously from all sides, set fire to the tower, and finally captured it. All of its defenders perished. If the reference here is to the same tower and the same bridge that were besieged from the start—and the context permits no other possibility—then the Franks would have had no further link with the north bank. Furthermore, it is impossible that they could have reconstructed such a bridge during the siege. But later we hear that Count Odo, from a sortie in the north, successfully drove through ("cacumina Montis Martis": "Montmartre") to the gate (Abbo, 2. 195-205), and when the emperor arrived, he moved into the city from this side. A number of scholars (Martin, Taranne, Dahlmann, Kalkstein) have therefore believed that the lost bridge tower was on the island's southern link. That is not only a very forced interpretation, but it is also opposed by the fact that the entire account of the siege would have to read differently if it were a question of the investment of the island stronghold, with the exception of the two bridgeheads. There are repeated references to the siege engines the Normans brought up and to the missiles they fired into the city. We are told on one occasion (Abbo, 2. 146-150) how, during a procession with relics around the wall, one of the relic-bearers was hit by a stone from a pagan, and another time (2. 321) we read of churches near the walls into which the Normans fled.

Consequently, we can bring unity into the account only if we succeed in linking the defense of the northern tower, particularly the account of the fiery rafts there, with the fact that an entire section of the city north of the Seine was also defended. I think it is possible to do so.

There is a source which states that Charles the Bald had a bridge built in Paris in 861 or 862;[4] whether or not this claim is erroneous does not concern us. "Placuit nobis extra praedictam urbem supra terram monasterii sancti Germani suburbio commorantis, quod a priscis temporibus Antisiodorensis dicitur . . . opportunum majorem facere pontem." ("We decree that outside the aforementioned city on the land of the monastery of Saint German dwelling in the suburb, which in former times was called Antisiodorensis . . . that it should be convenient to build a larger bridge.") This bridge outside the city on the terrain of the monastery of Saint-Germain-l'Auxerrois can only have been situated at the west end of the island, which at that time was supposedly not as long as today. The northern section of the city must have begun just a short distance to the east of that point. It was possible, therefore, for the Normans to place their fiery floats in the water between the northern suburb and the bridge and to drive them against the bridge with the help of the east wind.

Locating the bridge at this point even seems the only acceptable interpretation of the wording of the source, for the expression *"extra urbem"* ("outside the city") cannot refer to the city on the island but only to a part of the city on the north bank. It is, of course, only natural that there was a bridge outside the city on the island. The unusual aspect of this bridge was the fact that it did not link the city on the island with the city on the bank, where there was already a bridge, but it led from the island across to open land outside (downstream from) the city. That is why it was covered by a fortified tower.

This interpretation removes all the difficulties. The bridge closed the approach to the Seine between the two parts of the city. Although the suburbs naturally also had walls on the river side, the defense was very much simplified if the attackers were prevented from the start from attacking from the water. Consequently, the Franks attempted with all their power to hold the bridge and its tower. But even after they had been lost, nothing was yet decided. The strong attacks the Normans had made until then were certainly not exclusively against that tower but against the entire northern suburb near it. They concentrated on the tower because in its isolated location it seemed the easiest to overcome. But they were discouraged by the energetic opposition they encountered, so that, despite their success, they immediately thereafter changed the siege into a simple blockade, and, with the camp they now erected on the south bank as a base, they plundered the surrounding territory.

Consequently, even after the loss of the one bridge with its tower, which was only an outer defense, the Franks continued to hold parts of the city on the right and left banks of the Seine, which were linked to the island by bridges. Later, Abbo can truthfully sing (2. 232): "ballabant muri, speculae, pontes quoque cuncti." ("The walls, watchtowers, even all the bridges were protecting them.") Taranne, in *Le Siège de Paris par les Normands,* p. 258, interprets the passage in Abbo, 2. 160, which tells of the fight of the *urbani* (city dwellers) against the *suburbani* (those outside the city), as meaning that the Normans, the *suburbani*, must have held the parts of the city opposite the island. That is, of course, not necessary, just as it is not necessary to interpret the introduction to the poem (1. 10-19) as meaning that the entire city was situated on the island. In any case, there were walled suburbs (2. 322), and there is no reason to assume that they had been evacuated from the start. Saint-Germain-l'Auxerrois on the north and Saint-Germain-des-Prés on the south lay outside the walls.

(Added in second edition). W. Vogel, in *The Normans and the Frankish Empire* (*Die Normannen und das fränkische Reich*), 1906, p. 39, claims that the principal reason for the military superiority of the Normans over the Franks in the ninth century lay "less in greater personal courage than in the much stricter organization and the better developed tactics of the Norman armies at a time when the Frankish people's army was in a state of transition." Correctly understood, the crucial point in this sentence lies in the word "organization." The Normans came in clear-cut units; in a feudal nation, however, assembling a sizable body of warriors was not easy and always required a rather long time. This fact constituted the sense of "organization" in the feudal system. The better Norman "tactics" is a fantasy, and the "transition" in which the Frankish people's army was supposedly involved at that time was not a factor of weakness but quite the contrary. If the transition had not yet been completed, that is, if there had still existed remnants of the former warrior ability of the masses, it would have been all the easier to oppose the Normans. The critical point lay not in the fact that the Frankish people's army was "involved in transition," but that the transition was already completed.

NOTES FOR CHAPTER III

1. Regino, for the year 882: "innumera multitudo peditum ex agris et villis in unum agmen conglobata eos quasi pugnatura aggreditur. Sed Normanni cernentes ignobile vulgus non tantum inerme quantum disciplina militari nudatum tanta caeda prosternunt, ut bruta animalia, non homines mactari viderentur." ("A countless number of men on foot from the countryside and the villages massed into one column approached them as if about to attack. But the Normans, seeing that it was a low-born crowd not so much unarmed as deprived of training, overthrew them with so great a slaughter that dumb animals, not men, seemed to be killed.")

2. *Mon. Germaniae. SS.*, 2. 806. *Abbonis de bello Parisiaeo libri III, in usum scholarum recudi fecit G. H. Pertz* (*Abbo, On the Parisian War*, edited by G. H. Pertz). *Le Siège de Paris par les Normands en 885 et 886*, poème d'Abbon avec la traduction etc. par N. R. Taranne (*The Siege of Paris by the Normans in 885 and 886*, poem by Abbo with the translation etc. by N. R. Taranne), Paris, 1834. Another translation is to be found in Guizot, *Collection de mémoires relatifs à l'histoire de France*, Tome VI.

3. I have compared the following works of the numerous authors who have treated this siege in more or less detail: C. von Kalkstein, *History of the French Kingdom under the Early Capetians* (*Geschichte des französischen Königtums unter den ersten Capetingern*), Vol. I, 1877. E. Dümmler, *History of the East Frankish Kingdom* (*Geschichte des ostfränkischen Reichs*), 2d ed., Vol. III, 1888. F. C. Dahlmann, *History of Denmark* (*Geschichte von Dänemark*), Vol. I, 1840. F. Bournon, *Paris, Histoire*, etc., Paris, 1888. E. Monorval, *Paris depuis ses origines*, etc. F. T. Perrens, *Histoire générale de Paris*. Bonamy, *Mémoires de l'Académie des Inscriptions*, Vol. 17, 1759. Henry Martin, *Histoire de France*, Vol. II. Depping, *History of the Maritime Expeditions of the Normans and of Their Settling in France in the Tenth Century* (*Histoire des expéditions maritimes des Normands et de leur établissement en France au dixième siècle*), Brussels, 1844.

4. *Collection des Cartulaires de France*, Tome IV. *Cartulaires de l'église Notre Dame de Paris*, ed. M. Guérard, Tome I, 1850, p. 243. Also published in Baluzius, *Capit.* II, Column 1491, and Bouquet VIII, 568.

BOOK II

The Feudal State at the Height of Its Development

Chapter I

The Formation of Nations on the Remains of the Carolingian Empire

The strict concept of the state that was prevalent in antiquity was destroyed by the *Völkerwanderung*. While barbarian military leaders or kings took the highest powers into their hands by force, they were not capable of creating at once political systems based on concepts of unity. The strongest of all the new formations, the Frankish monarchy, as the repeated divisions show, did not rise above the concept of a dynastic family possession, and this possession was finally wrested from the original possessor by a newly risen family, the Carolingian.

Four successive great rulers from this family, Pepin the Mayor of the Palace, Charles Martel, Pepin the King, and Charlemagne, restored the nation, breathed into it something of a national concept, and finally extended it into the western empire. But after the death of Charlemagne, the Carolingian Empire collapsed even faster than the Merovingian had fallen.

The attempt that Charles's son made to hold the nation together through the law of succession of 817 failed. The centrifugal forces in the inconsistent makeup of the political system were too strong. Until now, the question has not really been raised as to why Charles's successors held out a shorter time than those of Clovis, since Charles, after all, passed on a nation that was much more powerful and spiritually higher than that of Clovis. There was no answer to be given to this question. But I think the answer is now apparent. The replacement of the general people's army by the army of vassals, which only got its start under the Merovingians, was already completed under Charlemagne. But the vassals, who were directly obligated to their feudal masters and providers,

placed the system of power, once the royal authority was shaken, in the
hands of the great families holding large territories, families that held the
positions of count. These families broke up the empire as soon as it had
been divided and brought into internal conflict under the sons and
grandsons of Louis the Pious.

From the ruins, a new kingdom arose. It was no longer a unified one,
but several different and varied types of kingdoms: Germany, France,
Burgundy, and Italy. All of them, however, had the common characteristic that the great families and the special territorial formations which the
Carolingian Empire had torn apart were no longer completely suppressed
in favor of an all-powerful monarchy.[1] On the contrary, they constituted the political system in conjunction with the newly risen royal
families. The feudal organization, under which the national concept was
divided into a hierarchy of rights at the upper, lower, and intermediate
levels, prevailed. The kings exercised only limited rights and would
no longer have been the equivalent of their title if they had not at
the same time possessed the position and powers of a duke. Only pale
shadows of the national concept arose or were preserved. It was not such
a national concept but the vassals' loyalty that built up the political body
and held it together.

In the eastern part of the former Frankish Kingdom, at first a number
of duchies were formed in conjunction with the old families: Saxony,
Bavaria, Swabia, Franconia, and Lorraine. As these dukes elected one of
their number, Duke Henry of Saxony, as king, or later paid obeisance to
him, there arose the German Kingdom.

The new kingdom was weaker than the preceding Carolingian
monarchy in that the king recognized the duchies as independent units.
Even when he later eliminated the old family of the duke and appointed a
new duke, he still had to leave the duchy itself intact. He was king not
because of a clear right of succession but only as a result of an hereditary
claim, which first had to be agreed to by the vote of those same dukes.
The restrictions that this procedure imposed on the royal power, however, worked to the benefit of the nation's armed forces. Charlemagne's
successors could not have been pleased when one of their counts had too
many and too skilled warriors, for that very situation made the count
himself dangerous. Even now this situation could arise, and that did
happen, but since the monarchy in any case was based on the cooperation
and free will of the most important nobles, and the king, who was raised
to his position by these most important vassals, reigned in consultation
with them, it was only natural that now at every level of the feudal
organization every effort was bent to the creation of an efficient

warriorhood—by the king, the dukes, the counts, and soon also by the bishops, each in his own right and at the same time for the benefit of the whole. It could only be through the step-by-step buildup of the feudal nation, in which each level is provided with a certain political independence, that the military power of which the Middle Ages was capable was brought to its fullest effectiveness. It was only the feudal nation from the tenth century on that politically was fully compatible with the principle of the individual fighters and quality warriors, as that principle had gradually developed since the Merovingian period.

At first glance, we do not recognize the difference between the new kingdom and the Carolingian, because the heirs of Henry I, first in the male line and then the female (the Salians), actually ruled in Germany for 200 years. But this rule in its inner spirit was different from that of the preceding dynasty because it continued not as the result of a clear hereditary right but by selection. Consequently, it accepted the existence of opposing and legally recognized powers and had to respect them. As with the throne, the high positions, the dukes and counts, were also not clearly hereditary from the legal viewpoint but as fiefs were only lifetime grants. In reality, however, they were usually passed on from father to son and approached closer and closer the principle of pure heredity. We may say that the feudal nation found its purest form in situations where, with respect to the throne and the fiefs, none of the various principles— hereditary right, election, or appointment—was dominant but they all formed a practical balance.

The obverse of this echeloned division of power, which was paralleled by the Church as a special political organization, was the resulting political disruption. All the partial sovereignties, each with a certain independent military force, constantly rubbed against one another. The Middle Ages was the period of almost uninterrupted civil wars. But it was precisely in these constant feuds that the military strength was increased, just as had the power of the small Greek city-states, whose victory over the Persians resulted from the preceding civil war between Athens and Aegina, as Herodotus remarked, which had caused them to build their great fleet. When it then became necessary in times of greatest emergency to pull everything together, great and decisive deeds and accomplishments were possible. In the German Kingdom, such accomplishments were all the more possible because there, above all the smaller powers, a monarchy was created and endured, and it formed the natural focal point and provided the natural leadership.

According to a source that is still often cited, the king who established the political bases for the German Kingdom, Henry I, also created a unique military system. He supposedly developed the Saxons as mounted troops, built fortified castles, and ordered that eight out of nine warriors were always to sow and harvest but were to deliver a third of their produce to the stronghold where the ninth warrior lived and guarded the fortifications and stored the supplies for his eight comrades. In this form, the entire account, to which has been attributed the most varied significance in its details, is to be regarded as a fable and eliminated from the critical writing of history.

Henry's great accomplishment was the political one, first the formation, or at least the further development, of the duchy of Saxony, and then the new, limited monarchy. The military system remained of the same type that had long been developing.[2] If, under his son, the great Otto, the impression developed that the warrior class, which accomplished so much, along with the fortified castles and strong city walls that protected the country, had been created by Otto's father, Henry, and if Widukind, who did loyal honor to the family of his prince, pointed out these facts, this is nothing more than a shortening of the perspectives that is often found in popular legends, as, for example, in the Persian accounts concerning their royal dynasty which Herodotus described. In Charlemagne's time, the Saxons and Friesians were already fighting on horseback, and they certainly did not forget this skill in the following century, with all its wars.[3] Since time immemorial, the horse was a part of the "*Heergewäte*" (army equipment) among the Saxons. They had already built fortified castles in the pagan period and had erected cities at least since becoming a part of the civilization of the Frankish Kingdom. Consequently, Henry can have done nothing other than develop and strengthen, from the physical and personnel standpoints, the military system he inherited. The legendary character of Widukind's account is particularly obvious in the statement that it was always to be the ninth man who moved into the fortified castle. The strength of the garrison of a fort in peacetime depends on its size and location, whether on the border or in the interior, but it can never be determined by the number of warriors who are present in the castle's area, which can vary greatly in size and population.

Furthermore, a full third of each year's harvest could not possibly be stored in reserve. Finally, it is least of all the warriors who live outside who must do the sowing and harvesting and must provision the castle, but rather the noncombatants, the peasants. Consequently, King Henry can never have issued a decree even somewhat similar to this one. It is also so much wasted effort to try to interpret into his training of Saxon horsemen something specifically new, such as the idea that Henry created light mounted troops or, on the contrary, heavily armed horsemen,[4] or that he taught them to execute close-order movements.[5] Widukind's account, written almost a half-century later, is to be completely eliminated as a direct, historical bit of evidence. It is nothing more than the reflection of the obviously recognizable great fact that, through the redevelopment and concentration of the political power, the military system was also fostered and developed qualitatively, and especially numerically. In this process, however, no new forms appeared.

The event of decisive importance in world history that sprang from this base was the victory of Otto the Great over the Hungarians on the Lechfeld. The victory enabled the Romanic-Germanic world to turn back the renewed assault of barbarianism and facilitated the formation of a German kingdom and with it a German people. We shall therefore devote a separate chapter to this battle.

In the western part of the Frankish Kingdom, developments were significantly different. In the first place, the Carolingians in this area held out for two generations longer. When the great dynasties controlling large territories finally broke away from them and elected the duke of Francia, Hugh Capet, as king, his dynasty was not capable of establishing a truly royal power over all of the West Frankish area, as Otto the Great did in Germany. For centuries, the royal crown on the head of the dukes of Ile-de-France remained not much more than a title and a political fiction. Nevertheless, the military organization was not significantly different from that in Germany. In Italy, too, it was the same.

THE FEUDAL MILITARY LEVY

We found that under Charlemagne the king did not levy the individual counties with specific numbers for the army but required either all their men from the warrior class or a specific quota. There were no bases for definite numbers, the counties varied greatly in size and wealth, and even the length of the march to the assembly point counted to some extent, since the more distant contingents could always suffer greater or smaller losses en route through sickness, desertions, fights with robber bands, and conflicts with local inhabitants. The king, who did not even have the necessary statistics as to how many men each county could provide, could therefore not demand specific numbers. Furthermore, the number of warriors was not even the most important consideration and the real burden. Men, even useful men, were probably not so difficult to find.[6] The decisive factors were the costly equipment and the accompanying provisions.

In the complete feudal nation after the tenth century, the levy took a different form, an easier one than in the Carolingian Empire. Precisely as the dukes and counts, and soon also the bishops and abbots, gradually lost the functions of officials and assumed those of princes, their contribution to the army was a matter of direct concern to them and it did not have to be supervised. With the advice of the princes at a diet, the king decided on the campaign and announced it, and the custom developed that each prince solemnly swore that he would come. This procedure seems to have been followed already on one occasion under Henry I,[7] and it continued to be the custom until the reign of Frederick II.[8] The number of knights and common serving men each prince then brought with him was his own affair, and since the weight of his advice in the king's council was directly proportional to the strength and skill of his contingent, this was a better guarantee than any supervision of numbers and inspections.

Consequently, in the army regulation that Frederick Barbarossa proclaimed at the Roncaglian Fields and repeated later, absence from a campaign was threatened with punishment, the loss of one's fief, but no mention was made of the case where someone came with too small a force. In the accounts of our sources, only seldom do we find a trace of an indication that an army strength was counted at all. For example, the *Royal Chronicles of Cologne* (*Kölner Königschronik*) include in their report on King Henry's (VII) invasion of the territory of the duke of Bavaria (1233) the fact that the royal army that assembled on the Lechfeld near Augsburg was found to be some 6,000 men strong.[9]

Instead of definite numbers, each prince therefore weighed the circumstances of each campaign as well as his own interests in order to decide the strength of his contingent.[10]

What a great deal of trouble the Carolingian kings took to establish some kind of standard that would determine the strength of each count's contingent and would oblige the count himself to levy and remunerate his subordinates! Nothing of the sort had been accomplished, and in the newly formed kingdoms the rulers were spared this trouble.

The historians of the nineteenth century tried again to reconstruct a military system from the evidence in the Carolingian capitularies, a task that necessarily remained as fruitless as had the efforts of the great Charles himself. In the same way, scholars have also attempted to find objective measures for the period of the Saxons, Salians, and Hohenstaufens, which would have allocated and prescribed the military burden for that period. The needs of the modern nation were transferred to the older period without sufficient understanding of the peculiar nature of the medieval nation. A modern nation is inconceivable without definite laws, organization, and regulations for the allocation of taxes and services. But we have not truly understood the medieval nation until we realize that it not only did not need such regulations but also could not even apply them. The feudal system meant a division of the highest sovereign powers into several echelons, each of which had a certain degree of independence and cooperated in national matters according to its own judgment, and not as a result of prescribed measures supervised from above. It is the real heartbeat of the feudal period that we feel in this matter. We cannot emphasize this point strongly enough.

But just as the modern nation does not rely exclusively on laws, decrees, and regulations but also in many respects has to depend on the good will and voluntary cooperation of its citizens, there were in the Middle Ages, on the other hand, circumstances and conditions where a fixed numerical levy did apply. It is both worthwhile and revealing to determine from the sources on just what occasions the numbers were mentioned.

The only great vassal of the German king concerning whose contingent the sources give a definite and permanent strength, 300 knights, is the duke, later king, of Bohemia. This was quite natural, since he did not belong to the German Kingdom and the German diet but was only attached to the German Kingdom as a foreigner, a Czech. This fixed contingent, if it already existed at that time, naturally did not prevent the Bohemian, in a case where he himself had the strongest interest, the battle on the Lechfeld, from bringing 1,000 men to his lord. As one of the most loyal vassals of Henry IV, he may also have often supported his lord with more than 300 men.

Similarly, Frederick I later imposed specific requirements on Italian cities. For example, his charter for the city of Lucca specified that the city was to provide twenty knights (*milites*) for the campaign to Rome and lower Italy, in addition to 400 lira in cash and *Fodrum* (food and fodder) for the court and the army.[11]

Sources from the time of Otto II contain a broad levy by numbers. In 981, probably from Italy, the emperor announced a mobilization order for battle against the Arabs. The bishops of Mainz, Cologne, Strasbourg, and Augsburg were each to send 100 men, and the bishops of Trier, Salzburg, and Ratisbon were each charged with providing seventy men. Other officials and localities were summoned to provide contingents as follows: Verdun, Liège, Würzburg, and the abbots of Fulda and Reichenau, sixty; Lorsch and Weissenburg, fifty; Constance, Chur, Worms, Freising, Prüm, Hersfeld, and Ellwangen, forty; Kempen, thirty; Speyer, Toul, Seben, Saint Gall, and Murbach, twenty; Cambrai, twelve;

the Duchy of Alsace, seventy; the duke of Lower Lorraine, twenty; Margraves Gottfried and Arnulf, Dukes Otto and Cono, and Count Hetzel, forty; other counts, thirty, twenty, twelve, and in one case, ten. Some of the vassals were ordered to accompany their contingents. In the case of Count Hetzel, who was to provide forty men, it was added that, if he himself came, he needed to bring only thirty men. The entire levy amounted to 2,080 to 2,090 men. From this source, it has been concluded that levies were always conducted numerically in this manner, and by chance only this one source has been preserved, or that there was also a definite roster for the kingdom indicating how many were to be provided from each area.[12] On the other hand, we can determine that this levy of Otto II was an exceptional case. If there had been a fixed roster, it would not have been necessary to specify the individual numbers but only to give the percentage. The listing of the numbers themselves clearly shows this to be an exceptional case. A whole group of princes, the duke of Upper Lorraine, all the Saxons, and the bishop of Utrecht were missing, and of the total, the clergy was to provide 1,482, while the laity sent only 598 to 608, not much more than one-fourth. It is impossible that the military burden was continuously divided so unevenly throughout the kingdom, especially since the clerical powers at that time still fell far short of the broad influence they assumed in the following centuries. Consequently, this levy was conducted under special circumstances and according to special viewpoints, primarily not for the campaign itself but undoubtedly only for the reinforcement of troops already stationed in Italy. This point also enables us to recognize the reason why specific numbers were prescribed on this occasion. It was necessary to give those princes who were summoned an indication of how much was expected from them under the prevailing circumstances. The usual basis for a levy, to appear with the manpower corresponding to the military forces in the area, could not suffice in this situation, where it was a question of a campaign in Apulia and a mere reinforcement. For example, the duke of Lower Lorraine had to know that only twenty men were required from him and no more. For special reasons, the princes of the Church had to bear a much heavier burden than the lay princes, many of whom were not called up at all. We can assume with certainty that such levies by specific numbers took place not only this one time but also quite often. If they had been the rule, however, they would finally have been drawn up as a definite system, a roster. But as we have seen, there is, for good reasons, not the slightest trace of such a roster.[13]

A treaty which Frederick Barbarossa made with Duke Berthold IV of Zähringen immediately after his election as emperor contains an interesting agreement as to numbers (1 June 1152).[14] Frederick promised to install the duke as the ruler of Burgundy, a throne to which he had certain claims, and the duke obligated himself to follow the king with 1,000 armored horsemen as long as Barbarossa was in Burgundy. But for Italy, he was to provide him 500 armored horsemen and fifty crossbowmen. For this obligation, he offered as a pledge his allodium, the castle of Teck with all its territories. This treaty may be regarded as an intermediate agreement between a feudal obligation and an alliance. Thus, it offers a transition to the treaties on mercenaries, which we shall discuss later and which naturally had to be based on definite numbers.

The relationship at the next lower level, between the princes and their subordinate vassals, was somewhat different from that existing between the king and his immediate vassals. At this lower level, no personal interest prompted a strong effort in the individual's contributions, and so here again we are at a point where numerical relationships are essential.

In keeping with their discretionary judgment, the princes summoned a number of their enfeoffed vassals or those without fiefs and their *ministeriales,* knights and serving men whose circumstances and qualifications were personally known to them, and placed the burden of equipping and supplying them on their areas. This discretionary judgment, both in the extent of the total contribution which they determined and in the allocation of this burden, gave free play to their whims, and since the burden was very heavy, this arbitrariness was very oppressive. For this reason, attempts had already been made early, certainly earlier than the occasion described in our source, to arrive at definite standards based on actual practice. We have original sources on this subject from a few monasteries and dioceses. We also have original indications of the duties and rights of the *ministeriales* vis-à-vis their lord.[15] A particularly graphic source from the monastery of Maurmünster in Alsace, which was under the bishop of Metz, reads as follows:

> When a campaign (*profectio*) of the king is announced to the bishop, the bishop will send an official to the abbot, and the abbot will assemble his *ministeriales*. He will inform them of the campaign, and they will assemble the following men and equipment and will turn them over to the indicated official on the designated day on the square before the gate: one wagon with six cows and six men; one packhorse with saddle and equipment and two men, the leader and the driver. If a cow or the packhorse collapses, the official shall provide a replacement from the property of the bishop. If the king moves the army to Italy, all the peasant farms

shall contribute for that purpose their usual taxes (that is, probably an entire annual rent as an extraordinary tax). But if the army moves against Saxony, Flanders, or elsewhere on this side of the Alps, only half that amount will be given. From these additional taxes the wagons and pack animals will be loaded with rations and other items necessary for the journey.[16]

If the individual contributions to be provided within each county were thus specified, this procedure also determined in a certain sense the total contribution of the county. But this does not contradict our point that no specific contribution was imposed on each prince from above. Even if the local specific determinations established certain limits for the contributions demanded by the prince within his area, that does not eliminate the possibility that he not only did not reach this limit on occasion but also that the limit was not specifically established everywhere in his area, whether in the cities or, especially, in the farm areas. Consequently, the prince continued to have a free hand, was able to make special expenditures from his treasury or from loans, and if he managed to assemble the physical resources from his area, he had no trouble finding horsemen and private soldiers who were ready to follow his banner.[17] Just as the princes gave the king a definite promise as to their contribution, so too did the vassals and *ministeriales* make such a promise to their princes.[18]

Those knights who possessed such an important fief that they could equip themselves for a campaign were also obligated to do so. In the thirteenth century, we still find in Germany and Italy traces of the regulation found in the Carolingian capitularies, that service was required for three months.[19] In France there is repeated reference to the fact that the vassal was obligated for a campaign of only forty days away from his fief.[20] This regulation has even been interpreted to mean that he was authorized to return home after forty days, a situation that nullified any real conduct of war, but in any case his lord had to assume responsibility for provisions in the broadest sense of the word for any extension of the period of service. If a fief was divided, the vassal was responsible for twenty days of service for a half-fief, ten days for a quarter-fief, and there were instances of even smaller fractions. Frequently, service was also limited to purely defensive situations or to the geographical limits of the lord's area.[21] With such limitations, the feudal military obligation made sense only if it served as nothing more than a base and introduction for mercenary military service.

A few provisions from the regulations for service of German knights may help to illustrate these conditions. The *ministeriales* of the archbishop of Cologne were obligated to serve under arms within the area of the diocese and also beyond its borders for the defense of the bishop's holdings, but they did not need to give further service unless they agreed.

For marches to Rome, those *ministeriales* who had more than 5 marks of annual income had to go along in person, with the exception of the bailiff and the chamberlain. Those with smaller incomes had the choice of making the march or giving half of their income from the fief as a military tax. The march to Rome had to be announced a full year before the departure.

The archbishop was required to give 10 marks (double the amount of a rather high annual income) to each of his *ministeriales* who made the march, along with 40 ells of fine cloth (*Scharlot*) with which to clothe his men. He was also to provide for every two knights a pack animal with full equipment and four horseshoes with twenty-four nails.

Beyond the Alps, each knight received 1 mark per month from the bishop. If this mark should not be paid and notice thereof to the bishop's officials did not remedy the situation, the knight laid on the bishop's bed a stick with the bark trimmed, which no one was allowed to remove. If there was still no payment, the knight went to the bishop in the morning, bent his knee, kissed the hem of the bishop's garment, and was allowed to return home without violating his honor and his duty.

In other regulations for such service, the individual provisions governing the obligation to participate in the expedition and the compensation to be made by the lord were expressed differently, according to the various customs.[22]

Instead of monthly pay, there were payments ranging from 3 pounds to 10 pounds for the entire expedition. The lord was also to provide horses, mules with equipment, and serving men, and to assume responsibility for rations.

In Reichenau, determination as to who was to participate did not depend on income but on the size of one's property.[23] It was different for different classes, and the lord was to decide whether the *ministeriales* were to participate or to pay. This service regulation also contained provisions concerning the division of any booty between the lord and the *ministeriales*.

In Bamberg the old method, which we know from the Carolingian capitularies, remained in force, namely, that the knights, instead of making a fixed payment, were arranged in groups of three. In each group, the two who remained at home were to equip the one who went on the expedition.

From these provisions, too, we see that it was a question of very small levies, and from this we may again judge whether the armies with which Charlemagne marched from the Elbe to the Pyrenees and beyond, and from the North Sea to Rome, could have been massive armies of peasants.

From the twelfth century on, conditions in Germany and France developed differently. In Germany, the monarchy became weaker, so that the contribution of each prince was left all the more to his own discretionary judgment. In France, on the other hand, a stronger, hereditary monarchy developed. This led to definite rosters of fiefs, but with such small contributions and such complicated provisions that very little could be derived from them.[24] Feudalism and definite numbers are by their very nature incompatible concepts.

EXCURSUS

MILITARY SERVICE OF THE PEASANTS

While the levy of vassals gradually replaced the ancient German people's levy in a long, slow development, even in the purely Germanic parts of the Carolingian Empire, the political concept of the general people's levy as an extreme measure of ultimate emergency in the form of a militia never completely disappeared. In the border areas, particularly Saxony, practical use of this procedure continued to be made from time to time for a long period. In the writings of Widukind, the difference that was made between the professional warrior class and the levy in the old sense still seems recognizable at times in the expressions used.

In 1: 21, King Konrad sees that Duke Henry is very strong "suppeditante fortium militum manu, exercitus quoque innumera multitudine" ("with a sufficient band of strong knights, also an army in countless number"). The difference between the *milites* and the body of the *exercitus* (army) seems to mean nothing other than the difference between professional warriors and the people's levy. The same distinction applies to 1: 36, where Bernhard is given "exercitus cum praesidio militari" ("an army with a knightly guard") against the Redarians, and 1: 38, where the "legio Thuringorum cum raro milite armato" ("levy of Thuringians with a few armed knights") was sent against the Hungarians. (See also 2: 3.) But Widukind is not quite sure and is not absolutely consistent in his terminology, as we see from the remarkable shift he makes in designating in the cited passage the Thuringian people's levy not by the word *"exercitus"* but with *"legio,"* a word having a specific military conceptual meaning. In 1: 17, he uses the expression "exercitus et militia" ("army and knightly service"), thus placing the two side by side. But in 1: 21, he tells of the indignation "totius exercitus Saxonici" ("of the whole Saxon army") with King Konrad, in which he undoubtedly includes the knights, directly adjacent to the passage in which they are excepted. In 1: 38, Henry wants to lure the Hungarians into the area of the *exercitus,* where the knights must have been meant primarily and at best the general levy only secondarily. Shortly before that, the word *exercitus* is used twice in the same broad sense.

It therefore seems to me that Schäfer goes too far in his interpretation when he understands Widukind's statement (3: 17) that Duke Konrad fought an indecisive battle "suppeditante fortium militum manu" ("with a sufficient band of strong knights") against the "*exercitus*" of Lorraine as meaning that the army of Lorraine was the general levy of that nation.[25] Konrad the Red would undoubtedly have broken up a simple peasant army with his knights.

Baltzer, p. 3, even believes that the peasants served on horseback. He interprets Thietmar (975-1018) as stating that the participation of dismounted soldiers in the war was unusual, and from this he further concludes that the peasants also served on horseback at that time. The correct conclusion, rather, is that they did not serve at all.

Least of all may we conclude, as Baltzer does, that the institution of the peasant service on horseback disappeared again under the Salians, because we read of "vulgus pedestre" ("a mass of foot soldiers") in the battle on the Unstrut. Of course, peasants were also levied in the internal wars of Henry IV. In the poem about the Saxon war (2: 130 ff.), it is said that the units assembled from all the villages and the peasant dropped his plow in order to fight against the king. (See also Chap. III, below.) Later, Henry also levied the peasants in South Germany for his own cause. But these levies achieved just as little as had those of previous generations against the Vikings. In the battle on the Unstrut, the Saxons were slaughtered by Henry's knights just as the Frankish peasant armies had been cut down by the Normans. The peasants who fought for the king in 1078 in Alsace and on the Neckar were not only completely defeated but were also castrated by their knightly opponents as a punishment for their insolence in daring to bear arms.

Guilhiermoz, pp. 346 ff., establishes the fact that, from the tenth century on, the sources treat the people as an unarmed, unwarlike crowd, but he believes that precisely at that time the regulations began to require military service from the peasants as well. He explains that the peasants formed the foot troops, whose arms were regarded as of such little worth that the men were designated as "*inermes*" ("unarmed"). No proof is necessary to show that this solution of the contradiction is impossible. Actually, there is no contradiction. For if we examine more closely the testimony from the eleventh, twelfth, and thirteenth centuries which Guilhiermoz cites on p. 387 for the military service of peasants, we find either that they do not speak of peasants (for example, the "hommes de la vallée d'Andorre" ["men of the valley of Andorra"], who wanted to provide one man from every house), or it is a question of the militia. Furthermore, the evidence which Ernst Meyer cites in *German and French Constitutional History* (*Deutsche und französische Verfassungsgeschichte*), 1: 123, Note 4, to the effect that only *one* man was to come from every house, specifically eliminates the possibilities of a peasant levy. Such a massive levy would be imaginable for only a few days and only in the immediate neighborhood.

In 1070, Otto von Norheim told his peasants that, since they could not fight, they could pray for him ("pro se, quoniam arma ferre non possent, supplicita ad Deum voto facere flagitavit").[26] It did not occur to him to use them to strengthen his forces, even though immediately afterward he had a battle and continued the struggle against the king throughout the winter. If the modern historians, contrary to this picture, recount a great deal about the achievements of the Saxon peasants in the battles against Henry IV, we shall see below in the accounts of the individual battles how little there actually is about this in the sources. Are we to assume, on the basis of those passages in Widukind, that there was once again a generation of military efficiency between two periods of little accomplishment? That is obviously impossible. The cited passages are no doubt partially only rhetorical embellishment. But we may also accept the fact that, just as there were instances of militia battalions serving at the time of the standing armies in the eighteenth century, so too King Henry I and others occasionally reinforced their units of professional warriors with levies of militia but that even this practice gradually disappeared, perhaps with the exception of border districts, where a certain degree of military spirit was maintained among the people. In the *Historische Zeitschrift,* 45: 205, Nitzsch stated:

> As late as the twelfth and thirteenth centuries, the general levy still took place in cases of overall danger in the districts north of the Elbe, enforced through the threat of having one's house burned and destroyed; at the end of the twelfth century, we find in the same area a legally recognized custom for the population to be levied in alternation for the siege of a castle under attack and that the successive levies relieved one another.

In an article entitled "The Saxon *Heergewäte* and the Holstein-Ditmarsisch Peasant Armament" ("Das sächsische Heergewäte and die Holstein-Ditmarsische Bauernrüstung"), *Jahrbücher für die Landeskunde der Herzogtümer Schleswig, Holstein, Lauenburg,* 1 (1858): 335, Nitzsch believed he was adducing proof that in the fourteenth century the peasants in the north were still serving on horseback and that, if this was no longer the case at the end of the fifteenth century, this difference indicated a significant change. The passages on which he bases his conclusions are partially worthless as evidence—for example, the account by the presbyter of Bremen (middle of the fifteenth century) concerning the horsemen of Count Klaus (100 years earlier)—or they only prove that there were also some mounted men in a militia levy, a point that is clear from the start. Nitzsch himself cites on p. 353 a levy of the Wilster March in the year 1342 which directly contradicts the account by the presbyter of Bremen, since only men and wagons and no saddle horses were required at that time.

Nitzsch believes himself justified in regarding as special proof that the peasants once fought on horseback the fact that the battle horse was counted in the Saxon *Heergewäte* and that there are a few indications that the peasants also had battle horses. Nitzsch believes that refers back to the period of Henry I, who "is supposed to have taught his whole people mounted warfare." But the indications that the battle horse was also part of the *Heergewäte* among the peasants are in any case only very weak, and, if one wishes to consider them as evidence at all, they do not prove that the horse was in general once a part of the *Heergewäte.* Finally, there is no basis for relating these situations to the time of Henry I. If that were possible, we could just as well go back to much earlier periods.

Most likely, a certain warrior spirit was maintained among the people in Prussia. The battle horse which the mayor was to provide in other places, for example, in Brandenburg, no doubt meant only the horse and not that he himself was to ride it.

As we shall see, in his battle against the Normans, King Harold of England made no use of a peasant levy because the Anglo-Saxon peasants had no particular interest in the struggle between Harold and William. It was probably only later that they realized it was a question of repelling foreign domination. The Saxons' uprising against Henry IV, however, undoubtedly had an element of popular participation. On the other hand, the peasants whom Henry later levied were no doubt likewise sufficiently inspired by the partisan spirit of that period to obey the summons. Consequently, these peasant levies are easily explained as exceptional phenomena.

On one occasion of dire emergency, in 1082, the margrave of the March of Austria is supposed to have mobilized the entire country, including even the cow- and swineherds, for defense against an incursion by the Bohemians.[27]

The Land Peace of 1156, however, expressly provided a punishment "si quis rusticus arma vel lanceam portaverit" ("if any peasant will have carried arms or lance") and ordered traveling merchants to attach their swords to the saddle,[28] and not to wear them on a sword belt, as the knights did.

If Otto I, in the *Poem of Roswitha* (*Gesta Oddonis,* v. 194), also mobilized a large number of common men in addition to his knights

Militibus suis summo conamine lectis
Necnon immodica tota de gente caterva
(His own knights selected with the greatest concern
And a large unit from the whole nation),

that is not to be understood as a militia. Rather, it means one of two things: either the real professional warriors were strongly reinforced by recruited men of the people, for even if the peasants and burghers as a group had neither a military obligation nor the right to bear arms, the warrior class was constantly supplemented by individual young peasants and burghers. Or, as is more likely,[29] the expression *"milites sui"* of the king in *Roswitha* means his own, directly obligated warriors, both vassals and *ministeriales,* the *scararii* (members of a *scara*) of the Carolingian period, *palatini* (soldiers of the palace) as they were called in the reign of Arnulf, or *aulici* (men of the court), as they were later named under Henry III,[30] in contrast to the men levied from the entire country whom all the counts led to the king.

The joke of Otto I in Widukind 3: 2, that he would lead so many straw hats against France, the likes of which neither Duke Hugo nor his father had ever seen, is incomprehensible, but it is completely impossible that he intended to terrify his enemy with a peasant army.

THE REFORMS OF HENRY I

The well-known passage in Widukind 1: 35 reads as follows: "ex agrariis militibus nonum quemque eligens in urbibus habitare fecit, ut caeteris confamiliaribus suis octo habitacula exstrueret, frugum omnium tertiam partem exciperet servaretque, ceteri vero octo seminarent et meterent frugesque colligerent nono et suis eas locis reconderent. Concilia et omnes conventus atque convivia in urbibus voluit celebrari." ("Selecting each ninth man of the country soldiers, he had him live in the cities so that he might build eight dwellings for his other comrades and might receive and guard one-third of all the harvest, and so that the others might sow, reap, and collect the harvest for the ninth man and store it in their places. He decreed that councils, all assemblies, and banquets be held in the cities.") Also, in Chapter 39, "cum jam militem haberet equestri proelio probatum" ("since he already had soldiers proven in mounted battles").

Dietrich Schäfer, in the *Sitzungsberichte der Berliner Akademie der Wissenschaften,* 27 (1905), 25 May, has recently discussed the first passage concerning the *agrarii milites* (country soldiers) and the construction of the castles. Whereas Nitzsch blithely states in *Deutsche Geschichte* 1: 306: "We do not know what *agrarii milites* means," Hegel understands it as meaning "those living throughout the country," Keutgen as "peasants with a military obligation," and Rodenberg, in *Mitteilungen des Instituts für östreichische Geschichte,* 17 (1896) : 162, as a reference to all freemen. Schäfer seeks to justify the opinion previously accepted by Köpke, Waitz, and Giesebrecht. He believes, namely, that the *agrarii milites* were the king's professional warriors who were settled on the land, that is, the *ministeriales.* All of Schäfer's arguments for this viewpoint seem convincing to me, but aside from the unrealistic point concerning the nine knights, he does not go into the question of the real counterargument, namely, that the eight *milites* who remain in the countryside are supposed to sow and harvest.

But here lies the basic difficulty, and it is insoluble. Schäfer has definitely proved that the *agrarii milites* were professional warriors. But they were also farmers; Widukind expressly describes them as such. Professional warriors, however, are not at the same time farmers.[31] Consequently, Widukind's account is not at all factually historical but only a legend. As soon as we consider it from this viewpoint, all its riddles are solved. For it occurs frequently and easily in a popular legend that several different events become confused with one another without the resulting contradiction being noticed. In Widukind's time, the contemporary situation, in which part of the warrior class, the Carolingian *scara*, lived in the castles as a standing garrison and a part lived on the land on fiefs, was projected into the recollection that formerly all freemen were at the same time warriors and farmers, and an explanation for the change in this situation was sought in a law of Henry I. In doing this, the *agrarii milites* of the older period (when they were still farmers) were grouped together with those of the newer period (when they were professional warriors). Thus, there arose the contradiction that the deliveries of provisions and tribute that were assembled in the castles and by means of which the castles received their provisions appeared to be contributions of the vassals settled on the land rather than those of the peasants.

An interesting legend similar to Widukind's account of the military arrangements of Henry I is to be found in the account already mentioned above of the presbyter of Bremen, who wrote toward the middle of the fifteenth century and reported:

> Rustici de parochiis Scenevelde, Hademersch, Westede, Nortorpe, Bornehovede, Bramstede, Koldenkerken, Kellinghusen cum inhabitantibus paludem Wilstriae, hi dicuntur veri Holsati. Et horum auxilio seniores comites Holsatie obtinuere triumphos. Ex his elegit comes Nicolaus certos viros, de magnis villis unum villanum, de parvis duabus villis unum. Hos, quando indiguit, habuit secum in armis. Nam dictus e. N. sic ordinavit, quod dicti rustici non offendebantur ab advocatis et quod equos valentes tenerent et arma haberent praesertim pileum ferreum, scutum et troyam sive diploidem, ferrea brachialia et chirothecas ferreas, circum amicti balteis latis et amplis. Rustici autem remanentes domi stabant expensas illorum, qui fuerant cum domino terre in campo usque ad reditum ipsorum in domos suos.
>
> (Peasants from the dioceses Scenevelde, Hademersch, Westede, Nortorpe, Bornehovede, Bramstede, Koldenkerken, and Kellinghusen along with the inhabitants of the marsh of Wilstria—these are called true Holsatians. With their aid the lord counts of Holsatia gained victories. Count Nicolaus [middle of the fourteenth century] selected from them reliable men, one villein from the large estates and one from two small estates. He kept them with him under arms when he needed them. In fact, Nicolaus so ordered that said peasants were not harassed by his representatives and that they should keep strong horses and should have arms, especially an iron cap, shield and *troya* or doublet, iron sleeves, iron gloves, and be girded with large wide belts. Peasants remaining at home, however, bore the expenses of those who had been with the lord of the land in the field until their return to their own homes.)

With respect to service on horseback, Waitz states in his *Heinrich I*, p. 391; 3d ed., p. 101 (cf. *Deutsche Verfassungsgeschichte*, 8: 112): "It is probable that Henry had his general levy serve on horseback or at least formed a corps of light horse from that levy." He specifically rejects the opinions of Köpke and Giesebrecht that these were vassals. But what would peasants on farm horses supposedly have accomplished as light horse against the Hungarians? Köpke and Giesebrecht are, of course, closer to the truth, except that it is not a question here of anything new but simply of a careful development of the interpretation of the source material.

In *Deutsche Verfassungsgeschichte,* 8: 114, Waitz himself says that the *"expediti equites"* ("battle-ready horsemen") which are mentioned quite often were not any special type of horsemen (and there is also no possibility of the existence of such special types). Lambert gives the correct explanation in the citation appearing in Waitz: "qui rejectis sarcinis et ceteris bellorum impedimentis, itineri tantum et certamini se expedierant" ("who, after their packs and the other baggage of war had been cast aside, had prepared themselves so much for the campaign and for battle").

NOTES FOR CHAPTER I

1. In "Les grandes familles comtales à l'époque carlovingienne," *Revue historique,* 72 (1900) : 72, Poupardin has shown that the number of these families was rather small. Most of them traced their origins to Austrasia and were located in the most varied parts of the kingdom. They were closely interrelated. They often had properties in very different regions. That point was very important in the divisions into the various nations, since a person who had fallen into disfavor could easily move to another part of the kingdom. For this reason, the kings would not tolerate a person's having fiefs simultaneously in various parts of the kingdom.

In "Social and Political Importance of the Control of Lands in the Early Middle Ages" ("Soziale und politische Bedeutung der Grundherrschaft im früheren Mittelalter"), *Abhandlungen der historischen-philosophischen Klasse der Sächsischen Gesellschaft der Wissenschaft,* Vol. 22, Seeliger has successfully explained, in my opinion, that the significance of the privileges for the formation of the great lords' areas has been exaggerated. The important aspect of the public power always remained with the counties, and it was from them, and not from the great domains, that the later authorities of the nation sprang.

This point alone also explains why such small differences are to be seen between the Romanic and Germanic areas, a point that Seeliger did not raise. He also passed over the fundamental fact that the position of count became a fief and why this occurred, but these points can easily be added to his explanation to complete the basic concept. This is not the place to go into the special controversies that Seeliger's studies have touched off.

2. In *Mitteilungen des österreichischen Instituts,* 17 (1896) : 165, Rodenberg quite correctly observes that Henry did not introduce anything completely new, but he holds fast to the idea that he did not just

simply revive Carolingian arrangements. It would also be a false concept to say that he only "revived old arrangements." In the first place, even a "simple renewal" always brings some changes of detail, and in the second place, the principal point is the great reinforcement of military power associated with the renewal, which was, of course, accompanied by very heavy new burdens (as, for example, the reorganization of the Prussian army by William I). The accomplishment was therefore an important political deed.

3. In this connection, see also the excursus of Chapter II, Book III, below, "German Combat Methods on Foot and Horseback," p. 291.

4. Waitz, *Heinrich I,* 3d ed., p. 101 and elsewhere.

5. Nitzsch, *Geschichte des deutschen Volkes,* 1: 306.

6. This point is not contradicted by the fact that the feudal lord held strictly to the obligation of his enfeoffed vassals to obey the summons for war. The law books also contain the strictest regulations on this point. But we already know from the Carolingian period that the strictness of the obligation did not mean that it always had to be accomplished in person. Rather, it could be satisfied with money, and for that very reason, and not because he would otherwise have had no men, the lord did not permit any modifications. The later supplements to the Roncaglian edicts of Frederick I required that the vassal provide a suitable substitute or pay half of the annual produce of his fief. Waitz, 8: 145. In the corresponding Saxon code, he had to pay only a tenth of his annual income, *Lehnrechte,* 4: 3. *Auct. vet.,* 1: 13. *Deutschenspiegel Lehnrechte,* 11. *Schwabenspiegel Lehnrechte,* 8. According to Rosenhagen, *Zur Geschichte der Reichsheerfahrt,* p. 59.

7. Waitz, 8: 100.

8. Baltzer, p. 23. Rosenhagen, p. 18.

9. *Annales Colonienses maximi. SS (Greatest Annals of Cologne.* Historians in the *M.G.* series), 17: 843, now *Chronica regia Coloniensis continuatio quarta (Royal Chronicles of Cologne, Fourth Continuation),* p. 265. "In campis Lici secus Augustam fere 6 milia militum in exercitu regio sunt inventa." ("In the area of Licum near Augusta almost 6,000 soldiers were found in the royal army.") The only other example of a counting of troops that I have noted is from the fourteenth century: Christian Küchemeister, *Neue Kasus Monst. St. Galli.* Abbot Berthold (1244–1272) moved to the aid of the count of Hapsburg against the bishop of Basel with recruited knights and soldiers "and brought him more than 300 knights and soldiers, all of whom were counted at Säckingen above Brugg." *Historischer Verein von St. Gallen,* 1 (1862) : 19.

10. We now see as pointless the frequently discussed controversy as

to whether only royal fiefs, or also fiefs granted by lords, or also allodia, carried obligations for military service under the king, and whether such obligations differed under varying conditions. (Weiland, "The Campaign of the Royal Army" ["Die Reichsheerfahrt"], *Forschungen zur deutschen Geschichte,* Vol. VII; Baltzer, *On the History of the German Military Organization* [*Zur Geschichte der Deutschen Kriegsverfassung*], Chap. 1, para. 3; Rosenhagen, "On the History of the Royal Army Campaign from Henry VI to Rudolf von Hapsburg" ["Zur Geschichte der Reichsheerfahrt von Heinrich VI. bis Rudolf von Habsburg"], Leipzig dissertation, 1885.) Anyone directly enfeoffed as a prince by the king was obliged to report with a troop of such strength as he himself determined and which he himself raised. It was up to him as to the extent to which he drew upon his fief and his allodia. Naturally, the king had no claim on the subvassals, but, on the basis of the royal levy, their lord ordered them to participate, or they were relieved of that responsibility through a contribution determined by custom and agreement. Allodial possessions within a county—a question that Heusler, *Deutsche Verfassungsgeschichte,* p. 137, still believes will never be solved—were also taxed by the count in accordance with custom, on the basis of the royal levy. Naturally, nobody was free from the military burden except in cases of specific privileges. The king placed the same requirements on his royal *ministeriales* that the princes placed on theirs. The conditions of those freemen of the kingdom who were not princes, conditions originating in the thirteenth century, form a special case which we need not consider here.

From the contributions which the cities made for the army campaigns, there developed the city taxes which the emperors later demanded from the free cities. These taxes give positive testimony that it was not just the royal fiefs that were called on for service to the emperor, a point that would, of course, be taken for granted under any circumstances. See Rosenhagen, p. 67, and Zeumer, *German City Taxes in the Middle Ages* (*Deutsche Städtesteuern im Mittelalter*).

11. Hegel, *Städteverfassungen,* 2: 191.

12. The last point represents Waitz's opinion. *Deutsche Verfassungsgeschichte,* 8: 133.

13. Baltzer, *On the History of the German Military System* (*Zur Geschichte des deutschen Kriegswesens*), Chap. 1, Sect. 5, "The Strengths of the Contingents," has already correctly recognized and given an excellent discussion of these conditions. I refer the reader to his work for the details and the cited passages. The only point on which I disagree is that Baltzer pictures the situation, as I have described it, as existing only from

Henry IV on, and he believes that in earlier periods definite numbers, differing according to the situation, had been required, as in the order of Otto II. For my part, I date the feudal organization, which only exceptionally necessitated the use of such specific numerical requirements, as early as the period of Henry I and thereafter.

14. Jaffé, *Bibl.*, 1: 514.

15. Bibliography on this subject is to be found in Brunner, *Principal Features of German Legal History* (*Grundzüge der deutschen Rechtsgeschichte*), 2d ed., p. 111, and Waitz, *Verfassungsgeschichte*, V, 2d ed., p. 342.

Of particular importance in this connection are the Latin and German versions of the *Laws for the Serving Men of the Archbishop of Cologne* (*Recht der Dienstmannen des Erzbischofs von Köln*), ed. Frensdorff, 1883, as well as the "constitutio de expeditione Romana" ("Ordinance concerning a Roman expedition"), although the latter, presumably a decree of Charlemagne, is fraudulent. According to Scheffer-Boichorst, *Zeitschrift für Geschichte des Oberrheins*, 42 (1888) : 173, repeated in the collection *On the History of the Twelfth and Thirteenth Centuries* (*Zur Geschichte des 12. und 13. Jahrhunderts*), 1897, this fraudulent document was composed around 1154 in the monastery of Reichenau in Swabia. The purpose was to specify, in the interest of the authorities, the obligations and rights of the *ministeriales* of the monastery, who were full of demands. Reprinted in *M. G. LL*, 2. 2. 2. See also "Das Weissenburger Dienstrecht" in Giesebrecht, *History of the German Imperial Period* (*Geschichte der deutschen Kaiserzeit*), Vol. II, appendix.

16. Schöpflin, *Alsatia diplomatica*, 1: 226. Waitz, *Deutsche Verfassungsgeschichte*, 8: 156.

17. When Ladislaus of Bohemia levied his men in 1158 for the march to Italy, they were initially very dissatisfied, but when he explained that those who did not want to go would be allowed to stay at home, while those who went on the expedition had the prospect of rewards and honors, they all eagerly accepted the call.

18. It is stated in this way in the "Service Regulations of Vercelli of 1154" ("Dienstrecht von Vercelli vom Jahre 1154"), published by Scheffer-Boichorst, *Zur Geschichte des 12. und 13. Jahrhunderts*, p. 21: "Illam securitatem, quam dominus fecerit regi secundum suum ordinem, illam securitatem debent facere vasalli super evangelio domino episcopo de expeditione Romana." ("That guarantee which a lord will have made to the king, according to his own rank, vassals ought to make to their Christian lord bishop in regard to a Roman expedition.")

19. On 7 November 1234, Pope Gregory IX required that a number

of German princes should march to join him in the following March "te personaliter decenti militia comitatum, quae in expensis tuis per tres menses praeter tempus, quo veniet et recedet... commoratur" ("you in person by the proper military service of the office of counts, which lasts at your expense for three months in addition to the time in which you will come and return..."). Huillard-Bréholles, 4: 513. In November 1247, Emperor Frederick ordered the Tuscan cities to send the knights their trimonthly pay. Huillard-Bréholles, 6: 576. A dubious document of Frederick's, supposedly dating from May 1243, confirmed to a certain knight Matthäus Vulpilla the property granted to his family by King William in return for providing "unius militis equitis armati per tres menses continuo infra regnum, cum necesu erit" ("one armed horseman for three months in succession within the realm when it will be necessary"). Huillard-Bréholles, 6: 939.

20. Guilhiermoz, *Essai sur l'origine de la noblesse*, p. 276, believes that the forty-day service was first introduced by Henry II for Normandy and was then extended to the other possessions of the Plantagenets. In other French areas, he believes, there developed the legal custom for military service to be provided from the start at the expense of the lord.

21. With respect to these conditions, see Boutaric, *Institutions militaires de la France avant les armées permanentes*, p. 126 ff. On p. 233, Boutaric mentions a "coutume d'Albigeois" ("custom of the region of Albi"), from Martène, *Thesaur. nov. anecdot.*, 1: 834, according to which a vassal who did not bring along the prescribed number of men to the levy had to pay, as punishment for each missing warrior, double the amount of the man's pay.

22. Waitz, 8: 162.

23. According to the so-called *constitutio de expeditione Romana, M. G. LL.,* 2. 2. 2.

24. Boutaric, *Institutions militaires de la France,* has collected the passages on this subject on pp. 191 ff. He says that complete lists of the feudal levies do not exist, but those that have survived show how small the obligations of the great vassals were. Under Philip Augustus, the duke of Brittany provided forty knights, Anjou forty, Flanders forty-two, the Boulonnais seven, Ponthieu sixteen, Saint Pol eight, Artois eighteen, Vermandois twenty-four, Picardy thirty, Parisis and Orléanais eighty-nine, and Touraine fifty-five.

From the time of Henry I (1152–1181), the counts of Champagne had lists made of their vassals, extracts from which have been passed down to us. Published in D'Arbois de Jubainville, *Histoire des ducs et comtes de Champagne,* Vol. II, 1860.

The first of these lists shows a total of 2,030 knights (*milites*). They provided the king with twelve bannerets.

Normandy had 581 knights in the service of the king and 1,500 in the service of the barons.

In 1294, Brittany had 166 knights (*chevaliers, écuyers et archers*), who were obligated to participate in the expedition. According to another source, there were 166 knights and 17 squires (*écuyers*). Brittany was obligated to provide only 40 for the king.

25. *Minutes of the Berlin Academy (Sitzungsberichte der Berliner Akademie)*, 27 (1905) : 6.

26. Lambert von Hersfeld. *SS.*, 5. 178.

27. Cosmas, 2: 35.

28. Waitz, 5: 403, Note 1.

29. Baltzer also understands it in this way on p. 29, and Waitz, 8: 126, at least considers this interpretation also (in contrast with his view on p. 108).

30. *Annales Altahenses* for the year 1044. *SS.*, 20. 799.

31. Widukind, 2: 30–31, recounts: "cum milites ad manum Geronis praesidis conscripti crebra expeditione attenuarentur et donativis vel tributariis praemiis minus adjuvari possent, eo quod tributa passim negarentur, seditioso odio in Geronem exacuuntur." ("Since the knights enrolled in the band of Gero the sheriff were wearied by frequent campaigns and could be supported less by gifts and fiscal rewards, and because they were sometimes denied their pay, they were enflamed by rebellious hatred of Gero.")

Chapter II

The Battle on the Lechfeld 10 August 955

The battle of Augsburg, or the battle on the Lechfeld, was the first national German battle against a foreign enemy. The battle of Andernach (876), in which the sons of Louis the German repelled their West Frankish uncle, had no other character than that of a dynastic feud. The true concept of a German political entity originated with the new dynasty, which freed itself from the overall Frankish Empire. The first battle in which this new nation proved itself, a battle in which warriors of all the peoples cooperated, was the victory over the Hungarians near Augsburg. We have a quite detailed account of the battle in the Saxon history of the monk Widukind of Corvey,[1] and there is a second account in the biography of Bishop Ulrich of Augsburg by a certain Gerhard, who participated in the siege and wrote as an eyewitness.[2] Various individual reports are also available, so that it is possible to establish with certainty a picture of this event.

After finally overcoming the great rebellion by his sons, King Otto returned to Saxony, where he received a report that the Hungarians, who had already marched through Germany once more during the civil war, had again invaded the country. The next report indicated that they were crossing through Bavaria south of the Danube, and they besieged the border city of Swabia, Augsburg on the Lech, which Bishop Ulrich defended with a unit of brave warriors. Gerhard describes how he aroused the courage of his men with a sermon on the psalm "Yea, though I walk through the valley of the shadow of death" and accompanied his men on a sortie wearing his bishop's vestments without helmet or armor.

Meanwhile, the king was assembling a large relief army. It was organized in eight units, or legions, as Widukind called them. One of these units was composed of the Bohemians (Czechs) with a reported strength of 1,000 men. Obviously, this number is supposed to indicate that it was a very strong contingent, as was also evident in another source which had their duke, Boleslaus, personally commanding them.[3] But the strongest contingent was King Otto's unit ("*legio regia*": "the royal legion"), consisting of the king's usual retinue of warriors, which could not have been very small, of a few Saxons, and probably those Frankish knights who were in the king's direct service and had joined him on the march. The main body of Saxon vassals had not been able to move out with the king, presumably because Saxony itself was engaged in a war with the Slavs. A more likely reason was that they would have arrived too late, since it was not even six weeks between the arrival of the first report in Magdeburg and the battle. For all the northern and western Saxons, this period was too short for the transmission of the summons, the mobilization, and the march to Augsburg. According to the sources, the entire army may be estimated at a strength between 7,000 and 8,000 men. It was certainly no larger; in fact, it was probably smaller. All were mounted. It would be incorrect to increase this number by allowing for those men accompanying the knights on foot or horseback who might possibly be counted as warriors. Most of these knights certainly had a serving man, and more prominent ones had several such men. These men also carried out combat functions under certain circumstances, but they did not figure in an open battle. An army of 7,000 to 8,000 mounted men, all of whom were trained professional warriors, was a quite powerful force, and Charlemagne probably rarely had such a force assembled as an army at one time, if indeed this ever happened.

We must pass over the question as to whether the strength of the Hungarians, which was naturally pictured as huge by the German chroniclers, was larger or smaller than that of the Germans; it was probably smaller.

A point of controversy which has been extensively discussed by scholars is whether the battle took place on the right or the left bank of the river.

Nothing can be concluded from the name Lechfeld, since local Augsburg historians applied this name to the plain south of the city on both sides of the river.[4]

There seems to be a clue in the report that the approach of the German army was treacherously revealed to the Hungarians by Berthold von Reisenburg. Reisenburg is situated on the Danube, 14 miles downstream from Ulm. Consequently, we might imagine that Otto crossed the river in that immediate area and approached Augsburg from the direction west-northwest. But closer investigation shows that this report has very little credibility. How should the Germans have known who informed the Hungarians of their approach? It is quite unlikely that the Hungarian king, whom they captured as he fled and then hanged him, was first interrogated on this point. While the main Hungarian army was besieging Augsburg, some of the Hungarian horsemen undoubtedly moved about in all parts of the country, and certainly this combat-tested people systematically observed the Danube. It is impossible that the large German army could have crossed this river without being noticed by the Hungarians, who did not need the help of a German for this information. The traitor Berthold was therefore probably nothing other than one of the typical traitors who are to be found in all the battles of world history, even the victorious ones, who play an important role in the popular fantasy: from the unknown person who gave a signal to the Persians at Marathon with a shield on a mountain to the miller who, by the movement of his windmill, revealed to Benedek the approach of the crown prince at the battle of Königgrätz. Even in the World War this superstition cost countless unlucky persons their lives, especially millers. Berthold von Reisenburg was the son of the Palatine Count Arnulf of the ancient Bavarian ducal family which Otto had deposed. We must leave aside the question as to whether he actually conspired with the Hungarians, but since nothing happened to him afterwards, that is very unlikely. With the credibility of this report, there also collapses the testimony for Otto's approach from west-northwest. We must not believe that, even though the report itself is to be eliminated, there would still be enough evidence remaining to show that the German army must have come from that area. The legend does not work in such a rational way. The Germans can have come from any other direction, and the legend could still have stigmatized Reisenburg as the traitor, once the attention and suspicion of the people were directed against him. If consideration of the Reisenburg situation has now been eliminated, there still remains as evidence for the location of the battlefield the passage in Widukind which relates that the Hungarians, when they learned of the king's approach, quickly crossed the Lech to meet him. Since we know from the bishop's biography that the Hungarians were besieging Augsburg and this city was situated on the left bank of the river and not even directly at the water's edge, the Hungarians must have crossed to the right bank in order to meet the king. In this case, the king would therefore have moved up from the east, from Ingolstadt or Neuburg. But this conclusion is not certain, since Widukind makes no mention of the siege of Augsburg. Furthermore, this siege was a very short one, perhaps lasting only two days. The Hungarians, coming from the east, had only just crossed the Lech. It would therefore not be impossible that Widukind, compressing these events, meant this first crossing of the river, and this, in turn, would mean that the battle took place on the left bank.[5]

The fact that Widukind also has the battle take place in Bavaria ("dum haec in Boioaria geruntur": "while this is done in Bavaria") is direct evidence for the right bank and must be given strong consideration—all the more so in that Swabia extended somewhat beyond the Lech opposite Augsburg and upstream from that city. Nevertheless, this point is not decisive, since we may have here a lapse of attention or uncertainty on the part of the Saxon monk concerning the geography of South Germany.

The direct statement, however, is confirmed by indirect factors that we find in Widukind's account. He reports the order of march of the eight units: the first three were composed of the Bavarians, the fourth unit consisted of the Franks under Duke Konrad, the fifth was the royal unit, the sixth and seventh were the Swabians, and the eighth was formed by the Bohemians. It would have been very unusual if the Swabians, who were familiar with the terrain, had not formed the head of the column if the march was made through their own territory. But instead of them, it was the Bavarians who headed the march, certainly for the reason that they were able to place those most familiar with the region at the head of the column without breaking up the natural units. Widukind goes on to say that the decision to do battle was taken when Duke Konrad arrived. If the assembly area of the army had been farther to the west, for instance, between Ulm and Dillingen, it would be difficult to understand why the Franks arrived later than the Bohemians. But if the assembly area was in the vicinity of Ingolstadt, it was quite natural that Konrad, whose family possessions were situated near Speyer and Worms, arrived so late. Even if the route from Speyer to Ingolstadt is about equal in length to the route from Prague, the Bohemian duke must have received the information and the summons much earlier. Finally, we are told by Ruotger, the biographer of Bruno, the archbishop of Cologne and viceroy of Lorraine, that the troops from Lorraine had not participated in the battle because they could not have arrived in time and had to protect Lorraine itself against an incursion. The last expression sounds suspiciously like an excuse, for the best protection for Lorraine was, of course, to defeat the Hungarians with the concentrated power of the kingdom. But if the army's assembly area was near Ingolstadt, the distance for the warriors from Lorraine was in fact too great, and in that case for the same reason that applied to the Saxons, they were not summoned.

This investigation as to which bank was the scene of the battle seems at first glance to be a matter of only local interest. Why is it important to determine so accurately the spot where the battle took place? We shall quickly see that this apparently minor question is significant in world history, for the location of the battle determines the strategic context, the strategic situation of the battle. But this battle also presents us with a problem in still another aspect.

Otto came with his army from the north, from the Danube. The Lechfeld is situated south of Augsburg, and, according to the statement of the eyewitness, Gerhard, the battle took place so far from the city that it could not be seen from the walls. Gerhard also recounts that the Hungarians, who up to that point were surrounding the city walls, moved out to meet their enemy as soon as the approach of the German army was reported. How then could the battle take place south of the city on the Lechfeld? How is the German army supposed to have moved so far southward?

Since the Hungarians moved to meet the Germans, the first contact must have taken place either to the north, or the northwest, or the northeast of Augsburg.

Gerhard says that this was not a very hard-fought battle. When the citizens of Augsburg saw the waves of Hungarians flowing back from the battle, their mass seemed to be changed to such a small degree that it was at first believed that there had been no battle at all. It appears as if the Hungarians had attempted to envelop the Germans with a unit of archers and attack them from the rear. This attack, however, was repulsed, and when the Hungarians then saw the mighty mass of German horsemen charging with sword and lance, they turned tail and rushed back to their camp south of Augsburg. Even if they recognized that the battle and the campaign were lost, they still had to try to rescue as much as possible of their train, their packhorses, the booty they had taken, and especially the women who surely were accompanying them in certain numbers on their expedition. To accomplish this, they had first of all to cross back over the Lech once again and then quickly cross the river one more time in order to reach one of the roads leading eastward, toward their homeland. If the first contact had taken place on the left bank northwest of Augsburg, the Hungarians would have had an open route for their retreat. Since the engagement was rather far from the river, they would have had an advantage over the heavy German horsemen, and there would have been no further significant fighting. The Hungarians, with the greatest possible speed, would have crossed the Lech, which, although it is a rushing stream and has deep spots, has very little water in August and does not form a significant obstacle. Then they would simply have ridden homeward. But the situation was completely different if the Germans came from the northeast, on the right bank. The first contact would have gone off quite easily for the Hungarians, but now the German army appeared on the Hungarians' withdrawal route, and at the passages over the river, on the Lechfeld, there now developed the actual battle, in which the Hungarian army, with its retreat blocked, was for the most part destroyed. We can imagine that the Hungarians rode farther and farther upstream in order to cross the river and that the German commander took pains to see that his warriors, too, spread their formation farther and farther along the entire Lechfeld and even beyond it, in order to finish their work of destruction. Even if the river offered no significant obstacle to crossing at many points, it is still probable that many Hungarians, caught in the pressure of the mass, fell into deep spots and, as the report reads, drowned. The unique aspect of the battle, then, is that it was divided into two separate acts, both as to time and place. Widukind's account to the effect that the battle, that is, the first engagement, took place in Bavaria is correct, and the fact that this was called the "battle on the Lechfeld" is also correct.

Now we have solved the contradiction that the German army came from the north and the battle was fought south of Augsburg.

A later source, of little validity in itself, can now be woven so well into this context that it gains credibility.

In a document of annals of the twelfth century, the *Zwifaltenses*, the location of the battle is given as a place named "Kolital." Nine miles from Augsburg, southeast of the road to Ingolstadt, between Dasing and Aichach, the village of Gallenbach and the farm Gollenhofen today are situated close to one another. It may be doubtful whether these two names stem from the same root, considering the different vowels, and we cannot establish a true etymological relationship with "Kolital." Nevertheless, the word "Kolital" cannot have been pulled out of thin air, and there is a similarity of sound. Consequently, we may imagine that it is a question of an oral account in which the name, inaccurately understood, was distorted and recorded in its changed form. That does not mean that the armies clashed precisely at the location of the present-day Gollenhofen, for place names can be moved in the course of centuries as a result of destruction and reconstruction. But the hilly terrain a half-day's march northeast of Augsburg, where the name Gollenhofen today still reminds us of a place called Kolital, must have been the battlefield for the first encounter.

Two other chronicles from the twelfth and thirteenth centuries name as the location of the battle a frequently mentioned hill 6 kilometers upstream from Augsburg on the right bank of the Lech. It was called

"Gunzenle," and today it has been washed away by the river. Everything points toward this place as the principal stage for the last act of the battle.[6]

But we have not yet reached the end.

When King Otto received the report of the invasion by the Hungarians in Magdeburg at the beginning of July, his first thought must have been where to decide on the assembly area of the royal army—north of the Danube, of course.[7] The dukes of Bavaria and Swabia had probably already given the order for the assembly of their knights on their own initiative.

It was impossible to know how fast and how far the Hungarians would advance in the period of about five weeks that it would necessarily take for the assembly of the army. At any rate, it could be assumed that they would initially remain south of the Danube and would not have crossed the Swabian border, the Lech, to any distance, if indeed they did not take position in front of the river. If the king selected the assembly area farther back in Swabia, possibly near Ulm or even farther westward, he could be certain of intercepting a further advance by the Hungarians. But if he had had this idea, it would be incomprehensible that he did not also summon the troops from Lorraine. At the beginning of July, when the summons was sent out from Magdeburg, it was impossible to foresee that the decisive battle would take place near Augsburg. Perhaps the battle would not occur east of the area of the Neckar or even on the Rhine. With these various possibilities, is the king supposed to have summoned the Bohemians but not the men of Lorraine? In Ruotger's work it appears as if Archbishop Bruno held his knights back on his own initiative, in keeping with his own judgment, but in view of the excellent relations between the archbishop and his brother, the king, it seems completely impossible for this decision to have been made without the king's approval. We must realize that, if the viceroy of the largest and richest of all the duchies (including also the Rhineland and the Low Countries) did not obey the summons to join the royal army because he wished to provide direct protection for Lorraine, which was, after all, quite distant from the theater of operations, that would have been not only disobedience but outright high treason. But all of this becomes clear as soon as we remember that we have now established the battlefield on the right bank of the Lech. This means, therefore, that the assembly area for the German army was not near Ulm in Swabia but somewhere in the vicinity of Neuburg or Ingolstadt in Bavaria. The German king, therefore, was following the strategic idea, not of taking position in front of the Hungarians in order to drive them back and out of Germany, but of assembling his army in such a way as to be able to attack them from the rear, cut off their retreat, destroy them, and prevent them from ever returning.

At Ingolstadt the king, arriving from Magdeburg, could easily and with the greatest speed join forces with the Bohemians, Bavarians, Swabians, and Franks. The Bavarians probably assembled in the vicinity of Ratisbon. The Swabians no doubt had their assembly area as far forward as possible, in the area of Augsburg itself, whence they withdrew to the north when the enemy approached, or they possibly assembled near Donauwörth. Quite naturally, the Franks arrived last, from the far side of the Rhine, with Duke Konrad. But the forces of Lorraine could not reach an assembly area so far to the east in time. However, they were given another mission. If the Hungarians noticed that a large German army was approaching from the rear, it was, of course, not impossible that they would withdraw to the west, in order to return home by way of Lorraine and the West Frankish Kingdom and Italy, as they actually had done in 932 and 954. That would have to be prevented by the troops of Lorraine, and they were capable of doing so. We may assume that Archbishop Bruno held his forces in readiness so that, in case of necessity, they could prevent the Hungarians from crossing the difficult barrier of the Rhine long enough for King Otto to arrive with the main army and attack them from the rear.

Consequently, although the knights of Lorraine did not participate in the battle on the Lechfeld, they still played an important role in the strategic concept on which the battle was based.

An apparently purely superficial, fortuitous point which the source has provided for us rounds off in an excellent way the picture we have composed and proves that Otto intentionally based the battle on a decision with a reversed front for the purpose of completely destroying the enemy. The last one to appear at the army's assembly area was the king's son-in-law, Konrad, with the Rhenish Franks. He had farther to march than the Bohemians, Bavarians, Swabians, and the Franks of the Main area. If the king had wanted to hasten the assembly, he could have gone one or two days' marches toward Konrad to join forces. Otto must have known what he was doing when, instead, he preferred to wait for Konrad farther eastward, on the withdrawal route of the enemy.

Gerhard goes on to tell us that the king spent the night after the battle in Augsburg and sent out messengers as fast as possible with the word that all the river crossings were to be occupied in order to intercept the flight of the Hungarians. Otto probably dispatched these messengers from the battlefield itself, and he presumably immediately detached a part of his victorious knights themselves, particularly the Bavarians, to carry out this mission. Then it was possible to block the retreat of the fleeing enemy perhaps on the Isar or the Inn, and it turned out that Hungarian leaders a few days after the battle fell into the hands of Duke Henry of Bavaria, who had them hanged. We may also consider in this same context the report that the Bohemians had an encounter of their own with the Hungarians, destroyed the enemy, and took their King Lele prisoner, an account that is found in the contemporary chronicle of Saint Gall.[8] This action could also have taken place on the Lech itself, where the victors might have appeared before the Hungarians had crossed, and the Hungarians either tried in vain to fight their way through or first turned off, intending to cross the river farther upstream, and were there attacked by the Bohemians.

The closer we study these details, the more we recognize not only that they all converge in the one decisive strategic point, the approach of the Germans from the east, but also to what a great extent the resounding success in the battle was determined by this strategy. We now suddenly see how mediocre is the idea of a battle with the approach from the west: the deed of a courageous body of knights still blemished by the fact that a whole duchy selfishly and shortsightedly withheld its cooperation. Nitzsch stated in his *Deutsche Geschichte* that Otto I appears in the sources not as a truly great warrior but as a great supplicant. Waitz, in his *Deutsche Verfassungsgeschichte,* 8: 174, mentions that, of all the emperors, the following demonstrated important qualities as army commanders: Arnulf, Henry I, Henry III, and Lothair. He does not include Otto I in this group, and Bresslau, in the *General German Biography* (*Allgemeine deutsche Biographie*), specifically denies Otto the qualities of a great commander. If the battle on the Lechfeld was fought on the left bank of the river, this concept would be correct. But now the deed of a courageous knight has become the deed of a great commander, and the absence of the Lotharingians from the royal army has become an outstanding strategem. Two generations earlier, Charles the Fat with an army levied from the entire Frankish Kingdom had been able to accomplish nothing against the Normans when they besieged Paris, and Otto's own father had paid tribute to the Hungarians. Our clerical historians may not have understood the situation themselves, and later scholars may simply have been imitating them when they repeated the title "the Great" that was accorded this emperor by his contemporaries, rather than feeling the significance of the title. But now we may say that Otto I truly belongs to those few kings whom world history has embellished with that title. Let us place ourselves in the position of the king when it was reported to him in Magdeburg that the enemy had suddenly invaded Bavaria. It was a

question not only of acting but also of acting with the greatest speed and
decisiveness. How difficult it was to assemble an army of vassals without
a rather long period of preparation! It was a matter of uniting Swabia and
Bavaria south of the Danube—from the Black Forest and from the
Alps—with Bohemia, Saxony, and Franconia, while the enemy army was
marching through these areas. Where was the ideal assembly point? Was
it not the most logical thing in the world to attempt to intercept the
enemy by taking position in front of him? Was it not the safest procedure
to bring up also the Saxons and the Lotharingians and thus unite the
forces of the entire empire, even if this caused the loss of somewhat
more time? How could one avoid the possibility that the Hungarians,
once they saw the strength of the approaching Germans, might avoid
battle and thus render useless the whole mighty mobilization?

All of these questions must have been raised at that time in Magdeburg, and we know how they were answered. It was decided not to
bring up the distant Saxons and Lotharingians, and the assembly point
was not designated on the lower Neckar, for example, but on the north
bank of the Danube in Bavaria between the mouth of the Lech and the
Altmühl, to which area the Bavarians and Swabians had to withdraw
before the Hungarians. The messengers who were dispatched and the
dukes were ordered to act with the greatest speed, possibly with the
words that were once used in a Carolingian document, to the effect that if
the order arrived in the morning, the march was to start that very evening, and if the order arrived in the evening, the march should start the
following morning. And woe to him who did not carry it out in that
manner ("terribile imperium": "dreadful command").[9] The king immediately started the march to the assembly area with the knights in his
retinue and the closest Saxons. The order was sent to Lorraine to defend
itself by occupying the Rhine.

The campaign was so planned that this time the Hungarians could not
avoid their fate if they did not succeed in defeating the Germans in the
battle on which everything was based. For the battle is the only true test
that decides whether the strategy has been correctly determined. If the
battle on the Lechfeld had been lost, the critics would have been heard at
once: Why did King Otto not wait until he actually had the knights of the
entire empire assembled, and why did he himself stimulate the courage
of the Hungarians to the point of despair by cutting off their retreat and
attacking them from the rear? Should one not build golden bridges for
the enemy?

Otto I was a great commander not only because he drew up his plan so
wisely, executed it with such speed, and was so well obeyed by his great

vassals, but primarily because he risked challenging the enemy and fighting the battle under these conditions.

EXCURSUS

CRITIQUE OF THE SOURCES

Widukind says of the *legio regia:* "princeps vallatus lectis ex omnibus militum milibus alacrique juventute" ("the chief vassal of all the thousands of knights and active youths selected"). Naturally, this is not to be understood as if individuals from all the small feudal contingents had been incorporated into a corps under the king's personal command. It is, rather, purely rhetorical glorification of those knights who were in the king's personal service. Immediately afterward it is said of the Franks, who under Konrad's command repelled the Hungarians' attack from the rear: "cunctantibus veteranis militibus gloria victoriae assuetis cum novo milite et fere bellandi ignaro triumphum peregit." ("While the veteran knights accustomed to the glory of victory were delaying, he gained the victory with the new knights almost ignorant of waging war.") This, too, is naturally nothing more than rhetoric—and unsuccessful rhetoric at that. The Frankish knights were probably no younger and no less combat-tested than the Swabians and Bavarians.

Widukind reports that on the last day "ducitur exercitus per aspera et difficilia loca, ne daretur hostibus copia turbandi sagittis agmina, quibus utuntur acerrime, arbustis ea protegentibus." ("The army is led through rough and difficult terrain, so that while the trees are protecting our columns an opportunity might not be given to the enemy of troubling them with the arrows which they use most fiercely.") That is the tactical wisdom of a fellow combatant who, as we can hope, was more courageous than perceptive, which was piously accepted by the good monk and repeated in his work. But the description of the terrain is effective.

Widukind recounts that on the last day's march the train for the entire army was placed at the rear of the column and covered by the Bohemians, because it was believed to be secure there. But, according to the account, this was not the case. The Hungarians reportedly crossed the Lech, enveloped the army, and attacked it from the rear. And they supposedly defeated the Bohemians and then the two units of Swabians as well, and captured the baggage. When the king saw that he had enemy forces both in front and behind, he sent out Duke Konrad with his Franks, and they drove the Hungarians off and took back all their booty.

This account suffers from such serious inner weaknesses that I would not risk incorporating it into an historical presentation. Since first the Bohemians, "the eighth legion," and then the seventh and sixth units were defeated, the army must still have been on the march. Nevertheless, Otto sent to their aid not the closest unit, the fifth, but the fourth. Consequently, this legion would first have had to ride by the fifth, while every minute was important. It is also hardly likely that the Hungarian enveloping force, which could only have been moderately large, was able to put to rout three-eighths of the German army.

Perhaps the situation was as follows: The army was already deployed, with the seven "legions" abreast and the Bohemians in the rear forming the rear guard and protecting the baggage train, when the sudden attack took place. Then it was logical for the fourth "legion," which was deployed in the center, to turn about and disengage the Bohemians. The report that the Swabians, too, were already fleeing, would then be a simple figment of Widukind's imagination, who pictured the units in column, one behind the other. But of course, this is only supposition. Possibly it is nothing more than a very insignificant event which Widukind's informants or he himself greatly inflated to bring higher honor to the king's son-in-law, who later found a hero's death in the battle.

I am not ready to say whether this engagement actually took place on the same day as the battle, as is now generally believed, or on the preceding day. Widukind himself may not have been completely clear on this point.

His statement to the effect that the king personally started the battle with his unit is, of course, not an historical fact, but it should be considered as a means of glorification. Incidentally, as an additional example of how little trust we may place in second-hand reports, let us observe that in the translation of Widukind in the *History Writers of the Earliest German Period* (*Geschichtsschreiber der deutschen Vorzeit*), published under the aegis of Pertz, Grimm, Lachmann, Ranke, and Ritter, with an introduction by Wattenbach, a whole sentence was completely omitted: "similiter septimam ac sextam aggressi, plurimis ex eis fusis in fugam verterunt." ("They were similarly attacked in the sixth and seventh units, and they fled after most of them had been scattered.")

Dietrich Schäfer, writing on "The Battle with the Hungarians in 955" ("Die Ungarnschlacht von 955") in the *Sitzungsberichte der Berliner Akademie,* Vol. XXVII, 1905, called attention to the passage in the *Annales Zwifaltenses* (*Annals of Württemburg*), SS., 10. 53, "Ungari juxta Augustam apud Kolital ab Ottone rega bello vincuntur 4. idus augusti, ubi ex nostris Cownradus dux et Diepolt frater santi Oudalrici occubuetunt." ("The Hungarians on 10 August at Kolital near Augsburg were defeated in battle by King Otto, where on our side Duke Conrad and Diepolt, the brother of Saint Oudalricus, died.") Schäfer identifies this "Kolital" as Kühlental, which is situated some 25 kilometers northwest of Augsburg on the left bank of the Lech on the eastern edge of the hilly terrain above the Schmutterbache. Etymologically, that is possible, but, aside from the direction, the 25 kilometer distance from Augsburg is obviously too great to allow us to place the battle there.

Schäfer convincingly establishes the point that the *"silva nigra"* ("black forest"), up to which the Hungarians, according to Gerhard, had supposedly laid waste to everything in this campaign, referred not to the Black Forest, but to the terrain at the foot of the Alps.

When I reconstructed the battle in the first edition of this work, I reached the same conclusions as now, but only by proceeding over detours and with little certainty, because there seemed to be lacking an absolutely reliable, contemporary account of the action as the "battle on the Lechfeld." It was a result of the outstanding work of Harry Bresslau that such an account was found while my volume was still on the press. In the *Historische Zeitschrift,* 93: 137, Bresslau proved that a vision reported in Gerhard's work on the life of Bishop Udalrich refers to this battle, a point previously doubted by scholars.

Alfred Schröder, "The Battle with the Hungarians in 955" ("Die Ungarnschlacht von 955"), in the *Archiv für deutsche Geschichte des Hochstifts Augsburg,* Vol. I, 1919, again took up the cudgels for the location of the battle on the left bank of the Lech. But the difficulties associated with this conclusion are still not resolved but only avoided or covered up.

Hefner-Alteneck, in his excellent work *Weapons, a Contribution to the Historical Knowledge of Arms* (*Waffen, Ein Beitrag zur Historischen Waffenkunde*), shows in Table IV a sword he owns which is of tenth-century origin and was supposedly found on the Lechfeld. It could, therefore, be a relic of the battle with the Hungarians. It is broad and long, with a rounded point, so that it was appropriate for hacking but not for piercing. The guard is larger than those of the older period, but it is still only of moderate size.

When this chapter was already at the printer's, I received the article "The Gunzenlee and the Lechfeld Battle" ("Der Gunzenlee und die Lechfeldschlacht") by Professor Eduard

Wallner in Augsburg, which appeared in the *Zeitschrift des historischen Vereins für Schwaben und Neuburg,* Vol. 44. Mr. Wallner was also kind enough to supplement his article with additional information through correspondence. His study is very valuable for the topography of the Lechfeld, and I have made extensive use of it in correcting my work. A point of special interest is the fact that "Gunzenlee," which today no longer exists, was actually 5 kilometers closer to Augsburg than has been previously assumed. Furthermore, I have had to eliminate the etymological relationship between "Kolital" and "Gollenhof," which would have been a linguistic possibility, since Mr. Wallner has shown that in a document of 1231 "Gollenhofen" was called "Goldenhoven." In any case, there does remain a linguistic relationship, since the "G" in the initial sound could have been changed to "K" in the mouth of a Bavarian, and the "ll" in the handwriting of the author of the *Zwifalter Annals* may have been dropped. The "*Tal*" ("valley") would be very appropriate in that hilly area containing numerous streams.

Once again I shall list the reasons that oblige us to divide the battle into two separate acts and to assume that the first took place in the vicinity of Gollenhofen, a half-day's march northeast of Augsburg, on the right bank of the Lech, while the second and decisive act occurred on the Lechfeld, close to the river, in the vicinity of Gunzenlee.

Widukind expressly says the battle took place in Bavaria, and this point is objectively confirmed by the fact that the Bavarians were at the head of the march column.

If the German army had assembled in Swabia, west of Augsburg, it would be difficult to understand why the Lotharingians were missing and the Rhenish Franks were the last to arrive. It would also be unclear as to why the king did not assign the Swabians, who were familiar with the area, to lead the column.

The most certain piece of information that we have on the battle is that the engagement took place so far from Augsburg that it could not be seen from the city walls. The retreat of the Hungarians was seen, however, and caused doubt as to whether an engagement had taken place, since the Hungarians seemed to have suffered no noticeable losses. If events of this type had occurred west of Augsburg, no large battle would have taken place. The Hungarians would have withdrawn across the Lech, which would not have been difficult for them, and Otto's order to block their crossings over the Isar and the Inn would have been senseless if he were still dealing with a very strong army. His order attests to a completely defeated enemy, with its units broken up.

Inasmuch as the Hungarians besieged Augsburg, which was protected on the east, west, and north by the Lech and the Wertach, the enemy camp must have been south of the city and therefore on the left bank of the Lech. They moved across the river to face the enemy in battle, consequently over to the right bank. If they did not intend from the very start to avoid the battle, they had no alternative. If they had awaited the enemy in their camp, quite close to the city, they would have been extremely hampered in their movements. And these movements were very important to them as mounted archers.

It is even less possible that the first contact took place south of the city, even if it could be imagined that the Hungarian camp was situated east of the city, that the Germans approached from Ulm, and that the Hungarians moved out in that direction to meet them. In that case, it would be incomprehensible that the withdrawal could have been seen from the city walls, but not the battle itself.

Count Dietbald, a brother of the bishop, left the city the night before the battle in order to join forces with the king's army (leaving behind, of course, as many men as were necessary to guard the walls). This point militates against the possibility that the king approached from the north, for in that case he would have come up so close to the city—or might even have passed it by—that Dietbald would have been spared his night march.

There remain only the directions northwest or northeast, and we have already seen why the northwest is eliminated, on the basis of the sources and objective analysis.

The vision of Bishop Udalrich, as reported by Gerhard, undoubtedly places the battle in the vicinity of Gunzenlee, about 6 kilometers upstream from Augsburg on the Lech, as Wallner proves. Gunzenlee is also expressly named by two later chroniclers. This combat at Gunzenlee cannot have formed the first act of the battle, for the Hungarians fled from the first encounter past the Augsburg city walls. This was, therefore, a special battle act, and it must have been a very important act. It would not have taken place if the Germans came from the west and the first encounter occurred on the left bank of the Lech. But it would have occurred easily if the Germans came from the northeast, the Hungarians had withdrawn to their camp from the first encounter, and the Germans then confronted them for the second time at Gunzenlee and blocked their retreat. That point is confirmed by Widukind's report that the Hungarians had crossed the Lech in order to confront the king and that the battle—that is, the first engagement—took place in Bavaria.

The specific, source-based, and analytical rejection of the many other hypotheses concerning this battle is to be found in detail in the *Delbrück-Festschrift* of 1908 from the pen of Karl Hadank (Georg Stilke, publisher). This work also corrects the widely held erroneous idea that Duke Konrad was struck in the neck by a Hungarian arrow when he loosened his helmet because of the heat. Actually, he opened up the gorget and his coat of mail.

EARLIER HUNGARIAN BATTLE

Liudprand *Antapodosis,* 2: 4, recounts a victory of the Hungarians over King Louis the Child. The Hungarians supposedly feigned flight and set up an ambush. Neither the author nor his account is reliable.

NOTES FOR CHAPTER II

1. *Mon. Germ. SS.,* 3. 408.

2. Gerhardi, *Vita S. Oudalrici (Life of Saint Oudalricus), SS.,* 4. 377.

3. Flodoard, *SS.,* III.

4. Steichele, *The Diocese of Augsburg (Das Bistum Augsburg),* 2 (1864): 491, and L. Brunner, *The Invasions of the Hungarians in Germany (Die Einfälle der Ungarn in Deutschland),* 1855, p. 38.

5. Attempts have been made to reconcile Widukind's report that the Hungarians crossed the Lech and the fact that they were already on the left bank with the assumption that the battle, nevertheless, took place on the left bank. This explanation is based on the assumption that the reference to the Hungarians was only to those who attacked the Germans in the rear before the actual battle and that, consequently, only a part of them crossed the river, only to cross it for a second time near its mouth, thus falling on the Germans from the rear. A special example of this belief is to be found in Wyneken in his *Studies on German History (Forschungen zur deutschen Geschichte),* Vol. 21, where he effectively corrects many of the errors made by others but in this case obviously falls from analysis

into pure harmonistics. Widukind's meaning is clear, namely, that the entire Hungarian army crossed the river to do battle, and not simply a part of the army crossed for the purpose of an envelopment and then returned. If anyone wishes to eliminate Widukind's testimony to the effect that the Hungarians crossed the Lech before the battle ("Ungarii nihil cunctantes Lech fluvium transierunt": "The Hungarians crossed the Lech River without any delay at all") in order to be able to place the battle on the left bank, the only consistent possibility is to assume, as I have done above, that Widukind, who makes no mention of the siege, meant the first crossing.

6. *Annales Palidenses* (*Annals of Pöhlde*), *SS.*, 16. 60: "ad clivum, qui dicitur Gunzenle" ("toward the hill which is called Gunzenlee"). *Chronicon Eberspergense* (*Chronicle of Ebersberg*), *SS.*, 25. 869: "Locus autem certaminis usque in hodiernum diem super fluvium Licum, id est Lech, latino eloquio nominatur Conciolegis, vulgares vero dicunt Gunzenlen." ("The site of the battle, however, on the river Licum, that is the Lech, is called up to the present day by its Latin name Conciolegis; the common people in fact say Gunzenlen.") Steichele, in *Das Bistum Augsburg*, 2: 491, reports that the hill no longer exists.

7. Widukind says that the king established his camp "in confiniis Augustanae urbis" ("on the borders of the city of Augsburg") and that the other contingents joined him there. That, of course, does not mean that the assembly area was in or beside the area belonging to the city of Augsburg, but only that it was in the vicinity of Augsburg, where the battle later took place. The assembly had to take place north of the Danube so that none of the contingents would be individually exposed to an attack by the swift Hungarians. Only after all the contingents were assembled did they move across the river, ready for battle.

8. *Annales Sangallenses majores* (*Annals of Saint Gall*), *Mon. Germ. SS.*, 1. 79. To judge from the short report in these annals, it would not be impossible to conclude that the engagement between the Hungarians and the Bohemians and the capture of Lele took place in a completely different campaign, possibly on the Bohemian border. But we may clarify this point through a report from the *Chronicon Eberspergense*, *SS.*, 20. 12, which is admittedly 100 years later and very distorted but also contains the same name, Lel, of the Hungarian duke who was taken prisoner by the Ebersperg garrison while fleeing.

9. Thus reads the imperial order as it was relayed by Archbishop Hatti of Trier to the bishop of Toul in 817. See p. 35, above.

Chapter III

The Battles of Emperor Henry IV

BATTLE AT HOMBURG ON THE UNSTRUT
9 JUNE 1075

We have three rather thorough accounts of this battle: one by Lambert von Hersfeld, one by Bruno,[1] and a heroic epic poem.[2] But the first two of these are tendentious and contradict one another on important points, while the third is purely rhetorical. Lambert and Bruno state that the army of Henry IV moved up completely by surprise and fell on the Saxons, but we do not know to what extent this is intended simply as an excuse for the defeat. We can no doubt attribute to rhetorical embellishment Lambert's statement that in their haste only a few of the Saxons had put on their armor and had stormed out through the "gates" as if they had had a fortified camp like the Romans. Very many of them supposedly remained north of the Unstrut and heard of the defeat before they knew about the battle. Nevertheless, the battle is supposed to have oscillated back and forth from noon until nine o'clock, and even then to have been decided only by the intervention of new units on Henry's side. Bruno is probably more accurate in this regard when he says the battle, while violent, was decided in a very short time, since on the Saxon side only three of the leaders were killed, whereas the royal forces, according to Bruno, lost eight of their leaders. Lambert's report of the numerous nobles from Swabia and Bavaria who were supposedly killed is no doubt just as erroneous as the report of the few who were not wounded.

It seems certain that this was purely a battle between knights, in which the most important princes fought in the forefront. Margrave Udo of the North March supposedly delivered such a blow with his sword to the head of his cousin, Duke Rudolf of Swabia, the later counterking, that Rudolf was saved only by the toughness of his helmet. And on other parts of the body the duke was reportedly covered with bruises. Margrave Ernst of Bavaria, who belonged to the king's army, was so critically wounded that he died. On the Saxon side, Count Gebhard of Supplinburg, the father of the later Emperor Lothair, perished. On the imperial side, it is not clear whether any foot troops at all were present. According to Lambert, the Saxon foot troops were in their camp during the battle. This was hardly intended—for why would they have brought the foot soldiers along unless they were simply the serving men of the train?—but this occurred because the mounted men stormed forward and decided the outcome of the battle so quickly. Bruno reports that a large part of the Saxons had already taken to their heels before the beginning of the battle.

Scholars have thought that these foot troops who were cut down en masse were a peasant levy. The *carmen de bello Saxonico* (*Song of the Saxon War*), *M. G. SS.*, 15. 2. 1231, describes thoroughly how the Saxon knights forcefully impressed the men of the people into military service and how these men themselves were then inspired with a warlike spirit, the farmers and the shepherds marched to war, wrought weapons from their tools, and left the countryside empty. But according to Lambert, the Saxons were described in the king's war council as an unwarlike people: "vulgus ineptum, agriculturae pocius quam militiae assuetum, quod non animo militari sed principum terrore coactum, contra mores et instituta sua in aciem processisset" ("an inept rabble accustomed to agriculture rather than military service, who, compelled not by a military spirit but by fear of their leaders, had entered battle contrary to their customs and traditions").

Despite these statements, it is quite impossible that the Saxon princes wanted to lead the peasant militia into open battle. The *carmen* is a poem full of fantasy. That point is particularly evident at the end, where it describes how the king followed up his victory by laying waste all of Saxony, capturing towns and castles. Few Saxons had any possessions left—"domus aut pecus aut res" ("house, herd, or property"). Actually, the king advanced with his army, marching around the Harz to the east, only as far as Halberstadt, and he then continued with a small retinue to Goslar but turned about on 1 July.[3] If in like manner we reduce the account of the general levy, we can interpret it as meaning that the Saxon princes, in addition to their knights, also took along on horseback quite a number of other useful men. But in particular they strengthened their forces with an unusual number of foot soldiers and in doing so, of course, sought out or recruited, equipped, and took along many who had not proven themselves.

Lambert's statement that the terrain did not allow the entire royal army to attack simultaneously and that consequently the units were deployed one behind the other, with the king in the fifth echelon and the Bohemians in the rear, should undoubtedly be rejected, for the terrain south of the Unstrut in no way forms an obstacle to a rather broad deployment of units of horsemen. Perhaps this description is based on a report concerning the order of march. The report by the monk Berthold of Reichenau (*M. G. SS.*, V) that 8,000 Saxons were killed in this battle is, of course, without any validity.

THE WAR BETWEEN HENRY IV AND THE COUNTERKING RUDOLF

While Henry IV was in Italy seeking a reconciliation with Gregory VII and doing penance in Canossa, the opposing German princes assembled in Forchheim in Franconia and elected as counterking the husband of one of the king's sisters, Duke Rudolf of Swabia (15 March 1077). But as soon as Henry, whose excommunication had been remitted, returned to Germany, so many counts and bishops joined him that Rudolf had to withdraw at once from South Germany. Rudolf moved back to join the Saxons, where the old hostility toward the king aroused the spirits of the people in his favor. But even if a decisive majority of Bavarians, Swabians, and Franks espoused the king's cause, these gentlemen were nevertheless not inclined to follow him at once into a battle that would decide between him and the usurper, but they wanted to settle the controversy over the throne with a peaceful agreement. Since such an agreement, no matter what the conditions, could only have ended, after all, with Rudolf's renunciation of his claim, he assembled his entire force and marched with a Saxon army up to the Neckar, after joining forces with the two dukes, Welf of Bavaria and Berthold of Kärnten, from the house of Zähringen. But despite these reinforcements, he was not strong enough to force Henry to do battle. He had to withdraw, and the winter and the following spring were spent in negotiations, a few wasting expeditions, and the siege of individual castles. Not until midsummer did Rudolf make a second attempt to bring on a decision by battle, and once again he moved out with the Saxons to join forces with the South German dukes.

THE BATTLE OF MELRICHSTADT
7 AUGUST 1078

Rudolf moved up through Thuringia, while the Swabian army under Dukes Welf and Berthold assembled between the Rhine and the Neckar.

But this time King Henry, too, had a large enough army. He moved out against the Saxons and met them near Melrichstadt, on the border between Thuringia and Franconia. According to Bruno's thorough account (Berthold's account is a completely confusing fable), the battle was fought purely as a battle between knights, with the result that on each side a part of the army was victorious while another part fled. That has happened in quite a few battles, but in a battle between knights, it has particular significance in that it is almost impossible to stop knights, once they have started to flee. Even with disciplined cavalry, it is very difficult to do so, and with knights it is not only more difficult psychologically, but particularly because it is impossible to take up a rallying position in order to clarify the situation by means of a delaying action. Except in very special circumstances, knights cannot wage a defensive battle. When the enemy moves toward them, they must either move against him or withdraw. Among those Saxons who acknowledged defeat at Melrichstadt and took to their heels was King Rudolf himself. He was recognized as a very courageous man. Actually, the battle was not lost for him, since his opponent, Henry, also abandoned the battlefield, and a Saxon contingent under Palatine Count Frederick finally dominated the field. Nevertheless, Rudolf had continued his withdrawal all the way to Saxony. Some of his princes were robbed and killed by the peasants along the way, or they were captured and turned over to King Henry. Even the victorious Saxons under Palatine Count Frederick could do nothing more than to take the booty and march homeward.

A later source, which may have been based on a definite report, the *Pöhlder Annals,* states that King Rudolf, on finding that he had fled before his own victory, could have died from despair.[4] Despite King Henry's defeat, it therefore appears that he succeeded in his strategic purpose of keeping the two enemy armies separated. We would expect that he would now have turned against the Swabian army, especially since the duke of Bohemia led fresh troops to join him. But whether it be that Henry's fleeing knights had also gone all the way home or that there were other reasons unknown to us, in any case Henry at first did nothing except to go to Bavaria, where finally in October he assembled a new army for a campaign of destruction against the possessions of his opponents in Swabia.

This event is highly characteristic of knightly warfare, and it may not be lightly passed over as Giesebrecht does when he states that Henry withdrew because otherwise he would have been caught between the two enemy armies. The Saxons had, after all, withdrawn, and even if they had returned soon, the king in the meantime could have defeated the South

German dukes. Floto, in his *Life of Henry IV* (*Leben Heinrichs IV.*), is just as far from the truth with his observation that the king could not pursue the Saxons because the South Germans, who had in the meantime defeated the peasants on the Neckar, would have moved in behind him. In this case, they would have played directly into the hands of the king, who could have turned back from his pursuit of the Saxons at any moment. In no way can Henry's action be explained by strategic reasons. Rather, the correct explanation can only be found in the nature of the knightly army (unless other reasons, completely unknown to us, played a role), which was no longer combat-ready, even after only a half-defeat.

BATTLE OF FLARCHHEIM
27 JANUARY 1080

Melrichstadt had had no immediate results for either side, but it was the king who won the eventual advantage to the extent that it was evident that Rudolf was too weak for a strategic offensive and that this conflict could not be ended by negotiations. These points now persuaded the adherents of the king to provide him enough help so that he could assume the offensive. He even undertook a winter campaign.

A number of the highest Saxon princes had lost confidence in the counterking and had abandoned his cause. Henry probably concluded, therefore, that if he now appeared suddenly, Rudolf would not be capable of opposing him in the open field.[5] But Rudolf, together with Otto von Nordheim, moved out to face him south of Mühlhausen in Thuringia. The Saxons took position on a rise behind a brook in order to attack the enemy at the moment when he was crossing the stream and moving up the hill. But Henry recognized the disadvantage of the terrain and moved around the position.

The partisan authors contradict one another concerning the result of the battle that now developed. Bruno and Berthold say that the Saxons were victorious and Henry fled. But according to Ekkehard (Frutolf) and the *Augsburger Annals,* the Saxons fled, and Duke Ladislaus of Bohemia, on Henry's side, even captured Rudolf's golden royal lance, which, by Henry's order, was thereafter always to be carried before the Bohemian dukes on formal occasions. But, Ekkehard goes on to say, during the battle a unit of Saxons attacked the king's camp, killed the squires, and carried off a great deal of booty. Then the king turned back to East Franconia and released his army.

At first glance, this explanation for the king's withdrawal sounds very much like an excuse to cover up a defeat, and certainly Henry did not win a true victory. But it is not entirely impossible that the course of the battle was similar to that of Melrichstadt and that Henry turned back less because at Flarchheim he was actually defeated than because he saw that his hopes to the effect that the Saxons would no longer support Rudolf were not fulfilled. That Henry was not actually defeated also seems apparent from the fact that Bruno says nothing about a conquest of the camp, and Berthold reports that the combatants were separated only as a result of nightfall. Nevertheless, he, of course, claims victory for the Saxons, for he says that Rudolf held out on the battlefield until midnight and then, only because of the intolerably cold weather, he sought shelter in the neareast village, returning to the battlefield at daybreak. Therefore, under no circumstances does there seem to have been any pursuit.

Berthold says that only thirty-eight men on Rudolf's side were killed "et hi omnes praeter duos de minoribus non de militaribus ensiferis cecidisse referuntur" ("and all these but two are reported to have fallen from the lesser troops, not from the knightly swordsmen").

BATTLE ON THE ELSTER
15 OCTOBER 1080

Not until after the engagement of Flarchheim did Pope Gregory break for the second time and definitively with Henry by excommunicating him once again at the Easter Synod of 1080. It was with this action that the military tension, too, reached its highest point. All illusions of a peaceful settlement, which until then had restrained a part of the forces on both sides, had now disappeared, and both sides could no longer have any other idea than to assemble all available forces and bring on as fast as possible a final and definite decision. After his experiences of the previous years, Rudolf knew that he was not strong enough for an offensive. The initiative fell to Henry as the stronger of the two opponents. Throughout the summer, he was still occupied with religious matters; he held a synod at Mainz and a second one, together with the Italian bishops, in Brixen, where he took the ultimate step and set up a counterpope. Then he turned his attention to Rudolf.

We are relatively well informed about the campaign and the battle by the thorough account of Bruno, who was perhaps present himself. But, of course, we cannot expect a complete account of the reasons in the report of the earnest priestly partisan author, even for the actions of the Saxon leaders, and, naturally, much less for those of King Henry.

The king's task was to unite the troops of West and South Germany with those of Bohemia and those of the margrave of Meissen, who had come over to his side. Henry took the dangerous route from Hesse through Thuringia, along the southern border of Saxony, in order to join forces with the other contingents on the Saale or the Elster. By a feint against Goslar, he succeeded in luring the assembled army of the Saxons at first in this direction, while the royal army was marching eastward via Erfurt. But the Saxons soon realized their error and turned to follow their opponent. They overtook him on the Elster. The Bavarians, coming from the south, perhaps already joined the king here.[6] The Bohemians and Meisseners were still on the far side of the river.

Bruno raises the question as to whether Henry may have intentionally drawn up his forces with their backs to the water so that they would have no chance to flee. The later local legend in the *Pegau Chronicle* shows that the battle took place near a place named Milsin (Mölsen) on the Elster (*"juxta Elstram"*). From this, there can be no doubt that the battle was fought directly on the river bank.

When Bruno further reports that Henry did not wish to delay the battle any longer, this statement apparently confuses the actual situation. Why then would he first have marched so far? Furthermore, the same author tells us that the king drew up his camp on the Elster against his will (*"nolens"*). If it had been within Henry's power, he would certainly have postponed the battle until the Bohemians and the Meisseners had joined him.

None of the sources gives us any indication as to what prevented the king from crossing the Elster, which, after all, forms no very significant obstacle. Since he had crossed the Saale south of Naumburg without being able to capture that city,[7] the logical route for joining forces with the Bohemians led in the direction of Zeitz. This point, as we shall see, is also consistent with the later events. Zeitz must have had a bridge across the Elster. Perhaps Zeitz, like Naumburg, closed its gates to the king, thus blocking his direct route, and before he had built his own crossing, the Saxons appeared on the scene.

We might still ask why Henry, if he could not cross the Elster and did not have his forces assembled, did not withdraw southward along the river. But once the Saxons had overtaken him, that move was no longer possible in an orderly way. Such a withdrawal might easily have turned into a flight. An army that depends almost entirely on close-combat weapons, and primarily on mounted men at that, finds it too difficult to fight delaying rear guard actions in order to gain time for an orderly withdrawal by the main body. Furthermore, south of the area where the battle must have taken place, the Elster makes a sharp bend to the west, which would have made very difficult a withdrawal before an army coming from that direction. Finally, it is possible that the reinforcing troops of Bohemians and Meisseners, on whose account the entire march from Hesse through Thuringia had been made, were already close by on the other side of the river. The *Pegau Chronicle,* which is, of course, of a much later date but still undoubtedly contained a local legend, even reports that the Bohemians participated in the battle. In view of Bruno's positive testimony to the contrary, we shall have to reject this point. But when that same chronicle goes on to tell how the duke of Bohemia rescued King Henry, covering his move through Bohemia, this point seems very likely and can hardly be pure fiction. The supposed participation of the Bohemians in the battle was probably concluded from the account of this flight and rescue, at a time when the details of the sequence of events were no longer accurately remembered. But we may now conclude that, if the Bohemian duke was able to rescue the king from the battle, he was perhaps already on the opposite bank with his advance guard during the battle. The direct possibility of joining forces with him caused the king to try to gain the necessary time by a maneuver, instead of withdrawing farther southward.

He therefore took up a position behind a swampy valley, where the Saxons could not attack him directly. According to Bruno, this swamp was called "Grona." We may assume that this name has been retained in the name of the village of Grana, or Grona, opposite Zeitz. There is a valley here that extends from west to east to the Elster, which formerly was presumably a swamp. The road on which Henry marched up from the Saale ran along the southern edge of this valley, crossed the swamp near the Elster with a sharp bend to the north, and led to the bridge at Zeitz. We can assume that the bridge was then at about the same place as today. Henry had, therefore, crossed this swamp and was in position on the north side, when the Saxons appeared behind him.

The Saxons were not able to cross the swamp in full view of the enemy, and Bruno says the knights shouted insults from one side to the other and scornfully challenged one another to come across.

Protected by the swamp, the king was momentarily unassailable. Although Zeitz blocked his direct passage over the river, on the other side the duke of Bohemia and the margrave of Meissen were approaching the city. Even if this threat did not open up the passage, it could not have been difficult for the king within a short time to erect a crossing outside the city, by·means of which he could unite his troops either on the one side of the river or the other.

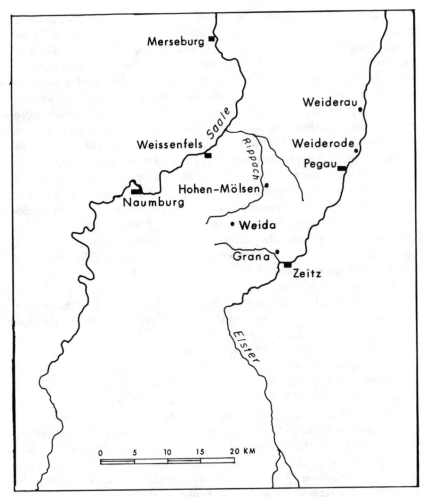

Fig. 2   BATTLE ON THE ELSTER

The Saxons, however, had the possibility of moving around the swamp on the west by moving back a bit on the road they had followed. Henry no doubt realized this but either estimated that such a move would require another day, which would have been enough for him to build a crossing over the Elster, or he himself could cross the swamp again to the south while the enemy was making his encircling move, so that once again the obstacle would have been situated between the two armies.

But King Rudolf and Otto of Nordheim realized what was at stake and were capable of dealing with the situation. Bruno recounts that, because many of the Saxon foot troops had fallen out from exhaustion during the pursuit through Thuringia, it had been ordered that all those knights who had weaker horses were to dismount and fight on foot. For what purpose were the dismounted men used? It was not that the knights had dismounted because their horses were no longer capable, but because they were to replace the missing foot soldiers. We know how much more valuable the mounted man was in open battle than the man on foot. The dismounted contingent that was artificially created here must have had a special purpose, a very important one, since Otto of Nordheim, the top man in the army after King Rudolf, assumed command of this unit. We may assume that the mission of this group was to occupy and block the crossings over the Grona Swamp, while the horsemen made the encircling move. During the battle, the foot troops themselves were to intervene from these points. The Saxon army was unquestionably considerably larger than the royal army, so that it could afford this division of its forces, which now obliged Henry to do battle and in a situation where he had no other retreat than into the river.

The dismounted troops were capable not only of defending the swamp but also of crossing it at spots that would have been impassable for mounted men.

The further sequence of events supports this supposition. The mounted battle that was fought with the opposing fronts facing east and west swayed back and forth. Some of the Saxons were reportedly already in flight, when Otto of Nordheim appeared from the south with the foot troops. Bruno says that Otto defeated a part of the enemy, drove into the enemy camp, prevented his men from plundering, and led them against the remainder of the enemy forces that were still fighting. He was victorious at each place. Such an accomplishment by dismounted men against knights *ceteris paribus* (with other things equal) is completely incredible. Everything clears up, however, at the moment we imagine that Otto crossed the swamp with his men while the outcome of the mounted battle was still in doubt. First, he drove off the defenders of the crossing point. Then he attacked the royal camp but was able to keep his men under control and led them into the mounted battle, which was now decided in favor of the Saxons as a result of these reinforcements. We may pass over the question as to whether the detailed actions occurred in this manner or somewhat differently. Our source, Bruno, obviously had no clear concept of these points. The principal point for us is the explanation of why the knights were ordered to dismount and why, fighting on foot, they were able to be the decisive factor in the mounted battle.

Although Henry was completely defeated and part of his army perished in the Elster, the scales remained even in that the victor, the counterking Rudolf, himself was killed. His right hand was cut off, and he had a serious wound in the abdomen, which caused his death. His gravestone can still be seen today in the Merseburg Cathedral. We can imagine how the proud knight, who at Melrichstadt "had fled before his own victory," had lost his royal lance at Flarchheim, this time had fought *"alsam er wuote"* ("as if he were raging"), to use the expression of the *Nibelungenlied*, to restore his fame after the battle on the Unstrut, and this knightly ambition now caused the king's death. His followers erected this inscription in his honor:

In the place where his men were victorious,
He fell as a holy sacrifice.
Living was for him the death
Which he suffered for the Church.

But Ekkehard wrote in his chronicle that, when Rudolf's severed right hand was brought to him, he reportedly said with a sigh to the bishops who surrounded him: "That is the hand with which I swore loyalty to my lord Henry; look you, who have allowed me to mount his throne, whether you have led me in the right way."

The final reason for the defeat of Henry IV was his march through Thuringia. If he had marched farther to the south, through Franconia, joining forces with the Bavarians, Bohemians, and Meisseners in the area of the upper Saale, and had then advanced with decisiveness, we do not know which side would have been the stronger. But as the king marched through Thuringia with half of his army, he came so close to the Saxons that they were able to attack him and force him into battle before he had assembled his entire army. In the final analysis, it may have been a question simply of a few hours, of a chance situation that held up to some extent the crossing of a medium-sized river like the Elster. We do not know what caused the king to choose his precarious route of march. We can only see, from the maneuver with which he lured the Saxon army in a false direction, that he was fully aware of the dangers of his undertaking. Presumably, it was concern for the problem of rations that caused him to establish the assembly point for all his contingents as far forward as possible. If Henry had succeeded in assembling the Rhenish, South German, Bohemian, and Meissen troops in one place, the army would no doubt have been unusually large and would have had great difficulty in moving as a unit. Furthermore, by marching through Thuringia with the contingents from the west, he spared his own regions and punished those of the enemy. It is also possible that he underestimated the strength and offensive power of the Saxons and relied too much on the effectiveness of his deceptive maneuver. All of these points are, of course, only suppositions, but they are suppositions that automatically arise from the nature of the warfare of that period, the circumstances, and the spirit of those involved. The constant difficulty of the conduct of war in all periods, namely, that large armies are difficult to move and to feed and that, if they are split or decreased in size, the small armies are defeated—in the period of feudal armies and barter economy, this difficulty was even greater than in other periods.

The fact that Henry IV failed in his attempt to overcome this difficulty helps us to understand why, in the Middle Ages, attempts to force great decisive actions on the battlefield with assembled large armies were made so seldom.

EXCURSUS

It is impossible to gain a picture of the battle on the Elster directly from Bruno's account alone. In order to make our reconstruction possible, it was necessary to draw in two other elements: the theoretical understanding of the value and significance of the armed branches, horsemen and foot troops, in this period, and the determination of the place and knowledge of the terrain on which the battle was fought. For knowledge of this latter point, we are indebted to a study by Dr. G. Landau in the *Korrespondenzblatt des Gesamtvereins der deutschen Geschichts- und Altertumsvereine,* 10. 5 (1862) : 38. In Floto's valuable book on Emperor Henry IV, the author arrived at a completely different picture of the battle, since he did not have available those two elements of the research. Furthermore, he also overlooked the strategic background of the battle, namely, that Henry did not yet have his forces assembled and was still seeking to avoid the battle, whereas the Saxons, with their superior forces, obliged him to fight. Consequently, Floto can explain the outcome of the battle in no other way than through the incomprehensible behavior of Palatine Count Henry von Laach, who initially was victorious with the wing of the royal army he was commanding but then called a halt and had the *Kyrie eleison* sung, instead of concerning himself with what was happening on the other flank.

Giesebrecht and Meyer von Knonau reject Landau's study and assume that the battlefield was about 5 miles farther to the north, on the Grunau stream near Hohen-Mölsen. The name *"Grunau-Bach,"* they say, is similar to "Grona," and also the local legend to the effect that the battle took place near Milsin naturally points to the place which today is called Mölsen. But the location of Hohen-Mölsen does not agree with Bruno's statement, which places Henry's camp and the battle directly beside the Elster. Hohen-Mölsen is almost 7 miles from the Elster. The other, later sources also place Mölsen on the Elster. The *Pegau Chronicle (M. G. SS.,* 16. 241) says: "Milsin juxta Elstram fluvium pervenerunt" ("They reached Milsin on the Elster"). The *Pöhlder Annals (M. G. SS.,* 16. 70) say: "Milsin juxta fluvium Elsteram" ("Milsin on the river Elster"). It is not impossible that Henry, coming from Naumburg, took the direction toward Pegau rather than Zeitz. But it would be incomprehensible if he moved back more than 5 miles to the Grunau stream from the Elster, where Bruno tells us he had already arrived. If the battle had taken place near Hohen-Mölsen, Bruno would not have been able to say that Henry intentionally drew up his army with its back to the river in order to heighten its courage. The fleeing men could not have been driven so directly into the river; they would have had enough space to move aside. A pursuit is not easily extended for some 5 miles. Consequently, there remains no other assumption but that the Milsin of the sources is not identical with the present-day Hohen-Mölsen. In contrast with this Hohen-Mölsen, which is located on the heights between the Elster and the Saale, at that time there must have been another Mölsen in the valley of the Elster, somewhat downstream from Zeitz.

Now the *Pegau Chronicle* goes on to say that the battle extended "a Milsin usque ad villam Widerhove" ("from Milsin up to the town of Widerhove"). In "Widerhove" Landau imagines the present-day village of Weida, which is situated north of the Grona valley on the edge of the battlefield. But the name undoubtedly is more closely related to Weiderau, which is about 2½ miles downstream from Pegau and almost 10 miles from the battlefield. If it were possible in other respects to place the battle on the Grunau stream near Hohen-Mölsen, a pursuit in the direction of Weiderau would be logical. But it is also logically related to a location for the battle north of Grana. It is true that the battle, or even the pursuit, cannot have extended from there to Weiderau. But royal troops could have gone that far in their flight. For, since the exit toward the south was blocked and in the east the river was directly behind the combatants, it is quite natural that part of the defeated forces withdrew northward and crossed the river farther downstream, in the vicinity of Weiderau. And even if this was only a small group, it is still natural that an account of this action would have been preserved in the Pegau Monastery, which is in the immediate area.

We cannot give much credence to the late legend or even to the name itself. The area is full of places with similar names—Weida, Weiderode, and Weiderau—and in the course of centuries, villages have often disappeared and been rebuilt in another place.

No matter how much or how little credence we attribute to this legend, the statement that the battle extended from Mölsen to Weiderau would still militate against identifying Mölsen with Hohen-Mölsen. For Hohen-Mölsen is some 2½ miles from the east bank of the Grunau stream, where the battle would have had to be fought.

According to Giesebrecht, lance points, spurs, and other items have been found in large numbers underground in the area of Hohen-Mölsen and near the village of Nödlitz. These finds can in no case be related to our battle, for their location is much too distant from the Grunau stream. Nödlitz is another 2½ miles southward from Hohen-Mölsen.

Most unclear of all is the question as to why the royal army could not cross the Elster. If the town of Zeitz blocked its passage—and this would be almost the only plausible explanation—we ask why Bruno made no mention of this. He obviously did not know it himself, for he gives two contradictory versions as to why the battle was fought here. In one case, he says that Henry wanted it and intentionally chose the field with his back to the river, but then he says that Henry had to establish his camp here against his will. It is evident that the second version is the right one. The reason for the first one is just as clear: the pride of the victors was not willing to admit that they had defeated only half of Henry's army at an advantageous moment but instead postulated a battle of equal knightly forces by mutual agreement. As we know ever since Marathon, the popular imagination has no inclination toward a strategic accomplishment whose triumph is based on making the opposing forces unequal. In this psychological mood, the factor of the closed bridge gate of Zeitz perhaps disappeared.

The authoritative monograph for this battle, which forms the base of my entire account, is the Berlin dissertation by Erich Topp (1904), published by E. Ebering. Recently, two other studies, by R. Wilcke and E. Zergiebel, Zeitz, 1919, have appeared.

BATTLE OF PLEICHFELD
11 AUGUST 1086

The rebellious princes were besieging Würzburg. Henry IV moved up with a strong army to lift the siege. The princes moved out 10 miles northward to meet him, and at the first contact the royal army took to its heels. According to the report by the monk Bernold (*M. G. SS.*, V), who was present, the victorious army lost only fifteen men killed, of whom only three were killed instantly; the others died of their wounds in the next few days. The army was reportedly 10,000 men strong, a very large number, as we know from other figures of this period. When Bernold adds that the royal army was supposed to have more than 20,000 men, we cannot place any credence in this number. The king's faction traced the defeat to treason. According to the *Annales Augustani* [*Annals of Augsburg*], the king's men immediately fled "utrum consilio an ignavia" ("whether by plan or cowardice"). See also the *Continuatur Scoti Mariani* (*Continuator of Scotus Marianus*), *M. G. SS.*, V, and the *Vita Heinrici IV.* (*Life of Henry IV*), Chap. 4, where this battle, however, is confused with the battle of Melrichstadt of 1078.

After the battle, the defenders of Würzburg surrendered, but later in the same year the city again fell into the hands of the king. The battle therefore was really inconclusive.

It is worthy of note that Bernold reports that Duke Welf and the troops from Magdeburg moved out on foot, having left their horses behind. No reason is given for this move. Could it perhaps have been a question of an ambush? We can draw no conclusions of importance to military history, since the entire event is too uncertain.

But it is also remarkable that, as Bernold tells us, the rebellious army had a banner wagon with it, similar to the Italian *carroccio*.

NOTES FOR CHAPTER III

1. Both in *M. G. SS.*, V and in the school edition.
2. *Carmen de bello Saxonico*, *M. G. SS.*, XV.
3. According to Lambert and Bruno.
4. The *Pöhlder Annals* (*M. G. SS.*, XVI) report as follows on a battle they place in 1080: "Rursus inter Heinricum et Rodolfum bellum gestum est, ubi Rodolfus percepto clamore suos occubuisse putavit et fugit. At ubi eventum rei didicit, se scilicet propriam fugisse victoriam, magis vivere quam mori recusavit." ("A battle was again waged between Henry and Rudolf, when Rudolf, after hearing a shout, thought his men had fallen and fled. But when he learned the outcome of the battle and that he obviously had fled his own victory, he was more reluctant to live than to die.") This probably cannot refer to any other event than Melrichstadt.
5. Berthold expressly stated (*M. G. SS.*, V) that Henry assured his retinue that this would be the case.

6. Bruno says nothing about this. But it might be concluded from these points that the *Pegau Chronicle* had Henry marching up via Weida (south of Gera, on the upper Elster). That is, of course, impossible in the light of Bruno's account. But since in any case Henry had also called up Bavaria, where he had a particularly large number of supporters, for the campaign, and these troops could presumably not march on any other route, the account in the *Pegau Chronicle* may be based on a positive legend that royal troops moved via Weida. Of course, it could also be that the village of Weida, situated on the battlefield, was the place referred to in this legend.

7. We cannot determine how close he came to Naumburg. Bruno's statements could be understood to mean that he made an attempt to take Naumburg by storm. But it is also possible that when he heard that the Saxons or their advance guard had already reached Naumburg, Henry crossed the Saale a day's march farther to the south. Perhaps only an engagement between reconnaissance forces took place before the town.

Chapter IV

The Subjugation of the Anglo-Saxons by the Normans

The history of the Anglo-Saxons, the race that developed from the Germanic peoples who settled in the British Isles, has already been mentioned and discussed in the general context. Nowhere else do we realize as clearly as here the original situation described by Tacitus and the gradual change. In the laws of King Ethelbert of Kent (about 600), the churls were still warlike free peasants. Violation of their domestic peace was punishable by a fine half as great as in the case of an eorl.

In Ine's *Book of Laws of Wessex* a hundred years later (about 700), the situation was already different. The Welsh, who had a place in the older nation only as slaves and serfs, now appeared in higher and better positions. We can see how the gradual conquest of the island by the Germans brought about a change from absolute enmity to treaty-based agreements. But even within the conquering people, the division into classes changed. We find churls who were in the service of a hlaford or lord, to whom they were obligated. But the members of the king's retinue, the gesiths, or gesithkundmen, had become the possessors of large estates. From them and from the former Hundred leaders (ealdormen, eorls) there arose a nobility. The mounted warriors, the thanes (*Degen, pueri*), in the service of the king and of these nobles, had double the wergeld of the churls. Consequently, the churl had already given up his full warriorhood.

A hundred years later, just when King Egbert had succeeded in uniting all the original minor kingdoms under his power (827), the attacks by the Normans (Danes) began, and they found the large Anglo-Saxon kingdom almost as defenseless as the Anglo-Saxons had previously found the inhabitants of the Roman province of Britannia. We see that the churls had lost their warlike skill and the thanes could not replace this lost strength.[1]

The opinion has been expressed that the Anglo-Saxon kingdom had a well-ordered military organization in that every area of five hides, or even units that were assessed at 20 pounds, had to provide one man in the levy, and this five-hide unit was further compared to those capitularies of Charlemagne which seem to prescribe a similar arrangement. But this concept neither is to be found in the sources, nor does it result in a really useful military organization. We have already seen that the Carolingian capitularies, too, which grouped three or four hides in a unit that was to provide one man, could have been implemented as written only temporarily at best. We have also seen that no effective action could ever have been accomplished by a levy of this type. Once the burgher-peasant frame of mind had pushed back the warrior spirit, the peasant militia no longer had any military value. We have on record a sermon of Archbishop Wulfstan of York, in which he bemoans the fact that ten Anglo-Saxons took to flight when faced by one Dane.

The analogy of the Anglo-Saxons and the Franks is to be found, rather, first of all in the fact that in both places a special warrior class developed from the general Germanic warriorhood. In Britain it was the thanes, and in the Frankish Kingdom the vassals. But while this Frankish warrior class was held close together by the great Carolingians, thanks to the feudal system, and developed a great military capability, at least as long as the entire system was inspired by a strong authority, the system of thanes among the Anglo-Saxons developed differently. The thanes, too, were in many cases given land and settled by their lords. This was not done, however, in accordance with strict feudal rules concerning the death of the lord or of the vassal but rather with a hereditary right that was only slightly limited. The normal property grant for a thane was five hides. Having thus become possessors of rather large properties, they were obligated for military service, but since there was no guarantee that they would maintain their military qualities, the warrior class was soon transformed into a simple class of large-estate owners who had no greater military capabilities than the simple owners of hides. We can clearly recognize this development from a few provisions of the law in which it was prescribed that anyone who had five hides, a helmet, coat of mail, and a sword embellished with gold was a thane. The same dignity was also granted to the merchant who had traveled abroad three times at his own expense. Consequently, the thanes became a class, a level in the social hierarchy in which the military origin was perhaps still recognizable but no longer effective.[2]

The technique of vassal warriorhood reached its peak on the Continent in mounted combat. In addition to the necessary weapons, it required not only a useful war-horse but also a skill that could be achieved only through complete dedication and constant practice. The mediocre warriorhood of the Anglo-Saxon thanes is indicated as much by the fact that they did not fight on horseback as by the provisions of the law. Even in the Anglo-Saxon heroic epic *Beowulf,* there is only a single reference to a war-horse. Of course, we must assume that King Harold himself and the prominent members of his court and of the country not only knew how to ride but could also fight on horseback. The number of such mounted combatants was so small, however, that, at the battle of Hastings, faced with the superior number of Norman knights, the Anglo-Saxons preferred to avoid completely any mounted combat, and they placed the mounted men in the ranks of the foot troops. Precisely the same thing was done at Marathon with the prominent Athenians, who normally served as mounted men, perhaps with the single exception of the commander. At Hastings, even King Harold himself fought on foot with his brothers in the midst of his housecarls.[3]

If the Anglo-Saxons were called up for war, according to the law, there could be nothing of a stricter nature. Each churl was still obligated to move out, and each thane was faced with such duty all the more strongly. But in reality, as had formerly been the case among the West Goths, despite all the provisions of their laws, there was no kind of organization. If the king issued a summons for war, his sheriffs could make demands on the individual estate owners, towns, and villages, demands for which certain standards had probably been established through custom. Either a few men were furnished or a payment was made. But, in the final analysis, the size and usefulness of the contingent that was assembled in this way depended on the skill and energy of the individual officials and the good will of their subordinates. Under no circumstances could very much be accomplished with the militia-like characteristics of such a mobilization. A certain military nucleus was formed only by warriors who had not settled on the land but were maintained at the royal court or in the retinues of the great earls, a group corresponding to the Frankish *scara.*

And so these people who had become unwarlike were first exposed to the frightful sufferings of the Viking raids. Then the raiders themselves settled in the land, and the two groups found themselves face to face. Under King Alfred the Great, the Anglo-Saxons rallied to such an extent as to assert their domination of at least a part of the island. Under his successor, and principally through the Church, Anglo-Saxons and Danes, closely related as they were, were successfully brought together into a political unity. Finally, however, the island could no longer defend itself against foreign domination. King Sven and his successor, King Knut of Denmark and Norway, subjugated all of England (1013). The chronicle reports that Knut had 3,000 housecarls, whom he led to war in the summer and billeted on the burghers in winter, where they frequently disturbed the domestic peace. The Burgundians, too, were supposed to have numbered no more than 3,000 when they established their kingdom on the Saône and the Rhône 600 years earlier. Once again, the Anglo-Saxons succeeded in casting off their yoke (1042), but then the Norman Duke William appeared on the scene and put an end once and for all to the independent Anglo-Saxon race and, by amalgamating it with the Norman-French stock, created the English people (1066).

William was the descendant and heir of the Viking Rollo, under whom the Normans had settled 150 years earlier. In that time, they had given up their Germanic language, had assimilated with the native population living among them, and had adopted the French language. They had maintained their warlike character, however, in the form of the Frankish feudal system and in the continual feuds that were associated with it. In this way, they were a remarkable blend of the cultural superiority of the Romanics and the warlike character of the Germans. At the Anglo-Saxon court itself, under the last king from the house of Cerdic, claims were made in favor of the Normans, and they evoked an Anglo-Saxon reaction against these claims and the preference that was shown to the Normans. The Anglo-Saxons sought to keep themselves apart from the Romanic-Germanic blending of races, even in the area of the Church. The Norman duke, as he prepared to seek the English crown, espoused the new religious orientation that was just taking place in Rome and arranged for Pope Alexander, the predecessor of Gregory VII, to present him a banner for his campaign.

It was precisely as a result of this relationship with the universal ideas and the cultural elements of the period that the Norman conquest was of such enduring importance in European history. The prerequisite, however, was that the Anglo-Saxons, despite the reinforcing power of the Danes that had been infused in them in the last few generations, had lost their military capability. The idea that this rich and fruitful land could become the booty of any brave leader must have been generally held. In the speech which the oldest reporter of these events, William of Poitiers, places in the mouth of the duke before the battle of Hastings, he has him telling his warriors that the English were often conquered, were without military prestige, and were inexperienced in battle. A somewhat later historian, Ordericus Vitalis, likewise has it said of them that they preferred to cultivate their land and enjoy themselves with feasting and the ringing of beakers than to seek battle. The army with which the Conqueror embarked was not at all simply his Norman feudal levy. It was rather a warrior group from a large part of France, which had entered the service of the duke for this undertaking in the hope of pay and booty. The Norman knights themselves followed him not so much as a result of their feudal obligation as for the sake of the war itself. It was not very different from earlier times in the Germanic primeval forests, where a prince who summoned men for a campaign always had enough volunteers from that warlike people—except that now it was not the masses themselves but the special class of warriors that had separated itself from the masses that formed the stuff of which the great military band was composed. Even independent lords, like Count Eustache of Boulogne, the father of Godfrey of Bouillon, joined this army with their retinues.

THE BATTLE OF HASTINGS
14 OCTOBER 1066

On the battle of Hastings we have very detailed epic accounts from later periods, from which many an English scholar is still trying to draw historical knowledge. This effort is completely wasted. Freeman's famous account of the battle of Senlac, as he unnecessarily names it, is the most curious mixture of pseudomilitary reflections (of course, he also bases his account on the advice of English general staff officers) and pseudocritical source studies. In this way, it is not possible to arrive at historically accurate concepts to any greater extent than it was possible to do so in Herodotus' account of the Persian wars or Plutarch's accounts of the battles of Marius and Sulla. But if we decide to move forward from the purely harmonistic presentation to an actual critical study, we can arrive at a picture of the battle that is not only credible but also confirmed. Our principal source is the account by the Norman cleric William of Poitiers, who was Duke William's chaplain and wrote his account a few years after the battle, on the basis of information from those who participated. He is thoroughly biased and embellishes his account freely, but a number of other sources enable us to check on him and to be assured that he may be trusted in his basic points. Of service to us as an historic source and historical evidence of a very special type is the Bayeux Tapestry, a piece of artistic embroidery no less than 70 meters long and half a meter high, in which the individual scenes of the battle are shown and explained by Latin inscriptions, unquestionably a work of the contemporary generation.

The Norman army may be estimated at about 7,000 men; it was perhaps somewhat smaller, but in any case not appreciably larger.

In one of the Norman sources the Anglo-Saxon army is given a strength of 1.2 million men. According to William of Poitiers, it was so large that it drank up all the water in the rivers that it crossed. The *Roman de Rou* is content with 400,000 men. But another source, likewise of Norman bias (William of Malmesbury), expressly says that it was a very small army ("Haroldus paucissimo stipatus milite Hastingas protendit": "Harold reached Hastings accompanied by very few knights"). The course of the battle itself leaves no doubt, as we shall see, that this is the truth.[4] We may estimate Harold's army at the most as being of the same strength as the Normans, but probably smaller—between 4,000 and 7,000 men.

The principal difference between the two armies was that the English consisted entirely of combatants on foot, while the Norman army was composed in part of mounted men. This fact is brought out so clearly and consistently in all the source accounts as well as the Bayeux Tapestry that it seems to be fully confirmed. Consequently, it was out of the question for Harold to meet his enemy on the plain; his units would immediately have been broken up by the Norman knights.[5] King Harold therefore chose a position on a broad hill, which his army covered in a rather tight formation. The position also had the particular advantage that there were rather steep slopes behind it, while in the middle a narrow isthmus led directly into a forest. In case of defeat, the Anglo-Saxons could flee on foot down the slope and into the forest, whereas the mounted men could not easily follow them.

The Normans were also superior to the Anglo-Saxons in their second weapon, the bow, the use of which, as in the case of the control of one's horse, required professional training and skill. The Bayeux Tapestry, once again in agreement with the accounts, shows veritable hails of arrows being launched by the Normans, while on the other side only a single archer is pictured. The dismounted combatants, who, like the Normans, were well-armored and equipped with various weapons— spears, swords, and especially axes—formed the nucleus of Harold's army. In addition, there were lightly armed fighters, some with shields and some without, equipped with javelins, pole-axes, and the like. This was, of course, not a peasant levy that might have been raised in addition to the housecarls and thanes. Such an army would have been as good as defenseless in the face of the Norman archers and horsemen, and it would necessarily have immediately taken flight. We must picture these lightly armed Anglo-Saxon troops as the squires and serving men of the actual warriors, who were stationed among the warriors. Initially, they perhaps ran forward a certain distance, launched their missiles, and then withdrew behind the armored combatants when the enemy approached.

The Normans moved forward against the hill in a broad front, with all three combat branches—horsemen, foot soldiers, and marksmen—side by side. The marksmen sprang forward somewhat to shoot at the enemy, with the advantage provided by the greater range of their bows and their numbers but with the disadvantage resulting from the higher position of the Anglo-Saxons, who were shooting at them from above. Now the mounted men, mixed together with the foot soldiers carrying close-combat weapons, stormed up the hill. But the advantage of the defensive position was so great and the momentum of the charge was so crippled by the slope that the defenders repulsed the attack. Some of the Normans were driven back down the hill, while others turned about when they were unable to penetrate the line, in order to launch the attack once again after a certain time, as was customary in this kind of mounted battle. Perhaps some of them had the idea that in this way they could lure the enemy behind them in order to turn against him on the more favorable terrain in the valley below. In this ebb and flow, during which the Norman archers found repeated opportunities to use their weapon, the Normans finally gained the upper hand. The strength of the Anglo-Saxons was limited, of course, to the defensive; but battles cannot be won with defensive action alone. The defensive is purely negative, while victory is positive. With extremely rare exceptions, the only defensive that can finally lead to victory is one that goes over to the offensive at the appropriate moment. We recognized this point in the first historically confirmed battle, at Marathon, where the Athenians, who were likewise not capable of opposing the enemy on the open plain, chose a defensive position but were led forth from it into the attack by Miltiades at the proper moment. Harold was not capable of doing this. His housecarls and thanes were brave men, perhaps as individuals more so than the Athenian burghers and peasants had been, but they formed no phalanx, no tactical body that was trained to move out as a unit on command. Individually or in small groups, here and there, the Anglo-Saxons, following their natural instinct, stormed out after the withdrawing enemy. In doing so they were not able to accomplish anything. The Norman army did not allow itself to be driven to flight by this movement, and as the advancing Anglo-Saxons came helter-skelter into the valley, they were ridden down and overpowered by the horsemen. It is possible that Harold intended that his men should not leave their position on the hill at all, but that was difficult to control, and even if it had been accomplished, it would not have saved the battle. For if the Normans, when they were repulsed, were not pursued, they reassembled, like the warrior group that they were, and tried again and again. Finally, there necessarily would have developed disorder at some point on the Anglo-Saxon front, a drive would have succeeded, and a number of horsemen penetrated the line. From that break, as more and more Normans pushed through, the Anglo-Saxon battle formation would have been split apart. The natural superiority of the mounted troops on the Norman side could be counter-balanced by the terrain advantage of the Anglo-Saxons only temporarily and not in the face of every possible circumstance. On the one side the superiority was a living, self-renewing force, while on the other side the advantage of the terrain was only mechanical and superficial, one that finally had to be overcome by the strong will of the attacker.

The reports leave no doubt that the battle lasted a long time and was hard-fought—proof that the Anglo-Saxon army was not composed of peasants. If it had been, they would either have overwhelmed the enemy with their mass or would immediately have taken flight. But a large part of the Anglo-Saxon army fought courageously and fell in the selected position, including King Harold himself and his two brothers. This death shows a warrior spirit and warrior concept of honor which the enemy cannot have surpassed. His superiority, however, lay in his professional training, mounted combat, archery, and finally probably his numbers as well.

The final and conclusive evidence that the Anglo-Saxon army was no peasant levy but a warrior class that differed from its Norman opponents only in its insufficient training and numbers is provided by consideration of the strategy.

When William landed in the Bay of Pevensey on 28 September, Harold was not at hand. He was in the north, where he was repelling a Viking attack led by his own brother, Tostig. Although William had no more than four to five days' march from the scene of his landing to London (56 miles as the crow flies), Harold did not return to his capital from his fighting in the north until the tenth day after the Normans landed (7 or 8 October). Consequently, William could have used that period for a major undertaking, perhaps even the conquest of London. The sources do not report why he did not do that, but we may probably imagine the reason. He was no doubt concerned that, with the capture of larger cities, his undisciplined troops would get so out of hand that he would not have all of them present for the battle that would finally have to be fought. Furthermore, of course, he did not want to appear as a conqueror and treat the country as an enemy, but he wished to be viewed as a legitimate candidate for the throne, who was presenting himself for election. But by remaining on the coast for these or similar reasons, the duke turned over the strategic initiative to his opponent. Instead of continuing the offensive that had started so well with his unopposed landing, William remained almost motionless on the coast near Hastings and thus left Harold time to make preparations. While our sources report that William laid waste to the surrounding area in order to force the enemy king into battle as a result of the suffering of his country, that point can only have been a concept of the crowd or the chroniclers and cannot have been the idea of the duke himself. The suffering of the small area which the immobile army could have laid waste could not possibly have lured the Anglo-Saxon king into a premature battle. If William had wanted to do that, he would have had to move forward and threaten London. Those instances of devastation, which, of course, also contradict the basic political idea of the campaign, William's candidacy for election, were presumably not even carried out at the special command of the duke but were the usual misdeeds of the requisitioning and plundering soldiers. In no case can they have had any strategic significance. The fact therefore remains that William left the initiative to his opponent and thus gave him full freedom of action to extend and complete his preparations. This point is all the more striking and significant in that the Normans could not even hold out for a long period. Even in his own country William had had difficulties with provisions, since he had had to wait a long time for a favorable wind. And if it was for this very reason that he now remained on the coast, in order to bring over supplies more easily, that still had its limitations for his large army. We recognize how important the question of rations was from the fact that on the Bayeux Tapestry riders are sent out to Hastings immediately after the landing to obtain provisions.

The duke's behavior, allowing the defender a free period of preparation after the surprise landing, would be completely incomprehensible if he had had to assume that the time would actually be used for such preparations—in other words, if there had been a question of a general levy. Even if we might imagine the population of England as very thin and the Conqueror's army as very large, a true general levy, even for only a part of the island, would necessarily have created an overwhelming superiority on the side of the Anglo-Saxons. The fact that William took no steps to prevent the formation of such a mass army by a rapid advance is sufficient proof that there was no question of such a levy and that, therefore, the military organization of the Anglo-Saxons was in the same condition in which we found that of the Franks at the time of the siege of Paris. Once we have understood this point, the Conqueror's strategy also becomes understandable. He knew that Harold had no forces to levy except his housecarls and the thanes, and then only to the extent that they were really useful and inclined to participate.

Here, too, the question arises as to whether the Anglo-Saxon army, composed in this way, could not have been considerably stronger on the day of the battle. A few sources, especially Florentius Vigorniensis (Florence of Worcester), expressly report that Harold could have been doubly or triply stronger if he had only waited a few more days. I unhesitatingly reject this information out of hand; it belongs to the belated bits of wisdom that always appear after every defeat and with which the defeated console themselves. (Florentius has an Anglo-Saxon bias.) It is true, of course, that the entire Anglo-Saxon military power was not assembled, for two great earls of the north, for whom it was presumably quite inconsequential whether Harold or William wore the crown, did not support Harold. But even with a longer delay, they would not have come, and if there was a prospect of any other reinforcements, we know how difficult it is to feed an army. It could easily happen that while Harold waited for some, the others, impatient and nearing the end of their supplies, could have returned home. In any case, we have no evidence that would authoritatively force us to attribute to the Anglo-Saxon king, who, after all, was quite aware of his weakness as shown by his choice of position, the monstrous error of going into the decisive battle before the assembly of his forces, even though he was strategically in complete control of the situation. Even if the entire Middle Ages contains frequent examples of knightly leaders dashing with wild daring but insufficient forces into a fight they could have avoided, and if Harold, too, could be considered similarly inclined, such a psychological causality is not appropriate here, since we see that the Anglo-Saxon king in no way dashed wildly against the enemy but only formed up for the battle in a very well-chosen defensive position. We must therefore assume that Harold had assembled whatever his kingdom was able and willing to provide, both quantitatively and qualitatively. Now, as a brave man, he did not hesitate to challenge his enemy in order to do battle to defend and save his crown and country. But the Norman believed himself to be so very capable of dealing with the Anglo-Saxon force that could be expected, and so superior to it, that, for the reasons stated, he could afford calmly to await developments, whether Harold used a somewhat longer or shorter period for his preparations.

EXCURSUS

REFERENCES AND CRITIQUE

The authoritative special study in the German language is the dissertation by Wilhelm Spatz, "The Battle of Hastings" ("Die Schlacht bei Hastings"), Berlin, 1896 (*Historische Studien,* published by E. Ebering). See this work for all the details.

The description of the battle by Edward A. Freeman is to be found in the third volume of his *History of the Norman Conquest of England.* As soon as it appeared, this account was critically dissected and rejected in England itself by J. H. Round. His review was reprinted in his work, *Feudal England,* London, 1895. In the *Revue historique,* 65 (1897): 61 ff., Round then took sides with Spatz and confirmed that Spatz, without yet being acquainted with his analysis in all the basic points, especially with respect to Freeman, had come to the same conclusions. Round believed that Spatz went too far in his critique in only small matters. This point is based partially on misunderstanding; for example, it was not Spatz' view that knightly armies, for lack of tactical units, had been without any leadership at all. But, of course, Spatz does not believe in the possibility of the feigned flight maneuver, whereas Round believes himself justified in holding fast to that point.

When Round's criticism appeared, public opinion in England was filled with such a belief in the scholarly authority of Freeman that his critic, whose scholarly superiority shines forth from every line, had the greatest difficulty even in having his reviews printed.

Very similar to Freeman's account, even though differing from it in numerous details, is the description by General Köhler in the first volume of his *Development of the Military Art and Conduct of War in the Knightly Period (Entwickelung des Kriegswesens und der Kriegsführung in der Ritterzeit),* 1886. Spatz correctly says of this work that one cannot help feeling a light vertigo when one hears of all these clever maneuvers which the Normans are supposed to have carried out.

Oman, in his *Art of War,* seeks a middle ground between Freeman and Round but basically agrees more closely with Round. Since Round himself did not go far enough in his critique, however, Oman does not come any closer to the mark.

It will be enlightening in many respects to assemble here the principal differences between the various accounts and to add to this comparison the reasons why Freeman's account is not acceptable.

Freeman refrains from giving any specific figure for the strength of the armies. Oman (p. 155) estimates the strength of the Anglo-Saxons at about 25,000 men, on the basis of consideration of the space. The hill on which they took position is some 1,500 meters long. If we estimate 3 feet per man, the front was between 1,700 and 2,000 men wide, and since they gave the impression of a very tight formation, they must have stood 10 to 12 men in depth. That would therefore result in about 25,000 men.

Against this estimate, it can be said that neither does the hill need to have been occupied right up to both ends, nor does the depth of the formation appear to be confirmed in the Norman accounts. The front may have been only 1,000 men wide, and the depth may have amounted to 6 men or even fewer.

Freeman says that Harold erected a palisade with three exits in front of his line. Köhler, p. 8, describes this palisade as follows: "A series of posts at certain intervals, dug in around each unit, which were inclined obliquely forward with their iron points directed toward the chests of the enemy horses, were planted firmly in the earth. . . . The posts were joined together by interwoven material up to a height of 3 or 4 feet apparently as a protection against the enemy's mounted troops, so that the horses, in order to get into the unit, first had to jump."

As Round has thoroughly shown, this whole idea is a fantasy that has its origin not in any historical source, but in Wace's *Roman*. General Köhler's picture of the posts planted firmly in the earth with their iron points directed against the chests of the enemy horses and bound together with interwoven material to a height of 3 or 4 feet, over which the knights' horses, galloping up the slope, were supposed to jump—this account may serve as consolation to historians that even men educated in their profession can imagine as possible some military actions that are actually out of the question. These points are all the less possible here, because the army that is supposed to have erected this fortification around itself is said by the same author to have numbered no fewer than 60,000 to 75,000 men and not to have arrived in this position until the preceding evening.

Oman seeks a middle ground between the account of the palisade, which has become so widely accepted, and the fact that it could not possibly have been erected in the one night by an army exhausted from its march and that the palisade is not mentioned in any of the contemporary sources. He believes that Wace, who wrote some ninety years after the event, could have had an oral legend or even a long-lost written account, and that it was not a question of a firm palisade but of a light woven work that was supposed to give more protection against the Norman arrows than to form an obstacle for the horsemen. Since the woven work had but little effect, the contemporary sources could ignore it in their accounts.

But if this woven obstacle was actually ineffective, then we, too, may leave it out of consideration in our study of the battle. Furthermore, if it was ineffective, the exhausted Anglo-Saxon army would hardly have taken the trouble to spend the night erecting it. In any case, the statement and the authority of a poet writing a hundred years later, with no intention of writing history but only of entertaining, are not sufficient to make us believe his account.

Even with those who believe in the Anglo-Saxon palisade, it plays no further significant role in the course of the battle. Rather, the central point of the action is the fact that the Anglo-Saxons were supposed to hold fast on the hill in a strictly defensive situation, in accordance with Harold's idea and his commands, but that William lured a part of the enemy from their good position by a feigned flight and then defeated them. Freeman believes the Anglo-Saxons would surely have won if they had followed Harold's command and had not left their hill. We do not know whether Harold actually gave such commands. But General Köhler has correctly observed that intending to win a battle with a purely defensive stance was an "unpromising beginning." Of course, without horsemen, they could not do otherwise. But once a portion of the Anglo-Saxons had rushed out after the Normans in pursuit, it would still have been better, as Köhler correctly observes, to pursue with the full force rather than to remain behind and let the army be wiped out piecemeal, as now happened. Consequently, Köhler considers this standing fast by Harold to have been as much of an error as Freeman does the movement forward in pursuit. In reality, we have to understand that there was no leadership in the confused melee of a knightly battle. It has even been said of modern disciplined troops that, once they are engaged in battle, they are no longer under the control of the commander. Accordingly, the general who has committed his last reserve has nothing further to do than to take up a rifle himself and join the fight. And this applies much more strongly to knightly armies than to disciplined troops. From the start of the battle on, knights were moved only by the instincts of the mass itself.

As Spatz has already effectively shown, it is, therefore, a purely fantastic concept that William lured the enemy from his position by ordering a feigned flight. How is it possible to pass on any commands at all in the heat and excitement of battle to thousands of men? How is it possible, in the mighty uproar, to see to it that they not only all hear and understand the order and act on it not only in like manner but also at the same time? But if they do not act simultaneously and with full understanding, how can one be sure that a large number will not take the "feigned flight" as the real thing and, animated by the saying that the devil takes the hindmost, actually flee? And we know that it is very difficult to turn fleeing horsemen around again.

"Feigned flight" is therefore a maneuver that can only be carried out by very small units that have been previously instructed on this action or are at least accustomed to obey the trumpet call unquestioningly, or by marksmen for whom this kind of action is normal procedure. The account of the battle of Hastings can only be based on events such as we have assumed in our account above, and the oldest and best description of the battle, that by William of Poitiers, also recounts nothing very different. He does not state that William himself ordered the feigned flight. He shows an actual flight taking place on one occasion and a feigned flight on two others, and he does not draw a direct reversal of the battle from those actions.

In the *carmen de bello Hastingensi* (*Song of the Battle of Hastings*), it is stated that when the Normans made their feigned flight, "rustica laetatur gens et superasse putabat" ("the rural folk rejoiced and thought they had won"). This may not be taken to mean, of course, that the Anglo-Saxon army was composed of peasants. Rather, it is only the scornful-symbolic expression of the poet with a Norman bias (probably Bishop Guido of Amiens) for the coarse ways of the Anglo-Saxon thanes in comparison with the finer Norman-French, with their better knightly technical training.

ANGLO-SAXONS AND ENGLISH

The Germans on the island of Britain called themselves, as far as we can trace back, "Engle" or "Angelcyn" (*cyn* meaning "family," "tribe"), and not Anglo-Saxons or Saxons. The expression "Anglo-Saxons" is principally of scholarly origin; it appears very rarely in the older sources. At the time of the Conquest, the contemporaries did not speak of Saxons and Normans, but of Angles and Franks, "Angli" and "Franci."

From the start, Freeman calls the nation and the people "England" and "English." He argues against the use of the word "Anglo-Saxon," because this gives the idea that the concept "English" originated only from a mixture of Anglo-Saxon and Norman. But, he says, ever since Hengist and Horsa, it was the same nation, which only took into itself certain foreign elements—Britons, Danes, Normans—but was not so strongly affected by them as not to be able to claim unbroken continuity.

The correct concept is the opposite one, namely, that the English people with their particular character and their particular language originated only as a result of the Norman conquest, the superimposing of a governing, French-speaking layer on the previous Germanic political system, which, to be sure, had taken into itself Romanic elements through remnants of the subjugated ancient British population and the influence of the Church. As small as was the number of Frenchified Normans and French who were actually settled by the Conqueror and his successors, they were still the rulers, whose character, customs, laws, and spirit enjoyed prestige, just as was formerly the case with the small number of Franks who took over the interior of Gaul under the Merovingians and were blended into a new unit with the subjugated population. If in England there continued to be more of the ancient Anglo-Saxon tradition than of the Gallo-Romanic in France, the process was still essentially the same. This relationship justifies our giving to the older period, by considering also normal speech usage, the name Anglo-Saxon rather than English, even though the expression "Anglo-Saxon" is not very accurately formed (since, of course, the Angles were a part of the Saxons), nor can it be based on the ancient sources.

THE HUNDRED AMONG THE ANGLO-SAXONS

Prothero, writing in the *English Historical Review*, 11 (1896): 544, has taken exception to my concept of the Hundred, stating that in England the Hundred did not appear until the reign of Edgar, in the tenth century. According to Prothero, it was, therefore, a new, artificially created division.

As remarkable as it is that the Hundred does not appear earlier in the sources, I can only consider that as a fortuitous circumstance. It is highly unlikely that such an organization was artificially created at one time. And it is especially improbable in that it was supposed to have happened so late. After all, the ancient kingdoms of the Heptarchy needed to have a link between the nation and the small village communities. While the larger ones were divided into several shires, that was not sufficient. These shires were still the size of the smaller kingdoms. The later counties were either such kingdoms or shires, and between them and the smallest settlements there is much too great a gap.

Jenks, in the same volume of the *Historical Review*, p. 513, "The Problem of the Hundred," believes he can prove from Westgotalag that in Sweden the *haeraed* (Hundred) was not only a juridical district but also a corporation, a unit that was not composed of a number of villages but, on the contrary, was divided up as a result of the formation of villages. I consider it doubtful that Jenks' proof is valid, but his conclusion would agree exactly with mine.

In his work referred to above, Prothero further opposes my theory, saying that the ealdor of the Hundred among the Anglo-Saxons was a lower official, in addition to and far below the ealdorman. He goes on to say that the latter was not the earl of the tenth century, who was rather the representative of the original independent kingdom. According to Prothero, there were but very few earls and ealdormen, even in the tenth century.

These points may well be correct, but they confirm rather than contradict my ideas. If in the tenth century earls and ealdormen were not yet identical, but the two titles existed side by side, the men with the simple title "ealdorman" were nevertheless estate-owners, such as were later generally called earls. How are such prominent men supposed to have acquired the name "ealdorman" if they did not have some actual relationship to the *Altermänner* of the ancient period, the *"majores natu"* ("greater by birth")?

If there sometimes existed, in addition to the prominent ealdormen, the lower position of the Hundred, ealdor, I must add to my description (Vol. II, pp. 35, 44, 47, 306) the fact that the two branches into which the original stem of the *Altermänner* (*hunni*) was divided, the prominent one and the common one, are not to be divided geographically but that among the Anglo-Saxons both positions existed simultaneously for a while.

GESITHS AND THANES

The gesiths corresponded to Tacitus' *comites* and the *antrustiones* of the Merovingians. The thanes were the same as the *pueri* of the Merovingian period. Just as in the case of the *vassi*, the thanes gradually grew and superseded the title "Gesith" (Gesithmann). Little gives an excellent explanation of this development in the *English Historical Review*, 16.4 (1889): 723. But when Little goes on to reject Stubbs' opinion that under Alfred the title "thane" was given to every owner of five hides of land and claims that the opposite is true, that is, that the normal grant to a thane amounted to five hides, I cannot agree with him.

THE FIVE-HIDE RULE

The incorrect concept of the significance of the Carolingian capitularies concerning the military obligation also had a misleading effect on the English organizational history. Recently, Maitland, in his very excellent book *Domesday Book and Beyond,* 1897, has again expressed the opinion that, as unclear as the Anglo-Saxon military organization was at the time of its fall, we can still accept as probable that the counties had to provide one man for every five hides.

Round, who had already broken up and destroyed this concept in all its bases in his study "The Introduction of Knights' Service into England" (*Feudal England,* 1895), has rejected, in the *English Historical Review,* 12 (1897): 492, an apparently new basis for the old concept, which Maitland believed he had found.

Completely aside from the silence of the sources, a simple critical consideration tells us that the five-hide rule is an impossibility. The wars and the military requirements were much too varied for such a unitary measure. A levy to drive off a small Viking band, to suppress an uprising, to punish a pillaging incursion of the Welsh—a partial levy of individual counties—and a general national levy for a large war, as, for example, under Alfred against the Danes who had settled on the island, or against the Scots—all of these were quite different. To require one man from every five hides would have been too much on one occasion and too little on another.

NOTES FOR CHAPTER IV

1. Major Albany's work, *Early Wars of Wessex,* 1913, has no scholarly value, according to the review by J. Liebermann in the *Historische Zeitschrift,* Vol. 117, p. 500.

2. Oman, *History of the Art of War,* to which I refer the reader for the cited provisions of the law, sees (p. 109) the reason for opening up the class of thanes in the hope of inducing the peasants and burghers to provide themselves with good weapons and strengthen the military forces. I cannot agree with this idea. A well-to-do burgher or peasant who procures fine weapons does not thereby become a useful warrior, and in case of war he might only be inclined to hide his weapons and reject his newly won status. Such minor measures did not create men of a caliber to oppose the Vikings. Consequently, as we have seen above, the laws can only be interpreted in the opposite sense, namely, that the former warrior status of the thanes had already disappeared and there remained only a civilian-social status into which the more prominent peasants and burghers tried to be admitted.

3. Stubbs, 1: 262, cites a source in Canterbury to the effect that there were no *milites* in England before the time of King William.

4. See Freeman, Vol. III, Appendix H. H., p. 741, for a listing of all the various estimates of the army strengths.

5. Compare the study on the changes in tactics in the preceding volume, Book IV, Chap. 2, p. 408, with the statements of Aristotle and Frederick the Great.

Chapter V

The Norman Military Organization In England

1066–1087	William I
1087–1100	William II, son of William I
1100–1135	Henry I, brother of William II
1135–1154	Stephen, nephew of Henry I by his sister
1154–1189	Henry II, grandson of Henry I by his daughter
1189–1199	Richard I, son of Henry II
1199–1216	John I, brother of Richard I
1216–1272	Henry III, son of John I
1272–1307	Edward I, son of Henry III

In the new Anglo-Norman kingdom, the military organization developed quite differently from that which we have seen on the Continent.

Duke William, to whom history has given the title "the Conqueror," did not take possession of the crown of England under this title. Rather, he presented himself to the Anglo-Saxons as a relative of their last dynastic king, Edward the Confessor, and perhaps even as having been designated by him as his choice for legal election to the kingship, since there was no adult heir at hand. Count Harold, who had first been chosen, had no right to the position, according to William, since a year earlier he had given William his solemn oath not to seek the throne. William therefore took over the reign after his victory, under the fiction of legitimate succession to the throne. He took nothing as conqueror, on the basis of military law, but only confiscated the properties of Harold's family and his supporters as the forfeited possessions of rebels. The great earls of the north, who had given no assistance to Harold at the moment of decision, rebelled belatedly, were likewise defeated, and increased the possessions of the king with their properties. In this way, William blended the principle of legitimacy with the practice of conquest and divided a large portion of the confiscated properties among some 300 men of his warrior retinue, about 40 of whom, the lords or barons according to the later title,[1] received very large domains, with the obligation of providing the king with knights from them. The number of these men obligated to serve (*servitia debita*), including those for whom the higher clergy were obligated, amounted all together to something under 5,000, and certainly no more than that. In order to provide the required service, the barons, for their part, took on subordinate vassals. But the number of secondary fiefs did not need to cover the number of men required, for the baron could also maintain knights at his court without settling them on the land, rather than to delay calling for them until the moment of need. They were known as those who were maintained at the lord's court ("*super dominium*": "without tenancy"). But the opposite also occurred in that secular as well as clerical lords for a variety of reasons maintained more knights than they were obligated to provide for the king.

A baron who had to provide as many as sixty knights already belonged among the most powerful of the earls.

The great vassals of the crown were exclusively Normans, while a number of Saxon names are to be found among the lesser royal vassals. A rather large number of Saxon names were included among the subordinate vassals as a result of the fact that Saxon thanes allied themselves with the conquerors and entered their service. The number of enfeoffed warriors in England under William, counting Saxons (also Danes) and Normans together, probably amounted to some 5,000,[2] of whom about a fourth may have come from the older population and three-fourths, that is, between 3,000 and 4,000, from the French-speaking knights whom the Conqueror had settled on the land. This number did not amount to anything like 60,000, as fable later had it and is sometimes even repeated today, or to 32,000, as some others have believed. In addition to the enfeoffed Normans, quite a number without fiefs presumably remained in Britain in the service of the king or of one of the lords. Even with these men, the number of warriors who were capable not only of conquering but also of continuously dominating a country previously occupied by a very warlike people with a population of 1.8 million souls, was very small indeed.

In time, the number of enfeoffed knights grew somewhat. When a census was taken in 1166, under the Conqueror's great-grandson, Henry II, it turned out that the number of knights with fiefs amounted to about 6,400. Both the secular and the clerical magnates had granted fiefs to so many vassals that they normally had more of them than the Conqueror had formerly required of them as knights for his levy. The reason was probably less that they wanted to have more warriors at their disposal to increase their own power, for they would, of course, have been able to keep them at their courts, and we see that, at the very time of the civil wars under King Stephen, very few new knightly fiefs were created. The reason for the large number of enfeoffed knights is probably to be sought rather in the fact that the knight possessing a fief was a more prominent man. Consequently, the barons created for themselves, by means of secondary fiefs, sacrificing portions of their possessions, a retinue that was socially higher and enhanced their brilliance and their ambition. They thus rewarded outstanding services among their loyal followers. We cannot measure the full significance of such a reward until we understand that it was not simply a question of material compensation, but of necessity in enabling the founding of a family, something that was denied to the warrior living at the lord's court. It is reported that among the dignitaries of the Church, ecclesiastic properties had been wrongly converted through nepotism into feudal grants as favors for relatives or friends.

There was no specified amount of land, such as five hides or some other measure, for a knight's fief. There was also just as little a standard governing the military burden imposed on the counties. Only in a very general way, in round numbers divisible by ten or five, did the king place his requirements on the great feudal lords, according to their possessions. The individual knights who held direct or secondary fiefs and were settled on the land had properties that differed extremely in size, even down to mere parcels. At a later time, when the concept arose that a knightly fief was to be considered as the equivalent of 20 pounds of annual income, even that was not much more than a theory.[3]

The large estates which the Conqueror granted were not situated side by side, but they were scattered throughout the kingdom, apparently with the conscious intention of preventing their consolidation into definite principalities, as happened on the Continent. Despite the existence of the great barons, this procedure enabled the Norman kings in England to have the counties regularly administered by officials, the sheriffs. That position did not become a fief. The name "earl" became a simple title. No doubt under the Conqueror's grandson, King Stephen, conditions at one time approached those of the Continent. The barons acquired magisterial authority and official positions, built castles, minted coins, and carried on private feuds, but Stephen's successor, Henry II, the first Plantagenet, was able to suppress all of that, to dismantle the castles, and to restore the strict royal authority. It was not only the wise distribution of the large estates that gave the monarchy constant superiority, but principally the national antagonism between the knightly class and the people, a situation that prevented their joining forces against the monarchy. In the following century, Ordericus Vitalis described the new noble class in England as "raw upstarts, almost crazed by their sudden rise, thinking they could do whatever they wanted." Against the tyranny of these foreign lords, the people had no other recourse than to the monarchy, and this situation lasted for generations before the two elements were blended into a new nationality. French remained the court language almost until the end of the Middle Ages. On this soil, the earl could not grow into a territorial prince, as on the Continent, and the counties continued to be administered by officials, while the warriors formed a knightly class based on feudal laws.

If we judge from what we have learned in the earlier chapters of this work, this situation would have resulted in a completely useless military organization. For a knightly army can be mobilized neither by officials nor by barons whose properties are not contiguous. Officials do not have that intimate personal relationship to the individual warrior which assures quality. Barons can only provide a levy if they have at hand the produce, services, and wagons of their properties.[4] The Frankish counts, too, had originally been simply officials, but the inherent natural laws of warriorhood had changed them into feudal lords, thus allowing them to provide reliable warriors with the resources of the county. Only on the borders, where it was completely unavoidable, had William the Conqueror allowed the formation of such tightly organized counties confronting the Scots and the Welsh, of the continental type, called "Palatinate." But even these palatinates were dissolved.

By keeping the public office of sheriff and the barony separated from each other, the Norman kings in England prevented the introduction of continental vassalage into England, neutralized any independence of the individual regions, created a large, strictly centralized kingdom—and nevertheless maintained the military system of their period, based on qualified individual warriors, by introducing a completely new element: money, pay, taxes.

While William did initially require that his vassals reinforce him by means of the feudal levy and that the most powerful among them each provide a specified number of subvassals, this method soon turned out to be impractical or impossible of execution. Even William himself, in 1084, on the occasion of a Danish raid, did not levy his vassals but proclaimed a tax, 6 shillings for every hide, and with this he sent mercenaries into the field. It is also reported that his son, Henry I, conducted his wars with mercenaries.[5] The chronicle says that Henry II led mercenaries into the field because he did not want to burden his knights, burghers, and peasants ("nolens vexare agrarios milites nec burgensem nec rusticorum multitudinem ... duxit solidarios vero milites innumeros": "Unwilling to trouble his landed knights or the city and rural populace, he led mercenaries, indeed countless knights").[6] This point is confirmed by his treasurer, Richard Fitz-Neal, in his accounting for the administration of the treasury, where it is stated: "mavult enim princeps stipendiarios quam domesticos bellicis apponere casibus." ("For the prince prefers in cases of war to bring in mercenaries rather than vassals.")[7]

And so it happened that when the Conqueror toward the end of his regime (1086) had the great cadaster of his kingdom, the Domesday Book, drawn up, all useful property in the form of lands, mills, forests, fish ponds, and the entire population according to classes were listed, but there was no indication of military obligations. This seemed so incredible in a feudal nation that scholars even thought there was not yet a feudal knighthood under the Conqueror but that it was first introduced under his successors. This concept was soon shown to be in error. Once we have understood that feudal warriorhood and mobilization by numerical measures are two concepts that are hardly related to each other, we are less astonished that the Conqueror did not have the military requirements listed in his cadaster.

Feudalism and vassalage therefore assumed a completely different significance in England than on the Continent. To be sure, the Conqueror made maximum use of the feudal concept for landholdings: he considered himself as the supreme owner of the entire country. Since that time, there has been no landownership in England which the possessor did not receive from a grantor. But this feudal sovereign authority applied only in property laws, in the laws of inheritance, and to the powers and fees of the lord. The real substance, military service, was at first supplemented and finally replaced by taxes.

Up into the period of the Edwards (Edward I, 1272–1307, was the great-grandson of Henry II), the mixture of feudal levy and mercenaries continued. The Magna Charta (paragraph 51) prohibited mercenaries, the powerful and dangerous force in the hands of the kings.[8] It happened that great barons declined military pay because they realized that their political position vis-à-vis the king was based on the feudal providing in kind of military service.[9] But the nature of things was stronger than this political reflection, and the mercenary system retained the upper hand.

It had been doubtful from the beginning as to how far the military obligation of the vassal extended. Charlemagne had been able to order a

Frankish count on the Loire with his followers to participate at his own expense in a campaign beyond the Elbe lasting for months, because the count, in his intermediate position between suzerain and official, was in a position to draw on the resources of the entire county. The English king could not require his barons to provide him their knights at their own expense for an unlimited time, possibly for a war on the Continent. Soon it was considered as a rule in England, as on the Continent, that a vassal had to serve forty days at his own expense, but whether such service could also be beyond the Channel remained controversial, and it was directly refused by the barons.[10] A war that was limited to six weeks could not be anything more than a feud between neighbors. Only in cases of uprisings, pillaging raids, and border feuds with the Scots or Welsh, therefore, was feudal service in the strict sense of the word required. But in other situations the service obligation was accomplished by means of a money payment. In a manner similar to the provisions of the Carolingian capitularies, several knights joined together to equip and furnish one combatant, thus forming the transitional stage between the two systems.

In 1157, Henry II conducted an expedition ("*maximam expeditionem*": "a very great expedition") against Wales, for which two knights in each group of three equipped a third one, "duo milites de tota Anglia tertium pararent."[11] In 1198 Richard I required that in each group of ten knights, nine would equip the tenth one for the campaign in Normandy.[12] In 1205 John made the same requirement.[13] Under Henry III it was required in 1230 that for every two plowlands, one man was to be provided for forty days at the expense of the community. Similar requirements were imposed on several other occasions under Henry III.[14] In practice, all of this must have amounted to satisfaction of the requirement through paying and recruiting the necessary men.

In the case of the Abbey of Saint Albans, we can trace the development in detail.[15] The abbot had six knightly fiefs, and each of these was divided among several subvassals. Whenever the king levied his army, the various landholders of each fief assembled and arranged to provide one knight. Sometimes they did this by hiring a knight or two sergeants, while at other times they selected one of their own number to perform this service and contributed toward his equipment and maintenance. A similar arrangement seems to have existed among the knights of Malmesbury.

From the time of Henry II on, we find direct proof of the arrangement of the "shield money" (*scutagia*), which was in any case much older.[16] It is not exactly a matter of explaining it as a simple "substitution" of money for the military obligation, so that on each occasion every individual baron or knight had the choice of either reporting for the levy or paying a specified amount. Rather, the kings maintained the principle that whoever did not report for the levy forfeited his fief, and he had to purchase his freedom from this charge by paying into the national treasury a fine of a sum to be determined. The debate over the feudal obligation also carries over into the concept of the general tax. Many of the details are still unclear. There remains the question of how much and to whom the subvassal paid when his lord did not report for the levy. But we can leave these doubts aside. The important point for the military organization was the substitution of a money payment for personal service, and the use, in turn, of this money for the recruitment and maintenance of mercenary knights.[17]

The military significance of the large domain is to be seen from this time on, therefore, in the manner in which the warlike spirit in this class was passed on through tradition, training, and practice, thus providing material for recruitment. The English knight took to the field and maintained the warlike tradition and skill as a result of his own decision concerning the pay to be received and not because of being levied by a suzerain. On the Continent, the count became the king's vassal and as such provided his feudal knights. Often there were even intermediate levels in this procedure, such as the duke above the count and the banneret below him. In England, the difference between the barons ("*tenentes in capite*": "tenants in chief") and their subvassals ("*subtenentes*": "subtenants") disappeared up to the point of a simple quantitative difference between the greater and smaller landowners. The statute *Quia emptores* of·1292 prescribed that in every feudal grant the new grantee became a direct vassal of the crown, a procedure that eliminated the intermediate feudal levels from the political-legal viewpoint as well. But militarily the original vassalage, based on the possession of large estates, was transformed in such a way that the barons took over the recruitment as condottieri. On the Continent, the count also led his men into the field. The English sheriff led them only when the militia was called up, but in the field the warriors, both knights and serving men, were led by the barons who had recruited them and who had the name, the personal prestige, and the resources for the initial equipping and the first payments, in accordance with their agreement with the king and in return for his pay.

The true feudal system was based on a pure barter economy. The modified version, as it developed in England under the Norman kings and their successors, the Plantagenets, was based on a combination of barter economy and money economy in that the nucleus of the warrior-

hood, the knightly class, was socially based on and supported by the
granting of land, while the active army was recruited and maintained with
money. The English kings were able to introduce this procedure as a
result of an economic change that had started in Europe. Just at that time,
we can perceive the early beginnings of a renewal of money economy
resulting from a considerable increase of precious metals. This increase
of the gold and silver in circulation, to which we shall return in the
chapter on the mercenary system, surprisingly does not show its first
effects on military organization in the area where nature provided and
offered these treasures, on the Continent, but rather in England, where
commerce brought a portion of these metals and the political development made it possible to use them. In the eleventh century, trade was
already quite significant. It was the period during which the cities in
Germany, under Henry IV, for the first time emerged as political powers. Cologne carried on a lively exchange with England, as did the
Flemish cities. The English chronicler Henry of Huntingdon (ca. 1155)
reported that England exported lead, tin, fish, meat, cattle, wool, and
coal to Germany. In return for these articles of general consumption, it
received silver from Germany.[18] On the Continent there was still no
central political power that would have been strong enough to control
the currency for its own purposes. The peoples were no longer accustomed to having taxes imposed on them. Only the most extreme power,
the frightful Vikings, had at times forced tribute from entire areas and
countries, amounts that were assembled through general contributions.
   England had suffered from this savage crew even more than the Continent, and the "Danish money" to pay them off had sometimes taken on
the character of a regular tax. When King Knut governed England, he
had paid his housecarls regularly and billeted them in winter. William the
Conqueror, when he prescribed taxes, was able to tie this to the tradition
of the "Danish money," even though that custom had disappeared in the
meantime. And the royal power of William's successors was strong
enough to develop gradually an entire system of taxation. For these kings
were the legal successors of the ancient Anglo-Saxon people's kings. But
they multiplied their power by grafting onto that ancient tradition the
concept of feudal hegemony which they brought with them. The English
king was now both the head of state and the possessor of the entire land.
The Anglo-Saxon people's monarchy had been limited by the witan. The
continental monarchies were limited by the immunity of the great vassals
and the trend toward hereditary status of the counties, while the English
monarchy was restricted by neither of these. While the Council of Barons (*consensus*) replaced the witan, its power in England, as we have seen,

had neither deep nor broad roots. Inasmuch as the Norman-French law, which the lords brought with them and under whose concepts they lived, had been superimposed on the Anglo-Saxon national law, it was within the power of the king, in cases of conflict, to decide which legal system would govern. Thus, the monarchy, as the central power, governed the counties through the sheriffs, proclaimed the laws, had land cadasters drawn up for the entire kingdom to serve as a base for taxes, imposed punishments, and granted favors in accordance with its own judgment. After the death of each feudal land grantee, the renewal of the grant called for payment of fees that were established in a purely arbitrary fashion. The king claimed the guardianship for all possessors of fiefs who were minors and used this for his own purposes. He married off the daughters of deceased vassals as he saw fit. There was developed a system of police fines (*amerciaments*) of such severity that it has been justifiably compared with the disciplinary element of the military force that occupied the country. By having the punishments graduated according to the fortune of the accused, very high fines could be imposed even for minor transgressions, simple oversights of formalities. No continental ruler would have been able to deal in this way with his subordinates, his eminent vassals, or even to have a Domesday Book drawn up. The sheriffs received the taxes of their counties in general tenancy. If the normal income, the "shield money," the fees, and the fines were not sufficient, then *"Hülfen"*—"support taxes"—and taxes of one-ninth or even one-fourth of one's personal property were prescribed.[19] Action against those in arrears in their payments was not limited to one's possessions. King John, the youngest son of Henry II, had a tooth extracted each day from a Jew who was unwilling to pay; when he had lost seven of them, he paid the 10,000 marks that were being required of him.

In brief, the English kings collected taxes in money and with this money created a special military system because, as a result of the conquest, they had the despotic power and the frightful pressure that were necessary to extract from the people the necessary means, which were very great, for the support of mercenary armies.

As early as the regime of Henry I, the youngest son of the Conqueror, we hear loud complaints about oppression and extortion and solemn promises of improvement. Henry II took certain measures, not to lighten the burdens as such, it is true, but to limit the sharpest edge, the arbitrariness in the assessments and valuations, especially by establishing jury commissions in addition to his officials. On one occasion he even dismissed all the sheriffs. When Richard I demanded in 1198 that 300 English knights should serve him for a whole year across the Channel, or that the body of knights should pay enough to be able to maintain that number at the rate of 3 shillings daily for each man, this requirement was said to be exorbitant.[20] While 300 knights seems to be a very modest number, the sum necessary for their upkeep amounted to 328,500 shillings, or 16,425 pounds, and that was a great deal. Under Richard's brother and successor, John, there finally arose from these demands the famous constitutional conflicts and the Magna Charta. Despite the successes that the barons won for a while in these conflicts, one thing remained true: the strongly centralized government which held the administration firmly in hand, raised taxes—either at its own discretion or with the agreement of the classes—and by means of these taxes placed armies of mercenary knights and common warriors in the field.

The mixture of mercenaries and knights in the English military organization soon completely overshadowed the feudal concept. If it had not been for the continuous wars that resulted from linking the English crown with great French fiefs (Normandy, Brittany, Poitou, and Gascony), the Norman knightly class settled in the British Isles would very quickly have changed into a peace-loving class of large landowners. But the wars that lured men with the promise of high pay maintained the warlike tradition, even though there was lacking that sharp control which, in keeping with the original concepts, allowed military fiefs to be granted only to actual warriors.

The eradication of the concept of a real military fief was accomplished so fast that already in the reign of the Conqueror's great-grandson, the son of his granddaughter Matilda, Henry II, we find a law that has hardly a trace of vassalage and bases the military organization purely on the concept of the citizen militia of the landowners.

The defense law or *Assisa de armis habendis in Anglia* (Assize of Arms) of 1181 prescribes that whoever held a knightly fief was to have armor, helmet, shield, and lance. Whoever owned more than 16 marks' worth of cattle or other mobile property was to have the same equipment; those with more than 10 marks' worth of property were to have a gorget, an iron helmet, and a lance, and all other freemen were to have doublets, iron helmets, and lances. No one was to dispose of these weapons in any way, and guardians were to keep them for their minor heirs until the latter were of age for military service. The traveling judges were to have the people classified in the various categories by juries, to read these provisions to them at the county assemblies, and to administer the oath to them. Anyone who did not attend the county assembly was to be ordered to go to Westminster, that is, to the royal court itself, where he would be informed of his status and be sworn. The judges were to publish the word everywhere that if a person did not maintain the prescribed weapons, the king would not be satisfied with a fine but it would be a question of life and death.

A proclamation by King John in 1205 prescribed that, in case of an enemy invasion, everyone was to hasten to the defense of the country, properly armed, at the first report. A landowner who did not come and was not excused because of illness was to lose his property forever for himself and his heirs. Those who did not own property were to be placed in bondage, with their heirs, and were to pay an annual poll tax of 4 *denarii*. No one was to avoid the levy because of poverty, for as soon as the army was assembled, it was to be fed at the expense of the king. The sheriffs and bailiffs were to publish this regulation everywhere at the markets and annual fairs, and they were responsible for reporting to the king anyone who avoided the levy.

A new defense law of Henry III of 1252 extended the regulations of 1181 by Henry II, going far beyond them. Whereas Henry II expressly prescribed only the arming of all freemen, Henry III called on everybody between sixteen and sixty years of age ("cives burgenses, libere tenentes, villanos et alios": "city-dwellers, free tenants, townspeople and others"). While Henry II had distinguished between only three classes, there were now five such distinctions. The highest class was required to serve on horseback. The next-to-last class was to be armed with bow and arrows in addition to the sword and dagger, and the last class, the possessors of the smallest parcels or of more than 40 shillings' worth of mobile property, needed to have only scythes, daggers, knives, and similar small weapons. Constables and high constables were to be placed in command of these levies.

These regulations may serve as an example of how little we may depend on laws, even when we have their original wording, as in this case, if we wish to learn the historical facts. While it is true that the Assizes of Arms formed the basis for the English militia that still exists today, this militia hardly ever played any role in either the older or the more modern military history. Despite the extremely severe punishments, the medieval regulations never came close to being carried out. The task of forming the classes, drawing up the lists, and enforcing and checking on the procurement of the weapons was much too detailed and too difficult, while the military value, even with the best execution, would have been much too small. As we have already seen, real wars are fought by troops with completely different organization. While the militia of all men between ages sixteen and sixty that was ordered by Henry III would have resulted in many hundreds of thousands, the decisive battles of even the following period were still fought by a few thousand men.

Gneist has compared the division of the entire English people into five classes of military obligation with graduated armament with the five classes of the ancient Roman century organization. The outward similarity is obvious, but the principal point is that we must understand the difference. That is, with the Romans it was a levy organization for a disciplined army, whereas with the English it was a question of a militia existing almost entirely on paper, something aside from the real warriorhood. Furthermore, it has now turned out that the famous Servian arrangement in classes was nothing more than a fiction of Cato's middle-of-the-road politics in the second century. (See Vol. I.)

While these military regulations had little practical significance, knowledge of them is still very important for us, first as documentation as to how little value such unorganized mass levies have, and then especially as an analogy with the similar provisions among the West Goths and the Franks that are known to us from the early Middle Ages. We do not know what the name "assizes" actually means; it is probably an abbreviation of *"sententia assisa,"* "assessment." Stubbs calls them simply "capitularies," in the sense of the Carolingian regulations, which they also are.[21] I am including the text below in order to facilitate this comparison. How extensively the Carolingian capitularies deceived scholarly research, and what pains we had to take to reduce their significance to the proper measure, because it first had to be understood that the letter of medieval law and real life not only did not correspond to one another but could actually be in direct contradiction of each other! In the Assizes of Arms of the Plantagenets, we see very clearly what was very difficult to recognize in the Carolingian capitularies because the sources of the thirteenth century are no longer as meager as those of the eighth, and they allow us to trace clearly the actual development step by step. But in this way the later period not only explains itself but also serves to confirm the interpretation of the earlier period, just as the Swiss account of the Burgundian wars provided a lodestar for the evaluation of Herodotus' account of the Persian wars.

EXCURSUS

ASSIZE OF ARMS IN ENGLAND
(STUBBS, *SELECT CHARTERS*, P. 153)
(SEE APPENDIX 4 FOR LATIN TEXT)

1. Whoever has a fief of one knight should have a coat of mail, helmet, shield, and lance, and every knight should have as many coats of mail, helmets, shields, and lances as he had knights' fiefs in his domain.

2. Indeed, whatever free layman will have had cattle or rent to the value of 16

marks should have a coat of mail, helmet, shield, and lance; truly whatever free layman will have had 10 marks in cattle or rent should have a hauberk, a cap of iron, and lance.

3. Likewise all burghers and the whole community of freemen should have a military tunic, cap of iron, and lance.

4. Let each of those swear, however, that by the festival of Saint Hilary he will have these arms and he will bear loyalty to the Lord King Henry, namely, the son of Matilda the queen, and he will keep these arms in his own service according to his own command and for the loyalty of the lord king and his kingdom. And no one who will have had these arms should sell them, neither should he mortgage, nor lend, nor deprive himself of them in any other way. His lord should not take these from his man in any manner, neither by penalty, nor by gift, nor by pledge, nor in any other way.

5. If anyone possessing these arms will have died, his arms should remain for his heir. If indeed his heir should not be of such age that he is able to use arms if necessary, the man who will have him in wardship would similarly have custody of the arms, and he would find a man who may be able to use the arms in the service of the lord king, until the heir should be of such age that he can bear arms and then he should have them.

6. Whatever burgher will have had more arms than it will have been necessary for him to possess according to his assessment should sell them and thus transfer them from himself to such a man who may keep them in the service of the lord king of England. And none of them should keep more arms than it will have been necessary to possess according to this assessment.

7. Likewise no Jew should keep a coat of mail or hauberk in his house, but he should sell them, give them away, or remove them from his possession in another manner so that they may remain in the service of the King.

8. Likewise let no one bear arms outside England except by order of the lord king; nor should anyone sell arms to anyone who may carry them out of England.

9. Likewise the justices should have it sworn by the knights of legal status, other freemen, and men of legal status of the Hundreds and of the cities, as many as they will have seen fit for battle and who will have the amount of cattle according to which it will have been necessary that he have breastplate, helmet, lance, and shield according to what has been said—namely, that they will mention all these of their Hundreds, neighborhoods, and cities, who will have 16 marks in either cattle or rent and similarly who will have 10 marks. Afterwards, the justices should have all those jurors and others list how much cattle and rent they had and what arms they ought to have according to the value of their cattle and rent. And afterwards in a general assembly they should have this assessment of having arms read before them and have them swear that they will have these arms according to the aforesaid value of their cattle and rent, and that they will keep them in the service of the lord king according to this aforesaid assessment in the command and faithfulness of the Lord King Henry and his kingdom. If indeed it will have happened that anyone of those who ought to have these arms is not in his county at the term when the justices will be in that county, the justices should set a date for him to appear before them in another county. And if he will have come to them in none of the counties through which they were going to go and he will not have been in that land, a date should be set for him at Westminster on the eighth day of Saint Michael, so that he may be there to swear his oath if he esteems himself and his property. And let it be com-

manded to him that he should have his arms by the aforesaid festival of Saint Hilary according as it pertains to him having them.

10. Likewise the justices should have proclaimed throughout all the counties through which they are going to go that whoever will not have possessed these arms according to what has been aforesaid, the lord king will punish him physically and in no way will he take land and cattle from him.

11. Likewise let no one swear against loyal freemen who do not possess 16 marks or 10 marks in cattle.

12. Likewise the justices should command through all counties that no one, if he esteems himself and his property, should buy or sell any ship to leave England, nor should anyone carry off timber or have it carried outside England. And the king ordered that no one except a freeman be admitted to the oath of arms. (*Gesta Regis Henrici Secundi Benedicti Abbatis: Deeds of King Henry II by Benedict the Abbot*, 1: 278. *Chronicle of Roger of Hoveden*, 2: 261.)

WRIT FOR THE LEVYING OF A FORCE. 1205.
(STUBBS, P. 281)
(SEE APPENDIX 4 FOR LATIN TEXT)

The King, etc. to the Sheriff of Rotelanda, etc. You should know that provision has been made with the approval of the archbishops, bishops, counts, barons, and all our loyal men of England that every nine knights throughout all England will provide for a tenth knight well equipped with horses and arms for the defense of our kingdom, and that those nine knights should provide for the tenth 2 *solidi* each day for his allowance. Therefore, we instruct you that, if you esteem yourself and your property, you should take care that ten knights from your bailiwick should be in London three weeks after Easter, well equipped with horses, arms, and their allowances, just as it has been stated above, and prepared to enter our service where we will have commanded and to be in our service for the defense of our realm as long as it will have been necessary. Provision has also been made that if foreigners will have come into our land, all together should oppose them with force and arms without any dispute and delay after word of their arrival had been heard. And if any knight, sergeant, or another tenant will have been found, who will have withdrawn himself from this duty, provided that he was not burdened by so great an illness that he was not able to come, the man himself and his heirs will be disinherited, and his fief will default to the lord of the estate to dispose of as he wishes, so that the disinherited and his heirs may never have any recovery of it. Indeed, if any knights, sergeants and others who do not hold land will have been found similarly to have shirked their duty, they and their heirs will become obligated to pay 4 *denarii* each year per person. They should not fail to come to the aforementioned assembly when they heard about it because of poverty, because from wherever they will have come to the army sufficient means will be provided from which they will be able to be sustained in our service. If indeed a sheriff, bailiff, or provost will not have presented to us by a list either written or oral those who will have shirked their duty, said sheriff, bailiff, or provost will remain at our mercy for life and limb. And therefore we instruct you that you should with haste have all these things proclaimed in the law courts throughout all your bailiwick, and in the markets, fairs, and elsewhere. And you should so apply yourself in performing that business that we do not have to punish you for your failure. You should also be in London on the aforesaid date and you should send a document from your area; and you should then have the names of the tenth knights written down and should have this list there. I witnessed this myself at Wintonia on the third day of April. (*Patent Rolls,* 1: 55).

ASSIZE OF ARMS. 1252.
(STUBBS, P. 370)
(SEE APPENDIX 4 FOR LATIN TEXT)

The provision has also been made that all sheriffs together with two knights specially assigned to this duty should make a circuit of their counties from Hundred to Hundred, cities and towns, and they should have convened burghers, free tenants, villagers, and others of fifteen years of age to sixty years of age, and they should have them all swear to bear arms according to the amount of their lands and cattle: namely, at 15 pounds' worth of land, a coat of mail, iron cap, sword, knife, and horse; at 10 pounds' worth of land, one hauberk, iron cap, sword, and knife; at 100 shillings' worth of land, one doublet, iron cap, sword, lance, and knife; at 40 shillings' worth of land and more up to 100, a sword, bow, arrows, and knife. Those who have less than 40 shillings of land should bear sickles, *gisarmes* (daggers), knives, and other small weapons; at cattle of 60 marks' worth, a coat of mail, iron cap, sword, knife, and horse; at cattle of 40 marks' worth, one hauberk, iron cap, sword, and knife; at cattle of 20 marks' worth, one doublet, iron cap, sword, and knife; at cattle of 40 shillings' worth and more up to 10 marks, sickles, *gisarmes,* and other small weapons. Also, all those who are able to have bows and arrows outside the forest should have them; those who are able to have them in the forest should have bows and pellets. (*Delbrück note:* I understand this last sentence to mean that the foresters were to have crossbows and bolts rather than bows and arrows.)

In all cities and towns, they should have sworn to bear arms in the presence of the elders of the cities and before the provosts and bailiffs where there are no elders. Indeed, in all the other towns a constable should be appointed or two according to the number of inhabitants and the provision of the aforesaid. In all Hundreds, in fact, a high constable should be appointed, at whose command all sworn to bear arms should assemble from their Hundreds, and they should be administrators to do that which pertains to preservation of our peace.

STATUTE OF WINCHESTER
EDWARD III, 1285
(Original text in French. The following passage is from the translation by Stubbs in *Select Charters,* p. 474.)

And further it is commanded that every man have in his house harness for to keep the peace after the ancient assize; that is to say, every man between fifteen years of age and sixty years, shall be assessed and sworn to armor according to the quantity of their lands and goods; that is to wit, from fifteen pounds lands, and goods forty marks, an hauberke, an helme of iron, a sword, a knife, and a horse; and from ten pounds of lands, and twenty marks goods, an hauberke, an helme of iron, a sword, and a knife; and from five pound lands, a doublet, an helme of iron, a sword, and a knife; and from forty shillings of land, a sword, a bow and arrows, and a knife; and he that has less than forty shillings yearly shall be sworn to keep gisarmes, knives, and other less weapons; and he that has less than twenty marks in goods, shall have swords, knives, and other less weapons; and all other that may shall have bows and arrows out of the forest, and in the forest bows and boults. And that view of armor be made every year two times. And in every hundred and franchise two constables shall be chosen to make the view of armor; and the constables aforesaid shall present before justices assigned such defaults as they do see in the country about armor, and of the suits, and of watches, and of highways, and also shall present all such as do lodge strangers in uplandish towns, for whom they will not answer. And the justices assigned shall present at every parliament unto the king such defaults as they shall find, and the king shall provide remedy therein.

REFERENCES AND STRENGTH ESTIMATES

The basis for a clear numerical idea of the Norman military organization is provided by the *General Introduction of Domesday Book,* accompanied by indexes, etc., by Sir Henry Ellis, in two volumes. London, 1833.

A true understanding of that organization, however, was first arrived at by J. H. Round in a series of articles that he collected in 1895 in the volume *Feudal England.* This work served as a basis for further development by Pollock and Maitland, *The History of the English Law Before the Time of Edward I,* 2d ed., 1898. See also Maitland, *Domesday Book and Beyond,* 1897. Also very worthwhile is the work *Domesday and Feudal Statistics,* by A. H. Inman, London, 1900. Although Gneist, in his *English Constitutional History (Englische Verfassungsgeschichte),* 1882, based his work on incorrect and unclarified basic concepts, he nevertheless made some very useful numerical estimates, pointing to the correct situation, on p. 103 ff. The most recent effective study is contained in the first chapter of "Studies on the Military History of England in the Twelfth Century" ("Studien zur Kriegsgeschichte Englands im 12. Jahrhundert"), by Douglas Drummond. Berlin dissertation, 1905. Publisher: Georg Nauck, Berlin.

According to the estimate by Ellis, the number of *"tenentes in capite"* ("tenants in chief") mentioned in the Domesday Book amounts to some 1,400. But among them are such a large number of unclear conditions of ownership and minor personalities (officials and the like) that Gneist, p. 104, holds that there are only 600 actual vassals of the crown, while Inman, p. 68, estimates as "capital tenants by knight service" only 300. In the same passage, Gneist establishes the fact that "among the minor vassals of the crown there were still a number of Saxon names" and among the subvassals "about half were Saxon names." Since many among the subvassals cannot be counted as of the warrior class, whereas the great majority of Normans who settled in England were undoubtedly warriors, I assume that a much higher percentage of the Saxon names in the Domesday Book were nonwarriors than was the case with the Norman names. The total number of subvassals in the Domesday Book is 7,871; therefore, counting the 1,400 vassals of the crown, there were at that time between 9,000 and 10,000 *tenentes* all together. But we can do very little with this number, as valuable as it may appear, since warriors and nonwarriors are not sufficiently differentiated. This situation is further complicated by the fact that, in the eleventh century, the term *miles* was not yet a knight in the later sense but often also included the completely subordinated serving man, as Ellis' *General Introduction,* p. 60, expressly points out in the entries in the Domesday Book. Since the Domesday Book contains nothing at all of the *servitium debitum* (service owed), Freeman even concluded that feudal knighthood did not yet exist at all under William the Conqueror but was introduced in England after his time. This idea, however, was contradicted by Round, who determined the existence of the *servitium debitum* from other sources for individual regions and lords, and, applying this result to all of England, estimated a total around 5,000. But Drummond, p. 18, correctly remarked concerning this estimate that the number was not of such great importance from a practical viewpoint as it might seem at first glance, since the feudal army was only very infrequently levied in this form. The number of *servitia debita* is consistent neither with the number of enfeoffed vassals, nor with the total number of warriors in England, nor with the strength of an army levied on this basis, since always there were undoubtedly a considerable number of warriors without fiefs in the direct retinue of the king, in addition to the contingents led by the barons and those warriors who were direct vassals of the king himself.

The number of enfeoffed warriors in England seems never to have been definitely determined during the regimes of the first Norman kings, since it was of no importance to the king whether a baron fulfilled his *servitium debitum* with enfeoffed warriors or those without fiefs. The first king who had the number of enfeoffed knights officially determined was Henry II, in 1166. Drummond's estimate gives this roster some 6,400 men, whom we can now consider as actual knights in the more narrow sense of the word that applied in the twelfth century. But even Henry II did not have this number established for the purpose of levying the army but to use as a better base for the creation of a taxation law than was offered by the old, completely arbitrary *servitium debitum* and the Domesday Book.

My assumption that there were all together under William I some 5,000 enfeoffed warriors in England is based on the one hand on a comparison with Drummond's count that there were 6,400 of them in 1166, and on the other hand on the fact that, in accordance with Gneist's account, about half of the 7,871 *subtenentes* in the Domesday Book had Saxon names. Certainly, a large portion of these Saxons were not warriors, and the same also applies to a small portion of the Normans.

There is no basic connection between the approximate number of 5,000 enfeoffed warriors at which I have arrived for 1086 and Round's estimate that the *servitium debitum* about the same time also amounted to about 5,000. This is a pure coincidence, and in fact not a complete one, since Round's figure is to be regarded as a maximum, while mine is not. Nevertheless, the two estimates support each other mutually to the extent that it results from them that the differences between the *servitium debitum* and the enfeoffments of knights undertaken by the individual barons were at times greater, at other times smaller, but in general they approximately balanced each other.

Among the at least 600 vassals of the crown estimated by Gneist, p. 104, instead of the 1,400 counted by Ellis, were 153 members of the clergy and 30 women.

The 8,471 *tenentes* given by Drummond on p. 8 are the total of Ellis' 7,871 *subtenentes* and the 600 *tenentes in capite* of Gneist's count. This total, however, does not present the correct picture, since the nonknightly *tenentes in capite* had already been subtracted, whereas this group was still included in the *subtenentes*. The total number of *tenentes*, therefore, must be estimated, in agreement with Inman, at between 9,000 and 10,000.

NOTES FOR CHAPTER V

1. "Lord" is an Anglo-Saxon word and means literally "bread-giver." The title "baron" came into England with the Conquest. It means the same thing as *homo,* "vassal," and originally applied to all those directly enfeoffed by the king, but it gradually became limited to the most impor-

tant men among them, the most eminent of whom were given the title of "earl."

2. The number of *servitia debita* that were provided by men not settled on the land, and the number of those who were settled, above and beyond the number of *servitia debita,* were therefore almost in balance, so that the number 5,000 appears in both cases. See p. 179.

3. Pollock and Maitland, *The History of the English Law before the Time of Edward I,* 2d ed., 1898, 1: 236.

4. In the battle Lincoln (1141), in which King Stephen was captured, he had a few earls on his side, who no doubt bore important names but had only a few men with them. One source, Gervasius of Canterbury, calls them "ficti et factiosi comites" ("false and factious earls"). They had no other connection with the counties whose titles they bore except that a third of the income from those counties was paid to them (Oman, p. 393). Consequently, it was probably less a question of bad will than a lack of resources that prevented them from providing the king better support.

5. Stubbs, *Constitutional History,* 2d ed., 1: 434.

6. Robert de Monte, for the year 1159, cited in Stubbs, p. 588.

7. *Dialogus de scaccario (Dialogue concerning the Exchequer),* written in 1178–1179. Cited in Stubbs, p. 588.

8. Section 51. "Et statim ... amovebimus de regno omnes aliegenas milites, balistarios, servientes, stipendiarios, qui venerint cum equis et armis ad nocumentum regni." ("And immediately ... we shall remove from the kingdom all foreign soldiers, crossbowmen, sergeants and mercenaries who will have come with horses and arms for the harm of the kingdom.")

9. Morris, *The Welsh Wars of Edward I,* p. 185, *passim.*

10. Pollock and Maitland, 1: 233, point out that the forty-day rule could hardly ever have had legal force but always remained only a theory. John of England once required eighty days. Recently, Guilhiermoz, *Essai sur l'origine de la noblesse française,* convincingly stated that it was Henry II of England who introduced the forty-day rule.

11. Robert de Monte, cited in Stubbs, *Constitutional History,* 1: 455.

12. Pollock and Maitland, p. 234.

13. Stubbs, *Constitutional History,* 1: 590.

14. Gneist, *Englische Verfassungsgeschichte,* p. 289, note (according to a manuscript in the Cotton Library).

15. Pollock and Maitland, 2: 252.

16. Pollock and Maitland, 1: 246.

17. The shift from personal service to money payments was, as Pollock and Maitland, 1: 255, suppose, the origin of the otherwise inexplicable reduction of the roster. In 1277, the clergy, who had had to provide 784 knights in 1166, acknowledged having hardly 100. The great earls did likewise. But the compensation for the individual knights was increased correspondingly. Morris, of course, explains this reduction differently in *The Welsh Wars of King Edward I*. On p. 45 f., he states that the reduction in the number of those to be provided was compensation for the extension of the period of service by several times the usual forty-day standard.

18. Cunningham, *The Growth of English Industry and Commerce*, 3d ed., 1: 196.

19. In 1294, the clergy provided one-half, the earls, barons, and knights one-tenth, and the cities one-sixth.

In 1295, the clergy provided one-tenth, the nobles one-eleventh, and the cities one-seventh.

In 1307, one-fifteenth was provided; that amounted to 40,000 pounds for all of England.

20. Stubbs, *Select Charters*, p. 255 (from Roger of Hoveden).

21. *Constitutional History of England*, 1: 573.

Chapter VI

The Norman Nation in Italy

To the Norman nation in England we now add the description of the Norman nation in lower Italy, which was founded somewhat before William's conquest of England and offers a number of analogies. Thus, the events help to explain each other mutually and to confirm the picture we have gained of them.

First of all, it is important to note that both nations were founded at almost the same time, for this fact gives new proof of the point that operations could be carried out at that time with such small military forces. When Duke William crossed the Channel to conquer England, he did not even have at his disposal the concentrated forces of his territories, but a part of them had already moved off to Italy. As we shall soon see, it was not a large number of Normans who made that journey, but in comparison with William's limited area, they were still a considerable force. On the other hand, if such a small number of warriors sufficed to establish a kingdom in Italy, this fact also leads to conclusions on England.

Whereas, in arriving at our numerical estimates, we had to depend in most cases on fortuitous reports and *a posteriori* conclusions rather than direct and reliable sources, we have for the Normans in Italy a few reports that are of direct use.

Forty Norman knights, returning from a pilgrimage to Jerusalem, arrived by chance in Salerno just as that town was about to succumb to the Saracens in 1016. The intervention of this courageous small unit was sufficient to free the city, and this event provided a reason for Normans to set out for lower Italy in increasing numbers to offer their military service. In lower Italy at that time, there were still a number of small Lombard duchies, counties, and independent towns, which were constantly engaged in alternating conflicts among themselves and with the Greek Empire, as well as with the Saracens, who had completely subjugated Sicily. The Normans came as mercenaries, at times to serve the

Greeks against the Saracens and at other times to fight for the Lombard noble families or regions against the Greeks. Finally, they became lords themselves, just as Odoacer or the Goths had once done in the Roman Empire. In the first two decisive battles, Olivento and Cannae, in which they defeated the Greeks (1041), their strength is given as 3,000 men and 2,000, respectively. Even this small number, however, was in no way made up only of Normans, but the Normans were supported by natives who had joined them against the Greeks. According to different reports, the Normans at Olivento were of a strength of 500 knights or 700 knights and 500 foot soldiers.[1] It is reported of Robert Guiscard himself that, at the start of his career, he had formed a unit of booty-seeking followers from the lowest classes of the Calabrian population, descendants of Roman tenant farmers and slaves, and with them he plundered the country.[2] The Normans, then, with their inherited Viking courage, formed only a nucleus around which assembled warlike men of every type, skilled in military action. The army of William the Conqueror, too, was thus formed not only of Normans but also of mercenaries from the territories of all the lords.

The oppressed population attempted on numerous occasions to get rid of this warlike lordly class by conspiracies and rebellions. Gaufredus Malaterra tells us on one occasion that they feared for their wives and daughters when the Normans were billeted among them.[3] But all their efforts were in vain. Finally, the strongest and most fortunate of the Norman adventurers, Robert Guiscard, succeeded in uniting under the hegemony of his family all of lower Italy and Sicily, which was wrested back from the Saracens. The Norman power also became so strong that they could oppose the German emperors. Robert Guiscard was able to drive Henry IV out of Rome, take Gregory VII under his protection, and even conceive the plan of defeating the Byzantine Empire and conquering Constantinople. When the army with which he crossed the Adriatic for this purpose is given as 1,300 Norman knights and 15,000 other warriors,[4] the latter number is certainly much exaggerated. It is a still more flagrant exaggeration when the same source reports that the army which Robert led against Henry IV had a strength of 30,000 foot soldiers and 6,000 mounted men. This conclusion follows from the fact that the main portion of this army, according to other testimony,[5] was supposedly formed of Saracen mercenaries, who could not possibly have been that numerous. If lower Italy had had such great military capability as to mobilize armies of 15,000 men, to say nothing of 30,000, it would be completely incomprehensible that the small number of Normans could have established their position of dominance. Even the 1,300 knights whom Robert reportedly led across the Adriatic against Byzantium certainly represent a maximum, but as such they still form valuable evidence of what great significance even a few knights had.

The political organization which the Normans created in lower Italy assumed very similar forms to that of their kinsmen in England. The reason for this similarity does not lie in a special racial or tribal characteristic of this people, but rather in the historical event. The political organization was built on the combination of knighthood with an administration conducted by officials and having a basis in taxation. The natural tendency, inherent in knighthood, for the development of a feudal organization with a hierarchical superstructure was restricted and suppressed in the Norman nations by the strong monarchy with its officials and taxes. Without such a strong monarchy, the dominance of a group of foreign warriors could not have been maintained. The Norman knights were inherently no less unruly and proud than their French or German counterparts, but they had to yield to the monarchy because without it they would have been forced again into a life of homeless adventurousness. As late as the year 1083, the Italian Normans felt so little attachment to their territory that, when the war which Robert Guiscard had so expectantly undertaken against Byzantium did not go well, and he himself had returned to Italy, a large part of the army was won over by the Greek emperor, Alexius, and deserted to him. When Robert himself died two years later (1085), the Norman garrisons that were still stationed in Greek territory also entered the service of their former enemy.[6]

Generations passed before the foreign, homeless warrior class was integrated into a new unity with the subjugated peoples. Even though feudalism was actually introduced, the knights still retained the characteristics of mercenaries rather than feudal knights.

The prince who developed this system to its point of highest perfection was the German Emperor Frederick II, the Hohenstaufen, son of the last Norman woman ruler, Constance.

The men of the warrior class, "those enfeoffed and those without fiefs" ("milites tam feudati quam non feudati"), as the chronicler says,[7] were probably also levied by Frederick II ("cum toto servitio quod facere tenentur": "with all the service they are bound to do").

But this actual feudal levy played only a very minor role. The warriors served almost completely for pay—the knights, the burghers, and the common soldiers who were recruited.

When Frederick II was preparing for the Crusade in 1227, he required that each knightly fief pay a tax of 8 ounces of gold and also that for every eight knightly fiefs one knight was to be provided and equipped.[8] Consequently, this was still the same system that we found in the Carolingian capitularies, except that here it was clearly stated that it was not a question of a group of peasants who were to equip one of their number, but of groups of knights. It was also stated that the taxes were to be paid not to the counts, but directly into the treasury of the king.

Frederick II theoretically cut the personal tie between direct vassals of the king and subvassals, on which the real feudal system was based. His book of laws specified that the king would also make the grants to the subvassals, and no one was allowed to obligate himself to any person other than the king. The link between the subvassal and his nominal suzerain now consisted only of a money payment of 10 ounces of gold. And, of course, the same development had marked the system of vassalage in the Norman nation in England.

EXCURSUS

THE BATTLE OF DYRRHACHIUM (1081)

Oman, p. 164, reports in detail on this battle because he sees in it the last engagement for 300 years in which actual foot troops like those of Harold at Hastings, and not dismounted knights or simple militia or marksmen, played a role, the last battle between the Anglo-Saxon battle-axe and the Norman lance supported by the bow.

Robert Guiscard had crossed the Adriatic and was besieging Dyrrhachium (Durazzo). Emperor Alexius moved up with a relief army that also included the Varangians who were in the service of Byzantium. Anna Komnena, 6: 6, describes these men who carried double-edged swords or battle-axes on their shoulders, as well as shields. She recounts that they dismounted from their horses and attacked the Normans in a closed formation. Initially, she reports, they had also thrown the Normans back, even though they did not wait until the mounted archers had worked the enemy over. But in this action they had become separated from the rest of the Byzantine army and were overcome by the Norman horsemen.

This description does not correspond as closely to the conduct of the thanes at Hastings as it does to the ancient German wedge. For the thanes at Hastings sought to win in a purely defensive action, while the Varangians at Dyrrhachium attacked like the ancient Germans.

But why did they dismount from their horses? The result shows that they were too bold in their attack. Perhaps it was only a question of insufficient cooperation with the other units of the Byzantine army. But since we are not clearly informed on this point and Anna Komnena is not such a reliable source, this battle can hardly be evaluated from the viewpoint of military history.

The other sources, too, which report on this battle, particularly the *Gesta Roberti Wiscardi* (*Deeds of Robert Guiscard*), *Mon. Germ. SS.*, 9. 369 ff., do not provide the answers to those questions.

NOTES FOR CHAPTER VI

1. *Lupus Protospatharius, Mon. Germ. SS.,* 5. 52, gives the strength for Olivento as 3,000. Gaufredus Malaterra, in his *History of Sicily (Geschichte Siciliens), Muratori, SS.,* 5. 533 ff., gives 500. William of Apulia, in his epic poem which he dedicated to Robert Guiscard's son (*Mon. Germ. SS.,* 9. 239 ff.), gives the number as 1,200. The reported strength for the battle of Cannae is given in the *Annals of Barri, Mon. Germ.,* 5. 51 ff. All these points are taken from von Heinemann, *History of the Normans in Lower Italy (Geschichte der Normannen in Unteritalien),* p. 359.

2. von Heinemann, *History of the Normans,* p. 113.

3. von Heinemann, p. 207.

4. von Heinemann, p. 311.

5. von Heinemann, p. 325.

6. von Heinemann, pp. 330, 333.

7. Ryccardus de San Germano, *M.G. SS.,* 19. 369, anno 1233. P. 376: "vocat ad se . . . omnes barones et milites infeudatos" ("he calls to himself . . . all barons and enfeoffed knights").

8. Ryccardus de San Germano, *M.G. SS.,* 19. 348: "statuens ut singuli feudatarii darent de unoquoque feudo octo uncias auri et de singulis octo feudis militem unum in proximo futuro mense Maii" ("decreeing that all vassals should give from each fief 8 ounces of gold and from every eight fiefs one knight in the next month of May").

Chapter VII

Byzantium

We last looked at the East Roman Empire when it had once again taken a mighty upsurge under Justinian, with recruited armies of barbarian mercenaries, had again destroyed the nations of the Vandals and East Goths, had again drawn Africa and Italy into the empire, and also had come close to retaking Spain. But the empire was not capable of maintaining itself in this position. The citizens were not willing to bear the tax burden which was necessary for the maintenance of mercenaries and tribute to assure the quiescence of dangerous neighbors. The catastrophe was finally brought on specifically because the throne was once again occupied by a man who was himself a military commander. Justinian had been exclusively a statesman. He had sent his generals out to war and had himself, as ruler, kept in hand and guided the various powers—the capital and the provinces, the Church, and the army, all in their various cleavages and factions. One would think that when his third successor, Mauritius (582–602), himself an outstanding and successful general, ascended the throne, the empire would necessarily have been more firmly and securely based. After all, it was only in this way that the situation reverted to the original concept of the imperial position. But there was not enough power for this complete return, for the essential base was missing: the legionary discipline. Mauritius, who seems to have been characterized by a certain doctrinaire trait,[1] attempted to bring the savage mercenary bands into a firmer military organization. He recruited his men to the maximum extent possible within his own empire rather than from foreigners, but when he required on one occasion, when they were fighting with the Slavs and Tatars, that they remain in winter quarters north of the Danube, they mutinied, an action that was also prompted by the fact that he could not even pay them what they were demanding. Since the citizenry of the capital also rose against him, he was murdered (602), just as previously, in the second half of the third century, the gallant soldier emperors from Pertinax to Aurelian and Probus had been killed.

Let us note what role the question of pay played in this last attempt to form a disciplined army. The number of troops was very small, since it was only with much effort and alternating success and failure that they succeeded in repulsing the barbarian hordes and their incursions. An emperor with the skill and perceptiveness of Mauritius was probably not lacking in willingness to satisfy the troops. Nevertheless, when he came into conflict with them on the question of certain deductions for weapons and clothing, his treasury could no doubt not afford more, because after Justinian's death his strict taxation system had been given up to gain the favor of the people. It had become impossible to obtain cash.

Consequently, the East Roman Empire also went over to a military system that closely approached the one with which we have become acquainted in the Romanic-Germanic west. Around the middle of the seventh century, the land was divided into a number of military districts called *themes* and subdistricts (*meros, turma*), and each district was charged with responsibility for raising and feeding a specified number of troops. The military and civil authority, which had been separated for such a long time, was now reunited for this purpose, as in the position of the Frankish count. Since the *themes* were given their names from the existing troop units, there can be no doubt that the units were distributed through the districts and were permanently assigned to them. Instead of being stationed on the border or in the capital and having their pay and rations brought there from the entire empire, a certain military force remained in each region and was there provided for with produce in kind or by being settled on the land. In case of war, a part of this force was sent to the aid of neighboring districts or to the field army.

The backbone of feudalism was formed by warriors settled on the land, except when it was a question of simple border guards. In the East Roman Empire, too, we find, from this time on, important moves in this direction, large-estate-holding families with their military manpower. We find a granting of properties for military service ("*ktēmata stratiōtika*": "soldiers' possessions"),[2] and there developed baronies, famous military families with large holdings, who were extolled by the common people in song and story. Such an epic account from the tenth century, *Digenis Akritas,* was again found recently.[3] The editors compare the hero, not inappropriately, with an occidental margrave.

Everywhere in the laws we also find analogies. In a manner very similar to that of Charlemagne, the East Roman emperors struggled against the annexation of the free peasant lands by the great families, the *dynatoi* (nobles), and that problem in this case was no more related to the true mass of peasants than in the Frankish Kingdom. In both areas, the mass of peasants consisted of unwarlike tenant farmers. The reference to the annexation of lands concerns, rather, those original warriors who gradually became civilianized and changed over to farming. Already in his day, Justinian issued decrees against this,[4] and in the tenth century several emperors conducted a systematic struggle against these abuses. They took the most radical steps, by simply declaring such accessions as invalid, and did not allow even the pretense of superannuation.[5] Two amending laws remind us of Emperor Lambert's decree of 898 (see p. 36 above), providing that *arimanni* were not to be given by the counts to their men as fiefs, by ordering that the soldier could not be used by anyone as a landed peasant (*"en paroikou logōi"*: "in the manner of a tenant") or for private services.[6]

A series of supplements specified the value that a soldier's property had to have. For mounted men and certain divisions of the fleet, it was to be 4 pounds of gold, and for the rest of the fleet, 2 pounds. Emperor Nicephorus Phocas established a firm minimum of 4 pounds and required 12 pounds for a heavily armed man, that is, a knight in the occidental sense.[7] If there were several heirs on hand, together they were to provide one man, according to the importance of their property.

As strong as the analogies with the Occident were, the Orient never arrived at the development of a complete feudal hierarchy. The barons were there, but there was no true knightly class, and the soul of occidental feudalism, the personal relationship of loyalty, the Germanic retinue as the all-powerful concept, was lacking. For a while, the Byzantine military organization found its closest similarity in that of the Norman-English. Certain elements of feudalism were linked with and incorporated in the organization for taxation and the system of officials. The levy was carried out in the form of recruitment, and we find, as in England, that induction into service was supplanted by a payment of money.[8] But since the useful elements in the interior of the empire were not numerous enough, despite the settling and immigration of barbarians, or they lost their warlike character too quickly, again and again the ranks were filled out by resorting to foreign mercenaries. Men from all the Germanic peoples, Slavs, Petchenegs, Magyars, Bulgarians, and even Turks, rubbed elbows here in the camp of the Byzantine emperor. Very special, important services were rendered for a long time by the Varangians, originally Swedes and Normans who had come across Russia to the Black Sea. The word "Varangians" means "allies" (*foederati*). All sorts of various elements were later known by this name. After William's conquest of England, supposedly that group included many Anglo-Saxons who had fled from England.

A reasonable picture of how a national levy sometimes looked in the tenth century is provided in an account by Johannes Skylitzes.[9] He recounts how the Turks time and again raided Cilicia and moved through the region, plundering and laying waste the land. Nicephorus Botoniates, the "Dux," assembled an army, but envy and negligence rendered all his efforts futile. The soldiers did not receive sufficient rations, took what was given to them, and then returned home, so that the barbarians were once again able to sweep through the land. Then a number of young men assembled in Antioch and were ready to fight with youthful courage, but since they were inexperienced in war, without war-horses, poorly armed, and meagerly fed, things went poorly for them, and they returned home unsung.[10] Botoniates attempted to repel the barbarians with his own retinue and a few mercenaries.

The events in a Frankish area were no doubt similar whenever the Normans or Hungarians invaded the country and also, for example, when Charles the Fat moved up to relieve Paris and accomplished nothing.

In the tenth and eleventh centuries, the Byzantine Empire again enjoyed a great upsurge. The Bulgarians were defeated once and for all. Basil II (died 1025) had the eyes put out of all the prisoners he had taken, reportedly 15,000, and sent them home by placing in charge of each group of 100 a man whom he had left one eye. When the miserable figures were led before their lord, he fell over unconscious and died two days later. Cilicia and Antioch were also recaptured from the caliphs by the Byzantines, and Armenia was incorporated in the empire. The empire now extended from the Adriatic to the Euphrates and beyond. I think that this change of fortune was associated with the fact that the money economy was again gradually beginning to take hold. Again we hear much about imposition of taxes and the gathering of taxes,[11] and taxation provided the possibility for hiring mercenaries. While in the western provinces, in Europe, natural produce was still being provided, which could only be used locally, in Asia the pay could once again be sent to the central treasury.[12] But more important than this slight change in the interior was the change on the enemy side. The Bulgarians had gradually lost their barbarian warlike power, and the same thing happened to the Arabs on the opposite border. As soon as the situation changed and new enemies appeared, the Byzantine renaissance was ended, and in the east the empire fell a victim to the Seljuks, and in the west it had great difficulty defending itself from the Normans.

It appears that we are excellently informed on the Byzantine military system, since we have a whole series of thorough, systematic writings from various centuries on the military organization of the Greek Empire. There are also many detailed accounts of wars and battles by contemporary authors. Emperor Mauritius (died 602) and Emperor Leo VI, "the Philosopher" (died 911), left thorough and systematic writings, and Nicephorus Phocas (died 960) left behind a valuable individual account. But the more we study them, the more doubtful it becomes as to how much of them we may accept. We have already observed in ancient history that the theoretical and systematic writings we have received from antiquity by no means agree with the events we read of in reliable historical sources. It seems incredible but is nevertheless a fact that the authors continue to repeat all kinds of theories related to the Macedonian phalanx, as if they had never heard anything of the Roman legion and its tactics. Not only these accounts, however, but also the description Livy has given us of the ancient Roman manipular tactics, Sallust's accounts of recruiting methods, and a large part of the accounts by Vegetius have proven to be either gross misunderstandings or even pure fantasy. The situation among the Byzantines was no different. On closer examination we realize that their individual accounts contradict one another. A very large part of the material they present to us must be regarded not as a record of actual practice but as fantasy and theory lacking any basis of truth, as simple repetitions and developments of those theories of the Alexandrians, who had previously systematized the Macedonian phalanx. William Louis of Nassau in the sixteenth century and Montecuccoli in the seventeenth made much use of Emperor Leo's *Tactics,* and the prince of Ligne in the eighteenth century collected this work with the regulations of Frederick the Great for his generals and claimed they were both superior to Caesar, since he had only given examples, while the other two prescribed regulations.[13] As we have seen, this praise was fully undeserved as far as Emperor Leo was concerned and is to be explained in the same way as the fame of Vegetius, who was also only a very limited mentality. (See Vol. II, p. 203.)

The Byzantine historical accounts of wars and battles, too—for instance, those by Bryennios and Anna Komnena—are in the highest degree fantastic and unreliable, but we may learn enough from the comparison and mutual control provided by these sources to be certain of the fact that a disciplined infantry like the Roman legions was just as nonexistent in the Greek Empire as in the Occident. In both places, the nucleus of the armies consisted of rather limited groups of heavily armed horsemen. The evidence against which all other testimony is to be measured as a standard is an expression by Nicephorus Phocas, which reads as follows: "The commander who has 5,000 or 6,000 of our heavy horsemen and the help of God needs nothing more." The historical evidence is in agreement with this statement, once we have eliminated with critical rigor everything that is not satisfactorily confirmed. Nicephorus Bryennios, too, describing the formation of the Corps of the Immortals under Emperor Michael III (1071–1078), estimates that the elements of their training consisted of their ability to manipulate their weapons and to ride.[14]

The principal difference between the oriental armies and those of the Occident lay first of all in the fact that the foreign barbarian mercenaries played a much larger role in the east than among the occidentals, who waged their own wars, and also in the fact that the mounted archers, along with the heavily armed horsemen, made up a large part of the army. After the defeat by the Seljuks at Manzikert in 1071, the role of the native warriors decreased strongly, and the empire seems to have depended almost exclusively on foreign mercenaries. When these mercenaries failed, Constantinople fell into the hands of the Crusaders (1204). After the restoration of the Greek Empire, the old military system was resumed.

Basically, then, it was the same military organization to which the Roman Empire had come in the third century and which we have met under Justinian in the war against the East Goths, with which the Greek Empire held its own for a thousand years longer. Despite interior disruption and ecclesiastic struggles, despite continuous military revolutions, palace revolutions, and usurpations, despite the most dangerous enemies on all sides, the Bulgarians (Huns) on the Balkan Peninsula itself and the Mohammedans coming from Asia, who as early as 654 besieged Constantinople for the first time, the empire not only held its own but even won great triumphs on a number of occasions and for a time extended its borders in the east once again as far as in the times of the ancient Roman Empire, up to the Tigris.

The question arises as to why the west, the Latin part of the old empire, was not able to defend itself against the barbarians and finally fell under their domination, while the Orient, the Greek portion, showed stronger vitality and toughness. It is out of the question that the Greek area should have been superior to the Roman politically or militarily as a result of its organization. Undoubtedly, the great families of the Byzantine nobility produced time and again excellent and mighty warriors who, at the head of their troops, whether these were feudal levies or barbarian mercenaries, accomplished heroic deeds. These families were no doubt partly of barbarian origin themselves, who had first become refined in Byzantium just as, of course, the Greek world from Alexander's time on had become more and more a Greek-speaking and Greek-thinking racial mixture. But, of course, in the Occident, in the area of the Latins, that was also the case to a possibly even higher degree, and the difference between east and west can therefore not lie in this point.

I believe the principal reason for the longevity of that portion of the Roman Empire that was transplanted onto Greek soil was a geographical one, that is, the incomparable military situation of Constantinople. Rome, an interior city on a medium-sized river, could not hold out against an energetic attack by a somewhat superior force. The emperors at times left the city in order to establish their seat in the more secure Ravenna. Constantinople, however, situated on the mighty stream of an arm of the sea, surrounded by water on three sides, was almost impregnable, even against greatly superior forces. Reinforcements and supplies from one side or the other could hardly be blocked by the enemy. If Rome became the capital of the world, it did not reach this position as a result of its economic advantages, which were only mediocre, but through politics and war. Consequently, its natural sources of assistance failed when it was no longer a capital city receiving the tribute of the various peoples. Constantinople, where the great land and water routes of world trade intersected, was not only a capital city, but it also contained within itself the greatest natural resources, which favored its defensive capabilities. It was besieged, without success, in 616 under Emperor Heraclius by the Persians, in 626 by the Avars, in 654, 667, 672, 717, and 739 by the Arabs, in 764 by the Bulgars, in 780 and 798 again by the Arabs, in 811 and 820 by the Slavs, in 866 by the Russians, and in 914 by the Bulgars.[15]

If Constantinople had once fallen victim to the varied barbarian peoples or around the year 700 to the Moslems, as Rome had previously been taken by the Goths and the Vandals, that would also have meant the end of the East Roman Empire, as it had with the west. But because the capital withstood all attacks, it served as a base time and again for the restoration of the empire, and in those periods when the enemies showed weaknesses, the capital city even led the empire again to victory and conquest. Byzantine history is no doubt the most remarkable alternation of weakness and success that world history has known. Again and again, the incursions and raids of the neighboring barbarians swept through the entire empire to the area of the capital itself—from the north, from beyond the Danube, from the east out of Arabia and the Euphrates region, through all of Asia Minor, and across the sea by pirates of every type. In these wars, a large part of the population was destroyed and eliminated, and barbarians took their places. The Bulgars and Slavs established themselves in the Balkan Peninsula at that time and founded their villages as far south as the Peloponnesus, but the empire survived and finally even drew these immigrants into its body and its organization, as Constantinople held out and maintained and passed on the ancient political system, the ancient political idea.

This concept finds a contradiction in the fact that Constantinople actually fell to the Crusaders in 1204. Yet, the empire held out, and after a half-century the capital city was won back by the province, thus enabling the empire in the ancient sense to be restored. But this episode can certainly be regarded as an exception from both viewpoints. In 1204, Constantinople was practically undefended—divided internally, ruled alternately by usurpers who destroyed one another mutually and were not capable of bringing in reinforcements from the provinces. But the Crusaders, in themselves a strong army, were allied with the Venetian fleet, which also blockaded the city from the sea. And so on that occasion the city fell, despite all its natural strengths.

The fact that the provinces then continued the opposition and finally drove off the enemies was not the deed of a stronger national Greek spirit or of warrior skill, but it is to be explained partly by ecclesiastic reasons and partly by the nature of the army of the Crusaders. If the conquering Franks had still been pagan barbarians, they would perhaps have remained the lords of Constantinople. The Greeks, like the occidentals, would have gotten along under this hegemony, while at the same time drawing the conquerors into their culture and their church. The Crusaders, however, imposed on the Greeks not only the yoke of their military might but also that of the Roman Church, which was introduced in the spirit of Gregory VII. The Greeks would have had to change completely their way of thinking if they had subjected themselves to this church. From this ecclesiastic opposition they drew their tough power of resistance, with which the Franks were all the less able to cope in that they themselves were far from possessing that inherent strength characteristic of a Germanic army in the *Völkerwanderung*. On their arrival, of course, in alliance with the Venetians, the Crusaders represented a very important force. But after their victory, when they established a count of Flanders as ruler, he had at his disposal only a small fraction of that force. He was obeyed by neither the Venetians, who claimed one and one-half fourths of the conquered empire, nor the great fief-holders, to whom large territories were granted. Clovis and his successors had ruled the Franks with a very different authority from that with which the Latin emperors in Constantinople ruled their knights. And so it happened that these occidental conquerors, although they were already in possession of the capital, were finally forced to withdraw from the Greek Empire.

EXCURSUS

A very instructive chapter in Oman's *History of the Art of War* is the one on the Byzantine military system, to which I am also indebted for a good bit of material. Nevertheless, I have arrived at quite different conclusions on important points.

Oman has correctly recognized that the Byzantine medieval military system, just like that of the Occident, was based on heavily armed horsemen (with the addition of mounted archers). Nevertheless, he accepts the statements made about the infantry, especially in Leo's *Tactics,* as Jähns, *Geschichte des Kriegswesens,* 1: 163, also did. But there can be no doubt that infantry did not exist, and the rules for its conduct are nothing more than the theoretical inheritance from ancient literature. For if the Byzantines had actually had infantry, as Alexander or the Romans had had, it would necessarily be mentioned in the battles and not only mentioned but it would necessarily have played a decisive role. Oman himself, however, has remarked quite correctly that the battles were fought almost exclusively by the mounted men; the infantry was presumably used for garrisons, ambushes, the blocking of passes, and the like. Jähns, p. 163, was also correct in finding it unusual that Leo gave the strength of the units, *meros* and *turma,* of the infantry as being just as large as the corresponding units of the cavalry. Oman, p. 188, notes that Leo gives us not nearly as accurate information of the armament and organization of the infantry as he does for the cavalry. Both of these points indicate that we are not dealing here with actual practice.

The given numerical estimates are consistent with this situation. On p. 182, Oman states that the *strategos* who was in command of each *thema* had some 8,000, 10,000, or 12,000 men, from which number between 4,000 and 6,000 selected cavalrymen could have been mobilized for the field army. This would have resulted in very large armies, since in the tenth century Asia Minor had seventeen *themen,* while Europe had eleven. On p. 221, Oman says that Asia Minor alone had a standing army of at least 120,000 men. This estimate is based on a combination of Leo's two statements that each *strategos* had two or three *turmarchen* under his command (Chap. 4, para. 45) and that each *thema* could provide 4,000 horsemen for the field army (Chap. 18, paras. 149, 153). This conclusion is numerically correct but methodologically unreliable, because Leo was an author given to too much theorizing for us to be able to arrive directly at an actual number from such a scheme. It is a good idea to clarify his type of theorizing with a few examples. In Chap. 17, para. 89 (and similarly in Mauritius), we find on one occasion a figure for the amount of space that 300,000 horsemen in a formation 600 horses wide and 500 horses deep would occupy, a figure to which Jähns (p. 155) correctly added an ironic explanation point.

In Chap. 14, para. 43 ff., Leo advises (as does Mauritius, Vol. IV, Chap. 3) laying out on the evening before a battle a ditch or pitfalls behind the position the army is to take up, or laying caltrops and leaving marked paths between them. Then the army is to withdraw via the marked paths in simulated flight, while the enemy runs into the ditches or the caltrops.

In Chap. 12, para. 55, Leo advises that the horsemen have banners on their lances in order to make an impression on the enemy from a distance. But since the banners would cause all kinds of disadvantages in the fight, they were to be removed as soon as the troops approached within a mile of the enemy.

These kinds of unrealistic speculations also lead to suspicions concerning his numerical figures, and Leo himself also directly contradicts Oman's estimate of the army strength, when he gives (Chap. 18, para. 153) the total number that can be assembled from the *themen* as only somewhat over 40,000 men. In Chap. 4, para. 62, he estimates that they had fewer men than the ancients, and the units (*tagmata*), seven or eight of which composed a *turma,* could not be as strong as 256 men. He bases his normal battle also on the assumption of only some 4,000 mounted men, a figure which in wartime had to be raised to double or triple that number if the enemy was very strong (Chap. 18, paras. 143-150). In another passage, he calls an army of between 5,000 and 12,000 men "*symmetron,*" a word we may translate as "normal" (Chap. 12, paras. 132-133) and also assumes a situation where the army could be still smaller.

The final proof that the Byzantine armies can have been of only very moderate strength is given by the army strengths for the Arabs and those of the Crusaders.

BATTLE OF MANZIKERT, 1071

In the battle of Manzikert, or Malasgard, in Armenia, the Seljuk Sultan Alp Arslan defeated Emperor Romanus IV, took him prisoner, and destroyed most of the Byzantine army. As a result of this battle, the Turks won Asia Minor. Oman also sees in this battle a turning point for the Byzantine military system, for the destruction of the army and the definitive loss of the Asia Minor *themen* eliminated the possibility of a national levy from that time on and forced the Byzantine Empire to depend exclusively on barbarian mercenaries. This concept is consistent with Oman's idea of the army strengths. He believes that at Manzikert Romanus had 60,000 men and his opponent 100,000. When we now find the report that a successor only managed with great trouble to assemble 10,000 men from the remains of the *themen* levies, this seems to mean that the country had become incapable of military action, since, of course, Asia Minor alone had previously provided 120,000 men.

This conclusion collapses along with the assumption that we have already destroyed. That is, the armies on both sides never had anywhere near the stated strengths, even at Manzikert. Indeed, even the 10,000 men who could still be assembled from the *themen* would seem to us questionably large, if the author had not expressly added that this corps had been assembled from the remains of the Asiatic levy and the mercenaries.[16] Nevertheless, this number is probably still too high.

I would also like to take strong exception to the description of the battle of Manzikert, as Oman pictures it. A study and review of the battle based on the sources would be desirable.

BYZANTINE MILITARY WRITINGS

On Mauritius, see Jähns, *Geschichte der Kriegswissenschaften,* 1: 152, and Krumbacher, *Geschichte der byzantinischen Literatur,* 2d ed., para. 262, p. 635. The *Stratēgikon* was edited by Scheffer. *Arriani tactica et Mauricii ars militaris* (The *Tactica* of Arrian and the *Ars Militaris* of Mauritius), Upsala, 1664. Krumbacher believes, for internal reasons, that this work is not derived from Mauritius. Oman, p. 172, ascribes it to Mauritius and dates it in 579, before he had become emperor. R. Grosse, *The Roman-Byzantine March Camp* (*Das römisch-byzantinische Marschlager*), p. 106, places it in the eighth century.

On Leo VI (886-911), see Jähns, 1: 160-70 and Krumbacher, *Geschichte der byzantinischen Literatur,* 1st ed., p. 350. The *Abridged Instruction of Tactics in War** or *Ordinance of Military Preparations** is printed best in *Meursii opera* (*Works of Meursius*), edited by Lamius, Vol. VI. 1745. Krumbacher characterizes this work as follows: "This work is a collection from older sources like Onosander, Aelian, Polyaenus, etc. It gives numerous notes, arranged by chapters, concerning the composition, equipment, and training of the army, etc., without much consistency." In his second edition, p. 636, he adopts the opinion that the work was written not by Leo VI but by Leo III, the Isaurian (718-741)—that is, that it was written under his aegis.

On Constantine VII, Porphyrogenitus (912-959), see Jähns, 1: 171. He was the son of Leo VI. The *Tactics* ascribed to him is actually the work of Constantine VIII (1025-1028), but it is mostly a word-for-word repetition of Leo's *Tactics* and contains very little original material. See Krumbacher, *Geschichte der byzantinischen Literatur,* p. 63. It appears also in *Meursii opera,* Vol. VI, edited by Lamius.

On Nicephorus Phocas (963-969), see Jähns, 1: 176; Krumbacher, p. 985; and Gustave Schlumberger, *Un Empereur byzantin au dixième siècle, Nicéphore Phocas,* Paris, 1890. 779 pp. 4°.

The work ascribed to Nicephorus Phocas is entitled *Peri paradromēs polemou (Concerning Skirmishes of War).* Edited by Hase, Bonn, 1828. On p. 169, Schlumberger says that the book was no doubt written at the emperor's behest but was not completed until after his death.

Jähns believes that, while the work was partially based on Leo, it was more independent than his. The character of the period of decline, however, he believes to appear emphatically in this work as well, since it shows no trace of military initiative. "Nicephorus did not expect the armies which he sent to the northern borders of his empire against the incursions of the barbarians to do anything more than to sit and observe or at most to do convoy duty. With this admission, of course, we find it recognized in the clearest possible way that they were willing to let the enemy lay down the law governing military action." Of course, this character of the book would stand in the strongest contradiction with the personal character of the author and his military deeds, which are also pointed out by Jähns himself. For this emperor was full of initiative and accomplished one conquest after another, especially that of Crete, which had become the focal point of a terrible Moslem piracy, and of Antioch (968).

Schlumberger, on the other hand, is entranced with the work. He gives a detailed analysis and writes (p. 173) as follows:

> I have taken great pleasure in reading these twenty-five chapters on the military art. They give a complete program for the border warfare of the tenth century. Everything that the most accomplished Byzantine *strategos* is to do at the head of his forces to oppose the invasion of a Saracen force, to paralyze its march or wreak a powerful vengeance for its depredations, is minutely presented as in a manual for the use of our officers at the War College. Every possibility is rigorously foreseen. For every problem the solution is given. When I had finished reading these pages, written in a barbarian Greek but vibrant with a unique patriotic ardor, with a profound love of matters dealing with national defense, and with a veritable warlike passion, I could picture passing before my eyes all these fights that had been so completely forgotten for such a long time but which were still bold, savage, punctuated with ambushes, surprises, prodigious rides, and which, during that centuries-long struggle between the Crescent and the Cross, thousands of times covered with blood the dark thickets, the steep defiles, the green slopes of old Mount Taurus. I heard again in my dreams the forced gallop of the Saracen mares in the night, bearing through the thick foliage their silent riders, their lance and shield gripped in their hands, bent over the pommel of their saddles, covering huge dis-

tances to strike like lightning at dawn a sleepy Greek village without defenses, almost holding their breath in order to escape the constant surveillance of the trapezites, those admirable Byzantine scouts. I saw again those unconquerable scouts of the Greek armies, veritable uhlans of the year 1000, accomplished artists in this kind of war unique in the world, a war of ruse against ruse, of ardent secret pursuit, of stratagems constantly discovered but constantly renewed, of lightning-like surprises, of hand-to-hand combats. I saw them once again with their cuirasse or coat of mail hidden under their thick outer garment, carrying out at a gallop with marvelous certainty and precision that same campaign of bold observations, of audacious reconnaissances of which the German horsemen of the War of 1870 are the most formidable modern representatives.

Yes, those were indeed the worthy predecessors of these uhlans who in our minds have remained the lugubrious personification of the invasion; such were those indefatigable Byzantine trapezites, whose dangerous service is described in detail by the editor of Nicephorus Phocas's *Tactics*. Theirs were the same immense and rapid rides by two horsemen in the middle of enemy territory in search of a definite piece of information. Theirs was the same scorn of danger, the same calm boldness, the same resolve, fixed and unique, to be able on their return, no matter what the cost, to give exact information to the leader who placed his confidence in them, to be able to inform him of everything he needs to know: the strength of enemy forces, the name of the officer commanding them, the direction they were preparing to follow, their probable destination. Theirs were, in order to obtain these facts, the same ingenious efforts, the same application of multiple ruses, the same perfecting of all the processes of gathering information, the same inventive genius, the same discipline aided by the same code of instructions, punctual, precise, complete, with the additional immense difficulty of all the resources that were lacking in that period of relative barbarism. Those persons are seriously mistaken who willingly believe that the eastern wars of that period consisted only of a succession of confused melees, of random collisions between savage hordes.

As much as this hymn to the "uhlans" of Byzantium differs from the judgment of Jähns, each man is still correct in his own way. What Jähns misses is, in fact, not there—that is, the strategy of a war of decision. But the work does not claim to treat such a war; it informs us about border warfare, guerrilla war, and in this area the conduct of war was not at all lacking in initiative and energy. Large-scale war, as it was conducted by the Byzantines of the tenth and eleventh centuries, did not correspond to the kind of war that is assumed here. This document deals precisely only with border warfare, and it is therefore not valid to draw from it a conclusion on the spirit of the times.

On p. 186, Schlumberger reports on a document attributed to Nicephorus Phocas that was not yet edited at that time, some passages of which have been published by M. Graux. These passages discuss the following points: one should not lead an army through country that has no water; one should not take along into the field any unnecessary mouths to be fed; and guides and spies are very useful in warfare.

On one occasion, Nicephorus Phocas demanded of a synod that it decree that all soldiers who were killed in war against the Moslems should be honored as martyrs. The clergy, however, Saint Polyeuctes the Patriarch, rejected the suggestion.[17]

(Added in the second edition). In 1917, a new edition of Leo's *Tactics,* edited by R. Bári, appeared in Pest, based on a renewed study of the relationship of all the works of Byzantine military literature. For a more detailed report on this, see L. Gerland in the *Deutsche Literaturzeitung*, No. 27-29 (1920).

NOTES FOR CHAPTER VII

1. We would be able to state this characteristic definitely if the *Strategikon* that has been passed down under his name was actually written by him. However, this is very doubtful. See pp. 193, 198, below.

2. Zachariä von Lingenthal, *History of Greco-Roman Law* (*Geschichte des griechisch-römischen Rechts*), 3d ed., p. 271, para. 63.

3. *Les exploits de Digénis Akritas*. Epopée byzantine du Xème siècle, publiée par G. Sathas et E. Legrand. Paris, 1875.

4. Zachariä von Lingenthal, *Geschichte des griechisch-römischen Rechts*, 3d ed., p. 265.

5. Carl Neumann, *World Position of the Byzantine Empire* (*Weltstellung des byzantinischen Reichs*), p. 58.

6. Zachariä von Lingenthal, p. 273, Note 916.

7. Zachariä von Lingenthal, p. 273. Neumann, p. 56, states that the threefold increase can be explained by the increased requirement for military preparations and performance. But such an increase can hardly have taken place; for a long time already, military service had meant service on horseback. But Neumann immediately adds that the increase indicated the intention of giving up the restoration of small landholdings as unsuccessful and unnecessary. This may well be correct.

8. Constantine Porphyrogenitus, *De administrando imperio* (*On Ruling the Empire*), Chap. 52. *Joh. Meursii opera* (*Works of John Meursius*), 6: 1110. For other evidence, see Carl Neumann, *Die Weltstellung des byzantinischen Reiches vor den Kreuzzügen*, 1894, pp. 68 and 69. Note, for example, from Constantine IX: "He paid large fees for soldiers."* Cedrenus, 2: 608.

9. *Excerpta Johannis Scylitzae Curopalatae* (*Excerpts of John Scylitzes Curopalates*), SS. Byzantini (Bonn). Cedrenus, 2: 662.

10. "Inexperienced in war, without horses, almost without arms and naked, and not even having daily supplies, they underwent many desperate straits and returned to their own land without glory."*

11. Neumann, pp. 60, 68. Gustave Schlumberger, *Nicéphore Phocas*, Paris, 1890, pp. 532-533. Krumbacher, *Geschichte der byzantinischen Literatur*, p. 985.

12. Neumann, p. 67, presumes that the west, more thickly inhabited by barbarians, lagged behind the east culturally and was therefore incapable of paying taxes in currency.

13. Jähns, *Geschichte der Kriegswissenschaften,* 1: 170.

14. Book IV, Chap. 4, Ed. Bonn, p. 134.

15. Taken from the listing in Hammer, *Geschichte des Osmanischen Reichs,* 1: 552, 674, which includes, however, a few cases that are not completely confirmed.

16. Nicephorus Bryennios, 4: 4, Ed. Bonn, p. 133.

17. Neumann, *Weltstellung,* p. 37. Krumbacher, p. 985.

Chapter VIII

The Arabs[1]

The barbarian horsemen whom the ancient Romans took into their service and from whom they formed their cavalry already included in an early period the Arabs, or Saracens. In Crassus's campaign against the Parthians, an Arab prince was already playing a role. It was Arab horsemen whom Emperor Valens led from the east against the Goths and who succumbed to the German charge at Adrianople in 378, an augury of later battles.

As with the Germans, the Romans once made a beginning toward the subjugation of the Arabs. Under Augustus, Aelius Gallus, governor of Egypt, moved out against them (26–25 B.C.) and succeeded in taking a large town, but he suffered heavy losses from hunger and sickness, and the Romans did not resume their offensive in this direction.

The Arabs, like the Germans in the west, were led into the areas of the civilized world as mercenaries, especially in the wars between the Romans and the Persians before and after Justinian's time. Finally, the moment arrived when they decided to take over the leadership for themselves.

But this procedure was carried out quite differently from the experience of the Germans.

The Germans had nothing and brought with them nothing but their warriorhood. They were still pure barbarians as they made themselves lords of the civilized world, which they largely destroyed in the process. The Arabs already had in themselves for a long time a double element: the warlike barbarian nomadic element, the Bedouins of the desert; and a city-dwelling, merchant citizenry with a considerable degree of culture. Both elements were held together by their common nationality, their language, and a common religious culture, which no doubt was intentionally fostered by the wise traders in Mecca in order to moderate and control the hostility and savageness of the Bedouins.[2] Jewish and Christian influences had been felt and had stimulated a religious impulse.

All of these elements and tendencies were brought together by Mohammed into a political-religious unity. Islam is not a religion like Christianity but a political-military national organization based on the power of religion. To carry through this comparison and recognize the fundamental difference, it is as if Arminius had been a prophet as well and had united all the Germanic peoples under his leadership.

As a warrior, a national leader, and a prophet, Mohammed organized from the Arab world a power that was almost suddenly at hand and with its irresistible force straightway overcame its neighboring countries on right and left: both Syria and Egypt, which belonged to Rome, and Persia, which was still involved with Rome in a struggle that constantly wavered back and forth.

In the countries of the Roman Empire which fell to the Germans, the ancient culture was maintained in the Church, and there developed in the Occident the continuously polarizing double element of the independent Church and the independent states. In Islam, the church and the state were one; the Prophet and his successor, the caliph, that is, his substitute, were the spiritual head and temporal ruler, the interpreter of the will of God and the military leader. The military strength of the Bedouin element, which had long been known and feared in the world, was multiplied by the religious teachings of fate (kismet) and of paradise, and military obedience was assured by the authority of Allah. "The best theology is to help God with the sword," was said even by the pious,[3] and the plundering Bedouins were glad to conform to a spiritual authority that threw the treasures of the civilized world into their laps. This spiritual authority added to the inherited warrior strength of the sons of the desert the element of discipline, which was able to go to such extremes as to prohibit the warriors from the use of wine.

In an Arab document on the military system, which, although it dates only from the fourteenth century, still goes back to the old traditions,[4] the obedience of the believers is described as follows (p. 28):

> Ibn Ishâk recounts in the *Campaigns:* When the man sent by God was leaving Wâdil Cafrâ and heard that the Kuraish were moving up against him, he asked his men for advice, and first of all Abu Bekr spoke very beautifully, and then Omar followed and also spoke very well, and then el-Mikdâd ben Amr rose and spoke: "Oh, ambassador of God! Go wherever you are ordered to go, and we shall be with you. We shall not say, as the children of Israel did: 'Go, you and your army, and fight. We shall remain here.' But we say: 'Go, you and your army, and fight; we shall fight side by side with you

both.' By him who has in truth sent you, if you desired to march with us to Birk el-Gimâd, we would fight our way there at your side, until you reached it." The man sent of God answered him: "Well spoken!" and he blessed him. Then he turned around and spoke: "And you men, too, give me your counsel." He was referring to the Ancâr (the citizens of Mecca who had gone over to Mohammed), because there was a significant number of them. Then spoke Sa'd ben Mu'âds: "It seems, Oh man sent of God, as if you mean us." "Of course," he replied, and Sa'd continued: "We have believed in you and held you to be real and recognized that everything you have taught us is the truth. In return, we have sworn and confirmed to you that we intend to hear and to obey. So go now, Oh man sent of God, wherever you are ordered to go, and we shall be with you. By him who has sent you in truth, if you wanted to cross this sea with us, we would jump in with you; not one of us would remain behind. We would have no objection if you wish to meet the enemy with us tomorrow. We are certainly steadfast in war and dependable in battle. Perhaps God will show you through us something to make your eyes rejoice. So march then with us under God's blessing." The man sent of God was pleased with Sa'd's speech, and he became very enthusiastic in his words, saying: "Up! Spread the good word, for God has promised me one thing from both factions. By God! It seems to me as if I already see the men stretched out." Omar spoke: "By him who holds my life in his hand, they will not fail to cut them down."

Before the time of Mohammed, the Arabs were divided into numerous tribes, like the Germans, and even more than them, in that socially opposing classes were also created among them by the development of towns. Through his system, the Prophet brought all of these tribes and classes together into a tight unity and with it created not only a great inner strength but also a very great cooperating mass. The Germanic peoples never worked together, and we have learned that the armies of the Goths, Burgundians, and Vandals which swept through the Roman Empire were very small. Arabia, too, like Germany, was thinly populated, but all the tribes and classes of the far-flung land now joined in a tight military force under a single hand. Mohammed himself is supposed to have assembled 30,000 men in 630 for a campaign against the Byzantine Empire, but this force came to a halt on the border and accomplished nothing.[5] Chalid, Abu Bekr's military commander, moved out against Persia with 18,000 men.[6] In the Bridge Battle in 636, where the Arabs were defeated by the Persians, they were reported to have had only 10,000 men.[7] Even in the decisive battle at Kadesia in 637, where they defeated the Persians, they were said by the "oldest and most reliable source"[8] to have had only 9,000 to 10,000 men, and in the battle of Dschabula shortly afterward, 12,000 men.[9] Judging from the army strengths with which we became familiar in Justinian's wars, these figures do not seem impossible. They are also not invalidated by the fact that, when the booty from Ctesiphon was divided, 60,000 men received their share. After the battle of Kadesia, reinforcements had arrived, but we must probably suspect primarily that, when the leaders reported the claims of their units, they very considerably exceeded the limits of truth. Judging from what we know of German lansquenet leaders in the sixteenth and seventeenth centuries, we can probably attribute to the extremely greedy Bedouins a three- or fourfold exaggeration. Nevertheless, it may also be, as more recent scholars assume, that the armies which defeated the Persians were larger than simply 10,000 to 12,000 strong. But we must take particular account of the fact that it was not the entire Moslem force that was operating outside the country but rather, at the same time, similar and perhaps even larger armies were fighting in Syria against the Greeks. In the battle of Adschnadein in 634, somewhat south of Jerusalem, where they defeated the Greeks for the first time, the Arabs are supposed to have had 25,000 to 30,000 men, although this estimate is, of course, uncertain.[10] In order to be sure of having the stronger force, they had moved up 3,000 more horsemen from the army that was operating against the Persians on the Euphrates, and these men had marched through the desert, carrying their water with them. Even if this estimate may be somewhat too high—the very fact that 3,000 more men were brought up from such a great distance argues against too high a number—the Greek Empire had for a long time not been capable of putting armies of anywhere near this size in the field. Let us remember that Justinian was able to send Belisarius with his 15,000 men against the Vandals and Goths only because he had made peace with the Persians for such a long time. Of course, the Arab sources are able to speak time after time of the manifold numerical superiority of the Greek and Persian armies, the hundreds of thousands, who were conquered and died under the swords of the believers,[11] just as the ancient Greeks had once written of the armies of the Persians that were conquered by Miltiades, Pausanias, and Alexander. In actual fact, the numerical superiority in all these cases was on the side of the victor.

By subjecting all of the warlike desert tribes to their command, the caliphs had at their disposal an inexhaustible supply of warriors and were able to send out simultaneously on all sides armies that were superior to their opponents. These were not simple mercenaries who mutinied as soon as they were not paid, but as God's warriors they endured periods of need and of self-denial in order within a short time to find the richest compensation in the conquered lands. Thus, they were able to sweep through the barren terrain of Tripoli in order to conquer Carthage, all of North Africa, and finally Spain, not meeting their master until they arrived at the Loire.[12]

The figures of 20,000 men, and even 40,000, who are supposed to have conquered North Africa, are surely too high. Such masses could not have been fed on the immense march through Tripoli, and a fourth of that number could have sufficed for that mission. At the same time, however, that Islam appeared at the Pillars of Hercules in the west, it was pushing forward in Alexander's tracks as far as Turkestan and India and was sorely pressing Byzantium itself.

The victors established themselves in the conquered lands as the ruling warrior class, like the Goths and Vandals in Italy, Spain, and Africa.

Already a well-ordered political organization themselves, they did not destroy the conquered civilized world to the same extent as the Germans. After a brief interruption, economic life continued as usual, the countries did not sink completely into a barter economy, as in the west, and the new political system was based on the principle that the subjugated unbelievers paid taxes in order to maintain the dominant warrior class.

The Germanic warrior class had had to spread across the entire country in order to have itself provided for by the produce furnished by the inhabitants, a situation that eventually resulted in the form of the fief, the feudal system. Since civilization, and with it the money economy, was not so radically destroyed in the Arab areas, their warrior class could be supported by taxes and pay and consequently did not need to be spread so extensively through the land. The conquerors remained together to some extent in large military settlements, especially in Kufa and Basra, which grew into cities.

But as we have seen especially in the case of the Vandals and Visigoths, a warriorhood based only on extension of itself and family tradition does not endure long. Among the Germans, that class disappeared all the faster the more it blended with the subjected peoples into a unit as members of a church. Among the Arabs, that class held out somewhat longer, since the conquered peoples mostly retained their religion and the ruling class remained more aware of its own individuality and consequently also of its warrior nature. In addition, the single spiritual-secular authority of the caliphate held the believers firm in their inherited system. After 200 years, however, the original strength which had been brought along from the desert was consumed and used up on the soil of civilization. The artificially blended elements of warriorhood and religion, which were already in conflict from the time of Mohammed's death on, were pulling away from each other. The caliphate had no certain principle of succession; theocracy is by its very nature not hereditary. The great dynasty of the Ommiads, which came into power after the assassination of Ali, the son-in-law of the Prophet, and of his sons, the Prophet's grandsons, was more representative of the warlike Bedouin element, while the following dynasty of the Abbassids (after 750) was more representative of the religious element. We could compare these two dynasties with the almost exclusively warlike Merovingians in the one case and the Church-related Carolingians in the other. The empire of the caliphs disintegrated under the successors of Harun al Raschid, the Abbassid, just as rapidly as the empire of Charlemagne fell apart under his successors. After the beginning of the ninth century, mercenary units replaced the believers. It was especially the Seljuk Turks who, adhering to the teachings of the Prophet, now provided the warriors, and soon their emirs and commanders made lords of themselves by leaving for the caliphate in Baghdad only the dignity of a spiritual representative. Large areas, Spain, and Egypt broke their ties with Baghdad and established themselves as special caliphates.

And so a situation arose in the east which was very similar to that in the west. Despite the teachings of the Prophet, the natural opposition of spiritual and worldly power also exerted itself in Islam. The Seljuk sultans were worldly rulers like the kings of the Occident, supported by their warrior class just as the latter were supported by knighthood, but the governing principles were basically very different. As Ranke has already remarked, however, one cannot see a significant difference in the outward aspect of rulers like Frederick Barbarossa and Saladin. From a purely military viewpoint, we may call the Arab and Seljuk warriors simply knights, who were under the somewhat closer control of their leaders, because of the unique direct relationship of religion to warriorhood in Islam, than were the occidentals.

As the strongest indication of Roman discipline, we have seen how commanders could require, after an exhausting day's march, that their soldiers still fortify their camp. The Arab author whom we have already cited required the same thing (p. 13):

As soon as the campsite is occupied, the emir orders first of all that a ditch be dug on the same day, without delay or hesitation.

This serves as cover for the army, prevents desertions, discourages attempts at surprise attacks, and protects against other dangers that could be caused by the cunning of the enemy and unexpected events.

I am inclined to doubt that this regulation was actually followed in the Arab army; at any rate, it was not carried out as systematically as by the Romans.

The combatants were primarily horsemen and individual fighters. The function of the leaders and the system of discipline were in no way of such a type as to form tactical units. We are reminded of the regulation of King Henry I of Germany concerning the maintenance of a close formation during the approach, when we read from the Prophet (Sura, 61. 4): "God loves those who fight for him in a battle order as if they were parts of a firmly assembled building,"[13] or when Chalid harangued his troops before the battle on the Hieromyces (636), ordering: "Do not fight as individuals against a people (the Greeks) who move against you in ordered units."[14]

Emperor Leo, in *Tactics,* 18. 49–50, describes the Turks as armored, mounted on armored horses, and fighting alternately with lances, swords, and arrows. The Arab document on the military system states:

The armament consists of a hard, durable armor, not too heavy and not too light, of a helmet with a connected cap under the helmet, two arm-guards, two thigh-guards, and two greaves. The war-horse must have a firm hoof and be strong in the breast, the forequarters, the neck, and the hindquarters. The equipment for combat consists of two strong bows, thirty arrows with straight, pointed tips, a hard middle piece, and iron wings, in a medium-sized quiver that is not so large as to become burdensome and to distract the attention, and not so small as to be unable to hold all the arrows and therefore unsatisfactory, of firm lengths of leather with firm seams and bands of real leather, of a quiver pocket with strong laces; a strong lance with a solid shaft, very straight, not extremely long but also not so short as to fail to fulfill its purpose, with a point of the best iron with many sharp edges, unusually hard, with a penetrating end; a straight javelin, a sharp, tempered sword, completely of iron with excellent effectiveness, or, short, easy to handle and sharp; a pointed, two-edged knife, a strong mace which neither exhausts the man fighting with it by its weight nor fails him by its lightness, in order to allow a mighty, penetrating blow; or a naked axe, sharpened on both sides, with a firm grip, with which one can break a strong weapon with one blow; of thirty stones in two bags suspended on the right and left of the saddle pommel. This is the equipment of a horseman ready for battle, and if any of it is missing, he is not completely equipped.

The last observation, to the effect that the warrior who does not possess all of the listed weapons is incompletely equipped, should probably be considered as a doctrinaire exaggeration by the author. This follows not only from the nature of things but also from the other comments by the author himself. Just before the passage quoted above, he prescribes that the completely armed warriors were to be placed in the first rank, those with less complete armament in the second, and so on up to the fifth rank. Consequently, the author himself assumes that the great majority of warriors will not be completely equipped. Furthermore, he then also assigns the soldiers to various fighting branches, according to their equipment: 1. horsemen with long lances; 2. horsemen with javelins; 3. horsemen with bow and arrow; and 4. horsemen who are completely armed.

The principal difference vis-à-vis the occidentals was the much more extensive use of bow and arrow, which is not really compatible with heavy equipment. The heavy equipment not only hinders the manipulation of the bow but also requires a strong horse, which, when it is also armored, cannot be so very fast. But if the horse is not fast, the marksman cannot be sure of avoiding close combat as long as he wishes, and so his bow hardly offers him any advantages. Therefore, what Leo seems to present as a single combat branch is divided into two branches, if indeed it was not always so: the armored close-combat warriors with armored horses, and the lightly equipped marksmen on light, fast horses. It was no doubt the age-old tradition of the Asiatics, and particularly of the people of the steppes, that had always caused them to nurture this fighting branch of mounted marksmen. When the Crusaders first became acquainted with them, they too adopted this branch and even carried over to the country of the knightly order, Prussia, the name they gave the mounted marksmen, *"Turkopolen."*

Nevertheless, this point does not represent a fundamental difference between occidental and oriental military systems but only a difference of a certain degree. When the occidental knights held a tournament in the Holy Land, it probably happened that Moslem knights appeared in the area and were finally invited to participate in the tourney. The fact that they jousted together is proof enough that the equipment, fighting style, and combat customs were very similar on both sides. The accounts of the

Crusades offer quite a number of indications that, despite all the religious and racial hatred, there was a certain similarity of the concept of classes between the Christian and Moslem knights.

On Palm Sunday 1192 at Akko, Richard the Lion-Hearted girded the son of Seifeddin with the sword. Seifeddin, son of Saladin, in the battle of Jaffa (5 August 1192), sent two war-horses to King Richard, who had hastened on foot to the scene of the battle. Richard gratefully accepted them and used them.

Christians and Moslems even entered feudal relationships with one another.

EXCURSUS

BATTLE OF SSIFFIN
(26-27 JULY 657)

After the assassination of Othman, the third caliph, Ali, the husband of Mohammed's daughter Fatima, was called to be caliph. He was the candidate of the pious and the representative of the hereditary right. But why should the Prophet's successor come specifically from his own family? Certainly Allah could also choose another person as his tool. Moawija the Ommiad, commander of the troops in Syria and representative of the savage, warlike Bedouin element, rose up against Ali. There seemed to be no other way to reach a decision than by force of arms. Ali was supported principally by the conquerors who had settled in Iraq, the territory of the Euphrates and the Tigris. His capital was the military colony of Kufa. Moawija lived in Damascus. They met one another in the area of Ssiffin on the Euphrates and took position in such a way that tribesmen were fighting against members of corresponding tribes: the Asd of Basra against the Asd of Syria, the Chath'am of Kufa against the Chath'am of Syria. Ali himself, surrounded by the men of Medina, who had come to join him, commanded the center. In keeping with the source, the battle is described by August Müller (p. 321) as follows:

> The strengths of the two armies were not very different; Ali's 70,000 horsemen opposed at the most 80,000 Syrians. They were also similar in that each side could boast of a special elite unit. A select unit had solemnly sworn to Moawija that it would either conquer or die. Among the Kufa forces were a number of the ardent pious, who were called "the Readers" because of their constant study of the Koran, and who also in other respects banded together and here formed three units under the command of Ibn Budeil, Keis Ibn Ssa'ad, and the old Ammar Ibn Jassir, determined men, including a number of the king's murderers, who had now transferred their repulsion for Othman with double intensity to Moawija. Ibn Budeil opened the battle with a mighty blow against the left flank of the Syrians. He succeeded in driving back Habib and with his "Readers" forcing a way into the middle of the enemy army, indeed almost in reaching the tent of Moawija. But then those who had taken the oath to Moawija moved in against them and forced them to withdraw; even the Medinans whom Ali sent from the center to assist and who on this occasion did not particularly distinguish themselves were unable to hold their own. In the meantime, things did not go too well on the left flank of the Iraki. On that part of the

field, the South Arabians of Ibn Dhi'l-Kala had made considerable progress, so that only the courage of a few men posted there from the Rabi'a tribes was still holding them firm. Then Ali himself intervened, assembled the men who were fleeing, and restored the battle. To the right flank he sent Malik with his horsemen who also succeeded in halting the incipient flight and cutting free Ibn Budeil and his "Readers," who had fallen into the most extreme danger. Now they moved forward again on the right, and in the renewed assault Ibn Budeil, who had pushed forward ahead of his men "like a ram," was killed. But Malik immediately took over the command and was able to push the men sworn to Moawija back again to his tent. Malik had already overcome four ranks of the courageous fighters when Moawija called for his horse and had already mounted it to flee when he by chance remembered an old masculine maxim, which stimulated his pride, so that he remained. Amr had been watching him; he said calmly to him: "Today the battle loud, then next the ruler proud." Now the body of sworn men carried out their obligation. Once again a unit of "Readers" from the other side under Ammar succeeded in moving in closely. "There you are, Amr. You sold your conscience for Egypt, now may it bring you your ruin!" cried out to the enemy the companion of the Prophet, who, despite his advanced age, was fighting like a lion, but even the sacrifice of his life could not win the victory. The two armies went on fighting without any prospect of ending the battle. Then Ali spotted Moawija from afar and cried out to his enemy: "Why do we allow the men between us to kill each other? Come here, I invite you to God's judgment! Whichever of us kills the other will be the ruler!" Amr urged Moawija to accept the challenge, but Moawija declined. "You know," he said, "that no one has opposed him whom he has not killed." And when Amr said that it was not very proper to shirk, Moawija angrily reproached him, saying: "So you want to rule in my place?" As a matter of fact, Ali's courage and skill were indeed too well known for Moawija to have anticipated much success from such an encounter. Thus, he can hardly be blamed for avoiding such an unequal individual combat.

Even the night did not separate the combatants; on various parts of the field the fighting went on continuously until morning—the second night of the fray that the victors of Kadesia had to endure. Finally, on the morning of the third day (10 Ssafar: 28 January 657), the moment of decision seemed to be near. Malik, who in the meantime had been confirmed in his command of the right flank, assembled all the horsemen whom he had at hand for a last great attack. He threw the opposing Syrians far back, all the way to their camp. In the center, Ali, seeing the victorious advance of his lieutenant, pushed forward with his foot troops against Moawija, who, after his left flank had given way, was in the greatest danger of being encircled from two sides. But the Prophet had once said: "War is a deceptive game." Perhaps there had already been prepared earlier for this case one of the most unseemly comedies of all world history, which again seems to have been the idea of Amr. As many Korans as could be found were held up on the lances, and they cried out to the Iraki that the solution to the quarrel between the believers was to be found here in God's book and not in mutual destruction. They said that they should stop the battle and establish a tribunal that would investigate the claims of Ali and Moawija in accordance with the word of the Most Highest and would settle everything. As laughable as was such a proposal at the moment the victory was already decided, and as obvious as was the objection as to why then it had not been made before all the bloodshed, it still did not fail to have its effect. The respect which the truly pious Moslems had for the Holy Book was so strong that under any circumstances they were necessarily impressed by the idea of having the decision drawn from this infallible source. This point was reinforced by the fact that the "Readers" were not only pious men but were also imbued with the ancient Arab sense of independence, for whose democratic attitude the thought of having those best acquainted with the revelation, as representatives of the community, make the decision on the Caliphate itself must have been very attractive. And so these men stopped fighting. Their example, however, was followed by a large number of others, whose motives must have been of a very different kind—traitors who, during the armistice, listened to the whispers of Moawija's emissaries, who had perhaps even taken over that role, which they were now not ashamed to play. At their head was no other than El-Asch'ath Ibn Keis, the Kindite, the traitor of his own people. He had never forgiven the pious men of Medina for having deprived him of his South Arabian kingdom. Now he seized the opportunity to help steal their victory from them and to enjoy a delayed revenge. He acted as speaker and urged Ali to call back at once Aschtar, who was continuing to fight on the other side, but to send El-Asch'ath himself to Moawija, so that they could come to agreement on the tribunal. From the first moment on, the caliph had reminded the "Readers" that they all knew well enough that men like Moawija, Amr, Ibn Abi Ssarch, and their comrades were enemies of the faith and of the Koran itself, so that this proposal could be seen as pure deceit, but his words were in vain. The blind fanatics and the traitorous mob pressed in on him with growing threats, and soon there were shouts that he would suffer the fate of Othman if he hesitated any longer. And so he was forced to decide to send a messenger to Malik. The bold cavalry commander was furious and was about to disobey the order, but finally, when he was threatened with the fact that Ali would be killed if Malik did not break off the battle, he yielded with a heavy heart. When he came in sight of the "Readers," he reproached them severely for their foolishness, saying that the battle was already won and they should let him return to his troops for just a moment, so that he could complete the destruction of those godless men, who had never inquired into the Koran. But it was all in vain. Supported in their pious obstinacy by the traitors, they maintained their demands. Ali, who was separated from his personal retinue by the bands of insubordinate men and who, despite all of his repeated shows of fearlessness in the battle, nevertheless yielded to the threat of murder and here as always, unfortunately, was incapable of making a strong decision, allowed himself to be forced to send Asch'ath to the Syrians—that is, to surrender himself and his cause.

   This account of the battle and its sudden end, a development that eventually ended with Ali's fall, has been objected to by recent critics, as far as I can see, on the basis of only one point: they have not believed in the improvised demonstration with the Korans but have presumed that this was the result of a deliberately planned betrayal. In his article "On the Opposing Religious-Political Factions in Ancient Islam" ("Ueber die religiös-politischen Oppositionsparteien im alten Islam"), Wellhausen took exception to this point and maintained that the story is not so very incredible after all. Among the pious followers of Ali, there had arisen, for good reasons, doubt as to whether the law was really on his side, whether he was the true caliph. Both armies were sensitive to the fact that it was foolish for the believers to want to destroy one another. We might remember how very reluctant the Franks under Louis the Pious and his sons were later on to let matters reach the extreme of actually shedding blood among themselves. Wellhausen therefore came to the conclusion that when the Syrian army held up the Koran, tied to the lance like a standard, this appeal to that which was commonly held as holy by both sides was capable of emphasizing the feeling that was already quite strong in Ali's army, namely, that there were also followers of the Prophet on the other side. This dominant sensation succeeded in forcing Ali to accept the armistice.

Wellhausen's arguments seem fully convincing to me, even in their details. But they still need a rounding out on the military side. Those who have not been willing to accept the truth of the source are correct to the extent that it appears completely impossible to effect such an outcome in the middle of a battle by having a number of men tie books to their lances, unless this action was agreed to in advance and the demonstration only served as a signal for its execution. Least of all is such action possible if one assumes such colossal armies as Müller does. Seventy thousand to 80,000 men on each side, mostly horsemen, occupy such a large area (if we assume that such numbers were at all possible) and make such a gigantic noise that it is impossible to arrive at any kind of agreement in the middle of a fight. But even much smaller armies—let us assume 10,000 to 12,000 men on each side—once they are engaged in battle, can no longer be controlled, stopped, and withdrawn. That is completely impossible.

If we now examine the account of the battle more closely, we soon realize that it has a completely legendary character. I do not believe one word of it.

Now the two armies, once they had come in contact with each other, supposedly did not move into battle but stood facing each other for fully two months, with maneuvering and skirmishing. This shows first of all that the armies were not so very large, since it would then have been impossible to feed them for such a long time in one place. But we must no doubt go one step further and eliminate the entire battle as a completely contrived bit of description and embellishment. As soon as they started their approach march, the armies were probably filled with the idea of avoiding mutual destruction if possible. Therefore, the meeting was never allowed to reach the point of a great battle. If such a battle had taken place, it could not possibly have been broken off in the manner described. There are more examples in world history where legend has blown up small encounters into great battles.

With this correction, and only with this correction, is Wellhausen's concept of the Islamic factions and Ali's fall acceptable, but then it becomes completely clear. It was not in the middle of a battle, but during the demonstrations being carried out by each army that Moawija's retinue tied copies of the Koran to their lances as symbols that they, too, were true believers. This action was understood on the opposite side, was discussed beside their tents in the evening, and gave the upper hand to those supporting a peaceful settlement, without the need for bringing a direct betrayal into the picture.

NOTES FOR CHAPTER VIII

1. In the *Cultural History of the Orient under the Caliphs* (*Culturgeschichte des Orients unter den Chalifen*), by Alfred von Kremer (Vienna, 1875), there is a chapter on the military system (pp. 203-255) in which the source reports are assembled quite completely but without analysis and without any military-objective understanding. I have not drawn anything from this work.

2. August Müller, *Geschichte des Islam,* 1: 31.

3. Wellhausen, "Die religiös-politischen Oppositionsparteien im alten Islam," *Abhandlungen der Königlichen Gesellschaft der Wissenschaften zu Göttingen. Phil. Hist. Kl.,* New Series, 5. 2. 10.

4. Edited and translated by F. Wüstenfeld in the *Abhandlungen der Gesellschaft der Wissenschaften zu Göttingen,* Vol. 26 (1880). This work consists in part of a translation and revision of Aelian's *Tactics* and must therefore, of course, be used with caution.

5. Müller, 1: 164.

6. Weil, *Geschichte der Chalifen,* 1: 30.

7. Weil, 1: 60.

8. Müller, p. 238.

9. Müller, p. 243.

10. Müller, 1: 252, note.

11. Müller, 1: 222.

12. Of course, not in one move. The events took place in the following sequence: in 641 the Arabs conquered Egypt; in 643 or 644 they took Tripoli. In 648–649 Moawija, as governor of Syria, built a fleet. The governor of Egypt did likewise. In 647–648 the latter, with 20,000 men, conquered Carthage but then left the country again. In the following decades, frequent raids were made from Tripoli into Tunis. In 683 the Arabs suffered a defeat, lost Tripoli, and were thrown back to Barca. In 696 Hassan arrived with 40,000 men and stormed Carthage. After a few reverses, when a Greek fleet was in action, the subjugation of the entire area up to the ocean was completed between 706 and 709. The Berbers joined Islam.

13. Cited by Wüstenfeld, p. 24. See also p. 27, where the temptation to break out of ranks in battle is expressly opposed with an indication for the necessary obedience.

14. Weil, 1: 42.

Chapter IX

General View of the Crusades

It is not very easy to determine the place of the Crusades in our work. In many respects, they form a unity from the military history viewpoint, as we see the same or very similar elements continuously struggling with one another. But they extend over such a long period—and a period in which significant changes took place—that it might seem advisable to divide up our study, both by time and by material. The peculiar conditions under which the occidentals had to fight in the Orient, and the unusual opponents with whom they fought, naturally produced special and new arrangements on their side also. When we now observe important changes in warfare in the Occident in the twelfth and thirteenth centuries, changes that show a relationship to the events of the Crusades, the question arises as to whether there is perhaps a causal relationship here, so that the progress would be based on the Crusades, or whether this was only a parallel phenomenon in which we would have to have the Crusades follow the developments in the west. There was, no doubt, a certain reaction of the Crusades on the circumstances in the Occident, but only to the extent that it accelerated and reinforced a natural development. I believe, therefore, that it will be best that I place the discussion of the military aspect of the Crusades, in the narrow sense, in the next book, in the overall context, and present at this point only the general features of the mighty movements we are to consider.

The formation of the feudal state in the Middle Ages, with various layers of authority and power, is not the only mark of the period. The period is characterized primarily by the Church, which extends over all of these loose political systems and intervenes in them. Our most correct concept of the Romanic-Germanic Middle Ages is not an array of German, French, English, and other kingdoms side by side, but, to borrow Ranke's expression, a spiritual universal state whose parts are formed by the individual kingdoms that are more or less firmly established units in themselves.

From the Church, which embraced the English, French, Spanish, Swedes, Danes, Germans, and Italians, and from the opposition of this unit to Islam, there sprang the Crusades, which, in keeping with this origin, were not conducted in accordance with rational-political motives but following a mystical pressure toward the conquering of a small enclave in the middle of the Mohammedan world, in the Holy Land.

Since war is a means of politics and in the final analysis the conduct of war is always determined by its political purpose, the mystical original basis made it impossible from the start to have a rational strategy in the Crusades. If the west had devoted only a part of the gigantic forces that were swallowed up in Palestine to the winning of border areas, there would certainly have resulted continuing successes. When Frederick Barbarossa moved down the Danube, the Greek emperor, whose empire was already filled with Latin elements, was greatly concerned that the Crusaders intended to take Constantinople, and the Serbs, Wallachians, and Bulgars offered to break away from the Greek Empire and become subjects of the Roman emperor. If only the Hohenstaufen had had such things in mind! Ranke adds. Barbarossa's son, Henry VI, died before he was able to implement such a policy, and perhaps he no longer had the forces for this purpose which his father would not have lacked.

But it is not necessary for us to delve into such possibilities. It is sufficient that we understand clearly the strategic lack of logic of the fundamental idea of the Crusades and that we understand their genesis. The mystical-transcendental trait of mankind is capable of developing a gigantic force, but the ability to direct this force to practical, down-to-earth goals is lacking, and the force is consumed fruitlessly.

The oath of the Crusaders obligated them to liberate the Holy Grave but not to live constantly in Palestine in order to defend it. A small number were ready to do so, so that the Crusades also signify a colonization, but surrounded as they were by Mohammedans, divided into several areas of control from Edessa (Urfa) to Jerusalem, they could only hold out by having a new army from the west make the endless voyage from time to time, bringing a temporary reinforcement, to the extent it was able to do so.

Concerning the basic question as to the strength of the armies of the Crusaders that the Occident sent against Jerusalem again and again for 175 years, we have again, as in the cases of Caesar's legions in Gaul and the armies of the *Völkerwanderung,* two groups of figures, which are mutually exclusive. According to the one group, they were armies of hundreds of thousands; according to the other group, the battles in the Holy Land were fought by a few thousand, including only a few hundred knights, and sometimes only by a few hundred men. The result of a systematic study by Hans Jahn is that, just as we have found in the other conclusions of this volume for the medieval armies, the armies of the Crusades, too, turn out to be quite small.[1] When Heinrich von Sybel published the second edition of his *History of the First Crusade* (*Geschichte des ersten Kreuzzuges*) in 1881, he found no other way of dealing with the figures reported in the sources than simply to repeat them, but without giving any guarantee of their credibility. But the sources for the first Crusade tell of 100,000 "loricis et galeis muniti" ("protected by coats of mail and helmets") and all together 600,000 "ad bellum valentium" ("capable for war"), as well as innumerable unarmed men (Fulcher) or 300,000 "pugnatorum" ("fighters") (Ekkehard). At the sortie out of Antioch, there were reportedly still 150,000 combatants (*bellatorum*) (Orderich). At that time, I found it surprising that before the battle of Dorylaeum this gigantic army had crossed a bridge in *one* day and then supposedly made a march. I estimated in an article in the *Historische Zeitschrift,* 47 (1882): 423, taking into consideration all the circumstances, that the highest imaginable total figure for the army was 105,000 men, of whom some 15,000 were actual combatants. By way of precaution, I added that this maximum estimate did not eliminate the possibility that the pilgrim army had a total strength of some 60,000 souls, including 10,000 fully armed men. Today there can be no further doubt that even this figure, especially the total of 60,000, but also the 10,000 warriors, is still considerably too high.

In a Marburg dissertation, "The Conduct of Battle of Occidental Armies in the Orient in the Period of the First Crusade" ("Die Gefechtsführung abendländischer Heere im Orient in der Epoche des ersten Kreuzzuges"), by Otto Heermann (1887), it has already been pointed out (p. 102) that the highest number of horsemen given for a battle in Palestine was 1,200, and the highest number of dismounted men was 9,000 (at Ascalon, 12 August 1099). After the end of the Crusade proper, the Christian army melted to 260 horsemen and 900 dismounted men all together, who could be assembled only with great difficulty. On three occasions 700 horsemen are mentioned, and in one case 1,100; the corresponding number of foot soldiers was 2,000 and 3,000. At one time, the total strength of the army is given as 8,000 men (at Ashdod in 1123), and I would like to add that I doubt whether this number was not strongly exaggerated.

As a result of these figures, all of the hundreds of thousands of which we heard earlier are just as surely eliminated as the hundreds of thousands of Gauls with whom Caesar obliges us are eliminated by his

remark concerning the Eburones (Vol. I, p. 512). If the Holy Land could
be defended with a few hundred knights, there must have been only a
few thousand who conquered it. But this figure of a few thousand is in
complete accord with the armies of the *Völkerwanderung,* as we have
gotten to know them, with the armies of Charlemagne, and with the
armies of the Normans, with which they lay waste Europe and finally
occupied the area of the lower Seine, England, and Naples. The small
size of the Christian armies corresponds to the army strengths of their
opponents. Byzantium had become unwarlike, and in the Caliphate,
where the Arabs had long since given up their primitive warrior strength,
the caliphs were reduced to spiritual figureheads, and power was in the
hands of Seljuk or Kurdish chieftains whose military units represented a
class above the unwarlike mass of the population, a class that was just as
small as the knightly class in the west. All the gigantic armies of the
infidels which the Christian authors show marching before us are the
same products of fantasy in the search for renown as were the massive
armies of Christian pilgrims products of fantasy in the enthusiasm of the
true belief.

The settling of Christian warriors in Palestine was on such a small scale
that in those times when there was no crusade bringing in a wave of
occidentals, the Moslems of Syria and those of Egypt must have been
considerably stronger. For this reason, the Christians would no doubt not
have held out so long if they had not received important continuing help
from the special organization of the knightly orders, the Templars, the
Knights of Saint John, and later also the Teutonic Knights. Whereas the
secular knights sought their strength in robbing, taking booty, and mur-
dering, as we read in the preface of the Templar regulations, the members of the order founded by Hugo von Payens (1118) wished to serve
the Church and justice and for the sake of spreading the true faith they
dedicated their souls as a willing sacrifice to God. Bernard de Clairvaux,
who personally participated in their creation, described the Templars in
1125 as follows:[2]

> They are not lacking in good discipline, either at home or in the
> field, and obedience is highly prized. They come and go in obedience
> to the nod of the grand master; they put on the clothing which he gives
> them, and they envy no one either his clothing or his nourishment.
> In both of these areas a surfeit is avoided, and care is taken only to
> fill basic needs. They live together joyfully and with moderation,
> without wives and children, and, so that nothing may be lacking in
> their evangelical perfection, without private property, in *one* house

and of *one* mind, taking care to maintain harmony in their bond of peace, so that a single heart and a single soul seem to reside in all of them equally. At no time do they sit unoccupied or mill about with curiosity. Whenever they rest from their battle against the infidels, which occurs but seldom, they repair their damaged or worn clothes and weapons so as not to be eating their bread gratuitously. They eschew chess and checkers, and they are opposed to hunting and no less strongly to hawking, which is such a favorite pastime elsewhere. They hate tricksters, rhymesters, all kinds of sensuous songs, and all actors as vanity and foolishness of the world. They do not go into battle wildly and unthinkingly but with caution and care, calmly, like the true children of Israel. But as soon as the battle has begun, they drive resolutely into the enemies, regarding them as sheep, and they know no fear, even when their numbers are small, trusting in the help of the Lord of Sabaoth. As a result, often 1,000 men are put to flight by one of them, and 10,000 by two. Consequently, they are a rare combination at the same time, gentler than lambs and more ferocious than lions, so that one is uncertain whether to call them monks or knights. But they deserve both names, for they possess the gentleness of monks and the boldness of knights.

No matter how much of this ideal picture we may reject in considering the realistic situation, the organization of knights in the form of monastic orders with their oaths remains an impressive phenomenon. Even if they produced no progress in a specifically military sense, we shall still have numerous occasions to take note of them and be occupied with their actions.[3]

NOTES FOR CHAPTER IX

1. "Army Strengths in the Crusades" ("Die Heereszahlen in den Kreuzzügen"), Berlin dissertation, 1907 (Georg Nauck, publisher). This work studies particularly the Third and Fourth Crusades.

2. *Opera St. Bernhardi* (*Works of St. Bernard*), ed. Mabillon, 1: 549. From the translation in Wilcken, *Kreuzzüge*, 2: 555.

3. The principal source for the knightly orders is found in the statutes with their later supplements, the various editions of which and all the related subject matter have been completely clarified only in the last few decades. See Schnürer, *The Original Regulations of the Knights Templars*

(*Die ursprüngliche Templerregel*). (In the *Studien und Darstellungen auf dem Gebiet der Geschichte,* edited by Grauert, 3: 1-2). Freiburg, 1903. *The Regulations of the Templars* (*La Règle du Temple*), Paris, 1886, contains a critical editing by E. de Curzon. With this edition as a base, the reading of this work has been made available to a broad public in the most praiseworthy way by a translation in the book *Die Templerregel,* translated from the Old French and accompanied by explanatory notes by Dr. R. Körner, Jena, 1902. As an appendix to his *Cultural History of the Crusades* (*Kulturgeschichte der Kreuzzüge*), Prutz reprinted the *Regulations of the Order of St. John,* in Latin. *The Regulations of the Teutonic Order, with all the Supplementary Laws and Customs* (*Die Regel des deutschen Ordens, mit allen nachträglichen Gesetzen und Gewohnheiten*) was published in exemplary fashion in the five texts in which it has been retained (Latin, French, Dutch, German, and Low German) by Perlbach, Halle, 1890.

BOOK III

The High Middle Ages

Chapter I

Knighthood as a Caste

The *Völkerwanderung* had meant neither the renovation of a segment of mankind sunk in depravity and senility by a vigorous, natural race with upright customs, nor the settling of Germanic farmers in place of Roman peasants, but the replacement of the Roman aristocracy based on municipal office, wealth, and education by an analphabetic, Germanic aristocracy based on an out-and-out warrior system. There is little connection between this aristocracy and the princely nobility of the original Germanic tribes, of which Tacitus speaks; in the Frankish Empire, the Merovingian dynasty is the only one that remained of that early nobility. The most vital roots of the new aristocracy are to be found in those families that acquired large possessions through the favor of kings and the fortunes of war and, most importantly, as counts and lieutenants of counts, came into possession of the reins of government. At the start, however, this new aristocracy is not a completely separate caste in the Frankish Empire. The word *nobilis* is used in the Frankish sources of the time as the equivalent of *ingenuus* for the freeman, which, in turn, is essentially the Frank, the warrior. From the mass of these socially and economically poor nobles, there arises the thin stratum that is to be regarded as the new aristocracy.

In the case of the Saxons, the original old Germanic, princely nobility continued to exist in a different way than with the Franks. When Charlemagne defeated them, they formed a caste that was strongly separated from lower groups, so that the meaning of the words when applied to Saxony is completely different from that of the strictly Frankish Kingdom. But this was only in the transition period; as the Saxon nobility assumed the responsibilities of the Frankish count, it, too, took on the character of an administrative nobility.[1] And it happened the same way in Bavaria, where, in like manner, some of the original noble families maintained their position.

In the final analysis, then, without being specifically defined and without having a positive, legally recognized significance, the nobility in the sense of aristocracy was composed in the whole Carolingian Empire of the great landowners, who also held the high court positions and the counties. At its lower edge, this concept merges into the concept of the freeman. And this concept, in turn, gradually loses its worth and meaning the more it deviates from equivalence with the concept of warrior, because on the one hand more and more unfree men assume the warrior status, while on the other hand freemen are giving it up and becoming farmers. Up to the eleventh century, we picture to ourselves the free as well as the unfree warrior status in the Romanic-Germanic countries as socially low and economically needy, that is, no different from the social stratum composed of the mass of city dwellers and peasants. A portion of their number lives at the direct disposition of their lord at the courts of kings, dukes, counts, bishops, and abbots, or as the garrison of the fortified castles; another portion lives in the country provided with small farms under the feudal system.

These relationships are mirrored in the literary sources of the period, where they speak not only of warrior status or mounted status in general (*militaris ordo, equestris ordo,*)[2] but also distinguish between the common warriors (*gregarii milites*) and the outstanding ones (*primi milites*)[3] or even warriors of the first, second, and third class.[4] Nevertheless, all these words do not constitute technical expressions or legal concepts.[5] It is not even to be assumed that the lowest stratum automatically comprises the unfree men, but there were in the lowest stratum surely also freemen, as, on the other hand, unfree men, without casting off their unfree condition, came to rather high social positions and passed them on to their heirs.

All of those who are constantly moving upward out of the lower warrior stratum approach, in doing so, the status of an aristocracy—one might even say of the ruling aristocracy. The Normans, who conquered England, lower Italy, and Sicily, were not by their lineage exclusively Nordics, but warriors of the most diverse origins who attached themselves to the nucleus formed by the Normans. The expansion of the hegemony of the German kings over Italy provided many a German knight the opportunity to attain higher position and property. The constant progress of the German colonization toward the east created ever-increasing areas for new ruling families. The French provided the largest contingent for the Crusades, which likewise included a colonizing movement. The Spaniards, on their peninsula, drove forward against the Moors.

As proof that the number of knights who originally possessed extensive property was very small stands the fact that, even today, the number of knightly estates in the Old German territory is very small; the great majority are in the colonial area, or, as it is called today, the East Elben region (*Ostelbien*).

The continuing expansion in which occidental knighthood is involved also brings that group higher socially. We observe how the social differentiations that we have previously known as purely *de facto* now begin to be legally fixed. The areas of demarcation that were formerly variable are now defined with clear-cut lines. First the higher nobility, and then, from the twelfth century on toward almost the end of the Middle Ages, the lower nobility also become stratified in distinct levels.

The economic base of the knightly class, except for those who were provided for at the lord's court, was the fief, which was not hereditary but was granted only for the lifetime of the vassal and was also recallable on the death of the lord (Vol. II, Book IV, Chap. 4). But if a suitable heir was available, it was natural that the fief be passed on to him. There developed from this practice an hereditary claim which tended more and more to become an hereditary right and in doing so not only strengthened the social position of this class but also raised it. Wipo, the biographer of Conrad II, tells us that this emperor "won the hearts of the knights (*militum*) to a high degree by no longer having the heirs deprived of those fiefs which their forebears had held for a long time." For Italy, he proclaimed in this vein a formal law forbidding feudal lords from shifting knights' fiefs into interest-producing or leased parcels, that is, peasant properties, or to require from the fief-holder more services than were customary. Their court was to be composed of colleagues of the same status as jurymen, and appeal to the emperor or the palatine count was authorized. This attitude on the emperor's part may be related to the repeated rebellions of his stepson, Duke Ernst of Swabia. In these conflicts, the emperor retained the upper hand as the Swabian vassals refused to obey the duke.

"We will not deny," they reportedly said to the duke, "that we have definitely promised loyalty to you against every one except him who gave us to you. If we were serving men of the king and our emperor and were given over to you by him, we would not be permitted to separate ourselves from you. But since we are freemen and have our king and emperor as the highest defender on earth of our freedom, we would lose our freedom if we abandoned him, which, as someone has said, no valiant man gives up, except with his life."

This account is probably not very reliable, for the quotation concerning freedom that one gives up only with his very life is taken from

Sallust's *Catilina,* with which the Swabian counts and knights could hardly have been familiar. But the basic concept is correct, namely, that in the hierarchical structure of the feudal state, the various levels gave mutual support and guarantees to their position and their prerogatives. The emperor governed with the advice of his princes, and the princes with the advice of their knights. In this way, authority and freedom were supposed to be in equilibrium. The knights exercised a limiting influence on the princely power, as the latter did on that of the emperor. For this reason, the emperor, for his part, had an interest in maintaining the position of the knights.

The form in which the lower nobility consummated its attainment of the social position was the ceremony of dubbing. If the act of dubbing was supposed to be related to the ancient Germanic custom of *Wehrhaftmachung* or *Schwertleite* (reception into knighthood), with the change in the whole system of warfare, the act took on another character. The *Schwertleite* applied to the young man who was being given arms for the first time, as soon as he appeared reasonably capable of handling them. The heavy equipment and the large horses to which military developments had gradually led no longer made it appear feasible to outfit with them a young man who had just emerged from his boyhood. He had to undergo a lengthy period of instruction, practice, and testing, during which his limbs were sufficiently strengthened, in order to wear this heavy equipment and to control his stallion. Instead of the old *Wehrhaftmachung,* which took place perhaps at age fourteen or even twelve, there appeared the dubbing ceremony, which was probably accomplished no earlier than the twentieth year, and often considerably later. Perhaps for a while both acts, the *Wehrhaftmachung* and the dubbing ceremony, existed simultaneously. The former, however, lost its significance, while the latter grew to a ceremony regarded as very important. The entire Christian knighthood formed a sort of fraternity; whoever was accepted into it took an oath to perform the duties of his station, and even the Church quite often lent its special blessing to the act. The symbols of the knight are the shoulder belt, the knightly waist belt (*cingulum militare*), and the golden spurs. As symbols of the warrior's position, we find the sword belt and the waist belt already appearing in the literature of the period in which the Germans supplanted the Roman legions. In the acts of a certain martyr Archelaus at the time of Constantine the Great, the saint is praised for having converted many soldiers, who then laid down their knightly waist belt (*cingulum militare*).[6] When Louis the Pious was forced to do public penance in 834 in the Cathedral of Reims and was supposed to be made a monk, it was specifically reported that he took off his knight's belt and placed it on the altar ("cingulum militare deposuit et super altare collocavit").[7] Each knight was authorized to raise one man to his own status through the dubbing ceremony. As long as this right was unlimited, admission was not difficult, and the class was open. Soon, however, we find restrictions providing that only those of knightly birth could receive the dubbing. King Louis VI of France (1137) is said to have ordered that, whenever anyone not of knightly birth was dubbed a knight, his spurs were to be stripped from him on a manure pile.[8] Frederick Barbarossa in 1187 forbade the sons of priests and peasants to accept the knightly belt.[9] His uncle and historiographer, Bishop Otto of Freisingen (1158), speaks disparagingly of the Italian cities, which dub the sons of craftsmen as knights.[10] The annexes to the statutes of the Order of Knights Templars, from the thirteenth century, deny the white cloak to anyone who is not of knightly birth and in addition expel him in case he should have been accepted on the basis of false information on this point.[11] At the same time, the feudal law establishes the material, far-reaching resulting rule that all who from their father or grandfather are not of knightly birth are not eligible to receive fiefs.[12]

The concept of the qualification for fief-holding is also expressed by the word *Heerschild* (feudal escutcheon),[13] which, on the other hand, is also used for the degrees of fief-holding qualification. Nobody may accept fiefs from a *Heerschild* comrade, since he would thereby be placing himself under him (*"Hulde"*: "in his grace"; *"Mannschaft"*: "in his ranks") through his vow. The first escutcheon is the emperor's, the second belongs to the princes palatinate, the third to the lay princes, the fourth to the counts, and thus the enumeration continued, somewhat differently in North and South Germany, up to seven escutcheons. The strict observance of this hierarchy was, however, soon bypassed, and by the fourteenth century it was already antiquated.

The dubbing, or accolade, as such, would have no significance as a confirmation of status, but only that of a personal distinction, since it had to be won on a personal basis. The distinctive feature was the condition that was joined thereto, the requirement for knightly forebears. That was the creation of an hereditary status which existed heretofore perhaps in practice but not yet on a legal basis.[14]

As a forerunner of this formation of a class resulting from the qualification to receive the ceremonial dubbing, let us examine a proclamation of Barbarossa at the start of his reign, the *constitutio de pace tenenda* (ordinance on keeping the peace), of the year 1156, where it is specified that only a person who has always been a *miles* by virtue of his parents' status is qualified for the duel.[15]

The new concept now completely supplanted the distinctions and values of free and unfree which for a long time had been intermingled. The unfree who belonged to the new knightly caste of knightly birth crossed over into the nobility, and their unfree status gradually faded away to such an extent that knights who were originally free voluntarily entered this status in large numbers.[16] Finally, the difference completely disappeared, although here and there, up until almost the end of the Middle Ages, a few traces of the former unfree condition were retained. If there had formerly existed on Germanic soil freemen who, as such, though nonwarriors, had held a higher rank than unfree knights, from the twelfth century on, the knight, whether free or unfree, won unconditional precedence over the common freeman.[17]

In order to arrive at the "nobility" in the modern sense, the ancient German warrior therefore had to work his way through the remarkable "chrysalis" stage, whereby he first recognized the fact that he was in an unfree status and in doing so mingled directly with the descendants of true unfree men. This class of unfree warriors and officials then raised itself to a ruling caste. Nevertheless, too much weight should not be placed on this transition through the unfree status. Actually, its real existence can be proved only in Germany; in France it was so unimportant that its existence could be completely denied.[18] In England there was no group of *ministeriales* at all, but the actual tyranny which the English kings exercised over their knights was much stronger than that of the German princes over their *ministeriales,* who, despite their theoretically unfree condition, formed a fraternity that was very conscious of its position, full of demands, and loudly insistent on its rights.

However significant the formation of this class might be, it is still not easy to grasp it in precise words in the course of its development. In the current language of today, we understand by a knight the outstanding and normally landowning warrior, precisely the class that took form beginning in the twelfth century and developed into the lesser nobility. From the point of view of military history, however, one must—or at least one *may*—designate as a knightly class the composite warrior group as it developed after the *Völkerwanderung* from the Germanic tribes that settled more or less in the Roman Empire or after the battle of Tours, as a result of the system of vassals and fiefs. This leads, however, to the awkward situation that from the twelfth century on the same word denotes a much narrower concept, a disadvantage which once again is historically justified, since the medieval language usage itself is also highly indefinite in this connection. As to the heart of the matter, there is no doubt that the strata in the warrior group which were formerly of lesser significance became more and more accentuated from the twelfth century on and that the designation "knight" was limited to a rather high social level. The lower warrior is called the "sergeant" (*serviens*) or the "*Knecht,*" and the expression "*Ritter und Knechte*" ("knights and sergeants") therefore becomes a frequently used form for the entire army. How strongly pure chance plays a role in these developments can be surmised from the fact that, in the German language, from the simple word "*Reiter*" ("rider," "horseman") there developed the distinguished word "*Ritter*" ("knight"), and the "*Knecht*" sank to the lowest level, while in English, with a precisely opposite result, the word "knight" is obviously related to "*Knecht.*" As an equivalent of the word *Knecht* stands the word *Knappe,* which has the same meaning etymologically, since *Knappe* is *Knabe* (boy) and *Knecht* also means originally nothing other than a young man. *Knappe,* however, gradually became identified with the young man who accompanied the knight as his servant and helper, especially when he himself was of a knightly family and was placed in his master's charge for the purpose of training as an apprentice. Finally, let it also be remembered in this connection that the German language has yet a third word with the same original meaning as *Knecht* and *Knappe,* the word *Thegn* (thane) or *Degen.*

The caste development in Romanic-Germanic Europe, therefore, occurred in the following manner. The invading, conquering Germans regarded as completely free men only warriors, which is really what they themselves were. That did not yet lead, however, to a real caste development, for the precise reason that it was still to too large an extent based on the ethnical antithesis. In the place of the ethnically based warrior group came the one that was based on the vassal system and fief-holding, which, as a result of this underpinning, transcended the contrast between free and unfree. There remained, however, the contrast between the professional, and essentially hereditary, warrior class and the nonwarrior class, and from this warrior class there developed both the higher and the lesser nobility.

The knight in the new sense, who was of knightly descent and had been received into the knightly fraternity through the ceremonial dubbing, therefore formed a warrior class within the warrior class. It is important, though in no way so easy, to understand how that was possible, since, in order for such a warrior caste to take form and assert itself, not only legal forms but also effectiveness in battle, a true superiority in

military action, were necessary. It is not difficult to understand how the
Germans at one time were able to take over the ascendancy in the
bourgeois, peace-oriented Roman World Empire, and also how the Vikings were able to do so later through military deeds in the world surrounding them, to project themselves into it as a warrior caste. How was
it possible, however, that this new knightly class now severed itself so
distinctly from its surroundings as to become eventually the ruling nobility? The answer is not apparent without further investigation. For neither
of the natural military qualities, physical strength and courage, is inherited so directly and in such a degree, nor does education have such a
molding force as not to be very frequently equaled and surpassed by the
innate qualities of sons of other classes of the same people, and especially
here where, side by side with the knightly class, stood the equally
hereditary class of military sergeants. Among these there certainly must
very often have been men who could hold their own with any knight in
physical strength, skill with weapons, and courage.

Since the ceremonial dubbing was associated with religious consecra-
tion and among the oaths which the young knight swore there appeared
also service to the Church, some have probably been prompted to believe that the origin of the new class was to be sought in the realm of the
Church. Knighthood formed a great, general Christian order, though, to
be sure, one so loose-knit that the word "order" seems to be applicable
only in a very exaggerated sense. But it has been believed that one
should look upon this institution as an imitation of the actual knightly
orders, the Knights Templars and the Knights Hospitalers, which had
been established in the east not long before, and the shaping of the
general Christian knightly order as a fruit of the religious exaltation of
the Second Crusade (1147). But it is easy to recognize that this leads us
in the wrong direction. If the entire phenomenon had no further meaning than that certain warriors spoke religious oaths in a ceremonial way
and wore certain religious insignia on their garments, that would have
been able neither to acquire significance in the history of the military art
nor to lead to the formation of such a powerful aristocracy, one which
asserted itself for centuries. Rather, it is clear that there exists here a
phenomenon in the sense of a very strong force in the area of the history
of the military art. Not until we have immersed ourselves completely in
the nature of the medieval military and have sought out its motivating
forces will we be capable of understanding the process of this development. For this purpose, we must start with the technical aspects.

The protective equipment with which the warriors were provided as
late as the time of Charlemagne—helmet, shield, coat of mail—were, as

we have seen, not yet so very heavy. The helmet had no visor; the coat of mail was an armored shirt that left the neck free. Throughout the entire Middle Ages we can observe how the armor became more and more complete and heavier.[19] Whereas in the older times warriors were often referred to in conjunction with the shield, as the principal protective arm ("*scutati*": "men with shields"), at the end of the eleventh century there arose, in place of this name, the designation "armored" ("*loricati*"), and finally, from the thirteenth century on, strength counts were based on armored steeds (*dextrarii* or *falerati cooperti*).[20]

The decision in a medieval battle was not brought about, as in the case of a Roman legion, by the steadfast maintaining of formation, the clever maneuvers, and the united force of disciplined and trained tactical units, but by the personal skill and bravery of individuals. Personal skill can, however, be reinforced to a high degree by the excellence of the weapons. The lance that does not splinter, the sword whose sharpness penetrates iron, the helmet, shield, and armor that are impenetrable— these things produce victory.

Again, as in Homer, the songs not only celebrated the heroes but also told of the invulnerability of their equipment, of the history and the special qualities of the sword "Balmung." It is not only the sword that very often has its proper name, but also other weapons of the knight.

The man with such weapons, with the complete heavy armor and practice in moving in this equipment, was superior, in individual combat, to the man with weaker armor. Nevertheless, he could not become the only warrior, for the heavy armor rendered him useless for many of the activities necessary in war. On foot, he could fight only with a certain awkwardness, with little movement away from a fixed position; it was difficult for him to mount up, to dismount, and to get up when he was unseated.[21] He could not pursue the foe to any appreciable degree. He could not use any kind of projectile weapons. In fact, he could not get along with one horse but, because of the heavy weight, had to spare his battle steed up to the last possible moment in order not to tire it out. In the meantime, he had to ride another animal and consequently needed not just one, but two or even three mounts (clearly seen in the sources since the eleventh century).[22] In the second half of the twelfth century, there began the practice of covering the horses with armor, something that, incidentally, was already reported of the East Goths in their battles with Belisarius.[23]

We, therefore, may still look upon the military in the Carolingian period and up into Otto's period as relatively uniform in its technology and weaponry, despite numerous small shadings of difference. At the same time, there arose gradually and ever more distinctly from the mass of warriors the superior group, which was in a position to procure the most costly and complete armor, with several horses and servants, and to practice in it. These knights were not capable of waging war alone; they needed at their sides the most varied types of assistance—not only personal servants and squires, but also light weapons, fighters on foot, and marksmen. In the transition from antiquity to the Middle Ages, we found that the various branches of the arms, infantry and cavalry, disappeared and were blended with each other. The same men fought both mounted and on foot, with projectiles and with close-combat weapons. That situation lasted for centuries. Now, once again branches of the arms took form, but of a completely different type than in antiquity. Beside the heavily armored knights were light horsemen, mounted archers, archers, and then also crossbowmen, on foot, and foot soldiers with close-combat weapons. If we should look only superficially, at the weapons alone, the difference from antiquity is perhaps not so apparent; then, too, there existed the same offensive and similar defensive weapons. In their deeper significance, however, the outwardly similar appearances were fundamentally different conceptually.

Most similar of all were the lightly armed foot soldiers, especially the archers; now, as previously, they were simply a supporting arm. William the Conqueror had already made use of them to an outstanding degree. In Germany up to that time very little use was made of them, but from the twelfth century on their importance grew steadily.

Originally, the Western Europeans had no mounted archers, and they could scarcely be found among the Romans. This was the ancient weapon of the Orient, of the Persians and the Parthians. Even the Crusaders first became acquainted with them through their enemies or at least learned to fear them and themselves hired such mounted men.

For a while fighters on foot with close-combat weapons seemed to have disappeared almost completely; particularly in Germany, there were many battles where there was no special mention of knights dismounting. They were purely mounted battles.[24] In the First Crusade and in the Crusades in general, there appear many dismounted warriors, but often probably only because the knights had no horses. Thereafter, however, they appeared gradually in the west in increasing numbers, and they constituted the fundamental difference from the armies of classical antiquity. In the latter, they formed the real nucleus; they were kept together in great masses, which, in time, were more finely organized, without giving up the weight of the mass effect. The Middle Ages did not possess such an infantry. The foot soldier, even with protective harness and piercing and cutting weapons, was not at all independent in battle but only an auxiliary of the knight.

For this reason, the knight, too, became different from the heavily armed horseman of antiquity. The *hetairoi* of Alexander the Great may have resembled quite closely the knightly concept of the Middle Ages in its earlier stage. The later knights of the Middle Ages, in the true sense of the word, were undoubtedly much heavier than the cavalrymen of antiquity had ever been. The mounted units of Hannibal and Caesar, barbarian mercenaries, more closely resemble the concept of modern cavalry than that of knighthood. The knight forms a combat branch of a very unique type, because none of the other arms—neither the light horseman, nor the dismounted fighter, nor the archer—can stand up to him man to man, and, consequently, the decision on the battlefield depends on him. It is very questionable that knights could have broken the mass of a Roman legion, but as for medieval foot soldiers, none of them could have withstood knights. The knight, therefore, by the type and power of his arms, formed the framework of the army. Recognizable from all about and at a great distance, he was the one to whom the private warrior looked for his example, whose spirit inspired the latter, whose influence also guided him. Origin, training, esprit de corps, and position strengthened to an extreme degree his concept of honor and his ambition; he had to be an outstandingly courageous man, for, if he was not, he was plainly despicable. We can see that it was not simply an artificially developed concept or an incidental matter that this arm of the military was at the same time an hereditary class. Without such a social nucleus, or, better expressed, without such deep social roots, it would have been difficult to assemble the elite troop which the heavily armed horsemen within a medieval army had to be. For the standing army, which becomes trained for the highest wartime accomplishment by virtue of its life in common and through its discipline, as in antiquity and again in modern times, did not exist in the period of the Middle Ages. Military training was the mission only of the family and the class. Thus, a military arm could become an hereditary class and an hereditary class a military arm.

Not incorrectly did Emperor Frederick II write to his son that he should send him knights, "for the fame of his empire and his own power resided in the body of knights" ("cum specialiter in multitudine militum decus imperii et potentia nostra consistat"). When Cologne, in 1368, renewed an old treaty of alliance, dating from the year 1263, with the count of Julich, the explicit statement was added to the effect that the fifteen squires, which the count was to provide in addition to nine knights, were to be "good men, born to the shield" ("guder Lude, zum Schilde geboren").[25]

The significance of this military arm finds its characteristic expression in the fact that the Latin authors simply called the knight "*miles*": he and he alone, the knight, is the real, complete warrior. The word which indicates private soldier in classical Latin now indicates the most outstanding one. In the writings of Richer, an author of the last part of the tenth century, the expression *milites peditesque* (knights and foot soldiers), is found for the first time, in about the year 995. We encounter the term very often thereafter,[26] as if the foot soldier was not at all a real soldier. Of course, the word never became a firmly defined, technically certain expression. When a medieval source says that an army numbered so and so many *milites,* we must therefore avoid concluding, without further investigation, that a certain number of other combatants were naturally there also—light horsemen, squires, common soldiers, archers, or other dismounted men. At least in the twelfth century, *milites* would also mean the ensemble of mounted combatants, where it is not expressly stated to the contrary, and whether an army consisted exclusively of mounted men or also had foot soldiers must first be definitely determined. With the passage of time, however, the word *miles* became generally limited more and more to the knight in the true, narrower meaning.[27]

The older warrior class, too, was in general hereditary, and its members for the most part married only among themselves. Nevertheless, a courageous young town dweller or peasant's son, or even an unfree man, could enter this class and establish a warrior famiy. On the other hand, sons from such families also crossed over occasionally to the life of farm or town. Now, as an upper stratum broke away from this open warrior class, finding at the courts of the princes, the counts, and the bishops, and at country seats, social centers of special culture and polished customs, the class itself broke away in a downward direction, and the breach finally became definitive.

At this point, I should like to call tbe reader's attention to a matter in the first volume of this work (Book IV, Chap. 1, pp. 256 and 265) connected with the most ancient Roman political system. A problem of ancient history which remains unsolved is the origin of the city aristocrats, of the Eupatrids in Greece, the patricians in Rome, and further, how it came about that this aristocracy proved to be so much stronger and more enduring in Rome than in any of the Greek cities. The solution I have given comes from linking the study of the ancient sources with that of the Middle Ages, just as we have found a clarification of the Persian wars in the wars of the Burgundians. Just as, in the Middle Ages, military achievement led to the formation of a class of nobility, everything points to the fact that a similar sequence of development occurred in antiquity, in prehistoric times. It has been customary for some time to speak of an "ancient middle age," and in Italy mounted combat, which plays such an important role in the formation of a knightly class, was of much greater significance than in Greece.

In the historic periods of antiquity, however, there no longer existed a knightly class, that is, a warrior caste which, as the most powerful individual warriors, formed the deciding factor in war. The patricians in Rome, and later the *optimates,* governed as a result of political strength and political organizations. The Roman consuls, unlike the German dukes and counts, were not the foremost fighters on the battlefield, but rather, burgomasters. Even when the professional soldier concept and the standing army had already completely replaced the ancient Roman citizen army, the army commanders, according to their own understanding, were not soldiers, but they remained primarily governmental officials. As provincial governors, the proconsuls and the propraetors also commanded the troops. On the contrary, the Germanic kings and their officials were originally warriors and retained this character even when, by virtue of their military positions, they controlled and administered the governmental organization in its entirety. The emperors and kings of the Middle Ages were knights; their entire courts consisted of knights. The princes and counts who possessed the lands were knights, and even the bishops and abbots were surrounded by knights and often enough took up arms themselves. According to Einhardt (in 778), Charlemagne placed members of his court (*aulici*) at the head of his troops. In this society, whoever was not a knight was a cleric; there existed no other type than these two. A king or other eminent person who laid aside his knightly belt thereby renounced completely his worldly life and was ready to withdraw into a monastery.[28] Even Rumold, the master of the kitchen in the *Nibelungenlied,* was "a highly selected *Degen.*" The warrior performed, on the side, all the higher functions not accomplished by the clergy. The incumbents of the positions at the courts and in the administrative organizations of the kings, princes, counts, bishops, and abbots formed the most outstanding group of the knightly class as a result of their higher position, their fortune, and their income.

The eminent Roman leaders at one time needed to be officials only, because they were able to exercise and to handle the power over the crowd as a result of the disciplined army units. The foremost leaders of

the Romanic-Germanic Middle Ages did not have at their disposal
trained maniples and cohorts; they could be leaders of the people only by
being at the same time the boldest fighters and the most powerful warriors.

In these circles, the age-old Germanic hero concept, described for us
by Tacitus, lived on, and it was cultivated and further nurtured in song
and story. On the one hand originally hard and melancholy, it became
more carefree in our particular period, while in the younger families
there was awaking a sensitivity for the beautiful, and they finally were
imbued with a knightly ideal for that which was beautiful. The knight
became refined through the self-discipline to which he committed himself, and courtly customs and the courtly love ideal served as his tutors.[29]
He placed his courage in the service of the concept of eternity which the
Church represented for him.

The knightly class, which at the same time formed the highest social
stratum, was the specific warrior class of the high Middle Ages but not
the only warrior group. As significant and valid as the birth status was as a
basis for the military arm, nevertheless, there naturally always existed
among the common warriors many who could perform the same feats—
all the more so in that the possessors of small fiefs who did not concur-
rently hold an official position in many cases did not move into the new
knightly order, but such families nonetheless belonged to the hereditary
warrior class.[30] Nothing prevented a military leader from outfitting with
knightly arms common warriors whom he knew to be personally qualified, whether they were the possessors of small fiefs or whether they had
won their freedom.[31]

From a practical viewpoint, in every army, in addition to the actual
knights, there also existed many—often *very* many—warriors armed like
knights.[32] Since it also came about, on the one hand, that, just as some
fought in knightly fashion without having received the accolade, so, on
the other hand, a man from the knightly class might also perhaps have
been serving in a lower branch of service or not in his own armor, but in
equipment loaned by his lord. So too the young men of knightly birth
who had not yet received the knightly dubbing, the squires, externally
appeared to blend into the group of light horse along with the common
light horsemen. The transitions of a social as well as a technical type were
very frequent, and the individual military branches and classes were,
from a practical viewpoint, less easy to distinguish from one another than
was the case from a theoretical viewpoint.[33]

The knightly class at first separated itself only very gradually from the
upper bourgeoisie in the cities, as it became a landed nobility. A consid-

erable portion of the warrior group had always lived in the cities. It is entirely wrong that the Germanic peoples who settled on Romanic terri- tory had settled in the countryside. As followers of counts, they had originally remained to a very large degree in the cities. The traveling merchant had to be not only a businessman but also an armed man, a part-time warrior. Of the warriors of the counts and bishops in the cities, it appears that not a few moved directly over into business. In the edict of the Lombard King Aistulf, of the year 750, and the ordinance of the bishop of Bremen (see above, p. 47), we find specifically named warriors "qui negotiantes sunt" ("who are businessmen"). Of those who remained in the profession of arms, the ones who possessed sufficient fortune entered the city administration and blended with the well-to-do mer- chant families to form the city patrician class.[34] In the edict of Frederick Barbarossa forbidding sons of peasants and ministers to be dubbed as knights, it is with deliberate intent that the question of the city bourgeois class does not arise.

However manifold and diverse the possibilities for transition on all sides are, it remains true that the nucleus of the medieval military system was formed by an essentially hereditary warrior caste. The frictions and impossible situations that resulted therefrom were adjusted in a practical way. The sons of knights whose inherited traits and training were not sufficient to meet the high demands of the position physically and spiritually were pushed off into the ministry and into the monasteries. The young men from other classes in whom the qualities required for knighthood were observable to an outstanding degree could first of all serve as squires and sergeants, and then also in a knightly manner with- out actually being knighted. Finally, even the law that only those of knightly birth could become knights was not an inviolable one. The emperor himself and the kings quite naturally dubbed as knights whomever they considered worthy of that honor, and already under Emperor Frederick II we find a formula by which the emperor could grant a dispensation to deserving persons.[35] Judging from the indignation that was quite often expressed in the literature of the day over the knighting of commoners, we can conclude that such an event was not too rare. Wirnt von Gravenberg, in his *Wigalois,* composed between 1204 and 1210, was already complaining: "May God strike down those who ever give a sword to him who cannot measure up to the knightly life, who from his origins is not born to it." In the second half of the thirteenth century, Seifried Helbling joked that it was as impossible to make a peasant into a knight with a shield and sword as to dedicate with the Church's blessing on Easter morning goat flesh instead of lamb's meat.

"Let the shield in this moment change into the earthboard of the peasant's plow, his sword into the plowshare, his knightly silken purse into a seedbag, the border of his belt into a hempen feeding halter." Ottokar von Steiermark jokes about the "clod-hoppers transformed into iron hats," and the glossary for the Saxon feudal law explains: "If a peasant is favored by the king and becomes a knight, and receives both knighthood and knightly rights, the king thereby goes against the law. If a peasant should become a knight, he still does not assume thereby the knightly manner."[36]

There is a well-known story of how a mounted soldier whom Emperor Frederick Barbarossa, because of a particularly courageous deed (at Tortona in 1155), wished to dub a knight, declined this honor, saying he was a man of low status and wished to remain in his own class.[37] Already at that time, therefore, the true knights must have differed so much in their customs and their whole way of life from the common man that it appeared painful to the latter, if he was of a modest temperament, to enter such a society, where he would have felt himself a stranger.

The formula that remained in use for some 800 years thereafter, that the people exist to work, the knights to fight, and the priests to pray, we find for the first time expressed in the poem of a French bishop to the Capetian Robert the Pious:

Triplex ergo Dei domus est, quae creditur una
Nunc orant, alii pugnant, aliique laborant.[38]
(Therefore the house of God is threefold, which is believed to be one.
Now some pray, others fight, and others work.)

The military training in the Middle Ages was almost exclusively of an individual nature.[39] The foot soldier learned nothing, the marksman learned to shoot, and the knight was trained from his early youth in riding and the handling of weapons, first in his family and then in the service of a lord. The entire, class-based training revolved about the weapons.

The English chronicler Roger of Hoveden recounts how King Henry II dubbed as a knight his third son Godfrey, duke of Brittany, and how the latter, full of ambition, thereupon practiced knightly exercises in order to emulate in military fame his brothers Henry and Richard the Lion-hearted.

For they were all of the same mind, that is, to be superior to others in the use of weapons, and they knew that one would not have the essential skills when they were needed unless they were practiced in advance. The boxer cannot step into the ring with confidence if he has never received a blow. He who has seen his blood flowing, who has felt his teeth cracking under an opponent's blow, who has lain on the ground with his enemy over him, and still has not lost his courage; he who has been thrown to the ground time after time, only the more staunchly to stand up again—he may go into battle with high hopes. For virtue grows when it is irritated, but a soul that gives in to fear has only fleeting glory. Blameless is he who, too weak to bear the burden, nevertheless hastens eagerly to assume it. The reward for hours of toil waits where the temples of victory stand.[40]

The main training areas are the princely courts, to which the sons of great families are brought for the purpose of training.[41]

Wolfram von Eschenbach describes in *Willehalm* the exercises on the square in front of the castle: "There between the palace and the linden trees one could see the children of the nobles jousting with spears against the shields, here by twos, there by fours, here charging against each other like oncoming waves, there sparring with clubs."

In the *Wolfdietrich* the training is described as follows:

> The three princes were taught many knightly skills: manipulating the shield, fighting with the sword, firing at the target, broad jumping, and gripping the lance well, and sitting straight in the saddle; and they mastered all these activities.

The Spaniard Petrus Alfonsi, at the end of the eleventh century, compares in his *Disciplina Clericalis* the seven free skills of the scholar with the seven knightly skills (*"probitates"*): riding, swimming, shooting with the bow, boxing, bird baiting, chess playing, and versifying.[42] (Wherein, strangely enough, there is missing precisely the most important, the use of the sword, whereas elsewhere even the serving up of foods and waiting on the table are mentioned as part of the training of the young knight aspirant.)[43] The jousts held before the assembled people form the culmination of the training, a practice that, nevertheless, dated from early times. As early as in Tacitus, they are referred to in speaking of the Tencteri ("lusus infantium, juvenum aemulatio": "the play of children, the rivalry of young men"), *Germ.,* Chap. 32. We hear of them at the court of the East Goth Theodoric,[44] and we have a detailed description of the games that Louis the German and Charles the Bald jointly put on in

Strasbourg in 842, when they had given each other their solemn oath.[45] Those participating rode straight for each other in bands and leveled their lances but did not strike each other, so that nobody was wounded. As the weapons gradually became heavier, these mock battles went one step further, and the participants actually struck with their lances and their swords, but with dulled weapons. The older type was called "*Buhurt,*" and the newer form, which originated in France, "jousting" (*Tjost*) or "sticking" (*Stechen*), and, especially when whole bands simultaneously rode down on each other, "tournament" (*Turnier*). It was in France that these armed games and the entire courtly life that went along with them were first established and whence they spread to other lands, including Germany. The Middle Ages themselves accepted the fact that a French knight, Godfrey de Preully, who was killed in the year 1066, had founded the practice of tournaments. Primarily, opponents sought to unseat each other with dulled lances, and this game was extremely dangerous. It led not only frequently to serious injuries, but also not infrequently to death, so that the Church intervened against the practice with repeated prohibitions and forbade these tourneys in solemn synodal resolutions under penalty of excommunication. The first of these injunctions dates from the year 1131, at the Council of Reims.[46] The knightly class, however, did not allow itself to be deprived of this, its peculiar sport, in the practice of which the spirit of the class showed itself most strongly and its members distinguished themselves most clearly from the common crowd. Here it had to be seen who the true knight was, who not only mastered the art of handling his weapons but also did not flinch before danger, even for the sake of a mere game. It appears that, with the passage of time, the conditions and forms became even sharper. They used not just dull lances, but also sharp ones, which were perhaps prevented from entering too deeply by a metal crosspiece, or relied on the fact that the thin lance would splinter rather than penetrate the strong shield and armor of the opponent. But then strong shafts were also used, and it even happened that actual enemies would challenge each other to life-and-death battles in these tourneys.

When entire bands, and, on occasion, individual pairs, rode directly down on each other simultaneously, they sought to ride directly toward and then around each other, which always caused at least serious bruises.

The approach ride was always quite short and even the common charge was not, for example, to be compared with the modern attack of a massed squadron. That would have required quite different prerequisites, particularly a long period of practice together, and not just fleeting clashes. This amounted, therefore, only to a proliferation of individual fights.[47]

The cities, too, loved and practiced tournaments. Emperor Frederick II once forbade the Lübeckers to hold tourneys,[48] because of the disorders that accompanied them (even "violationes matronarum et virginum": "violations of matrons and virgins"), but the citizens of Magdeburg, according to the *Schöppenchronik,* in 1270 invited all the merchants to a tourney which the knights wished to hold. In 1368 the citizens of Constance traveled to Zurich for a "sticking."[49] Not until the fifteenth century were the patricians forced out of the tourneys, probably because, since the victory of the guilds, their position had undergone important changes politically. They were obliged to obey the Council, which was often composed of more guildsmen than patricians, to pay taxes, and to do guard duty like other citizens. Many of the proudest patricians, since they were no longer the ruling class, left the cities and moved to the country.[50]

A particularly weak point in this military system was the aspect of discipline. In fact, I am inclined to doubt whether we can use this word here at all, since it has for us strong technical concepts. Knighthood had no tradition of a system of discipline. The roots of the medieval warrior class we have found in the Germanic peoples' armies, which moved into the Roman regions and settled there. Of the organization and hierarchy of these peoples' armies, we have said that they had, in fact, no military discipline, but that nevertheless their whole social and political structure actually produced, to a certain degree, something similar. Thus, there existed in the feudal state, too, a peculiar organization and hierarchy, command and obedience, without which elements—masses if one will—simply cannot be moved. But it was not what we call discipline, not what the Roman legions had and what modern armies have once again. Discipline rests on the power to punish which stems from the power to command, a power of punishment that unconditionally subordinates to itself the individual will and produces a habit that, as such, is constantly effective. The most difficult point in any disciplinary system is not so much the subordination of the masses, but the mastery of the general over his subordinate leaders. More recent military history is filled with interior conflicts within the armies, which are created by the opposition of the generals to the high command. How weak, however, was the power of a medieval prince over his most important vassals, in comparison with the modern military hierarchy! Even the oath of allegiance which the vassal took toward his lord did not contain the concept of unconditional obedience. There has come down to us the form of the oath which the Italian communes and bishops swore to Frederick Barbarossa when he restored the kingdom in Italy in 1158.[51] They did not swear, for example, to listen to, accept, and carry out every command, but only that command which the emperor should give in the exercise of his rights. True enough, there existed in the case of refusal to obey the possibility of a withdrawal of the fief, but this would perhaps lead to civil war. The vassal expected rewards from the "generosity" of his lord and could forfeit these through insubordination and disobedience, but the fear of losing rewards and of falling into disfavor with one's lord is very much less effective than the fear of that punishment, heavy and direct, which can increase in seriousness even to immediate execution, as is provided in the organizational system that we call military discipline. No doubt the knight was conscious of owing obedience to his master, but the very spirit of this warrior class produced an opposition that easily overstepped the limits of this obedience. It was certainly thought in the true spirit of the knight when, in the *Nibelungenlied*, Volker scornfully said to Wolfhart, as the latter referred to the command of his lord: "He who keeps his hands off everything that is forbidden to him is too fearful."

A modern researcher has expressed the opinion that the spirit of insubordinate independence which prevented the development of a disciplined tactical unit first appeared in the period of declining knighthood: "Not until the search for pleasure, brusqueness and selfishness, broken promises, craftiness and disloyal actions of every type had taken the place of those shining virtues of the good old days was it possible for that false ideal of the knight to spring up, of the knight who bends his will before that of nobody, even the highest authority." Whoever leafs through books of German history soon finds that, even here, the idea of the "good old days" is misleading. As long, of course, as the powerful monarchy of Charlemagne existed, we hear, and even not so rarely, of conspiracies, but the existing authorities reacted forcefully and overcame the resistance. From the dissolution of the Carolingian Empire on, however, even with the most imposing restorers of the royal power, we encounter again and again the "spirit of insubordinate independence which refuses to bend its will before anybody, even before the highest authority." As early as the period of the reign of Charlemagne's grandsons, there began the series of constantly repeated uprisings of sons against the father, of dukes against the king, of counts against the duke, of the nobles among the Saxons and Bavarians who preferred to go over to the heathens in excommunication rather than subordinate themselves. How vainly Otto the Great went to great pains to appease that old friend of his house, Duke Eberhard and his Franks, when he was obliged to punish them for a breach of the peace of the land. The saga that extols the battles of Duke Ernst of Swabia against his father probably was not incorrect in blending in his person that of his predecessor, Duke Ludolf, who had also once fought against his father, King Otto. Let nobody raise the possible objection that these events were all related to the highest, most noble ranks and that a different spirit could have reigned in the lower ranks of warriors. It is an inviolable law that discipline starts at the top and extends from there downward. Where the colonels and generals are mutinous, so are the troops. It is impossible that in knightly circles one would have had a different concept of the military authority of the counts than that existing among the counts with respect to the king's authority. From the period of Barbarossa we have examples not only of princes but also of private knights who disregarded a command of the emperor.[52] The history of the First Crusade shows us at every step how painfully even the most urgently needed leadership and organization was accomplished, from case to case.

"Quales constringit nulla potestas, Crimina si fugiunt quae regum sceptra coercent" ("No power checks men of that sort, if they flee the crimes that constrain the authority of kings")—so sings the French Bishop Adalbero of the "*nobiles*" who are "*bellatores*" ("warriors")[53]— verses that, with Schiller, we might translate: "Only the soldier is a free man." We have seen above that the backbone of the knightly class, the *ministeriales,* were legally and socially unfree. Is it a question here of various elements within the knightly class or a difference between French and German knights? By no means. But the complexity of human existence is such that content and form can oppose each other in a complete contradiction.

At any rate, the greatest obedience existed still in the knightly orders, where a strict punishment system held sway and precise rules regulated both the service and the life. For example, in order to spare the horses, the Knights Templars were forbidden to gallop without special permission (Chap. 315). Whoever failed to put on his mail shirt, but put it instead in a bag, was obliged to have a sack of leather or woven wire (not cloth) and could not tie the sack on without permission but had to carry it in his hand (Chap. 322). The punishments were: to eat the common meals sitting on the ground; giving up the white cloak; imprisonment; expulsion from the order. In one case, because a brother had replied to a commander, on receiving an order, "Just be patient, I'll do it in a minute" ("espoir, je le ferai"), he was stripped of the uniform of the order by unanimous vote of the chapter because he had not obeyed on the spot (Chap. 588).

With the mass of soldiers (*Knechte*), discipline was no doubt exacted forcibly with a stick,[54] but even here we must picture the standard of obedience more as that of the servant to his master rather than of the soldier to his superior.

Emperor Frederick I issued at the beginning of his reign in 1158 a field regulation, which has come down to us and has also been referred to on occasion as an "article of war," although it does not deserve this title. It does not contain disciplinary regulations at all, but principally only a certain prohibition against disorder and quarreling among the men at arms. It was forbidden in brawls to call out the battle cry, which would call one's comrades to his assistance. One was to run to separate the brawlers not with swords, but only with defensive arms and clubs. Whoever found a wine keg was not to let it run out, so that fellow soldiers might also have some of it. It was established to whom the game which was brought down on the hunt would belong. It was specified that nobody would have a woman with him. Whoever did so anyway was to lose his armor ("omne suum harnasch": "all his own equipment"), and the woman's nose was to be cut off. But disciplinary regulations are always easily proclaimed but difficult to enforce, even by the mightiest emperor. In the very same year in which this "peace" was solemnly proclaimed, Frederick was obliged to remove a large number of prostitutes from the camp.[55]

Real discipline is in general so much an artificial product that it cannot be created at all without a whole system of exercises. As the best means therefor, that drill has always proven itself which brings the man, with every movement of his body, into the hand of his superior. This kind of drill was completely unknown in the Middle Ages, and even the apparently so strict measure by which the warrior gave up his freedom and became not only a vassal but *ministerial* of his military lord did not create a true military obedience—what we would call subordination.

A warrior class that feels itself to be the holder of power and that is not restrained by strict discipline exercises its power in daily life also, in contacts with the working classes and even among its own members. This warrior class had evolved from the barbarians, who had scornfully struck down in ruins and trampled on the ancient civilized world in the *Völkerwanderung*. In the civil wars and feuds of the feudal state, there remained the acceptance of blood-spilling and of the destruction associated with the conduct of war. In the service code (*Dienstrecht*) of Bishop Burchard of Worms, dating from the beginning of the eleventh century, it is recounted that in a single year thirty-five subjects of the diocese were struck down by their fellow men without having any guilt. In a case of insult, taking the law into one's own hands was the custom and the established rule.[56] The more important feudal lords who went so far as to build themselves their own strongholds, from which they could defy even their count or their lord, soon found themselves tempted to oppress the peasants of the surrounding region and to exact tribute from traveling merchants or to plunder them completely.[57] The social development toward more proper amenities of life brought relief in that the social class gave itself a certain education, facilitated and created an economic order and the blossoming of a new cultural life. The songs of the *Nibelungenlied* were nurtured in the milieu of the knights of Frederick Barbarossa and of Henry the Lion and their sons. A completely individual branch of world literature, the songs of the troubadors and the *Minnesang* were the intellectual product of this warrior class. "If war," said Ranke, "aroused every possible breaking out of passion, of crudeness, and of brute nature, knighthood correspondingly had the destiny of saving the true human being, of tempering strength by custom and the influence of women, of transfiguring power through a religious orientation." Often enough, however, this civilizing power of the knightly class's education broke down, even in the case of knights, and the unoccupied, wandering warrior turned time and again to the robber's life. Human nature is thus: the same class created for itself the ideal characters of Siegfried and Parsival, produced Walter von der Vogelweide and the robber knights. This paradox is also reflected in tradition and in history. On the one hand, the rawness and the lack of freedom in feudalism are complained of and condemned, while on the other hand knighthood is romantically glorified. In fact, both concepts are linked with any consideration of all historical points of view. In the *History of the Cavalry* by the English Lieutenant Colonel Denison, translated and annotated by Brix, lieutenant colonel in the Royal Prussian War Department (1879),[58] the following description concerning knighthood (p. 126) is cited from an older book:

Toward the middle of the tenth century, a few poor noblemen, united by the necessity for a justified defense and troubled by the excesses of the many sovereign powers, took to heart the suffering and tears of the people. They swore to each other, in the eyes of God and Saint George as witnesses, that they would devote themselves to the protection of the oppressed, and they took the weak under the protection of their swords. Simple in their clothing, strict in their customs, humble in success, steady and unperturbed in failure, they very soon gained an extraordinary reputation. The gratitude of the people, in their simple and trusting joy, embellished their feats of arms with miraculous reports, lifted their courage, and blended in their prayers their magnanimous liberators with the heavenly powers. It is so natural for those who are oppressed to deify those who bring them consolation.

We have already come to know the weakness of the feudal state against barbarian enemies, as soon as the latter appeared in any numbers— Vikings, Saracens, Magyars. We shall realize this weakness even more clearly when we see to what a small degree, even inside the country, the royal power was able to impose itself and its laws, and especially to suppress the feuds and robbery. The feudal German Kingdom reached the apogee of its power and expansion under Henry III, son of the mighty Conrad, himself a great-grandson of Liutgarde, daughter of Otto the Great. Under Henry III, the cathedral dean of Liège, Anselm, wrote the biography of his Bishop Wazo (1041–1048) and recounted in a special chapter the steps Wazo took against the robber knights in his diocese. This account gives us such a comprehensive picture of the state of security in the empire, even under the most powerful rulers, of the nature of the struggles resulting therefrom, and of the difficulty of building an effective authority—for, as the knight stood with respect to the prince, so stood the latter with respect to the king—that I should like to insert Anselm's account in its entirety here.[59] It reads as follows:

Piety, compassion for the helpless, and the laments of the poor moved the bishop to rise up from his mildness and his peaceful situation and come to their aid, in the conviction that nothing could be holier or more pleasing to God than that he curb the wild rage of the robbers in their suppression of the innocent people. A large number of them had built strong refuges for themselves in swamps or on cliffs, in their reliance on which they plundered the surrounding area, crushed the inhabitants of the region into unbearable servitude, and raged far and wide, laying waste to the countryside. The chosen vessel of the Lord resolved to level these strongholds, which had always been destructive but were now especially so, and to free the countryside from these armed robberies of which it had become so tired. Filled with the spirit in which Samuel had once cut down the Amalekite Agag and Elias the priests of Baal, our hero, contenting himself with a small following of knights, began the siege of first this stronghold, then that one. The robbers, trusting to their walls and swamps, refused at first to believe there was any danger, railed at our men and called them demented to think that they could capture a habitation protected by nature itself. Our men, however, stimulated by their outstanding leader, each worked harder than the other at making revetments and fasces and opened passages for themselves. With ardor and back-breaking effort, they conquered nature, transformed the swamps, previously known only to fish and frogs, into firm ground, and built the engines that were to bring ruin to the robbers. Then, working day and night in reliefs, they launched stones against the castle, and the bishop himself was present and urged them on with song and prayer. Soon, since no relief got through to them, the robbers surrendered, with the proviso that no harm would come to them, and the castle was razed to the ground. In this way, one after the other of them fell. I also wish to mention, however, that in the sieges, often with 1,000 men, often more, seldom fewer, the bishop, in keeping with the custom of the ancient Romans, paid a salary ("cottidianos sumptus praebebat": "he supplied their daily needs") to the knights (*armatis*), allowed the common soldier (*gregario militi*) to butcher cattle which was not necessary for plowing, and the owners were fully reimbursed, so that even in such emergencies no injustice might be done.

So much for Anselm.[60] In France, where not even a strong kingdom existed, the Church sought to help and proclaimed the *Treuga Dei,* the Truce of God, in which it was specified that at least on those days that had been sanctified in sacred history, from Thursday evening until Monday morning, all feuding was to be forsaken and safety was to reign in the land. The Truce of God was then carried over also into Burgundy and to certain parts of Germany. Later, efforts were made from time to time to assure civil peace by the proclamation of a general peace throughout the country for a specific period or at least through the decree that a feud was to be announced three days before the start of hostilities (Frederick Barbarossa, about 1186). No "eternal peace" was attained, however, until the reign of Emperor Maximilian (1495), at a time when knighthood, feudalism, and the Middle Ages had all ended.

EXCURSUS

SCHWERTLEITE (RECEPTION INTO WARRIORHOOD) AND DUBBING

Knowledge of the difference and significance of these two acts has very recently been impressively furthered by Guilhiermoz, *Essai sur l'origine de la noblesse française,* (1902), p. 393 ff., but certain important points have still remained doubtful to me. With the old Germanic tribes, the qualification for military service undoubtedly took place very early, in the fourteenth, and possibly even in the twelfth, year of age. Guilhiermoz claims that it was not until the twentieth year, but his evidence is not convincing. He is very right, however, in pointing out that, in the Middle Ages, there existed several stages of recognition of maturity, following closely one on the other, which were linked with the ceremonies of the *capillaturia,* the haircutting, and the *barbatoria,* the shaving of the beard. The knightly dubbing can probably not be associated with the old qualification for military service, since it assumes a full-grown man, but it would be conceivable that it replaced a later act, the *barbatoria,* and, whereas the knight's belt (*cingulum militare*), originally and into the eleventh century, was bestowed at the time of the qualification for military service, this ceremony may have been deferred in the twelfth century to the second act and joined with the knightly dubbing. As long as the *cingulum militare* was linked to the qualification for military service, it could not also have had, of course, a status-conferring effect, but this could undoubtedly have been the case with the second act, where the full, heavy knightly armor was put on, which only the well-to-do man possessed and as a rule only the man of knightly status wore. The result was that this act was regarded as the really important one and was formally executed, whereas the qualification for military service, the *Schwertleite,* which was formerly held to be the more important, now took a secondary position. One can see here an interrelation between the technical—the heavy armor and the strong steed— and the social.

Schröder (*Deutsche Rechtsgeschichte,* Section 42, p. 430) believes that the distinction between knights and squires did not develop until the thirteenth century; however, he simply does not attribute a real significance to the act. He assumes that, in comparison with the knightly dubbing, the *Schwertleite* with the bestowal of the knightly belt at the moment of entering military service continued to be the important act. "Aside from rare exceptions," he says, "the *Schwertleite* was always carried out for a group, normally in conjunction with important court functions in the course of which a tournament would give the young knights at once an occasion to prove themselves in their new profession." If it is true, however, that the young knights had to show their skill in a tourney immediately after the ceremony, then the act could no longer have been identical with the old qualification for military service. For the heavy tourney armor of the twelfth and thirteenth centuries required a full-grown man with long practice. One might, of course, imagine that, in addition to the real tourney, a sort of special youths' game was arranged. That possibility, however, seems to be ruled out by the fact that Henry VI, when he was formally inducted as qualified for military service, in Mainz in 1184, was nineteen or twenty years old. It is also recounted of a son of Henry the Lion and a son of Duke Leopold of Austria that they had already fought in the wars before they became knights.[61]

Consequently, I believe that one must interpret the ceremony in Mainz in 1184 not as the *Schwertleite* in the old sense, but as the knightly dubbing. I offer no opinion as to whether or how long two formal ceremonies, one upon entry into the squire's status, the old qualification for military service, and the second the knightly dubbing, which was often deferred quite a long time, continued to take place.

Roth von Schreckenstein, pp. 215 and 224, contradicts himself on the matter of knightly dubbing and qualification for military service.

This question has recently been treated by W. Erben in "Schwertleite und Ritterschlag" in the *Zeitschrift für historische Waffenkunde,* 1919.

THE NORTH GERMANS

In the Northern Germanic countries—Denmark, Norway, Sweden—military organization naturally has its own history. Dahlman, *Geschichte von Dänemark,* 2: 308 ff. and 3: 50, treats the subject thoroughly. See also the recently published Berlin dissertation of Büchner, "Die Geschichte der norwegischen Leiländiger," 1903. I have not checked on these two works.

NOTES FOR CHAPTER I

1. See Richard Schroeder, *Zeitschrift für Rechtsgeschichte, Germanische Abteilung,* 24. 347, "The Old Saxon People's Nobility and the Landowner Theory" ("Der altsächsische Volksadel und die grundherrliche Theorie").

2. Richer, for the years 930 and 888. *SS.,* 3. 584. Bonitho, Jaffé 2: 639.

3. Wipo, Chap. 4.

4. Bruno, Chap. 88. Cosmas II, Chap. 25, for the year 1087. A document of Emperor Lothair of the year 1134 distinguished between "ordo equestris major et minor" ("greater and lesser equestrian rank"), cited by Schröder, *Deutsche Rechtsgeschichte,* p. 430; "milites tam majores quam minores" ("greater as well as lesser knights"), *Gesta Consulum Andegavensium* (*Deeds of the Counts of Anjou*), ed. Bouquet, 10. 254; "milites plebei" ("soldiers of the people") in Raymond of Agiles, *Recueil des histoires des Croisades,* 3: 274.

5. This is correctly expressed by Waitz, 5: 439, where still more examples are cited (also p. 398, Note 4). When he adds, however, that it cannot be said with certainty with which meanings the expressions were used, I can see no basis for this doubt. Legal meanings, everybody agrees, are not intended; the factual, social relationships that are meant, however, are entirely clear. Source citations are also to be found in Köhler, *Ritterzeit,* 3: 20.

6. Cited by Harnack, *Militia Christi* (*Service of Christ*), p. 84, note: "ut plurimi ex ipsis adderentur ad fidem domini nostri Jesu Christi derelicto militiae cingulo" ("that most of them should be added to the faith of our Lord Jesus Christ after the belt of military service has been given up").

7. *Gesta Cons. Andegavensium,* ed. Bouquet, *Recueil,* 10: 254. It is recounted that the inhabitants of a castle under attack "cingulis militaribus accincti armisque protecti ad pugnam se more militum castrensium paraverunt" ("girded with military belts and protected by arms, they prepared themselves for battle like the knights of a castle") and made a sortie. The knight's belt plays a role in this incident, in that it creates the deceptive appearance that knights are coming and attacking.

The purple or scarlet cloak which is often mentioned (Abbo repeatedly; Ruotger, *vita Brunonis,* Chap. 30, *vita Heinrici IV,* Chap. 8; *Chronicle of Monte Casino for the Year 1137*) I am not willing to count, as does Baltzer, p. 5, as a specific part of the knightly garb, since it is expressly stated that, when the knights are too poor, they must be satisfied with the cloak in its natural color. (*Vita Heinrici IV,* Chap 8.) We also read (Guiart, 2. 698 cited in Alwin Schultz, 2: 313, Note 3) that the knights on taking the cross, renounce any elegance in their clothing and put on simple, dark garments. They were not willing, however, to lay aside a symbol of their rank, but only the elegant attire.

8. At any rate, that is what one finds often recounted in modern works, although I have not been able to find the original source therefor, and in works on legal history nothing on such an order is to be found, no more so than in the special works on Louis VI. Daniel, *History of the French Militia (Histoire de la Milice Française),* 1724. Boutaric, *French Military Institutions (Institutions militaires de la France),* 1863. Boutaric, *The Feudal System. Review of historic questions (Le régime féodal. Revue des questions historiques),* Vol. XVIII, 1875. Glasson, *History of the Law and Institutions of France (Histoire du droit et des institutions de la France),* 1891. A. Luchaire, *Manual of French Institutions, period of the direct line of Capetians (Manuel des institutions françaises, période des Capétiens directs),* 1892. Luchaire, *History of the Monarchical Institutions of France (Histoire des institutions monarchiques de la France),* Tome III (also under the title *Studies on the Acts of Louis VII* [Etudes sur les actes de Louis VII], 1885). Luchaire, *Louis VI, Annales de sa vie,* 1890.

9. "De filiis quoque sacerdotum dyaconorum ac rusticorum statuimus, ne cingulum militare aliquatenus assumat, et qui jam assumserunt, per judicem provintiae a militia pellantur." ("We also decree concerning the sons of priests, deacons, and peasants that they should not assume the knightly belt to any extent, and those who have already assumed it should be banished from military service by the judge of the province.") *LL,* 2. 185.

In the dispensation statement under Frederick II, we read: "nostris constitutionibus caveatur, quod milites fieri nequeant, qui de genere militari non nascuntur." ("Let it be decreed by our ordinances that those who are not born of a knightly family should not be able to become knights.")

10. *Gesta Friderici II,* 13: "inferioris conditionis juvenes, vel quoslibet contemptibilium etiam mechanicarum artium opifices, quos caeterae gentes ab honestioribus et liberioribus studiis tanquam pestem propellunt, ad militiae cingulum vel dignitatum gradus assumere non dedignan-

tur." ("They do not think that young men of the lower class and craftsmen of the contemptible, even mechanical arts, whom other nations banish like the plague from the more honorable and freer pursuits, are worthy to assume the belt of military service and the ranks of offices.")

According to Daniel, *De la Milice Française,* p. 33, in the *Ligurinus,* Gunther, on the other hand, has the emperor act in this way: "Utque suis omnem depellere finibus hostem posset (possit), et armorum patriam virtute tueri Quoslibet ex humili vulgo, quod Gallia foedum Judicat, accingi gladio concedit equestri." ("And so that he might be able to repel all of the enemy from his territory and to guard the country by strength of arms, he granted that all of the low populace, which France judges hideous, to be girded with a knight's sword.")

Had the *Ligurinus* itself not been preserved, this passage would appear completely puzzling to us—and so it should serve us (especially old historians and classical philologists) as a warning as to how seriously and how easily one can be led into error by a second-hand source. Daniel, for example, whose work in other respects is quite thorough, slipped up for once here and ascribed to the emperor what Gunther actually has the Italians doing (Book II, verse 151 ff.); here too, then, he simply adheres to his source. The "*Gallia*" in his verses, in keeping with the well-known linguistic usage of the Middle Ages, includes Germany also.

11. Curzon, *Rules of the Templars* (*La règle du temple*), Chaps. 337, 431, 586.

12. Vetus auctor de beneficiis, 1. 4: "rustici et mercatores et omnes qui non sunt ex homine militari ex parti patris et avi jure careant beneficiali." (The old author on benefices, 1. 4: "peasants, merchants, and all who are not the sons of a knight by their father and grandfather should abstain from the beneficial oath.")

13. Concerning the original meaning, see Waitz, 8: 117.

14. Schröder, *Deutsche Rechtsgeschichte,* p. 430, believes the distinction between knights (as a result of the dubbing ceremony) and squires (*Knappen*) had come into force only since the thirteenth century but had never actually attained a legal significance.

This line of thought is too specifically juridical. The dubbing, as such, did not have, it is true, a directly legal effect, but only as the result of such an act could the distinction become fixed which finally led to the formation of the petty nobility.

15. *M.G. LL,* 2. 103. 10: "Si miles adversus militem pro pace violata aut aliqua capitali causa duellum committere voluerit, facultas pugnandi ei non concedatur, nisi probare possit, quod antiquitus ipse cum par-

entibus suis natione legitimus miles existat." ("If a knight will have wanted to fight a duel against a knight because of a breached peace or any capital offense, the opportunity of fighting should not be granted to him unless he should be able to show that from ancient times he with his parents is by birth a knight of legal status.")

16. The Bamberg Service Law, at the end of the eleventh century, specifies that a *ministerial* whom the bishop does not invest with a fief may enter the service of another but may not allow himself to be bound by a fief "cui vult militet, non beneficiarie, sed libere." ("Let him serve for whom he desires, not as a man enfeoffed but as a freeman.") Such a provision already indicates an extensive weakening of the concept of the unfree condition.

17. The finer distinctions and developments in the various generations and regions are passed over here. Zallinger, in *Ministeriales and Knights* (*Ministeriales und Milites*), 1878, believes, for example, he has proven that in the regions under the Bavarian law the *ministeriales* or serving men (*Dienstmannen*) had in the thirteenth century assumed a special position clearly above the common *milites* and no longer regarded the latter as of equal birth. Only the monarchy and the princes were allowed to have such outstanding, though unfree, serving men (*Dienstmannen*). This latter group later became completely intermingled with the free nobility in the status of lords or property holders.

18. For example, by Guilhiermoz. Against him, E. Mayer, in *Zeitschrift für Rechtsgeschichte, Germanische Abteilung,* 23 (1902): 310. In connection with this controversy, I invite the reader's attention to Chap. 435 of the statutes of the Knights Templars: "One does not ask a knight if he is servant or slave of no man, for since he says that he is a knight by birth, of a legal marriage, if he is truthful, he is by his very nature free." In Germany this condition could not have been met.

19. Even if it should be correct, as Böheim in *Manual of Weapons* (*Handbuch der Waffenkunde*), p. 12, claims, that around the year 1400 there took place a lightening of the protective equipment, nevertheless that would only have been a momentary trough in the constantly rising tide. But the fact itself is doubtful and in any case not yet fully established. Böheim himself says shortly thereafter, p. 14, that at the start of the fifteenth century the protective arms were strengthened.

20. Baltzer is quite correct about this, on p. 52 ff. If in the meantime an enumeration by helmets (*galea*) also appears, that follows the same direction as the general development but does not directly bring it on. The account mentioned by Baltzer on p. 56, to the effect that knights, in order to fight more easily, had taken off their armor, is explained cor-

rectly by Köhler as being not for the purpose of fighting but for the pursuit. Even so, I would prefer to regard this account not as a historic fact, but as "trimming." The first use of *"dextrariis coopertis"* ("covered war-horses") was found by Köhler (3. 2. 44) in the year 1238.

21. Giraldus Cambrensis, *Expugnatio Hibernica* (*The Conquest of Ireland*), *Opera* 5. 395. "Cum illa nimirum armatura multiplici sellisque recurvis et altis difficile descenditur, difficilius ascenditur, difficillime cum opus est pedibus itur." ("Certainly with that multiple armor and a high curved saddle it was difficult to dismount, more difficult to mount, and most difficult to go on foot when necessary.") The author died about 1220.

22. Köhler, 3. 2. 81. From the statutes of the knightly orders it is clear that, wherever it is a question of knights with several horses (*"equitaturis"*), this means those horses which the knight himself rides— just as, today, the cavalry officer has several mounts—and not, for example, those horses which he provides for his followers. See Curzon, *La règle du temple*, Chap. 77, p. 94. *Statutes of the Knights Hospitalers*, Chaps. 59 and 60; in Prutz, *Cultural History of the Crusades* (*Kulturgeschichte der Kreuzzüge*), p. 601. *Statutes of the Teutonic Knights*, Perlbach, p. 98.

23. Baltzer, p. 59. According to Köhler, 3. 2. 77, Viollet-le-Duc is said to have claimed that protective covering was not placed on knights' steeds until the end of the thirteenth century.

24. Waitz, 8:123, says correctly: "Of course, there was never a complete lack of foot soldiers, only that they were employed mostly in defensive situations . . . or in a war where everybody who could bear arms was used, whereas they participated only exceptionally in army expeditions."

25. Ennen and Eckertz, *Sources for the History of the City of Cologne* (*Quellen zur Geschichte der Stadt Köln*), 4. 488. 560.

26. Roth, *Dignity of the Knight* (*Ritterwürde*), p. 98. Suger, too, in the description of the battle of Brémule in 1119, uses the expression that King Henry "milites armatos ut fortius committant, pedites deponit." ("He placed the foot soldiers in reserve so that the armored knights might engage more bravely.") The *Gesta Francorum* (*Deeds of the Franks*), Chap. 6, on the battle of Dorylaeum in 1097: "Pedites prudenter et citius extendunt tentoria, milites eunt viriliter obviam iis." ("The foot soldiers skillfully and rather quickly cocked their crossbows and the knights courageously attacked them" [the Turks]). Fulcher, p. 393: "milites sciebant effici pedites." ("The knights knew how to become dismounted combatants"), (1098). Likewise, in the report on the battle of Ascalon in 1099: "quinque milia militum et quindecim milia peditum" ("5,000 knights and

15,000 foot"). Gervasius Dorobernesis, *Chronica de rebus anglicis* (Gervasius of Canterbury, *Chronicles of English History*) for the year 1138: "milites et pedites" ("knights and foot troops"). Also *Gesta Consulum Andegavensium* (*Deeds of the Counts of Anjou*), *Recueil des Histoires des Gaules* (*Collection of Histories of the Gauls*), 11. 265. Pope Innocent IV to Cardinal Reiner in 1243 (Huill. Bréholles, 6. 131): "cum pro defensione civitatis militia minus necessaria videatur, pedites autem utiliores esse noscantur." ("Whereas a band of knights is less necessary for the defense of a city, foot soldiers are known, however, to be more useful.")

27. Zallinger, *Ministeriales und Milites,* p. 4: "The expression *miles* is used in the original sources in the most varied senses and serves alternatively in the course of time as the normal indication of individual knightly classes, according to whether the importance of the knightly way of life or of knightly birth might appear as particularly characteristic or determining for a class. Thus, it is frequently found in an earlier period with the sense of a free vassal, whereas later it is used predominantly for the unfree knight. Furthermore, by *miles* is meant particularly the man who has already been knighted, in contrast to the squire who is simply of knightly birth."

Waitz, 5: 436, gives a series of citations from which it can be concluded that in the older period the *ministeriales* and the unfree warriors in general, as well as the free ones, were designated as *milites*. He then continues: "The royal chancellery distinguishes between *miles* and *serviens*," but he does not touch on the decisive question as to how long this distinction had been in effect, whether any contrary examples are to be found, and on how broad a basis or how long this usage was also observed in the chronicles.

Köhler, Vol. I, Section IX, claims that in Spain and Italy the light horsemen also were called *milites* over an extended period, whereas in France and Germany from the twelfth century on the expression *miles* had the exclusive meaning of knight.

Fulcher, *Historia Hierosolymitana* (*History of the Jerusalem Campaign*), 2: 31 (Mignet. 155, p. 886), recounts concerning the battle of Ramleh: "Milites nostri erant quingenti exceptis illis qui militari nomine non censebantur tamen equitantes. Pedites vero nostri non amplius quam duo milia aestimabantur." ("Our knights were 500, except those who were not counted of knightly rank but ride horses. Our foot in fact was estimated at not more than 2,000.")

Frederick II had promised the pope to maintain 1,000 *milites* in Palestine for two years at his own expense, and he sent Hermann von Salza, the grand master, to Germany to recruit them. In his letter of 6 December 1227 appears: "Misimus magistrum domus Theutonicorum pro militibus solidandis, sed in optione sua potentem, viros eligere strenuos et pro meritis personarum ad suam prudentiam stipendia polliceri." ("We sent the master of the house of the Germans to hire knights, but having the power in his choice to select strong men and to promise pay at his discretion according to the merits of the individuals") It is difficult to imagine that Hermann, in carrying out this mission, limited himself strictly to men who had already been knighted or that he knighted the recruits who had not yet been so elevated. Rather, it must be assumed that he took, even for heavy mounted service, qualified soldiers. The word *miles,* therefore, is not to be taken here in its strictest sense.

28. The quotations are in Waitz, 5: 400, Note 5.

Guilhiermoz, p. 429, Note 41 says: "We know that in the Merovingian and Carolingian periods the high officers of the palace, including those who had the most unwarlike responsibilities, were given military commands in time of war," and he presents evidence thereof. It is more correct to express this idea, as we have done, in the opposite way: not that possessors of peacetime positions received military command positions, but that warriors were placed even in the most peace-oriented posts, except those held by ecclesiastics.

29. Gustav Roethe, *German Heroes (Deutsches Heldentum),* address given in Berlin, 1906. G. Schade, publisher.

30. Köhler, 3. 2. 123, seems to me to present this correctly.

31. Köhler, 3: 91, speaks of an order of Louis IX prohibiting the squire (*écuyer*) from wearing body armor, hood, or arm bands. For this point, he relies on Daniel, *Milice française,* 1: 394, where nothing of this sort is to be found. It appears that he meant the passage in Vol. I, p. 286, where Daniel, on the basis of a treatment by Ducange, cites a ceremonial tourney from the period of Louis IX, wherein the squires were supposed to wear no trousers of mail, no covering of mail over the bacinet, and no "bracheres" (I believe that by this word he means brassards or sleeves of mail.)—Consequently, this has to do only with tournaments. In war, the idea of decreasing artificially the effectiveness of the armor because of class jealousy would simply appear to be too absurd.

Köhler, 3. 2. 67, is also in error when he concludes (citing Niedner and Alwin Schulz), from the *Partenopter* of Konrad of Würzburg, v. 5225 ff., that the squire was not allowed to wear the sword on a sword belt, but like a merchant on his saddle, since his lady had begged him not to buckle it on: "ê sie, daz viel reine wîp ze ritter in gemachete" ("before she, the very pure lady, made him a knight").

32. *Chronicon Hanoniese (Chronicle of Hainaut),* M.G., 21. 552, says

of a count of Hainaut that he joined the king of France "cum 110 militibus electis et 80 servientibus equitibus loricatis in propriis expensis venit et ibi et in reditu in propriis expensis semper fuit." ("He came there with 110 selected knights and eighty sergeants as armored horsemen at his own expense and on his return it was always at his own expense.")

Köhler's citation, 3. 2. 39, from Gislebert *SS.*, 21. 520 is incorrect. The same Gislebert reports on p. 522 that Baldwin of Hainaut in 1172 came to the assistance of his uncle Henry of Luxembourg "in 340 militibus et totidem servientibus lauricatis et 1,500 clientibus peditibus electis" ("in 340 knights and just as many armored sergeants and 1,500 selected men-at-arms on foot").

33. We even find cases where men of knightly birth disdained receiving the ceremonial knighting and had to be forced to it by their lords. Count Baldwin of Flanders announced in 1200 that the son of a knight who had not become a knight by age twenty-five was to be regarded as a peasant. In France, in 1293, it was required, under penalty of punishment, by the twenty-fourth year of those noblemen ("nobiles saltem ex parte patris": "nobles at least on their father's side") who had 200 pounds of income from their property, 160 of it as inheritance. Guilhiermoz, pp. 231, 477. In Zurich this was required by the thirtieth year. Cited in Köhler, 3. 2. 65. In the thirteenth century, the English kings made a fiscal measure of it.

34. Köhler, 3. 2. 6 and 3. 2. 135, claims that the city knights did not count in the warrior class because they did not belong to a vassal group, were not vassals or *ministeriales.* That is conceptually false; one can be a warrior without being an enfeoffed vassal.

35. Roth, *Ritterwürde,* p. 197. Strangely enough, the raising to the nobility did not come about in France until the end of the thirteenth century. In 1271 Philip III raised a goldsmith to the nobility. Warnkönig and Stein, *French Political and Legal History (Französische Staats- und Rechtsgeschichte),* 1: 250. Daniel, *Milice française,* 1: 74.

36. The last quotations are from von Wedel, *Germany's Knighthood (Deutschlands Ritterschaft).*

37. Otto von Freisingen, *Deeds of Frederick II (Taten Friedrichs II.),* Chap. 18: "At ille, cum se plebejum diceret, in eodemque ordine velle remanere, sufficere sibi conditionem suam." ("But he, since he said he was a commoner and wanted to remain in the same rank, and his own class was enough for him. . . .") In the *Ligurinus,* 2. 580, the story is recounted in the following way:

Strator erat de plebe quidem nec nomine multum
Vulgato, modica in castris mercede merebat.

(There was a common groom, to be sure not a man of well-known name,
And he worked for small wages in the castle.)

Frederick wants to give him (v. 610)

titulos et nomen equestre
Armaque, cornipedesque feros, cultusque nitentes.
(titles and knightly name
And arms, wild horses, and beautiful clothes.)

38. According to Guilhiermoz, *Essai sur l'origine de la noblesse française*, p. 372. As a precursor of this formula, Guilhiermoz cites a letter from Pope Zacharias in the year 747 to the mayor of the palace and later king, Pepin, in which he says: "Laymen and warriors have as their calling the defense of the land, priests the giving of counsel and praying." The pope does not mention the people, the common mass, at all. They form, in the sources of that day, the unwarlike, unarmed species ("imbelle, inerme vulgus"), which the warriors are to protect like cattle from the wolves.

39. Rust, "The Training of the Knight in the Old French Epic" ("Die Erziehung des Ritters in der altfranzösischen Epik"), Berlin dissertaion, 1888, adds nothing new.

40. Eodem anno (1178) rex Angliae pater transfretavit de Normannia in Angliam, & apud Wodestocke fecit Gaufridum filium suum, Comitem Britanniae, militem: qui statim post susceptionem militaris officii transfretavit de Anglia in Normanniam, et in confinibus Franciae & Normanniae militaribus exercitiis operam praestans gaudebat se bonis militibus aequiparari. Et eo magis ac magis probitatis suae gloriam quaesivit, quo fratres suos, Henricum videlicet regem, & Richardum Comitem Pictavis in armis militaribus plus fiorere cognovit. Et erat his mens una, videlicet, plus caeteris posse in armis: scientes, quod ars bellandi, si non praeluditur, cum fuerit necessaria non habetur. Nec potest athleta magnos spiritus ad certamen afferre, qui nunquam suggilatus est. Ille qui sanguinem suum vidit; cuius dentes crepuerunt sub pugno; ille qui supplantatus aduersarium toto tulit corpore, nec proiecit animum proiectus; qui quotiens cecidit, contumacior surrexit, cum magna spe descendit ad pugnam. Multum enim adiicit sibi virtus lacessita; fugitiva gloria est mens subiecta terrori. Sine culpa vincitur oneris immensitate, qui ad portandam sarcinam etsi impar, tamen devotus occurrit. Bene solvuntur sudoris praemia, ubi sunt templa Victoriae.

Hoveden, ed. Stubbs, 2: 166. According to Stubbs, the maxims are all from Seneca.

41. See Rabanus Maurus below in the chapter "Theory," Book IV.

42. The preceding citations are from von Wedel, *Deutschlands Ritterschaft,* and Alwin Schultz, *The Courtly Life (Das höfische Leben),* 1: 170.

43. Cited in Guilhiermoz, *Essai sur l'origine de la noblesse française,* p. 433, Note 60.

44. Roth von Schreckenstein, *The Knightly Dignity and the Knightly Class (Ritterwürde und Ritterstand),* p. 167, as taken from Ennodius.

45. Nithard, 3: 6.

46. Alwin Schultz, *Das höfische Leben,* 2: 108.

47. There are two thorough and fruitful source studies on tournaments: F. Niedner, *The German Tournament in the Twelfth and Thirteenth Centuries (Das deutsche Turnier im 12. und 13. Jahrhundert),* Berlin, 1881, and Becker, *Armed Games (Waffenspiele),* Düren Program, 1887.

48. 24 July 1230. *Huill. Bréholles,* 3: 202. Only fragments of this document have survived.

49. *Konstanzer Chronik.* Mone, *Collected Sources (Quellensammlung),* 1: 310.

50. Roth von Schreckenstein, *Ritterstand,* p. 661.

51. Rahewin, III, Chap. 19.

52. Otto Morena, p. 622. 1160 on the Adda. In 1161, before Milan, the duke of Bohemia and the landgrave of Thuringia on one occasion refused obedience to the emperor and left him to move alone into battle.

53. Cited in Guilhiermoz, p. 358.

54. In the Templars' statutes it was expressly forbidden for a knight to strike servants who were in service through piety (Chap. 51). It was permissible to strike a slave (*esclaf*) with one's stirrup leather when it was deserved, but it was forbidden to injure or maim him or place him in neck irons without higher authority (Chap. 336).

55. According to Rahewin, Book III. See Elsner, *The Army Regulations of Frederick I of the Year 1158 (Das Heergesetz Friedrichs I. vom Jahre 1158),* Program of the Matthias Gymnasium in Breslau, 1882.

56. Hälschner, *Prussian Punitive Law (Preussisches Strafrecht),* 3: 212.

57. *Continuatio Reginonis (Continuation of Regino)* for the year 920: "Multi enim illis temporibus, etiam nobiles, latrociniis insudabant." ("In those times many in fact, even the nobles, engaged in robbery.") Further citations are to be found in Baldamus, *The Military System under the later Carolingians (Das Heerwesen unter den späteren Karolingern),* p. 18 ff.

58. See my review of this book in the *Zeitschrift für Preussische Geschichte und Landeskunde,* 17: 702.

59. *M.G. SS.*, 222.

60. From this account it can also be seen how transitory and uncertain the meaning of the word *"miles"* still was at that time. In the first instance, where it is a question of the bishop's contenting himself with a few *"militibus,"* it is obvious that "knights" are meant. Later, where the author wants to distinguish between knights and the common levy of troops conducting the siege, he calls the former *"armati"*—"heavily armed ones"—and the latter *"milites gregarii."* Since they were often more than 1,000 strong, it is impossible that they could all have been professional warriors. Apparently, the bishop had his own military organization reinforced by the militia (*Landsturm*), the most useful peasants and peasants' sons. The same situation has already been reported to us, in fact, concerning the Burgundian King Gundobad and the king of the Goths, Totila (Vol. II, p. 391).

61. Baltzer, p. 7.

Chapter II

Military Aspects of Knighthood

In keeping with the progress of our studies to date, in the first and second books of this volume, we have observed the medieval military system principally from the viewpoint of the history of military organization and have sought to bring it into focus in a series of campaigns and battles.

Then, in the preceding first chapter of Book III, we have treated the unique class differentiation in knighthood, and in doing so we have entered a period in which the military system and military actions became significantly more complicated than previously. The transition was gradual, but the difference was nevertheless so great that we were able to divide the Middle Ages into distinct periods. At this point, it is also appropriate to insert a general study to establish a theory on the combat methods and strategy of knighthood. This task, of course, was not only already touched on in the preceding chapter but was also basically accomplished, since the status of the knightly class was indeed based on its method of combat. But now the question must be approached in its entire breadth from the opposite viewpoint, that of the existing class formation, and it must be followed through in detail. This is a more difficult task than in the corresponding earlier parts of this work, where certain periods of time and stages of development could easily be separated from one another, definitely isolated, and characterized with certainty. The Middle Ages does not offer such specific partitions.

The partition we have made lies in general in the twelfth century, but characteristics of each of the two periods are at times present in the other, and the development proceeds continuously. Thus, the various centuries can, no doubt, be distinguished from one another, but still not in such a manner that they can be definitely separated from each other. Through the entire Middle Ages in the broadest sense, from the *Völker-*

wanderung until almost the end of the fifteenth century, the basic features remained the same. The last real knightly battle of which we have a thorough description, the battle of Montl'héry between Charles the Bold and Louis XI, in 1465, could have been fought in a very similar way between Emperor Henry IV and his counterkings, or even between Clovis and Theodoric. For a while I wondered whether I should not put aside chronological considerations and present the very lively and clear account of the battle of Montl'héry, which we have received from the pen of Comines, who personally participated, in direct conjunction with the battles under Emperor Henry IV, in order to show how closely the events of the fifteenth century resembled those of the eleventh century. In the end, I did not do so because there are, after all, differences in the details that will only become clear in the course of our observations. Nevertheless, I would like to recommend that the reader jump ahead at this point and read the chapter on the battle of Montl'héry, in order to have the full impression of the similarity and to gain thereby a better perspective of the events of the earlier Middle Ages that have come to us in a form that is less realistic and less lively.

In addition to the similarity of basic features of the military system in the entire Middle Ages, we naturally also find a number of differences, variations, and special formations that show us quite different pictures, so that the similarity almost disappears in the fullness of the events. But we must seek to grasp it. We shall go about our task by keeping the twelfth and thirteenth centuries in view but with the idea in the back of our minds that many things were also similar earlier, or, on the other hand, remained so up into the fifteenth century, despite the progress toward the mercenary system and in weaponry. Where the boundaries lie is to be found, to the extent that this is at all possible, in the individual case from the individual accounts of battles and campaigns and from studies that have preceded this chapter or will follow. In considering the individual points, we must remember again and again to take into consideration the special conditions in the Crusades and their reaction on the Occident.

As we must now begin anew, we recognize that Charlemagne's warriors and those of Otto the Great were predominantly horsemen with good but not extremely heavy armor protection, who also fought on foot under certain circumstances. There were practically no foot soldiers, as such, or marksmen. After this warriorhood became more sharply differentiated by combat branches from the eleventh century on, the question arises as to how the various weapons cooperated in battle. Two basic formations were possible: the forming of each arm in itself into larger units, such as heavy horsemen, light horsemen, dismounted marksmen, dismounted close-combat weapons; or the grouping of supporting arms around the principal arm, the knights.

Both types occurred, but the first one only as a matter of expedience. The dominant form in principle was the second, the arranging of supporting weapons around the knights. This point is clear in the battle accounts, and it follows from the nature of the weapons. None of the three other types could compete with the principal arm, the knights, and each of them would have been lost at the moment in which it came into contact with knights under equal and normal conditions.

The horseman mounted on a light horse with light armor or even almost no armor at all could not afford to risk a clash with the horseman on a heavy, armored horse, covered from head to foot with impenetrable armor.

The marksman armed with the bow or crossbow might hope that his missile would hit the charging knight or especially his horse in an unprotected or weaker spot in his armor and put him out of action. But the chances of doing so were rather slim, and the possibility of launching several bolts or arrows against an attacker was seldom used, since the marksman did not wait until the attacking horseman was quite near, which would have meant almost certain death for him, but sought to save himself while a certain interval still gave him hope of doing so. Consequently, a body of dismounted marksmen, positioned alone in the open field, without some kind of special protection in the terrain, could not oppose knights. We shall treat in a special chapter the particular phenomena that the Anglo-French wars of the later Middle Ages brought to a head in this area.

The Occident itself did not develop mounted archers. This arm was encountered first of all among the Hungarians, but then very particularly so in the Crusades. We shall come back later to the special advantages and disadvantages of these weapons. Let us only note here that they cannot compete in general against knights with lance and sword.

The greatest chance of standing up to the knight lies with the foot soldier armed with a close-combat weapon, who is cool and agile enough to avoid the shock of his opponent and then attack him or his horse from the side. But this applies only in the case where one individual is opposing another. Rather large units can close ranks and ward off with their extended spears a penetration by the knights. But if the unit does not hold very firmly together, or if there develops at any point an opening into which the knights penetrate, the foot soldiers are lost. If a unit really holds fast against knights, then the question arises as to whether the knights can bring up marksmen. Roman cohorts in such a situation would have gone over to the offensive—the only means of finding their salvation. Medieval foot soldiers, however, could not do that (action of this kind is reported only occasionally, as a special exception), because this would require a cohesiveness and a training in closed movements which they did not have. In those cases where the steadfastness of foot soldiers in medieval battles is especially praised, their action normally did not go beyond a defensive repelling of knights. For an independent offensive of nonknightly foot soldiers against knights, I find in the entire Middle Ages, before the period of the Hussites and the Swiss, only one or two certain examples: the battle of Courtrai, in 1302, where the Flemish cities were victorious over the French; and perhaps the battle of Bannockburn, in 1314, where the Scots were victorious over Edward II of England. Everything else that foot soldiers did, whether in battle as marksmen, or in mixed combat, or in passive resistance in a closed mass, remained within the sphere of a supporting arm.

This is the truly decisive factor of the period, at which we have already arrived a number of times and to the importance of which we must point again and again. In Rome the horseman was not considered the equal of the legionary ("nequaquam par habetur": "by no means is he considered equal") in combat.[1] In the Middle Ages, it was said: "One hundred horses are worth as much as 1,000 men on foot."[2] The foot soldier of the Middle Ages was only an auxiliary, on the same basis as the light horseman or the marksman.

Under normal circumstances, the supporting arms are best used in such a way as to give maximum support to the effect of the principal arm, which, of course, brings about the final decision. They can exercise this effect to a certain degree from the flanks, but they are most effective in the form of mixed combat, which is already known to us from antiquity. Therefore, since the formation of the various combat branches, this was the actual, normal combat form of the Middle Ages.

Before we observe more closely this mixed combat form in its varied possibilities, let us note the relationship between the tactical and institutional developments—in other words, the origin and the social character of the supporting arms.

The supporting arms had a triple root. First, they were those parts of the ancient warrior class that did not move up to true knighthood but developed in another direction. Second, among the city burghers with their awakening independence, new elements entered the warrior class, fighting as spearmen and marksmen. And third, they came from the retinue, the train of the earlier warrior, the squires (apprentice knights), and mounted serving men, who had not yet become combatants before the twelfth century. Even at that time, they were not completely un-armed, and they were also occasionally used for secondary military pur-poses, like the Greek *psiloi* (unarmored light infantry) and the ancient Roman light troops, but they were not to be counted as actual warriors in open battle and did not follow their lord into the fight. With the growing distinctions within knighthood itself, this situation changed. While the heavily armored man was a powerful warrior, he was still so limited that he could very well use the support of a more lightly armored man in battle also. If those were special types of troop units, then the same could be said of the serving men from the knight's retinue, especially the shield-bearer. Since we find that the name of the shield-bearer, *scutarius* (from which, the words *escuyer* and *esquire*), was often applied to warriors of lower rank, we can probably conclude that this combat branch de-veloped from both elements, the original noncombatants in the knight's retinue and those parts of the ancient warrior class that did not rise to true knighthood. The former became combatants, while the latter re-mained what they had been or more likely moved farther back as they were given for their equipment only whatever was left over. The dif-ference between these two elements appears smaller if we understand that the knight was never an individual but rather the follower of a lord, the member of a larger group. It was up to the feudal lord to decide whether to keep the common warriors together more for his own use, or to assign them to individual knights as shield-bearers and combat support men.

In antiquity there was frequent mention of the mixed combat of horsemen and foot soldiers. The Boeotians used this combat method, and Caesar improvised a special unit for this purpose before the battle of Pharsalus.[3] Vegetius (3. 16) states that even the best horsemen could not hold their own against such a mixed unit. Caesar pictures the ancient German mixed combat for us in *Bellum Gallicum,* 1. 48: "There were 6,000 horsemen," he recounted of Ariovistus' army, "and there was the same number of very agile and courageous foot soldiers, each one of which had been selected from the entire army by a horseman for his protection. The two men fought as one. The horsemen moved back to the foot soldiers, and the latter hastened to the assistance of the horse-men when they were in a perilous situation. If a mounted man fell seriously wounded from his horse, the foot soldiers surrounded him to protect him. If a quick advance or a hasty withdrawal became necessary, the foot soldiers, as a result of their training, developed such speed that by holding on to the horses' manes they could keep pace with the horses."

Medieval combat cannot have taken place in just this manner. The knights were much too heavy and too cumbersome, and the foot soldiers had very little training and did not have the relationship of comrades with the knights but were subordinates or even strangers. Nevertheless, the cooperation was similar.

The classical citation for the nature and the sense of knightly mixed combat is found in a speech made to his warriors, according to Saba Malaspina, by Charles of Anjou before the battle of Benevento in 1266. The king advised his men to seek to hit the horses more than the men, saying that, once they were caused to fall, the foot soldiers would dispose of the knights, who would be immobile in their heavy armor. For that reason, every knight should have one or two foot soldiers accompany him, and if no others were available, they should use mercenaries, for as battle-hardened men they knew how to strike down horses as well as dismounted riders.[4]

The first example of the participation in this manner by foot soldiers in mounted combat is given by the historian of the Crusades, William of Tyre, in his account of the battle of Merdy-Sefer in 1126. Later we find similar accounts quite often, for example, in the battle of Arsuf (1191), in the battle of Bouvines (1214), and in the battle of Cortenuova (1237), in which the shield-bearers (*"armigeri militum"*: "squires of the knights") captured the fallen enemies and tied them up.

The marksmen ran in front of the knights or stayed off to the side of them and sought as skirmishers to cause the enemy as much damage as possible before the actual clash. On one occasion (1264) we find an account of a case of mutual support in the Prussian War.[5] Henry Monte, the leader of the Natangi, was fighting with the knights before Königsberg. With his spear, he wounded a knight, Henry Ulenbusch, who was just drawing his crossbow (*balistam*). A foot soldier (*famulus*) of Ulenbusch wounded Monte with his small spear ("cum modica lancea"), so that Monte had to withdraw. To be sure, this case is not typical in that the knight himself was acting as a marksman. But we find a theoretical observation on the value and the cooperation of the various weapons in the work of an English chronicler, Giraldus Cambrensis, who recounted the conquest of Ireland by Henry II (around 1188).[6]

He says that the Gallic method of warfare, under which he also understands the methods brought to England by the Normans, although it was preferred in his country, was very different from that of the Irish and the

Welsh. For in England they sought an open plain, while the Irish and Welsh chose broken terrain; in the one case the field, and in the other the forest. The one side protected itself with armor, while the other did not want to be burdened. This one side was victorious through steadfastness, and the other through its agility. In the plain, the complete, heavy armor, both doublet and iron, served as protection, but in narrow areas, whether forest or swamp, where the foot soldier gets along better than the horseman, the lightly armed man had a far greater advantage. For against unarmored men, who always either conquer or flee at the first clash, light weapons are also sufficient. But if one wishes to pursue them through narrow, unlevel terrain, one is necessarily impeded by his heavy arms. For with his complicated armor, seated in his high, arched saddle, the horseman can mount or dismount only with difficulty, and it is most difficult of all for him to move on foot.

Consequently, in all the Irish and Welsh campaigns, the Irish and the Welsh, who had grown strong in their local feuds, were best. In Irish battles, archers were always supposed to be assigned to the knights. For if the Irish attack the heavily armored men with stones and escape from them through their agility, and then come back, one must be in a position to answer them with arrows.

Least of all can we recognize from the sources how the cooperation of the heavy, fully armored knights with lightly armed horsemen took place in combat. In small skirmishes, where only a few knights were present, no difficulties would result from such cooperation, but the larger the groups became, the more the supporting weapons limited the space available to the knights and the less helpful they could be for them. To be sure, the regulations of the Order of Knights Templars (Chap. 179) prescribed that when the knights went into battle, a part of the squires was to lead the packhorses to the rear, while another group under the control of the gonfalonier was to follow the lords into the battle. But that too much was expected in having the insufficiently armored squires dash into the knightly battle is shown in other chapters (172, 419), where every brother knight and fully armored man who withdrew from the battle as long as the banner was waving was threatened with disgraceful expulsion from the order, whereas the unarmored man was given the option, when his conscience told him that he could neither help nor hold out, to withdraw without reproach. Since that was no doubt the most frequent case, the statutes of the Teutonic order did not have the rule that the squires were to follow into the battle, but they prescribed, rather, that the squires were to assemble under a banner and wait until their lords returned from the battle.[7] The little assistance that their participation could offer in the battle was offset by the danger that if they had to withdraw under pressure, a panic could ensue which might also seize the knights. In every respect, foot soldiers could accomplish more and cause less harm. They could help their lord in many ways, were less exposed to the danger of being directly attacked by the enemy knights, and could withdraw and run away without infecting the knights.[8]

At numerous places in his work, General Köhler holds that in the thirteenth century there were not yet any mounted armed servants in the retinue of a knight, or at any rate, if any were present, they were not combatants. In this respect, Köhler goes too far. These men were undoubtedly there and always had been in larger or smaller numbers. They were also combatants in that they were used for secondary purposes, armed foraging, laying waste enemy areas, and the like. They were also real combatants in smaller fights, where they supported the knights. But the practice of having them regularly follow the knights into battle developed only very gradually.

Toward the middle of the fourteenth century, the assignment of individual support branches to the individual knight finally led to the formation of the concept of the *"gleve"* or "lance," by which term one understood a knight with his accompanying men. The individual knight, of course, still appeared in combat, and he was called a "one-man team," but as a general rule, the strength of a force was counted by *gleves.* Of course, that was a very indefinite concept. There could be as many as ten men in a *gleve,* both horsemen and foot soldiers, but once again this is a new proof as to how strongly the knight was regarded as the decisive arm, namely, that the strength of armies was reckoned by *gleves.* Whether the individual *gleve* numbered more or fewer quasi-combatants was not particularly taken into consideration. The knight in the *gleve,* on the other hand, was not only the knight in the strictest sense of the word, the knight by birth, the nobleman who has been dubbed a knight, but he might also be a nobleman who was not yet admitted to knighthood, as well as a soldier in knightly equipment. The stricter the social distinctions became and the further the formation of a lesser nobility progressed, the smaller the number of true knights became. While many descendants of warriors who had gone into the field as "sergeants" and "knechts" in the twelfth and thirteenth centuries now entered the noble class, many who had not maintained themselves in their fiefs moved downward into the mass of common people. Consequently, the group of true knights always needed to be filled out with soldiers who, as selected, proven men, together with the knights could accomplish more or less the same deeds. Since the word "knight," which in the twelfth century had not yet completely lost its flexibility, was now quite strictly limited to the true knight, the nobleman, the entire mounted levy was now referred to by the expression "knights and men" ("Ritter und Knechte").

The theory of mixed combat, as we find it confirmed in the sources since 1126 but which we can undoubtedly assume to have existed since time immemorial, wherever a variety of weapons was at hand, now allowed numerous special arrangements for the composition of the arms, whether by type and occasion, or in accordance with special concepts and commands of the leaders. The progress of combat itself led to a variety of forms and compositions.

We find the arrangement in which the marksmen precede the horsemen, seek to cause the enemy the greatest possible damage before the clash, and at the last minute withdraw between the knights' horses, which have left very wide intervals between them. It is understandable that this assistance was used but was not considered to be of decisive value. Battles were sometimes fought without it, for the time in which the marksmen did their work could only be very short and their success could not be very great. On the other hand, the approach ride of the mounted men was somewhat impeded whenever the marksmen tended to group together by chance here and there, or did not withdraw fast enough through the intervals and around the flanks.

The foot soldiers armed with a spear probably moved out in advance only when there was a question of removing an obstacle, such as a fence. In general, they followed the knights and became involved in the battle from the rear. A case such as that in the battle on the Elster (1080), where part of the knights dismounted in order to approach the enemy from a side that was impassable for horsemen, was, of course, a completely different situation and does not belong in this context. Aside from such special combinations, the strongest effect that the dismounted spearmen had was when they formed a tight unit and thus provided a refuge and cover for the knights in dangerous moments. I find this function theoretically attributed to foot soldiers for the first time in Vegetius,[9] and then again in Emperor Leo. In his *Tactics* Leo advises (Chap. XIV, para. 20) that if the enemy force is composed of horsemen and one has only a weak contingent of foot soldiers on his own side, one should form this unit 1 to 2 miles behind the horsemen and order the horsemen, if they are thrown back, to withdraw not directly but in a curving movement around these foot soldiers and assemble behind them.[10]

The first practical example of this type of combat seems to be reported in the poem about Robert Guiscard.[11] A quite certain example for the manner of execution as well is provided by the description of the battle of Dorylaeum (1097) in the First Crusade. There, of course, the dismounted combatants may have been for the most part knights who no longer had horses, but we also find this method used quite systematically in the Crusades. Gautier, the chancellor of Prince Roger of Antioch, who has left us very valuable reports, says in his account of the battle of Hab (1119), that the dismounted combatants were drawn up behind three units of horsemen in order to cover them and to be covered by them.[12] They had arrived at this method because the ratio of dismounted men to horsemen was quite different in Syria than in the west, for most of the horses brought from the homeland died during the voyage, and replacements could not easily be found. According to the report of the princes to the pope, which was, of course, greatly exaggerated in all respects, the knights in Antioch had only 100 horses left. It is obvious that the need was very great, since the sources representing daily journals repeatedly mentioned that horses had been taken as booty. In the statutes of the knightly orders, there is frequent mention of horses that were sent from the homeland, the expensive transportation of which would undoubtedly have been spared if there had been enough suitable horses available in Syria. Consequently, in the Crusades, dismounted spearmen played a much more important role than in the Occident, not as a matter of principle or because particularly skillful men were developed there, but as a simple matter of necessity.

It cannot be proven and should not be assumed that this experience had a direct effect on the west, although in the following generations new forces appeared in the theater of military operations. These forces seemed to be well suited to provide the knights assistance of this type—namely, the burghers, and especially those of the Italian communes. But there is really only a single example where one can observe this questionable phenomenon with definite success, the battle of Legnano, which we shall discuss in the special chapter concerning the Hohenstaufen-Italian conflicts.

There is a similar account from the battle of Bouvines (1214), but only as an episode and not the decisive factor, and it is obviously described with poetic hyperbole.[13]

A unique but similar type of action is provided by the battle of Northallerton (1138), where an English militia levy, by placing a number of dismounted knights in the first rank, repelled the charge of a Scotch army, but without finally going over to the offensive itself.

In general, the method remained in which the foot soldiers, either as marksmen or as spearmen, sought to support the knights directly in the mixed combat. An excellent example of how such action could be carried out successfully is offered by the victory of the inhabitants of Strasbourg over their bishop at Hausbergen in 1262.

If squires and foot soldiers without sufficient armor came into the middle of the melee, they were still not necessarily lost. If a knight attacked them, they could run away, as we have seen in the example of the Templars, without forfeiting their honor. But a knight always attacked another knight at first, since only that action could be decisive in the battle, and it therefore became a point of honor. In the battle of Bouvines, 300 light horsemen reportedly attacked the Flemish knights, but the knights did not consider it worth the trouble to move from their position. They struck down the unarmored horses of their opponents and then rode forward to seek out enemy knights and do battle with them. Heelu, who celebrated the battle of Worringen (1288) in song, has a sergeant cry out (v. 4954): "Each man take aim at one of the enemy lords and don't let up until you have struck him dead. If their army was so large that it reached to Cologne, they would still be beaten, once their lords are dead."

As important as the support which the auxiliary arms, especially marksmen and spearmen on foot, occasionally gave to the knights might have seemed, we should not forget that this was still only supporting action. It did not change the basic fact that the knights formed the decisive arm. Whenever we state this thesis, we cannot emphasize too strongly that, according to the medieval viewpoint, the best army, the ideal one in open battle, was always the army composed purely of heavy horsemen. If, despite this preeminence, the auxiliary arms appeared to be increasing constantly in importance, that was only because they were more readily available than the heavy horsemen. Especially in the feuds of the smaller powers, dynasties, and cities, which could provide only a few heavy horsemen and actual knights, the great majority of combatants often consisted of the support arms. But the great decisive battles of the kings seem frequently to have been purely mounted battles, as, for example, Tagliacozzo, Marchfeld, and Göllheim. It even happens quite frequently that an account specifically says that the foot soldiers who were present did not participate in the battle but were left behind.

The question remains as to how the knights themselves were formed for battle. The reports on this point from various battles differ greatly. The Byzantine Emperor Leo, in his *Tactics* (XVIII, para. 88), says of the Franks that they were negligent and without skill, forethought, or caution. Consequently, they also paid no attention to orderly formations, especially among their mounted men. But order and disorder are relative concepts, and just before the foregoing passage the same eminent author reported that the Franks went into battle with their front aligned and in closed formation.[14] Without any kind of orderly formation, neither the Franks nor any of the various peoples that succeeded them would have been able to move their troops to the enemy.

When we read that before his battle with the Hungarians[15] King Henry I gave the order to his Saxons that no one was to try to dash forward with a faster horse ahead of his flanking man, and therefore all clashed with the enemy at the same moment, this is the same thing that the Byzantine emperor reported. It should be regarded not as unusual or an innovation but as renewed emphasis on a regulation which, as logical as it was, was easily and often ignored.

We have also found the same warning above (p. 209) in the work of an Arab military historian. We find the regulation again in the rules of the order of Knights Templars (Chap. 162): "No brother may attack without permission or ride out of his rank" ("Ne nul frère ne doit poindre ne desranger sans congié"). The Teutonic order had a similar regulation.[16]

But good order and uniformity were not natural to knighthood, where everything was based on the individual person, his personal honor, personal fame, and personal courage. On the contrary, the natural trend was for the individual to break out of rank and dash forward. Therefore, completely at odds with King Henry's order, we find quite often in the epics that in the attack a special hero charges ahead to break into the enemy, and his men follow him.[17]

But what is esteemed in poetry is not on that account tactically correct. Therefore, the historic sources, differing from the songs, sometimes praise the fact that an army went into battle in good order, but they often also point out a defeat resulting from a lack of order.[18]

The unit leader or captain whom we occasionally encounter in the epics, and who apparently had the mission of aligning the knights in order, is never found in the actual history.[19] We are told on numerous occasions that knights did not make their attacks like modern cavalry, depending on shock action, but that the rule was to ride forward slowly.[20]

Of course, larger contingents and entire armies had to be divided into sections that were based on the feudal hierarchy, even if they were often quite different in size.[21] We can imagine these units as being either deep or shallow, formed up side by side or in column. Despite the innumerable battle accounts that we have, the sources give very little direct information on these formations. Actually, only a single one is really accurate and detailed, and it is from a period in which so many new factors had already appeared in the conduct of war that we must be very hesitant about drawing direct conclusions from it concerning the High Middle Ages without further study. This was the encounter at Pillenreuth in 1450 between Margrave Albrecht Achilles and the Nurembergers. Gunpowder had already long been in use, and the combat of marksmen with bolts and arrows had also undergone a much stronger development. But the conditions of mounted combat in this encounter were so similar to those of the thirteenth century that we can study in this event a series of characteristic qualities of medieval knightly battles without danger of injecting false concepts.

THE ENCOUNTER AT PILLENREUTH
11 MARCH 1450

This encounter is thoroughly described in a collection of the Nuremberg burgomaster, Erhard Schürstab,[22] who personally participated as commander and also had the best information on the enemy, since a large number of noblemen from Albrecht's retinue were brought into Nuremberg as prisoners.

Albrecht had challenged the Nurembergers by letting it be known that he would fish in their pond at Pillenreuth, two hours south of the city. They were welcome to come and help him catch and eat the fish; he would be waiting for them. The Nurembergers issued the call for a general levy and arrived with 500 horsemen and 4,000 men on foot, armed with crossbows, muskets, and spears.[23] At that time the city had 20,000 inhabitants and was sheltering an additional 9,000 of its rural subjects who had taken refuge from the ravages of war inside the city walls. The city had also taken mercenaries into its service, including the knight Kunz von Kaufungen, who later gained fame as a robber prince, and Heinrich Reuss von Plauen, who was in command of all the Nuremberg forces. The margrave had 500 horsemen.[24]

Let us skip the details of the formation and the battle. The point of interest to us here is the formation of the main units of knights on both sides. Heinrich von Plauen called on the "noble and manly" Heinz Zenger, with four other knights, to form the point. "The five held the point in the first rank." The second rank was formed of seven knights, the third of nine, and the fourth of eleven. Then came the mass of common soldiers, and the last rank was composed of fourteen "honora-

ble men" (patricians) of Nuremberg, "who held the formation together."
The knights of the leading ranks are all specifically named. The unit
numbered 300 men all together. Whether the rearward ranks numbered
eleven or perhaps thirteen or fourteen men is not clear, and this point is
not important. In any case, the unit was between twenty-two and
twenty-five men deep.

Translated into modern terms, the formation would therefore correspond approximately to a regiment of lancer-cuirassiers of three squadrons in line, each squadron four files wide, with the commander and the
captains and the lieutenants at the head and as file closers.

A modern cavalryman who might be told that a colonel led his regiment into combat in this way (for it should be noted that this was not a
march formation but a formation for battle) would undoubtedly reply
that the man belonged either before a court martial or in the madhouse.

This account is so important specifically because the closer we examine
it, the better we can recognize and demonstrate the fundamental difference between cavalry and a group of knights. For the origin of our
evidence guarantees that we are not dealing with a fantasy, and the fact
that we do not have here simply a whim of Heinrich von Plauen is made
clear when we learn in the same source that Margrave Albrecht drew up
his principal unit in the same manner. (In this case, too, the knights in the
individual ranks are specifically named.) In other passages similar formations are reported or prescribed.[25]

The unique aspect of the formation is the narrow front (fourteen files
at most) and the point at the front. Let us observe first of all the narrow
front, which corresponds to the great depth. Let us imagine that the
opponent, on the other hand, with an army of equal strength, formed in
two, or even three or four ranks. Then, in the movement into contact, he
would swing in from both sides against the opposing flanks. The horsemen in the deep column would not be able to swing their horses suddenly from their original direction to face the attacker. They would be
struck in the side by the enemy lances without being able to defend
themselves. Would this loss be offset by advantages provided by the
depth of their formation? With foot soldiers, the depth of the mass
produces a forward pressure which either rolls back or penetrates a
weaker enemy. But this effect does not take place in a mounted unit.
This fact was already known to the ancient theoreticians. Aelian says in
his *Tactics* (Chap. 18, para. 8) that a deep formation of horsemen does
not have the same advantage as a similar formation of foot soldiers, since
the rear ranks of horsemen cannot press the others forward, as the foot
soldiers can. By pressing closely against the men in front of them,

horsemen would not form a single heavy mass. On the contrary, if they tried to press together, they would excite their horses and throw them into confusion.

For the above reasons, modern cavalry regulations prescribe exactly the opposite of the formation of the knights at Pillenreuth. They state:[26] "The line is the only combat formation of cavalry in close order. Therefore, an attack is never made in columns (or at best only as an expedient, where time and space are not available for deployment), since an enemy cavalry unit of equal strength formed in line has the advantage as a result of this formation." "The success of the attack depends primarily on the weight of the shock and the use of cold steel. These weapons can be used by all simultaneously in the linear formation, whereas only a small part of them can be used in column. The line also has the important advantage over a column of equal strength of having the greater width forward, which enables it to envelop the enemy with its extended wings and to attack him in his flanks, his weakest points. Cavalry that is attacked in the flank is just as lost as cavalry that stands in place and awaits the enemy."

Consequently, even if a column like those at Pillenreuth should penetrate the enemy front with its point—and this is not even certain—no advantage is won, since the main part of the regiment, defenseless against the double flanking attack, is destroyed in the meantime.

But a knightly battle is completely different from a modern cavalry battle.

Just as in a modern mounted battle, the winning of the flanks was of special importance in a knightly battle, but it could not be done so easily, because all movements were much slower. The horses were not pressed into a more lively pace until the unit was already very close to the enemy, and even then the advance remained so moderate that a horseman could still turn his steed to face an opponent coming from his flank. The deep column at Pillenreuth was, therefore, not so planned that the mass was to stay in this formation during the battle, a procedure that would make it impossible for the large majority to use their weapons. But it must be assumed that, at the moment of the approach ride, the rearward ranks continuously extended on the right and the left so that the deployment took place, so to speak, during the approach ride and the clash. Contrary to the present situation, that was possible because the movement was so slow, and it was advantageous because, as a result, the close formation of the attack was guaranteed. Certainly it would have been better in theory if the deployment had already been completed in advance, but then it would have been necessary to move forward on a broad front, and that is very difficult. It requires a degree of training and drill which these loose units did not have. An approach ride on a broad front lends itself particularly to the development of intervals, which can become dangerous.

The *Themes for Instruction in Tactics,* which we have already cited, states (p. 46) that the cavalry must be capable of great mobility. "The line does not have this capability, since changes of direction from the line are awkward, and furthermore, passable terrain broad enough for the linear formation can only be found now and then. Therefore, the cavalry needs the column for maneuvering. In addition to greater mobility on the terrain, the column must also offer the fastest and simplest deployment into line." Associated with the fastest possible deployment from the column into line which is required in the foregoing passage are a maneuverability and training that the "knights and men" ("Ritter und Knechte") simply did not have—hence, their approach ride at a slow pace and in a deep column, from which the line was supposed to develop of itself no sooner than the moment of contact.

Now we can also understand the unusual "point." If the unit was drawn up simply in a uniform, deep column, let us say twelve men wide and twenty-five men deep, the first ranks were exposed to the danger of being outflanked at once by an enemy in a somewhat broader formation. But by having each successive rank extend by one man, that man protected the flank of the preceding rank without at the same time being exposed to the same danger himself. But the danger did not extend farther than five or six ranks. At the moment of contact, the following ranks were already automatically flowing over so broadly that they met the enemy flanking movements. If it was desired that the gradual broadening of the column be continued all the way to the rear, then the principal advantages of the narrow formation, the easy and certain control, would again be lost.

The purpose of the approach ride in a deep column, then, is that the whole mass can be brought up to the enemy in this way uniformly drawn up in close formation. The knights in the rear also held firmly in the formation the less dependable common soldiers. Not until they were engaged in the battle itself, or very shortly beforehand, did the mass extend widely enough for the individual to be able to use his weapons. Reducing the first rank to five men had the advantage of allowing the column to be controlled easily, and the gradual broadening provided flank protection for the foremost ranks just as today an overlapping second echelon protects the flanks of the first.

A front deployed in line against such a column would have the disadvantage of being very difficult to control and of meeting the enemy in a loose formation, with intervals. Its advantage, the outflanking capability, would not be effective, since the rearward ranks of the enemy column would constantly be extending, would already be opposing them, and with the slowness of the movements on both sides, would have enough time for this encounter. The only ranks that were really exposed to being flanked were protected by this point formation, which logically led to the extending movement forward of the rearward ranks on right and left.

Modern cavalry is effective as a unified tactical body by means of the tightest possible shock action and with special effect from a flank, since a unit in close formation cannot defend itself from a side attack. The knights' formation in column did not mean a closed shock of special massiveness and strength. It was simply an approach formation from which the combat of individuals then developed.

If that was the unquestionable purpose of the formation at Pillenreuth, the composition of the point seems somewhat too theoretical—one might even say doctrinaire. For it is clear that the two horsemen on the right and left of each rank who overlapped the preceding rank could hardly hold their horses back at a definite horse's length, but rather, at the moment of clash, they would already be in the first rank, to the extent that the varying temperaments and speeds of the horses and the varying degrees of eagerness among the knights permitted the retention of any kind of straight line at all. We can therefore leave aside the point as a disappearing overrefinement in actual practice, with which the contemporaries played, so to speak, for only a short time.[27] The important and decisive point is the approach ride in a deep column (*acies, cuneus,* wedge, point, as they are called in the sources), which stands in the strongest contradiction to cavalry theories.

If we leave aside the decrease in the number of files in the foremost ranks as a point of finesse that was unimportant in practice, there still remains the approach ride in a very deep column. We have found this procedure so well confirmed by the nature of knightly combat that we may assume without further investigation that this practice also held true in the earlier centuries of this epoch.

The formation in column, however, was not the only normal one. The advantage that could be gained through outflanking action with a broader and more shallow formation was always kept in mind, even if not decisive, and we have clear evidence that this polarity was recognized and that on occasion the use of the line could even be preferred to the column. In the battle of Worringen (5 June 1288), Ian von Heelu (v. 4918) tells us that during the move forward Seigneur von Liedekerke shouted out: "The enemy is extending so much to the flanks that, before we know it, we shall be surrounded. It would be good if we should move farther apart and let our unit become more shallow." But Heelu rejects that as a custom in tourneys, which was not suitable for serious combat, and he shows Liebrecht von Dormael, one of the most outstanding knights of Brabant, as representing the opposite viewpoint. When he heard the cry "shallow," he shouted angrily: "Deep, deep and narrow! Each man as close as possible to the next man, and we shall gain honor this day!" Now everybody shouted: "A tight formation! Tight! Close together!"

In the battle of Bouvines (1214), on the other hand, William the Briton tells of a Frenchman who formed all his knights in one rank and said to them: "The field is wide; spread out, so that the enemy will not surround you. It is not proper that one knight use another as his shield."[28]

Finally, as a special characteristic of a broader and more shallow formation, we must note the fact that it alone made possible the cooperation of foot soldiers in mixed combat. If the horsemen moved up in such a tight column as at Pillenreuth, it was impossible for either marksmen or spearmen to support them. They would have been trampled by the horses of their own men. The great mass of the Nuremberg foot troops, even the marksmen, at Pillenreuth followed in their own units quite far behind the horsemen, and they therefore served only as a backup force. If it was desired that foot soldiers actually participate in battle, the horsemen had to be drawn up in a very loose formation, and that occurred automatically when they approached on a broad front. But if they rode forward with a depth of twenty to thirty horses, where everybody then pushed forward, a horseman from the rear would move forward into any opening that was wide enough.[29]

As strong as was the theoretical difference between the formation in a pointed column and the formation in line (*en haye*), both formations could nevertheless exist side by side and could even be used one beside the other in the same battle, since, I repeat, they were only approach formations and not combat formations. Even when the approach was made in a deep column, it can be assumed that at the start of the fight the column extended into a line, because each individual sought to be in a position to use his weapons. The difference which remains lies in the fact that the men approaching in column will form a very much more narrow, more closed front than men charging forward from a distance who are already deployed in line.

Of course, with very large armies, several columns had to be formed, which deployed side by side with a certain interval. If they remained one behind the other, the last ones would, of course, not make contact with the enemy until very late or perhaps even not at all.

A certain difference between the later and earlier periods may have been caused by the fact that in the fifteenth century the ratio of knights to common soldiers had become very small. Consequently, the tendency to form masses that were held together by the knights could have increased.

Starting with the early period, we hear again and again of rivalries for the "first contact," and this appears to contradict the formation of the various columns side by side. As early as in the battle on the Unstrut (1075), the Swabians won their point that this right belonged to them from olden times, and since this account is reported by two independent sources (Lambert and Berthold), we may consider it as accurate. Before the battle of Sempach (1386), we hear of this once again, and bodies of knights claimed this as their historic right in certain areas.[30] What kind of significance would this right have had if the various units from different regions deployed side by side?

The answer probably lies in the fact that battles very frequently began before the armies were completely deployed. In these cases, the unit that first moved out of camp and made contact with the enemy entered the fight before the others, even though the latter did not hold back behind them but, moving from their march column or from their camp, tried to reach the side of the foremost unit as quickly as possible. Therefore, they moved into contact with the enemy and into the fight by echelons. It happened very often that the first ones to enter the battle were the only ones engaged in the fight, since the battles often were not actually fought to the finish, but they were decided at the first clash, because one side, realizing its inferiority, considered its cause to be lost. It was therefore an enviable advantage for a knightly unit seeking fame to be in the point during the deployment for the battle, even though ideally the units were positioned side by side.

In the Crusades, we find documentary evidence for the belief that the concept of the "first contact" was maintained in the side-by-side formation of the contingent columns as the result of an attack in echelons, which, of course, meant a formation in line of columns that developed only gradually. In the battle of Athareb (1119), Gautier tells of a corps (*acies*) of Saint Peter that had the right to move out ahead and make the first contact with the enemy.[31] This unit was followed by those of Gaufrid and Guido, but they did not support the attack of the first corps. Instead, when they saw the success of that corps, they attacked other

enemy units and defeated them in like manner. This account allows no
other interpretation than that the three units moved into the battle in
echelons.[32]

It was probably specifically in the Crusades that this echeloned method
of attack was recognized as a principle, because in those campaigns the
enemies were mainly mounted archers. They naturally started their part
of the battle as soon as possible; the most favorable period for them was
the span of minutes during their opponents' deployment. If in the Occident the first unit deployed often dashed forward from sheer impatience
and a knightly lack of discipline, there was present in the Orient a practical reason for doing so, namely, the losses a unit necessarily suffered
from the archers if it did not close with them as fast as possible. How the
knights complained in the battle of Arsuf, saying that they were being
sacrificed to the enemy without any defense when Richard the Lion-
hearted, for good reasons, did not give the signal for the attack! And how
the Turks, also according to the report we have on them by Boaeddin,
Saladin's historiographer, dispersed when they were attacked by the
knights with their lances! It is similarly reported that as early as in the
battle against the Hungarians by Henry I in 933, the Saxons charged so
quickly that the enemy had no time to launch a second volley of arrows.[33]
Otto von Freising recounts that in the battle with the Hungarians in
1146, Duke Henry Iasomirgott, by the speed of his attack, overcame the
Hungarian archers and destroyed them but was himself then defeated by
the knights of the king of Hungary.[34]

With these accounts, we already have the important points concerning
the relationship of knights to mounted archers.

Mounted archers were the age-old combat arm of the Central
Asians—Persians, Parthians, Huns, Arabs, and Turks. They formed a
frightful arm, as was shown by the repeated victories of these peoples,
but only under certain conditions. These mounted archers would have
been able to offer much less resistance than they actually did to the
Crusader knights, who charged against them with lance and sword, if
they had not finally been armed with close-combat weapons in addition
to the bow. They were thus not very differently armed than the occidentals, and, with a sufficient superiority of numbers, they would also have
been able to engage in close combat. The mounted archer can develop
his full capabilities only where a broad plain allows him the freedom to
withdraw at will and then move forward again as soon as the enemy is
tired and gives up the pursuit. We must therefore seek the origin of this
combat branch in the steppes, where the weapon was so advantageous
that the armies were willing to accept the great trouble and hard work

necessary for training and practice to the point of the needed skill. Once this skill has been gained and passed on as a matter of tradition, the arm can be transposed to other regions. The Crusaders recognized only too soon the harm that these horsemen caused them, and they sought to provide security against these weapons by taking Turks into their own service. In the year 1115 we find the first "Turcopoles," but the defenders of the Castle of David in Jerusalem, who entered the service of Raymond of Toulouse after the capitulation, may already have served as a corps of mounted archers. Emperor Frederick II had Saracen archers on foot and on horseback in his army in his Italian campaigns. The Occident itself did not develop the mounted archer arm amidst its mountains, forests, and swamps, since that arm had only a limited use there and could be created only with a great deal of effort.[35]

The opinion has been expressed by some, and General Köhler, especially, has based his entire work on it,[36] that knightly armies customarily formed and fought in three echelons. This concept is to be rejected, for in no way does it apply to knightly armies. We shall return to this point after we have traced the progress of the development up to the transition of knights into cavalry and have determined what is to be understood technically by "echelons."

Very often a battle was already decided at the first clash, the first moment, when one side admitted defeat and fled. If that did not happen and the encounter developed into a longer fight, the mission and the honor of the knight was the *Kêre,* as it was called in the Germanic heroic epics, that is, the act of riding through the enemy combat unit, turning around and riding through again, while continuously fighting, as Caesar has already recounted of the Gallic knights (*Bell. Gall.,* 7. 66).[37] But the extension of this act of riding through and back into a "constant rolling action" ("*roulement perpétuel*") by entire sections (echelons), drawn up one behind the other, is a fantastic embellishment which in no way can be reconciled with the idea that the individual "echelons" were columns with a depth of many ranks.[38] We may also ascribe more to the romantic than to the historical those accounts of the armistice that was occasionally declared in the middle of a fight to give the combatants a chance to renew their strength,[39] or accounts that a knight would interrupt the fight in order to give his opponent the accolade.[40]

As we may conclude from the basic principles of knightly combat, it is not very important how many units were drawn up side by side or one behind the other in any individual case, or how deep and broad the individual units were. The decisive points were the number, the skill, the confidence of the individual and his neighbor in the fact that they would make contact with the enemy with a certain uniformity. The formation resulted almost automatically from the number of combatants on hand and the space provided by the terrain. The greatest tactical significance is to be found in those reports to the effect that a unit was designated to offer assistance wherever it was needed, that is, to serve as a reserve. This is not to be confused, however, with the modern reserve, which is supposed to bring on the final decision. If two modern armies of equal strength meet and the commander of one sends his whole force into the fight, while the other holds back, let us say, one-third of his force, he is assuming that his two-thirds, even though weaker, will suffice to carry on the battle for a considerable time and to break up the tactical formation of the superior enemy force to such an extent that an attack by troops in good order will finally decide the battle. In a knightly army, breaking up the formation played much too small a role to offset the disadvantage of fighting at first without the participation of one unit. A reserve that does not intervene until after the main body is as good as defeated would accomplish little more, and the commander would be blamed for having committed his troops to battle piecemeal. Consequently, the purpose of a reserve in a knightly army was quite different from that of a modern reserve—that is, by withholding a unit for a short time, to have the possibility of committing it wherever a thinly held position, a weakness, has by chance developed, while the enemy is perhaps closely formed and strong at precisely that spot. From the modern viewpoint, then, it is not so much a question of a reserve but of a withheld echelon.

Those cases where it is actually reported that in a battle the side that was already victorious was defeated by the sudden intervention of the enemy's reserve, for example, at Tagliacozzo, are too uncertain in their source documentation to permit conclusions as to the principles involved. In these cases, it was probably a question not of a planned maneuver but of fortuitous events. In particular, no commander would intentionally first allow the main body of his army to be defeated with the hope of then being able to strike with his reserve the scattered and disordered victors. The plan can always be based only on the idea of having the last troops intervene while the outcome is still undecided.

Committing the last echelon is the final possible act of leadership. Once the commander ordered or the various leaders agreed as to which position each banner was to take, the kings and dukes themselves joined in the fight and sought their fame in the knightly tradition rather than in the exercise of command.[41]

If we have recognized the true type of medieval combat and the medieval battle in many individual fights between knights, only superficially controlled to a certain degree, along with the support of the other arms, this determination of the typical occurrence has still not completely exhausted all the possibilities. Certain situations are imaginable—and we find examples of them—where either the knights find it appropriate to fight on foot or the supporting arms provide a special and stronger effect than usual.

Whether or not we should designate this kind of combat as the tactics of knighthood is merely a play on words. According to Clausewitz's definition, tactics is the employment of combat forces for the purpose of the battle. By this definition, a knightly army undoubtedly also had its tactics. If we consider that certain dispositions had to be taken with respect to the formation of the units and had to be suited to the circumstances, that a reserve was withheld and then committed, that commands were issued concerning the deployment and advance of the marksmen and the foot soldiers, and that under certain circumstances the marksmen or foot soldiers were even assigned a special mission, then we see that there was also a kind of tactics in the sense of a certain art of leadership. But these accomplishments were always so small that basically those who have denied that knightly armies had any tactics are correct from a practical viewpoint.

Viollet-le-Duc once said: "To assert that feudal armies were devoid of any tactics is almost the same as saying that a country has no literature because one does not understand its language."[42] This French scholar believed, therefore, that scholars simply did not yet understand how to find and interpret the secrets of medieval tactics in the sources. Since then, many efforts have been made to solve the problem that he thus posed and to complete the lacuna in our knowledge, but nothing of value has developed.

Of course, it is not difficult to infer one concept or another from the medieval sources. But for our purposes these sources are of a very questionable nature.

Most of the medieval authors, once they go into detail, had no sense of recounting what really happened or what seemed credible to them, but they painted and embellished, particularly when they were describing the tensest and most exciting of all events, the battle. It would perhaps not have been worth their trouble to portray the real events. From the start, their accounts make no other claim—or, we may also say that they claim to be a combination of fact and fancy. For antiquity also, of course, we have historical sources of this type, which modern historians continue to use carelessly, but we also have a few real writers of history, who enable us to recognize the true circumstances. In one case at least—and it is a particularly important one—for Cannae—we are in a position to compare both types of sources with each other. I cannot recommend strongly enough that the reader practice this kind of comparision by studying in detail the description that Appian has given of the battle of Cannae so that we may be prepared for those cases where the true historical source is missing. This procedure is particularly necessary for the Middle Ages, since the spirit of the period was whimsical and uncritical, the writers were seldom of very high status, and finally, the use of the Latin language, a foreign tongue for them, provided a particularly dangerous source of aberration of reality. References from ancient authors were constantly woven into these accounts, and their words introduced concepts and images that did not fit the conditions of the times. Rahewin, Barbarossa's historian, did not hesitate to copy his account of the siege of Crema, with all its details, the division of the army into seven contingents, and the like, directly from Josephus' account of the siege of Jerusalem by Titus. In the tenth century, the French monk Richer recounted in great detail and elegant language a whole series of military events, for example, King Odo's battle against the Normans in 892. But his descriptions are pure fantasy.

With this attitude on the part of the authors, individual source reports, no matter how exact they might appear, signify very little. Only by comparing the reports against each other throughout the entire period can we gain accurate ideas of the typical events.

Recognition of the knightly combat methods also makes it clear why the Middle Ages never considered establishing true military discipline. For the direct military purpose, nothing would have been gained through military discipline. After all, the decision in battle always rested on the knights. Wherever they held out and as long as they held out, they were the mainstay, the nerves, and the skeleton for the other arms as well. But knighthood was based on the most highly developed concept of personal honor, which would have gained nothing from strict discipline and would perhaps even have suffered from it. For the knight, it was not enough that the army be victorious. He wanted and needed to have his personal share in the victory as well, for personal distinction was the governing ideal in his life, and that concept was opposed to discipline and made of him an individual combatant. This caused the Byzantine Emperor Leo to say that the attacks of the Franks on horseback and on foot were violent and irresistible in their toughness.[43] No doubt, battles were lost because knights, with obstinate foolhardiness, disobeyed a command, but those were exceptional cases that occur even in the best disciplined armies. In view of the extremely small measure of leadership for which there was room in knightly armies, as we have seen, these kinds of lapses cannot be regarded as very weighty. The principal disadvantages of a lack of discipline would probably have been the disorder in pursuit and the mania for plundering first of all, instead of pursuing the enemy. In the First Crusade, it was determined on one occasion that any one who plundered before victory was complete would have his ears and nose cut off.[44] Before the battle of Bouvines, Philip Augustus announced that he had erected a number of gallows and would hang anybody who was caught plundering before victory was completely won.[45]

Greed for booty also stimulated efforts to take prisoners, who could promise a ransom. This tendency was multiplied by the constantly developing class spirit of knighthood, which recognized the opponent as also being a brother in the order, almost a comrade, whom one's natural feelings sought to spare and protect from the extreme sacrifice. Such humane sensitivities are very dangerous for the truly warlike spirit, and we find them already at a very early date. Orderich recounts that, in the battle of Brémule (1119), where Henry I of England defeated Louis VI of France, only three of the French knights were killed, while 140 were taken prisoner, "because they were clad completely in iron, and from fear of God and a feeling of comradeship, the men on both sides spared their enemies."[46] Giraldus Cambrensis reported in like manner 100 years later that, in addition to other differences between the Welsh and the knights, the former were intent on killing, while the latter were more interested in taking prisoners. Later, in the battles of the Austrian knights against the Swiss, we hear the complaint that the coarse peasants killed their enemies instead of capturing them.

Clear pictures from the military life and warfare of the knights are provided in many passages of the statutes of the knightly orders, especially the Templars.[47]

Whenever a unit intended to establish camp, a space for the chapel was marked off with strings. Then positions were indicated for the grand master, the dining tent, the provincial commander, and the quartermaster. The other brothers did not select their positions in the area until the cry sounded: "Gentlemen brothers, encamp in God's name!" (Chap. 148).

No brother was allowed to go so far from the camp that he could not hear the call or the bell signal. One of his two squires always had to remain close by, while the other went in search of wood and fodder (Chap. 149).

The knights were not to saddle up or mount before the command was given. They were to check carefully to see that none of their equipment was left lying about. On the move, each one was to have his squires with his armor ride in front of him and those who led the horses (for each knight had three or four horses) behind him,[48] and no one was allowed to leave his place in the column except to test his horse for a moment. Under penalty of expulsion from the order, no one was allowed to attack or to ride out of his rank without command (Chaps. 162, 163, 166). Whenever they went into battle, the marshal took the banner in his hand and ordered from five to ten knights to form closely around him and protect the banner. These brothers surrounding the banner were to slash away at the enemy as best they could and were not permitted to separate themselves from the banner or to move away, whereas the other brothers could attack forward and in the rear, right and left, in short, wherever they believed they could harm the enemy (Chap. 164).[49] A commander carried a reserve banner wound around his lance, which he unfurled whenever anything happened to the main banner. He was therefore forbidden to strike with the lance around which the reserve banner was bound, even if he had an opportunity to do so (Chaps. 165, 241, 611).

Even if a knight was very seriously wounded, he was not permitted to abandon the banner without authority (Chaps. 419, 420). Even in case of a defeat, the knight was not allowed to leave the battlefield, under penalty of permanent expulsion from the order, as long as the banner was still waving. If his own banner was lost, he was to attach himself to that of the Knights Hospitalers or to another Christian banner. Not until all of them were beaten was the brother knight permitted to seek safety wherever God counseled him to go (Chaps. 168, 421).

Just as it was possible above, from the formation in column at Pillenreuth, here, too, it would be possible from these rules of the order, to understand the entire difference between a knightly force and cavalry by comparing those rules with modern regulations. Among the knights, we do not find the slightest indication of drills in riding in close order, deploying, or wheeling. The only kind of control was limited to the prohibition of leaving ranks and attacking individually without command—a prohibition that need not even be mentioned in a cavalry regulation—and the instructions for the protection of the banner. The control of the battle, therefore, aims at nothing more than making contact with the enemy uniformly, and after the battle has begun, to fight it through with the utmost fierceness by means of holding the banner high.

That is opposite of the teachings of the modern cavalry tactician. Today the rule is: "The breakthrough is the real combat act of cavalry, that which brings on a direct decision.[50] Only in the case of doubtful success in the breakthrough will the following melee bring on a special turn of events." The modern regulation goes on to say: "Cavalry is never weaker than after a successful attack," and it places particular stress on the necessity for quickly reassembling and, where possible, keeping individual units in close formation throughout.[51] With knights, the unit around the banner serves the same purpose, to a certain extent. But there is no question of assembling or of signals and commands during the fight. And there is nothing concerning flanking movements in the attack or defense against such enemy movements, nor do we find second echelons or reserves, for the decision lies in the fight, the hand-to-hand melee. And there, no further leadership exists; the fight is left exclusively to the knight himself, who may harm the enemy wherever and however he can.

The essence of cavalry is the closely formed unit under the control of its leader. The signal "Assemble," therefore, plays such an important role in their drills that the horses automatically start to run toward the spot from which they hear it sounded. Knights had nothing to do with such drills and signals, and the trumpet had nothing to do with them.[52]

Earlier studies on the conduct of war in the Middle Ages were naturally always guided by a certain tendency to seek analogies to modern occurrences, in order to clarify the past. The result of our study is to bring to light primarily the fundamental *difference* between medieval warfare and all modern methods, as well as the difference from ancient warfare. A unit of knights was very different from a squadron of cuirassiers with lances. Let us clearly recognize once again why the tactical concepts with which we became familiar in the military history of antiquity no longer appeared in the Middle Ages.

The skill of the ancient commanders can be seen from their utilization of the special advantages of the offensive and the defensive, the special strengths of each weapon, and the unique conditions of the terrain. They knew how to turn these factors to their advantage, while avoiding the associated disadvantages.

At Marathon, we have seen how the commander held his entire army on the defensive up to a specific moment. Later, we saw again and again how certain parts of an army were assigned to the defensive in order to permit a superior concentration of force at another point for the offensive. This kind of action was not possible for a mounted army, since horsemen have no defensive but can only act offensively.

With this situation, tactical use of the terrain also faded into the background. Knightly armies could fight in no other way than on a plain.[53] With them, resting a flank on a terrain feature may possibly have had some meaning under certain circumstances, but this was of very minor importance.[54] A knightly battle quickly turned into a general melee in which flanks and front no longer played any role. The task of the leaders was not so much that of securing a good feature on which to rest the flank but of obtaining sufficient space for the movement of the mounted units.

While in the Middle Ages and in antiquity the various combat branches gave each other mutual support, in the latter period it was only by way of assistance to the knight by the marksman, the foot soldier, and the light horseman. We cannot speak of any tactics of combined arms, because the three support arms did not have independent significance. There was no question of having the marksmen or foot soldiers hold up an enemy attack, in the manner of a phalanx or a legion, in order to allow the knights in the meantime to make an enveloping movement. These support arms were much too weak.

Consequently, the tactical mission of a mounted army was completely different from that of a Greek or Roman army. The grouping of the various arms did not have the purpose of mutual support, which is necessary for the true tactics of combined arms, but all the other arms served only the one decisive combat branch, the knights. Only their needs and characteristics determined the battlefield and the conduct of battle, and since they had no defensive capability and could utilize the terrain in only a very one-sided way, clever tactical combinations were not possible.

The central point around which everything revolved and on which everything was oriented was the low worth of foot soldiers with close-combat weapons. Rüstow has stated the point in this way: "The importance of the foot soldier declined because he was not respected." But why was he not respected? Among the Romans, the legionary was considered more important than the horseman. Certainly the dismounted soldiers sank all the lower in prestige once they had lost their ancient standing, and now this arm was neither given any special attention nor did the best and most capable men feel attracted to it. But the decisive reason for the change was the loss of the tactical body. The medieval foot soldier was only the man himself and not a member of a close-knit, disciplined cohort. Consequently, it is unjust to reproach the foot soldiers for not being of any value. They could not be any more than they were; we could almost say that they were not supposed to be anything more, since, of course, the knights were supposed to be and claimed to be the decisive arm. The dismounted men, even when there were many of them, were therefore in no way superfluous, but they were useful and hardly dispensable as support for the knights, even in battle, and they were absolutely necessary and indispensable outside of battle, especially in sieges.

At this point, let us once again assemble and consider the effects which the Crusades had on the combat methods of the occidental knights.

The first effect was that they encountered an arm that was practically new to them, the mounted archers. Furthermore, they themselves, when they were unable to replace the knights' horses, had to bring the foot soldiers into combat in a very different way from that which had been customary and necessary in their homeland. Both of these points necessarily led to far-reaching results. Mutual support by the various combat branches had to be studied and developed carefully. The application of mixed combat was developed in principle and fostered, and efforts were also made to adopt the arm of the mounted archers. In order to defend themselves against the sudden attacks by the mounted archers, the Crusaders had to give much greater care to their march formation than was normal for them in the west. It is often mentioned that they moved in three parallel columns in order to be ready to fight at once on all sides—a procedure which, of course, was possible only in areas that offered the necessary road net and freedom of movement.[55]

EXCURSUS

GERMAN COMBAT METHODS ON FOOT AND HORSEBACK

On the question as to whether and how extensively German knights from the ninth to the thirteenth centuries fought on foot or horseback, Baltzer, p. 98 ff., has assembled a series of bits of evidence that are in direct contradiction with one another. King Arnulf's warriors dismounted in 891, when they stormed the Norman fieldwork, and in 896, when they climbed the walls of Rome. In the battle on the Elster against Henry IV in 1080, Otto von Nordheim had part of the Saxon knights fight on foot. The same thing occurred in the Bleichfeld battle in 1086, and before Damascus in 1147, under Conrad III, "facti pedites, sicut mos est Teutonicis in summis necessitatibus bellica tractare negotia" ("They became foot soldiers, just as it is the German custom to conduct military affairs in the greatest crises"), says William of Tyre.[56] In the battle of Bouvines in 1214, William the Briton (*Philippis,* X, v. 680) has King Philip Augustus saying: "Teutonici pugnent pedites, tu, Gallice, semper eques pugna." ("Let the Germans fight as foot soldiers. You, Frenchman, should always be a horseman in battle.") Robert Guiscard's biographer says that the Germans were no special horsemen.[57] The Byzantine John Cinnamus praises them for being superior to the French in dismounted combat (Baltzer, p. 47, Note 5). To this we should also add the fact that Emperor Leo (886-911) also said of the Franks in his *Tactics* that they loved dismounted combat just as they did fighting on horseback.[58] It is quite often reported of individual knights that, in order to fight, especially in moments of extreme peril, they sprang from their horses.

On the other hand, the Germans boasted that they were better horsemen than the Italians (Liudprandus, *Liber Antapodosios* [*Book of Repayment*], 1. 21 and 3. 34). The annalist of Fulda says that, on the occasion of the battle with the Normans in 891, the Franks actually fought on horseback. The Byzantine Emperor Nicephorus is reported to have told

Liudprandus that the Germans were skillful neither on horseback nor on foot, and the Bohemian Cosmas (2. 10) says that the Germans were not accustomed to fighting on foot. In another passage, Baltzer (p. 3) interprets Thietmar of Merseburg (976-1019) as meaning that for him the participation of foot soldiers in war seemed to be unusual.

Baltzer compares the various passages and concludes that, even a long time after mounted service had become customary among the Germans, they were still not fully capable in that kind of fight. The performance of their mounted men, according to him, was not brilliant.

Both factual analysis and consideration of the sources point to rejection of this conclusion. As early as Caesar's times, the Germans were excellent horsemen, and against Charlemagne, the Saxons, in particular, fought on horseback. In a Carolingian capitulary (see p. 33 above), the Friesians were also described as horsemen. It is completely impossible that among a people for whom the art of riding had always been native and in whom there was a knightly class that constantly practiced this skill, ability in mounted combat was not highly developed. Baltzer believes that the horseman who felt completely in his element on horseback would only dismount and fight on foot when such action was completely unavoidable, and the more questionable the situation, the more difficult it was for him to decide to do so. This cannot be said to apply generally. The superiority of the horseman is important principally when fighting in a group. One hundred knights on horseback are undoubtedly much more valuable than 100 fighters on foot in the open field; a large part of the foot soldiers would immediately be overridden. Before the battle of Courtrai, the commander of the French, the count of Artois, supposedly said that 100 horsemen were as valuable as 1,000 men on foot.[59] In individual combat, however, a skillful foot soldier may very well be able to hold his own with a horseman, and, as curious as it seems to us, there are many reports in the history of warfare of horsemen who dismounted in battle, for example, even among the Cossacks[60] and also in antiquity.[61] If one is perhaps inclined to explain this phenomenon among the Romans, of whom it is endlessly recounted, as resulting from their lack of horsemanship, this explanation is not confirmed in the sources. It fails completely when, quite to the contrary, we read in Polybius (3. 115) that, in the cavalry combat of the battle of Cannae, Hannibal's horsemen, whose quality as cavalry is above any questioning, sprang from their horses and, instead of making normal attacks, overcame the Romans in this barbaric way, as Polybius expresses it. On a number of occasions (*Bell. Gall.*, 4. 2 and 4. 12), Caesar reported the same action on the part of the Germans, who were noted as particularly capable horsemen. The same action also occurs in the battle with the Saxons in the *Nibelungenlied* (str. 212).

Furthermore, a man who considers himself as lost, who will or can no longer flee, and intends to die while still fighting to his utmost ability, gladly jumps from his horse for this purpose and fights on foot. For if he remains on horseback, he can be brought down and made defenseless if his horse is wounded, whereas on foot he is dependent only on himself. The most positive of all statements on this period is that of the *Annals* of Fulda concerning the battle with the Normans: "Francis pedetemptim certare inusitatum est." ("It is unusual for the Franks to fight cautiously.") Baltzer seeks to explain this away by saying that the remark perhaps applied only to the Franks in the narrower sense or to the Lotharingians. This objection is completely arbitrary, for the author was speaking not of the men from Lorraine, but of the Franks, and why in the world are the Lotharingians supposed to have been especially good riders?[62] With limitations of this kind, one can, of course, turn any statement into its opposite. Nevertheless, I have nothing against this procedure; we must simply apply it to all such statements in order to recognize that all of them are unreliable. In every single one of them, it is possible that some kind of tendency, which is not now apparent to us, some error, a mere mood, led to a completely false judgment. That is why we have the phenomenon of assembling pieces of evidence of equally good apparent credibility which directly contradict one another. In these cases, we cannot arrive at a solution simply through analysis of the sources. We must resort to objective analysis, which looks at the periods from an overall viewpoint. How dangerous it is to build our concepts on isolated statements, we have learned specifically in the chapter on the origin of the feudal system. By depending on a few such isolated reports, scholars had formed the opinion that the Franks in the *Völkerwanderung* were still only dismounted warriors. From this they allowed themselves to be drawn on a false trail in a question of such cardinal importance as that of the beginning of the feudal nation.

Consequently, it is not on the basis of individual bits of evidence that are completely unreliable and contradict each other, but on a basis of critical testing and weighing of the individual sources in the overall context and comparison with the total process of development of warfare that we reach the conclusion that, from the *Völkerwanderung* on, the art of mounted combat was nurtured and very highly esteemed among all the Germanic peoples. Only among the Anglo-Saxons does mounted combat really seem never to have been developed, a situation that perhaps resulted from the fact that they had brought few if any horses with them across the sea. Indeed, a real warrior class among them was developed to only a very limited extent. But the true knight, who was developed on the Continent and was also brought over to England by the Normans, was a fighter on foot as well as on horseback, and if he fought on foot, that does not mean in any way that he was not skillful enough in mounted combat. Widukind's praise of Duke Conrad the Red (3.44) must apply to every real knight: "dum eques et dum pedes iret in hostem, bellator intolerabilis." ("Whether he goes against the enemy as a horseman or a fighter on foot, he will be an irresistible warrior.")

KNIGHTS AND COMMON SOLDIERS (*RITTER UND KNECHTE*)

It seems quite apparent that the knightly class in the narrower sense broke away as a lesser nobility from the older, general warrior class. It is also quite clear how this took place. It is more difficult to understand how the lower warrior group, beneath the knightly class, was composed and continued its existence, especially the foot soldiers. In this area much research remains to be done. The particular question arises as to the extent, the beginning period, and the manner in which those who accompanied the knights on horseback and on foot were or became combatants.

Baltzer, p. 78 f., believes that, until the eleventh century, knights for the most part still had no squires or shield-bearers with them, since, for example, as is often mentioned, they themselves went out foraging. I would like to interpret this observation somewhat differently. As we know, from the *Völkerwanderung* on, even the most outstanding men in the army were not just commanders but also fighters. From the kings and dukes downward to the mass of horsemen, there were intermediate levels and transitional positions. Certainly at a very early period, the custom of having a servant along applied even to the common mounted soldiers. But they were still private soldiers who also went out foraging themselves, and often they had no servant, or he was with the baggage train, where he led packhorses or drove a wagon. But the men of the knightly class, who gradually worked up to a higher status, naturally had with them at the least an arms- or shield-bearer and in most cases several serving men as well.

Baltzer then also determines that the number of squires increased after the middle of the eleventh century. They were often mounted but were armed only for cases of emergency and were used only for secondary military tasks or, by way of exception, in combat.

It is difficult to determine Köhler's opinion on the formation of the combat branches in the Middle Ages and their relationship with one another, since the author contradicts himself in various passages of his work. He does hold fast to the idea that the followers of a knight were originally unarmed and dismounted and did not accompany the knight into combat. Nevertheless, from the beginning of the period which he treats, there supposedly existed, in addition to the knights, a special combat arm of light horsemen. From the eleventh century, foot soldiers, too, supposedly played a significant role from time to time, and mention was even made both of dismounted soldiers who followed the knights into combat and of independent units of foot soldiers. The *gleve* or lance—that is, the theoretical assignment of supporting arms to the individual knight—was supposedly not formed until after the middle of the fourteenth century.

I agree with Köhler's point that the men accompanying the knight did not originally follow him into combat,[63] even though each man no doubt had some kind of weapon.[64] Whether or not one of the knight's followers once had an old horse was a matter of chance and had no significance, either for military purposes or for the movement of the army. Köhler did not sufficiently distinguish between the two questions as to whether the knight had a mounted serving man and whether this man on horseback normally followed him into battle. The answer to the first question is clearly yes; in the twelfth century mounted and armed men were to be found in the group accompanying a knight. The man whom Barbarossa wished to dub a knight before Tortona (1155), and who declined this honor, was called "*strator*" (groom); that is, he was a mounted servant,[65] for he carried "an axe of the kind that this sort of man normally had on his saddle."[66] In 1158, the Brescians made a sudden attack on Bohemian "*scutiferi*" (shield-bearers) and took their horses away from them.[67] Therefore, if these "*scutiferi*" were mounted, it was no doubt also the "milites et scutiferi" (knights and squires) who in the same campaign moved about through the countryside, conquering, destroying, and burning down castles and villages.[68] There was documentary evidence of a "*servus equitans*" (mounted serving man) in the so-called *Ahr Service Regulation*,[69] and Köhler's attempt (3: 1: 17) to explain away this evidence is so contrived that it does not seem to me worthy of contradiction. On the other hand, the textual correction which Köhler undertakes in the *Weissenburg Service Regulation* of 1029 seems to me to be correct, so that this evidence falls away.[70]

But in 1240, Emperor Frederick II ordered that twenty knights, twenty marksmen, and twenty serving men, *all mounted,* should go to Sardinia.

In the treaty of the count of Savoy with Genoa (*Annales Januenses* [*Annals of Genoa*] *SS.,* 18. 158) it is reported: The count is to receive 16 pounds per month "pro milite cum donzelio armatis et duobus scutiferis" ("for a knight with an armed page and two squires"). Furthermore, the noble Lord Lotharingus of Brescia was in the army "cum militibus 50, quorum quisque erat cum duobus equis et cum tribus scutiferis et donzellis bene armatis" ("with 50 knights, each of which had two horses, three squires and well-armed pages"). There was also present another man "cum saumerio et duobus scutiferis" ("with a pack-horse and two squires"). Köhler, 3: 2: 87, translates the word "*donzellus*" by "noble serving man" (*Edelknecht*), and he gives for the word "*scutiferi*" "other serving men, probably younger sons of knightly families." Obviously, this is completely arbitrary. It is possible, however, that all the horses were for the knight, and the serving men went dismounted into the battle.

In 1239 a treaty was concluded between the pope and Venice, by the terms of which the city was to provide "300 milites et pro quolibet milite dextrarium unum, roncinos duos, scutiferos tres cum armis" ("300 knights and for each knight one war-horse, two packhorses, and three squires with arms"). Köhler, 1: 10, assumes that the three horses were for the knight and the *"scutiferi"* were on foot. That may very well be correct; otherwise, there would have had to be at least four horses.

If the mounted and armed serving man in the twelfth and thirteenth centuries is thus accounted for, this still does not prove that he followed his lord on horseback into combat, especially into the full-scale battle. For that reason I would prefer at least not to contradict Köhler's point that this practice did not become customary until the second half of the fourteenth century.

And with the question of the mounted servants there arises also that of the independent light horsemen.

It is an unquestionable fact that warriors have always been distinguished among themselves by their arms as well as their rank, but the differences are not of a type and not so great as to constitute separate, different combat branches. If that were the case, the difference would necessarily be much more obvious in the many battle accounts.

In this respect, Köhler makes all kinds of sharp distinctions in matters which in reality were not at all so clear-cut. In doing so, he falls into continuing contradictions with himself and strongly defends assertions that have no real significance. Instead of arriving at greater clarity through these sharp distinctions, we end up by no longer understanding what he really means. The principal passages in question are the following:

In Vol. II, p. 14, it is said that in the twelfth century the knight's servants were unarmed and dismounted. The same statement appears in 3: 2: 83.

In Vol. III, 2, 87, we read that in the thirteenth century the custom arose of having the noble serving men (squires, *scutiferi, armigeri*) accompany the knights into battle on foot.

But in Vol. III, 3, 249, it is stated that in the twelfth century the custom arose of having the men on foot accompanying each knight take arms and go into battle with him.

In Vol. I, p. IX, we hear that the *gleve* (or lance), consisting of the knight and two light horsemen accompanying him, was introduced for the first time in France in 1364 and in Germany in 1365. The same point appears in the *Göttingische gelehrte Anzeigen,* 1883, p. 412. See also Köhler, 3: 2: 89, where it is specifically emphasized that, until the introduction of the *gleve,* the knight did not have a mounted retinue.

In Vol. II, 14, however, it is stated that, after 1240, one of the two servants of the knight, both of whom were already armed, was now given a mount. When it is added that the two servants were not combatants, this avoids, of course, a direct contradiction of the previously cited passages, but we still ask why the servants (of whom it is expressly stated that they were unarmed in the twelfth century) were now provided with weapons in the thirteenth century.

In Vol. I, p. IX, and Vol. III, 2, 24, we hear that the light horsemen normally formed the first echelon.

But in 3: 2: 75 it is stated: "The horsemen of the Middle Ages fought in close-ordered groups that were formed of the lightly armed men and in which the knights formed only the point and the last rank, and, if their number was sufficient, the flanking files also, and thus they inclosed the unit of light horsemen.... Not until the fifteenth century did the French develop the formation 'en haye,' formed of the heavily armed men, behind whom stood the lightly armed horsemen." In Germany, this formation reportedly never became customary, but the closed unit remained.

See also Köhler, 1: 193, note.

In Vol. II, foreword, p. VI, Köhler speaks of the effective levies of foot soldiers and their influence on the battle formation, troops whose presence followed uninterruptedly after

Senlac (1066). Particular mention is made of the Saxon foot soldiers of the eleventh century, the Brabantines of the twelfth, and the foot soldiers of the German cities in the thirteenth century.

According to Vol. III, 3, 248, the importance of the dismounted men in the Occident lasted only briefly, during the end of the twelfth century and the beginning of the thirteenth, and it originated from the experiences of the Third Crusade. It is said that the Germans even had to experience the events of 1197 before they, too, were willing to accept this change. Köhler sees in this rise of the foot soldier in this period the most important influence that the Crusades exercised on occidental warfare.

On p. 274, it is said that previously there had been only a few traces of foot soldiery in the west. On p. 378, the Normans, at least, are pointed out. The Brabantines of the twelfth century, whose importance is strongly emphasized elsewhere, were apparently overlooked by the author in these passages.

On p. 309, it is not the Third Crusade but the Crusades in general, in which the tactics with foot soldiers were developed. The battles of the First Crusade at Antioch and Ascalon are named as models adopted by the west.

On p. 307, it is said that the importance of the foot soldier reached its peak at the beginning of the thirteenth century (as we have seen above, it first started at the end of the twelfth, after the Third Crusade), and afterward it gradually declined.

On p. 272, we find that the mounted men were dependent on the support of the foot soldiers in the wars of Frederick II also.

In 1: 219, we hear that the dismounted men of Frederick II, the Saracens, stood on the two flanks at Cortenuova, "as was customary in Italy for a long time afterward."

In 3: 3: 275, however, Köhler says that in the thirteenth century there was no organizational tie with the mounted troops, and therefore even Cortenuova, for example, the principal battle of Frederick II (1237), must be regarded as a mounted battle. On p. 334, we hear that Frederick II, through his disdain, allowed the foot soldiery to sink to a miserable role.

We find on p. 308 that the foot soldiers played a role in Germany for only a short time, at the beginning of the thirteenth century, and in France their importance was of even shorter duration. Of German foot soldiers and the Brabantines we hear nothing more in the course of the thirteenth century (p. 309). The only mention is of dismounted men belonging to the cities.

But on p. 378 the author states that communal troops never played the role of "infanterie de ligne."

In 3: 2: 145 and 3: 3: 308, it is stated that the worst period for foot soldiers began toward the middle of the fourteenth century. In Italy, mounted service prevailed exclusively.

On the other hand, we are told in 3: 3: 275 that foot soldiers appeared independently in the fourteenth century.

We hear on p. 310 that not the firearm but only the spear was able to give the foot soldiers an independent position. But the spear supposedly first came into its full importance with the Swiss and did not appear in its full significance until the Burgundian wars, that is, at the end of the fifteenth century.

On pp. 329, 334, and 377, the battle of Certomundo (1289) and other battles of the period are supposed to have been of the highest importance—indeed, "epoch-making"—for the history of the infantry.

The author admits (p. 320) that the accomplishments of the foot soldiers were not so outstanding as to demand continuing respect. But we hear in 1: 429 that Emperor Frederick

II did not come upon the idea of foot troops, as they had already existed previously, because he lived in the attitudes of his period. "It was the knightly pride, which tolerated no other type of warrior beside itself." This exclusive outlook of knighthood had the saddest effects, according to Köhler. In a similar vein, 3: 2: 327 and 3: 3: 307, 316–318, it was the class spirit of the knights, and in 2: 310 even the deterioration of knighthood, that were responsible for the suppression of the foot soldiers.

It is demonstrably false in these passages primarily that there was originally an independent arm of light horsemen in addition to the knights. Such light horsemen are never to be found as an independent combat branch in the sources of the older period. The passages which Köhler cites for this point (3: 2: 11 and 3: 2: 29) are not conclusive.

In the *Annales Altahenses* (*Annals of Niederalteich*) for the year 1042 (*SS.,* 20. 797), there is mention of knights and common soldiers, but nothing allows us to interpret them as separate combat branches.

In the *Chronica monasterii Casinensis* (*Chronicles of the Monastery of Cassino*), *SS.,* 7. 818, it is recounted of a fight of Henry the Proud at Benevento in 1137: "Set cum scutiferi ducis in prima acie terga vertissent, dux eventum fortunae alteratum perpendens, praecepit militibus ut fluvium transvadentes montem in quo civitas sita erat ascenderent et ab Aurea porta civitatem invaderent." ("But when the squires of the duke in the first unit had fled, the duke, judging the changed outcome of his fortune, ordered his knights to cross the river, to climb the mountain on which the city was located, and to attack the city via the golden gate.")

In this passage, Köhler understands the "*scutiferi*" as the light horsemen who formed the first echelon. That is obviously impossible. The existence of a "first echelon" presupposes a second one, which follows it. But if the first echelon is in full flight, the second one cannot move in any other direction, completely unconcerned with the first. If the expression "*scutiferi*" here should mean any kind of special unit at all, then the word "*acies*" certainly does not mean "echelon," but at most "battle unit." This is very unlikely, however, for we would then necessarily hear much more often of this kind of separation of horsemen into combat branches if such a difference had been suitable for medieval warfare. Rather, the most likely interpretation of this passage is that "*acies*" means "fight." The shield-bearer squires were sent out foraging, were suddenly attacked and defeated (in which account we can just as well interpret "in prima acie" as "in a first engagement" or "at the beginning of the fight"), and thereafter the duke had the city attacked by the knights from another direction.

Still less definitely is it said that "*expeditissimi equites*" ("the least encumbered horsemen") who were sent out for a pursuit represent a special combat branch.

In the *Chronicle of Moyenmoutier* from the eleventh century (*SS.,* 4. 59), a distinction is made between the unit of the *loricati* (men with coats of mail) (30), which the abbot had to provide, and the *clypeati* (men with shields). (See Waitz, 8: 116.) In his 3: 2: 31, note, Köhler agrees with Baltzer that the *loricati* and *clypeati* are treated as separate corps. But this is not indicated in the wording of the source.

There is just as little basis for concluding that there were separate corps of horsemen from the *Annales Colonienses majores* (*Greater Annals of Cologne*), *SS.,* 17. 209, for the year 1282, where it is said of Italy: "occiderunt de inimicis suis 1300 clipeatos, praeter alios qui armis gravibus utebantur." ("Of their enemies, they killed 1,300 men with shields in addition to others who used heavy arms.") Perhaps these *clipeati* were foot soldiers.

A Livonian document from the year 1261 (cited by Köhler, 3: 2: 45) states that the knight was supposed to have sixty hides, the "*probus famulus*" (good sergeant, or squire) forty, and the "servus cum equo et plata" (attendant with horse and plate-armor) ten hides. Again, we have the various types of arms, but it does not follow from that that they formed different corps.

In four passages (1: 175; 1: 219; 2: 15; 2: 17) Köhler speaks of "light weapons on armored horses." That is an obvious impossibility. All four passages stem from the document of the Teutonic order of the year 1285 (*Cod. Warm.*, 1. 122, cited by Köhler in his 2: 15, Note 3): "sepedicti teodales et eorum heredes in dextrariis faleratis et armis levibus erunt obligati deservire." ("The above-mentioned vassals and their heirs will be obligated to serve on armored horses and in light armor.") This document is probably to be understood as meaning that the light weapons were to be drawn up *beside* the armored horse.

In close relationship to the preceding explanations are the repeated discussions of the meaning of the words *"scutarius," "scutifer,"* and *"armiger,"* which appear in the most varied places in Köhler's work. *"Scutifer"* and *"armiger"* are apparently supposed to be essentially the same,[71] but a sharp distinction is made between *"scutifer"* and *"scutarius"* (3: 2: 37, note).

In 2: 11, the *"scutarii"* are indicated as the men in the knight's retinue, so far do they stand above the serving men of the baggage train (*lixae*). The *scutarii* were therefore "the body of men which the knight had with him to serve him" (3: 2: 86). Of the same meaning as *"scutarius"* are the expressions *"donzellus," "damoiseau," "valetus," "servus,"* and *"serviens"*; the *"garcio"* and the *"bubulcus"* were also *"scutarii."*

The *"scutifer"* and *"armiger"* both referred to a serving man of noble birth or apprentice knight; therefore, they also belong in the broader concept of the *"scutarii"* (3: 2: 86).

"Scutifer" also means, however, the trained man of knightly birth who still had no fief, and the heavily armed man (sergeant?) in possession of a fief (3: 2: 19), and finally also the light horseman of unfree status (3: 2: 31; see also 3: 2: 24).

We see that the attempt to distinguish between *"scutarius"* and *"scutifer"* melted away in Köhler's hands.

And what Köhler has to say about dismounted units and their development is, of course, so full of contradictions that it eliminates itself. His most telling passage is probably the one which states: "The dismounted units, wherever they appeared in the knightly period in conjunction with horsemen, were only a supporting arm and therefore at that time not an arm in the modern sense" (3: 3: 306).

Once again, by way of summary, I say that, despite the actual differences in the weight and quality of the arms and the still greater differences in the personal status of the warriors, up until the twelfth century warriorhood still formed in theory a single group. It was not until the twelfth century that a distinction arose between actual combat branches. The very heavily armed body of knights split away and formed at the upper level the knightly class in the narrower sense. New elements of lesser military value entered the body of warriors, but principally only as foot soldiers. The men accompanying the knight, who were previously noncombatants, gradually assumed the character of combatants and, according to the circumstances, followed their lord into the fight. From this it follows, with respect to numerical estimates, that until the eleventh century *milites* and combatants were identical. From the twelfth century on, we must be more careful, and often we cannot arrive at simple estimates for the number of combatants, because the boundary between combatants and noncombatants was fluid.

I will not risk stating definitely when it was that the concept of the *gleve* as a group formed of a heavily armed horseman with several supporting fighters developed. As Köhler claims, the *name* may not be older than 1364, but the idea goes back at least into the twelfth century. Jähns, in his *Geschichte der Kriegswissenschaften*, 1: 295, sees in it from the start the characteristic element of feudal armies. He calls the combination of a knight with a marksman, which originated in the Crusades, a "double *gleve*." But there are no sources for this.

The difference between the various horses of the knight, the *dextrarius* (war-horse) and the *roncinus* (packhorse), should not be taken as absolute. Even the *dextrarius* can on occasion be ridden by the squire or can carry baggage. The principal point is that the knight always had a fresh horse at his disposal. If he had three horses, of which he himself used one, his squire another, and the third served as a packhorse, the last one was the fresh horse, since the baggage was normally much lighter than a rider.

NOTES FOR CHAPTER II

1. *Bell. Hispan.*, Chap. 15.

2. This is what the count of Artois called out before the battle of Courtrai (1302) (*Spiegel historial*, IV, Chap. 25):

Thus spoke Artois quite haughtily:
I am glad that they are formed thus;
We are on horseback, and they on foot.
A hundred horse and a thousand men
Are all the same.

3. Thucydides, 5. 57. 2. Xenophon, *Hellenica*, 7. 5. 23. Harpokration. Perhaps also Polybius, 11. 21. Indirectly associated with this is the dismounting of horsemen in the fight. See the preceding excursus and Vol. I, p. 538.

4. Potius equos quam homines offendatis, feriatis et cum gladii cuspide non cum acie ita quod equis hostium vestris ictibus succumbentibus, nostrorum peditum promta manus sessores equorum taliter prostratos ad terram et prae armorum gravidine lentos liberius excipiet et trucidet. Reguletor et aliter in primo conflictu probitas vestra. Singuli militis singulos juxta se pedites habeant, aut duo quilibet, si valeat, etiamsi non possit habere alios, quam ribaldos. Hos enim tam pro conficiendis equis hostilium, tam pro conterendis iis

You should hit the horses rather than the men, and you should strike with the tip of your sword, not with the edge, so that while the horses of the enemy are falling under your blows, the ready band of our foot soldiers may more freely catch the riders of the horses and kill them, thus lying on the ground and slow by the weight of their armor. Otherwise let your fitness be directed on the first clash. Every knight should have a foot soldier beside him, or two if he can, even if he should not be able to have other than grooms. In fact, experience of

qui excutientur ab equis, experientia pugnae valde necessarios et utiles esse probat. Muratori *SS* (L. A. Muratori, *Writers of Italian History*), 8. 823.

battle strongly proves that they are necessary and useful for destroying the horses of the enemy as well as killing those who will be shaken off by their horses.

5. *Dusburg Capitulary*, 104 (99). *SS. Rer. Pruss.*, Vol. I.

6. *Expugnatio Hibernica. Opera* V. (*Rerum Britannicarum Medii Aevi Scriptores*) (*The Conquest of Ireland. Works* V. [*Writers of British History of the Middle Ages*]), p. 395. I have already cited a passage from this work above.

Novi vero, quamquam in terra sua milites egregii fuerint, et armis instructissimi, Gallica tamen militia multum ab Hibernica, sicut et a Kambrica distare dinoscitur. Ibi namque plana petuntur, hic aspera: ibi campestria hic silvestria; ibi arma honori, hic oneri; ibi stabilitate vincitur hic agilitate; ibi capiuntur milites, hic decapitantur; ibi redimuntur, hic perimuntur.

As in truth I know, although knights were outstanding in their own land and most learned in arms, French military service, however, is known to differ greatly from the Irish as well as the Welsh. And in fact there level areas are sought, here rough; there open fields, here forests; there armor is an honor, here a burden; there they conquer by steadfastness, here by nimbleness; there knights are captured, here they are decapitated; there they are ransomed, here they are killed.

Sicut igitur ubi militares acies de plano conveniunt, gravis illa et multiplex armatura, tam linea scilicet quam ferrea, milites egregrie munit et ornat, sic ubi solum in arcto confligitur, seu loco silvestri seu palulustri, ubi pedites potius quam equites locum habent, longe levis armatura praestantior. Contra inermes namque viros, quibus semper in primo fere impetu vel parta est statim vel perdita victoria, expeditiora satis arma sufficiunt; ubi fugitivam et

Therefore, just as when knightly units assemble on a plain, that heavy multiple armor, obviously linen as well as iron, offers the knights outstanding protection and decorates them, so where they fight only in a confined area, a forest or a swamp, where the foot soldiers rather than the horsemen have the advantage, light armament is by far preferable. In fact, against unarmored men, by whom almost always in the first attack victory is

agilem per arcta vel aspera gentem sola necesse est gravi quadam et armata mediocriter agilitate confundi.

Cum illa nimirum armatura multiplici, sellisque recurvis et altis, difficile descenditur, difficilius ascenditur, difficillime, cum opus est, pedibus itur.

In omni igitur expeditione, sive Hibernica sive Kambrica gens in Kambriae marchia nutrita, gens hostilibus partium illarum conflictibus exercitata, competentissima; puta formatis a convictu moribus, audax et expedita, cum alea; Martis exegerit, nunc equis habilis, nunc pedibus agilis inventa; cibo potuque non delicata, tam Cerere quam Baccho, causis urgentibus, abstinere parata. Talibus Hibernia viris initium habuit expugnationis talibus quoque consummabilis finem habitura conquisitionis. Ut igitur

"Singula quaeque locum
teneant sortita decenter,"

contra graves et armatos, solumque virium robore, et armorum ope confisos, de plano dimicare, victoriamque vi obtinere contendentes, armatis quoque viris et viribus opus hic esse procul dubio protestamur. Contra leves autem et agiles, et

immediately gained or lost, lighter equipment suffices. When they fight a swift and nimble nation in a confined or rough terrain, it is necessary that some heavily armed and moderately armed be confounded by their quickness.

Of course, with that multiple armor and high curved saddles it is difficult to dismount, more difficult to mount, and most difficult to proceed on foot when necessary.

Therefore in every campaign, whether the nation is Irish or Welsh, reared on the borderland of Wales, the nation is practiced and most capable in the hostile conflicts of this area, pure by the habits formed from its way of life, bold and ready with risk, found expert with horses at one time and quick on foot at another as the conflict demands, not fastidious in food and drink, and prepared to abstain from bread as well as wine when affairs are pressing. With such men Ireland faced the beginning of the campaign and complete with such men Ireland was going to face the end of the conquest. Therefore, so that

"all things properly allotted
may have their place,"

we declare without hesitation that against heavily armored men relying only on the strength of force and the aid of arms, and hasten-

aspera pedentes, levis armaturae viri taliumque praesertina exercitati congressibus adhibendi.

ing to fight on a plain and to gain victory by force, there is also need here of armored men and strength. Against light-armed men and quick men, however, traversing rough terrain, light-armed men trained in the effectiveness of such matters must be used for battle.

In Hibernicis autem conflictibus et hoc summopere curandum, ut semper arcarii militaribus turmis mixtim adjiciantur. Quatinus et lapidum, quorum ictibus graves et armatos cominus oppetere solent, et indemnes agilitatis beneficio, crebris accedere vicibus et acscedere, e diverso sagittis injuria propulsetur.

In Irish battles, however, you must greatly see to it that archers should be added in mixed fashion to knightly units since by benefit of their quickness they can safely attack and retreat repeatedly, and they may inflict injury with stones, by the blows of which they are accustomed to attack the heavily armored, and in a different manner with arrows.

7. *Gewohnheiten,* Chap. 61. Perlbach, p. 116.

8. Gislebert, *Chron. Han. M. G. SS.,* 21. 522, describes a fight between Count Baldwin of Hainaut and the duke of Burgundy (1172). Baldwin armed his *"armigeri et garciones"* ("squires and grooms") so that they could defend themselves as foot soldiers. Delpech, 1: 306, understands that for this purpose he had them dismount. This point has been rejected by Köhler, 3: 2: 83. There is no indication that they were mounted. And even if they should have been mounted, it was perhaps correct, as we have seen, to have them fight on foot. The passage reads as follows:

cum comes Hanonienis in parte sua quinque terre sue milites secum haberet, et ex adversa parte eum duce Burgundie Henrico quamplures in superbia nimia, servientibus peditibus stipati, advenirent, comes Hanoniensis vivido ac prudente animo assumpto de armigeris suis

When the count of Hainaut on his side had five knights of his domain with him and on the enemy side a great many in excessive arrogance accompanied by sergeants as foot soldiers came against him with Henry the duke of Burgundy, the count of Hainaut, quickly hitting upon a

et garcionibus clientes pedites ordinavit et eos quibus potuit armis quasi ad defensionem contra multos preparavit militibusque multis ex adversa parte constitutis viriliter restitit et eos expugnavit.

sensible idea, ranged his squires and grooms as men-at-arms on foot and equipped them for defense against the many with what arms he could. After the many knights of the hostile party had been deployed, he resisted them bravely and defeated them.

9. It is noteworthy in several respects that Vegetius (2. 17 and 3. 14) attributes this passive-defensive role to the infantry. He cannot have derived this from the classical Roman authors, for, of course, it was precisely through its offensive, its closed attack, that the ancient legion was most effective. If Vegetius explains this in the opposite manner, then he has taken that from his own contemporary period, and that is again proof that the true Roman method of warfare no longer existed in his time and that warfare then already had the character of the Middle Ages. This point has already been correctly observed by Jähns, *Geschichte der Kriegswissenschaften,* 1: 186. It has, of course, been known for a long time that Vegetius had no sensitivity for the various periods. It would be a work of the highest value if someone succeeded, through a very careful analysis, in differentiating the various elements of his work from one another. But will that ever be possible?

10. In another passage, Chap. XVIII, para. 69, it is recommended, on the contrary, that the horsemen be placed behind the foot soldiers when opposing the Turks. It is not clear how that is intended.

11. The passage in *Gesta Roberti Wiscardi* (*Deeds of Robert Guiscard*), I, v. 260 ff., which is interesting in a number of respects, reads as follows:

Artmati pedites dextrum laevumque monentur
Circumstare latus, aliquod sociantur equestres
Firmior ut peditum plebs sit comitantibus illis.
His interdicunt omnino recedere campo
Ut recipi valeant, si forte fugentur as hoste.

(The armed foot soldiers are instructed to surround the right and left flanks, and some horsemen are joined to them so that the mass of the foot soldiers may be stronger with their support. He absolutely forbids them to retreat from the field so that they can be rescued, if they should be put to flight by the enemy.)

12. "Tribus aciebus antepositis manus pedestris, ut has protegat et ab his protegatur, retro sistitur." ("The band of foot soldiers stood in the rear with a triple battle line drawn up before it to protect them and to be protected by them.") In the edition by Prutz, *Source Contributions to the History of the Crusades* (*Quellenbeiträge zur Geschichte der Kreuzzüge*), 1: 44.

Radulf, *Gesta Tancredi* (*Deeds of Tancred*), Chap. 32 (*Recueil des Historiens des Croisades. Occidentaux: Collection of the Historians of the Crusades. Occidentals,* 3: 629) reports of the fleeing Turks: "nec fuga gyrum senserunt, adeo fugere est sperare salutem." ("Nor in their flight did they even think of turning, to such an extent to flee is to hope for safety.") According to the account, this refers to horsemen whom we cannot imagine as forming a tight group. That can perhaps be explained by the fact that the poet in his holy inspiration inadvertently attributed to the horsemen a picture from the actions of the fighters on foot.

13. William the Briton, *Philippis,* Book XI, verses 605–612 (Duchesne, 5: 238):

In peditum vallo totiens impune receptus
Nulla parte Comes metuebat ab hoste noceri
Hastatos etenim pedites invadere nostri
Horrebant equites, dum pugnant ensibus ipsi:
Atque armis brevibus, illos vero hasta cutellis
Longior et gladiis, et inextricabilis ordo
Circuitu triplici murorum ductus ad instar
Caute dispositos non permittebat adiri.

(After retreating safely so often to his rampart of foot soldiers, in no way did the count fear to be hurt by the enemy. And in fact our knights dread to attack foot soldiers with spears, while they themselves fight with swords. They have short weapons; the others indeed have a spear longer than knives or swords. And their unbreakable formation drawn up in a triple circuit like walls did not permit those cautiously disposed to come near.)

14. At least, I would like to translate paragraph 86 in this manner. ("Ison de to metōpon tēs parataxeōs autōn poiountai kai pyknon en tais machais": "They make the front of their battle line even and closely ordered.")

15. Liudprandus, *Antapodosis,* 2. 31.

16. Perlbach, p. 117.

17. Hartung, *The Ancient German Days of the Nibelungenlied and the*

Gudrun (*Die deutschen Altertümer des Nibelungenliedes und der Kudrun*), p. 505, compares *Gudrun,* 647. 2, 1403. 1, and 1451. 1 with *Nibelungenlied,* 203 and 204. 2210.

18. See Berthold on the Saxons in the battle on the Unstrut, 1075; Ekkehard, p. 223, on a battle in the Crusade of 1096; and the defeat of King Baldwin of Jerusalem at Ramleh in 1102, as described by Fulcher.

19. Hartung, p. 503, and Lexis' and Grimm's dictionaries give only a very few passages for these words.

20. Otto von Freising, 1. 32: "Dux . . . secus quam disciplina militaris et ordo exposuit, non pedetemptim incedens sed praecipitanter advolans in hostem ruit suis gregatim adventantibus et dirupto legionum ordine confuse venientibus." ("The duke . . . otherwise than as knightly training and rank lays down, charged, not proceeding cautiously but flying headlong at the enemy with his men advancing like a herd of cattle and coming in disorder after the formation of the units had been disrupted.")

Baldric, *Historia Jerosolimitana* (*Recueil des Historiens des Croisades. Historiens Occidentaux*), 4. 95: "Sagittarios et pedites suos ordinaverunt et ipsis praemissis pedetemptim ut mos est Francorum, pergebant." ("They drew up their archers and foot soldiers and with themselves in the lead they proceeded cautiously, as is the custom of the Franks.")

Heelu, verse 4898 ff., describes the approach ride in the battle of Worringen as follows: "As the opponents were moving up against each other, they went about this matter so calmly, at a leisurely pace, coming from the two sides as if they were men riding along with their brides in front of them in the saddle."

Guiart, too, in his account of the battle of Mons-en-Pévèle, verse 11494 (cited by Köhler, 2: 269), says that each unit rode up slowly and in closed formation—"Each group moves along at a slow pace, advancing together as in a square."

21. Emperor Leo says, para. 80 ff., the Franks do not form up on horseback or on foot by regiments or squadrons with specific strengths, but by families and groups of companions ("not in a determined size and formation, either sections or divisions as the Romans, but according to tribes and by kinship and attachment to each other, many times even by sworn agreement"*).

Waitz, *Deutsche Verfassungsgeschichte,* 8: 179, believes that individual source passages indicate an organization by thousands, so that every thousand men formed a special unit, and that would undoubtedly mean a thousand horsemen, even if perhaps not always or not completely heavily armed horsemen. Such a group was, according to Waitz, designated as a "*legio,*" and this name also applied to the tactical unit formed for battle.

That is a false concept. A thousand horsemen form such a powerful force that they cannot be designated as a tactical unit, and such a formation with fixed numbers is not consistent with the nature of feudal contingents under their feudal lords. Emperor Leo had a more accurate conception of it. Widukind's strength figure for the battle on the Lechfeld, insofar as the number 1,000 is concerned, is merely a number, and the expression "legion" is a scholarly embellishment.

Among the Normans, we find a faint trace of an organization in groups of ten warriors. It is reported that Tancred of Hauteville had ten knights under him at the court of the count of Normandy ("in curia comitis decem milites sub se habens servivit"). Gottfried Malaterra, *Migne,* CXLIX, 1121. Furthermore, the knightly services which William the Conqueror required of his most important vassals were always divisible by five or ten.

The Knights Templars were grouped in "squadrons" ("*eschielle*") whenever they took to the field (*Regulations,* Chap. 161). I have never been able to determine how strong an "*eschielle*" was.

In the Crusade, Emperor Frederick I divided his army into units of fifty. How strange such an organization, which seems to us natural and indispensable, was to a medieval army is best indicated by the special attention Ansbert gives to this measure in his report (*Fontes rerum Austriacarum, Abteilung I, Scriptores: Sources of Austrian History, Section I, Historians,* 5. 34):

Interea serenissimus imperator ut fidelis et prudens familiae domini dispensator de statu sanctissimae crucis exercitus in dies sollicitus, praefecit eidem pentarchos seu quinquagenos magistros militum, ut videlicet universi in suis societatibus per quinquagenarios divisi singulis regerentur magistris, sivi in bellicis negotiis, sive in dispensationum controversiis salvo iure marschalli aulae imperialis. Sexaginta quoque meliores ac prudentiores de exercitu delegit, quorum consilio et arbitrio cuncta exercitus negotia perficerentur, qui tamen postea

Meanwhile the most serene emperor, as the loyal and wise steward of the royal house and anxious every day about the state of the crusade, placed pentarchs or fifty masters of the soldiers in charge of it, clearly so that all divided in their companies by the commanders of fifty might be governed by a master both in military affairs and in disputes over orders by the reserved right of a marshal of the imperial court. He also selected sixty better and more prudent men of the army by whose counsel and judgment all affairs of the army might be ac-

solertioris cautelae dispensatione et certi causa mysterii pauciori numero designati sedecim de sexaginta sunt effecti.

complished. But afterwards, by an ordinance of rather clever caution and by reason of a definite plan, they were assigned by a smaller number and were made sixteen from the sixty.

22. Edited by Karl Hegel, *Chronicles of the German Cities* (*Chroniken der deutschen Städte*), Vol. II, 1864.

23. As shown on p. 485. According to the report on p. 203, there were only 400.

24. According to Albrecht's letter, *City Chronicles,* 2. 495, there were 450 "riding horses" and "about 50 *'Drabanten'*."

25. Köhler, 2: 695, drew from Dlugoss, *Hist. Polon,* 11. 240, edition of 1711 (incorrectly, of course) the fact that the Poles rode up in this formation at the battle of Tannenberg.

But in his *Military History of Bavaria* (*Kriegsgeschichte von Bayern*), Würdinger, who used Archivalien as a reference, reported, at the battle of Hiltersried in 1433, where Duke John of Neumarkt or Neunburg defeated the Hussites, exactly the same formation of the knights as at Pillenreuth, giving their names. The banners were placed in the third rank. According to a study that District Assessor Reimer in Neunburg sent me, however, there was no report of a wedge formation. The knights apparently were stationed on foot at the point of an assault column that attacked the Hussite wagon stronghold.

The formation with a point is prescribed as a regulation, so to speak, in Elector Albrecht Achilles' instructions to his son John for the campaign against the duke of Sagan, the so-called Preparation of 1477. Quoted in Jähns' *Manual of the History of Military Science* (*Handbuch von Geschichte der Kriegswissenschaften*), p. 979 ff., and *Kriegsgeschichte,* Document of the Supreme General Staff, 1884, Book 3. In the formation prescribed here, the banners were placed in the eleventh, fourteenth, or nineteenth rank.

26. *Themes for Instruction in Tactics in the Royal Military Schools* (*Leitfaden für den Unterricht in der Taktik der königlichen Kriegsschulen*), 2d ed., 1890, p. 45. *Drill Regulations for Cavalry* (*Exerzier-Reglement für die Kavallerie*), (1895), No. 319-331.

27. The "point" did not occur before the fifteenth century.

Each group moves along at a slow pace,
Advancing together as in a square,

says Guiart, verse 11494, in his description of Mons-en-Pévèle (1304), cited by Köhler in his 2: 269. The first example of the point is perhaps the formation of the troops of the Dauphiné "en pointe" in the battle of Mons-en-Vimeux in 1421, cited in Köhler, 2: 226, note. Recommendations for the formation with a point in documents of the fifteenth and sixteenth centuries are to be found in Jähns, 1: 328, 738, and 740. At the end of the fifteenth century, under Maximilian, the formation was surely squared off again. Leonhard Fronsperger speaks of the "pointed" battle formation as an obsolete one (Köhler, 3: 2: 251). We already find a formation of horsemen in a wedge or rhomboid in antiquity mentioned in Aelian, Chap. 18, and Asclepiodotus, Chap. 7. Among the reasons for this, which are probably theoretical fantasies, at least in part, it is also stated that control and wheeling actions are easier than in the squared formation. As far as control is concerned, this is obviously correct. With respect to wheeling actions, I understand that as meaning they did not need to make any true wheeling motion but could easily turn half-right or half-left by changing the rhomboid into a square.

28. "Istos in una et prima acie posuit et dixit illis: campus amplus est; extendite vos per campum directe, ne vos hostes intercludant. Non deceti ut unus miles scutum sibi de alio milite faciat; sed sic stetis, ut omnes quas, una fronte possitis pugnare." ("He set them in one battle line and said to them: The field is big; extend yourselves across the field in a straight line so that the enemy may not cut you off. It is not proper that a knight make a shield for himself from another knight. But you should thus stand that all are able to fight on one front.")

29. Köhler, 2: 226 and 3: 2: 253, believes that the formation in line first occurred in the fifteenth century. I see no basis for this assumption. Wherever mixed combat took place, the linear formation must have gained ground. Boutaric, p. 297, makes the general statement: "The knights fought 'en haye,' that is to say, in a single line; the squires were drawn up behind them."

30. Baltzer, p. 106, cites two pieces of evidence for this.

31. Prutz, *Quellenbeiträge*, p. 29: "acies... beati Petri a dextris antecedens, cujus juris est antecedere et primum hostes percutere" ("the unit of the blessed Peter going ahead on the right, of whose privilege it is to go first and to strike the enemy first").

32. This valuable observation had already been made by Heermann, p. 85, and Köhler has also agreed with him. Nevertheless, the battle finally ended in a serious defeat.

33. Liudprandus, *Antapodosis*, 2. 31.

34. *Gesta Friderici*, 1. 32.

35. Köhler, 3: 1: 95, has assembled a few passages, wherever they occur. Edward III of England, especially, formed in 1356 a guard of mounted archers. In the index volume, among the supplements, the author also added another passage from *Wigalois*. I would also add the treaty of alliance of the Lombards, *Murat. Ant.*, 4: 490. But even in England they never became a real arm. In the fifteenth century we do find many archers on horseback, but this was only a means of transportation for them; in battle, they dismounted.

The Saracens of Frederick II are considered by Köhler to have been exclusively dismounted archers. But it is expressly stated in *Annales Parmenses majores* (*Greater Annals of Parma*), SS., 18. 673, that in 1248 before Parma the emperor had "balistarii tam equites quam pedites" ("crossbowmen on horseback as well as on foot").

36. Köhler, 1: 5 and 3: 3: 355. Up to the tenth century, he says, they had fought in a single echelon, but from the eleventh century on, in three echelons.

37. Köhler, 2: 35, assembled a few examples, but they show basically that such combat techniques were used less in actual practice than in the heroic accounts, and they succeeded still less often.

38. Köhler, 1: 468, and 2: 13.

39. Köhler, 2: 42.

40. Daniel, *Histoire de la milice française*, p. 82.

41. Only seldom do we find that a king remained behind the front, as, for example, at Ascalon in 1125, cited by Heermann, p. 120. Or old King Iagiello of Poland at Tannenberg in 1410.

42. Viollet-le-Duc, *Rational Dictionary of French Furniture from the Carolingian Period to the Renaissance* (*Dictionnaire raisonné du mobilier français de l'époque carlovingienne à la renaissance*), 6: 372.

43. This is how I prefer to translate the Greek expression "sphodrōs kai akataschetōs hōs monotonoi": "violent and unstoppable like obstinate men"). (*Tactics*, para. 87). See Mauritius, p. 269.

44. Before Ascalon, 12 August 1099. Albert of Aachen, 6. 42, as cited in Röhricht, *History of the First Crusade* (*Geschichte des ersten Kreuzzuges*), p. 200, Note 8.

45. Richer of Sens, M.G. SS., 25. 294.

46. Orderich, 12. 18: "ferro enim undique vestiti erant et pro timore Dei notitiaque contubernii vicissim sibi parcebant nec tamen occidere fugientes quam comprehendere satagebant." ("for they had been dressed completely in iron and mutually spared each other according to fear of God and acknowledgment of their brotherhood in arms; they did not endeavor so much to kill those in flight as to capture them.")

Giraldus, *Opera,* 5. 396: "ibi capiuntur milites, hic decapitantur; ibi redimuntur, hic perimuntur." ("There knights are captured, here decapitated; there they are ransomed, here they are killed.")

47. See p. 221, Note 3, above.

48. The provisions of the Teutonic order, which followed the pattern of the Knights Templars, state in the "Customs," Chap. 46 (Perlbach, p. 111), that on the march the knight was to have his squire ride in front of him so that he could keep a close watch on his armor.

49. The provision in the Teutonic order was quite similar (Perlbach, p. 117): "Nullus frater insultum faciat, nisi prius vexillum viderit insilisse. Post insultum vexilli quilibet pro viribus corporis et animi, quidquid poterit exercebit et redibit ad vexillum, cum viderit oportunum." ("No brother should make an attack, unless he will have seen the banner charge first. After the attack of the banner each will employ whatever he can according to the strength of his body and spirit, and he will return to the banner when he will have seen it opportune.")

50. Meckel, *Tactics,* 1: 50.

51. "The weakest moment for the cavalry is immediately after carrying out an attack. This pause cannot be eliminated fast enough, and order, calm, and a closed formation cannot be restored quickly enough, in order that a unit be in a position to face any eventuality." *Instructions* by Major General Carl von Schmidt, Berlin, 1876, p. 152.

52. I cannot remember reading in any medieval source anything about signals in battle. The Knights Templars gave signals in camp with a bell. According to Gautier (Prutz, p. 27), before the battle of Athareb, Prince Roger ordered that at the first trumpet call everybody was to don his equipment ("audito primo sonitu gracilis"—that was a kind of trumpet), at the second trumpet call they were to assemble, and at the third they were to appear for service of worship. Afterwards, as they went into battle (p. 29), the Christians moved forward "gracilibus, tibiis, tubisque clangentibus" ("while the trumpets, pipes, and horns were sounding"). Duke John of Brabant, too, ordered before the battle of Worringen that the trumpets should blow to signal the manner in which they should attack or fight, in order to encourage his men. The *"ministrere"* stopped their blowing when they saw the ducal banner sink but started blowing the trumpets again when it was raised once more (Ian von Heelu, verses 5668, 5694, pp. 211-212). From this passage, Köhler (3: 2: 340) concluded that this was a normal custom and that the trumpeters were near the banner in order to indicate where it was, even if it was obscured by dust. This conclusion goes too far in every respect. Ducange quotes from the *Vita St. Pandulfi,* n. 15: "illam tubam, quam ad significandum proelium

tubare significavi" ("that horn which I gave the sign to blow to indicate battle").

53. In his work on the conduct of battle of occidental armies in the period of the First Crusade, Heermann determined (p. 103) that all the battlefields in that area whose terrain forms are recognizable (Dorylaeum, Lake of Antioch, Antioch, Ascalon, Ramleh (1101), Joppe, Ramleh (1105), Sarmin, Merdj-Sefer, Athareb, and Hab) are plains and that in all the source accounts there is hardly a trace of terrain difficulties or battles in towns or woods.

Emperor Leo, *Tactics*, 18. 92, says that broken terrain was disadvantageous for the Franks in mounted combat, because they normally made a strong shock action with their lances. Of course, this strong blow is not to be understood in the modern sense.

54. This comes into consideration particularly against mounted archers, and therefore in the Crusades. Heermann (p. 103) traces this back to the tactics of the Moslems, who, with their great numerical superiority, always tried to envelop the Christians. This great superiority of the infidels is to be dismissed as a Christian fable; the reason is to be sought, rather, in their differing armament.

55. Heermann says in his introduction that we can get to know the knightly method of warfare best and most accurately from the early period of the Crusades. In the later Crusades, the occidentals possibly had borrowed from the orientals, whereas they must have won their first victories with their original tactics. Furthermore, we also have broader source accounts of those events, accounts that are much more meager for events in the west. As logical as this idea may seem, it is nevertheless not correct. The peculiar new conditions of combat were present right from the beginning, at Dorylaeum, and the Crusaders had to try to adapt to them.

56. Book XVII, Chap. 4. Basel edition, 1549, p. 397.

57. *SS.*, 9. 257. *Gesta Roberti Wiscardi*, 2. 154.

58. Leo, *Tactics*, 18. 84; "Chaiousi de mallon tēi pezomachiai kai tais meta elasias katadromais." ("They take more delight in infantry battle and in attacks with a charge on horseback.") The Greek word *mallon* does not mean "more" but "very." I would like to translate this passage as: "They were accustomed both to fighting on foot and to charging on horseback."

59. Guiart, p. 299 above, Note 2.

60. In the seventh and eighth supplements to the *Militär-Wochenblatt*, 1894, there is reprinted a diary of Captain von Kinsingen for the year 1812, where it is stated on p. 277 that, when Cossacks attacked an

isolated company, "It was curious that, in this hand-to-hand fight, most of the Cossacks jumped from their horses and fought on foot"—and with their lances, at that!

61. Fröhlich, *Contributions to the History of the Romans' Conduct of Warfare* (*Beiträge zur Geschichte der Kriegführung der Römer*), 1886, p. 60, assembled eleven passages on this subject from Livy. And I will add Polybius, 11. 21, where the interpretation of the text, of course, is questionable, and *Polyb. Fragm.* 125 (Dindorf), where it is reported that the Celtiberians jumped down from their horses for combat.

62. In my opinion, the passages on which Baltzer, p. 99, Note 11, bases his conclusion have no validity as evidence.

63. Heermann, too, p. 101, has proven this for the period of the First Crusade.

64. Köhler, 3: 2: 39 and 83, cites passages indicating that *armigeri* and *garciones* were armed, and he concludes from this that they were normally unarmed. This conclusion goes too far; the reference is undoubtedly only to heavy defensive arms, which they had not had and with which they were now provided.

65. "rex Chonradus . . . papae . . . stratoris officium exhibuit." ("King Conrad . . . held the office . . . of the pope's groom.") Bernold 1095, cited by Waitz, 6: 194.

66. Otto von Freising, *Gesta Friderici*, II, Chap. 18.

67. Otto Morena, *M.G. SS.*, 18. 603.

68. Otto Morena, p. 606. Otto von Freisingen, *SS.*, 20. 398.

69. Lacomblet, *Book of Source Documents* (*Urkundenbuch*), 4: 792.

70. Reprinted in Giesebrecht, *Deutsche Kaiserzeit*, 2: 686.

71. 3: 2: 50. But, of course, in Vol. II, p. xi, a distinction is again made between them.

Chapter III

Mercenaries

We have recognized as erroneous the idea that an individual man ever went to war at his own expense. That was possible only for very short distances and a very short time, in feuds with neighbors, but not in the wars of large nations with which we are dealing. Starting with Clovis, warriors who took to the field had to be equipped and fed by a larger organization or an important lord. The lord who primarily organized campaigns in this manner was the count, and whether the count chose the warriors whom he led from his enfeoffed vassals or those without fiefs and his inherited common soldiers or also took wandering knights and soldiers who came to him and who seemed useful to him did not make any significant difference in their performance. In addition to their rations, the lord had probably always had to give something in the way of cash money even to his own men, and from the twelfth century on, this amounted to quite a bit. We have given a few samples above (p. 103) as to how much the *ministeriales* received for a march to Rome. The transition from a levy of vassals and *ministeriales* to a mercenary army was therefore much easier from a practical viewpoint than it might seem from the conceptual contrast between the two types. In a certain measure, both of these presumably always existed side by side. As early as the tenth century, it is recounted of a Venetian doge, either Vitalis or Urseolo, that he had recruited mercenaries in Lombardy and Tuscia and for this reason was killed by the burghers of Venice.[1] In 992, Count Fulco of Anjou sent against Duke Conan of Brittany an army composed "both of his own men and of mercenaries."[2] At the time of Emperor Henry III, Pope Leo IX recruited troops in Germany for use against the Normans in lower Italy.[3] The army with which William the Conqueror crossed to England in 1066 consisted of mercenaries for the most part, and we have seen how quickly those elements of the feudal organization which were, of course, only in part taken over to England by the Normans changed over completely there into a mercenary system. And soon we find the same phenomenon on the Continent. In the wars of Henry IV, money was already playing a considerable role. The subsidies which the emperor in Constantinople paid to the German emperor so that the latter would keep the Norman Robert Guiscard off his neck were used by the German for his own military purposes. We also hear quite often that the king loaned money and his cities paid him taxes. Under his son, Henry V, we hear for the first time mention of the insatiable gullet of the royal treasury ("regalis fisci os insatiabile").[4] In 1106, the duke of Lorraine sent *Gelduni* to the aid of Cologne,[5] and, under Frederick Barbarossa, the Brabantines formed a very important part of his armed forces. The army which Archbishop Christian of Mainz led across the Alps in 1171 consisted mostly of Brabantines. In 1158, the Genoese recruited marksmen to fight against the emperor, and Byzantium recruited in Italy "milites qui solidarii vocantur" ("knights who are called mercenaries"), to quote the expression of the German, Ragewin (4. 20). It was not just primarily Germanic areas from which these mercenaries came, but there is also mention especially of Aragonese, Navarrese, and Basques. They were also called *coterelli, ruptuarii* (marauders), *triaverdini, stipendiarii, vastatores* (ravagers), *gualdana* (or *gelduni:* band of vagabonds), *berroerii* (sergeants, armed servants), *mainardieri, forusciti* (exiles), *banditi* (banished ones), *banderii, ribaldi* (rascals, vagabonds), and *satellites* (attendants, retainers).[6]

Feudal warriorhood was a product of the barter economy. It could not have happened that, in addition to this military system and from it, there developed again a mercenary system, unless a certain degree of money economy had again sprung up. And associated with this change was the fact that a certain amount of precious metal was in circulation.

The supply of precious metals must have constantly decreased in the period of the *Völkerwanderung,* during which normal mining ceased completely, and in the period of the first Carolingians the supply must have been at its lowest point.[7] But as early as the eighth century new sources are supposed to have been discovered. Gold was panned in the French and German rivers, and in Poitou much silver was obtained again through mining as early as the Carolingian period. Silver was found in the ninth century in Alsace and the Black Forest, beginning with the tenth century in the Tyrol, Steiermark, and Carinthia, and particularly in Bohemia and the Saxon Erzgebirge, and from 970 on in the Harz Mountains. Starting at about the same time, and perhaps even earlier, gold was obtained in Bohemia, Salzburg, Hungary, and Siebenbürgen, principally areas that the Romans had been able to exploit only little or not at all.

Even if individual dates for the beginning of these mining successes are uncertain, and the periods of truly rich exploitation only came later, the increase from the twelfth century on was still so significant that it must have started even considerably earlier. The monk Abbo, in his description of the siege of Paris (886), was already complaining (Book II, verses 605–609) about those knights who would only wear clothing trimmed with gold. A similar picture is given us by the biographer of Archbishop Brun, brother of Otto the Great, whose knights strode about in purple and gold ("inter purpuratos ministros et milites suos auroque nitidos vilem ipse tunicam induxit": "Among the officials clad in purple and his soldiers shining with gold, he wore a common tunic.")[8]

It is impossible to determine from the individual sources whether the mercenaries were foot soldiers or men who fought on horseback in knightly fashion.[9] In any case, at a very early period knights in the strictest sense of the word also accepted service as mercenaries.[10] When King Ladislaus of Bohemia levied his men in 1158 for a campaign into Italy, the chronicler tells us that they were initially very dissatisfied. But when the king explained that those who were unwilling would be allowed to remain at home, while promising rewards and honor to those who participated, they all pressed forward to join up. At an earlier time, a very unproductive fief or simply food and shelter at the court had formed the compensation for military service, but now that cash money and affluence had generally increased, military service, too, offered the possibility for higher gains and profit. The feudal base did not disappear to the same degree in Germany and France as it did in England, but conditions nevertheless gradually approached those in England. Fiefs and the knightly class were no longer the direct agents of military service, but they retained their significance principally only through the fact that they represented and perpetuated a class that constantly provided excellent material, an ideal source for the recruiting of mercenary warriors. We might well say the significance of the social roots, the class basis of the knightly branch, manifested itself most strongly through the fact that, although the military system turned more and more toward mercenaries, a system in which one strong, brave, experienced man was just as good as the next one, nevertheless knighthood held its own as a class and precisely in this period was transformed into the lesser nobility.

The parallel phenomenon was the growth of a tendency among those possessing knightly fiefs to transform themselves into a simple class of large property owners.

In the "Little Lucidarius" (also called "Seifrid Helbling"), between 1283 and 1299, the squire tells his lord that at the court one no longer discusses Parsifal and Gahmuret but milch cows and commerce in grains and wine.[11] In the next century, the Austrian poet Suchenwirt has the following words spoken by a knight who has never left his home area:

Here I stay like another cow
And I am a home-bound child.

As early as the twelfth century, the mercenary system was so widely developed that there were famous mercenary leaders, who can be considered as precursors of the later condottieri. The first of these was William of Ypres, an illegitimate son of Philip of Flanders, it seems. He married a relative of Pope Calixtus II, became lord of Sluys, and in England was named count of Kent by King Stephen. The bands at the head of which he waged war, now here and now there, were composed of horsemen and foot soldiers, and the chronicle describes his position as "quasi dux fuit et princeps eorum" ("as if he was their duke and prince").[12] If William of Ypres himself was a prominent knight, another man, William of Cambrai, who is named as a leader of the Brabantines, was a former priest. But most of these leaders were probably of knightly origin or at least rose into the top social class by acquiring fiefs and prestige. The chief of another band, Mercadier, a Provençal, was the principal support of Richard the Lion-Hearted when Richard returned from captivity, and he supposedly was a personal friend of the king.

With the passage of time, there developed as a link between the feudal military system and the mercenary system the practice of concluding definite monetary agreements between great powers, such as kings or cities, on the one side, and princes and lords on the other. This meant that the latter, with the fixed nucleus of warriors whom they supported and recruited, their supplies of weapons, and their own experience and authority, obligated themselves to provide specific numbers of men, whether it be for a definite campaign or for an eventual emergency. Henry I of England, son of William the Conqueror, concluded the first treaty of this type in 1103, with Count Robert of Flanders, who obligated himself to provide for the king 1,000 knights with three horses each, in return for 400 marks of silver annually. The treaty was spelled out in very precise detail. It was not valid against Robert's suzerain, the king of France. The count was to have his knights ready forty days after receiving notification. The king of England was to send ships to pick them up. As long as the Flemish were in England, the king was to provide their rations and replace their losses in materiel just as for his own retinue (the "family"). The treaty was strengthened by having the barons and castellans of the count of Flanders recognize their obligation to the king of England in a special document. Fifty years later, in 1163 [*sic*], the treaty was renewed by the successors on both sides.[13]

An interminable number of such agreements were concluded later, especially by German free cities with neighboring dynasties.[14]

The advantages of leading into the field, instead of feudal knights, mercenary knights who, providing one could assemble their pay and pay them promptly, were completely under control, were obvious and great for a prince—so much so that in the thirteenth century in France feudal lords preferred to sell vacated fiefs to burghers, who paid for them, rather than place on the land a new knight who was to serve in return.[15]

We have seen how easily the true, wealthy knight became a robber. Naturally, the common, homeless mercenary soldier was even much more inclined in that direction. The areas through which they marched on the way to war already suffered seriously as a result of the very weak disciplinary authority in such an army, but the worst situation occurred when these men were released after the end of a war and moved through the country on their own. Armed as they were, they remained together in bands, harassed and ravished the inhabitants in the most extreme degree, and spared neither churches nor monasteries. From the start, of course, these were the most brutal, coarsest elements of the population, whose nature was inconsistent with civilian life and peaceful enterprise, who answered the recruiting call and in the lawlessness and savagery of war shed every restraint and every sense of compassion. The chronicler Hermann of Reichenau tells us about one of the first mercenary armies of which we hear, the one which the strict, energetic Pope Leo IX had assembled in 1053 to oppose the Normans, one composed of adventurers and fugitive criminals. Even the kings who made use of these bands had to search later for means of freeing their countries from them. Emperor Frederick and Louis VII of France concluded a treaty on 14 February 1171 in which it is stated that they met personally with many barons and mutually obligated themselves never to tolerate in their kingdoms the "reprobates" who were called Brabantines or *coterelli*. Neither was any vassal to tolerate them unless a man had taken a wife in his region or had entered his service on a permanent basis. Anyone who broke this agreement was to be excommunicated and interdicted by the bishops, he was to replace all damages, and the neighbors were to hold him to this by force. If the vassal was too powerful to be forced to do this by the neighbors, the emperor himself was to carry out the punishment.[16]

The Lateran Council of 1179 provided for the most severe ecclesiastic punishments against all "Brabantines, Aragonese, Navarrese, Basques, and *triaverdini,*" and also against those who hesitated to take arms against them.

There are also reports of a few cases in which they were forcefully done away with. The Brabantines under the priest William of Cambrai, who for a time had also served King Henry II of England, seized the castle of Beaufort in the Limousin, from which they lay waste the surrounding area. In 1177 they were finally defeated there by Count Ademar and the bishop of Limoges, and all of them were slain.[17]

In 1183 a large band of Brabantines was destroyed at Charenton; a large "Alliance for Peace," under the command of a certain carpenter Durand, had been formed in Auvergne to destroy them.

But when this alliance for peace turned against the lords, the latter, themselves now allied with the Brabantines, destroyed the rebellious plebeians.

EXCURSUS

A FEW REFERENCES TO MONEY AND SOLDIER'S PAY

There has been preserved the draft of the treaty which Saint Louis was willing to conclude with the doge of Venice in 1268, but which was not executed because the king finally came to an agreement with the Genoese. In this *contractus navigii* (shipping contract),[18] Marcus Quirinus promises the king, in the name of the doge of Venice, fifteen ships for 4,000 horses and 10,000 men, if the king undertakes the passage between the Feast of Saint John and the New Year. Twelve ships were to have a crew of fifty sailors, but the "Roccafortis" and the "Santa Maria" were to have 110, and the "Saint Nicholas" was to have eighty-six. As rent for the "Roccafortis" and the "Santa Maria," the king was to pay 1,400 marks each (that is, some 56,000 Reichsmarks), for the Saint Nicholas 1,100 marks (44,000 Reichsmarks), and for the twelve others, 700 marks each (28,000 Reichsmarks). And so the rent for the ships alone was to cost almost a half-million Reichsmarks in our currency. A knight with two servants, one horse, and one groom was to pay 8½ marks (340 Reichsmarks) for his passage (*navigium*), including their rations. A knight alone was to pay 2¼ marks (90 Reichsmarks) for a covered spot (*placa cooperta*) between the middle mast and the poop deck. A squire (*scutifer*) was to pay 7 ounces (35 Reichsmarks) for an uncovered space (*placa discooperta*); the groom and the horse were to pay 4½ marks (180 Reichsmarks). For a place between the middle mast and the prow, a pilgrim was to pay 3 3/4 marks [*sic. This should apparently be 3/4 mark—Trans.*] (30 Reichsmarks), rations included. The necessary wood for cooking was to be furnished.

Philip Augustus gave each knight three gold pieces per month. Richard the Lion-Hearted announced before Acre that he would give four gold pieces per month to each knight who would enter his service. The gold pieces in question were probably byzantines. At the time of Saint Louis 1 byzantine was worth 10 *livres tournois,* and Natalis de Wailly gives the value of the *livre tournois* as 20 francs, 26 centimes. Consequently, a byzantine was worth 202 francs, 60 centimes. By this reckoning, Philip Augustus paid 607 francs, 80 centimes per month, and Richard even paid 810 francs, 40 centimes. For the period from the Feast of Saint James (25 July) to Easter, Joinville, since he had sacrificed all his possessions in conjunction with his captivity, demanded of King Louis IX 1,200 pounds, and for each of the three knights whom he had recruited, 400 pounds. If we assume that these pounds were *livres tournois,* Joinville received 24,312 francs, and each of the knights received 8,104 francs. If the reference was to *livres parisis,* the amount rose to about 30,396 and 11,132 [sic] francs, respectively. In this case, the pay would have risen quite significantly in a period of fifty to sixty years, for Philip Augustus paid only 7,293.60 francs per year, the generous Richard 9,724.80 francs, and Louis IX had to grant his knights annual compensation of 10,805 (or 13,509) francs. And Joinville even received 32,416 francs (or 40,528) annually.

A table showing the pay scales for warriors of every kind from 1231 to 1785 can be found in D'Avenel, *Histoire économique,* 3: 664–680.

Interesting statistics on pay are also given in Köhler, 1: 167.

In the pay agreements of the counts of Flanders with the kings of England of 1101 and later years, each knight is assumed to have three horses (Rymer, *Foedera,* 1: 1).

NOTES FOR CHAPTER III

1. Petrus Damiani, *Vita Romualdi (The Life of Romualdus), SS.,* 4. 848 (written ca. 1040).

2. Richer, IV, Chap. 82: "exercitum tam de suis, quam conducticiis congregabat." ("He assembled an army from his own men as well as from hirelings.")

3. Hermannus Contractus, *SS.,* V, for the year 1053.

4. Waitz, 8: 238, 402, 411.

5. *Annales Hildesheimses (Annals of Hildesheim), SS.,* 3. 110.

6. Mikulla, "The Mercenaries in the Armies of Emperor Frederick II" ("The Mercenaries in the Armies of Emperor Frederick II" ("Die Söldner in den Heeren Kaiser Friedrichs II." Berlin dissertation, 1885, p. 5.

Ducange questions whether instead of *"triaverdini"* we should not read *"triamellini,"* a word supposedly derived from the name of a certain type of dagger.

7. Peschel, "On the Variations of Relative Values Between the Precious Metals and Other Commercial Goods" ("Ueber die Schwankungen der Wertrelationen zwischen den edlen Metallen und den übrigen Handelsgütern"), *Deutsche Vierteljahresschrift,* 4 (1853): 1.

Soetbeer, "Contributions to the History of the Monetary and Minting System in Germany" ("Beiträge zur Geschichte des Geld- und Münzwesens in Deutschland"), *Forschungen zur Deutschen Geschichte,* Vols. I to VI and 57th Supplementary Volume to *Petermanns Mitteilungen,* 1879.

Lexis, article "Gold" and article "Silver" in the *Dictionary of Political Science (Handwörterbuch der Staatswissenschaft).*

Waitz, *Heinrich I.,* Excurs 15, "On the Reported Discovery of Metals in the Harz under Henry I" ("Ueber die angebliche Entdeckung der

Metalle im Harz unter Heinrich I"). According to Waitz, mining in the Harz under Otto I is definitely confirmed by Widukind and Thietmar; it is still questionable as to whether it really went back to the time of Henry I. Inama-Sternegg, *German Economic History from the Tenth to the Twelfth Century* (*Deutsche Wirtschaftsgeschichte des 10. bis 12. Jahrhundert*), 2: 430 f.

The values for grains estimated by Peschel are obviously unreliable, and his opinion that a decrease of metal supplies can be observed in Europe from the fourteenth century on is certainly incorrect.

Soetbeer, 2: 306, thinks he has found indications that there was still much cash money on hand under the Merovingians. This opinion no doubt needs to be researched further.

The Florentine guilder was minted from 1252 on.

Helfferich, *Money and Banks* (*Geld und Banken*), 1: 87, says: "In the face of an almost complete cessation of production of precious metals and a heavy flow of such metals to the Byzantine Empire and the Far East, an unusual decrease in the supply of precious metal in Western Europe apparently took place in the fifth, sixth, and seventh centuries." It does not seem to me to be proven that precious metal flowed away from the west specifically to the Byzantine Empire; at least, there was only a shortage and no superfluous amount there either. But the general decrease in the Roman Empire must have started much earlier, and in the third century A.D. it was already leading to the catastrophe. See Vol. II, p. 212 ff.

8. Ruotger, *vita Brunonis* (*Life of Bruno*), Chap. 30.

9. Delpech, 2: 43, believes the Brabantines were horsemen. Köhler, 3: 2: 148 ff., says they were foot soldiers, but he gives no basis for his opinion. When he expresses surprise on p. 152 that they disappeared after the battle of Bouvines and we later find only national levies and soldiers of the cities in Germany as foot troops, this point is at odds with his opinion that the Brabantines were already such a highly developed infantry. Furthermore, on p. 147, note, he himself cites an English source, Gervasius Dorobernesis, *Chronica de rebus anglicis* (*Chronicles of English History*) of the year 1138 to the effect that William of Ypres, the first of the historic mercenary leaders, commanded "milites et pedites multos" ("many knights and foot soldiers"). Furthermore, in the treaty between Barbarossa and Louis VII of France of the year 1170 (Martène, *Veterum scriptorum . . . amplissima collectio: Largest Collection of Ancient Writers . . .* , 2: 880), express mention is made of the "Brabantiones sive coterelli" (*"Brabantines or coterelli"*) as "equites seu pedites" ("horsemen or foot soldiers").

10. Gislebert, *SS.,* 21. 844. Baldwin presumably had "milites auxilia-tores, qui quamvis non essent solidarii, tamen in expensis ejus erant" ("auxiliary knights, who, although they were not mercenaries, were nevertheless on his payroll").

11. 15. 100, cited by Roth von Schreckenstein, p. 352.

12. Gervasius Dorobernesis, *Chronica de rebus anglicis.*

13. The first treaty is reproduced in Rymer, *Foedera,* 1: 7, and the second one on p. 22. In the conditions governing the pay are provisions that do not seem to be consistent. In the obligation of the barons, it is stated that those who receive 30 marks "pro feodo" (as "fief") were obli-gated to provide 10 *milites,* and so forth. But the total amount for 1,000 knights was only 400 marks. But in the renewed treaty of 1163, 30 marks was the agreed amount for every ten knights.

This agreement forms an intermediate type between a treaty covering compensation and a political treaty, in that the count excludes in the first case service against his suzerain, but secondly, in case his lord himself should attack England, he obligated himself to serve him only to the extent of not forfeiting his fief.

"Tam parvam fortitudinem hominum secum adducet quam minorem poterit ita tamen ne inde feodum suum erga Regem Franciae forisfaciat." ("He will bring with him so small a force as he can so that he may not, however, forfeit his fief to the king of France thereby.")

14. Köhler, 3: 2: 155, has assembled a number of these treaties.

15. Boutaric, p. 1138.

16. *M. G. LL.,* IV Constitutiones I (*Records of Germany, Laws IV, Ordinances I*), 331, and Martène and Durand, *Veterum scrip-torum... amplissima collectio* (*Largest Collection of Ancient Writers*), 2: 880. The rulers consented "inter cetera de expellendis maleficis hominibus, qui Brabantiones sive Coterelli dicuntur tale fecimus utrimque pactum et statutum. Nullos videlicet Brabantiones vel Coterellos equites seu pe-dites in totis terris aut imperii infra Rhenum et Alpes et civitatem Parisius [*sic*] aliqua occasione et uerra retinebimus." ("We have made the following agreement and regulation among other things concerning the expulsion of criminals who are called Brabantines or Coterelli: we shall not keep on any occasion and in war anyone, namely, Brabantines and Coterelli, whether horse or foot, in all the lands of our empire within the Rhine, the Alps, and the city of Paris.")

17. H. Géraud, *The Highwaymen in the Twelfth Century* (*Les Routiers au douzième siècle*), Bibliothèque de l'Ecole des Chartes, 3 (1841): 132.

18. According to Alwin Schultz, *The Courtly Life* (*Das höfische Leben*), 2: 316.

Chapter IV

Strategy

What we have said about the concept of tactics in the Middle Ages applies also to strategy. Strategy—that is, the use of combat for the purposes of war—did, of course, exist, but only seldom in the sense of an art.

We have seen that the military accomplishments of the feudal nation were generally small. The armies were small in numbers, had but little discipline, and were not even obligated to serve for an unlimited period.

Charlemagne's might was based on the huge extent of his empire and his sweeping monarchical authority. His truly military accomplishments, as is shown by the slow and limited progress against the Saracens and the interminable Saxon wars, were only very small. We hardly dare to speak of strategy in these campaigns, and the kingdoms of his successors were soon completely powerless. The two great kings of the Saxon dynasty, Henry and Otto, had again created in the eastern part of the Carolingian Empire, through a compromise with the other great feudal families and the dynastic autonomy, a strong central power, and Otto did succeed, to be sure, in inflicting a great defeat on the Hungarians on the Lechfeld by assembling all the forces of his kingdom. But the military power of the new kingdom was nevertheless in no way great and not even very reliable, since the partial independence of the great vassals constantly challenged the authority of the crown and the peace of the country. In the battle on the Lechfeld we have assumed Otto's army to have been no larger than 6,000 to 8,000 men. Only by recognizing the full significance of this number do we understand the successes of the pagans. It was only partially through military strength but very significantly as a result of the entry of the Normans and the Magyars into the Christian civilized area that the dangers from the pirate armies of north and the armies of horsemen of the Asiatic nomads were eliminated.

Nothing is more characteristic of medieval warfare than the feud between Emperor Otto II and his cousin, King Lothair of France, in 978.

The mighty German king, lord of Germany and Italy and Roman emperor, had to flee from his capital, Aachen, when the almost powerless king of the West Franks suddenly approached. While he succeeded in quickly assembling an army in order to avenge himself and arrived before Paris, he could accomplish nothing against the fortified city and had to turn back, suffering considerable losses during his return march.[1]

Nor were the armies of the Salian and Hohenstaufen emperors significantly larger than the army of Otto the Great on the Lechfeld—since we have here several reliable sources, a supplementary confirmation of our estimate of Charlemagne's armies, for in view of the increasing population and the improved economic life in these centuries, the armies had in any case not become smaller.

Those things that differed in this period in the elements of the conduct of war were related to political developments.

As the feudal nation took on more definite form, it resulted that all the half-independent levels that were thus created, princes as well as cities, were concerned with insuring their own security with fortifications. The cities strengthened their walls, and on the hills and mountains there rose almost impregnable castles. The edifices of the kings themselves took on a different character. While the Merovingians and Carolingians had built their castles on the open plains, the kings of the Saxons, Salians, and Hohenstaufens built their castles on hills or spots protected in some other manner, so that they could be defended.[2]

As a result of this situation, the power of the defense grew vis-à-vis the offense. It became easy for a weaker force to avoid a decisive battle, whereas it was now more difficult for the stronger opponent, even if he won a victory, to benefit from it. For besieging every individual city and castle was hard work, and there were countless numbers of them. The powerful German emperor Frederick, who had also been joined by many Italians, required more than half a year to reduce the small city of Crema (1160).

Instead of a true siege, we quite often find recourse to the system of a loose blockade; the enemy city was surrounded by forts that cut off its commerce with the outside world. By this means, the Normans in lower Italy forced the Greek cities to surrender,[3] and Barbarossa twice reduced Milan without resorting to an actual siege and attack in force. But this kind of action requires that one's own forces be held together for a very long time, and the medieval feudal armies were only seldom capable of that.

The final decision in all the large Hohenstaufen wars, even in Barbarossa's defeat of Henry the Lion, and in the struggle between their two sons, Philip and Otto, was eventually more dependent on the partisan-ship or the change of sides of the great vassals and the large cities than on military actions. This taking of sides, while no doubt influenced by mili-tary successes, was still not dominated by them. For that reason, on a few occasions in this period we find a distribution of forces and a suspenseful tension in their employment of such a kind as to produce a true strategy, as, for example, in the way in which Otto the Great brought on the battle on the Lechfeld and in the war of Henry IV against the counterking Rudolf of Swabia. As the various elements—political, strategic, and tactical—constantly influence one another in war, so there appeared in these battles tactical factors such as we hardly observe anywhere else. On the other hand, the later wars of the great Hohenstaufens, despite innu-merable actions, do not offer anything similar. The effect of the victory at Hastings in bringing the large Anglo-Saxon kingdom under the domina-tion of the Normans with a single blow and on a lasting basis was closely related to the completely undeveloped political situation of the country. The German kings were not able to establish a similar mastery of Italy (even though their enemies did not risk offering them any opposition in the open field), because Italy, Romanic as it was, nevertheless had in its independent communes and in the universal institution of the papacy stronger powers of resistance than did the Germanic kingdom of the Anglo-Saxons. The Italians even finally succeeded in defeating the em-peror in open battle, but it is well to note that the defeat at Legnano (1176) did not have any significant meaning in the final decision. It was a chance battle, which was brought on by the fact that the emperor, with much too great confidence, intended to lead his contingents arriving from Germany through the region of Milan, from Como to Pavia, passing the city at a distance of only a few miles. The Milanese took position with their allies on this route to oppose him, and the Germans fell victim to their numerical superiority. But the truly decisive point was that the emperor, after his falling out with Henry the Lion, was only able to bring from Germany very limited forces, whereas Milan had much stronger backing by the other Italian communes than in the earlier wars. Even without the defeat of Legnano, Frederick would still have had to agree to a reasonable treaty. The fact that the Milanese, despite their victory, were willing to concede him many points shows that they did not overes-timate the significance of that victory.

The great victory of Emperor Frederick II over the Milanese and the Lombard alliance at Cortenuova in 1237 also had practically no results.

Was the Middle Ages perhaps ignorant of the theory that, in war, open battle is the truly decisive action, and that the first law of strategy, therefore, is to assemble and unite all of one's fighting forces on the battlefield? It is interesting to hear that knighthood did not lack insight on this point. In a French chronicle, the *Deeds of the Counts of Anjou* (*Taten der Grafen von Anjou*), Lisaeus the seneschal says to his count, Godfrey Martell, when the latter was besieging Tours in 1041 and a relief force was approaching:

> It is better that we should fight united rather than be defeated separated from you. Battles are short, but the gain from victory is great. Sieges last a long time and accomplish their purpose only with difficulty; battles subject peoples and cities to you, and those who are defeated in battle disappear before their enemies like smoke. If the battle is won and the enemy defeated, you will have the mastery of the situation and also Tours.[4]

In the same spirit, Saladin, when the large armies of the Third Crusade were approaching, had the walls of many Syrian cities razed in order to reinforce his field army with their garrisons. Totila, the East Goth, had also done the same thing.[5] But those were exceptions and were to remain as such. Throughout the entire Middle Ages we find the opposite principle predominant, the exploitation of the strength of the defensive in fortified places, since the conditions seldom existed where one could really exploit victories in the open field. Feudal armies were too small and too weak for that purpose. Even battles for the relief of a siege, which offered the attacker the advantage of being able to move against the siege army in a very unfavorable position, are only seldom to be found.

Just as the battle was tactically not much more than numerous small combat actions, for which one only needed to decide to act, so, too, were the strategic considerations not much more than implementation of political decisions. Since there was usually nothing significant to decide concerning the "how" of a battle, there remained only the question as to whether one believed his force strong enough to fight or not. The commander who did not feel strong enough sought a fortified place, and the enemy then had only to decide whether or not to besiege it. That might have depended on a number of circumstances, and the decision may have often been very difficult. But it was not truly of a strategic nature in the higher sense of the word, that is, in the sense of an art. Equipment, march order, and concern for provisions may have required a high degree of prudence and energy, but they can only be regarded in a certain relative sense as strategic actions.

Even the ultimate decision to fight a battle was not a strategic one in the Middle Ages in that it was not a decision of the commander in the full sense of the expression. In a disciplined army, a battle is fought by having the commander so order. A medieval commander did not have enough control over his army for this purpose. He could fight only when not simply he himself but his entire army was willing to do battle. Even in disciplined armies, the confidence of the mass of troops in the outcome is a very important factor; in a medieval army, it was impossible to fight at all without this factor. It is a very characteristic phenomenon, which was reported twice by Widukind (1. 36 and 3. 44), before a battle of the Saxons against the Slavs and before the battle with the Hungarians on the Lechfeld, that each warrior first vowed to assist the commander and then the warriors solemnly vowed to help each other. Elsewhere, too, we find mention of a similar formal obligation directly before a battle, even among the Moslems. The unified will that has to govern the whole body was not provided by the organization of the army as such, which decides everything according to the will of the commander, but it had to be created and guaranteed for each occasion.

This condition, the great dependence of the commander on the mood and the will of his army, also no doubt contributed to the fact that battles were so rare in the medieval wars. Wars were almost interminable, and in many years there were no battles, for it was necessary that a feeling of superiority exist at the same time in both opposing armies, unless one of the armies fought only as a matter of necessity, because it could not avoid combat. Even a modern commander normally does not fight without counting on victory. But he perhaps fights even against an unquestionably stronger foe because he hopes to offset the inferiority of his army by his leadership and utilization of the terrain. As we have seen in our consideration of the question of tactics, the medieval commander had no such prospect; he fought only when he himself and his army were convinced of their own superiority.

Characteristic of knightly warfare and the difficulty of basing real strategy on it is the phenomenon of how often it happened that the side that was defeated tactically still managed to attain its strategic purpose. The nature of things requires that whichever side has defeated the enemy army first will probably accomplish its other purpose. But a knightly army was under the control of its commander to such a small extent that the relaxing of tension that normally occurred after a victory, and especially one in which losses had been heavy, often could not be overcome. This forced the commander to give up the further pursuit of his plans. We have established this point on a number of occasions in the wars of Henry IV, and we shall find still more examples of this situation.

In the Middle Ages, we do not find heroic deeds of commanders like those of Miltiades at Marathon, Pausanias at Plataeae, Epaminondas at Leuctra, Hannibal at Cannae, Scipio at Naraggara, and Caesar at Pharsalus, except perhaps on the Lechfeld. The decision of William the Norman not to move immediately on London after his landing in England, but to await the enemy on the coast and keep his forces assembled there, may also be regarded as an act of strategy that had a strong basis as a result of the extent and importance of the victory that followed. However, it is only after a certain amount of reflection that we reach the point of using the word "strategy" in this situation. In the war between Henry IV and Rudolf, a certain degree of strategic thought is no doubt visible, but since no great decisive action resulted from it, it does not stimulate our full interest. A number of artfully and cleverly arranged sudden attacks, such as the attack by Frederick II against the Milanese at Cortenuova, can be considered to be in the realm of strategy, but they lack the high style found in the Lechfeld battle.

It would be a complete misunderstanding if one therefore concluded that personal character, as such, was of relatively small importance in the medieval army. On the contrary, precisely because techniques and with them the art of tactics and strategy had no real substance, the personal character of the leader had to accomplish all the more. Theoretically, the genius of the strategist appears in the phenomenon where he brings on battles and wins them through his tactical skill. In the Middle Ages, battles were almost always possible only when the opponent, too, wanted them. Such a direct zeal among the forces on both sides existed only seldom, and only seldom can this situation exist. The strength and talents of the leaders were needed in other areas, principally in maintaining the unity of the loosely structured feudal nation.

The German Empire collapsed again and again and was reestablished again and again according to the man who stood at its head, disappeared, and returned. In this kind of situation, personal character means everything.

NOTES FOR CHAPTER IV

1. *Annales Altahenses* (*Annals of Niederalteich*) for the year 978: "relictis in alia ripa fluminis victualibus cum plaustris et carucis et pene omnibus utensilibus, quae exercitui erant necessaria." ("After all the supplies had been left behind on the other bank of the river with the wagons, carts, and tools that are necessary for an army...."). The enemy took all of this from the Germans and inflicted many losses on them.

2. W. Weitzel, *The German Imperial Castles from the Ninth to the Six-teenth Century* (*Die deutschen Kaiserpfalzen vom 9. bis 16. Jahrhundert*), Halle an der Saale.

3. Heinemann, *History of the Normans in Lower Italy* (*Geschichte der Normannen in Unteritalien*), p. 120.

4. *Collection of the Historians of the Gauls* (*Recueil des historiens des Gaules*), 11. 266:

> melius est nos convenire et pugnare, quam nos a vobis separari et superari. In bellis mora modica est, sed vincentibus lucrum quam maximum est. Obsidiones multa consumunt tempora et vix obsessa subjugantur municipia: bella vobis subdent nationes et oppida, bello subacti evanescent tamquam fumus inimicis. Bello peracto et hoste devicto vastum imperium et Turonia patebit.
>
> (It is better that we make an agreement and fight rather than be divided from you and overcome. In battles (wars) a delay is insignif-icant, but the conquerors have the greatest gain possible. Sieges take a lot of time, and besieged towns are conquered with diffi-culty: battles (wars) should put nations and towns under your sway and those subjugated by battle (war) vanish like smoke for their enemies. After the battle (war) has been finished and the enemy defeated, a great empire and Tours will lie open.)

In this context, the word *"bellum"* is to be translated as "battle." The fact that the work from which we have extracted this passage is late and unreliable as a historic source does not make any difference for us, of course, since we are concerned not with the authenticity of the sene-schal's speech but with the confirmation of the fact that such reflections did occur in the Middle Ages.

5. Vol. II, p. 378.

Chapter V

The Italian Communes and the Hohenstaufens

At the collapse of the Carolingian Empire, several great territorial dynasties, called margravates, similar to the German duchies, were formed in Italy just as in Francia. But then the cities in Italy developed into independent political powers much faster and more strongly than on this side of the Alps, and these cities played a greater role than the Italian princes.

In Italy, a particularly large number of the members of the warrior class had always lived in the cities. This situation did not change even under the feudal system that developed in accordance with the Frankish pattern. In a document of the bishop of Modena of the year 998, mention is made expressly of the agreement by the knights and the people of the city, in addition to the approval of the ecclesiastics.[1] Under Emperor Henry III there was once a long civil war between the knights (*milites*) and the people (*plebs*) of Milan. The knights had to leave the city, and they attacked the city from without by erecting six forts in front of the six gates. Henry finally subdued the conflict by threatening to send 4,000 knights, and the Milanese guaranteed amnesty to their emigrants.[2]

In 1067 the factions in Milan concluded a treaty in which they established, as punishment for violations, payments of 100 pounds by the archbishop, 20 pounds by one of the *ordo capitaneorum* (rank of the prominent citizens), 10 pounds for the *vassorum* (vassals), and 5 pounds for *negotiatorum* (merchants).

Under the Lombard kings and the Carolingians, independent communes were not yet possible, since, on the one hand, the monarchy was still too strong, and on the other hand, in the cities themselves, the unity of the classes was still too weak. Not until the end of the ninth century did the loosening and dissolution of the royal power begin to create, along with the formation of the dynastic territorial powers, the possibility for independent cities. With independence, there grew a unified sense of citizenship, a communal patriotism that bound the classes together and reawakened the warlike spirit in the previously unwarlike classes.

We can leave out of consideration at this point the manner and forms in which independence was finally achieved.[3] The important point for us is the drawing together and blending of the classes, especially the warrior and burgher classes. In any case, living together in the cities necessarily led in many ways to a blending of the classes, and warriors adopted civilian professions without giving up their status as freemen and warriors. Indeed, we have already learned of warriors under the Lombard kings who were at the same time merchants. On the other hand, under the feudal organization, too, the general national levy was useful for defensive purposes, watch duty, and defense of the walls, and it was so employed.

According to a report which, to be sure, is of a later period and has little reliability, we find that, as early as the beginning of the eighth century, Ravenna and three other cities of the Exarchate had risen in a conflict with the emperor in Byzantium, and their entire citizenry was organized militarily.[4] At the time of Otto the Great, it was still possible for Luidprandus, in the pride of the ruling Lombard people. to write: "We scorn the Romans so much that we know no greater way of abusing our enemies than by saying 'Romans' to them, signifying with that expression every kind of coarseness, cowardice, and vice."[5] But the national paradox, which was at the same time a professional paradox, had already started to die off. Remnants of the Lombard language held out in the north of Italy until the eleventh century but then disappeared. (See Vol. II, p. 440.) The Romans, whom the Lombards had considered as only half-free, moved gradually into the status of freemen,[6] and the citizenry as a unified element defended the freedom of the city commune.

We must study the accomplishments of the city military system which originated in this way in the wars of the communes against the Hohenstaufen emperors.

THE FIRST SUBJECTION OF MILAN (1158)

The hegemony of the Germans over Italy had almost ceased under the first Hohenstaufen kings. Conrad III had not even succeeded in being crowned emperor. When his successor, Frederick I, began his reign by establishing peace in Germany through reconciliation with the Guelphs and, supported and accompanied by Henry the Lion, by again gaining the imperial crown for himself, it soon developed that in order to rule Italy he would have to subdue that country by force. The feuds of the individual communes and princes offered him the prospect that a large number of them would be ready to join him from the start in order to escape their closer enemies. For example, Piacenza assumed the obligation in 1158 of supporting the emperor with 100 knights and 100 archers during the entire siege of Milan and also with 100 marksmen for one month. The German princes and knights gladly crossed the Alps with the prospect of rewards and domination that were held out to them.

The great campaign was undertaken in the seventh year of the new reign (1158). The march took place via four different crossings: The dukes of Austria and Carinthia, with the Hungarians, through Friaul; the emperor himself with the Bohemians and many princes and bishops via the Brenner Pass; others through the Rhine valley and over the Splügen Pass; and the duke of Zähringen, with the Upper Lotharingians and the Burgundians, through the Rhone valley and across the Great Saint Bernard. There is no doubt that the total army was of significant size, but the assumption that there were 10,000 knights, whose number supposedly grew to 15,000 knights and a total strength of 100,000 men when joined by the Italians, was a strong exaggeration.[7] Although the Italians did not risk opposing them in the open field, as strong as the army was by contemporary standards, it was still not large enough to conduct a true siege of Milan or even to surround the city completely,[8] a mission that could not have been difficult for 100,000 men, or 50,000, or even 30,000. While on several occasions sudden attacks were attempted, such as the storming of a gate, those efforts did not succeed. The army had to resort to laying waste the fields and cutting off supplies to the city, actions that reduced the city to submission in the course of a month. (The emperor appeared before the city on 6 August, and the capitulation took place on 7 September.)

THE SECOND SUBJUGATION OF MILAN (1159-1162)

After having been forced into submission in September 1158, Milan rebelled again at the beginning of 1159. The emperor was obliged to await reinforcements from Germany before he could undertake military action in earnest. He decided first to besiege Crema, but as small as the town was—only a little more than a mile in total circumference—it still required fully half a year, from 2 July 1159 to 26 January 1160, to subdue the place, and there were not enough forces left over to undertake any larger project at the same time. The emperor himself, Henry the Lion, Duke Welf, and a considerable number of the foremost German princes were present, but the inhabitants of Crema not only defended themselves most courageously, throwing back several attacks, but they also made sorties, and against Milan itself only a few wasting marches were undertaken, some of which led to successful skirmishes. The inhabitants of Crema were finally granted a capitulation with free conduct.

While Frederick was besieging little Crema, he was so involved that the Milanese risked besieging the castle of Manerbio on Lake Como.[9] The emperor detached 500 knights, who, together with a levy from the counties of Seprio and Martesana, drove off the Milanese. It is 62 kilometers from Crema to Manerbio (Erba), and therefore between two and three days' march. And it was easily possible from the area of Crema to cut off the besiegers of Manerbio from Milan. How weak, then, Frederick must have been, that the Milanese could risk this siege!

But the capture of Crema had already been such an extreme effort for the knightly army that it could not proceed immediately to a second one. First of all, the emperor had to release his army, and in the summer of 1160 the Milanese, for their part, went over to the attack and conquered a number of imperial castles. This led to a larger encounter in the open field.

THE BATTLE OF CARCANO
9 AUGUST 1160

After most of the German troops who had forced the capitulation of Crema had returned home, the Milanese besieged the castle of Carcano, some 23 miles from Milan and about 5 miles east of Como. They had all their troops as well as knights from Brescia and Piacenza. In order to relieve the castle, the emperor moved up with his German and Italian reinforcements and intended to assemble his army, portions of which were approaching from opposite directions, between Carcano and Milan, so as to cut off the besiegers from their own city. Even before he had all his contingents assembled, he moved in a foolhardy manner almost directly to the camp of the Milanese, apparently intending not to allow the enemy under any circumstances to leave that position unbeaten. But he had underestimated his opponents. They realized that they were lost if they allowed themselves to be cut off from their base in that manner, and so they decided to attack the relieving army at once.

The Milanese foot troops that moved against the German knights could not stand up to the attack of the latter. Their formation was broken up, they suffered heavy losses, and they lost the *carroccio*. On the other flank, however, the left wing of the imperial army, the Milanese knights and their allies, presumably assisted by another unit of their foot soldiers, were victorious over Frederick's Italian knights and foot troops, and when the two victorious flanks assembled again, the emperor realized he was too weak to risk a second fight. Undoubtedly, the Milanese had been considerably stronger from the beginning, and at the end of the fight the emperor reportedly had only 200 knights left. Nevertheless, the Milanese, too, were unwilling to risk a new attack immediately, especially since it began to rain heavily. They withdrew into their camp and thus enabled the emperor to withdraw without opposition. He moved back toward Como, in which direction the defeated parts of his army had fled.

Of course, by withdrawing, the emperor separated himself from troops that were moving to join him from Lodi and Cremona, 280 knights, and the Milanese took advantage of the opportunity to surprise them and cause them heavy losses when they approached and were quite close to the emperor. The remainder were saved by Frederick, who personally rushed to their rescue.

Despite their victory, the Milanese lifted the siege of Carcano a few days later (20 August), since they feared a resumption of the emperor's attack. We see then that Carcano belongs to that category of encounters, so frequent in the Middle Ages, in which the side that was beaten in combat still attained its strategic objective, which in this case for the emperor was the relief of the castle of Carcano. Compare Melrichstadt and Flarchheim.

As a warning of the dangers in the use of source statements, let us add the report of the Milanese Annals in the version of the *Codagnellus,* which has been more or less accepted as reliable by historians up to now. The author, who wrote some seventy years after the battle, recounted (*SS.,* 18. 369 ff.) that in the summer of 1160, supported by the Placentians, the Milanese had moved out against the emperor, who was laying waste their country. They had reportedly taken with them the *carroccio* and 100 wagons constructed by Master Guilelmus in the form of a shield, which were provided in the front and all around with scythes. They supposedly placed these wagons in the front line, the *carroccio* with the marksmen in the second line, the knights (*milites*) with the colors and other standards in the third line ("cohort"), and the Placentians in the fourth line (*quarto loco*). When the emperor heard that, he was overcome with fear and withdrew in the night.

In the battle of Carcano, the Milanese placed in their first echelon (*acies*) all their warriors up to the age of forty, a total of 1,500. In the second echelon were all the warriors up to fifty years of age, who also numbered 1,500. In the third echelon stood all the older men, those who were particularly experienced in war, and their total was 1,000. They formed the Placentians and Brescians beside the common soldiers in order to give the latter a fixed support and protect the *carroccio* ("juxta populum, qui confortarent et manutenerent populum et auxilium praestarent populo ad carocium manutenendum et defendendum": "beside the crowd, who might strengthen and support the people and offer them aid for holding and defending the wagon"). The first two echelons of the Milanese were defeated, and the emperor pressed in on the foot soldiers (*populus*), who were tightly pressed around the *carroccio*. Then the unit of the old men, which had remained hidden to that point in a valley, stormed forward. Along with them the troops surrounding the *carroccio*, who attacked as rapidly as a war-horse ("populus cum caroccio qui impulsus a populo ita velocissime currebat ut destrarius"), also took up the offensive, and the emperor and his men took to their heels and were defeated.[10]

THE INVESTMENT OF MILAN

It was not until the spring of the following year (1161) that sufficiently large reinforcements arrived again from Germany and allowed the emperor to move directly against Milan. The strengths of a number of contingents have been reported in a relatively reliable manner.[11] Duke Frederick of Swabia had over 600 knights ("ultra sexcentos milites bene armatos"), Archbishop Reinald of Cologne had over 500, and the son of the king of Bohemia, together with a duke, his uncle, had 300 (*equites*).

While Henry the Lion was also in Italy at the beginning of the siege, he was not mentioned in the battle accounts, and in any case he returned to Germany before the fall of Milan. By way of comparison, however, we may point out that, according to a reliable report, he had appeared at Crema two years earlier with 1,200 knights, while his uncle, Welf, had 300.[12]

If princes like the duke of Swabia and the archbishop of Cologne, who were so powerful and so close to the emperor, as well as being staunch allies, provided no more than 600 or 500 knights for the army, and Henry the Lion, the incomparably most powerful of all the German princes, the master of two duchies, provided no more than 1,200 knights, then the total German strength cannot have exceeded a few thousand knights. The army of 1158 was probably stronger than the armies of 1159 or 1161. At any rate, a comparison of the campaigns with one another justifies our concluding still more specifically than previously that the number of 10,000 knights for the year 1158 was strongly rounded off at the upper extreme.

Although numerous other contingents from Italy from the communes and princes now joined the emperor, another siege of the rebellious city was not contemplated. Frederick contented himself with completely laying waste the immediate surrounding area of Milan in a ten-day campaign (May–June 1161). Then he released the Italian contingents, and from a camp on the Adda, he cut off the supplies to the Milanese. Anyone who transported food to Milan was threatened with having his right hand cut off; this punishment was actually carried out against twenty-five burghers of Piacenza on a single day. In the fall, part of the German princes and knights were sent home. The remainder sufficed to hold the Milanese in check and to prevent any large-scale transport of provisions into the city. As a further means of intimidation, the emperor did not shrink from the cruel procedure of having prominent prisoners blinded and mutilated and sending them back into the city. Thus, after nine months of holding out, the city was finally forced by hunger, terror, and hopelessness to surrender unconditionally (1 March 1162).

BATTLE OF TUSCULUM
29 MAY 1167

The Romans moved out en masse, knights and common soldiers, against Tusculum, which Archbishop Reinald of Cologne occupied while the emperor was still besieging Ancona. Archbishop Christian of Mainz came to the aid of his colleague. The ensuing encounter produced nothing of tactical significance. The account by Otto of Saint Blasien (*M.G. SS.*, 20), to the effect that Christian specified which men were to fight at first, which ones were to fall on the enemy flanks, and which were to be held back as reserves and aid the others ("qui primi committunt, qui consertos hostes a latere irrumpant, qui subsidia pondere proelii laborantibus ferunt"), was nothing but rhetorical embellishment. It contradicts the better reports, according to which Christian's troops, exhausted from their long march and suddenly attacked by the Romans, initially gave way and were only disengaged by the intervention of the troops of Cologne, who fell on the rear of the Romans. Faced with the united imperial forces, the Romans took to flight, at first the knights and then also the foot troops, and they suffered very heavy losses. The Germans were supported by several Italian counts.

This encounter is interesting because of the confirming source report that the Romans, despite their very great numerical superiority, were defeated because, as the chronicler of Lodi, himself an Italian, reported, they "feared the Germans more than others."[13] We are reminded once again that Belisarius once declined to lead the Roman burghers into combat against the Goths, although they had volunteered for that service, because he feared they would not hold fast.

The battle is also interesting because of the account in the same source to the effect that the Germans rushed into the battle singing aloud "Christ is risen," as was their custom. Although the Lodi author is an excellent, reliable reporter, I can still not overcome a certain inner doubt as to whether this report can be believed. Of course, these are the same knights who marched out to liberate the Holy Sepulcher and who formed the Nibelungen characters. Therefore, it may well be possible that on some occasion a bishop fighting at their head dashed into the battle shouting "Christ is risen." And in the Crusades this may really have become a custom, but it is difficult to imagine the German knights singing this battle song as a general practice in these wars of the emperors and popes. The words read: "signo dato maximis vocibus cantum Teutonicum, quem in bello Teutonici dicunt videlicet 'Christus qui natus' et cetera omnes laetantes acriter super Romanos irruerunt." ("After the signal had been given, all at the top of their voices taking delight in other things and in the German song which the Germans sing in war, namely, 'Christ who was born,' firecely overwhelmed the Romans.")

The annals of Egmond Monastery on the North Sea in the diocese of Utrecht also tell of this victory and report that the German knights attacked with "Teutonic fury." This expression had already been minted in antiquity by the poet Lucanus with respect to the Teutones. In the Middle Ages, it was used for the first time by Ekkehard in 1096, in a pejorative sense, as it was also later used by authors to indicate in some cases frenzy and folly, and in other cases bravery.[14]

Archbishop Reinald wrote a letter home concerning his victory,[15] and it may serve as an example of how careful we must be when using the sources. He gives the strength of the Romans as 40,000 at one time, and another time as 30,000. He reports that 9,000 were killed, 5,000 were taken prisoner, and hardly 2,000 returned. The number of knights (*milites*) from Cologne was no greater than 106 (according to the text of the *Cologne Annals,* 140). The bishop states that not a single one of their men was lost ("nostros omnes sano et integro numero recepimus": "we recovered all our men with their number full and intact"). All other contemporary sources which report on this battle differ from this one and from one another, obviously giving completely arbitrary figures for the Romans' losses.[16]

We need not doubt the great numerical superiority and the heavy losses of the Romans, since Cardinal Boso gives a similar report in his *Life of Pope Alexander III.*[17] And it is probably correct that Reinald had no more than 106 (or 140) knights. Christian, too, no doubt had no more than a few hundred knights, and, in addition, both bishops had their sergeants and mercenaries (Brabantines), so that they commanded a total of a few thousand warriors at most. But the estimate of 30,000 to 40,000 Romans is, of course, a huge exaggeration. Reinald's statement that he did not lose a single man would make the whole victory appear somewhat questionable, even if we did not have reason to suspect boastfulness on this point. The chronicler of Lodi, who also states that the Romans were twenty times stronger than the imperial army, nevertheless states that on both sides many were wounded and died.

An interesting point in Reinald's letter is the definite distinction between classes, which is expressed in the remark that the knights had turned over the great amount of booty to the mercenaries and sergeants and had been content themselves with the fame of their victory.

The result of this victory was the capture of Rome by the emperor.

Otto of Saint Blasien gave a completely fantastic account of the entire battle. I am quoting it completely below (from the translation in the *History Writers of the Early German Period* [*Geschichtsschreiber der deutschen Vorzeit*]), in order to reinforce our sense of critical analysis. This report of the account of the battle also served as a basis for the descriptions in the *History of Pope Alexander III* (*Geschichte Papst Alexanders III.*) by Reuter and the *History of the City of Rome* (*Geschichte der Stadt Rom*) by Gregorovius. It reads:

> In the year 1166 since the birth of Christ, Emperor Frederick, after settling the conflict between the princes, as we have mentioned, and restoring good order to the situation in Germany, assembled an army from all parts of the empire and led it into Italy, crossing the Alps for the fourth time. Then he crossed the Apen-

nines, and, leading his army through Tuscany,[18] he turned to the
March of Ancona, and surrounded the rebellious city of Ancona
with a siege. In the meantime, Reginold, the archbishop of Cologne, who had previously separated himself from the emperor on
imperial business, turned against the castle of Tusculanum near
Rome, as he was returning with his corps to rejoin the emperor, in
order to take care of the situation there. When this was reported in
Rome by messengers, the Romans, whose strength was estimated
as 30,000 armed men, moved out from the entire city and suddenly
besieged the archbishop in the castle, to the dishonor of the emperor. As soon as this was reported to the emperor at Ancona, he
assembled the princes and asked them whether or not he should
give up the siege of Ancona and go to the aid of the archbishop. A
few of the princes, most of them of the laity, who feared the spread
of unfavorable rumors that would result from a lifting of the siege,
advised against it. Angered by this agreement of the princes, because the lay princes had such small regard for him and his colleagues or abandoned them in danger, the stately archbishop of
Mainz, Christian, called together his men and others whose aid he
could enlist by pleas and rewards.[19] He assembled 500 knights and
800 mercenaries, appropriately equipped for war, and moved out
toward Tusculanum against the Romans, in order to relieve the archbishop. When he arrived there and had pitched his camp opposite the Romans, he sent emissaries to them to request peace for
that day only to allow his army to rest, recalling the virtue of the
noble attitude that was characteristic of the ancient Romans. In this
way, he hoped to win his demands from them. But the Romans
themselves, completely unlike the ancients in this and all other
respects, answered that they would not grant his request but arrogantly threatened that on this day they would give him and his entire
army to the birds of heaven and the wild animals of the earth to
eat.[20] Giving up the siege, they formed 30,000 warriors in line of
battle against 500 German knights. But the archbishop, completely
unshaken by the answer he had received from them—for he was
not inexperienced in the troubles of war—with great energy encouraged his men for battle by promises and threats. Even though
their number was very small in comparison with their opponents,
he knew they were battle-hardened fighters. He warned them in
noble words that they could not place their hope in flight, since
they were too distant from their fatherland and the emperor's army
to be able to flee, but, mindful of their inherent courage and of the

cowardice that was natural to their enemies, they should fight for their lives with all their strength.

But when he saw that the knights were filled with German fury (*"animositate Teutonica"*)—for his exhortation had injected a certain invincible courage in their hearts—he formed his lines and specified precisely which ones were to fight at first, which were to break into the fighting enemy forces from the flank, which ones were to bring help to those in trouble in the fight, while he himself took position where he could bring help with the most highly selected men. And now he moved into the fight against the Romans with raised banners and widely deployed cohorts, placing his hope in God. The archbishop of Cologne, however, armed himself and the garrison of the castle and all his men, a number estimated as 300 well-armed knights, in order to be able to give help under any circumstances, and he remained calmly in the castle until the start of the battle. After the battle had begun and the lances were broken at the first clash of the armies, the fight was carried on with swords, while the archers on both sides obscured the light of day with their arrows as if they were snow flakes. And behold, the archbishop of Cologne, breaking out of the castle with his eager knights, attacked the Romans from the rear and pushed against them courageously, so that they were surrounded on all sides, attacked from front and rear. While the Romans therefore were fighting only with the weight of their mass, Bishop Christian with his men penetrated their battle line from the flank, tore the middle of their formation apart, and covered with blows the enemy that was thus skillfully separated into three groups. After many had been killed and a number taken prisoner, the defeated Romans took to flight and, pursued by their conquerors up to the city, they were cut down in the bloodiest slaughter. After they had called back their knights from this butchery, the bishops returned to the battlefield and spent that night celebrating with the greatest joy.

In the morning the Romans hastened out to the battlefield to recover the corpses of their fallen. They were driven to flight by the bishops, who sent their knights out against them, and returning toward the city, they barely escaped death. Finally, they sent emissaries to the bishops to beg that they be allowed, for the love of Saint Peter and respect for Christianity, to recover their dead. The bishops granted this plea on the condition that they would count the number of men on their side that were killed or captured in this battle and would report this to them personally in writing with a

sworn guarantee of their truthfulness, and that they could peacefully recover their dead for burial only after complying with this
condition. When they went about this accounting, they found the
number of some 15,000 of their men who had been killed or captured in this battle. After receiving permission, they buried the
remains of their dead, which they recovered with loud lamenting.

BATTLE OF LEGNANO
29 MAY 1176

After futile peace negotiations and hopes for peace, in the spring of
1176 Barbarossa was awaiting reinforcements from Germany in order to
resume the war against the Milanese. In addition to his personal retinue,
with which he was waiting in Pavia, some 18 miles south of Milan, he had
a mercenary army in Italy, under Christian of Mainz, which was fighting
with the Normans on the border of Apulia. We can assume that the
emperor summoned this army, which on the sixteenth of March won a
victory at Carseoli near Rome, for the decisive battle in the north. This is
all the more probable because Henry the Lion this time had declined to
help, and the German army was therefore smaller than previously. But
we do not have a report as to where Christian actually was when the
approach of the Northmen became known. Perhaps he was already close
to Pavia, but it is also possible that he was still at some distance. In any
case, the emperor had the task of uniting the German army that was
approaching on the road through Disentis, Bellinzona, and Como, directly to the north of Milan, with those parts of the army farther south, at
least as quickly as possible with those at Pavia. If the German army,
instead of taking the Lukmanier Pass, had chosen an easterly pass, for
example the Brenner, to cross the Alps, the juncture of the armies would
have offered no difficulty. The sources do not report why the emperor
did not so order. It was presumably because the approaching princes, the
archbishops of Cologne and Magdeburg, the bishops of Würzburg,
Worms, Münster, Verden, Osnabrück, Hildesheim, and Brandenburg,
the counts of Flanders, Holland, Saarbrücken, Duke Berthold von
Zähringen,[21] and the landgrave of Thuringia, all but three of whom were
coming from Western Germany, as well as the Hohenstaufen knights
from Swabia, wished to avoid the detour over one of the more easterly
passes. And so the enemy stronghold, Milan, now lay directly between
the corps that were to be united.

Frederick decided to take over personally command of the approaching troops, and, detouring around Milan, he hastened toward Como to

meet them. He intended to return by about the same route and lead the army to Pavia. But the Milanese realized the danger to which they would be exposed if the emperor united all his forces. The situation was somewhat similar to that existing before Carcano, and the Milanese again adopted the same decision: to attack the emperor before he had all his forces together. They exhorted their allied cities to send reinforcements and moved out against the Germans, blocking their route to Pavia.

The battle was brought on as the two armies on the march encountered each other at Legnano, some 14 miles northwest of Milan. The Milanese knights riding at the head of the column were thrown back by the Germans, and a number of them fled past the foot troops who were following them. These foot troops had perhaps just started their march from the camp they had occupied during the night, or they were possibly just about to start out when the rush of the fleeing knights and the pursuing Germans reached them. The foot soldiers, however, were not drawn along in the flight, but were successful in standing fast in a large, close-ordered mass, holding up their shields against the Germans and pointing their lances at them. Some of the knights, who had jumped from their horses, were also in this mass. According to one source, it appears as if the camp were surrounded by a trench or canal, probably not completely but, in any case, on several sides, and this greatly aided the defense. In any event, the pursuit was broken up by the opposition of the closed mass of foot troops. We hear nothing about the marksmen whom the emperor might have brought up, either because there were only very few of them, or because the burghers of Como, who were marching with him and among whom there were marksmen, were still too far back.

As the German knights were now attempting in vain to penetrate into the mass of Milanese foot soldiers, the fleeing Milanese knights were brought to a halt when they encountered the knights of Brescia, who were just arriving from their long march to assist the capital city of the league. They realized that the outcome of the battle was still undecided, that the fight was still raging around the dismounted troops, and they decided to assist their sorely pressed brothers, who, if they received no support, would certainly be defeated in the end. The German knights, who were involved in combat with the Milanese foot troops, suddenly found themselves attacked again, and in their flank, by enemy knights. Encouraged by this development, the Milanese foot soldiers may also have gone over to the offensive; they were now significantly superior in numbers. And so the Germans, who, with the men of Como, may have been some 3,000 to 3,500 men strong, were defeated.[22] The emperor himself escaped with great difficulty to Pavia, but we do not know how he succeeded in this, since he had disappeared for a time.[23]

PHILIP OF SWABIA

We have seen how small the forces were that actually fought against one another in the Italian wars of the mighty Barbarossa. It was extremely difficult for the lord of three great kingdoms to overcome the opposition of a single fortified city.

When an opposing faction now chose Otto, the son of Henry the Lion, as a counteremperor against Barbarossa's son, Philip, we have the same phenomenon; that is, that the Hohenstaufen, on whose side stood by far the larger number of the German princes, could still not suppress his opponent.

The campaigns were carried out as simple wasting expeditions. In the eighth year of this conflict, 1205, after almost all of Germany had recognized Philip, he conducted a campaign against Cologne, which was still siding with Otto and which he himself was defending. Although Philip had several dukes with him, he was not able to carry out the siege of Cologne.

In 1206 Philip conducted a second campaign against Cologne, with a reportedly very large army. But the men of Cologne, under Otto's leadership, dared to move against him in the open field. They had no more than 400 knights and 2,000 dismounted men. Even when this army was almost completely destroyed at Wasserberg by the imperial army (27 July 1206), Cologne still did not capitulate immediately, and Philip did not move to besiege the city. Instead, after negotiations lasting for months, he granted the city the mildest possible conditions.

The reason for this is no doubt that the princes, after Cologne had reported its willingness to give up, would not have been available for a siege. In the conduct of the city they saw not a rebellion, which would have to be punished for reasons of principle, but a feud, a phenomenon that was unavoidable under the institution of the elective monarchy—a simple, so to speak constitutional, incident.

At the moment when Philip finally seemed to be gaining the upper hand after ten years of struggle, he was assassinated.

EMPEROR FREDERICK II

The difference between Emperor Frederick I and his grandson, Frederick II, in the Lombard conflicts, was that the latter only seldom received support from Germany, but, in return, he had the basis of his power in Italy itself, in the birthright of his mother, the Kingdom of the

Two Sicilies. The German princes were no longer ready to march across the Alps in rather large numbers and with considerable expenditure of their resources, since the idea of gaining rewards and honor in the service of the empire had already lost much of its attractiveness since Barbarossa, and the dynastic concerns of the individual princely houses had replaced the imperial concept and now filled the minds of those lords. Frederick II also gradually brought back into his power the lower Italian kingdom, which, after the death of Emperor Henry VI (1197), had fallen into anarchy during the period of the regency. Frederick then sought to restore the rights of the empire in upper Italy, which were due him as king and emperor and which had also fallen into disregard in the meantime. If his policy had succeeded, the result would presumably have been a united kingdom of Italy detached from the German Empire.

Frederick's first attempt to place the bridle of his domination once again on the communes of upper Italy, in 1226, was a failure. Ten years later, when he had created an advantageous position for himself by his willingness to yield to the claims of territorial dominance by the princes in Germany and had assured himself of reinforcements from them, he began the decisive conflict, the end of which he did not live to see.

Whenever Barbarossa or the emperors before him had appeared with the German army south of the Alps, the Italians had not risked meeting them in the open field. Whenever there was a fight, and especially when Barbarossa was defeated, at Carcano and Legnano, his troops were only parts of the army which the Milanese skillfully attacked in close formation before those contingents joined with other corps, as they intended. In general, the Lombards had always relied on the defensive strength of their fortified cities. They moved out with an army of allies against Frederick II in the open field, but not with the intention of fighting. Rather, they wanted to prevent him from besieging and capturing strongholds through their maneuvering and positions in the terrain that was intersected by rivers and canals. The first year (1236) they succeeded with this type of maneuvering. In the second year the emperor himself returned once more to Germany and came back across the Brenner with 2,000 knights in the fall. He persuaded Mantua to defect from the Lombard alliance and threatened Brescia by moving against it from the southeast. In order to cover that city, the Lombard army took up a position near Manerbio, behind the small Lusignolo River, a position so protected by streams that the emperor was unable to do anything. When November came to an end, he could do nothing else but release those contingents from the cities that were loyal to the empire, who were not willing to stand by any longer.

But the emperor was able to exploit wisely this very situation in order to achieve the desired decision at the last moment and to strike his opponents a deadly blow.

BATTLE OF CORTENUOVA[24]
27 NOVEMBER 1237

When the Lombards saw that the emperor was releasing his city contingents and that he himself, moving westward, crossed the Oglio in order, as it appeared, to go into winter quarters at Cremona, they, too, decided to return home. They had achieved their purpose of defending Brescia. The direct route from their position toward Crema and Milan would have led them across the river at a distance of only one day's march from the place where Frederick himself had gone over the Oglio (Pontevico). Prudently enough, they swung still another day's march farther toward the north, almost to the foot of the Alps, in order to avoid an encounter. But the emperor himself had immediately marched up along the river, and the Lombards, who were peacefully encamped at Cortenuova, in the district of Bergamo, suddenly found themselves attacked. Since the imperial troops had to make a rather long march, the battle did not begin until late in the day. The advance guard of the Lombards was thrown back by the emperor's knights. That part of the Lombard army which did not immediately take flight, seized by panic, assembled around the *carroccio*, which stood, as at Legnano, in a position protected by a ditch or canal. Frederick's knights could not storm this position. It would have been a task for the Sarazen archers to open up an approach for them. According to a few sources, the archers did participate in the fight and emptied their quivers. But since the emperor makes no mention of their action in his own reports on the battle, which have been preserved, their effectiveness cannot have been very great. Perhaps they were not very numerous, or they did not arrive on the battlefield until very late. In any case, the battle could not be fought through to a decision on that day. The emperor commanded the knights to rest overnight without removing their armor, so that they could continue the fight on the following day.

The Lombards, however, did not await the renewal of the battle. During the night, more and more of them took to their heels, so that the flight finally became general. They left the *carroccio* in the lurch and took along only the cross of the flagstaff, which they broke off. Even this, however, was finally abandoned and was captured by the emperor's troops. The entire camp fell into their hands, and many more Lombards were either killed or captured during their flight.

According to a kind of official bulletin, the *Encyclical to the Loyal Men of the Empire (Encyklika an die Getreuen des Reiches)*, which has been preserved under the name of Peter of Vineis, the imperial army was more than 10,000 men strong when it started the march into the battle.[25] Consequently, it would have been considerably larger previously, since a number of city contingents had already been released. Judging from what we have previously heard of knightly armies, this number seems to be very high, and the tenor of the account does not seem to exclude the possibility that the number was stated as very high in order to prove the emperor's strength. In any case it was not a question of the opposite effect, stating the number too small in order to increase the fame of the victor. Since the 10,000 *"sui exercitus"* ("of his own army") were not indicated as horsemen or otherwise defined, we are to understand this as the number of all combatants in the broadest sense.

When their alliance was renewed in 1231, the cities of Lombardy had agreed that the army of the alliance was to be 10,000 men on foot, 3,000 knights, and 1,500 marksmen.[26] We can assume that the actual strength of the army that was still assembled at the finish of the campaign, at the end of November, was considerably less than the maximum agreed number, if indeed the latter strength was ever reached—perhaps amounting to only half the prescribed strength, especially in foot soldiers.[27] It was not unnatural, therefore, that the alliance sought to avoid battle in the open field, since the emperor was superior both in numbers and presumably in the quality of his warriors.

Since we are dealing here with a large action, in which both sides had committed their entire strength, it is very valuable for us to have strength estimates for both sides which are positive and sufficiently reliable to permit us to say with certainty that there were no more than about 10,000 combatants, all told, on the two sides.

CONTINUATION OF THE WAR AFTER CORTENUOVA
1238–1250

As great as was the emperor's victory and as heavy as was the defeat of the Lombards at Cortenuova, the battle did not produce decisive results. Although the Milanese did sue for peace, they were not willing to accept the unconditional surrender that Frederick demanded, and so the war continued without having been significantly influenced by Cortenuova.

Far from the idea of now besieging Milan itself, Frederick was not even able to capture Brescia in the following year.

Although the emperor had at his disposal the significant resources of the strictly administered Kingdom of the Two Sicilies, although a not inconsiderable number of large Italian communes and powerful princes were fighting at his side and supporting him with all their forces, and although Germany, too, sent him important help in the first years, his strength still was not sufficient for an energetic and effective conduct of the war.

The war was conducted through mere wasting campaigns, sudden attacks and storming of castles, and occasionally the siege of a city of moderate size, which normally did not accomplish its purpose unless a faction favoring the besieger was able to act effectively within the besieged city itself. The decisions depended not on military deeds but on the changes of sides which caused cities and princes to shift their support from one side to the other. But such shifts occurred all the more easily because in most of the cities there were factions that were struggling for dominance and sought support either from the emperor or from the alliance of the cities and from the pope. Consequently, the varied, shifting undertakings in each year were governed more by political than military motives. Clashes and encounters, even rather large-scale fights, occurred quite often, but their success was always very small, even when one side suffered heavy losses, since there were not enough forces to carry out sieges in the grand style.

SIEGE OF PARMA
1247–1248

Köhler assumes that Parma had some 80,000 inhabitants. That is certainly much too large a number. Today the city has 50,000 at most. The section of the city on the left bank was, by Köhler's statement, considerably smaller at that time than at present, and that part of the city on the right bank was, in any case, no larger than today.[28] According to the *Annals of Parma,* Emperor Frederick II had 10,000 men himself,[29] and that would already have been an army of very important size. In any event, in this statement from the camp of the opponent, we have the maximum number we can assume.

Frederick went about the siege by setting up a fortified camp opposite the smaller part of the city that was situated on the left bank. He named the camp "Vittoria," and from it as a base he lay waste the area surrounding Parma and sought to prevent the arrival of reinforcements.[30] But the main part of the city was not surrounded, and the besieged city itself had significant fighting forces at its disposal. Its allies, especially the Mantuans, who appeared on the Po with a fleet, brought powerful assistance to the besieged city. The emperor, therefore, had no prospect of really defeating it; at best, he could gradually wear it down. Köhler estimates that if the emperor had wanted to surround the city completely, the circumvallation would have had a circumference of about 5 miles and would have required a garrison of 40,000 men. If we assume that the estimate for this circumference was not too high, certainly the figure for the garrison was excessive, for the circumvallation, of course, did not have to be garrisoned with equal strength at all points. It would have been sufficient if impregnable forts had been erected on all the access roads and a ditch with palisades prevented the free movement of the besieged. In this case, the emperor would also not have needed the special covering corps at Guastalla. The fact that Frederick, who was, after all, an experienced warrior, instead of doing that, contented himself with that partial blockade seems to me sufficient proof that he was too weak to encircle the city and that his army can therefore have been of only a very moderate size.

In the winter the emperor released the contingents from Bergamo, Pavia, Tortona, and Alessandria, and detached some of his troops to Treviso and Alessandria. The troops that remained with him consisted of 1,100 horsemen, 2,000 foot soldiers from Cremona, and an unspecified number of Saracens. Consequently, the total can hardly have exceeded 5,000.

One thousand more men were detached from this total, and the emperor himself had ridden off to hunt with 500 horsemen, when the Parmesans made a sortie on 18 February.

Köhler has made it clear that the sortie was not premeditated. Basically, the Parmesans intended only to conduct an expedition up to the Po against King Enzio and had designated about half of their men for that purpose. The other half moved out only with the mission of covering their rear. Then it happened that the emperor's troops, without command and without their complete equipment, allowed themselves to become engaged in a melee with those who had moved out of the city. This fight turned out so badly for them that their pursuers penetrated into the Vittoria camp along with the pursued, and they captured the camp. According to the Parmesans' own report, they killed 1,500 men and captured 3,000. But the report in the *Placentine Annals,* according to which 100 knights and 1,500 foot soldiers were captured, is no doubt closer to the truth.

If the emperor had had a larger force in Vittoria, such an attack could probably not have succeeded. But a force of 5,000 to 6,000 men was in itself not too small to carry out the strategic plan Frederick was following. Even if the defenders of Parma were perhaps more numerous, they could still not capture the enemy fortification of Vittoria and could gradually be harassed from that base. In about this way, the Normans had besieged Paris in an earlier day, and the Milanese knights had besieged their own city. Even Barbarossa had not actually surrounded Milan but had only laid waste the entire surrounding region and had blocked the accesses. Those actions had sufficed to bring about the capitulation in about nine months. Frederick II was much weaker, even in relation to the beleaguered city, which was certainly much smaller than Milan. Barbarossa dominated upper Italy to such an extent that he actually starved Milan into submission without any serious attempt being made from the other side to help the city. But in 1247, so many communes were in arms against Frederick II that he had to fight not only against the city but just as seriously against its allies. Nevertheless, the emperor would perhaps have reached his goal if the lack of discipline and the foolishness of the soldiers during the chance absence of the emperor had not given the Parmesans the unexpected opportunity for their destructive blow. Consequently, the emperor is not subject to reproach for an undertaking that was poorly planned and led from a strategic viewpoint, but rather for his lack of foresight in personally leaving his camp on a day when its garrison was very much weakened by the detachment of troops.

This result is also important with respect to earlier events. If the emperor had still been able in the autumn of 1247 to assemble a large army, it is difficult to see why he did not make such an effort at a time when his victory of Cortenuova gave him an advantage and with which he could have won final success. In 1247 he had at his disposal no special new resources at all. On the contrary, he was weakened by numerous decreases in his forces. But if we accept the fact that his forces were much reduced already, his conduct becomes completely understandable.

Whereas this more or less fortuitous defeat damaged the cause of the Hohenstaufen emperor very much for the moment, the outcome of this battle had as little lasting result as his victory at Cortenuova had had earlier.

IN RETROSPECT

If we consider from the viewpoint of the history of the art of war these battles of a period of almost 100 years, we quickly realize that the Italian cities did not produce an infantry of the type of the ancient units, the Greek phalanx and the Roman legion. While the foot troops did occasionally play a significant role, especially at Legnano, it was still not the decisive role. No matter how numerous they were, they still remained only an auxiliary arm for the knights. Even if the direct source statements concerning the course of the battle of Legnano should appear not certain enough or as capable of various interpretations, the following events lead to a clear conclusion and leave no doubt. If the foot troops at Legnano had had an effect like that of ancient infantry, there would have been some kind of further development from this action. But there was nothing of this sort. The Milanese did not draw from their victory the faintest conclusion that they now possessed a new, superior method of warfare and no longer needed to fear the German emperor. Instead, they made peace with very modest conditions, and in the next generation, as in the following ones we shall study, their methods of warfare did not differ in any way from those of other countries in either the preceding or the following century.

Consequently, the Italian communes did not produce a citizen warriorhood such as that of Athens and Rome in olden times, where the entire citizenry had moved out en masse and fought battles in accordance with the strictly observed principle of universal military obligation. Completely aside from the question as to whether the necessary warrior skills would have existed, there was lacking the one true prerequisite that was peculiar to those ancient republics, that is, the political unity of city and country, the close cohesion of burghers and peasants. Not so much the city dwellers of Athens and Rome as the peasants, peat diggers, and fishermen of Attica and the inhabitants of the rural tribes around Rome formed the mass of the phalanx and the legions. But while the Italian peasant villages were no doubt dominated by the cities, they did not form a unified body with them and were not fellow citizens of the city inhabitants. The communes themselves, despite their republican character, always retained for the most part the knightly military organization. How military service was determined in detail has not been reported. In general, this probably did not go beyond a mustering of volunteers, but in times of great danger or great political excitement, a considerable portion of the citizenry was probably called to arms, at least for short expeditions and especially for defense of the walls. For the latter purpose, the general military obligation may also have been put into practice.

For the waging of war in the field, however, horsemen equipped in the knightly manner, reinforced by marksmen and spearmen, were sent out.

As those elements which felt a natural warlike inclination joined the traditional warriors for these campaigns and developed along with them, this resulted, as long as the entire group was inspired by a lively communal patriotism, in a very useful and skilled military body. They dared to stand up even to the German knights who were led across the Alps by their kings, even if the proud Germans made fun of the carpenters and craftsmen who were knighted in Italy.

THE *CARROCCIO*

We have learned that the military system of the Italian communes was of the knightly type and remained so, but with the special quality of having the foot troops play a stronger role in mixed combat, and sometimes even a much stronger role, than elsewhere in that period. But this did not go as far as forming a true infantry of firm tactical units, such as the phalanx and the legion. We can regard the *carroccio* as a kind of substitute for the missing tactical units. The *carroccio* was a heavy wagon, drawn by eight oxen, on which a high pole with a banner was erected. At the top there was also probably attached the monstrance with consecrated hosts. On the wagon stood priests. This sacred object has been aptly compared with the Israelite Ark of the Covenant. We know the weakness of loosely formed foot troops when opposing horsemen. The *carroccio* behind the front was intended to form a focal point, visible from afar, where any men who were temporarily driven from their position or had become confused could assemble again. The wounded, too, moved to the *carroccio* or were brought there to be absolved by the priests before their demise. We may assume that, before each battle, it was again emphasized to the warriors that they should not abandon the colors but in the most critical situation should group themselves around the sacred vehicle and save it or perish with it. The spirit of determination and confidence in victory, which was naturally present in a well-ordered and efficiently led legion (which, of course, also had its field standards), was artificially stimulated by the *carroccio* and heightened by the religious character of that symbol. We find such a banner wagon mentioned for the first time in Milan in 1039, that is, precisely at the time when the Italian communes were being formed through the amalgamation of the classes and elements of the citizenry that had long been unaccustomed to warriorhood were again taking up arms. Archbishop Heribert armed, as the source expresses it, all "a rustico ad militem, ab inope usque ad divitem"[31] ("from peasant to knight, from poor to rich"). The Church, therefore, stood as patron as early as the first appearance of the municipal symbol (at least the first one that is reported in the sources). The later alliance of the Church with the communes contributed still more strongly toward giving the *carroccio* an ecclesiastic character. We find it north of the Alps especially in armies that had a close relationship to the Church. The opponents of Henry IV had the *carroccio* in the battle of Bleichfeld in 1086, the English militia under the archbishop of York in the battle of Northallerton in 1138, and Richard the Lion-Hearted in Syria in 1191. It was also present with Otto IV at Bouvines in 1214, with the troops of Cologne at Worringen in 1288, and the forces of Mainz in 1298 at a siege of Alzey. With the Italian communes, it was undoubtedly standard equipment whenever the citizens took the field throughout the twelfth and thirteenth centuries.[32]

BATTLE OF TAGLIACOZZO
23 August 1268

To the battles of the Hohenstaufen emperors with the Italian communes, I am adding a discussion of the battle in which the last representative of that great dynasty, Conradin, went down to defeat, no longer in combat against the burghers, but against the French Prince Charles of Anjou, whom the popes had called to drive the Hohenstaufens from their hereditary kingdom, Naples.

The original and principal source for the usual account of this battle is the description of a French monk, Primatus, who probably wrote in the monastery of Saint Denis near Paris. Villani took his material principally from this source, and all the later scholars—Raumer, Schirrmacher, Delpech, Köhler, Busson, Hampe, Oman—have taken this account as their base, with some small deviations in details. Recently, however, Roloff has shown, on the basis of better and earlier sources, that this account is unreliable in every respect.[33] What we can say of this battle with historical certainty is to be taken principally from the *Ghibelline Annals* of Piacenza and from the brief reports of Charles of Anjou himself.

In all the battle accounts, there appear on both sides nothing but horsemen. The foot troops that are occasionally mentioned therefore played only a very insignificant role, perhaps taking no part in the fight.

Since the *Placentine Annals* also state that the combined army of Conradin and his ally, Henry of Castile, senator (burgomaster) of Rome, was stronger than that of their opponent, that seems to require acceptance. But I am not ready to rely completely on that statement, especially since the complete lack of foot soldiers in the battle accounts seems suspicious to me. Roloff considers as credible the reports that Conradin had between 5,000 and 6,000 horsemen, while Charles had 4,000. If we call these horsemen knights, we are already going beyond the true concept of the knight. Many of that number had undoubtedly not only not been knighted but were also simply common horsemen, who, even though provided with more or less heavy armor, were still not of knightly birth.

The course of the battle was such that, at first, Conradin's troops, the combined Germans, Spanish, and Italians, were victorious. But then, when they had been spread out and had given up any kind of close formation, they were defeated by the intervention of a French reserve under King Charles' personal command.

It is not clear from the sources what Charles' intention was or how he succeeded in holding out this reserve, apparently concealed. We can only speculate on that point. Of course, it is out of the question that Charles, from the start, intentionally had the larger part of his army fight a losing battle, planning to fall upon the disorganized victors with his hidden reserve and win the day with his orderly formation. If a smaller force could conquer a larger one through such a simple stratagem, that would have occurred quite frequently. Wherever a reserve is held out, the intention can only be to intervene while the outcome is still undecided. A later attack would be very easily repelled by the enemy, even if only a very moderate-sized unit remained in close formation and ready for action, thus forming a nucleus for the rallying of those troops who were momentarily scattered but still several times more numerous.

Roloff clearly describes the situation of a victorious knightly army as follows:

> Let us imagine a battle between two knightly armies. Several thousand individual combatants start with hand-to-hand combat at about the same time. After a certain time, the weaker side begins to yield. At this point, some of the victors naturally press against their withdrawing enemies while others jump from their horses to bind up their wounds, to rearrange their armor that has been damaged in the fight, to change horses, to finish off or capture an opponent who has been thrown to the ground, or to tear from him some valuable piece of armor or weapon. Of course, there did not exist any order to prevent such individual plundering and resting and to force the knight to remain constantly equipped and ready for anything. Such a situation, which was inevitable in any victory of a knightly army, undoubtedly detracted from the combat value of the army, and a body of troops that attacked at such a juncture necessarily enjoyed important advantages, even if it was considerably weaker. Many

dismounted knights would be almost defenseless against the attacking horsemen, and the army being attacked would be spread over a broad area, so that the attackers would perhaps initially encounter no opponents of equal birth. They could then progressively wipe out the enemy forces. How the battle would develop in case of such a sudden attack would depend on the special circumstances; if the troops under attack were greatly superior in numbers, it is not impossible that they might accept combat and fight their way through to victory. Since the knight was an individual combatant and could easily turn in any direction, it would not make much difference if the sudden attack took place from the flank or the rear. The critical point was always the question as to how many knights were not ready for battle at the moment of the attack and how widely scattered they were.

Roloff goes on to say that Charles must have attacked the Hohenstaufen army at such a moment of beginning disorganization. That was very advantageous, but, let us repeat, it was still only a coincidence, brought on perhaps by the fact that the main body of the Angevine army had been defeated and put to flight faster than Charles had estimated. There is no doubt that a hard battle still followed, but we do not know why this fight ended in a victory for the French, for the sudden appearance of the fresh troops and their well-ordered formation against the very superior numbers of the enemy, buoyed up in morale as they were by their victory, do not suffice of themselves to be regarded as decisive without some further factor. Perhaps, as Roloff supposed possible, there was much mistrust among the three nationalities of Conradin's combined forces, and panic broke out because they suspected treason when fresh enemy troops suddenly appeared?

In any case, there is little to be learned from this battle from the viewpoint of military history, since the sources do not inform us of the two principal factors—why and how Charles of Anjou formed his reserve or his ambush, and why he was so successful with it—and mere speculation leads us no further. We can only draw the negative conclusion that echeloned formations were not customary at that time, since Conradin's army, if it had had a second echelon, could not have been so completely disorganized.

As a contribution to the critique of medieval accounts, we may also mention the following details from Roloff. Henry of Castile reportedly allowed himself and his Spanish troops to be drawn so far from the battlefield in the pursuit that they did not return until Charles had conquered the Germans there. Then there was a third phase of the battle. While this division of the battle into separate acts would seem to be a likely explanation for the victory of the smaller army, Roloff points out, on the basis of source analysis and objective criticism, that it is fantasy. In the alleged third phase of the battle, the Spaniards supposedly held fast like a wall, so the French could not penetrate into their formation. But Erard of Valery, who was the hero of the legend, knew what to do. With thirty knights, he feigned flight, and the Spaniards, thinking that all the French were fleeing, started to pursue them and so broke up their close formation. Then the French drove into their mass for individual combat, but their efforts were in vain, for the Spaniards' armor was impenetrable to cut and thrust. Then the French moved in close to their opponents and seized them by their arms and shoulders to throw them from their horses. And since they were more agile in their light chain mail than the Spaniards in their heavy plate armor, they were successful. After fighting bravely, the Spaniards were completely defeated.

Anyone who is at all alert to military legend will immediately recognize it here. If men wearing lighter armor could so easily overcome heavily armored troops, we would undoubtedly have more frequent reports of this kind, and heavily armored warriors would not have existed so long in military history. But Roloff also shows this to be mere legend from analysis of the sources by pointing out that Primatus had already given a very similar account of the battle of Benevento two years earlier, except that there the living wall was formed not of Spaniards, but of Germans. It is not clear why the Germans should have fought differently at Benevento than at Tagliacozzo, and Andreas of Hungary, who thoroughly described the battle of Benevento a few years later, knew nothing of such an interesting detail. The origin of the account is simple; it is always reported about those with whom the French had the fiercest or last battle. The most closely involved, oldest sources in Italy itself say nothing of such details. The legend did not arise until later, at a distance from the battle. The returning knights, from whom Primatus in Saint Denis heard his stories, related the fantasy that, with ruses and great effort, they first had to break up the formation of the mighty men whom they had conquered in Italy, before engaging them in hand-to-hand combat. And, as is the case in exaggerated accounts, they made the impenetrability of the Spanish armor appear so great that they actually detracted from the warrior skills of their enemies; for after all, what kind of enemies are those who can be overcome with bare hands? Should the battle-hardened Spaniards not have meanly used their swords or daggers to cut the fingers of those who were reaching for their arms and shoulders to throw them from their horses? Knights could only be defeated by lightly armored or unarmored warriors if one knight was attacked by several men, and even then the knight would be overpowered not because of his good armor, but in spite of it. This may also have happened at Tagliacozzo.

If we look more closely, we see that these warriors who were incapacitated as a result of their heavy armor are much older acquaintances of ours. After all, how did the Greeks explain the victory of their supposedly inferior numbers at Salamis? The Phoenicians, the most experienced sailors of all the nations, had allegedly built such large and heavy ships that they were unable to steer and control them correctly.

If we compare Roloff's conclusions on the course of the battle of Tagliacozzo with those accounts that have been commonly accepted until now, which differ from one another only in details, we once again find proof as to how little can be learned from analysis of the written sources alone, without objective critical analysis. How proud our historiography has been precisely of the exactness of the methods applied to analysis of the medieval sources! And with all its exactness, *modern, critical* scholarship has until now produced such fantastic descriptions of Tagliacozzo as did ancient historiography on Xerxes or about the Cimbri and Teutones.

EXCURSUS

ITALIAN INFANTRY

In his dissertation, "The Tactics in the Lombard Wars of the Hohenstaufens" ("Die Taktik in den Lombardenkriegen der Staufer"), Marburg, 1892, Julius Reinhard Dietrich systematically defended the concept that the Italian cities produced a true infantry and that it was the decisive factor against the Hohenstaufen emperors. This study was based on the most painstaking analysis of the sources and is therefore very valuable, although the basic idea, and consequently the detailed conclusions, must be rejected. It is actually a kind of counterargument to my *Persian and Burgundian Wars* (*Perser- und Burgunderkriege*). The opposition between the two exists, however, only in the fact that it is derived from a fundamental misunderstanding.

In the *Perser- und Burgunderkriege*, I established for the first time the polarized antithesis between the tactical body and the system of individual combatants. Dietrich questions this distinction. "For the unity of will in a group of warriors," he says (p. 5), "actually finds its expression when two warriors stand back to back to ward off a larger number of opponents, or when several fighters group themselves so closely that each man's right chest is covered by his neighbor's shield." That point is correct, but it obscures the decisive factor. After all, it is a question not of an absolute distinction but of a diametric one; that is, a group of knights and a squadron of cuirassiers are very similar and yet basically different in that the former possesses a very low degree of unity and a very high degree of individual quality, while the latter has a very high degree of unity and much lower degree of individual quality. A group of knights with no unity at all, no kind of leadership, is just as unimaginable as a cuirassier squadron with no courage and no skill in the use of weapons. But there is no doubt that in one case the one factor predominates, while in the other case the other factor is predominant. A cuirassier squadron is in no way the simple evolutionary development of a group of knights, as Dietrich would have it, but something significantly different in that certain characteristics are gained while others are lost. Dietrich argues against me as if I had denied the knightly armies any organizational coherence, any kind of leadership or capacity to be led. He points out quite correctly that there was also a certain leadership in the medieval armies, but then he refers to the sections and groups in these armies as tactical units and thus eliminates the specific character and the differences between the armies of this period and those of antiquity and the modern era. There are, of course, numerous source passages that read more or less as if procedures in medieval armies were completely or almost completely like those of today, but anyone who is misled by this to the extent of overlooking the differences misses the main point. Radulf tells us that, in the battle of Dorylaeum, Tancred and his brother William, moving over from the defensive, attacked the Turks and sought to drive them from a hill dominating the terrain. Boemund, the overall commander, reportedly denounced this as foolhardy and tried to hold them back, because such individual undertakings endangered the good order of the army. Heerman, p. 17, and after him, Dietrich, p. 20, claimed that that "indicated the high degree of self-denial that was required, even of the most important and bravest men," and they drew conclusions as to subordination and discipline. I would like to turn this little story around and show that it is evidence in support of my thesis. Boemund's reproach, to the effect that individual attacks carried out at will endangered the situation of the entire army, was no doubt expressed a thousand times, but that is still no proof that there existed a discipline that prevented such actions. Indeed, if the story of Boemund and Tancred only went farther, like the Roman legend of the Consul Manlius and his son! But no; Tancred pays no heed to the command, his brother William is killed in the fight, and Boemund takes no action beyond his theoretical reproach! Nothing could show us more clearly how foreign the true concept of subordination and discipline was to knightly armies.

Dietrich's other pieces of evidence are of the same type. On p. 24 he writes:

> From this stern reproach, which is concerned with untimely attacks, foolish undertakings of individual leaders and groups, disorderly and uncoordinated advances, insubordination and arbitrary actions, we can conclude there was a strict military discipline. I simply invite the reader's attention to Frederick's utterance concerning the count of Bubingen's foolhardiness before Milan in 1158, the widely blamed, overhasty advances of the Genoese on Tortosa in 1148 and Ventimiglia in 1221, the disorderly encounter of the Pavians and Milanese before Tortona in 1155, which was due to the lack of agreement between the leaders, the battle of Lodi in 1195, the senseless advance of the Piacenzans against the Pavians in 1213, but, foremost of all, the battles of Castelleone, Cortenuova, and Tagliacozzo.

All these bits of evidence of insubordination are supposed to be proofs of discipline because they were reproached! Dietrich continues:

> Against this concept, there stands the incident of the "*miles explorator*" ("knight scout") of the Pavians (1157), who was captured by the Milanese and released after chevaleresque negotiations, and the discretion with which the enemies avoided leaving their camp and attacking (against the will of the leaders). In 1160, during the siege of Farah, the German *milites*, with very few exceptions, stayed out of the battle

on the emperor's orders, as also happened in 1161 before Milan during a battle between the Pavians and the Milanese. One word from Gregory of Montelongo, the allied commander, sufficed to hold back the battle-eager Piacenzans from pursuing Enzio.

Here, for once, we fortunately have a few examples of obedience to the commands of leaders, and this no doubt also occurred quite often, but I think that the very tone of the account shows us how uncertain this kind of subordination was. We are told that the command of the emperor or the commander was sufficient to cause the knights, admittedly with some exceptions, to obey. But after all, what kind of concept of command authority and discipline is it when the commander's word does *not* suffice to evoke obedience?

NOTES FOR CHAPTER V

1. "cum consensu . . . Canonicorum ejusdemque civitatis Militum ac populorum" ("with the agreement of the *Canonici* and of the knights and of the people of the same city").

An agreement drawn up in Modena in 1106 also distinguishes between *"milites"* and *"cives"*. Hegel, *History of the City Organizations of Italy (Geschichte der Städteverfassungen von Italien)*, 2: 174.

2. Arnulph, Chap. 18, *SS.*, 8. 16 ff.

3. Handloike, *The Lombard Cities under the Hegemony of the Bishops and the Rise of the Communes (Die lombardischen Städte unter der Herrschaft der Bischöfe und die Entstehung der Kommunen)*, Berlin, 1883.

4. Hegel, 1: 252. Hartmann, *History of Italy in the Middle Ages (Geschichte Italiens im Mittelalter)*, 2: 2: 80; 2: 2: 117.

5. *Relatio de Legatione Constantinopolitana (Report on the Embassy to Constantinople)*, Chap. 12.

6. Hegel, 2: 31. In a charter of Henry III for Mantua, there appears the expression "cives videlicet Eremannos" ("inhabitants, namely warriors"), which Hegel, 2: 143, interprets as meaning that the burghers were declared to be warriors (*"Eremannos"*).

As evidence from the other side of the narrowing of the distinction between the classes, we may cite Emperor Lambert's law of 898: "Ut nullus comitum arimannos in beneficio suis hominibus tribuat." ("That no count should grant to his own men warriors in a benefice.") If the emperor had to take the *"arimannos,"* that is, the free warriors, under his protection in this manner, then they were under a pressure that necessarily lessened the distinction between them and the burghers and peasants.

7. According to the *Gesta Friderici in Lombardia (Deeds of Frederick in Lombardy)*, p. 30 (*M.G.,* 18. 365), there were 15,000 knights ("milites

fuerunt appretiati quindecim milia") before Milan; according to Ragewin, 3: 32, there were about 100,000 men ("circiter 100 milia armatorum vel amplius"). These two figures were then combined in the manner indicated above. The *Annales Sancti Disibodi* (*Annals of St. Disibodus*), M.G., SS., 17. 29, give only 50,000 men ("Teutunicorum seu etiam Longobardorum" ("of Germans and also Lombards"). See Giesebrecht, *History of the German Imperial Period* (*Geschichte der deutschen Kaiserzeit*), 6: 259.

    8. Ragewin, 3. 34.

    9. Ragewin, 4. 58.

    10. The accounts of the battle of Carcano in the narrative works of Raumer, Giesebrecht, Prutz, etc. are all inaccurate, especially since they did not eliminate the fables of the Codagnellus. The documentary basis for my account is given in the "Contributions to the Military History of the Hohenstaufen Period" ("Beiträge zur Kriegsgeschichte der staufischen Zeit") by Benno Hanow. Berlin dissertation, 1905. The account in Köhler, 3: 3: 124, is mostly fantasy.

    11. Otto Morena, *M.G. SS.*, 18. 631.

    12. *Annales Weingartenses Welfici* (Welficius, *Annals of Weingarten*), *M.G., SS.*, 17. 309. The duke of Bavaria and Saxony reportedly went to the emperor's aid "in mille ducentis loricis" ("about 1,200 men in mail"). Welf: "in trecentis loricis Deuthonicorum" ("about 300 mailed Germans").

    13. The complete passage from Otto Morena reads as follows: The Romans flee "tum quia forte justitiam non habebant, tum etiam quia postquam in campo exeunt, non sicut sui majores fecere, faciunt, imo vilissimi sunt, tum etiam qui Teutonicos magis timebant quam alios" ("then because they did not, as it happened, have justice, then also because after they went out on the field they acted, not as their ancestors did; rather, they were most worthless. Then also they feared the Germans more greatly than others"). What does the word *"justitia"* mean here? The "just thing"? Or "the correct way and manner," that is, of fighting?

    On this point I turned to the prominent scholar of medieval Latin, Paul von Winterfeld, who since then has been prematurely lost to the field of scholarship, but he did not know the answer either. He wrote to me:

> From the purely philological viewpoint, it also seems quite unlikely to me that *"justitia"* should mean the "just thing"; for this is not a biblical expression. I have looked through the article on *justitia* in the concordance but have only found the expression

"habeas justitiam coram deo" ("You should have justice in the presence of God"), in Deuteronomy, 24, 13.

But now can "the correct manner" be the right interpretation? That would, after all, be very colorless, but there is also an idea associated with it which seems to oppose this meaning: "tum quia forte iustitiam non habebant", as well as because they are of no value (or rather: "or because"?). What do you understand here by "the correct way"? In any case, "*forte*" means this "single instance" in contrast with the word "in general" of the other clause. I have the feeling that the word "*justitia*" is a corruption, but I do not know how to emend it. "Fiduciam" would fit here, but, of course, it is too extreme a change.

14. Dümmler, *Sitzungsberichte der Berliner Akademie,* 1 (1897): 112. Lucanus, *de bello civili* (*On the Civil War*), 1. 256. *Annales Egmondani* (*Annals of Egmunda*), SS., 16. 453.

15. Gedr. Sudendorf, *Registrum,* 2. 146.

16. All of these various figures, arranged in numerical sequence, are clearly presented in Varrentrapp's *Christian von Mainz,* p. 38.

17. *Liber pontificalis* (*The Papal Book*), ed. Duchesne, p. 415.

18. That is incorrect. The emperor did not go through Tuscia but penetrated into Romagna from the north.

19. This entire scene is pure fiction, since Christian was not with the emperor before Ancona but had moved from Genoa through Tuscany and was not far from Reinald. It was only afterward that the emperor heard of these events. See Varrentrapp, *Christian von Mainz,* p. 28 ff.

20. Not a word of this is to be believed. See Varrentrapp, *loc. cit.*

21. Wyss, in the *Allgemeine Deutsche Biographie,* 540: 2, doubts whether Duke Berthold von Zähringen really participated in the battle and was taken prisoner, but his view seems to be contradicted by Giesebrecht, 6: 530. Giesebrecht, 6: 528, considers it possible that Margrave Dietrich von der Lausitz also took part in the battle. But we only know from an undated document which was probably not written until December 1176 that he was then at the emperor's court, but that does not permit any conclusion as to his whereabouts in May.

22. According to the *Gesta Friderici in Lombardia,* ed. Holder-Egger (*Annales Mediolanenses majores: Greater Annals of Milan*), the army that had come across the Alps numbered 2,000 men, that is, knights. This number is not to be divided in half, as if only half of the men were knights (Giesebrecht), nor can it be multiplied as if there were naturally

additional combatants of lower rank. According to the *Gesta Friderici,* the emperor himself had led 1,000 knights from Pavia, and according to Gottfried von Viterbo, this number was 500. In addition, there were the men of Como, who hardly numbered more than the 500 men who supposedly were killed or captured (*Gesta Friderici* and *Continuatio Sanblasiana ad Ottonis Frisingensis chronicon* [*Sanblasianus' Continuation of the Chronicle of Otto of Freysingen*], SS., 20. 316).

23. The standard source study for Legnano is the previously cited dissertation by Hanow.

In the *Deutsche Literaturzeitung,* No. 26 (1 July 1905), Güterbock reproached Hanow for not taking into account in his work the *Chronicle of Tolosanus.* In fact, this work should have been expressly mentioned, but only for the purpose of rejecting it as unimportant. It was written about a generation later and is either erroneous or confusing in all the figures that can be checked on. The other points for which Güterbock reproaches Hanow are either unsubstantiated or obviously false. See the *"Entgegnung"* ("Reply") and *"Antwort"* ("Answer") in the *Deutsche Literaturzeitung,* No. 31. Also *Historische Vierteljahresschrift,* 1911.

The account which Köhler, 1: 69 ff., gives of the battle is based on uncritical contamination of the various source reports and especially on the completely unreliable Gottfried von Viterbo; much of this is also mere fantasy. Effectively opposed to these descriptions are the remarks of the same author in the note in his 3: 3: 122. Here it is not the critical scholar of the source documents who is speaking, but the practical, experienced soldier.

24. The standard study for Cortenuova is the dissertation by Karl Hadank, Berlin, 1905. Publisher: Richard Hanow. 63 pp.

25. "ultra decem milia sui exercitus secum trahens . . . signa direcit victricia" ("taking with him over 10,000 of his own army . . . he arranged the signals of victory").

26. *Annales Placentini Guelfi* (*The Guelph Annals of Piacenza*), M.G., SS., 18. 453. They promise one another help, "militum, peditum et balistariorum" ("of knights, foot soldiers, and crossbowmen").

27. According to the *Ghibelline Annals of Piacenza,* Piacenza alone had provided 1,000 knights. But if we accepted this figure and also estimated the other allied contingents correspondingly, it would not be understandable why the Lombards so anxiously avoided battle with the emperor. Perhaps those 1,000 men were Piacenza's total contingent.

28. The fact that Riccardus di San Germano speaks of 60,000 inhabitants has, of course, no validity as proof.

29. *Annales Parmenses majores* (*Greater Annals of Parma*), M.G., SS.,

18. 673: "decem milia militum cum innummerabili populo diversarum gentium" ("10,000 knights with a countless crowd of different nations"). The events indicate that the "*milites*" are to be understood not simply as "knights" in the narrower sense, but as combatants.

Earlier, scholars believed they had still another strength estimate worthy of consideration in the work of Salimbene, who was personally in Parma at the start of the siege, who gives the emperor 37,000 men. But it turns out that this number resulted from an error in reading. Salimbene only says that the emperor's army was huge, and he cites Chapter 37 of Ezekiel. This "37 Ezekiel" was interpreted as 37,000. *M.G., SS.,* 37. 196.

Of course, sources that speak of 60,000 men (Schirrmacher, 4: 441) are not worth repeating.

30. Collenuccio, from Mainardino of Imola, as cited in Scheffer-Boichorst *On the History of the Twelfth and Thirteenth Centuries* (*Zur Geschichte des XII. und XIII. Jahrhunderts*), p. 283, describes the camp: "This 'town' was 800 rods long and 600 rods wide, and the rod was of 9 yards; and it had 8 gates and deep, wide ditches all around." The emperor himself had written to Mainardino: "civitatem (Parmensem) civitatis nostre, que vires obsistentium ab hyemalis temporis quantalibet tempestate tuebitur, nova constructione vel oppressione comprimimus." ("We are now besieging the city (Parma) by depredation and by the recent construction of our own fortified camp, which will protect the strength of the besiegers from the adverse weather of winter, however great.")

31. Arnulph, *SS.,* 8. 16.

32. The source passages concerning the *carroccio* have been assembled and discussed by Muratori in *Antiquitates,* 2: 489. See also Waitz, 8: 183; San Marte, *Zur Waffenkunde,* p. 323; Köhler, 1: 185, 2: 147, 190, 3: 2: 344. The opinion that the idea for this originated in the Orient does not seem to me to be proven.

33. "The Battle of Tagliacozzo" ("Die Schlacht bei Tagliacozzo"), *Neue Jahrbücher für das Klassische Altertum, Geschichte und Deutsche Literatur,* 1903, Section I, Vol. XI, Book 1, p. 31.

Chapter VI

The German Cities

The military system of the German cities, like that of the Italian cities, was based on the body of knights residing in those cities, whose class was filled out by the men who had become rich merchants and whose group tended to blend with the warrior class. As Roth von Schreckenstein has already correctly stated,[1] service on horseback was first provided by the knights living in the city. Later, however, this service included all those men who had sufficient means for this purpose. We might doubt whether such property ownership provided a sufficient guarantee for military usefulness, but on the one side we must consider the class tradition, which maintained the concept of knightly honor, and on the other side the warrior element to be found in the merchant class of a period in which public legal security offered very little protection, and finally the possibility of having oneself represented by a mounted soldier. There are very frequent examples of burghers also being referred to as knights.[2] In his *Constitutional History of the German Free Cities* (*Verfassungsgeschichte der deutschen Freistädte*), 2: 186, Arnold says: "Half of them were knights who, like these, possessed fiefs from ecclesiastic and secular lords, served in armor on horseback, and enjoyed all the privileges of knighthood. And half of them were burghers who had their actual residences in the cities, carried on trade and commerce, and pursued municipal interests."[3]

In Strasbourg, Magdeburg, Zurich, and other cities, the burghers serving on horseback were called *Konstafler* or *Konstofler* (constable: the same word as *connétable,* that is, *comes stabuli* ["count of the stable"]). In 1363 the Strasbourg *Konstafler* provided eighty-one *gleves,* the guilds twenty-one, the boatmen five, the storekeepers four, the wine merchants four, etc. Emperor Louis the Bavarian required that the free cities accompany him over the mountain to his coronation, with a body of horsemen, "in accordance with ancient custom."[4]

In Italy, as we have seen, the long struggles against the Hohenstaufen kings did not produce any truly military citizenry. The accomplishments which the masses could point to here and there were by their very nature limited and temporary. And in Germany there was even less opportunity and occasion to develop a military spirit among the citizens. Even after the guilds began to dispute the hegemony with the great families and to vie with them for positions on the councils, there was still not much in the way of military accomplishment. The never-ending feuds with the neighboring princes and knights did just as little to develop an effective, specifically urban, military organization. The mass of common citizens no doubt also armed themselves and possessed or gradually assumed certain military characteristics, but they still remained only a support force for the knights, particularly as marksmen,[5] in which capacity they also gained fame in the emperor's service. In the chronicle of Arnold of Lübeck, burghers with military skill resulting from long practice were once praised,[6] and they moved out often enough, especially against robber knights, but those were small-scale fights rather than war. In the fourteenth century, it happened that the guild members moved out on wagons, with six of them seated on each vehicle. But as early as 1256 it was decided at a meeting of the city council in Mainz to hire mercenaries to the extent possible.[7] They not only recruited common soldiers or knights but also made treaties with lords and knights of the surrounding area, who obligated themselves to provide continuing help in return for payment.

These agreements with mercenaries became characteristic of municipal military systems on all sides. In 1263 Cologne made an agreement with Count Adolf of Berg in the form of a defensive and offensive alliance. The count became a citizen and obligated himself to help the city with nine knights and fifteen squires on armored horses in return for 5 marks in Cologne pennies daily. In return, Cologne was to help the count with twenty-five men from the foremost families, armored and mounted on armored horses. Similar treaties were made with Counts William and Walrum of Jülich and Dietrich of Katzenellenbogen. Even 100 years later, this treaty was renewed almost word for word.[8] In a similar way, the city of Worms obtained obligations from the counts of Leiningen.[9] How unmilitary the citizenry of Cologne and of Worms must have seemed to themselves, when they claimed such assistance! To think that such treaties were made for a mere twenty-four or twenty-five men! But these were knights, and twenty-five knights were not such a small number. I remind the reader of the care with which Charlemagne issued regulations as to whether one of his counts might be allowed to leave two or four of his warriors at home. These capitularies are not understandable until we realize that the Carolingian military system, too, was based on a warrior class of knights and not on peasant levies. The unmilitary aspect of the masses was the natural complement of a knightly class, and so the men of Cologne, for their part, also promised to provide assistance to the alliance, not with a levy of burghers, for example, but with armored horses.

If the burghers moved out at all, at any rate they were not willing to go any farther than a distance that would allow them to be back home the same evening. On one occasion, in 1388, the Rhenish and Swabian cities made a decision expressly to this effect.[10] The regulations that were often announced, to the effect that the burghers were to maintain weapons, and the types of weapons in question, and that reviews in armor were to be held in order to check on compliance with these regulations, never had a truly practical significance.

The detailed accounts and descriptions that we have, especially those from the history of the city of Cologne, for example, in the rhyming chronicle of Master Gottfried Hagen,[11] often present the situation to us in very clear pictures. But the battle of Worringen (1288), which is celebrated in legend as a victory of the Cologne burghers over their archbishop and his knights, does not belong in this context since the men of Cologne played only a secondary role in the battle.

BATTLE OF FRECHEN
1257

In 1257, a struggle broke out between the city and its archbishop, Conrad von Hochstaden. After a few engagements had taken place, the archbishop had all the roads leading toward Cologne occupied and cut off access to the city by land and water, in order to force it to surrender from hunger. One of the lords who was in the service of the city as an ally, Dietrich von Falkenburg, took command of the burghers and called on them to move out and drive off the enemy, saying it was a disgrace for the city to allow its roads to be blocked by 400 of the enemy. The citizens promised to follow him, and at Frechen they attacked the forces of the archbishop. According to Hagen, the men of Cologne were victorious when Falkenburg himself, who had initially held back and spared his forces, brought on the decision. But, as Ennen remarks, the succeeding events in no way give the impression that the forces of Cologne had won a real victory. If the archbishop's troops were really no stronger than 400 men, that point would make the military ability of the men of Cologne appear in a very unfavorable light. We may probably

assume that Dietrich, in order to encourage the burghers, greatly under-
stated the strength of the opponents. But this still indicates that the city's
military accomplishment was only of a minor nature.

INTERNAL STRUGGLES IN COLOGNE

The same conclusion is to be drawn from the accounts of the internal
struggles of the burghers. Under Conrad's successor, Archbishop Engel-
bert II of Falkenburg, the guilds, stirred up by the bishop, once rebelled
against the hegemony of the great families. They banded together and
planned to attack the residences of the nobles. This led to heated combat
in the streets, in which the patricians held the upper hand and carried out
a great blood bath, especially among the weavers. Despite the narrowness of the streets of Cologne, the knights fought on horseback. Hagen
recounted again and again how they spurred their horses on and broke
the chains with which the guildsmen tried to block the streets. Since the
number of knights and their supporters can only have been quite small,
their personal military superiority over the mass of burghers must have
been all the greater.

Of a quite similar nature was a battle that took place a few years later in
the streets of the city, on the occasion of a conflict between the two
prominent families, the Overstolzen and the Weisen. As a sequel to this
dispute, the Weisen, who were beaten and driven from the city, made a
plot to take the city by surprise. A poor cobbler, who had his house
under one of the arches of the city wall, agreed, in return for a sum of
money, to dig a hole under the walls big enough for a horseman to ride
through. Duke Walram of Limburg, the count of Cleve, and the seigneur
of Falkenburg promised to move into the city through this hole with 500
men on the night of 14 October 1268. The duke actually carried out the
plan, entered the city through the subterranean passage, opened the
nearest gate, and then moved in with his entire unit. But the Overstolzen
were warned in time, the citizens joined them, and in a heated fight, in
which a number of members of the prominent families were killed, the
attackers were pushed out or captured.

ENGAGEMENT AT HAUSBERGEN
8 MARCH 1262

On this very interesting fight between the Strasbourg burghers and the
troops of their bishop, Walter von Geroldseck, we have two reports from

the opposing sides. On the bishop's side, there was Richer, the author of a history of the monastery of Senone in the Vosges (*M.G. SS.*, 25. 340), who was a contemporary of the event, since his work closes with the year 1265. The second account, from the pen of an unknown author, dates from a generation later, around 1290. It was written out in Strasbourg and is apparently not of primary credibility—all the less so in that the text available to us was perhaps touched up here and there at a later time and is not a completely accurate reproduction of the original. Nevertheless, this *Conflictus apud Husbergen* (*Battle at Hausberg*), as it was formerly called, and *Bellum Walterianum* (*War of Walter*), as it is now called, is a very valuable piece of evidence, from the viewpoint of military history. For, although some of the individual points are of a legendary nature, the author apparently had the events recounted to him by men who participated. Some aspects of the account are of such concrete clarity as to have been produced only by a real reflection of the life and the manner in which a battle of that period was fought. The Strasbourg chronicler Fritsche Closener of the fourteenth century, who was one of the first men to write history in the German language, could do nothing better for the history of the bishop's conflict, in which Rudolf of Hapsburg, the later emperor, was also involved, than simply to translate that old Latin account.[12]

The war between the inhabitants of Strasbourg and the bishop went on for a rather long time in the usual way, as the two sides plundered and burned the villages and the bishop blocked the accesses to the city. The chronicler Richer reported that all of Alsace was depopulated and laid waste, and the people were sunk in sadness. Since the knights with property in the country were on the bishop's side, he had arranged a signal system to call them together as soon as the burghers moved out. If the bells were sounded in Molsheim, 14 miles west of Strasbourg, the bells in the nearest villages started to ring and passed on the call through the entire countryside.[13]

When the townspeople moved out on one occasion to destroy a tower near Mundolsheim, about 5 miles north of Strasbourg, on the road to Hagenau and Zabern, the bishop had the alarm sounded and moved up with his troops to attack the burghers on their return march. Those burghers who had remained behind came to the aid of those who had marched out and joined them some 3½ miles west northwest of the city, at Hausbergen. "Herr von Zorn, my very dear comrade," said the aged knight, Reimbold Liebenzeller, burgomaster of Strasbourg, who was in command of the initial sortie, to Nicolaus Zorn, who led up the reinforcements, "in God's name, welcome. In all my days I was never so anxious to see you as I am now."[14]

The burghers lined up in battle order ("ordinantes acies suas": "arranging their own battle lines") and encouraged one another, especially the
foot soldiers, to whom they said: "Today be strong in spirit and fight
fearlessly for the honor of our city and for the everlasting freedom of
ourselves and our children and all our descendants." Two knights were
specifically charged to teach the foot troops ("populo seu peditibus":
"the multitude of the foot soldiers") how they should fight, and the
burghers promised to obey them.

When the bishop's knights saw the size of their enemy, they reportedly
were hesitant to risk the attack. But when they warned the bishop, he
reproached them as being cowards, saying they were free to leave if they
wished. Then, for the sake of their honor, they remained, and although
they anticipated being killed, they nevertheless rode into the battle, the
chronicler tells us.

A Strasbourg patrician, Marcus of Eckwersheim, a youth who had not
yet been knighted, dashed out in front of his own force with his lance
poised. One of the bishop's knights named Beckelarius took up the
challenge and rushed to meet him. Both lances were splintered, and the
clash was so strong that both men were thrown to the ground with their
horses, and both horses were killed. Friends rushed out from both sides,
and the troops from the city rescued their man and killed his opponent,
Beckelarius.

Now the general encounter of the knights developed, and the men of
Strasbourg soon had the upper hand, because the entire mass of burghers
on foot, armed with spears, pushed into the battle and struck down the
horses of their opponents, so that soon all of them were lying on the ground.
Reimbold Liebenzeller had instructed them simply to keep on jabbing
with their spears, even if they should strike the horse of a friend, for the
burghers were, after all, close to home and could also return on foot.
This passage, which was quite seriously emphasized at some length in our
source, was probably intended humorously by the old knight. But, in any
case, it is very valuable for us as a picture of mixed combat of knights and
spearmen.

The bishop's knights fell prey to the greatly superior numbers and the
cooperation of the two arms because they were left in the lurch by their
own dismounted spearmen. The Strasbourg crossbowmen, instead of
likewise being used as support troops in the knightly combat, had been
withdrawn from the main body and formed up before the start of the
fight in such a way as to prevent the bishop's foot troops from coming to
the aid of his knights. Unfortunately, how this was possible is not clear in
our source. When the burghers made a swing in the direction of the city

in order to move around a ditch, the bishop supposedly thought they intended to withdraw from the battle. He therefore moved out with his horsemen ahead of the foot troops and attacked before the foot soldiers had moved up.

The Strasbourg marksmen, however, could not have moved in between the enemy knights and their dismounted troops. We could perhaps imagine that the marksmen had occupied a height in front of the formation of their own troops and the bishop's men moved up along the foot of that ridge. The knights did not allow themselves to be held up by the crossbow bolts, but the foot soldiers were frightened back by them. Of course, on closer examination this concept, too, seems hardly tenable, since the bishop's forces would hardly have come through a low pass when they could easily have moved outside the range of the Strasbourgers, which was certainly not very great. We must no doubt eliminate this entire episode as mythical, especially since our source gives the marksmen a strength of only 300 men, while the bishop's foot troops were said to be 5,000 strong. Even if this foot soldiery should have been only 1,000 or 800 men strong, how could 300 marksmen, so far from the main body of their army, have successfully opposed them? It would necessarily have been a very miserable body of spearmen that would not have been confident of overrunning a smaller number of marksmen in the open field. Perhaps the nucleus of the account is that the Strasbourg marksmen, drawn up on both flanks, successfully fired from there on the bishop's spearmen, who were directly following their knights. This action was then exaggerated to such a point that they presumably completely prevented them from participation in the battle of the knights.

The principal point, in any case, was a very strong numerical superiority on the part of the Strasbourg forces, which the bishop, who was of a knightly family and himself participated in the battle as a "pious knight" and had two horses killed beneath him, did not believe to be a cause for fear.

The bishop was defeated, sixty knights were killed, and seventy-six were taken prisoner. The report that the Strasbourgers had lost only one man, who was initially only captured but then killed by the bishop's forces in their rage over the defeat, is too strong a contradiction of the entire character of the battle to be credible. If it is really true that the knights of the valiant bishop rushed into the battle "for their honor's sake," even though they anticipated death, then the sixty knights who fell were also men who would not sacrifice their lives in vain. Furthermore, the battle was not a short one, for after his first horse had been killed, the bishop was placed on another one, lost it also, and escaped on a third.

The fame of the men of Strasbourg themselves would have been lowered by such a victory without bloodshed. The fable is no doubt to be explained by the fact that our account was not written until a generation later. The oral accounts of the battle in Strasbourg placed particular and indignant emphasis on the fate of the butcher Bilgerin, whom the defeated enemy had led off as an unwounded prisoner and then murdered. The concentration on this story overshadowed the others who were killed, so that eventually Bilgerin was named as the only one who had died.

EXCURSUS

We have based our account of the battle exclusively on only one of the two sources, the *bellum Walterianum*, because this account, although late, still has a strong basic plausibility in its favor. But, as we have already done quite often, especially in the battle of Cannae, as a valuable example of source analysis, we wish to give here the word-for-word translation of Richer's account. Since Richer lived not far from the scene of these events and wrote his account very soon afterwards, we would presumably have no hesitation in accepting his report if there were no other source at hand.

Here is what Richer wrote:

As Bishop Walter, with the army he had assembled from all sides for his protection, was waiting in one of his castles, called Dachenstein, the Strasbourg forces moved out of their city one day, ready for combat. When the bishop heard this with his knights, he declared war on the Strasbourgers ["cum suis armatis argentinensibus bellum indixit"; the expression is not entirely clear, since Richer had already recounted how both sides were laying waste to the region and burning it. Perhaps the author meant that he commanded his men to make ready to battle]. But the men of Strasbourg moved against the bishop and thus entered the battle. The Strasbourgers had arranged to have made for themselves battle-axes, which the French call "*haches danaises*," with which the burghers assaulted the bishop's men so strongly that neither shield, nor helmet, nor armor, nor any other kind of protection could defend against them. Furthermore, while the battle became so fierce and the two sides fought with murderous violence, the army of Strasbourg received reinforcements. For, since the battle was taking place near the city, the garrison and the citizenry, seeing their men engaged in the heat of the battle, rushed confidently to their aid, furiously assaulted the bishop's army, and cut down everything in front of them. When the lords and knights of the bishop's army realized there was no salvation for them, they preferred to live as prisoners of the Strasbourgers rather than to die in the battle. And so the burghers led them, disarmed, into their city. The citizens of Strasbourg, believing that God was aiding them in this fight, fell upon the battle group in which the bishop was posted and from which he was seeing the defeat of his men, destroyed the unit and killed the bishop's horse, so that the bishop himself fell to the ground. But a few of the knights who were around him lifted him onto a horse and persuaded him to leave the battlefield. The Strasbourgers then killed as many of the enemies as they wished and led others as prisoners into the city. . . . The number of prisoners was reported to have been eighty; the number of those who died in the battle could not be definitely determined.

So much for Richer. We can see that all the important aspects of the fight—with the exception of the superior number of the Strasbourg force—have disappeared. I invite the reader's attention particularly to the Danish battle-axes, which supposedly led to the victory of the burghers. It can be assumed that the men of Strasbourg had many new weapons made at the outbreak of the war and that battle-axes were included among them. But we must reject the point that this specific weapon was supposedly so effective in this battle, since, in that case, the Strasbourg source itself would have reported something on that point, and we cannot see why this fearful weapon would not then always have been used with such success. Rather, as the Strasbourg account stated, the decisive factor was certainly the mass of spearmen who supported the knights of the city and struck down the enemies' horses, as well as the superiority in marksmen, even though it is not clear as to how they were so effective. The emphasis placed on the battle-axes in the account from the bishop's side, instead of the points enumerated above, can be taken as an ideal example of the observation that authors like to concentrate on special aspects of such actions, even when, as in this case, it was the superiority of numbers that led to the decision in a normal way in a typical battle.

NOTES FOR CHAPTER VI

1. *The Knightly Dignity and the Knightly Class (Die Ritterwürde und der Ritterstand)*, p. 502.

2. Roth, p. 470.

3. See *Bremer Urkundenbuch,* edited by Ehmk and Bippen, Vol. I, No. 172. In 1233, Archbishop Gebhard promised the citizens of Bremen:

Cives Bremenses mercatores non tenebuntur ad archiepiscopi Bremensis expeditionem, ni voluerint, exceptis illis mercatoribus qui vel tamquam ministeriales vel tamquam homines ecclesiae ab ecclesia sunt feodati, quorum quilibet ad expeditionem ecclesiae evocatus servicium suum per unum hominem poterit redimere, competenter armis instructum.

(The merchant inhabitants of Bremen will not be obligated for the campaign of the archbishop of Bremen unless they will have desired to be, with the exception of those merchants who either as officials or as men of the Church have been enfeoffed by the Church, of which each one called out for the campaign of the Church will be able to fulfill his obligation through one man suitably equipped with arms.)

See Donandt, *History of the Bremen Municipal Law* (*Geschichte des Bremer Stadtrechts*), 1: 111.

4. H. Fischer, "The Participation of the Free Cities in the Imperial Campaign" ("Die Teilnahme der Reichsstädte an der Reichsheerfahrt"), Leipzig dissertation, 1883, p. 14. The first march to Rome in which they actually participated, of course, did not occur until 1310. P. 29.

5. Lindt, "Contributions to the History of German Military Organization in the Hohenstaufen Period" ("Beiträge zur Geschichte der Deutschen Kriegsverfassung in der Staufischen Zeit"), Tübingen dissertation, 1881, p. 28, cites several passages for this point, the earliest being from the year 1114.

6. 1204 "collecta multitudine militum vel etiam civium, qui propter continuas bellorum exercitationes gladiis et sagittis et lanceis non parum praevalent" ("after a crowd of knights and even inhabitants had been assembled, who, on account of their continuous military exercises with swords, arrows, and lances, were sufficiently capable . . .").

7. Arnold, 2: 241.

8. Ennen and Eckertz, *Sources for the History of the City of Cologne* (*Quellen zur Geschichte der Stadt Köln*), Vol. II, No. 449, p. 165, and Vol. IV, No. 488, p. 560. See also 3: 232. Arnold, *Constitutional History of the German Free Cities* (*Verfassungsgeschichte der deutschen Freistädte*), 1: 443.

9. Arnold, 2: 243.

10. "Not many of the gentlemen joined me, since they were anxious to be able to return home again on the same day and could not remain out overnight." Königshofen, *Chronik deutscher Städte* (*Chronicle of German Cities*), 9. 845. Vischer, *Studies in German History* (*Forschungen der deutschen Geschichte*) 2: 77. Köhler, 3: 2: 381.

11. Master Godefrit Hagen, city clerk for the period, *Rhymed Chronicle of the City of Cologne from the Thirteenth Century* (*Reimchronik der Stadt Köln aus dem dreizehnten Jahrhundert*). With notes and glossary in accordance with the only ancient manuscript. Edited completely for the first time by E. von Groote, city councilor, Cologne on the Rhine. Published and printed by M. Du Mont-Schauberg. 1834.

12. This document is printed in the *Fontes rerum Germanicarum* (*Sources of German History*), by Böhmer, Vol. III, and recently edited by Jaffé in the *SS.*, 17. 105. See also Wiegand, *Bellum Walterianum* (*Studies in Alsatian History* [*Studien zur Elsässischen Geschichte*], I), Strasbourg, 1878. Roth von Schreckenstein, *Herr Walter von Geroldseck*, Tübingen, 1857.

13. Roth, p. 40, assumes that the bishop had distributed his men throughout the region up to about Schlettstadt, Rheinau, Zabern, and

Hagenau. Some of these points are more than 18 miles distant from the assembly point at Molsheim.

According to Richer, the bishop's troops had not initially assembled but were concentrated at Dachenstein.

14. From Closener's translation. The Latin text reads: "Bene veniatis, dilectissime domine Zorn; nunquam in tantum desiderabam vos videre."

Chapter VII

The Conquest of Prussia by the Teutonic Order

In the history of the Crusades, the Church, and the Occident, the knightly orders played a very significant role, and in this work we have often made reference to them. But not in the sense, for example, that they filled a special page in the history of the art of war or had produced unique forms.

Nowhere do we see that their performances were different from the normal picture of the period, as we might have expected from their discipline, resulting from their oath of obedience. On the contrary, it is specifically in the regulations of these orders that we can find the clearest features of the knightly methods of waging war and fighting. The number of true knights, considered as combatants, was always much too small for such effects to have been produced by the order. Their significance and their success resulted from the organization which was made effective by the rich goods and contributions that came streaming to them in all countries of the Latin Church for the purpose of the fight for the Holy Land.

In one place, however, one of the orders, the Teutonic, gained an enduring success of immeasurable significance.

The mighty German Empire required 300 years, or if we reckon from the time of Henry I, more than 200 years, to subject once and for all the humble Slavic tribes between the Elbe and the Oder and to assimilate them. If we keep this length of time in mind, we are not surprised that the Poles were not able to overcome their pagan neighbors to the north, the Prussians between the Vistula and the Memel, but finally called the Teutonic Order to their aid from Germany.[1]

We are not very accurately informed of the history of the unusual establishment of a nation and the colonization that resulted from this turn of events. The actual reporter for this period, Peter Dusburg, did not live until 100 years later. But we can clearly recognize the military principles that governed during this conquest.

The order did not possess the standing army with which Caesar, when he subjugated Gaul, established himself in the middle of the country and defeated and with invincible force suppressed every instance of disobedience. The order was also lacking in armies of vassals, like those of Charlemagne, which, led forth when necessary, in coordination with politics, gradually wore down and broke the resistance of the Saxons. The direct power of the German order, when it subjugated Prussia, and simultaneously Livonia and Courland, was only small. It did not become a great power until after it had become ruler of these countries. Strangely enough, the number of members of the order has not been recorded for any period in the source documents and cannot be determined.[2] In the thirteenth century it was certainly never more than a few hundred, or, at the very most, 1,000. The strength of the order lay in the fact that it was the representative of the great ideas of the period, it united Church and knighthood organically within itself, and, as their champion, it had not only Germany but the entire Occident, so to speak, backing it up. The papacy, with its Crusade bulls and Crusade sermons, and the warlike nature and desire for adventure of princes and knights brought to the order such a strong and constant flow of forces that it was finally able to accomplish a task in which emperors and kings could have had their forces drained away and from which Poland had weakly shrunk in fear. The Crusades to Jerusalem were not able to achieve a lasting political success, but the small brook that branched off from this mighty stream and took its course toward the corner of the Baltic Sea flowed upon a fruitful field and had a telling effect on world history, lasting up to the present day.

First, the knights established the fortified castle of Thorn in the devastated Polish border country on the Vistula (1230 or 1231). From there they moved down the Vistula and built other strongholds: Kulm, Marienwerder, and Elbing (1237). Then they moved along the Frisches Haff and built Balga on its shore (1239). Scholars have thought that they had moved along the border with the plan of surrounding the Prussians, so to speak, but that was not the reason. There was never a strategic, coordinated move from two separate bases. Rather, the decisive factor was that all these installations were on the water and could remain in contact with one another and with Germany by the water route. As soon as they had moved down the Nogat to the Baltic Sea, they established contact with the German seaports; Elbing was to some extent a colony of Lübeck. When Margrave Henry of Meissen, who had become the richest prince as a result of the newly discovered silver in his Erzgebirge, once visited the order while on a Crusade, he did the order a greater service than through his knights, by presenting it with two warships, the "Pilgrim" and the "Friedeland," which gave the order domination of the Frisches Haff.

From their castles on the water, the knights then pushed other fortified places into the countryside, most importantly Rheden, Bartenstein, and Rössel. This step-by-step advance—so completely different from Charlemagne's procedure in Saxony—did not result from an abstract strategic principle but was suited to the special conditions and strengths of the order. The order itself was too weak for an offensive, but time and again Crusaders came, often great princes with a mounted retinue—the margraves of Meissen and Brandenburg, the landgrave of Thuringia, the duke of Braunschweig, a bishop of Merseburg, a prince of Anhalt. Each time such reinforcements were used to strike a blow at the pagans and move farther forward into the country, establishing permanent fortifications. In this way, with the castles as bases, the Prussian peoples along the Vistula were subjugated first, the Pomesanians, the Pogesanians, and then the Ermelanders. According to the sources, there was also a battle on the Sirgune (Sorge) in 1236, but we may doubt that it was very important or whether it even took place. The principal factor, in any case, is to be seen in the installation of those fortified places.

That is the principal point because, in all such colonial conquests, it is not so much the first subjugation, which often enough can succeed rather easily by surprise and deception, that is the deciding factor, but rather the effective overcoming of the rebellion which is sure to follow as soon as the subjected people has become familiar with the foreign hegemony, with its changes and its pressure. In 1242, the twelfth year of the conquest, the first great rebellion broke out, and it lasted eleven years, until 1253. It was survived and overcome not with field armies and open battles but because the Prussians were not able to conquer the fortified places of the knights and thus drive them out of the country. Again and again, pilgrim warriors aided the knights, participated in offensive moves with them, and helped them build a new fortified support base deep in the interior, at Christburg. The papal legate, Jacob of Liège, finally mediated a peaceful settlement with a part of the rebels (7 February 1249), and this document is still in existence at the present day. The conflict broke out again, and the knights even suffered the serious defeat of Krücken (23 November 1249), where fifty-four members of the order were killed. But finally all the rebels accepted the peace.

The order immediately resumed its expansion activity. Supported by a

Bohemian unit which King Ottocar had personally led up, the order established a fortified place at the mouth of the Pregel, Königsberg (1254). For contact with Courland, Memel (Memelburg) had already been founded at the mouth of the Kurisches Haff, and Kreuzburg had been built in the interior. There then followed Labiau on the Kurisches Haff (perhaps this was not until somewhat later), and farther in the interior on the Pregel, Wehlau. From these and a few other places, there was completed the subjugation of East Prussia, which for the most part was already no longer inhabited by actual Prussians, but by Lithuanians.

In 1260, six years later, the second great rebellion broke out after the knights had suffered a serious defeat at the hands of the Lithuanians, at Durban in which 150 knights of the order, foremost among whom were the Livonian Master Burchard von Hornhausen and Marshal Henry Botel, were killed (13 July 1260). Pomesania, the area directly on the Vistula, remained loyal this time, but the five interior districts of Samland, Natangen, Ermeland, Pogesania, and Barten revolted in a well-planned conspiracy and selected captains, or dukes as we might call them, who then waged a fifteen-year war with great determination. One of these captains, Henry Monte of Natangen, like Arminius in Rome in an earlier day, had received his education and probably even his Christian name in Magdeburg. In the field, the Prussians repeatedly held the upper hand, especially on one occasion in the Löbau, where the Vice Grand Master Helmerich was killed, along with forty brothers of the order, and the entire Christian army was destroyed (13 July 1263). In general, the war was fought in repeated plundering and wasting expeditions on both sides, which brought the Prussians up to the walls of Thorn and led to their destruction of Marienwerder. But the final decision was once again brought about by the struggle for the fortified places. The Prussians captured the interior strongholds, except for Christburg. While their skill at siegecraft was only very small, even though they had learned something about the use of engines of war from their enemies, they sealed off the castles with counter-strongholds, which were garrisoned by alternating units, and thus succeeded in starving them out. Just as the Roman garrison of the fort of Aliso, with the remnants of Varus' army, had once held out for months against the Germans and finally, when their food supplies were exhausted, had slipped out and successfully covered the 90 miles to the Rhine, the garrisons of the order's strongholds in Prussia finally saved themselves by distracting their besiegers from their alertness and secretly withdrawing.

In this way, the garrisons of Heilsberg and Braunsberg escaped to Elbing and the garrison of Wiesenburg (north of Rastenburg) escaped through the desert area in the south to Poland or Sassen. Diwan, the captain of the Bartens, pursued them when he became aware of their withdrawal, and he finally overtook them with thirteen men whose horses had held out for that long move. But when he himself was wounded in the fight, the others gave up the struggle and the pursuit.

Events did not turn out so fortunately for the garrison of Kreuzburg, which was discovered during its nocturnal escape and was cut to pieces.

Bartenstein withstood the blockade until the fourth year. Finally, its situation became so desperate that its garrison could only be saved by secret flight. They prepared for this flight artfully by remaining completely quiet and hidden for a few days within the walls, so that the Prussians believed that the stronghold had been abandoned. When they approached, they were suddenly received with shots and were driven back with heavy losses. For the withdrawal, the garrison was divided into two smaller groups, one of which took the road toward Königsberg (some 40 miles), while the other followed the road toward Elbing (70 miles). A blind, crippled brother of the order remained behind, rang the bell regularly at the prescribed hours, and thus deceived the enemy, who were more careful as a result of their latest loss, into thinking that the place was still occupied. When they finally decided that the Germans had really disappeared, the latter were already far away without any traces. Both groups succeeded in reaching Königsberg and Elbing.

The order had not been able to do anything to relieve all these strongholds. But the forts along the water, Memelburg, Königsberg, Balga, and Elbing, held fast. The rebels did not risk approaching Thorn and Kulm. Balga, and especially Königsberg, were strongly besieged. At Königsberg the Prussians even tried to block the river by building a bridge over the Pregel, but the knights destroyed the bridge, and rations, reinforcements, and finally even relief were brought to them via the water route. On one occasion, it was the two counts of Jülich and Berg who drove off the Prussians (22 January 1262). In 1265 there arrived a duke of Braunschweig and a landgrave of Thuringia, and they enabled the brothers to take up the offensive again from Königsberg.

The end of the second great rebellion appears to have come about like that of the first; the Prussians were not really defeated but were outwaited. Two of their captains or dukes, Henry Monte of Natangen and Glappe of Ermeland, had fallen into the hands of the knights through deception and perhaps also some kind of treachery by their compatriots, and they were hanged. A third leader, Diwan of Barten, was killed at the siege of Castle Schönsee. The Prussians realized that, even though they had caused so much damage to the conquerors and had captured and destroyed so many towns, farms, and strongholds and had killed the inhabitants, they were still unable to drive the enemy out of the country. And so Skumand, the duke of the Sudauens, in the extreme southeast, after having fought most bravely for a long time and extending his campaigns into the Kulm region, decided to yield. Despairing of everything, he had already moved out with his men to Lithuania, but then he turned back, renounced paganism, and recognized the hegemony of the knights. Other leaders did likewise, and in 1283, the fifty-third year after the founding of the stronghold of Thorn, the subjugation of Prussia was considered as completed.

We are inclined to ask whether the Romans might not have been able to master the Germans in this way and introduce their political system. The difference lies, first of all, in the fact that their task was a much greater one. After all, Prussia was only a very small region in comparison with Germania, and even if the latter was most certainly only very thinly populated, the population of Prussia may have been even sparser. Even the most advanced posts were not too distant from the secure double base of the sea and the Vistula. During the entire struggle, the Poles were allies of the order. While the dukes of Pomerania (Pomerelia) were at times very hostile to the order and direct allies of the Prussians, they finally were pacified not simply through military force, but, as princes who already belonged to the Christian cultural world, through diplomatic means, the intervention of crusading princes. If we add up the resources which Germany and partially also Poland and the entire Occident employed for the subjugation and Christianization of Prussia, they necessarily appear gigantic in comparison with the small area involved. As we may never forget, the struggle lasted a total of fifty-three years, whereas Caesar had completely conquered and pacified the huge territory of Gaul up to the Rhine in eight years. The intensive, faster drive to victory like that of Caesar in Gaul is certainly the method that requires the smaller expenditure, everything considered. The order could not proceed in that manner because it was too weak, and the flow of its resources was always only drop by drop. The question as to why the Romans did not overcome Germania by using the method of the knights therefore breaks down as follows: If they had absolutely wanted to subjugate the land and were willing to apply the necessary resources, they would have had to proceed by using Caesar's method. It was impossible for a Roman emperor to conceive of proceeding in the expensive method followed by the order. At the first defeat, they would immediately have taken up the war on a full scale. But we have already seen why this kind of warfare was no longer possible after the recall of Germanicus and why Germanicus was recalled.

NOTES FOR CHAPTER VII

1. The best comprehensive account is that of Karl Lohmeyer, *Geschichte von Ost- und Westpreussen*, 1st Section, 2d ed., 1881. The work of A. L. Ewald, *The Conquest of Prussia by the Germans (Die Eroberung Preussens durch die Deutschen)*, four volumes, 1882-1886, is based on a variety of sources. The second great rebellion by the Prussians is treated thoroughly and well by Köhler in the second volume of his *Development of Military Organization and Conduct of War in the Knightly Period (Entwickelung des Kriegswesens und der Kriegführung in der Ritterzeit)*.

2. Whether the remark, from Dusburg or the chronicle of Oliva, that the order numbered 600 lay members in 1239 is reliable cannot be determined.

Chapter VIII

English Archery. The Conquest of Wales and Scotland by Edward I

The importance of the bow in the warfare of the earlier Middle Ages appears in a remarkably uncertain light, not really recognizable in the sources, and, to the extent that it is recognizable, hesitant and variable. Among the original Germans, we find practically no mention of it in the sources (Vol. II, p. 49), but the Goths and other Germanic peoples of the *Völkerwanderung* appeared as archers so extensively that Vegetius was able to write that the Romans fell prey to their hail of arrows (Vol. II, p. 230). The bow is prescribed in the Carolingian capitularies, but it appears only very seldom in the source accounts of the period, and there is no doubt that we must think of the German knights as using lance and sword almost exclusively. On the other hand, in the battle of Hastings, the Normans made extremely effective use of their archers. But the Crusaders found, when they were dealing with the Turks, that the latter were superior to them as marksmen, and the Crusaders created their own combat arm of mounted archers following the example of the Turks. We hear that an important part of the armies of Emperor Frederick II in Italy was composed of the Saracen archers, but, according to the accounts, no marksmen were active in the battles that Frederick's son and his grandson fought and lost against Charles of Anjou.[1]

In addition to the bow, the crossbow gradually came more and more into use.[2] The German word for this weapon, *Armbrust,* has nothing to do with either "arm" or "breast," but it is a vulgar etymological shifting of the Middle Latin words *arcubalista, arbalista*. In antiquity it already seems to have been known not simply as a missile weapon, but also as a hand weapon. It is pictured on a relief of the fourth century A.D., to be found today in the Museum of Le Puy, and Vegetius, Ammianus, and Jordanes seem to mention it. In the actual Middle Ages, the first trace of it appears in a miniature illustration in a bible of Louis IV, of the year 937. Anna Komnena is supposed to have mentioned it under the name "Tzagra" as a unique weapon of the occidentals, and the weapon appears in a not completely understandable way in a decision of the Lateran Council of 1139.[3] But since the historiographer of Philip Augustus claims it was Richard the Lion-Hearted who first introduced it to the Franks and the Goddess of Fate supposedly wished that the king might die by this very weapon,[4] it must therefore still have been rather rare in the twelfth century.

The increase in protective armor led to the corresponding change in offensive weapons. As early as in the *Introduction to Archery (Anleitung zum Bogenschiessen)* from the time of Justinian,[5] it is recommended that arrows be shot diagonally against an opponent, since the shield could not be penetrated by an arrow from directly in front. The bolt of the crossbow had a much stronger penetrating force than the arrow, so that the crossbow would seem to be the ideal missile against heavily armored knights. Nevertheless, it was adopted only very slowly and never completely replaced the simple bow but only existed in addition to the bow. It was finally once again even defeated by the bow. After a long period in which the bow appeared only occasionally and temporarily, we have the remarkable phenomenon that in the fourteenth and fifteenth centuries it suddenly assumed a completely overriding importance in the English armies. How did it happen, how was it possible that such an ancient weapon, whose use was known for thousands of years and whose techniques could probably not have been increased any further, suddenly took on such importance?

In his *History of the Art of War,* Oman has already recognized that the origin of this rejuvenation of the bow is to be sought in the reign of Edward I of England and his Welsh wars. A later work on these wars by John Morris, which is of the greatest value concerning all aspects of the warfare of this period, has also thoroughly treated the origin of this weapon.[6] Morris, just as Oman did before him, proceeds from the report that it was customary earlier to pull the bowstring back only to the chest, whereas at this time the string of the longbow was pulled back to the ear.[7] I do not wish to repeat this account word for word, for the fact that the farther one pulls the string, the stronger the shot, cannot have been any new discovery, and there were, of course, strong men also in the earlier periods. Furthermore, we literally find the same account 700 years earlier in Procopius (see Vol. II, p. 346), where he intends to prove that the use of the bow became so general in his time. If there were periods and peoples who used the short bow and not the longbow, and, at that, peoples who were so famous as marksmen as the Persians and Parthians, there cannot have been such an important difference between the various forms. Good marksmen have certainly always bent their bows as strongly and as far as their physical strength allowed. With a slight modification, however, Morris's idea becomes correct. If we may proceed from the concept that bows and arrows existed for thousands of years and the technique of their use could not be surpassed, nevertheless this technique was not always maintained at the same high level. If we find in the Middle Ages periods and peoples to whom archery was hardly known and great battles were fought without marksmen, this no doubt means that the techniques both of manufacture and use of this weapon had retrogressed. Morris very nicely points out how at the end of the nineteenth century, along with speeds in rowing competition that had never previously been achieved, the construction of such an ancient instrument as the boat also experienced great new improvements and refinements. Zeal in the practice of an art always goes hand in hand with the production of constantly improved instruments. Consequently, it is a question not of the introduction of something completely new, whether it be the longbow or the custom of pulling the bowstring back to the ear, but rather of an improvement, starting at a given point, of the fabrication and use of the missile weapon that naturally and automatically resulted from greater and more intensive appreciation of the weapon that had previously been neglected. Thus, the techniques in the use of the weapon were raised to a level that had no doubt already been reached earlier but that now seemed to be new to the contemporaries. The perfected technique was, therefore, not the cause but the result of the phenomenon in military history of the rejuvenation of the bow, a result which then reacted, of course, on the cause: The greater the accomplishments, the stronger the inclination to use this weapon.

The real question, then, is whence came the momentum for the renewed acceptance of the art of archery at this particular time and specifically in England.

The origins are in the Welsh wars of King Edward I (1272–1307), which ended with the final subjugation of Wales and the unification of that country with England. The preceding great decisive actions on English soil, the battles of Lewes and Ewesham, in which Henry III, father of Edward I, fought with his barons, still showed practically nothing in the use of marksmen, as was also the case in the battles of Benevento and Tagliacozzo of that same period. Edward had already participated in those battles as crown prince and had then made a Crusade to the Holy Land, where he probably became familiar with the Turkish archers and their effectiveness. According to an unconfirmed source, he was even wounded by a Turkish arrow. Having mounted the throne, he established for himself the mission of subjecting the Welsh, who in their mountain fastnesses had withstood all the storms, first of the Roman occupation of the island, then the Anglo-Saxon, and then the Norman, in their Celtic heritage and ancient barbaric military skill. It was Edward's intention to put an end to the constant border wars and the suffering of the neighboring counties. Little could be done with knights amidst these forests, heights, and ravines. In the north, the Welsh were still fighting principally with the spear, according to the ancient custom, like the Germans described by Tacitus, whereas in the south, where they had already come under English-Norman hegemony and influence, archery was well developed. As early as two generations before Edward I, a political author and historian, Giraldus Cambrensis (also called Gerald de Barri: died about 1220), had recommended how the Welsh could be defeated. Gerald himself was the grandson of the Norman constable of Pembroke and the daughter of a Welsh prince. He was proud of both sides of his family tree and showed appreciation of the achievements of both sides. He praised the knights and described the combat methods of the Welsh, pointing out how, lightly armed as they were, they sometimes attacked aggressively and at other times withdrew stealthily and nimbly into their inaccessible mountains and forests. Gerald therefore recommended that support troops be obtained from those Welsh tribes that were already subjected or allied, and that the archers be combined with the knights. "Semper arcarii militaribus turmis mixtim adjiciantur."[8] ("Archers should always be mixed in with the companies of knights.") In this way, with combined troops, Ireland had just been conquered. Indeed, it was precisely in this way that William I had earlier overcome the Anglo-Saxons. But the fact that Gerald recommended this as something unusual and recognized the French combat method only in the knight armed with the lance is an additional proof that in the meantime the methods of William the Conqueror had in fact fallen into decline. In the Assize of Arms of Henry II of 1181, the bow is not mentioned at all as a weapon.[9]

The immediate need for combat in the mountains therefore led Edward I to take up again and develop the art of archery, which had been passed down but neglected and not widely enough known. The first elements for this renewal were taken principally from the counties bordering Wales, for whom this war was a matter of life and death and tradition, and from those Welsh themselves who entered English service and accepted English pay. With the simple feudal levies, nothing would have been accomplished, despite greater use of the missile weapon. The rule that vassals were obligated to serve only forty days was in effect at that time. Indeed, there were still shorter periods of service; it happened that only three weeks were sometimes required, or it is reported that a levied warrior was obligated to serve only as long as the rations he brought with him lasted. He would bring along a ham, would try to consume it as quickly as possible, and would then return home.[10] But Edward knew that only a war waged as seriously as possible could lead him to his goal. We know that in the Norman nation the vassal levy had always been filled out and even replaced by mercenaries. Edward now based his war completely on paid mercenaries and used the levies only as a secondary measure or combined both.[11] For example, he ordered all enfeoffed men of the knightly class (with more than 40 pounds of possessions) to be prepared for a call-up for three weeks and to enter the service and pay of the king for three more weeks after the end of the first period. "Ad eundum in obsequium nostrum et morandum ad vadia nostra ad voluntatem nostram quandocunque super hoc ex parte nostra per spacium trium septimanarum fuerint premuniti"[12] ("to enter our service and to remain on our payroll, according to our will, whenever, in addition to this, they were prepared at our expense for a period of three weeks"). Uncompensated service was required in the warrior's own county or march, but pay was received as soon as the action crossed the border. In the case of large undertakings, as, for example, an important siege, the national levy was also paid in its own area after an initial uncompensated period of three days' service.[13] Edward also brought in experienced warriors from Gascony to fight alongside English mercenaries, and he waged war continuously, even through the winter. Morris has completely explained and very graphically described the conduct of this war by referring to the vast source material, the royal commands, mercenary payments, etc. We are continuously reminded of the campaigns of the Romans in Germany and of the Teutonic Order in Prussia. Edward's principal concerns were the establishment of communications and the provision of rations. Like Germanicus and the German knights, he used the water route, both the sea and the rivers, for these purposes, and he brought up ships from his five ports. Just as Domitian had conquered the Chatti by laying out 180 kilometers of road through their territory (Vol. II, p. 157), now Edward paid woodsmen, who opened access routes through the Welsh forests.[14]

Although Edward had his country strongly behind him for these wars and made the greatest efforts, the armies he raised were hardly any larger than those we have previously become familiar with in the Middle Ages. When the war began in 1277, the king had war-horses brought from France—over 100, according to a specific report.[15] For our part, we note this number as proof that 100 "dextrarii et magni equites" ("war-horses and great horsemen") was at that time already a quite significant number.

Morris (pp. 80 ff.) reckons that there were at most 2,750 knights under Edward I, including all those who were obligated to become knights. He therefore assumes that if there were two other horsemen for each knight, then the largest number available in England—but, of course, never all levied at the same time—was some 8,000 horsemen.

Morris estimates (p. 132) the maximum strength of the dismounted troops in 1277 at 15,640 men, but of that number not many more than 6,000 were English, while more than 9,000 were allied Welsh. This large combat force was assembled for only a very short time.

In 1282, in the second war, the foot troops amounted to 8,600 men, including some 1,800 Welsh. The total number of horsemen, knights and serving men, was between 700 and 800.[16]

In the winter, as a result of losses and desertions, this army shrank very seriously. But the losses were replaced by the arrival of mercenaries from Gascony. At the outbreak of the war, no more than twelve mounted crossbowmen and forty of the same on foot had been required of the seneschal of that country that had been inherited by King Edward.[17] But now there came a body of troops which Morris (p. 188) has been able to reckon from the pay rosters at exactly 210 horsemen and 1,313 foot soldiers. Their principal weapon was the crossbow; these reinforcements brought along 70,000 bolts in barrels and baskets. From the high amount of their pay, we realize that these crossbowmen were regarded as elite warriors.[18] With these reinforcements, Edward fought through to final victory.

According to Morris's estimate (p. 105), no more than a total of between 2,000 and 3,000 men were engaged in the two larger battles of the Welsh wars.[19]

If we look back to the fact that Emperor Frederick II and William the Conqueror were previously shown to be the leaders who had many marksmen among their troops, it is clear that the marksmen appeared each time that a great commander raised an army through his strong central powers. But it was the feudal levies that got along without marksmen. Commanders recognized their value and prized them, but they could only have such soldiers when they paid for them (or at least were able to promise pay, as in the case of William the Conqueror). The vassal and the individual knight did not train or like to have marksmen in his retinue, not as if he did not value highly the technical aspects of this weapon and its effectiveness, but, as we have already recognized, a remarkable tension existed between the concept of the feudal knight and the use of marksmen, since the latter had a relationship to the high command and its mercenary payments, a relationship at odds with the nature of knighthood.

The sources do not indicate directly why Edward I finally chose the bow as the weapon for his marksmen at a time when the crossbow was highly regarded and he himself used it extensively. The French scholar Luce, in his *Bertrand du Guesclin* (p. 160), believes that one needs but to glance at the crossbows of the fourteenth century in our museums, "so massive and complicated to manipulate," to understand that they could not advantageously compete with the English bows, but that seems to me to go too far. The crossbow gained acceptance in competition with the bow and continued to hold its ground in this rivalry despite the English victories. If the one weapon had the advantage of simpler handling and faster firing, the other had a much stronger penetrating force. It was therefore not a question of something absolutely better on one side or the other but of different kinds of advantages and disadvantages that did not compensate for one another. In this connection, scholars have already appropriately compared the simultaneous use of bow and crossbow with the competition between the flintlock (musket) and the rifle in the first half of the nineteenth century. The musket could be loaded and fired much faster, but with less accuracy; the grooved rifle was hard to load but more accurate. This problem was not solved until the discovery of the breech-loader, which combined the advantage of rapid loading with that of accuracy, but no solution was found to the dilemma between the bow and the crossbow.[20] Juvénal des Ursins said of Duke John of Brabant in 1414: "He had 4,000 crossbowmen, each armed with two crossbows and served by two strong soldiers, one of whom held a large shield, while the other primed the crossbow, so that one was always ready to fire."

I think that the reason why Edward I developed the bow, while his predecessor Richard the Lion-Hearted, had preferred the crossbow, lies in the fact that Richard was fighting against knights, whereas Edward's opponents were the Welsh, who wore only insignificant protective armor. Once the bow had proven itself so well in these wars and the following conflicts with the Scots, the English kings, as we shall see, retained it for the French wars and found ways to develop it to its most favorable effectiveness.

With the help of the numerous and skillful archers who supported the knights, and thanks to an energetic administration which made possible the continuous waging of war, and finally owing to a well-regulated system of rations and supplies, Edward I succeeded in definitively subjugating the Welsh mountaineers in the course of a few years. The military force he created in this conflict then also brought him victory over the Scots.

BATTLE OF FALKIRK
22 JULY 1298

The Scots under William Wallace had taken up a position with their front protected by swamps. Their army consisted of four large units of spearmen, between which marksmen were posted. The knights, of moderate strength, were drawn up in the rear.

Edward moved up against them with a very strong army, principally knights and marksmen. Some of the Scots were also fighting on his side. The swamps in front of the Scots afforded them no protection, as the English moved around them on the right and left. In the face of the onrushing superior enemy forces, the Scottish marksmen immediately broke ranks, and the horsemen fled without striking a blow. Then the English knights fell upon the units of spearmen, but they did not succeed in penetrating into the thick forest of spears that were held out against them. Then King Edward ordered his knights to withdraw and his marksmen to shoot into the thick masses of Scots. The English spearmen supported them by picking up fieldstones and throwing them into the helpless mass. Soon the Scottish units were so exhausted that they offered no further resistance, and the knights were able to break up their formations. A general slaughter then began.

According to the smallest estimate, the Scots had 1,000 horsemen and 30,000 foot soldiers. The principal source, the otherwise sensible and reliable canon of Gisburn, Walter Hemmingford, gives a strength of 300,000 dismounted men. Oman is inclined to accept the figure of 30,000 as possible, but this number, too, seems to me grossly exaggerated, even though we may assume that the large units of spearmen consisted principally of peasant militia.

Köhler's belief that the Scots had tied themselves to one another is based on an erroneous interpretation of the words "Scotos lancearios, qui sedebant in circulis cum lanceis obligatis et in modum silvae condensis" ("the Scottish spearmen, who were standing in circles with their spears held together and thick like a forest"). The word "*obligatis*" simply means with spears "united," "closely held together."

Morris estimates a total of some 2,400 English mounted men, instead of the 7,000 given in a chronicle.[21] There were eight earls and a bishop, with their men, and mercenaries of various types, especially Gascons and Welsh, precisely those whom Edward had only recently subjected and who were now fighting in his service.

Köhler's belief that a combination of foot troops and horsemen, such as we see here in the English army, was never before to be found in military history may rather be reversed. This was the normal composition of a knightly army, such as the Persians led against Greece and like those we have observed ever since the *Völkerwanderung* and throughout the entire Middle Ages. But the marksmen attained such great effectiveness because Edward was, first of all, very strong in this arm, and second, because the four large Scottish masses, in their purely defensive stance, offered the marksmen such an unprecedentedly favorable target. The Scottish masses were, in the final analysis, nothing other than the formation of Harold's Anglo-Saxons at Hastings, who were likewise defeated by William's marksmen and knights. The difference was that the Scots were not completely without horsemen, but this difference disappears when we see that these mounted men immediately took flight. A further difference lies in the fact that Harold's warriors were drawn up in a single, closed, shallow mass, whereas the Scots were divided into four deep groups. This difference could be explained by the presence of knights, who were supposed to push through the units, and perhaps also by the larger number of marksmen, who could not have been drawn up in front of a single phalanx, and finally by the different quality of the spearmen. Harold's soldiers were professional warriors, whereas at least the majority of the Scots were militia. The latter type of unit had to take a deep formation in order to achieve the necessary steadfastness; the professional soldiers took up a shallower formation in order to allow more individuals to participate in the fight. And many of them fought not with the spear, but with the more effective battle-ax. The Scottish units, with their great depth, remained in a purely defensive situation, extending their spears on all sides.

The unusual aspect of the battle of Falkirk, therefore, is to be found to a much higher degree on the side of the Scots rather than the English. Nowhere else in the Middle Ages do we find such great masses of foot soldiers who do not immediately break ranks when attacked by knights.

On a smaller scale, however, the phenomenon of a cohesive unit of foot troops which cannot be broken up by knights but is overpowered by marksmen no doubt occurred quite often, as, for example, at Bouvines in 1214 and Cortenuova in 1237.

EXCURSUS

I wish to add a few extracts on finances and army strengths from Morris's book. In 1283, after nine months of war, the king's financial resources were exhausted. According to the final accounting that has been preserved, the war cost almost 100,000 pounds (98,421 pounds), including the construction of strongholds. It lasted fifteen months.

In the same year, an account informs us, the king had to provide replacements for 200 shields, 140 lance shafts, and 120 lance points that were lost in his service (p. 83).

Edward made many efforts to raise money through loans. See W. E. Rhodes, "The Italian Bankers in England and the Loans of Edward I and Edward II" ("Die italienischen Bankiers in England and die Anleihen Eduards I. und II.") in *Historical Essays by the Members of the Owen College, Manchester,* ed. Tout and Tait, 1902.

In 1295 Edward levied 25,000 foot soldiers, archers, and crossbowmen from certain counties. In the statute of Winchelsea, he had ordered a public review.

On p. 97 f., Morris explains that Edward was hardly so sanguine as to believe that one could create soldiers through such regulations. He presumably hoped that by levying such a large mass, at least usable men would come and would form an acceptable corps. But even this hope was fulfilled to only a small degree. Those who came deserted later. It was a Falstaff's guard. To help cover the shortage, criminals were inducted.

Hemingburgh gives the strength of the earl of Surrey, who won the battle of Dunbar in 1296, as 1,000 mounted men and 10,000 foot soldiers, whereas Edward himself had a larger force at Berwick. Morris, p. 274, estimates the entire army as being of the size Hemingburgh attributes to Surrey's corps.

Morris, p. 286, says that the largest army which he found mentioned during this period was the one mobilized against Scotland in the spring of 1298. It was composed of 28,500 foot troops and 750 mounted men. But this army was assembled for only a moment. Seven thousand men were immediately sent back, and the remainder of the army quickly shrank in size. It probably consisted in part of militia. Edward gave up the idea of fighting with the remnants of this army, had the men return home, and in the summer he formed another army, with which he won the battle of Falkirk.

Morris, p. 310, has drawn up the following table showing the status of the foot troops in a campaign in 1300:

Levied for June		In Carlisle 1 July	In Caerlaverock 10–15 July	Remaining in August
5,000	Yorkshire	2,912	2,932	919
2,000	Lancastershire (including Blankenburn)	267	1,327	1,026
2,000	Cumberland		940	346
3,000	Nottinghamshire and Derby	386	900	289
3,000	Northumberland		788	570
1,000	Westmorland		732	31
16,000		3,565	7,619	3,181

Levied for June		In Carlisle 1 July	In Caerlaverock 10–15 July	Remaining in August
	Ireland	306	361	306
	Chester		307	167
	Staffordshire	137	216	188
	"Garrison" of Lochmaben		487	430
	"Garrison" of Roxburgh		103	93
	"Garrison" of Berwick			785
		4,008	9,093	5,150

We see, says Morris, that the counties provided less than one-fourth of the actual number initially required of them, a week too late, and eventually less than half of the total requisitioned.

NOTES FOR CHAPTER VIII

1. Slingers, *fundibularii*, are mentioned in *Continuatio Reginonis* (*Continuation of Regino*) for the year 962. *Casus Sancti Galli Continuatio* (*Continuation of the Chronicle of St. Gall*), 158.

2. See Jähns, *History of the Development of Ancient Offensive Weapons* (*Entwickelungsgeschichte der alten Trutzwaffen*), p. 333 ff.

3. In Jaffé, *Regesta pontificum Romanorum* (*Register of the Roman Popes*), p. 585, the decision (No. 29) reads as follows: "artem ballistariorum et sagittariorum adversus Christianos et catholicos exerceri sub anathemate prohibent." ("They prohibited, on pain of damnation, the skill of crossbowmen and archers to be exercised against Christians and Catholics.") On the basis of this *Regesta,* we find it stated quite often (for example, in Demmin, *Military Weapons* [*Kriegswaffen*], 2d ed., p. 100, and also Waitz, 8: 190) that the council had forbidden the use of the crossbow among Christians as too deadly a weapon. Since the *sagittarii* (archers) are mentioned in a line with the *ballistarii* (crossbowmen), that cannot possibly have been the intent of the council. In Mansi, Tome 21, p. 534, the decision reads as follows: "Artem autem illam mortiferam et Deo odibilem ballistariorum et sagittariorum adversus Christianos et catholicos exerceri de caetero sub anathemate prohibemus." ("We prohibit, however, on pain of damnation, that deadly skill of crossbowmen and archers, odious to God, to be practiced by another against Christians and Catholics.") Hefele, *Concil. Geschichte,* Vol. V, 2d ed., p. 442, interprets this as referring to a kind of tournament of competitive shooting at persons. San Marte, p. 188, claims that it refers to poisoned arrows and bolts. I prefer Hefele's interpretation.

4. Guillemus Brito, *Gesta Philippi regis* (William the Briton, *Deeds of Philip the King*), Book II:

Francigenis nostris illis ignota diebus
Res erat omnino, quid Balestarius arcus
Quid Balista foret.
(In those days, what a Balestarius bow was
And what a Balista was
Were completely unknown to our Frenchmen.)
Has volo, non alia Ricardum morte perire
Ut qui Francigenis ballistae primitus usum
Tradidit, ipse suam rem primitus experiatur
Quamque alios docuit im se vim sentiat artis.
(I wish that Richard, who first related
The use of the crossbow to Frenchmen,
Die by no other death,
And he should feel the force against himself
Which he taught to others.)

5. Köchly and Rüstow, *Greek Military Authors* (*Griechische Kriegsschriftsteller*), 2:2:37, 201. (See Vol. II, p. 346.)

6. *The Welsh Wars of Edward I, A Contribution to Medieval Military History based on Original Documents,* by John E. Morris, M.A., formerly of Magdalen College, Oxford. With a map. Oxford at the Clarendon Press, 1901.

7. Morris, p. 34.

8. Morris, p. 18.

9. Oman, p. 558.

10. Morris, p. 88.

11. Morris, p. 74.

12. Morris, p. 37.

13. Morris, p. 95.

14. Morris, p. 105.

15. Morris, p. 115.

16. Morris, p. 178.

17. Morris, p. 155.

18. Morris, p. 87.

19. Edward I also had a military retinue which received pay and rations as follows: bannerets, 4 shillings per day; knights, 2 shillings; sergeants (*servientes, valetti, scutiferi*), 1 shilling.

In 1277 the number of knights amounted to some forty; later there were undoubtedly more. The sergeants numbered about sixty in 1277, but that was probably only a part of the group. Horses and weapons were provided for them. Each man had to maintain two soldiers and three horses. Quite a number of them were crossbowmen. In peacetime they formed small units as castle garrisons; in wartime their number was greatly increased.

20. Oman, p. 558, is of the opinion that the longbow, which from the time of Edward I replaced the short bow in normal use, also surpassed the crossbow in penetrating power. Presumably, then, a great technical stride forward had been made with the introduction of the longbow. I cannot agree with this viewpoint. If it were correct, the continuing use of the crossbow into the sixteenth century would be incomprehensible.

George, too, in *Battles of English History,* p. 51 ff., devoted himself to a thorough study of the remarkable phenomenon of the bow and its overpowering effectiveness. He, too, sees the longbow as a decisive factor. According to him, it was invented in South Wales. The earlier periods had known only the short bow.

George finds the advantages of the longbow and of the manner in which it was used in England in three factors. First, it was held vertically and not horizontally like the short bow, and it could therefore be pulled back much farther; second, in doing so, one could give the longbow greater tension; and third, the marksmen could aim better along the arrow that was thus pulled farther back. While the range of an arrow's trajectory was 400 yards, the normal range in practice, according to George, was a furlong (one-eighth of an English mile, or approximately 200 yards).

Why Richard the Lion-Hearted, in spite of these advantages, preferred the crossbow, and why the longbow actually remained peculiar to the English, appears to George to be a "mystery."

21. *The Welsh Wars of Edward I,* pp. 79, 82, 313.

Chapter IX

Individual Campaigns, Battles, and Engagements

In the following paragraphs, I give a summary of those battles and combat reports or strategic relationships that seem to me to be particularly useful, either from the objective point of view or that of source analysis, to support the ideas presented in the preceding chapters, or that had to be discussed in order to eliminate misunderstandings and false conclusions to which they could lead, even if they are not of sufficient interest for a full discussion.

BATTLE OF TINCHEBRAI
28 SEPTEMBER 1106

This battle between King Henry I of England and his brother, Robert of Normandy, deserves mention because a false interpretation of the sources has given rise to the opinion that on both sides the knights dismounted for the fight. That would have been such an unusual procedure in that period that it would deserve the greatest notice. But a thorough special study by Drummond has left no doubt that it was a question of nothing more than a "completely normal battle of the twelfth century."[1] Since King Henry was besieging a castle that Robert moved to relieve, Henry also had foot soldiers in his army. But he did not have these dismounted troops participate directly in combat. Instead, he held them in reserve behind the knights, apparently to provide a mainstay and rallying point for assembling the knights in case of a possible flight. In order to give greater stability to the foot soldiers, the king himself, with his retinue, had dismounted and remained with them. Nevertheless, as a result of their numerical superiority, his knights were victorious without this assistance.

The first, second, and third lines of knights ("prima, secunda, tertia acies") need not be considered, according to the explanations given above (p. 277), as units formed one behind the other.

BATTLE OF BRÉMULE
20 AUGUST 1119

In this battle, too, we hear of dismounted knights on the side of Henry of England, who defeated Louis VI of France as a result of the steadfast stand of this unit. Drummond has attempted to bring sense into the source account, but he finally had to explain that the sources, after all, did not present an early example of a much later development, as seemed to be possible, but that we are possibly dealing here with a purely fantastic description. Of the 900 men who took part in the battle, 500 on Henry's side and 400 under Louis, supposedly only three were killed, but 140 French were taken prisoner by the Anglo-Normans, because the knights on the two sides spared each other. (See p. 287, above.)

ENGAGEMENT AT BOURGTHÉROULDE
26 MARCH 1124

This fight developed when royal troops blocked rebellious knights from a narrow pass, which the knights then tried in vain to force open. Their horses were killed by the defenders' arrows, and eighty were captured, but not a single knight was killed.

In order to defend the pass, the king's knights had, of course, dismounted. It is worthy to note and interesting from the viewpoint of source analysis to observe that our reporter, Ordericus Vitalis, stated as the reason for their dismounting that it was done in order to make it impossible to flee and also to strengthen the spirit of the troops.[2]

THE BATTLE OF THE STANDARDS AT NORTHALLERTON
22 AUGUST 1138

King David of Scotland made an incursion into England and had levied for this purpose both the Germanic vassals of the lowlands and the barbarian Celts of the highlands. The militia of the threatened counties was called to arms to oppose the savage destruction and burnings carried out by the invaders.

The aged archbishop of York had himself carried around on a stretcher in order to stir up the men of the levy and raise their courage. A *carroccio* was prepared, on which the banners of Saint Peter of York, Saint John of Beverley, and Saint Wilfred of Ripon were placed together. At the point of the flagstaff was a silver casket with a consecrated host. All the men fasted, confessed, received absolution and communion, and swore mutual loyalty and steadfastness. They took up a position on a hill near Northallerton, north of York, to await the enemy attack, and the knights dismounted and formed as the first rank of the phalanx of the militia. King Stephen of England was not personally on the scene, but he had sent knights to support the army. The numerous archers stood in the mass of the phalanx. It may well be that a portion of them initially took position in front and then moved back behind the knights in order to shoot between them from the rear or over their heads.[3]

We have four reports of authors quite close to the events, and they agree quite well with one another. One of them was by Richard the prior of the Abbey of Hexham, close to the Scottish border, written before 1154. Another account was written by Abbot Aelred of Rievaulx (died in 1166), who in his youth had lived at the court of King David of Scotland and now lived quite close to the battlefield.

The battle probably progressed in this way: After a wild assault by the Gaels and an attack by a unit of knights under Prince Henry of Scotland had been thrown back, the rest of the Scottish army gave up the attack and withdrew without being counterattacked. It is also possible that Prince Henry, with a few knights, penetrated through the left flank of the English phalanx but was too weak to attack from the rear.

This battle is very famous in English legend and is embellished with myths and exaggerations. The Scots were supposedly greatly superior in strength, and between 10,000 and 11,000 of their men were reportedly killed. We may assume that it was in fact the English who were stronger, for a militia, whenever it does succeed at all in assembling, is numerous. The weakness normally lies in the lack of military skill, and this battle is in fact extremely interesting in that the militia units were actually made capable of standing fast by the bishop's persuasiveness and the resources of the Church, the *carroccio,* and the mixing of the knights with the mass, in which they formed the first rank. Of course, these means were effective only to the extent that they enabled the militia to stand fast and repulse the enemy attack—an analogy to Legnano, but not to the Athenian militia at Marathon, which made its own attack on the run.

BATTLE OF LINCOLN
2 FEBRUARY 1141

This battle, too, is remarkable because foot troops fought on both
sides, in the one case burghers and the other peasants, who had their
morale boosted by dismounted knights. The battle ended, probably as a
result of treason, unfavorably for King Stephen, who had also dismounted and was taken prisoner by his rebellious barons.[4]

THE BATTLES AND ENGAGEMENTS OF THE FIRST CRUSADE

These battles have been analyzed in careful and methodical study in
the dissertation of Otto Heermann, "The Combat of Occidental Armies
in the Orient in the Period of the First Crusade" ("Die Gefechtsführung
abendländischer Heere im Orient in der Epoche des ersten Kreuzzuges"), Marburg, 1887. Consequently, I can omit many details here by
referring the reader to this valuable work, even though, like the work of
Dietrich on the Lombard wars, which has been discussed above, it is
based on erroneous objective assumptions and is theoretically false.
Heermann speaks of infantry and cavalry, regiments, squadrons, and
officers among the Crusaders and therefore misunderstands the basic
military concept of that period, the fundamental difference between the
knightly military system and modern disciplined troops. It is not simply a
question of a disagreement over terminology that Heermann, for instance, used modern terms when he would have done better to avoid
them, or that he gave these modern concepts a somewhat broader interpretation than is customary. Rather, it is a question of an absolute,
objective antithesis, which in every sentence, so to speak, not only influences the interpretation of the sources but dominates them. All the
skillful formations and maneuvers which Heermann, with his assumption
concerning the character of the troop units, has interpreted from the
sources, and which he could rightfully so interpret up to a certain degree,
must simply be eliminated, since it is precisely the theoretical assumption
that does not apply, since knights were not "cavalry," but, despite some
external similarity, were very different. Of course, this cannot be derived
from individual battle accounts but only from the entire sequence of developments from the decline of antiquity up to modern times.

If we now eliminate, however, all these false pictures, concepts,
assumptions, and conclusions from Heermann's study, it still contains a

very useful nucleus. As a supplement to Heermann, I would like to single out the factors that are of importance for our purposes.

As particularly appropriate, I point out Heermann's remark on p. 105, that the battles were very short. Somewhat at odds with this observation and certainly incorrect, of course, is his overall characterization (p. 121):

> A marked wavering of the fight, the breaking up of several units or echelons, the complete or partial inclosing of the whole army, and then the relieving attack by the reserve, under the leadership of the highest commander, against the point where the enemy was applying the greatest pressure, and the final victory—all these points formed the repeated characteristic features of most of the battles.

The author was led into error particularly by his idea of the great numerical superiority of the Turks, a point on which there is no basis for believing the Christian authors.

BATTLE OF DORYLAEUM
1 JULY 1097

The Crusaders were attacked on the march. The knights, thrown back by the superior Turkish forces and pursued by the arrows of the mounted archers, fled back to the foot troops, who were placed farther to the rear and had pitched a camp. The foot troops provided protection for the knights ("militaris fugae impetus pedestrem conculcat tarditatem, isque vicem densissima pedestrium hastarum sylva nunc fugam impedit, nunc extinguit"[5]: "The rush of the knights' flight trampled the slow-moving foot soldiers, and this in turn by its very thick forest of foot troops' spears at one point hindered their flight and at another point checked it"). The mass of foot troops and knights, which we must picture as rather confused and closely pressed together, was strongly attacked by the Turks. The knights led the defense by making sorties, "jamque nobis nulla spes vitae . . . tunc proceres nostri . . . pro posse illis resistebant et eos saepe invadere nitebantur, ipsi quidem a Turcis fortiter impetebantur" (Fulcher) ("and now we had no hope of survival . . . then our leaders . . . resisted them as they could and were often striving to attack them. They were themselves certainly assaulted strongly by the Turks").

The Christians were finally rescued when the other half of their army, which was marching on another road, 2 miles away, hastened to their aid. As these knights approached, the Turks took to flight.

BATTLE BY THE LAKE OF ANTIOCH
9 FEBRUARY 1098

The Christians were besieging Antioch. A relieving army approached, and it was decided that the Christian knights, numbering only 700 horsemen, would move out to meet it, while the foot troops were to guard the camp.[6]

The small army of knights was sufficient to throw back the enemy with the impact of their heavy shock action.

Heermann emphasizes the point that the Christians spread out over the entire plain, which was probably rather narrow at that time, and thus prevented the Seljuks with their superior numbers (Raimund gives them 28,000 horsemen!) from enveloping them. But, at the same time, the Christians were supposed to have been drawn up in three echelons. With only 700 horsemen, that is a contradiction. Köhler, 3: 3: 159, has already raised this objection, pointing out that there is nothing about echelons in the better sources, and that it was only a simultaneous attack of the five units (Boemund remained in reserve with the sixth unit) that enabled them to succeed.

ACTION AT THE BRIDGE GATE OF ANTIOCH
EARLY MARCH 1098

This fight was brought on by a sortie of the Christians, who were now besieged in the city they had just captured. Of special note is an episode concerning the participation of the foot troops. Raimund recounts that a Provençal knight, Isuardus of Gagia, had stirred up the zeal of 150 foot soldiers for combat after they had prayed to God on their knees. Then, with a shout of "*Eia,* you warriors of Christ!", he led them into the fight. Reportedly, other groups had done likewise.

DECISIVE BATTLE BEFORE ANTIOCH
28 JUNE 1098

Despite the many reports by eyewitnesses that we have on this battle, the decisive points still remain so very much in the dark that little of military value is to be learned from it.

The Christians took the city, with exception of the citadel, when a large relief army under Karbogha, the emir of Mosul, approached. Instead of forming for a battle against him in the open field, the Christians allowed themselves to be surrounded in Antioch, reached the point of starvation, and in desperation finally rallied their forces for the battle, which they won without difficulty. The Holy Lance, which was found under an altar when its whereabouts were revealed to a monk in a dream, had again filled the army with confidence and the will to win. We could perhaps emphasize this event as an example of that peculiarity of knightly armies which has them fighting, not like disciplined troops, simply through obedience to commands, but only when the proper mood is present or is stimulated in each individual. But even if the story of the Holy Lance is very characteristic, it is perhaps not sufficient by itself to explain the situation, since we hear that, on the other side, in Karbogha's army, there was great dissension, mistrust, and treachery. Thus, the decisive reason for the victory after such long hesitation is perhaps to be sought here.

According to the usual interpretations of the sources in Sybel, Kugler, Heermann, Oman, and Köhler (3: 2: 170), the Christians deployed by moving across the Orontes bridge. But they then formed up, not with their rear, but their flank, toward this bridge, as one group after another deployed by wheeling toward the right (in Sybel, toward the left). But that seems to me completely unbelievable, or in any case incomprehensible. Why then did Karbogha, who was in position with his army in the immediate area, allow the Christians to carry out such a deployment before his eyes? It was, of course, correct and logical that he would not prevent the march across the bridge from its very start, but why did he allow the entire army to cross instead of having his horsemen attack when perhaps half of the enemy was still crossing and involved in the cumbersome deployment toward the flank? He would certainly then have overcome the enemy, driven them back onto the bridge, and there, where everything would have been jammed up, he would have destroyed them. Did Karbogha have some special reason for not doing so? And how could the Christians have exposed themselves to such a possibility?

The distribution of the combat arms was the well-known one. The foot troops, principally archers, were in front, and the knights, whose number had been increased with horses taken as booty in the city, were behind. But they then broke out to the front and decided the outcome of the battle.

The strength, sequence, and relative positions of the various units need not be considered as important, as Heermann does, and least of all may we say that the eight ranks that were formed were drawn up in four echelons. They all deployed side by side, and the attack began by echelon, starting with the units closest to the river. But this point had no further significance.

The front extended from the Orontes to the mountain and was 2 *miliaria*—that is, at least 2,000, and perhaps 4,000, paces long. Consequently, the individual battle groups had either deployed from the start in a line with a depth of only a few ranks, since the Christians had 2,000 horsemen at most, or they had formed with very wide intervals between units.

One source (Raimund) says that they had as wide an interval between one another as the clergy in procession.[7] Köhler interprets that as the interval between the individual units, whereas Heermann takes it to be the interval between individual knights. Heermann's interpretation seems to me the more logical one.

As was reported in all the sources, the foot troops marched out in front of the knights. Nevertheless, we find that during the battle foot troops were attacked by the Turks *behind* the knights. Heermann, pp. 121–22, concludes from this, probably correctly, that the foot soldiers had moved to the rear through the knights and assembled there. But he incorrectly supposes that the archers then shot their hail of arrows at the enemy over the heads of the horsemen. That would have been much too dangerous for their own riders and horses in the melee.

Of particular interest is the episode which Raimund also recounts, to the effect that a unit of these same foot troops, attacked in the rear by Turks, formed in a tight cluster and held out, "pedites facto gyro impetum hostium sustinuerunt viriliter." ("After forming a circle, the foot troops stoutly checked the attack of the enemy.")

BATTLE OF ASCALON
12 AUGUST 1099

Shortly after the conquest of Jerusalem, the Crusaders had to move out against an Egyptian army that had landed near Ascalon. In order to be ready to meet a sudden attack from any direction, the army, which was divided all together into nine columns, marched along in three parallel columns. Heermann, like Delpech, pictures the columns as linear formations, but not only would it have been very difficult to march in this way, but also the flanks would have been much weaker than the front, a situation they obviously wanted to avoid. Consequently, we can probably imagine the individual columns as quite similar to those at Pillenreuth. Since, according to the best source (Raimund), the army numbered 1,200 horsemen, each column had an average of 133. As they prepared for the battle, the rear columns deployed beside the foremost ones. The *Gesta* expressly report that the princes were in position side by side. The Moslems did not meet the attack but immediately fled.[8] Heermann, who believes that in the formation of the columns three by three there was already a battle formation of three echelons (and not a simple order of march), reconciles this in such a way that the three echelons were not formed one behind the other, but obliquely, with the second unit in front, the first to its right rear, and the third to its left rear. That may actually have been the case, but then we need not call these "echelons" but can see in the formation a deployment that is not completely finished. Köhler, too, p. 178, rejects Heermann's concept but is himself not clear, probably as the result of a slip of the pen. (In Note 6 it is initially said that the ranks were formed *behind* one another, whereas at the end it is said they were placed *beside* one another.) According to Köhler, 3: 3: 339, the echelon battle formation and combat method could not be used during the Crusades in the Orient because of the foot soldiers.

Raimund says that, in addition to the 1,200 mounted men, the Crusaders had 9,000 foot soldiers. These troops consisted of marksmen and spearmen, and they moved out in front of the horsemen, who then pushed through them for the attack.[9]

It is difficult to imagine how the horsemen were able to move through such a mass of foot soldiers. It is also difficult to understand that with such a one-sided numerical ratio, the horsemen still appear to have been the only decisive arm. Presumably the strength given for the foot troops is much too high. It is true, of course, that the letter from the Crusader princes to the pope states that the Christian army had 5,000 horsemen and 15,000 foot soldiers. But since the same letter attributes 100,000 horsemen and 400,000 foot troops to the king of the Babylonians (as it calls the sultan of Egypt), and since we cannot very well imagine where the Crusaders, who at Antioch were reduced to a few hundred horses, are supposed to have gotten 5,000 useful knights' mounts, we shall prefer in any case the estimate given by Raimund, who was present at the battle as the bearer of the Holy Lance (reducing even his number concerning the foot soldiers). And we shall regard the strengths given in the princely letter as proof that even the numbers in official documents are not always reliable.[10]

ENGAGEMENT AT RAMLEH
7 SEPTEMBER 1101

Heermann, p. 58, seeks to understand from the sources a clever, obliquely echeloned formation, even though the Christian army under King Baldwin numbered only 260 knights and 900 foot soldiers, and the latter stayed behind and did not actually participate in the fight. Since there is mention of *"anteriores acies"* ("anterior battle lines"), and the expression *"in capite"* ("at the head") is used of the victory and *"in cauda"* ("at the tail") of the defeat, the sources actually seem to say this. Nevertheless, this interpretation has correctly been rejected and contradicted by Köhler, who otherwise, of course, defends the echelon formation (3: 2: 186).

ENGAGEMENT AT RAMLEH
MAY 1102

King Baldwin attacked a greatly superior Egyptian force with his knights alone, and he was defeated. Fulcher criticizes him for attacking without an orderly formation and for not awaiting his foot troops. Since the knights alone had been victorious at the Lake of Antioch in 1098, Heermann, while rejecting more extreme interpretations by Delpech (pp. 66, 124), concludes that the significance of the "infantry" had increased since that time. This is an inadmissible conclusion, for the different outcome can, of course, have resulted from the fact that the opponents in the second case were better or more numerous.

Very little is to be concluded from the reproach with which authors normally tend to remember a defeated commander.

ENGAGEMENT AT RAMLEH
27 AUGUST 1105

Here, too, Heermann seeks to interpret his ideas of the oblique echelon formation from the sources, but he himself admits there is no persuasive proof for this interpretation.

BATTLE OF SARMIN
14 SEPTEMBER 1115

BATTLE OF ATHAREB (BELATH)
28 JUNE 1119

In both these battles, Heermann points to an echeloned attack, and Köhler agrees with him. In the chancellor of Prince Roger of Antioch we have a very good source. His work also constitutes documentary proof that the concept of "first contact" or a "forward battle" does not imply that the units were formed one behind the other (see p. 280).

BATTLE OF HAB
13 AUGUST 1119

As at Ascalon, the Christian army marched in a three-by-three column formation and was attacked simultaneously from several directions. A few of the columns were defeated and broken up. But finally the Christians claimed the victory for themselves. They were 700 horsemen and a few thousand foot troops strong.

The Crusaders marched in nine columns, three beside each other and three behind one another, in order to be able to face in all directions at the same time. Heermann describes these columns as linear formations. For the reasons given on p. 406, above, that is impossible. The individual columns, whose strength at Ascalon was reckoned by Heermann to average 133 horsemen each, and at Hab at fewer than 100 horsemen each (in addition to foot soldiers), must have had a similar formation to that of the army at Pillenreuth. This is also Köhler's opinion (3: 2: 211).

BATTLE OF HAZARTH
1125

In his sketch, Heermann shows the foot troops behind the knights. There is no apparent reason for this. And in the text, p. 98, it is stated that the foot soldiers were already engaged in combat when the knights attacked.

BATTLE OF MERDJ-SEFER
1126

William of Tyre reports that the foot troops killed the fallen and wounded enemies with their swords, blocked the route of those who were fleeing, and helped up those of their comrades who had fallen from their horses.

BATTLE OF HITTIN
4 JULY 1187

A quite detailed account of this battle has been given by Groh in "The Collapse of the Kingdom of Jerusalem" ("Der Zusammenbruch des Reiches Jerusalem"), Berlin dissertation, 1909. This contains confirmation of my concept of the relationship of the knights to the foot soldiers and the squires.

BATTLE OF ACRE
4 OCTOBER 1189

The archers and crossbowmen moved out in front of the knights.

BATTLE OF ARSUF
7 SEPTEMBER 1191

The battle in which Richard the Lion-Hearted, who was attacked by Saladin while on the march along the seacoast from Acre to Joppe, won a brilliant victory is thoroughly discussed by Köhler, 3:3:234, and by Oman, p. 305. Köhler bases his account principally on the report of Benedict of Peterborough. Oman shows that this report, as soon as one considers the topography of the battlefield, cannot be reconciled with the three closest bits of evidence—King Richard's itinerary, his letter to the abbot of Clairvaux, and Boha ed din, Saladin's historiographer. The report is therefore to be rejected as a source.

Consequently, Köhler's account seems untenable. We must immediately reject the strength of the Crusaders, which Köhler gives as 100,000 men. His opinion, that this particular battle is especially appropriate as a confirmation of his basic concept of medieval tactics, would still appear unfounded to me, even if his account itself were unassailable.

ENGAGEMENT AT JAFFA
5 AUGUST 1192

Richard the Lion-Hearted was attacked by a force of Mamelukes and Kurds with a reported strength of 7,000, while he himself had only fifty-five knights, of whom only fifteen were mounted, and 2,000 foot soldiers, mostly Genoese and Pisan crossbowmen from the fleet. He formed a line of spearmen, who placed one knee on the ground and held their spears pointed toward the horses' chests. The crossbowmen were formed behind them, facing the intervals between the spearmen, with the order to fire continuously while a second man with a crossbow stood behind, cocked the bow, loaded, and handed the weapon forward. Thus the hail of bolts flew out without interruption. The Moslems surged forward, unit after unit, but they did not risk attacking. They accomplished nothing with the missiles which they themselves shot while riding forward, but they suffered considerable losses. Finally, Richard attacked them with his knights, forced his way among them, slashing and cutting, and personally pulled the earl of Leicester and Ralph Mauléon, who were surrounded and in danger of being captured, safely out of the melee. And thus the fight continued for hours. Finally, the Turks withdrew, leaving 700 men and 1,500 horses on the field, while the Crusaders had lost only two men.[11]

Oman finishes his repetition of the source account with the expression: "So well had their battle formation protected them." I cannot agree with this conclusion. If it were possible to ward off a greatly superior enemy of recognized courage by such a simple method, it would have been used more often. The figure for the Turkish losses immediately shows us that we are dealing here with a picture painted in strongly exaggerated colors. A line of spearmen, even backed up by a double line of crossbowmen, is much too weak an obstacle to frighten off a determined, well-equipped mounted force, and Saladin's warriors were both brave and well armored. If the figure of 7,000 Turks were anywhere near accurate, the account would still not prove the impregnability of Richard's battle formation, but only the fact that on that day the fighting spirit of the infidels was very dull. Presumably, the attackers were a unit of only very moderate size, mostly light horsemen, who probably attempted a few times to see if their approach would frighten the Christians and perhaps create panic in their ranks, but who did not risk an actual attack.

In addition to the *Itinerary,* which Oman used, there is also a report by an eyewitness, Ralph of Coggeshale (ed. S. Stevenson, Rolls Series, p. 45). According to his account, the king had eighty knights but only six horses and one mule.

Commilitones suos . . . stricte et conjunctim ordinando disposuit (rex), ut unumquemque juxta latus alterius firmiter collocavit, ne quis aditus perforundi cuneum suum in ipsa congressione ex spatii vacuitate pateret hostibus. Pauca autem ligna, quae ibidem reperta

fuere ob tentoria construenda ante pedes singulorum quasi pro
antemurali jussit collocari.

([The king] posted his fellow knights... by arranging them
tightly together, and he stationed them steadily each at the side of
the other so that no avenue of cutting through his unit in battle
might lie open to the enemy from empty space. And a few pieces of
wood, which were found at the same place for constructing tents,
he ordered to be placed before the feet of each man as *chevaux-de-
frise.*)

Finally, Richard made a sortie, keeping his marksmen in front, and he
was victorious with the loss of a single knight.

FOOT TROOPS IN THE CRUSADES

Like Heermann, Köhler 3: 3: 209, believes that a skilled body of foot
troops developed from the school of war itself during the Crusades. He
says that these foot troops were already gaining attention at Antioch and
Ascalon, after they had proven to be very weak at Dorylaeum. At that
time there was no useful foot soldiery at all in the Occident. He goes on
to say that the reason for the development of foot troops is to be found in
the necessity of protecting the mounted men against the Turkish archers.
The historical relationship in this observation seems to me to miss the
mark.

There is no proof that the foot soldiers who fought at Dorylaeum were
worthless. Whether it be that these troops consisted of mounted men
who had lost their horses or whether they were marksmen and spearmen
from the start, in any case we can and must suppose that the lords in
whose service these men made the campaign had selected men who
would be useful in battle. Indeed, on all sides the Occident offered
enough opportunity for schooling in warfare.[12] The beginning of the
battle automatically led to Boemund's making an initial drive with his
knights. It is possible, although not certain, that in doing so he took along
no foot troops whatever, since Fulcher expressly points out concerning
this fight that the Turkish army was composed exclusively of horsemen,
while the Christians had both arms, foot troops and mounted men.

The knights were defeated, with or without support from foot soldiers.
They streamed to the rear and were taken up by the mass of foot troops,
who stopped the flight with their outstretched spears (Radulf). The entire mass now stood fast, and from it the knights made sorties and short
advances.

Even in later periods, the spearmen did not accomplish any more than this in unfavorable combat actions. This situation did not change until the time of the Swiss and the Hussites.

It must be simply by accident that none of our sources mentions anything of missile weapons among the Christian foot troops. This can presumably be explained by the great effort to picture as impressively as possible the dangerous situation of Boemund's army, which was pressed on all sides by the mounted Turkish marksmen. If mention had been made of the Christian archers, who held off their enemies with their shots, the danger would not have appeared so extreme, and the rescue by Godfrey and the others would not have seemed so miraculous. Since we know how well the Normans were able to use the bow on other occasions and also that marksmen participated in later battles of the Crusaders, they were undoubtedly not completely absent at Dorylaeum.

Finally, Köhler's opinion that the Crusaders were obliged to develop foot troops in order to protect their mounted units from the Turkish archers shows a complete lack of understanding of the nature of the medieval combat branches. The only protection that exists for the horseman with a close combat weapon against the archer, mounted or dismounted, except for the knight's armor, lies in his fastest possible assault of the archer, preventing him, by the approaching threat, from getting off more than a single, very inaccurate discharge of his weapon. That knights could be supported effectively by assigning to them both marksmen and spearmen is proven on many occasions, not simply in the Crusades. But we may not express that idea by saying that these foot troops provided them protection.

The increased importance of the foot troops in the fighting in Syria, which was indeed more pronounced than in the Occident, was undoubtedly based on no other factor than the shortage of horses.

BATTLE OF MURET
12 SEPTEMBER 1213

King Peter of Aragon came to the aid of the count of Toulouse, who, as an Albigensian, was hard pressed by the Crusaders under Simon de Montfort. Peter besieged the fortified city of Muret, on the Garonne above Toulouse. Simon drove into the beleaguered city, made a sortie, and drove the besiegers, who were caught napping, to flight.

Since we happen to have many accounts of this event, it has been treated in many different ways. But it has no special significance from the viewpoint of military history, unless it be as a result of the many curious theories on medieval tactics that were built specifically on this battle.

The sources report that Simon formed his knights into three *ordines*, or *acies*, or *batailles* in the name of the Holy Trinity. A source reports the same action by King Philip Augustus at the battle of Bouvines. From this report, Köhler (1: 144, cf. p. 105) concludes "that by *'ordines'*, 'echelons' are meant, is evident from the remark on the name of the Holy Trinity." The conclusiveness of this analysis must be doubted until we have some clearer explanation of the analogy between an echeloned formation (i.e., one behind the other) and the Holy Trinity.

The same author reckons Montfort's army at a strength of hardly 800 horsemen, less than half of whom were knights, and Peter's army as some 40,000 strong, of which 38,000 were foot troops. On p. 101 he adds: "Nevertheless, we must carefully avoid saying that he (Montfort) opposed 40,000 men with 800 horsemen, because the foot troops can hardly be counted as participating in the battle. According to William Brito, furthermore, the heretic prince even had 200,000 men."

Finally, Köhler says (p. 116) that the Crusaders' losses amounted to one knight and seven sergeants, while their opponents lost 20,000.

To him who has been endowed with a credulous attitude, it makes no difference whether he has spent his life at the study desk or in the practice of the profession of arms.

Recently, this engagement has been treated by Dieulafoy in "La bataille de Muret," Paris, 1899, 44 pp. *Mémoires de l'Académie des Inscriptions,* Tome 36. Review by Kiener, *Deutsche Literaturzeitung,* No. 26, 23 June 1900.

ENGAGEMENT AT STEPPES

13 OCTOBER 1213

This action, between the duke of Brabant and the bishop of Liège, is thoroughly discussed by Köhler, 3: 3: 283, and Oman, p. 444. There were spearmen in the center on both sides; those in the army of Liège were burghers. Nevertheless, they did not enter the fight until the battle of the knights was already decided. Up to that point, they were to provide protection for the knights in a withdrawal.

The difference between Köhler and Oman is that Köhler says the knights were victorious on both flanks, while Oman shows only the left flank as victorious.

BATTLE OF BOUVINES
27 JULY 1214

The older accounts of this battle have been overtaken by the dissertation of C. Ballhausen (Jena, 1907. J. W. Schmidt). I am therefore reducing the discussion I included in my first edition, but I cannot agree with
Ballhausen's concept of some important points. The extensive treatment
by Delpech in *La tactique au XIIIième siècle,* Vol. I, despite all its apparent erudition, can still only be rejected *in toto* with Molinier, *Revue
historique,* Vol. 36, p. 185.

Emperor Otto IV had assembled, with his allies, at Nivelles, south of
Brussels, while Philip concentrated his forces at Péronne. As they moved
forward, the two armies initially passed by one another, and this went so
far that they finally circled completely around each other and Philip was
in position to the north, near Tournai, while Otto was to the south, near
Valenciennes. These marches can no doubt be explained in no other way
than that neither side knew anything of the advance of the other. (I
cannot agree with Ballhausen's opposite opinion on this point; the reasons he gives for Philip's advance on Tournai are not sufficient.) As each
learned the whereabouts of the other, they both turned about. Philip
moved back from Tournai along the route on which he had moved up,
via Bouvines, in the direction of Lille, consequently moving away from
the enemy. Otto, on the other hand, moved toward his enemy.

As Philip, on his march from east to west, was crossing the bridge near
Bouvines over the small stream named Marque, he received word that
the Germans were advancing toward him and were skirmishing with a
detachment sent out in that direction. Philip immediately ordered that
the troops who had already crossed the bridge should turn about, because he intended to accept the battle. It can hardly be assumed that it
would have been impossible for him to have the army cross the bridge
without any significant involvement with the enemy, for even though a
considerable part of his force was probably still on the near side, the
emperor's army still needed quite a long time to deploy. Ballhausen's
belief that Otto planned to cut off Philip's rear guard is not clear to me.
From the strategic viewpoint, Philip's decision was extremely dangerous,
for he was fighting with an almost completely reversed front, with the
bridge of Bouvines behind him as his only route of withdrawal, for the
Marque was expressly reported to be impassable elsewhere. The fact that
Philip nevertheless accepted battle in this position can therefore only be
explained by his complete confidence in victory, the fact that he thus had

time to deploy systematically, and his considerable numerical superiority in at least the decisive arm, knights, a point specifically reported.

It is true, of course, that in the morning the king had taken up the withdrawal, instead of moving toward the emperor for the battle, and this change of heart is curious. Nevertheless, we are not dealing here with an absolute contradiction. For in the morning Philip had only decided neither to remain in Tournai nor to move toward the emperor for battle. But the situation was now different in that the emperor was moving toward him, a fact that he did not yet know in the morning.

On the other hand, Otto's attack against the king, despite his smaller forces, is probably to be explained by the fact that he hoped and believed he would be able to attack the French on the march, with their forces divided by the river. It is expressly reported that he voiced his astonishment when he saw them drawn up before him in battle formation.

It is not completely illogical that the emperor did not then withdraw from the battle, since he could assume that, as soon as the Germans turned back, the French would go over to the attack, and that would immediately have meant certain defeat. In this situation, therefore, it was better to retain at least the advantage of morale inherent in the attack and take a chance on having good fortune in the battle.

If that is the strategic basis for the battle, then the outcome is to be explained in the same way. The emperor was defeated, since his assumption that he would attack the French on the march while they were divided by the river did not apply. The king was victorious because he was considerably stronger and he met the enemy's attack in good order—in fact, in better order than that of the attackers, of whom it was specifically reported that their approach march was carried out in a disorderly way.

We do not have reliable strength estimates for the two armies. Scholars (for example, Schirrmacher) previously accepted the figures of Richard of Sens, giving Otto 25,000 knights and 80,000 other warriors. Hortzschansky believes that Philip had 59,000 men (2,000 knights, 7,000 squires, 50,000 foot soldiers) and that Otto had 105,000 men (5,500 knights, 19,500 mounted squires, and 80,000 foot troops). He himself finds it puzzling (p. 41) that it was possible for the emperor to be defeated with such a numerical superiority.

Köhler reckons the strength of the French at 2,500 knights, 4,000 light horsemen, and 50,000 foot soldiers; he gives the Germans only 1,300 to 1,500 knights but says they were very strong in the other arms. Oman's estimate is smaller, but he too believes that Philip had perhaps 25,000 to 30,000 foot troops, while Otto had 40,000 men in that category.

In all these estimates, including even those of Oman, the strength of the foot troops is undoubtedly much too high. The general descriptions of the chronicles with their "countless masses" really mean nothing at all, as we have learned from numerous examples. From Mortagne on the Scheldt, where Otto took up the march on the morning of the twenty-sixth, he moved in an arc via Villemaux-Froidmont around the forest which lay along his direct route, a distance of a full 14 miles to the battlefield. Even for an army with excellent march discipline, it is a real accomplishment to deploy after such a march with 50,000 or even only 40,000 men and fight a battle on the same day. For an army of undisciplined mercenaries, burghers, and knights, this seems to me hardly possible, as Molinier has already observed.

I do agree with Ballhausen that neither of the armies was stronger than 8,000 men. It seems certain that Otto had no more than 1,300 to 1,500 knights. Philip did have more. It is also possible that the two armies were only about 5,000 men strong, for the individual contingents, whose strengths are given in a number of places in the sources, were all very small.

Most important of all, the nature of the battle itself contradicts the assumption that the foot troops were so abnormally strong, for they accomplished nothing on either side. Winkelmann's statement that the French burghers had had the stimulating consciousness of fighting "pro aris et focis" ("for hearths and homes") is taken from thin air. Nothing is to be found in the sources of any kind of decisive cooperation by the communal troops Philip had in his army. The cities presumably provided the king with a number of marksmen who fought in the normal way in conjunction with the knights. In like manner, the Flemish cities had furnished their contingents for Otto's army.

The losses on the French side seem to have been very small. An English source from a slightly later date, the *Chronicle of Melrose,* even claims that only three French knights were killed. We must assume that the losses were in fact very small, since otherwise more names of the honored dead would have appeared in the sources. Seventy knights and 1,000 foot soldiers of the emperor's army were supposedly killed, and a large number were taken prisoner—according to one source, 127 knights; in another source, 131; and in the third source, 220 knights, including five counts and twenty-five bannerets.[13] If, because of this, John of Cyprus calls the battle "durissima pugna, sed non longa" ("a most difficult battle, but not long"), it seems to me that Oman goes too far when he assumes a duration of three hours. I prefer to believe that the battle was decided almost at the first clash, which did not, however, take place simultaneously on all parts of the field. The low figure for the losses of the victors is stronger testimony here than the statements of all the authors. There is always very little credence to be given to the reports of the authors on the duration of a fight, since the beginning and the end are very indefinite concepts, and they allow a particularly broad area for the natural tendency to exaggeration. In one passage (*Gesta,* 311), William Brito says that the units of burghers arrived in the center before the beginning of the battle and, moving through the knights, had formed as marksmen in front of them. In another passage (*Gesta,* 312), he states that the burghers did not arrive until the fourth hour of the battle. Are we perhaps to imagine that the two centers stood by watching the battle on the one flank? Or did it even happen that, if one side was not yet finished with its deployment, the other side waited for them in friendly fashion? Even if the individual units in a knightly army naturally did not often attack simultaneously, the time intervals can, nevertheless, only have been very moderate, assuming that on the two sides they did not hasten forward from the march column, attacking successively.

Our principal source for this battle is William Brito, who was present as the chaplain of the king of France and described the events both in prose, in continuation of Rigord's account, and in verse in his *Philippis.* Köhler disagrees with him completely; while, on the one hand he has a very high opinion of him as a reporter (p. 118), he reproaches him for having no understanding of the tactical relationships and thereby contributing to the impression that in the battles of the Middle Ages individual combat was predominant (p. 135). Actually, the error is on Köhler's part. Oman, p. 471, note, correctly points out that of the division into three echelons, which Köhler understands from William's account, not only is nothing of the sort said by William, but by the nature of his account such a formation is specifically excluded. And with this point, Köhler's entire concept of the battle collapses, just as in the case of the battle of Hastings.

The count of Boulogne, who fought on the emperor's side, had 700 (according to another source, 400) Brabantine foot soldiers in his pay, in addition to his knights. He had these foot troops form a circle into which he withdrew whenever he himself became exhausted in the fight. When the battle was lost and all the rest of the emperor's army was already in flight, this unit was still holding fast. The French knights did not risk penetrating into the line of outstretched spears. But finally, when reinforcements arrived, the dismounted unit was overpowered, the Brabantines were cut down, and the count was taken prisoner.

Since the source for this scene is the heroic epic *Philippis,* we may not weigh the individual factors on the gold scale. But the more accurate they may have been, the more they would indicate the inferiority of the foot troops of the period. A chronicle expressly praised these Brabantines as being on a par with the knights in their military skill and courage ("pedites quidem, sed in scientia et virtute bellandi equitibus non inferiores": "foot soldiers to be sure, but not inferior to the knights in the knowledge and courage of waging war"). Nevertheless, their actions were purely defensive, and although they were a rather large unit, they served no other purpose than to provide a certain degree of protection for a few knights. We must pass over the question as to whether their unit was finally directly broken up by an attack by the knights, or perhaps had already been worn down by marksmen. The principal point is that even this body of troops, which is praised by our source for being particularly skillful, exercised no kind of independent, active effectiveness in the battle.

In fact, however, we may probably not be justified in going so far. I believe we may be allowed to presume that the scene in question forms only the final act of the fight, when the battle was already lost, and the defeated soldiers were trying at this point only to sell their lives at the highest possible price. At the start of the battle, they may well have advanced along with the knights.

This is expressly reported in the same battle concerning the foot soldiers of Emperor Otto in the center, who drove back the French marksmen of the communes and penetrated into the body of knights up to King Philip Augustus himself, who was pulled down from his horse. Of course, this event did not occur as an isolated action, as a number of scholars have understood it, where the knights remained halted behind them, but it was carried out in the general action with the knights.

Ballhausen believes, without any real basis, that Otto's army, including the English, was of approximately equal strength to the French and that the principal reason the imperial army was defeated was that it was fatigued by the long march. I cannot, however, believe in the long flanking march and the site of the battle at the place where Ballhausen claims to establish it.

BATTLE OF BORNHÖVED
22 JULY 1227

The source reports have been assembled by Usinger in *German-Danish History* (*Deutsch-dänische Geschichte*), p. 428. Those reports that are worthy of credence do not contain anything from which we could learn something on the sequence of the battle. The Danish sources attribute the defeat of their king, Waldemar, to the treachery of the Dithmarschen, who were on the Danes' side but suddenly attacked them in the rear.

The mythical aspects of the battle are to be found in Hermann Korner and in Lambeck, *Rerum Hamburgensium libri* (*Books of the History of Hamburg*), 2. 37. On a vow of the burgomaster of Lübeck, the sun supposedly shone suddenly in the eyes of the Danes, so that they could no longer see.

Hasse, "The Battle of Bornhöved" ("Die Schlacht bei Bornhöved"), *Zeitschrift für Schleswig-Holsteinische Geschichte,* Vol. IIV [*sic*], is without any important conclusions from the military viewpoint.

BATTLE OF MONTE APERTO
4 SEPTEMBER 1260

With the help of 800 German horsemen, the Sienese were victorious over the Florentines.

There is much to object to in Köhler's account, 3: 3: 289. In particular, the number of 30,000 men on foot and 3,000 on horseback, which he attributes to the Florentines, in accordance with the sources, is certainly much too high. As the battle progressed, the principal role by far was played by the German horsemen, who were divided into four groups of 200 men each. Four groups of 200 men each could not possibly have determined to such a great extent the whole course of the battle if the enemy army had been 33,000 men strong. And the losses of the Florentines, given as 10,000 killed and 11,000 captured, must be greatly exaggerated.

In Köhler's opinion, which may well be correct, the combat participation by the burgher levies on foot consisted principally of their role as marksmen.

BATTLE OF LEWES
14 MAY 1264

Simon de Montfort, at the head of the English barons, defeated King Henry III, whose troops were also commanded by his brother, Richard of Cornwallis, who had been selected as king by the Germans, and by Henry's son, the later King Edward I.

Both armies were composed of horsemen and foot troops, but foot troops played no active role in the accounts. It appears to have been a mounted battle.

Oman, p. 415, gives an excellent analysis and correctly rejects as a hopeless exaggeration the figures of the sources, which give the armies 40,000 and 50,000 men, respectively (which Köhler, 3: 3: 303, accepts).

BATTLE OF WORRINGEN
5 JUNE 1288

A quarrel had erupted over the succession of the count of Limburg. Two large alliances faced each other, one under the leadership of Duke John of Brabant and the other under Archbishop Siegfried of Cologne, both old rivals for the dominant position in Lower Lorraine. On this war and the battle that finally decided its outcome, we have a thorough account in the rhymed chronicle of Ian van Heelu, which was composed shortly afterward in honor of the victor, the duke of Brabant.

In this battle Köhler has found the most remarkable tactical phenomena. The fact that part of the duke's forces, the knights of Count von Berg, did not enter the battle until late is supposed to have resulted in a combination such as the greatest command genius could not have produced more favorably (p. 176). And this supposedly achieved an even higher significance through the fact that the battle formed the point of departure for the development of a combat method that came into its own in the later German battles. On the next page, to be sure, we learn that the same thing had already occurred at Muret and Tagliacozzo, and finally, a few sentences later, that this combat method extended back into the twelfth century.

There can hardly be any question of a special combat method in this battle. It is admittedly noteworthy as a result of a certain maneuvering by the units of knights and the actions of the foot troops on both sides. It is possible that the final decision resulted from the fact that the archbishop's foot troops, despite the *carroccio* in their midst, did not hold fast, whereas the foot soldiers on the other side, burghers of Cologne and peasants from the mountains, moved against the flank and the rear of the archbishop's knights. But this cannot be clearly recognized, since our only thorough source, Heelu, was obviously concerned with concentrating the spotlight on the Brabantine duke. A special study by Richard Jahn (Berlin dissertation, 1907) has attempted with great perspicacity and careful attention to detail to construct a picture of the battle from

Heelu's poem. But I cannot overcome my doubt as to whether such complicated planning and movements could have taken place in a knightly battle. Even though the author may have construed somewhat too much "tactics" from the poetic pictures, in any case this attempt to reconstruct the battle from a tactical viewpoint here where we have, for once, a very detailed contemporary account of a knightly battle is very valuable. This attempt was undertaken very carefully, with admirable knowledge and complete mastery of the subject matter, and, despite my reservation stated above, I can only recommend Jahn's study for further investigation and imitation. Perhaps in this way we can still manage to arrive at a somewhat fuller understanding of medieval combat procedures.

Concerning the "*konroots*" into which Heelu has the knights divided, Jahn explains that they contain an actual approach to the organization of the squadron. But, as a result of the knightly concept that stood in opposition to such an orderly formation, they had no real effectiveness.

According to Jahn's conclusions, Heelu used the names "squire," "sergeant," and "serving man" (*Knappen, serianten, Knechte*) interchangeably for all who were not knights.

The battle is valuable to us as a result of two of Heelu's expressions, which we have already used in our general observations of knightly warfare: the specific testimony of the slow approach ride by the knights, "as if they had a bride in front of them on the horse," and the dialogue as to whether one should attack "thick" (*dick*), that is, in a deep and close formation, or "thin" (*dünn*), that is, loosely spread out.

In addition, we also find that fine old story, that Archbishop Siegfried, who was finally defeated, had brought with him the chains with which his prisoners were to be bound. (See Vol. II, p. 124.)

BATTLE OF CERTOMONDO
11 JUNE 1289

Köhler, 3:3:329, calls this battle, in which the Florentines defeated the Aretians, "epoch-making" in the military history of the Italians. I cannot see the basis for this importance. The fact that the foot troops were placed partly beside the horsemen and partly behind them, which Köhler, p. 337, sees as the innovation in this battle, is nothing special. That the Aretian foot soldiers, as Köhler recounts, crept on all fours under the horses of the Florentines and slit open their bellies with long knives from underneath, I must regard as a fable until it is explained why the horses of the Florentines neither moved nor trampled on the crawling men, nor why the horsemen did not spear them from above. That the Florentines finally drew up their wagons in the form of a wagon fortification behind the front may also have often taken place with wagons on other occasions. As far as the tactical importance is concerned, that is, that the troops were "held together," or in plain words did not turn tail, this story belongs in the same military recipe book as the long knives with which the troops slit open the horses' bellies from underneath.

BATTLE ON THE MARCHFELD
26 AUGUST 1278

Köhler (2: 106) assumes that the Germans in the army of Rudolf of Hapsburg had 2,000 horsemen, including 300 knights with armored stallions, while the Hungarians had at least 30,000 horsemen, including 1,000 with armored horses, and 23,500 foot soldiers. Since he believes at the same time that the foot troops did not participate in the battle but remained in the camp, Rudolf would have enjoyed a huge superiority of numbers, and it would be difficult to explain why the battle wavered for so long and Ottocar supposedly came so close to victory. But all the figures are completely unconfirmed chronicle reports. A particularly remarkable feature of this battle is the fact that the foot troops on the two sides are not mentioned in the numerous accounts, so that the battle was apparently purely a mounted combat. The Hungarians were for the most part mounted archers.

Köhler's thorough account is the painting of a fantasy contaminated by the various sources on which it draws.

Nor are the various other attempts to treat this battle satisfactory. See Ottokar Lorenz, *Historische Zeitschrift,* Vol. 42 (1879). Same author, *German History in the Thirteenth and Fourteenth Centuries (Deutsche Geschichte im 13. und 14. Jahrhundert)*, Vol. 2. Oswald Redlich, *Rudolf von Habsburg,* 1903. Perhaps a renewed special study will succeed in shedding more light on this important event.

ENGAGEMENT AT CONWAY
JANUARY 1295

Nicholas Trevet or Trivet, a Dominican in Oxford (died 1328), described a victory of the English over the Welsh at Conway in January 1295 in the following words:[14]

When the count of Warwick heard that the Welsh were assembled in large numbers on a certain plain between two forests, he took a selected corps of armed men, along with crossbowmen and archers, attacked the Welsh in the night, and hemmed them in on all sides. The Welsh planted the ends of their spears in the ground and directed the points against the attacking horsemen in order to protect themselves against their assault. But the count placed a crossbowman between every two horsemen, and when the largest part of the Welsh spearmen had been laid out by the bolts from the crossbows, the count attacked the remainder with his mounted troops and caused them, it is believed, heavier losses than any they had suffered in the earlier wars.

BATTLE OF GÖLLHEIM
2 JULY 1298

The reports we have on this decisive battle between the German King Adolf of Nassau and the counterking, Albrecht von Habsburg-Austria, make it appear to have been purely a battle between knights. We hear nothing either of foot troops or of marksmen. The strengths of the armies are unknown.

Albrecht is supposed to have ordered that the horses be struck down. Consequently, the number of dead horses was supposedly so large that their corpses piled up to form walls, behind which the Bavarian knights continued the battle on foot, with their princes in the forefront. That may well be just as much of a fable as the report that Albrecht had the points of their swords especially sharpened for more effective thrusting.[15] And the description of the Bavarians, who were unable to move, at least having been able to take a momentary rest, for the reason that their horses were struck down,[16] can hardly be a reflection of reality. Knights whose horses are struck down hardly wait quietly to see what will happen next, and their opponents would not allow them to rest, even if they took cover behind the dead horses.

NOTES FOR CHAPTER IX

1. "Studies on the Military History of England in the Twelfth Century" ("Studien zur Kriegsgeschichte Englands im 12. Jahrhundert"), by J. Douglas Drummond. Berlin dissertation, 1905.

2. According to Drummond.

3. Aelredi Abbatis Rievallensis (Aelred, abbot of Rievaulx), *Historia de bello Standardii* (*History of the Battle of the Standard*), p. 338. "strenuissimi milites in prima fronte locati lancearios et sagittarios ita sibi inseruerunt ut, militaribus armis protecti . . . Scutis scuta junguntur" ("The most vigorous knights placed on the front line, so inserted spearmen and archers that, protected by the arms of the knights . . . shields were joined to shields").

4. According to Drummond.

5. Radulf, *Gesta Tancredi* (*Deeds of Tancred*), Chap. 22.

6. "Ut pedites castra servarent et milites hostibus obviam extra castra pergerent" ("so that the foot soldiers might guard the camp and the knights might proceed against the enemy outside the camp"). Raimund. According to the *Gesta,* "pars peditum" ("part of the foot soldiers").

7. "Procedebamus ita spaciosi, sicut in processionibus clerici pergere solent et re vera nobis processio erat." ("We were advancing in so loose a formation, just as clerics are accustomed to go in processions, and in fact we had a procession.")

8. Letter from the princes to the pope.

9. Heermann, p. 52, Note 2.

10. Furthermore, the character of this letter as an official document is not absolutely certain. Hagenmeier, *Studies in German History* (*Forschung zur deutschen Geschichte*), 13: 400, believed he could show that Raimund himself was the author of the letter. The difference in the figures for the army strengths would not stand in the way of this interpretation. These numbers are only very vague estimates, which the same man can have stated very differently at various times, after speaking with various people.

11. According to the *Itinerarium Regis Ricardi* (*Itinerary of King Richard*), VI, paras. 21-24. Edited by Stubbs in the *Rerum Britannicarum medii aevi Scriptores* (*Writers of British History of the Middle Ages*), p. 415. Oman, *History of War,* p. 316.

12. Of course, we could base a conclusion on the worthlessness of the foot troops on the express testimony of Raimund of Agiles, who says that, when the knights moved out before Antioch for the battle by the lake (9 February 1098), the foot troops were left behind in front of the beleaguered city. "Dicebant enim, quod multi de exercitu nostro imbelles et pavidi, si viderent Turcorum multitudinem, timoris potius quam audaciae exempla monstrarent." ("They said in fact that many of our army, cowardly and afraid if they saw a crowd of Turks, presented examples of fear rather than boldness.") But these kinds of statements are not

objective evidence. Furthermore, some of the foot troops did move out with the knights (according to the *Gesta*), and that same day the rest of them successfully repulsed a sortie of the besieged forces.

13. Köhler, p. 156. Oman, p. 477.

14. Morris, p. 256. Oman, p. 561.

15. Köhler, 2:206-207. On the basis of the *Regensburg Annals, M.G. SS.,* 17. 418.

16. Köhler, 2:210.

BOOK IV

The Late Middle Ages

Preface

The fourteenth and fifteenth centuries brought a series of innovations in warfare which in some areas significantly modified the picture of medieval warfare we have formed up to this point, so that we must now once again establish a dividing line. These innovations were not of such a type as to be new forms resulting from constant development of the old ones, nor are they related to one another in an organic context. Actually, they are individual phenomena that either die out again, like the highly developed combat methods of the marksmen and the employment of dismounted knights in conjunction with marksmen, or that do not achieve their full importance until centuries later, like the rise of firearms, or the comet-like phenomenon of a victory of burgher and peasant foot soldiers over a knightly army, or the unique emergence of the Hussites. As important as all these events were in themselves, no fundamental change in warfare resulted from them. The principal features with which we have become familiar remained the same until the end of the Middle Ages, or they emerged again and again, hardly unchanged. Consequently, I am arranging my material in such an order as to allow us to observe the special phenomena of these centuries one by one in their theoretical significance and their historic individuality and causality, and then examine several campaigns and battles, which will show us that military events are repeated again and again, events that could have occurred in about the same way in the thirteenth and twelfth centuries or even earlier. This is proof that these changes did not represent a continuing progressive development, but rather a series of individual phenomena.

The real historical progress proceeded, in the final analysis, only from a single place and a single point—the Swiss. I am therefore removing them from the chronological sequence and treating them in a special book.

Chapter I

Phalanx Battles. Burgher Forces and Militia Levies

BATTLE OF COURTRAI
11 JULY 1302

Much as we heretofore have heard of foot troops in the Middle Ages, nevertheless, when they were on the victorious side, they always played only a secondary role, even at Legnano, or they were defeated by knights fighting in conjunction with marksmen. The first battle to give us a different picture was the battle of Courtrai.

Although the County of Flanders was of the Germanic language area, it had become a part of the Romanic western kingdom at the breakup of the Carolingian Empire. Its counts, however, had assumed a very independent stance until Philip the Fair drove them out and annexed the country to the crown. Cities and peasants now rebelled against this domination by the French. A popular leader in Bruges, Peter König, brought the masses into action and drove out the royal garrisons, and he was joined by a series of smaller cities and groups of peasants. Ghent, the most powerful city beside Bruges, remained divided. The aristocratic faction, the Leliaerts as they were called, remained loyal to the king, but they could not prevent the democrats under Jan Vorlut from moving to the aid of the citizens of Bruges. As overall commanders of the rebellion, however, there appeared a younger son of the imprisoned count, Guido, and a grandson, Count William of Jülich, who, although he had become a priest, did not let that prevent him from following the inherent warlike tendencies of his nature. The two counts, still young men about twenty-five years of age, took over the command, apparently not by virtue of their right as representatives of the native ruling family, but on the strength of an agreement with the popular leaders—a curious alliance between feudalism and democracy, reminiscent of the command position of Miltiades at Marathon.

The Flemish were still laying siege to two castles occupied by the French, Cassel and Courtrai, when a large French relief army under the captain general count of Artois, brother-in-law of King Philip, approached. The Flemish gave up their siege of Kassel and concentrated all their forces at Courtrai, whose burghers had also joined the insurrection. Artois marched up before the city, no doubt thinking that his mere appearance would suffice to persuade the Flemish citizen army to withdraw and would relieve the castle. But the Flemish were convinced that if they were to save their country, they would have to fight a battle, and they were resolved to accept battle here and now, before Courtrai. If they had withdrawn and demobilized their army, the French would not only have relieved the castle and laid waste the low country, but they would perhaps also have captured the cities, even Bruges, which was only weakly fortified. They could count to a much higher degree on supporters within the citizenry itself than the Persions could in Attica long before.

The fortified castle or stronghold of Courtrai, which the French intended to relieve, was situated on the Lys, at the northern corner of the city, and on the right (south) bank, like the city itself. In order to block access to the castle, the Flemish army took position in the angle between the city and the river, with the city on their right, stretching southward, narrow and extended, along the river. To their left was a monastery on the river bank, and in front of them was a rather deep creek, the Gröningen, with partially swampy banks. The position offered no route for retreat; if the burghers were defeated, they would be pushed into the river close behind them. Men who accepted battle here were determined to win or die. The formation they took up was described as "acies longa valde et spissa" ("a very long and thick battle line"), "pariter adunati et densati lanceis adjunctis" (*Annales Gandenses*) ("joined together and closed up with their spears brought together") (*Annals of Ghent*). "Brugenses unam solam fecerunt armatorum aciem praemittendo balistarios deinde homines cum lanceis et baculis ferratis alternatim postea reliquos" (*Genealogia Comitum Flandrensium*) ("The men of Bruges made only one unit of their armed men by putting in front their crossbowmen and then alternately in the rear the rest of their men with spears and iron-tipped staffs"). (*Genealogy of the Counts of Flanders*); "drawn up in thick, closed order" (*Chronicle of Saint Denis*). The formation, then, was like a phalanx and was no doubt at least 600 meters long, perhaps even longer. The marksmen, who were not very numerous, were deployed in front of the line, and the main body was armed with spears and *goeden-*

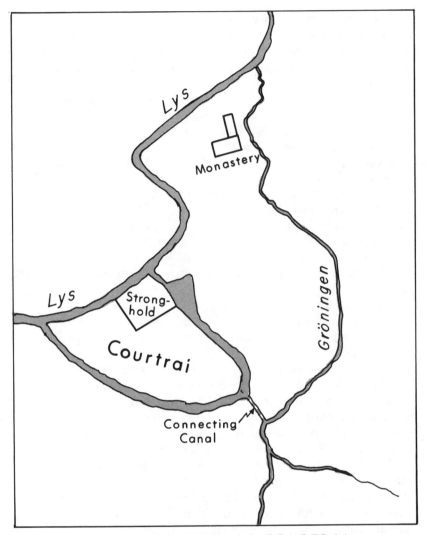

Fig. 3 BATTLE OF COURTRAI

dags, a kind of halberd, and probably only partially with defensive armor. The two commanding counts with the ten or so knights of their retinue had dismounted and joined the phalanx, so that nobody was on horseback. The obstacle in front of their line, the Gröningen stream, which, according to Villani, was 5 ells (yards) wide and 3 ells deep, was strengthened artificially by the installation of pitfalls and probably also the deepening of shallow spots.

A unit under the command of Johann von Renesse, a knight of long military experience, was formed as a reserve behind the phalanx. Another unit, composed of the burghers of Ypres, was drawn up facing the castle to prevent the garrison from attacking the phalanx in the rear during the battle.

The count of Artois, who is described as a brave warrior who had proven himself in five or six battles, recognized the strength of the enemy position, which was difficult to attack from the front and could not be enveloped on either the right or left flank. He hesitated for a few days, encamped about a mile south of the city. Were the burghers really willing to risk battle in their position with no withdrawal route? To be sure, the French commander, in order to maneuver them out of position, could have moved on Ypres or directly against Bruges, laying waste the countryside as he went. But in the meantime, the garrison of the castle of Courtrai might well have been obliged to surrender, and it was doubtful as to what success other maneuvers would have, whereas a victory right here would have decided the war and destroyed the enemy in a single stroke.

Artois therefore decided to attack.

His Genoese crossbowmen and Spanish javelin-throwers moved out in front, the knights followed, unit beside unit, and a rather small detachment remained in reserve.

The crossbowmen and javelin-throwers drove back the enemy marksmen and fired on the phalanx, which was apparently drawn up quite close behind the Gröningen. Their fire was so effective that the phalanx could not stand up to it, but the counts succeeded in leading it in good order a short distance to the rear. The French marksmen could not follow them over the Gröningen in order to approach them again, since, on the other side, they would have been too exposed to the danger of a counterattack. Therefore, the count of Artois gave the signal for the crossbowmen to fall back and the knights to ride forward to the attack. Since the enemy foot troops had withdrawn some little distance from their frontal obstacle, he could hope that his horsemen could work their way across the stream and have enough room on the other side for their charge. Although the withdrawal of the marksmen through the forward movement of the knights created a certain amount of disorder and a number of the Genoese were trampled, that was probably almost always the case when these two arms worked together, and it could not have any influence on the progress and outcome of the battle.

At this point, however, something new and completely unprecedented occurred. At the moment when the knights were preparing to complete the difficult stream crossing, hindered by the water course, the swampy banks, and the obstacles artificially laid out by the Flemish, the enemy phalanx suddenly went into motion, dashed forward, and fell on the knights with furious cutting and thrusting. The knights were hardly able to use their weapons and were not at all able to take advantage of their unique strength, the shock action of their heavy steeds, which normally broke up and overthrew enemy foot troops.

Undoubtedly, the two Flemish counts had trained their burghers in this tactic in advance and now gave them the signal at the proper moment. After the marksmen had withdrawn, each of the knights, who were no doubt far outnumbered, found himself attacked by several enemy foot soldiers simultaneously. The knights were soon overcome and were killed in large numbers. It had been ordered in advance that whoever granted mercy or took booty before the outcome of the battle was decided was to be cut down immediately by his comrades.

Only in the center did the knights manage to cross the Gröningen quickly enough and attack and push back the enemy phalanx in the normal manner. But the reserve under Johann von Renesse, which the Flemish had prudently held back, moved in and restored the situation. The battle now ended in complete disaster, even for those knights who were initially victorious, since they were obliged to withdraw across the Gröningen. There they were easily overtaken and subdued. The count of Artois himself reportedly wanted to surrender to a warrior monk, William of Süftingen, but since he spoke in French, the Flemish shouted to him: "We do not understand you," and they struck him down.[1]

A sortie attempted by the castle garrison was easily repulsed by the corps from Ypres that had been drawn up for that purpose. The reserve which Artois had held out under Saint Pol was unable to rescue or to assist.

Villani reported how extremely proud the Flemish were of their victory at Courtrai, where one man with his *goedendag* had dared to stand up to two mounted knights. The author added that he recounted this in such detail because it was new and marvelous.

The Flemish claimed to have removed from the fallen knights and taken as booty 700 gilded spurs; they therefore named their victory the "battle of the golden spurs."

EXCURSUS

The standard study for Courtrai is the Berlin dissertation "The Battle of Courtrai" ("Die Schlacht bei Kortryk") by Felix Wodsak, published by Karl Arnold, Berlin-Wilmersdorf, 1905. It also lists all the earlier references.

Wodsak estimates the strength of the Flemish at some 13,000 men and that of the French at 5,000 horsemen and 3,000 marksmen. These figures are probably not too far from the truth, although the bases for the estimates are very uncertain.

In the work of the Flemish poet Velthem, our principal source, and that of Villani, the same list is to be found (after the correction of obvious errors), which gives the strengths of the individual French contingents, leading to a total of 7,500 horsemen. But the agreement between the two sources should not be regarded as confirming the reliability of the figures. Both authors base their work on a common original source, which, however, like Herodotus's figure for the strength of the Greeks at Plataeae, stems from only a very vague estimate. Wodsak reduces the 7,500 to 5,000 by assuming there were 2,500 *gleves* of three horses each, one of which was ridden by a groom who was not a combatant. It is doubtful, however, that this was the meaning of the source. The pay records for the year 1317, which Wodsak cites on p. 42, in which the knight appears with three horses, may be interpreted as showing that this group included a heavily armed horseman, a light horseman, and a mounted groom, but the sources which speak of 7,500 horses at Courtrai certainly mean 7,500 mounted combatants, knights, and soldiers. Of course, this does not eliminate the possibility that there were only 5,000, a number that already represented a powerful fighting force.

Wodsak took great pains with his terrain study, but he is not always completely clear. With his work, he included a sketch that was based on a map by Deventer from the sixteenth century, of which our own sketch is a simplified copy. But the scale is missing. From the one that was later given to me by the author, I estimate that the distance from the mouth of the Gröningen in the Lys to the castle was exactly 1,000 meters, the width of the city along the Lys was 600 meters, and the length of the connecting canal was 150 meters. The changes in the terrain that have been caused by cultivation in this area were obviously very significant. Wodsak believes that the Flemish were formed from the connecting canal up to the monastery, and he states the length of this position as about 1 kilometer (p. 41). But the scale indicates that the distance between those two features amounted to more than 1 kilometer. But even with 1 kilometer, Wodsak's estimate would result in a phalanx only seven men deep, and that seems to me to be too small. It is not impossible, however, that we might assume the length of the phalanx to have been considerably shorter, without creating any serious change in the overall picture.

As I have already assumed in the foregoing text, the right flank probably rested, not on the connecting canal, but on the city wall, and on the [left] flank the monastery may have been situated somewhat farther upstream, or the terrain may have been further limited by swamp or monastery walls.

According to the chronicle of the monk William (Matthaeus, *Veteris aevi Analecta* [*Selections of the Ancient Period*], 2. 557), the Flemish did indeed rest their right flank on the connecting canal ("loca magis commoda studet discernere et fossam antiquam suo lateri sociare": "He was eager to discern a more suitable position and to join the old ditch to his flank"). But the chronicle is of a late date, and the pushing forward of the right flank up to the canal is too illogical to be believed on the strength of that sentence. Why should the Flemish have moved out in front of the city fortifications? The men who were posted there would have been much too exposed to the enemy crossbowmen. Furthermore, the wording of the chronicle can be quite easily reconciled with our concept; that is, the canal was useful to the Flemish flank, even if the flank rested on the city wall, especially at the moment when that flank moved forward on the offensive toward the Gröningen.

Of course, this interpretation is at odds with Wodsak's explanation of why it was precisely in the center that the French knights were initially victorious. That is, he believes that the center was farthest from the Gröningen because of the bend in that stream. Consequently, we might say, the knights in that section had the most time to cross the stream and form for an orderly attack, which then succeeded until the Flemish reserve moved in. If, then, the right flank of the Flemish was formed farther back, the same argument would apply there, but without the same result.

Nevertheless, this point does not constitute a counterargument against my concept. All kinds of other conditions, of course, such as the possibility that the stream was easier to cross in the middle, may have played a role in determining why the Flemish center yielded while the flanks were immediately victorious.

On p. 30, Wodsak quotes from the "excellent chronicle": "Ende de Vlamingen liegen oostward om te commene ter zyde, daer gheen gracht en was." Whether he interprets this passage correctly is very questionable. It apparently means that the Flemish extended toward the east up to a point where there was no longer any *"Gracht,"* that is, canal or stream. What then was there? Perhaps swampy terrain? I confess that the passage is not clear to me.

Navez, in his *Study on Courtrai (Untersuchung über Courtray)*, Brussels, 1897, p. 23, discusses the controversy over the *goedendag.* Some scholars (De Vigne, Köhler) believe that this weapon consisted of a shaft surmounted by an iron point, while others (Paulin, Paris, Viollet-le-Duc, Hardy, Demmin) believe it had the form of a halberd. In the museum at the Haler Gate in Brussels, there is a weapon similar to a halberd (No. 37, eighth series of the catalog), which Viollet-le-Duc has claimed to be the *goedendag.* (Hermann Van Dnyse, *Catalog of the Arms and Armor of the Museum at the Haler Gate [Katalog der Waffen und Rüstungen des Museums am Haler Tor]*, p. 130). M. Van Walderghem ("The Truth about the 'Goedendag' " ["Die Wahrheit über den 'Goedendag' "], *Annalen der Gesellschaft für Archäologie in Brüssel*, 9: 305), believes it was made of a plowshare attached to a shaft. Navez believes that the problem is not yet solved, but the following explanation seems to him to be almost without doubt the correct one:

In his opinion, the best description of the *goedendag* appears in William Guiart's *Branch of the Royal Lineages (Branche des royaux lignages)*. It is very logical that this description is the most accurate one; Guiart was a soldier (crossbowman) in the French army that moved into the field against the Flemish and fought at Mons-en-Pévèle. Consequently, he must have been completely familiar with the weapons of the men against whom he had fought and who had wounded him with these weapons at the attack on la Haiguerie. Guiart says that the *goedendags* are:

> Grans bastons pesans ferrez
> A un long fer agu devant.
> Long, heavy shafts reinforced with iron
> With a long, sharp iron point.
>
> *

This sharp iron head made it possible to carry out spear thrusts, since the man who used the *goedendag* was able

Ferir sans s'aller mocquant	To strike without moving
Du bout devant en estocquant	By stabbing with the point
Son ennemi parmi le ventre	His enemy in the belly.
Et le fer est agu qui entre.	And the iron that penetrated was sharp.

The *goedendag* was therefore a long pike, and it was used in the way all pikes were manipulated, that is, by thrusting (*estoquant*). It had the unique feature of being heavy enough ("bastons pesans") to be used as a club.

Cil baton sont longs et traitis	The shafts are made long
Pour férir à deux mains faitis.	To strike with both hands.

Navez believes that, although this last verse means that the weapon was manipulated with both hands, it can also mean "thrusting" and not "hitting." He therefore considers the *goedendag* to be a pike.

BATTLE OF BANNOCKBURN
24 JUNE 1314

This battle is the complete antithesis of the battle of Falkirk (1298) and a counterpart to the battle of Courtrai. The Scots, who had been subjugated by Edward I, rebelled again and acclaimed Robert Bruce their king. Edward II, who was involved in conflict with his own barons, was not able to intervene for a long time, but finally he marched up with a large army. Robert withdrew before him to a point a short distance before Stirling (where the castle was still occupied by the English), a number of miles north of Falkirk. There he took position on the high left bank of the small river Bannockburn, a position with both flanks resting on swamp or forest, which could not easily be enveloped or outflanked. The open front was only about a mile in length. Approximately in the middle, an ancient Roman road led across the deep valley of the Bannockburn toward Stirling. The valley of the Bannockburn is not quite 2,000 paces wide; the height on which the Scots were formed rises between 186 and 240 feet above the valley floor.

The formation of the Scots was quite similar to the formation at Falkirk: four large units of spearmen, with the small body of horsemen behind them.[2]

Oman recounts the course of the battle as follows: Robert had strengthened the frontal obstacle formed by the deep, swampy river valley, which was already a formidable obstacle in itself, with concealed pitfalls that he had installed on the slope leading up to his position.

Despite all the obstacles, the English knights stormed up the slope and attempted to break up the Scottish units. But the huge mass of Englishmen, probably 10,000 horses and 50,000 to 60,000 men on foot, were unable to move on the narrow terrain. Most of them did not reach the enemy at all but stood still, inactive. Most important of all, however, the marksmen could not be brought forward through the horsemen to face the Scottish spearmen. A unit of marksmen which succeeded in moving around the Scottish flank was driven back by an attack of the Scottish knights under the command of Marshal Robert Keith. The decisive action was finally brought about by the Scottish train soldiers, who appeared on the flank of the English, giving the impression, through colored cloths which they tied to their spears, that a new army with its banners was arriving, shouted loud battle calls, and thus created panic among the English knights.

That this last twist is simply a legend needs only to be expressed to become clear. Even if we assume that the English knights were so timorous, where are the Scottish soldiers supposed to have come from, since, after all, the terrain on both flanks of their army was impassable? The real problem is why the English did not first have the Scottish units of spearmen worn down by their marksmen, as they had done at Falkirk, before sending in the knights against them. The explanation that the Scottish knights drove them off, whereas at Falkirk they themselves took flight, is not sufficient, for why did the English knights at Bannockburn not come to the aid of their marksmen and first of all drive away the small number of Scottish horsemen, instead of involving themselves in vain with the units of spearmen? That can perhaps be explained by the fact that the Scottish units formed a closed phalanx, whose flanks were so well protected that at most a few marksmen, but no horsemen, were able to envelop them. But, as at Hastings, they could, nevertheless, also have had the marksmen do their work in the front. Furthermore, it does not even appear that flanking action was so impossible, for it is reported that on the day before the battle a group of 800 English knights moved around the left flank of the Scots up to a point near Saint Ninian's Church, which was situated behind the middle of the Scottish front, and these knights were reportedly driven back only after heavy combat.

Lord Hailes, Lingard, and Pauli believe that the Scots had taken position, not behind the Bannockburn stream, with their front facing south, but with their left flank against the cliffs of Stirling and their right flank resting on the Bannockburn. In this case, their left flank, of course, could not have been enveloped, but their right flank was all the more exposed. Furthermore, this northeasterly orientation of the front does not agree with the source account to the effect that the morning sun was shining in the faces of the English. It seems to me there can be no doubt as to the topographic basis of the position of the Scots behind the stream, with their backs toward Stirling, as we have seen in Oman's account above.

The solution is perhaps to be found once again in the army strengths.

Up to the present time, it has been generally assumed that the English army was by far the larger. The Scottish chronicle by Fordun (died about 1384) gives the English 340,000 men on horseback and as many more on foot, for a total of 680,000. Most of the more modern historians have accepted a strength of at least 100,000 men, and even Oman, as careful as he is, believes, as we have seen, that he must assume as many as 60,000. This number even appears to have a documentary basis. That is, there have been preserved the levy orders of Edward II to a number of sheriffs and barons. Not only the English and Welsh, but also the Irish and even the Gascons were supposed to provide their contingents for this war. As usual, the summons for the knights do not give any numbers. In addition to the knights, however, "*pedites*" were levied, with a definite number specified for each district: York, 4,000; Lancashire, 500, etc. All together, twelve English counties, a number of border barons, and Wales were to provide 21,540 men. That was about one-third of the country. If we now also assume, Oman argues, that the south sent fewer men for this campaign in the far north, the entire army can probably not have been smaller than 50,000 to 60,000 men.

Against this argument, I would like to point out that, first of all, it is not stated that the south provided any men at all for this war, except the knights and their retinue. The Welsh were called because, as semibarbarians, they were supposed to be particularly skilled in warfare and especially useful in mountain combat. But it is neither proven nor credible that a mass levy was sent to Scotland from Southern England.

But it is also certainly a mistake to establish the army strength automatically as even anywhere near the number levied. We may not carry the concepts of modern administrative exactness over even to the sixteenth century, much less the fourteenth. That the sheriff of York was charged with sending 4,000 men is still no proof that he sent even half that number.

If we examine the levy letters more closely, our doubts increase. The summons to the Irish is dated 22 March. The levies for the *pedites* have the date of 27 May, and the men were already supposed to be at Berwick on 10 June. According to the context, it is possible, of course, that this was simply a repetition of an older order. But the rationale speaks for the fact that these reinforcements were only now decided on, for it is stated that the foot troops were needed because the Scots had established themselves "in locis fortibus et morosis (ubi equitibus difficilis patebit accessus)" ["in a strong, inaccessible position (where a difficult approach will expose the horsemen)"]. But whether this was simply the repetition of an earlier order and a strong warning or was the first order, it cannot be assumed that fourteen days after the order the mass of men levied was really assembled at the assigned place on the Scottish border. Indeed, it does not appear impossible that this order was issued zealously but was never actually carried out. For if such a force had been present at Bannockburn, it would necessarily have showed itself and accomplished something in one way or another. They had been called up to close with the Scots where the horsemen could not come to grips with them. Now the Scots had such a position. And these foot troops supposedly stood inactive behind the knights instead of enveloping the Scottish flanks through the woods and around the swamp?

Of course, this then brings up the other contradiction, that the levy for the foot troops was proclaimed but that the leaders then went into battle without awaiting their arrival. But there was no time to wait. The campaign was intended to relieve Stirling Castle, and the commandant, Sir Philip Mowbray, had arranged a capitulation with the Scots, agreeing to surrender Stirling in case he was not relieved by the feast of Saint John, and that was precisely the day of the battle.

In the king's knightly retinue, from the start there may have been a difference of opinion as to whether or not they should burden themselves with the militia. After all, their military value was only small, and a number of knights may have taken the position that they would be more trouble than they were worth, so that the campaign went ahead without much delay, even if only a few foot troops had reported.

All these points lead me to believe that, while it is not proven or provable, it is still quite possible that the English army was primarily the usual knightly army, and that the superiority in numbers was on the side of the Scots, who, in the midst of their own country, had assembled a real mass levy for the defense of their national freedom.

If we accept this point, the course of the battle becomes understandable. The Scots had very good features on which to rest their flanks, and the knights made no attempt at envelopment, since all their strength was demanded by the frontal attack. The envelopment by marksmen only was beaten back by the Scottish knights, who were formed behind the phalanx.

The decision went against the attackers, contrary to what had happened at Hastings and Falkirk, but similar to Courtrai, because the frontal obstacle, the swampy stream, the slope, and the pitfalls were extremely difficult for the knights and caused them many losses, flanking action was impossible, the lack of free movement did not permit the usual cooperation between marksmen and knights, and finally, Bruce presumably led his closed mass, with its superior numbers, forward to counterattack.

A theoretical superiority of the Scots or the Scottish system of warfare over the English was not established by Bannockburn. Even after this brilliant success, as Oman correctly points out, Robert Bruce avoided open battle with the English. In 1321 he even allowed an English army to move again to Edinburgh and only sought to maneuver it out again to the countryside by cutting off its supplies.

BATTLE OF ROSEBEKE
27 NOVEMBER 1382

Just as the Greek burghers and peasants had once conquered the Persian knights, the Flemish and Scots conquered the French and English knights by their masterful utilization of the terrain. But the Greeks soon went on farther and no longer shied away from fighting with the Persians in the open field. Of Bannockburn we have already heard that it was not the starting point for a superiority of the Scots, and Courtrai was not followed by any further similar victory. Instead, eighty years later, the battle of Rosebeke proved that, as soon as the advantage of the terrain was taken from the burghers, the upper hand remained, as previously, with the knights.

The political origin and character of this fight differ from those features at Courtrai to the extent that this time the count of Flanders was not on the side of the burghers, but on that of the king. Under the leadership of Philip of Artevelde, Ghent rebelled against the ruler of the country, Count Louis, won the other Flemish cities over to its side, partially with kindness and partially by force, and drove out the count, to whose aid the young King Charles VI of France moved up to subdue the rebels. Duke Philip of Burgundy, the son-in-law of the count of Flanders and later his successor, had been the intermediary in the alliance, while Philip of Artevelde sought an alliance with the king of England. This political difference between the conditions of 1382 and 1302 also made itself felt in the strategy.

Artevelde besieged the city of Oudenarde on the Scheldt, 25 kilometers above Ghent, which a French knight was obstinately defending for the count. Not until six months had passed, in the middle of November 1382, had the king of France reached the point of assembling a relief army and leading it forward from Arras.

Although it is reported that Artevelde had powerful artillery, he had, nevertheless, not really besieged Oudenarde, but had sought to starve it into submission and had protected the siege army against an external attack by entrenchments.

The French council of war (Constable Olivier Clisson and three of the king's uncles), which met in Seclin on 17 November, therefore had to decide whether he should move up along the Scheldt for a direct attack on Artevelde and his troops, in order to relieve Oudenarde, or whether he could cause the enemy by a diversion to give up the siege, lure him out of his fortified position, and perhaps force or inveigle him to a decisive battle somewhere else. Probably remembering the bad experience of Courtrai, they decided, as serious as the plight of the beleaguered troops in Oudenarde already was, to avoid a direct attack and instead to make an incursion into Western Flanders. If Artevelde had been able to rely implicitly on the Flemish cities, he would probably not yet have needed to give up his position at Oudenarde. If the cities closed their gates and the French laid waste only the flat land along the border, instead of attacking the rebellious burghers and freeing their beleaguered compatriots, the morale advantage would undoubtedly have been on the side of Artevelde. But, of course, the count, the legal hereditary lord of Flanders, was also in the king's camp. Ancient dependence and fear of the great French army, and probably also envy of Ghent and of Philip of Artevelde himself, combined to make the mood in the cities very uncertain. It appears that Artevelde wanted to defend the Lys, which protected Flanders from this side, but the French succeeded in crossing the river at Comines, upstream from Courtrai, and Ypres and a series of other communities immediately surrendered to the royal army.

If Artevelde had remained at Oudenarde, the French army would have proceeded to Bruges, would have captured this city, which was very divided in its sympathies, and then Artevelde's army would simply have broken up. He now had no other choice than either to withdraw to Ghent, hoping to hold out there but sacrificing the rest of Flanders, or to lead his army from Oudenarde against the French army and to appeal to the god of battles. This would mean a simple, open field battle, with the two sides meeting on even terms. For if the Flemish leader had tried to seek out a position somewhere between Ypres and Bruges, as strong as his forebears had had at Courtrai and as he himself no doubt had skillfully laid out before Oudenarde, such positions would not so easily be found, in the first place, and if the terrain should by chance offer such a position, nothing would prevent the French from enveloping it instead of attacking, and from maneuvering the Flemish out of the position and

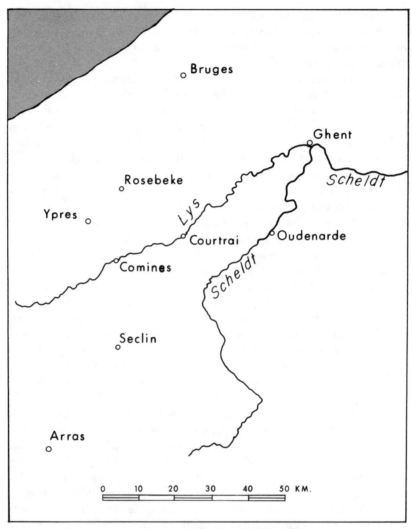

Fig. 4   BATTLE OF ROSEBEKE

attacking them in a more favorable place. For the position Miltiades had taken at Marathon and the one the Flemish took at Courtrai, there was necessary not only the sharp eye of the commander, who found the position and selected it, but also the entire political-strategic combination, which forced the enemy to attack the chosen position. The French who invaded Flanders in 1382, after they had once renounced a direct relief of Oudenarde, had a completely free choice as to which route they might wish to take to move through the open country, and they did not need to attack any position that seemed too strong to them. Consequently, the defenders did not have the possibility of forming in a specific, advantageous position and calling out to the enemy: "Either attack me here or go home." This time it was, rather, a question of a simple battle in the open field which would be fought only if neither of the two sides had too strong an ally in the terrain. The burghers and peasants who had won at Courtrai with the help of this ally were now obliged, if they did not wish to admit defeat without a battle, to show they also dared to face the knights under equal circumstances.

Philip of Artevelde, the "Protector of Flanders," as he called himself, was courageous enough to demand such a decision, and the burghers dared to follow him into this battle.

With their spears and *goedendags,* the Flemish formed a tightly knit phalanx that did not now await the attack, as had been done at Courtrai, but resolutely moved out to meet the advancing enemy. As we must expressly point out, this was their only chance to win the battle. If they had awaited the French attack without such flank cover as had been available at Courtrai and also without horsemen to defend their flanks, everything would have been lost from the start. Artevelde, therefore, showed himself to be a skillful and brave soldier by proceeding accordingly and taking up the offensive himself. After the two armies had already camped not far from each other some 10 miles northwest of Ypres on the night of 26-27 November and had reconnoitered each other's positions on the following morning, they made contact in fully deployed battle order near the village of West Rosebeke.

The constable had placed all his foot troops in the center, and in order to strengthen them against the attack awaited from the Flemish, he had had all the knights stationed in the center dismount, except for the young king himself and the closest members of his retinue.[3] This center, however, was only supposed to hold up the fight. The main blow was to be carried out simultaneously from the two flanks by the knights who had remained mounted.[4] With this arrangement, he could not fail to win. "They are ours. Our common soldiers would be able to defeat them," the constable reportedly said to the king, when he returned from his reconnaissance and reported that the battle was imminent.

At first, after the cannon had been fired, the shock action of the phalanx, which moved in close order down a slope, succeeded in pushing the French back a little distance. Froissart wrote: "The approaching mass, with its spears and poles, looked like a forest," and he says that it fell on the enemy like a boar. And the Monk of Saint Denis also conceded that the French had yielded one and one-half paces.

But the French did not allow themselves to be completely thrown back and driven to flight. Thus they had already won, for now the mounted men drove from both flanks into the Flemish phalanx, and that action also brought to a halt the push in the front. We are reminded of the battle of Cannae. Since the Flemish were not victorious, they were cut down in large numbers. Quite a number of them were reportedly squeezed to death when the terrified mass pulled more closely together. One of the victims was Philip of Artevelde himself, whose corpse was later found among the dead on the battlefield, presumably without any wound.

There are no reliable statements concerning the strengths of the armies that fought on both sides at Rosebeke, and there are not sufficient bases for estimates.

The battle is of the greatest importance for European history, less from a positive point of view than from a negative one. If the Flemish had been victorious at Rosebeke, the French cities, which were already causing the greatest difficulties, would immediately have refused any further obedience to their king. The possibility that burgher armies could defeat knightly armies in the open field, once demonstrated, would have produced other similar events and would thus have given a completely different direction to the social development of the Germanic-Romanic peoples.

EXCURSUS

The sources on Rosebeke were buried under veritable mounds of fables and biased attitudes and were first brought to light in the Berlin dissertation of Frederick Mohr (Georg Nauck, publisher, 1906). This same work has also eliminated all the fantastic constructions with which more modern scholars have tried to establish the course of the battle.

Of particular interest from the viewpoint of source analysis is the report given by Froissart concerning the council of war in Seclin on 17 November. One of the participants, the seigneur de Coucy, is supposed to have suggested that they attack the enemy at Oudenarde, moving along the Scheldt, which would be used for bringing up provisions. The constable supposedly replied that it would be doing the enemy too much honor if they made a detour. Rather, as brave warriors, they were obliged to move directly to the enemy and therefore invade West Flanders.

In reality, it was, of course, Coucy's proposal that led directly against the enemy main force, and the constable, with better strategic insight, lured the enemy to West Flanders from his fortified position by means of the diversion via Comines.

Consequently, we have here a case where the author, our source, heard something quite correct but, because he himself understood too little of the situation, later, in writing out the account, he confused the two speakers and their motives. A glance at the map suffices to make us realize this. General Köhler, however, in his thorough discussion of the battle in *Warfare of the Knightly Period (Kriegswesen der Ritterzeit)*, 2: 574 ff., has simply copied this nonsense.

BURGHER FORCES AND MILITIA LEVIES

The battle of Rosebeke shows us why nothing of a lasting nature, no enduring superiority of the burgher foot troops, resulted from tendencies toward general arming of the citizens, which at Legnano at least contributed to the success, and at Courtrai led to a great, completely independent success. They remained simple episodes. No doubt, we continue to find that burghers were levied, moved into the field, formed contingents, and even fought successful battles on occasion, but toward the end of the Middle Ages, the military strength of the burghers appears not to have progressed, but to have moved back and collapsed again. There were numerous military ordinances in the German cities, but finally the cities fought their wars with mercenaries, so that, for our purposes, it is superfluous to list these regulations in detail.[5] The test of the capabilities of the German cities, which shows them to be unsatisfactory, is the battle of Döffingen (1388), the description of which I am including in the following book which deals with the Swiss, for the sake of contrast and mutual clarification. The victory of the Nurembergers over Albrecht Achilles at Pillenreuth has already been discussed above (p. 275), and it has appeared as a purely knightly combat. Italy was completely under the domination of mercenaries. The English militia never achieved a real military significance. In France, the kings specifically rejected burgher levies, since they accomplished nothing and only got in the way.

According to Froissart, Philip VI explained in 1347 that in the future he intended to use for war and lead into battle nothing but noblemen. This report says that the burghers were nothing more than ballast, for they melted away in close combat like the snow in the sun. Only their marksmen and their money were still useful. For the rest, they should remain at home, take care of their wives and children, and carry on their business. For warfare, the only men of value were the noblemen, who had learned military skill from their youth and were raised for that purpose.[6]

In such utterances, it has no doubt been customary to recognize the haughtiness of the nobles or the envy of the knights, who were not willing to share with the burghers the pay, which at that time had indeed risen.[7] But, in reality, it was probably not very different from the way it was presented in King Philip's angry description.

Despite Rosebeke, it was in Flanders that burgher levies logically lasted the longest and were most used. The bordering counties, too, Brabant, Hainaut, which were finally united with Flanders under the hegemony of the dukes of Burgundy, still provided their lords contingents in the fifteenth century. But the very element that carried the victory at Courtrai and that necessarily would have constituted the strength of these military forces, if they were to have a future before them, the mass levy equipped with the close-combat weapon—that element disappeared, and the burgher contingents were principally companies of marksmen, and consequently only a supporting arm for the knights, as in France.[8]

EXCURSUS

A clear picture of the campaign of a burgher levy is provided by the following description of the campaigns of Regensburg against the Hussites in 1431:

> First of all, they drank the "Saint John's cup," and then they moved out. The point was formed by Captain Soller with 73 horsemen. These were followed by 71 crossbowmen with their battle colors, and then 16 marksmen with their muskets. These men were followed by the chapel wagon with the chaplain of the Ah church, and behind them came the blacksmiths, leather workers, the tin-smiths, roasters, tailors, cooks, and butchers, all together 284 men with 6 muskets and their accessories, 330 pounds of stones for the muskets and 220 pounds of lead balls. Forty-one wagons carried powder and lead for the contingent, 6,000 arrows, 300 fire arrows, 19 muskets, cowskins for the stalls and tents, and a supply of grain for six weeks. The provision wagons were loaded with 90 oxen, 990 pounds of cured meat, 990 pounds of lard, 1,200 pieces of Terminierer cheese, 80 dried cod, 56 pounds of tallow candles, and also vinegar, olive oil, pepper, saffron, ginger, two cartloads of 73 buckets of Austrian wine, and 138 buckets of beer. The expense for the campaign amounted to 838 pounds, 3 shillings, and—pence.[9]

Special mention is also due to the army regulations by which a number of princes in German areas sought to organize a popular military force. The counts of Württemberg strengthened their forces with peasant levies in their conflict with the cities (1388). Similar steps were taken by the palatine counts, the dukes of Bavaria,[10] and others, but especially the dukes of Austria, who were obliged by the Hussite wars and the battles with the Hungarians to take special steps to strengthen their forces.[11] At the very start of the Hussite wars (1421), Duke Albrecht V had a list drawn up of all the men in his country between the ages of sixteen and seventy who were capable of military service. According to a levy of 1431,[12] which was no doubt based on earlier similar ones, one man was to be provided for every ten households, the man who had the greatest agility and physical strength for military service, and he was to be provided with all the necessary equipment by the nine men who remained at home, who in the meanwhile also had to take care of his work. Those men who were left over after the division into tens in any single lord's area were to be combined with those of other areas. The armament and equipment were exactly prescribed to the smallest detail. Of every twenty men, three were to be armed with muskets, eight with crossbows, four with spears, four with flails, and they were also to have an iron helmet, a coat of armor or a doublet, metal gloves, and a sword or a knife. Each group of twenty was to have a wagon. The landowners and officials who withdrew men from the levy paid heavy fines, part of which went to the duke and another part to the field commander.

Similar levies were proclaimed quite often in Austria. On some occasions one man was to be provided from thirty "settled men," or twenty, fifteen, ten, five, and even three, but most often it was one of twenty or one of ten. Sometimes more men were called from those areas situated closest to the danger than from more distant areas.

This formation of groupings was very similar to those of the Carolingian capitularies; we might even assume a tradition that was never completely interrupted. But after we have understood that the Carolingian regulations applied not at all to the entire mass of peasants but to the warrior class, the possibility of such a connection disappears. The Austrian levies are related, rather, to the militia duty which, of course, at all times and places existed in addition to the real military organization, even if it was of very small practical effect. According to the capitularies, armies were to be formed to move hundreds of miles into the field for the summer. The Austrian levies only served for local defense or perhaps on occasion for a short push across the border, as, for example, on one occasion to break up and render harmless a large robber band in the Hungarian area (1449). The analogy of the formation of groups has no historical continuing relationship with the Carolingian capitularies, but it arises from the same need, namely, to link the levy with an assessment of taxes, a form of tax collection that we have encountered again and again and that can be applied just as well to a class of warriors, lords, or vassals as to peasants and burghers.

According to the oldest version of the Austrian political law, which was probably drawn up in 1237, in case of emergency each man was to move out with his lord, whose "housed man" he was (that is, from whom he held his house and courtyard), or he was to give him a war tax amounting to the annual income from his land.[13]

Nothing, then, has been reported of any really military accomplishments by these Austrian levies.

An engagement in which we hear for once of the success of levied peasants is that of Seckenheim (1462), which I shall discuss in connection with the Swiss.

ENGAGEMENT AT REUTLINGEN
14 MAY 1377

The account of this battle says that Count Ulrich of Württemberg blocked the withdrawal of the Reutlingers, who had been engaged in pillaging, close to their city, but he was defeated because a group of the burghers who had remained at home attacked him from the rear through a gate that was normally blocked off. In a special study by Johann Jacobsen, *The Battle of Reutlingen (Die Schlacht bei Reutlingen)*, Leipzig, 1882, this entire account is shown to be mostly legendary. Jacobsen also doubts that the count with his knights fought on foot, as Königshofen reports. Von der Au, *Critique of Königshofen (Zur Kritik Königsho-*

fens), p. 18, as well as Schön, *Reutlinger Geschichtsblätter,* 1899, p. 5, agree with Jacobsen. Consequently, this engagement is unusable from the military history viewpoint.

NOTES FOR CHAPTER I

1. *Spiegel historiaal,* IV, Chap. 33:

Then he (Artois) wanted to surrender to them
And so he said: . . . .
The Flemish shouted: We do not know you.
The count called out in French:
I am the count of Artois.

. . . .

They (the Flemish) said: Here is no nobleman
Who can understand you.

2. Oman, from whom I have also taken the terrain conditions, gives on p. 570 a very clear and tactically correct presentation, but I cannot accept it, since the sources on which we must depend seem to me very unreliable. The principal source is a heroic poem by Archdeacon John Barbour of Aberdeen, *The Bruce, or the Book of Robert de Broyss, King of Scots,* written between 1375 and 1377, and consequently not until almost two generations after the battle. There is another poem written sooner after the event but not offering much information. The author was the Carmelite monk Baston, who accompanied King Edward in order to celebrate his deeds but who, when he became a prisoner of the Scottish king after the defeat, was then obliged to celebrate the battle on that king's behalf. (Lappenberg-Pauli, *Geschichte von England,* 4: 243). The English sources, Geoffroy Baker of Swinbroke (died between 1358 and 1360) and the *Chronicle of Lanercost,* of which this part was probably the work of a Franciscan monk of Carlisle, contain only meager information.

3. The reason why the French knights in the center dismounted is not given directly in any source, but we may interpret the words used by the Monk of Saint Denis as we have done. He says: "The horses themselves were removed from the view of the combatants, so that each one, losing any hope of escaping the danger by fleeing, would show more courage."

4. We can conclude from the sequence of the battle itself that this was the sense of the French formation. That this epoch was capable of

such a tactical idea is shown in the report on the battle of Othée (1408), by Monstrelet, where the questionable maneuver is described with exact clarity: "When that other dismounted company, much larger . . . intends to invade your land and fight you, those on horseback, experienced in battle and in good order, will move up quickly and attempt from the rear to separate you and break up your formation, while the others are assaulting you from the front."

5. There are available quite exhaustive writings on this subject: Mojean, *City Military Arrangements in the Fourteenth and Fifteenth Centuries (Städtische Kriegseinrichtungen im XIV. und XV. Jahrhundert)*, Program of the Gymnasium of Stralsund, 1876. Von der Nahmer, *The Military Organizations of the German Cities in the Second Half of the Fourteenth Century (Die Wehrverfassungen der deutschen Städte in der 2. Hälfte des 14. Jahrhunderts)*, Marburg dissertation, 1888. Mendheim, *The Mercenary System of the Free Cities, especially Nuremberg (Das reichsstädtische, besonders Nürnberger, Söldnerwesen)*, Leipzig dissertation, 1889. Baltzer, *From the History of the Danzig Military System (Aus der Geschichte des Danziger Kriegswesens)*, Program of the Danzig Gymnasium, 1893. G. Liebe, *The Military System of the City of Erfurt (Das Kriegswesen der Stadt Erfurt)*, 1896. P. Sander, *The Municipal Economy of Nuremberg (Die reichsstädtische Haushaltung Nürnbergs)*, 1902, in which the second section of Part II treats the military organization in detail.

6. Froissart, Tome IV, p. 270: ". . . that he no longer wished to wage war with men other than nobles and that it was a complete loss and a hindrance to lead into battle the men from the communities, for in the hand-to-hand combat those men melt like snow in the sun. This had happened at the battle of Crécy, at Blanquetagne, at Caen, and in every place where these men had been led. And so he did not want to have any more of them except the crossbowmen from the fortified cities and the good towns. As to their gold and their silver, he wanted much of both to pay the expenses and the compensation of the nobles, but that was all. The common men had only to stay at home to protect their wives and children, carry on their business and their trade, and that should be sufficient for them. It was up to the nobles alone to practice the profession of arms that they had learned and in which they had been trained since childhood." (Extracted from Luce's citation in *Bertrand du Guesclin*, 1: 156).

"What do we want with help from these shopkeepers?" Jean de Beaumont reportedly said in 1415, when the city of Paris offered reinforcements. *Religieux de St. Denys,* Book 35, Chap. 5.

And Monstrelet writes in his chronicle: "The masses of the communes, even though they may be very numerous, can hardly offer resistance against a number of nobles accustomed to battle and proven in the profession of arms."

7. Michelet, *Histoire de France*, 3: 299.

8. Guillaume, *History of the Military Organization Under the Dukes of Burgundy* (*Histoire de l'organisation militaire sous les ducs de Bourgogne*), *Mém. cour. de l'Académie Belge*, 22(1848): 94.

9. Würdinger, *Military History of Bavaria, Franconia, the Palatinate, and Swabia from 1347 to 1506* (*Kriegsgeschichte von Bayern, Franken, Pfalz und Schwaben von 1347–1506*), 1: 182, from Gmeiner, 3: 23.

10. Würdinger, 2: 313.

11. Franz Kurz, *Austria's Military Organization in Older Times* (*Oesterreichs Militär-Verfassung in älteren Zeiten*), 1825. Meynert, *History of Military Organization* (*Geschichte des Kriegswesens*), 2 (1868): 11. Werunsky, *Austrian Imperial and Legal History* (*Oesterreichische Reichs- und Rechtsgeschichte*), 1896, p. 158 ff. W. Erben, *The Levy of Albrecht V of Austria against the Hussites* (*Das Aufgebot Albrechts V. von Oesterreich gegen die Hussiten*), *Mitteilungen des Instituts für Oesterreichische Geschichtsforschung*, Vol. 23 (1902).

12. According to Erben in the cited work—not 1426.

13. Werunsky, *Oesterreichische Reichs- und Rechtsgeschichte*, p. 158.

Chapter II

Dismounted Knights and Marksmen

BATTLE OF CRÉCY[1]
26 AUGUST 1346

The kings of England strove to unite the two large islands under their scepter, to join Wales, Scotland, and Ireland to their country. In the same way, the kings of France attempted to gain actual domination of the feudal principalities, which were subordinated to the crown practically in name only. But each of the two neighboring kingdoms sought to hinder the other in its beginnings to prevent it from becoming too powerful, so that the areas whose separatist independence was threatened found in their need a protector in the rival of their oppressor. The Scots adhered to the king of France, and the Flemish to the king of England. The continuing struggle between England and France was at the same time in both areas a struggle between the central monarchy and the separatism of the regions. This opposition, in turn, was interwoven in numerous ways with constant class strivings and dynastic rivalries and alliances. But this struggle was pushed to its highest point when the older line of the Capetians died out and King Edward III claimed the French crown for himself and his successors against Philip of Valois. Philip's claim to the throne was based on his position as cousin in the male right of succession, whereas Edward, as son of the previous king's sister, had the closer, female right of inheritance. Gascony also belonged to him under any circumstances, as a result of his ancestry.

A naval victory which the English won over the French fleet at Sluys in 1340 had given Edward control of the sea. He could land wherever he wanted, and in 1346, persuaded by a refúgee French nobleman, he chose to land in Normandy. Since the French had directed their main force against the areas of the English king in Gascony, the English were able to capture without difficulty a number of Norman villages, which they plundered. That had the effect of a diversion on the southern theater of operations and disengaged the English fighting there, who were already in great danger. As the French king now turned with his troops against Edward, the English king decided to march overland to the area of his ally, Flanders. It is possible that he did not make this decision voluntarily. He had allowed some of his ships' captains to sail home with the sick and wounded and the booty that had been taken. But all the other captains, without permission, also made this journey, so that the English army was suddenly cut off from the homeland and was forced to attempt to reach friendly territory by land. King Philip tried to catch the army on the march. While he did not yet have all his troops assembled, he had his men destroy the bridges that Edward would have had to cross, thus forcing him to take long detours, while the French king assembled more and more of his contingents.

As a result of extremely clever maneuvering, and favored by fortune, Edward succeeded in crossing both the Seine and the Somme. When he had thus moved far enough to the north as to have a means of retreat open to him in case of defeat, he took position for battle facing his pursuer.

It is estimated that the English army at Crécy numbered between 14,000 and 20,000 men. This strength seems to be confirmed by the fact that the royal treasurer, Walter de Wetewang, drew up a roster for the siege of Calais, which followed the battle, a document that has been preserved. Wetewang's list shows 32,000 men. If we deduct the reinforcements that did not join the army until after the battle, the result is about 20,000. This strength seems so high that I cannot suppress a certain skepticism, but it is not impossible.[2]

Whether Philip VI was able to assemble an army of the same strength or even stronger during the six weeks following Edward's landing in Normandy on 12 July is not known. Those troops that had previously been fighting in Gascony and were marching up as fast as possible had not yet arrived. Even if the French army should have been smaller than that of the English, Philip's decision to accept battle would still be quite understandable, since he was certainly superior in the number of knights, and the continuing withdrawal of the English gave the impression they were fleeing and raised the confidence of the French.

If the meeting had resulted in a normal knightly battle, in all likelihood the French would have been victorious.

But the genius of Edward III created a new form of tactics, an employment of weapons that the Middle Ages had not previously seen, so well suited to the terrain and the strategic situation as to overcome all the knightly courage of the French.

The English army was composed in very large part of archers. In the normal battle reported in the sources, the marksmen formed a supporting arm for the knights. On relatively accessible terrain, marksmen, operating on their own, could not compete with a similar number of knights. If the knights drove forward speedily, they necessarily overran the marksmen before too many knights or horses had been put out of action by the arrows. But in the certain knowledge that the knights would soon be in their midst and that they would then be lost, the marksmen normally did not continue to use their weapons up to the last moment but sought to save themselves by fleeing before the knights could even arrive within the most effective range. Consequently, the task of the tactician was to hold his marksmen firmly in line up to the last moment, as they kept up a constant fire. For this purpose, King Edward ordered his knights to dismount and form on foot with the marksmen and the spearmen. If they had remained on horseback, they would have been able as individuals to accomplish more at the start of the hand-to-hand battle, but this direct achievement by the knights was now not intended to be the principal action. The main mission of the knights at Crécy was to imbue the mass of common warriors with steadfast morale, and this was done to a much higher degree when the knights fought on foot like the common soldiers. A small number of knights on horseback among the mass of archers and spearmen would not have given the latter any security. The common man would not have lost the feeling that the number of knights was too small to accomplish much, and if things went badly, they would dash off on their horses, leaving the masses to pay for the defeat with their blood. Indeed, it is expressly reported of no small number of medieval battles that the lords saved themselves and the foot soldiers were mowed down. As unknightly as that might sound, it still may not be branded simply as cowardice; after all, the knights would no longer have been able to save their men but could only die with them. The mood of the times did not lend itself to this solution. Once the battle was lost, even the brave man was allowed to flee and to use whatever means of salvation were at hand. And the mounted man could, of course, escape more easily than the man on foot. But the confidence of the foot soldier necessarily rose to its highest point whenever he saw the mounted man, with all the advantages of his arm, voluntarily give up those advantages. The knight took his name from the fact that he preferred to fight on horseback and was most effective in that position; his technical superiority depended on his horse. At Crécy, it was not the terrain that forced him to give up his best means of combat, as was the case in some other battles. It was the psychological-spiritual factor which opposed the technical-physical factor and overshadowed it. At a very early period, we are able to observe this tension in individual cases: When Caesar led his untried legions into his first battle against the Helvetii, he had his own horse and the horses of all his high officers led away, and he directed the battle on foot. This undoubtedly greatly increased the difficulty of his orderly control, but it was the most effective means of steadying his freshly levied legionaries against the savage assault of the Helvetii. In the battle of Strasbourg in 357, the Alamanni even demanded that their own princes dismount and fight on foot with the common soldiers so that, in case of a possible flight, they would not be able to save themselves before their men. In a fight against Godfrey of Louvain in 1170, Count Baldwin of Hainaut dismounted in order to arouse the courage of his men,[3] and in the late Middle Ages we frequently find similar actions.[4]

Edward, then, by placing his dismounted knights among the archers, succeeded in utilizing the volleys of arrows in a very different way from other knightly battles. The marksman continued shooting until the last moment, with the full certainty that, if the enemy knight still succeeded in approaching him, he would be able to move a few paces to the rear, and the dismounted knight beside him would necessarily take up the fight.

But Edward was able to increase this effect even further. He did not take up his position squarely across the road on which the French were moving up. Instead, he sought out a position where a ridge ran along parallel to this road on the left and was covered from a French attack by thick woods and a very steep slope on his right flank. Consequently, in order to close with the English, the French first had to deploy toward the left flank of the English in order then to attack up the hill. We know now, and King Edward also knew, that it is not so easy to restrain knights once they are facing the enemy. It would have required a very well-disciplined army to have the first columns that swung around from their march order to face the enemy line halt directly facing the enemy until the last elements had also moved up into the battle formation. Edward could therefore count on the fact that his flanking position would lure the enemy into piecemeal attacks to a much greater extent than would have been the case with a frontal position, where the approach march can be observed from afar. Each individual attack, however, offered the English the advantage of strengthening the effect of their arrow volleys time after time

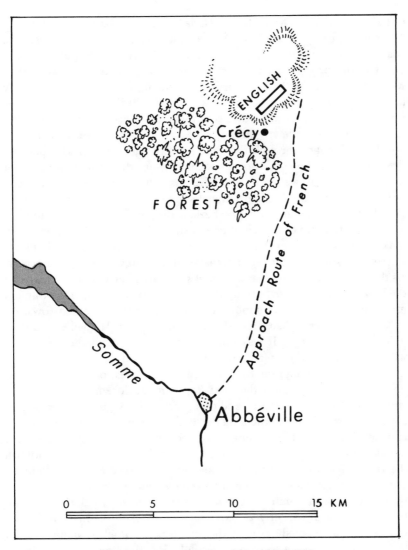

Fig. 5 BATTLE OF CRECY

as the arrows could be shot at the charging horses and men not only from the front but with still greater effect from the side.

Finally, the shape of the formation also deserves attention. Froissart reports that the archers had stood "in the form of a *herse.*" This expression, which has puzzled many, means nothing other than what we today

call the form of a chessboard. *"Herse"* means a "harrow" and also a
"portcullis" or a "palisade." We see no recognizable comparison in
"palisade" or "portcullis," but the image of a "harrow" is especially suitable. For the prongs can neither be very close together, because they
would then heap up the earth in front of them, nor can they be directly
placed one behind the other, because they would then open up too few
furrows. Instead, they are either so arranged that each of the ones in the
rear is always somewhat to the side of the preceding one, or the harrow is
not drawn straight through the field but obliquely, thus accomplishing
the same effect. And so, in order to allow more than one rank to fire at
the same time, Edward did not have his following ranks cover down
exactly but had them overlap somewhat and shoot through the intervals.
I shall pass over the question of whether it is possible in this way to have
more than two ranks fire simultaneously.[5] The third, fourth, and fifth
ranks probably shot only when rather thick masses were approaching and
were still at some distance so that they could be hit with a high trajectory.
As they came closer, the rearmost ranks of marksmen could no longer hit
them, but they served to back up the foremost ranks, to replace wounded
men immediately, and to supply replacements for bows and arrows.

King Philip's army had spent the night in and near Abbéville, about 12
miles south of Crécy. It was not until three o'clock in the afternoon,
while he was on the march, that Philip received the report that the
English were awaiting him, drawn up in battle formation. He decided to
postpone the attack until the next day, but the foremost troops were
already in sight of the enemy, and those farther back pushed ahead when
the news spread. And so the king decided to bring on the decisive action
at once. First, he had his Genoese crossbowmen move up, but they were
not able to accomplish much against the English archers in position on
the ridge. The fight did not become serious until the French knights,
charging through their crossbowmen and overrunning a number of them,
sought to break through the enemy formation in the usual way. If there
had first been an orderly deployment and the entire mass had then
charged simultaneously against the English, the English arrows would
hardly have been able to stop the assault. But the French moved up in
individual actions, just as they arrived on the battlefield, with one charge
following another and only at a moderate speed, because of the slope.
Participants in the battle claimed to have counted fifteen or sixteen
attacks. Each time the entire hail of arrows from the long front converged
on each individual group, and even though many arrows were not effective against the armor of the knights and their horses, nevertheless so
many of that huge number of arrows found their mark that only a few of

the charging knights broke into the enemy ranks.[6] Having arrived there, they were struck down by the English knights and spearmen. The principal attacks were naturally directed against the English right flank, which was closest to the line of the French approach march. In command on that flank was the prince of Wales, the Black Prince, who was only sixteen years old. At one point his situation became so serious that his father sent twenty more knights from the center to assist him. This minor reinforcement sufficed to drive the French back, since the number of them that had entered hand-to-hand combat was also only very small.

King Philip himself came so close that his horse was shot out from under him, but then he recognized the impossibility of winning the victory and left the battlefield with a small escort.

The courage of the French nobles who carried out the attacks is shown by the list of the dead; at their head was the blind King John of Bohemia, count of Luxembourg and father of Emperor Charles IV. Also killed were a brother and a nephew of King Philip, the counts of Alençon and Blois, Duke Raoul of Lorraine, Count Louis of Flanders, Count John of Harcourt, Count Simon of Salm, Count Louis of Sancerre, Count John of Auxerre, Count John of Granpré, and in addition eighty-three bannerets and some 1,200 knights.

King Edward's victory belongs to the category of victories won in a purely defensive fight, which are very rare in military history. The king had strictly forbidden any pursuit, and he even ordered that there be no advance, so that his foot soldiers would not be exposed to a possible sudden mounted attack in the valley.

The archers with whom Edward III won the battle of Crécy were introduced into the English military system by his grandfather, Edward I, as we have already seen. This did not constitute a theoretical innovation but only a renewed acceptance and strengthening of forms inherited from the past. Indeed, William the Conqueror had been strong in archers, and Emperor Frederick II even stronger. The emphasis which Edward I placed on this weapon, while it brought him his conquests of Wales and Scotland, still did not change anything in the conduct of battles and did not give the English any permanent superiority over their enemies. These archers did not prevent Edward II from losing the battle of Bannockburn, and with it, Scotland. And when Edward III first took up the great war against France in 1339, he had no idea at all of being able to defeat his enemy as a result of the numbers and accuracy of his archers. In fact, he made alliances and mercenary contracts with numerous German princes and lords, such as the counts of Berg, Mark, Limburg, Holland, the count palatinate, the margrave of Brandenburg, the dukes of Jülich, Geldern, Brabant, and even with the emperor himself, Louis the Bavarian. Huge taxes had to be raised in England in order to pay these princely condottieri. In addition to the large sums approved by parliament, the king also forcibly impressed much more money. He had a tax placed on the wool that was intended for export and took large loans from the Hanseatic merchants, to whom he gave in return privileges that were harmful to his own subjects. A number of the princes of the lower Rhine, who could not be paid the agreed sums in cash, were granted instead export agreements for specified quantities of wool. The rich abbeys, too, had to provide assistance from their treasuries. But as important as was the army that was assembled in this way, Edward still accomplished nothing when he invaded France in 1339. While King Philip VI did move against him with his levied forces, Philip still avoided battle, and Edward did not feel strong enough to force the issue. Philip had rightly estimated that the English-German army could not be kept assembled for long. After a short time, the princes stated that they had provided enough, and Edward had to turn back without having accomplished anything.

In the seventh year of the war, when Edward crossed the sea for the second time with a large army, he did not have the German knights, who were replaced by archers whose number was all the greater. But although the army this time was an essentially national English force, it was nonetheless a mercenary army. The necessary resources were obtained by the most oppressive taxes, as the levy was once again carried out in the manner of the Carolingian capitularies by levying the service-obligated men and then allowing them to furnish substitutes.

If the English king had not been able to force a decisive battle during his first invasion, he can have counted all the less on doing so in 1346, when his contingent of knights was so much weaker. If he perhaps originally intended to go directly to Gascony, his purpose in any case was no other than indirectly, by means of a diversion, to disengage his castles under siege in Gascony and his troops fighting there.

Finally, the battle was only brought on by the fact that the French king, encouraged by the continuing withdrawal of the English, had confidence in his strength and decided to attack them in their position, something he had not done in 1339, when the two armies faced each other in a similar situation at Buironfosse.

The unprecedented effectiveness developed by the English bows at Crécy we have attributed to the special tactical conditions which the situation and the commander had created for this battle. This point is not directly reported in the sources; they describe and emphasize the advantage of the bow as such, the fast rate of fire, and the effectiveness of the arrows. But the success at Crécy cannot have been due to the bow itself, for it would not then be understandable how the crossbow could have been just as important as the bow both before and afterward, and why the bow did not play any greater role in the earlier centuries of the Middle Ages. For this battle, we do not have any truly expert witness, who might have perceived the relationships and examined them in detail. We have only the statement of general agreement that the arrows flew "like snowflakes," which we must accept as a fact and seek the explanation for ourselves. A number of sources, including no less a one than Villani, who apparently also felt the need for an explanation, report that the English had formed up in a wagon barricade. Others (Rüstow) have interpreted the sources as meaning that the English had thrown up a small embankment in front of their position, which protected them as they shot at the knights. But a comparison of all the reports among themselves leaves no doubt that there was nothing in the way of such protection for the marksmen. It was, therefore, nothing but the skillful leadership of King Edward which determined the formation of the archers and gave them steadfast morale by placing knights and spearmen among them. But on the other side, it was not any lack of determination on the part of the French knights which caused them to lose the battle, but their lack of discipline, which led them into the enemy fire and to their defeat in small groups rather than as a cohesive whole.

It will help us to reach a clear understanding of the whole situation if we ask why Emperor Frederick II, of whom it is also reported that he was very strong in archers, did not fight any similar battle. After all, he was certainly the man to hit upon such an idea. The answer is found in the fact that Crécy was a defensive battle. If one intends to stay on the defensive, then the enemy comes into consideration just as much as one's own forces. The extremely confident and powerful French knights rode against the English formation just as they had ridden against the formation of the Flemish at Courtrai in 1302. But such a spirit did not exist among the knights of the Italian communes. From the start, their efforts were not directed—in fact, *could* not be directed—toward conquering the emperor in open battle. Rather, they sought only to outlast him and not allow themselves to be beaten by him. They would fight battles only if such good opportunities arose as had previously been the case at Carcano and Legnano. Consequently, the initiative and the offensive were entirely on the emperor's side. But Edward limited himself to harming his enemy by laying waste and plundering the flat lands or, on one occasion, to capturing a city that was not sufficiently defended, and he left it to the enemy to attack him.

Of course, the formation at Crécy was not an improvisation. The defensive power of the bow had no doubt already frequently been used on a small scale in terrain that was accessible only with difficulty. We have examples of this as early as the twelfth century in the engagement at Bourgthéroulde (1124) and the battle of Jaffa (1192). It also appears that Crécy had two direct precursors: the battle of Dupplin Muir (9 August 1332), where a number of exiled Scots under Edward Baliol, with Englishmen and foreign mercenaries who had invaded the country, were victorious over a Scottish force under the regent, earl of Mar; and the battle of Halidon Hill, near Berwick (19 July 1333), where Edward III himself was victorious against the Scots under the regent, Archibald Douglas.[7] The combination of dismounted knights with the archers appears in both battles, and one of the English sources, Baker of Swinbroke, says expressly of Halidon Hill that the English learned to fight on foot there in a manner different from the customs of their fathers, and to save their horses for the pursuit. This final pursuit on horseback, which we do not find at Crécy, supposedly took place at Halidon Hill, and that battle would be more important in that respect from the military history viewpoint than Crécy itself. But the reports on those battles do not seem to me reliable enough to receive the main focus of our attention in the study of military history. It is especially questionable as to how large the forces engaged actually were, and it is difficult to understand how the Scots could risk an attack against the position of the English at Halidon Hill. Crécy remains the historically reliable large battle in which the combination of dismounted knights and marksmen won the victory. The choice of the battlefield for this battle on the flank of the enemy approach march seems truly inspired, a position that was undoubtedly planned to foster the piecemeal attacks of the enemy, which then also increased the effectiveness of the archers.

Edward took advantage of his victory at Crécy to besiege Calais, which finally surrendered to him, but only after a very obstinate defense of no less than eleven months. On one occasion King Philip moved up with a large army to relieve his loyal city. But as the French approached, Edward had moved in reinforcements, so that he finally had fully 32,000 men. Philip was not willing to risk attacking such a force, especially after his experience at Crécy; instead, he moved off again empty-handed and left the city to its fate.

But even Edward, with his mighty force, still contemplated nothing further than the capture of Calais. For even if he had succeeded, with the most extreme straining of the resources of his widespread kingdom, in assembling such an unprecedented force as 32,000 men formed in the Middle Ages, it was still beyond his capabilities to maintain such a force for a considerable time and to carry on operations with it. Even after the capture of Calais, the English continued the usual activity of nothing more than wasting expeditions, which kept them so occupied that in the meanwhile Scotland again freed itself of the English domination.

BATTLE OF MAUPERTUIS
19 SEPTEMBER 1356

Ten years after Crécy, Edward, the Black Prince, the son of Edward III, won a very similar victory over the French. But first of all, we must again eliminate the large numbers reported in the sources. According to the accepted special study by Karl Lampe,[8] the English had between 1,600 and 1,800 knights, 2,000 archers, and a number of foot soldiers, while the French had 3,000 knights. With this superiority in the number of knights, the French moved against the prince, who was laying waste the land along the Loire far and wide. The prince withdrew until he found a suitable position. The king hesitated to attack, since he was still receiving reinforcements, and he thought it possible that the prince would have to withdraw because of a lack of provisions. Negotiations concerning a peace treaty were initiated. Then the prince feigned a movement to the rear; the French advance guard allowed itself to be lured immediately into an attack. It came under the hail of arrows of the English archers, was put to flight by the attack of the English knights, and in its flight spread panic in the main body of the army, which was still encamped in the rear. In order to save their honor, King John ordered the French knights to dismount and fight on foot. After resisting the enemy attack for a long time, he himself and his retinue were taken prisoner.

Maupertuis was therefore a defensive-offensive battle brought on and carried out with great skill by the Black Prince. The English mercenary warriors (even though half the knights were from the Gascon levy) were under better control by their commander than were the French feudal knights. Because of this, all the courage of the French was to no avail.

BATTLE OF AGINCOURT
25 OCTOBER 1415

In its strategic background, the battle of Agincourt shows still more similarity to Crécy than does Maupertuis. Again the English king, Henry

V, landed in Normandy and moved toward Flanders. Again the French sought to block his crossing of the Somme, and since they succeeded in doing so at the mouth of the river, Henry was obliged to march more than 100 kilometers upstream, almost to the source of the river, to a point where the river bends to the north. The French had to march around the bend, whereas the English had the shorter route on the inside, so that they arrived before the French and crossed the river. In 1346, after crossing the Somme, the English brought on the battle by halting their march, facing about, and taking a position in which they awaited the pursuing French. In 1415, by marching northward five more days parallel to the English line of march, the French succeeded in gaining a lead on their enemy and blocking his route, so that the English were obliged to attack.

The situation was therefore the direct opposite of what it had been at Crécy, and the battle promised to be of the greatest interest from a tactical viewpoint. For the strength of the English tactics of combined dismounted knights and marksmen at Crécy lay in the defensive; but now the question was, how would they succeed on the offensive? For their position, the French had chosen a narrow area between two forests, an area that was no wider than 500 meters, according to some reports. Henry V appears to have hesitated and perhaps wavered for half a day as to whether he should risk the attack. But then he presumably told himself that if he tried to move around the French, they would once again form in front of him or attack him on the march and would in the meantime also reinforce their troops, so that it was best to risk the battle at once.

The principal task of an account of the battle is to make it clear how the English were victorious over the brave French knights, even though this time they were without all the advantages that accounted for their victories at Crécy and Maupertuis, and even though the sources, including the French, are agreed in assigning the English a decisive inferiority of numbers. None of the earlier accounts has been able to solve this riddle. My account is based on a special study by Friedrich Niethe.[9]

The first point is whether we are to accept the numerical superiority of the French and not preferably presume that the English were more numerous. Of course, the sources are unanimous in stating that the French were much stronger, but even the French sources which we have were not friendly but hostile toward the defeated side. We do not have any report representing the viewpoint of the Orléans faction, the Armagnacs; all the sources are from the opposing factions. Furthermore, we shall also learn in discussing the Hussite wars that even the strength figures of one's own side are sometimes exaggerated after a defeat, and in the case of Agincourt the facts indicate very clearly that this was the case. If the French had felt strong enough to attack the English, the moment for such action would have been immediately after Henry's crossing of the Somme, where the two armies stood facing each other at Péronne. But the French allowed Henry to move by them and sought to stop him by the somewhat clumsy stratagem of challenging him to a knightly battle. This behavior hardly allows any other explanation than that they wished to gain time, because many of their contingents were still missing. But since Henry, in keeping with the English tactics, did not choose to attack, the two armies marched along for five days almost directly side by side. It was an out-and-out race; if Henry gained a lead, he had the choice of either moving without a battle to Calais, which belonged to him, or of turning around and offering battle to the French, as his ancestor had done at Crécy. But if the French gained the lead, they would force the English to fight an offensive battle, which was at odds with their tactics. Henry made the most difficult marches without granting a single day of rest to his troops, who had already been marching continuously for fourteen days (starting 8 October at Harfleur). Finally, the French proved to be faster—but at the price of preventing their reinforcements from catching up under such march conditions. The constable, d'Albret, may have consoled himself with the thought that the movement toward the north at least brought them closer to the duke of Brabant, who was on the way with reinforcements, and when the French took position at Agincourt, his arrival was no doubt expected hour by hour. We learn, however, that in the end only the duke himself appeared at the last minute on the battlefield, while his knights took no part in the fight. All these points force us to the conclusion that in the six days following the crossing of the Somme by the English, the French had received no significant reinforcements and that they were therefore also weak at Agincourt, and not strong, as stated in the sources. The fact that Henry was still hesitant about attacking them is sufficiently explained by the defensive character of the English tactics. Niethe estimates a strength of some 9,000 men for the English, including 1,000 knights, and between 4,000 and 6,000 men for the French.[10] He assumes that Henry did not have any dismounted spearmen but, aside from the armored horsemen, only archers, who also carried some kind or other of close-combat weapon in addition to their bow.

In keeping with their defensive plan, the French had some of their knights dismount; the crossbowmen were formed with them and the foot soldiers. But since such a formation in a purely defensive action would have been exposed without protection to the fire of the numerous English archers, two sections of mounted knights remained on the two flanks, so that, in case the English archers actually risked moving up, they could counterattack and ride them down.

This formation seems to have been well planned, but it suffered from basic errors. It was based on the assumption, quite correct of itself, that in the open field archers cannot withstand a mounted attack. But it is also a question of the strength of the two sides. The French mounted units that were supposed to attack the archers were only a part of the French army, and in their advance they encountered the total strength of the English, whereas the main part of their own army waited inactively in the defensive position. The battle plan of the French, therefore, resulted in splintering of their forces. The strategic situation had imposed the defensive on the French. If they had been anywhere nearly as strong in marksmen as the English, they would have been able to win despite their smaller total strength. But the French were very weak in this arm,[11] and the defensive is a very poor form of combat for an army with close-combat weapons. The proper action for them would have been to move over into the attack with both their mounted troops and their foot soldiers at the moment when the English marksmen were close enough. This action was apparently prevented by the preconception that they had to stay on the defensive to the maximum extent. But the impossibility of a purely defensive action in the face of the English missile weapons was responsible for the partial offensive by the mounted troops, which could not be successful under these circumstances.

It would probably have been even more appropriate to attack the English somewhere during the preceding days of marching, since the French army, by its composition, was simply unsuited for the defensive. Henry had also foreseen that possibility and therefore had equipped all his archers with stout, sharp poles about 2 meters long, which, in case of an approach by the enemy horsemen, they were to set up in front of themselves in the form of a palisade, in order quickly to form a protective barrier. We shall see how the English, even though they were now obliged for their part to go on the offensive, still made use of this expedient.

Previously, whenever knights had moved into battle together with marksmen, the marksmen had been followed by the knights on horseback.

Now King Henry had his knights dismount and take position among the archers. In this way, he applied to the offensive the combat method that the English had already tested in their defensive battles. The reason for this change is to be sought in the numerical relationship of the two combat branches. Henry probably had eight times as many marksmen as knights. If the knights remained on horseback, from the moment of their charge on, the marksmen would have been left out of the action. That had been acceptable and logical when the marksmen, by their numbers, formed only a supporting arm and the decision depended only on the knights. In cases like the present one, however, where the marksmen made up the bulk of the army, the knights had to operate in closest conjunction with them, and that was only possible when they dismounted, no matter how uncomfortable it was for them to march in their heavy armor. In order to prevent them from becoming completely out of breath, the forward movement was interrupted by a halt.

When the English had approached within range of the enemy, the archers drove their sharpened poles into the ground in front of them. It is difficult to imagine how that was possible, since the French knights could well have moved to the attack at any moment, and they could not afford to lose a single second and a single bow, so to speak, from that short period of fire. Furthermore, any further advance by the English themselves was hindered by the stakes. But since this is reported by two sources independent of one another, and it is also specifically stated that the French horsemen charged over the poles, we will have to believe it and find the explanation in the fact that the French, obsessed by their defensive concept, allowed the English enough time to shift this part of their defensive tactics into the offensive. And presumably it was not the entire front that was covered by this palisade, but only a few stretches of the line on the flanks opposite the horsemen, perhaps a bit to the rear, before they had arrived within the actual range of the French. Consequently, the English had their center advance so that their hail of arrows against the French foot troops would force the knights to attack, leading them then into the volley of arrows from the withheld and palisaded English flanks.

Whatever the case, the huge mass of English archers, joined with their dismounted knights, succeeded, just as at Crécy, in repulsing the charge of the few hundred French knights. Then, as the riders or the riderless horses, many of whom were wounded, rushed to the rear and created disorder and discouragement among their own foot troops, who were just starting to move up or were even still standing in position, the English drove forward resolutely into their formation, with even the marksmen now brandishing their close-combat weapons. The French could not withstand the charge and were overpowered. Faced with the superior mass of English arrows, the French marksmen had already withdrawn into the rear echelon at the start of the fight. Many eminent lords perished or were captured, both in the hapless mounted attack and later in the dismounted battle, where any possibility of fleeing was eliminated for the dismounted men in heavy armor.

As at Salamis and Tagliacozzo, here too we have the account (Walsingham) that the French knights in their tight armor had not been able to move sufficiently and were therefore defeated by the lightly armored English without difficulty, so that one would have to conclude that a man in armor was less capable in battle than the man without armor.

RESULTS

After the events of the battle of Crécy, it seemed that the English tactics of combined marksmen and dismounted knights was useful only on the defensive. But at Agincourt Henry V moved up to the offensive with these same tactics. That was only possible, however, under the very special circumstances of this particular battle. No new tactics developed from this, and it is not correct, as some have believed, that the English foot troops formed the transition to modern infantry and that Edward III should therefore be considered its real creator.[12] On the contrary, this combined phalanx of marksmen and knights has remained only an episode, despite the brilliant successes it repeatedly won, and modern infantry grew from a completely different root, with which we still have to become acquainted. In the final analysis, the archers, spearmen, and knights of Edward III and Henry V were no different from the other archers, spearmen, and knights of the Middle Ages, except that certain of their characteristics were exploited ingeniously and to a particularly high degree, as new combat forms were created by the large increase in the number of archers and the better discipline of the knights. The dismounting of the knights, which was necessary in this development, was technically no progress, however, for the knight gave up the strength of his horse, and the phalanx of knights and marksmen continued to be incapable of withstanding a sufficiently strong attack by mounted knights in the open field. Movement on foot was so difficult for the knights that later, when it was planned to maneuver in this manner, it had to be specified how often halts were to be made during the advance to give the knights time to catch their breath. Olivier de la Marche, the steward of Charles the Bold, recounts on one occasion that the Burgundian knights were so exhausted from marching on foot that their pages had to hold them under the arms to prevent them from falling over.[13]

Nevertheless, we find that in the second half of the fourteenth century the practice of having knights dismount for battle actually became a custom. It was as if they used their horses only as a means of transportation and no longer as a resource for battle, except when they mounted up again for the pursuit or sought to reach their horses, which the squires had been holding, in order to take flight. The reason for this practice was not based on the technical factor but is to be found only in the increase in the psychological factor which had first of all led to dismounting for the defensive. The seriousness of the battle had risen to its highest point as a result of this procedure. Knights who sprang from their horses during the battle were burning their bridges behind them; in doing so, they were showing that they intended to win or to die. This heightening of the morale factor was probably able to compensate, and even overcompensate, for the physical disadvantage—all the more so as the number of knights became smaller and that of the common foot soldiers larger, and the latter were thus given increased morale by the dismounted knights and were presumably imbued with new confidence. We can say: After the common mercenaries had become so much more numerous than the knights that the direct, physical accomplishment of the knights became only a secondary factor, it became advisable no longer to utilize the spiritual force of the knights directly, but to apply this factor indirectly by raising the morale of the common mass.

Of course, it also happened (battle of Bullegneville, 1431) that the Burgundian knights refused to dismount. Finally, under threats from the Picards and the English, it was decided that every man, regardless of his status, had to dismount or be punished by death.[14]

I believe that we have also found here the reason why knights dismounted so much less frequently in the early Middle Ages.

The psychological factors that have been discussed are of a permanent nature, and we can say that they could have been utilized just as well in the Carolingian or the Hohenstaufen period. But in order to set this force free, there had to be postulated on the one hand the increasing numbers of common soldiers, especially the marksmen, and then there had to be the impulse that came from Crécy and the following English victories. It originated with the English because with them the knights were better disciplined and under the control of the commander, who was thus put in a position to carry out the innovation. And once the great success of dismounted knights had become obvious as a practical procedure, all thoughts automatically turned in this direction. It not only became a custom, but it even became something of a mode to demonstrate one's knighthood by separating oneself from his horse. This would probably explain why a French prince, the duke of Brabant, brother of the duke of Burgundy, who, accompanied by only a few knights, did not arrive at the battle of Agincourt until the last moment, sprang from his horse in order to fight with the others, and in the same manner, and was then immediately killed by the English. His grandfather, King John of France, had founded the Order of the Star, in memory of the legendary King Arthur. The members of the order were obliged by the statutes never to flee more than 4 arpents, by the individual's estimate.[15] This condition is so absurd that it can hardly have been followed from a practical viewpoint, but the fact that it could be established at all shows that the heightened knightly concept of honor at that time was close to becoming a caricature. A few steps further and they would have arrived at the hara-kiri of the samurai, the Japanese knights. We must be reminded of such excesses in order to be able to understand such an inherently unnatural procedure as the knights' dismounting for battle as a matter of principle, even in the attack. But finally these actions were so contrary to nature that the custom did not completely prevail, and we continue to find from time to time mounted battles or battles in which at least some of the knights remained on horseback.[16] How often and to what extent the natural limit for dismounting—that is, either difficult terrain or the desire to serve as backbone for the foot soldiers—was actually exceeded is difficult to determine, for the sources tend to speak of dismounting in situations where it did not take place at all or was at least not general.[17]

Even if only a significant episode, we may still regard the dismounting of knights for battle as a precursor of the modern period to the extent that this procedure represents a certain transition to the later officer corps. The officer in the modern sense no longer fights at all personally but only sees to it through discipline and example that the mass of men fight. In this psychological effect on the mass of common warriors, we have, of course, also recognized the principal reason for the dismounting of the knights; for the sake of this effect they gave up an important part of their own personal accomplishment with their arms.

NOTES FOR CHAPTER II

1. The standard monograph on the battle of Crécy is the Berlin dissertation by Richard Czeppan, published by Georg Nauck in 1906. The other accounts by Rüstow, Jähns, Pauli, Köhler, and Oman vary remarkably from one another, depending on the extent to which they follow one source or another. But Czeppan may well have definitively

clarified and decided all the significant questions. Several convincing observations on the effect of the bow and arrow are to be found in Köhler, Vol. III, foreword, p. xxxvi. Forerunners of the battle of Crécy are discussed by Tout, *English Historical Review,* 19 (1904): 711.

2. In a review of the book by Wrottesley, *Crécy and Calais,* which contains the source passages in question (*English Historical Review,* 14 [1899]: 767), Morris calls attention to the fact that the 32,000 men had been together only a very short time when King Philip threatened the English with his relief battle. Morris estimates that at Crécy Edward had 4,000 mounted men (knights and soldiers) and 10,000 archers.

3. "Ut sui videntes eum peditem, non relinquerent, sed cum eo tam equites quam pedites ad bellum animarentur." ("So that his own men, seeing him on foot, might not desert, but horsemen as well as the foot soldiers might be inspired with him for battle.") Gislebert, *SS.,* 21. 519.

4. In the Hussite war, the foot soldiers once refused to attack, saying: "If we are hard pressed, you ride away, while all of us have to stay." The knights had to dismount and fight on foot. According to Johann von Guben, p. 64, cited by Wulf in *The Hussite Wagon Barricade* (*Die hussitische Wagenburg*), p. 37.

5. See above, p. 411, the formation of the English under Richard the Lion-Hearted at Jaffa in 1192.

6. Comines says concerning the battle of Montl'héry (ed. de Mandrot, 1: 31): "The most important thing in the world for battles is the archers, but let them number in the thousands, for they are worth nothing in small numbers, and let them be men with poor mounts, so that they will have no regrets in losing their horses, or let them have no mounts at all."

7. Both these battles are discussed excellently by Oman, *History of the Art of War,* p. 581 ff. Dupplin is described on the basis of a study by Morris, *English Historical Review,* 1897. Halidon Hill is thoroughly described in Tytler, *History of Scotland,* 2: 32 and 454, on the basis of a presumably ancient manuscript, whose credibility, however, is not proven.

8. Berlin dissertation, 1908.

9. Berlin dissertation, 1907.

10. The Englishman Walsingham believes the French had 140,000 men.

11. That is specifically attested to by Saint Rémy, who was present at the battle.

12. That is the opinion of Luce, for example, in *Bertrand du Guesclin,* 1: 147.

13. In the engagement at Termonde, 1452. Olivier de la Marche, I, Chap. 25.

14. Monstrelet, II, Chap. 108.

15. Luce, *Bertrand du Guesclin et son époque,* p. 169. The knights vowed "that they would never flee in battle more than 4 arpents by their estimate, but they would rather die or have themselves taken prisoner."

16. A certain survey of the decisive battles is provided by M. de la Chauvelays in *Dismounted Combat of the Cavalry in the Middle Ages* (*Le combat à pied de la cavallerie au moyen-âge*), Paris, 1885. To be sure, the author is very uncritical, and the individual facts are in no way reliable. M. T. Lachauvelay, *Guerres des Français et des Anglais du XIième au XVième siècle,* 1875, seems to be the same author, despite the different spelling of the name.

17. For example, Thwrocz, *chronica Hungarorum* (*Chronicles of the Hungarians*), reports erroneously that the French knights at Nikopol in 1396 attacked on foot.

Chapter III

The Ottoman Turks

We have seen how the natural warlike strengths of the Arabs were replaced after a few centuries by those of the Seljuk Turks. Even before the Crusades had ended, the oriental world was overrun by the Mongols under Genghis Khan. But despite his mighty military deeds and those of Tamerlane, who followed in his footsteps, we can pass over both of them in our present context.[1] On the other hand, the peculiar military organization of the Ottoman Turks which sprang up from the ruins deserves a description.

They were not really a branch of the Turks, like the Seljuks, but, blended from the most varied elements, they were the band of followers of a great military leader, Osman (1300), and his no less warlike successors. And, of course, the Normans, too, were of a mixture of many strains.

The Ottoman Turks did not begin differently from other nations that had been founded before them in the Orient and the Occident. As mighty warrior horsemen, they subjugated areas and spread over them as a military fraternity or a warrior class. The original system of the Arabs (p. 207), in which the warrior group was supported by a national treasury that was filled by the taxes of the subject peoples, had already been changed by the Arabs themselves into forms that were similar to occidental feudalism and gradually became even more similar to that institution. Individual warriors were assigned areas whose taxes came directly to them and over which they exercised a certain jurisdiction.[2] First the Seljuks, and then the Ottomans, continued that system. But there were still significant differences in comparison with the Occident. As best I can see, we may describe them somewhat as follows. First of all, the Ottoman fiefs were always appraised and distinguished according to their monetary value. Second, it was much longer before the fiefs became hereditary. Consequently, in the third place, the official position, the government administration, was not taken over by those holding fiefs but remained with the sultan. The Ottoman nation, therefore, was more similar to the Anglo-Norman state than to the European-Continental. In neither place did true feudalism develop completely. But the Ottoman feudal system at its peak also differed significantly from the Anglo-Norman, because the fiefs, the *timar,* classified by their value, were actually granted again and again and not intimately associated with the families of the holders, belonged, so to speak, to the entire fraternity of warriors, the *sipahi.* The young man, as the son of a great fief-holder, did not inherit his father's domain but started with a simple warrior's fief. If he then distinguished himself, he was awarded larger fiefs. As much as the power of the sultan over the enfeoffed warriors, the *timarli,* was strengthened in this way, we nevertheless hear of hesitation even among them when they were supposed to obey the summons to war. In one of the subjugated areas, Serbia, it has been estimated that there was one enfeoffed *sipahi* for about every 40 square kilometers. In addition to the *timarli,* the sultans also had in their immediate retinue the *Sipahi* of the Gates, their life-guard, which we may compare to the Frankish *scara.* In addition to the horsemen, there were also dismounted spearmen, the Asaben, who, however, as was the case in the Occident, showed no outstanding accomplishments. As we see, even though these institutions had their own peculiar oriental stamp, there was nothing in them that distinguished this national system significantly from the other contemporary states. Osman's empire, if it had been based simply on the *sipahi* holding fiefs and those without fiefs, would hardly have produced the intensive vitality that caused it to overshadow so strongly the preceding Moslem nations.

The troops that gave the Ottomans their special characteristic and established and maintained their hegemony for centuries were the janissaries.[3]

The janissaries, "new troops" (*Jeni dscheri*), established in about 1330, were dismounted archers, like the English archers of the same period, but organized completely differently. They were a standing disciplined force. The English archers were also professional warriors, but mercenaries who, recruited for the purpose of a short-term war and discharged again after the peace treaty, either returned to a civilian trade or sought service with another lord, or moved through the country as robbers and vagabonds. The janissaries, who were also initially recruited, remained together permanently in the service of their sultan. Their ranks were reinforced by boys who were levied among the subjugated Christians, forcibly torn from their families, converted to Islam, and trained for the military profession through a strict education. The janissaries did not marry and had no family but lived in their indissoluble comradeship, which was at the same time a troop unit and an economic community. Each ten men formed a file and a tent group, which had its common cook kettle and its common packhorse. Groups of from eight to twelve such files formed a company, an *"oda,"* under the orders of a commander. In the fourteenth century, there were sixty-six *odas* of janissaries, which we may estimate at a total strength of about 5,000 men. Mohammed II, the conqueror of Constantinople, added thirty-three *odas*, the *"Segbans,"* and later a further 100 were added, the *"Jagas."*[4]

The prerequisite for the coherence and the character of this body was the absolutely reliable and regular system of rations. The Ottoman sultans continuously obtained the resources for this system from their subjects whom they had conquered by the sword, something which no Christian monarch was able to do at that time. The degree to which the janissaries were based on the organization for rations can be recognized in the grotesque titles of the officers' responsibilities. The commander of the *oda* was called the *Tschorbadschi Baschi,* that is, the "distributor of soup"; another was called the "chief cook"; and a third was "quartermaster." The noncommissioned officers were called "camel drivers." *"Oda"* itself means the "room" where the comrades slept together, and it was probably also called *"orta,"* that is, "stove," on which they did their cooking in common. The kettle was considered to represent the sanctity of the troop. In addition to the small kettle for the file, the entire *oda* had a large common kettle in which each Friday the pilav, the national dish of rice and mutton, was brought for Allah's warriors from the sultan's own kitchen. Each janissary had his wooden spoon pinned to his felt cap.

Not only the military spirit but also the religious spirit of Islam was nurtured from the start among the janissaries. The dervish order of the Bektaschy participated in the founding of this troop, and Bektaschy dervishes accompanied the janissaries into war as chaplains, as well as singers and jesters. The warriors wore the monk's felt cap with the insignia of a white, hanging strip of cloth, which was supposed to remind one of the fluttering sleeve of the dervish giving his blessing. Presumably the education of the youthful replacements lay principally in the hands of these dervishes.

Forgetting their parents and their home, these warriors knew no fatherland but the seraglio, no father or master but their great lord, no will but his, no hope but in his favor. They knew no life but that of strict discipline and unquestioning obedience, no occupation but war in his service, no purpose for themselves but possible booty in life, and in death, paradise, which in Islam is opened by battle.

In the monastic life of the barracks, discipline was so strict that nobody was allowed to spend the night outside. The younger men served the older ones without speaking. Anyone who was punished was to kiss the hand of the man who, with his face concealed, carried out the punishment.

In their equipment and their personal skill the janissaries were about the same as the English archers, but their discipline enabled them to accomplish still greater deeds. While we hear that spearmen (*Asaben*) were assigned to them at times, in order to fend off the horses of the enemy, nevertheless that apparently happened only exceptionally. The *Asaben* were not warriors of a higher status who were to support the morale of the archers, as the knights did; on the contrary, they were men of lower status. The janissaries were steadfast enough to confront any attacker on their own—not to such an extent, of course, that they could have opposed a free attack by knights in the open plain. Bows and arrows could not accomplish that. But they knew how to erect light earthworks in front of them and to dig trenches, behind which they awaited the attack. They left it to the knights, the *sipahi,* to carry out the offensive.

BATTLE OF NIKOPOL[5]
25 SEPTEMBER 1396

Earlier, I have pointed out the extraordinary importance of the site of Constantinople, which, in addition to its natural security, enjoys the wealth and the resources of a trade center and route junction (p. 195). This strength of the city is also to be seen in the fact that the Turks had already taken the entire Balkan Peninsula before they finally captured Constantinople. Almost a hundred years passed between 1356, when they first established themselves in Europe, and the fall of the imperial city in 1453. During this century, Adrianople was the capital of the Padishah, from which he subjugated the Serbs and the Bulgars.

At that time, through marriage with a daughter of the Hungarian dynasty, the son of Emperor Charles IV, Sigismund, the elector of Brandenburg, who was himself to wear the imperial crown later, became king of Hungary. He recognized the danger that was threatening not only his own kingdom but also the entire Occident and used his ties to provide assistance from all quarters. Since Sigismund, as count of Luxembourg, was descended from a French-speaking family, he also had long-standing friendly relationships with the French. His grandfather, King John, had been killed in the battle of Crécy. Now Pope Boniface IX, who was recognized in Germany, Italy, and England, summoned all of Christendom and had the Cross preached.

The success was so great as to be matched only by the Crusades. The youthful count of Nevers, a son of Duke Philip of Burgundy, took command of a brilliant expeditionary force of French knights. Venice promised ships. Germans, English, Poles, and Italians sought service under the command of the Hungarian king. Among the German princes were a count palatine, Ruprecht, and Burgrave John of Nuremberg, and with them were also city knights from Strasbourg. The grand master of the Knights Hospitalers, which at that time had its headquarters on Rhodes, joined the forces with his knights, and the prince of Wallachia, Mircea, sent reinforcements. The French alone numbered some 1,000 knights and squires, for a total of perhaps 2,500 men with their support troops. The entire Christian army may have been between 9,000 and 10,000 horsemen strong, of which, after the march losses and the garrisons left behind, some 7,500 may have taken an active part in the battle—such a powerful army that the pride and the confidence with which the knights made this journey and went into battle against the infidels appear quite understandable. We hear nothing of foot troops. The march was made along the Danube, while a transport fleet carried along the provisions on the river.

They presumed not only to drive the Turks completely out of Europe, but even to win back the Holy Sepulcher. Sigismund is supposed to have said that if the heavens fell in, his army would be capable of carrying the weight on their lances. What humans, then, should they fear?

At the Iron Gate, they crossed the Danube but did not move into the interior, toward Adrianople, where it would have been difficult to feed the mighty army, but moved on farther along the Danube, accompanied by the supply fleet. By capturing the Bulgarian cities, they were certain of luring Sultan Beyazid with his army and could then fight the desired decisive battle against him.

Vidin surrendered without resisting. Rahowa was taken after five days, as the Bulgarian population rose up against the Turkish garrison. But Nikopol was strongly defended, and the Crusaders had still not succeeded in capturing it after sixteen days, when the approach of the relief army was reported.

Beyazid was in position before Constantinople when he learned that the Crusaders' army was marching up. He seems to have taken some time to make his preparations, in order to let the Christians move farther into the region. Then he marched from Philippopolis through the Schipka Pass via Tirnova, that is, swinging around toward the east, apparently because he found on that side of Nikopol terrain that was particularly well suited to his tactics. He marched so rapidly that he himself appeared almost at the same time as the messengers who reported his arrival in Tirnova (90 kilometers as the crow flies from Nikopol). On the evening of 24 September, he pitched his camp only 5 to 6 kilometers away from the Christian army. The Christians were in position before the city, in the Danube valley, while the Turks were on an undulating plateau rising above the river valley toward the southeast, something over 2 miles wide and bordered on the right and left by steep slopes.

This sudden appearance of the Turks immediately put the Christian army into a very bad situation. If they had only had a day's notice, they could have moved onto the open plateau to meet the Turks, but now they had to move in full view of the enemy from the valley, from which a ravine led up to the plateau. On that day they had, to be sure, already halted the siege of the city, because a few reports had arrived concerning the approach of the relief army, but they had not realized that it was close enough to cause them to move out against it at once. It was not until that night that Sigismund went to the French to agree with them on the deployment and the battle plan. Presumably, this discussion resulted principally in a quarrel as to who would have the honor of striking the first blow, but it is possible that a question of tactics was hidden behind the question of etiquette. If Sigismund wanted his Hungarians to be in the lead for the approach march, he may well have been more concerned with their armament than with this honor. For ages the Hungarians had continued to have mounted archers, and they were therefore particularly suited for starting a battle. But the French insisted that it was their right to lead off, and they won their point. One by one, the various contingents and nationalities moved up through the ravine onto the plateau.

The janissaries awaited them in a position they had protected and strengthened by a light palisade, just as we have heard of the English archers at Agincourt. It does not seem impossible that the English actually copied that from the janissaries; after all, English knights did take part in this battle and were witnesses of the Turkish success. For the rest, the battle is more similar to Crécy than to Agincourt. The Turks had a favorable defensive position for their archers, and the Christians allowed themselves to be lured into attacking this position piecemeal, rather than with their assembled mass. Beyazid had had his horsemen skirmish in front of the janissaries' position, while he, with his *sipahi,* remained concealed behind a hill. As the French arrived on the plateau and saw the small number of Turkish horsemen and the archers behind them, they could not be restrained. They charged against the enemy, thinking either that he was no stronger than the troops they saw or that they were surprising him while he was still deploying. In vain Sigismund again sent word to them that they should wait until the whole army was in position.

The French knights easily pushed back the Turkish horsemen, who drew them within range of the janissaries. Then, after horses and riders were exposed to the heavy hail of arrows, the padishah appeared on the hill at the head of his *sipahi* and met the proud French knights with crushing blows. We may assume that space had been left on the right and left of the janissaries to allow the *sipahi* to attack without riding down their own archers. With greatly superior numbers, they simultaneously fell on the French from all sides and had soon completely surrounded them.

When Sigismund appeared with the Hungarians, the Germans, and the other contingents and entered the fight, the French were already done for, and soon the Turks completed their victory over the Crusaders' army.

We must leave aside the point as to whether the total strength of the Turks was greater than that of the Christians. The sources, which run as high as 400,000 men (*Annales Estenses: Annals of Este*), do not give us any reliable basis for an estimate.[6] The excellent coordination on the Turkish side and the ingenious leadership, both tactical and strategic, would be completely sufficient to explain their victory, in view of the complete lack of leadership on the part of the Christians. But a considerable numerical superiority may also have been involved, so that we can estimate the strength of the Turkish army between 11,000 and 12,000 men. Because of the steadfastness of the janissaries without support from the knights and because of the offensive of the Turkish horsemen, this victory, in its skill and power, was even more brilliant than the victories of the English at Crécy and Agincourt.

This comparison is all the more appropriate in that not only the tactical actions but also the final reason for the victory were the same in all three instances. Each time it was a victory of the army of a strong monarchy over an unmanageable feudal army trusting only in its courage. King Sigismund himself bore the least guilt for the unsatisfactory leadership, for he hardly had command authority over his Hungarians, much less over the French. But since the sultan had his troops much more highly disciplined and under control than was the case with Edward and Henry, his victory was also much greater than theirs.

The Christian army, with the broad Danube, enemy territory, and the closed city, whose garrison made a sortie, all in its rear, was as good as destroyed.[7] The count of Nevers was captured by the Turks; King Sigismund escaped in a ship and sailed down the Danube, eventually reaching home via Constantinople and Dalmatia.

If the surge of the Ottomans did not overrun the Occident immediately after the battle of Nikopol and Constantinople even continued to defend itself, that was due to the Mongol Tamerlane, who eight years later defeated and took prisoner the brave Beyazid in a great battle at Angora in Asia Minor.

NOTES FOR CHAPTER III

1. For a while it was even believed that the Mongols had to be credited for an outstanding role in the history of the art of war, particularly since there exist theoretical concepts that supposedly stem from Tamerlane. But in the final analysis their accomplishments were no different from those of other nomads, and Tamerlane's principles were without real content. For a summary of these points and applicable references, see Jähns, *Handbuch*, p. 698 ff. The battle of Liegnitz, 1242, in view of the legendary nature of the source, gives us nothing new, as far as I can see, on the history of the art of war.

2. P. A. von Tischendorf, *The Feudal System in the Moslem Nations, especially in the Ottoman Empire. With the Book of Laws of the Fiefs under Sultan Ahmed I (Das Lehnswesen in den moslimischen Staaten insbesondere im osmanischen Reiche. Mit dem Gesetzbuch der Lehen unter Sultan Ahmed I.)*, Leipzig, 1872.

3. Heinrich Schurtz, "The Janissaries" ("Die Janitscharen"), *Preussische Jahrbücher*, Vol. 112 (1903). Leopold von Schlözer, *Origin and Development of the Ancient Turkish Army (Ursprung und Entwickelung des alttürkischen Heeres)*, 1900. Ranke, *The Ottomans and the Spanish Monarchy (Die Osmanen und die spanische Monarchie)*, *Werke*, Vol. 35.

4. The *Segban* were supposedly formed from the sultan's hunting retinue. The report that this body was 7,000 men strong was, of course, a great exaggeration. And with this point there also collapses the idea that an *oda* numbered more than 200 men and the resulting ideas concerning the file and the tent group. Schurtz, p. 459. Under Selim I, 1512–1520, the janissaries are supposed to have been only 3,000 men strong, but in 1550 they were supposedly 16,000. Schurtz, p. 454. In that case, the "3,000" would no doubt refer only to the original 66 *oda*. On p. 459, Schurtz states that under Mohammed II the janissaries numbered 12,000.

5. The standard special study is the Berlin dissertation "The Battle of

Nikopol" ("Die Schlacht bei Nikopolis"), by Gustav Kling. Published by Georg Nauck, 1906.

6. Kling estimates the Turkish strength between 16,000 and 20,000 men. That would then be more than twice the strength of the Christians. Based on the numbers given by Schurtz, discussed in Note 4, above, he assumes a strength of only 3,000 men for the janissaries but believes that dismounted irregulars were also present, for whom the janissaries had formed the nucleus. I would prefer to eliminate completely these "dismounted irregulars"—Beyazid would hardly have brought along any troops other than quality warriors—but I would assume a greater strength for the janissaries.

7. Characteristic of the loose manner in which chroniclers treated army strengths is the fact that Königshofen gave the strength of the Christian army as 100,000 men but stated its losses as 200,000.

Chapter IV

The Hussites

For the military system of the Hussites, I shall first repeat the description given by Max Jähns in his *Manual of a History of the Military* (*Handbuch einer Geschichte des Kriegswesens*), p. 891 ff.

We read that the Taborites were divided into two groups, those remaining at home and those serving in the field. The former group carried on handwork and agriculture and provided the necessities of war, while the latter group only waged war. But it appears that the groups alternated in these activities.

Ziska's combat methods were completely logical. In his army there was no question about knights and coats of arms, or of jousting skills and courtliness. But counterbalancing this lack was all the more careful concern for the peculiarities of the terrain.

They zealously exploited every resource of the art of fortification, both by use of earthworks and especially by outstanding development of combat with battlewagons. This was Ziska's principal method of blending the defensive and the offensive in that effective and unprecedented method that aroused the amazement of all his contemporaries.

The wagon stronghold was a mobile fort whose individual members, the wagons, bound to one another with chains, moved along in columns. Two horses pulled each wagon, one of them in the traces and the other in front on ropes. The maneuvers were controlled by signal flags, which were raised on the leading wagon and the last wagon of each file. The practiced skill of the Taborites in the ingenious intricacies and evolutions of their moving fortresses proved to be unusually great. Usually the wagons formed four "lines" (columns), two outer ones (*krajni*) and two inner ones (*placni*). The files of the *krajni* were longer in the front and rear than those of the *placni,* and these extended lines of wagons were called *okridli* (flanks). They were intended, according to the circumstances, to be bound together, in order, with a single movement, to convert the march order into the form of the closed camp (*tabor*). But one could also form the most varied shapes with them, even while in motion, especially those of a V, C, E, or Q.

When the mobile fort was to be transformed into the closed *tabor,* the horses were unharnessed, the wagon shafts were placed against the preceding wagon, and they were firmly chained together. The horses remained close to the wagons so that at any moment they could be hitched up again, since the Hussites liked to move suddenly from the defense into the attack. They were in the keeping of the shield-bearers (*paveseni*), with whose shields the narrow spaces between the wagons were covered. On each wagon stood four threshers, who were practiced at swinging their iron-tipped flails twenty to thirty times a minute, as well as warriors armed with long hooks and a number of archers, crossbowmen, and musketeers. Lengthwise under each wagon there hung a plank that was capable of stopping small projectiles. Behind the wagons, in the alleys of the camp, columns of armed men were drawn up, ready to relieve the wagon fighters. Finally, in the alert area, the reserve was in place, ready to break out through a sallyport as soon as the repulsed enemy showed any weakness.

Pope Pius II (Enea Silvio Piccolomini), a contemporary of the Hussite wars, gives a picture of the combat methods of the Taborites which, while insufficient, is still graphic. He says:

> They camped in the field with their women and children, who accompanied the army, as they had a large number of wagons with which they drew up a wall-like fortification. When they moved out for battle, they formed two lines of these wagons, which enclosed the foot troops, while the horsemen remained outside without moving off to any distance. If the battle was about to begin, the drivers, at a signal from their captain, quickly encircled a part of the enemy army and formed an inclosure with their vehicles. Then their enemies, squeezed between the wagons and cut off from their comrades, fell victim either to the swords of the foot troops or the missiles of the men and women who attacked them from above, from the wagons. The mounted troops fought outside the wagon stronghold but moved back into it whenever the enemy threatened to overpower them, and they then fought dismounted as if from the walls of a fortified city. In this way they won many battles and gained the victory. For the neighboring peoples were not familiar with such combat methods, and Bohemia, with its broad and level fields, offers good opportunities to align carts and wagons, to spread them apart, and to bring them together again.

For this was apparently the most frequent procedure, and it stands out even more clearly in another passage from Piccolomini. He reports:

> As soon as the battle signal was given, the drivers developed their movements against the enemy, according to certain figures or letters that had previously been indicated to them, and formed alleys which, well known to the trained Taborites, became a hopeless labyrinth for the enemy, from which he could find no exit and in which he was caught as in a net. If the enemies were broken up, cut off, and isolated in this manner, the foot troops easily completed their full defeat with their swords and flails, or the enemy was overcome by the marksmen standing on the wagons. Ziska's army was like a many-armed monster which unexpectedly and quickly seizes its prey, squeezes it to death, and swallows up its pieces. If individuals succeeded in escaping from the wagon maze, they fell into the hands of the horsemen drawn up outside and were killed there.

In December 1421, when Ziska was surrounded on Taurgang Mountain and seemed to have a choice only between surrender and death, he bound his battlewagons together with chains, placed selected warriors on them, and moved down the mountain. In this way, he broke through the enemy, who did not risk attacking the moving fortress but yielded irresolutely, and Ziska escaped to Kolin.

One year later, Ziska undertook a campaign into Hungary. The Hungarians avoided battle, and the Hussites withdrew. Subjected to constant attacks from all sides, the wagon stronghold, several hundred vehicles strong with numerous guns, moved along for six days through plains and forests and across mountains and rivers. But as often as the Hungarians sought to attack the rolling stronghold, each time they were repulsed.

The preceding description by Jähns is based in its principal points, according to the author's own statement, on Enea Silvio Piccolomini, Pope Pius II, who was not only a contemporary but also had close relationships with those best familiar with the Hussite system. He was active at the Council of Basel, and he was close to Cardinal Cesarini, who personally led the last Crusade against the Hussites and who, at his request, had received an explanation of the Hussite military system during the peace negotiations from the Bohemian Captain Procopius. Enea Silvio was in Bohemia himself and even in Tabor, and in later years he himself had negotiations with surviving leaders of the movement. We cannot wish for a better informed witness than the pope-author, and even if he himself was not critical, his reports have passed through the sieve of well-trained historical critics. Jähns did not take his description in its principal points directly from him but through the intermediary of the Bohemian historian Palacky. Even the most recent author of the period, Professor Loserth, in his *History of the Later Middle Ages* (*Geschichte des späteren Mittelalters*), p. 490, gives the same account in brief. In his later work, *History of Military Sciences* (*Geschichte der Kriegswissenschaften*), 1: 303, Jähns stood by his earlier account and provided further support for it from the sources. For the offensive maneuvering of the wagon forts, he refers especially to two passages in Caesar, where that author already reported the same thing on the part of the Helvetii and the Germans.[1]

Palacky, the historian of Bohemia, believes that Nicolaus von Huss and Ziska, "possibly also with assistance from other experts, drew up a new system for the conduct of war that harmoniously blended in a unique way the ancient experiences and principles of the Romans with the latest advances in the art of war, based on the use of gunpowder."[2]

If the original sources had been lost, it would certainly be very difficult for historical criticism to take a stand against such a generally accepted historical description. Jähns was a Prussian general staff officer and professor at the Kriegsakademie, his *Manual of the History of the Military* (*Handbuch der Geschichte des Kriegswesens*) was dedicated to Field Marshal Moltke, and his *History of the Military Sciences* (*Geschichte der Kriegswissenschaften*) was written under the aegis of the Munich Historical Commission. He bases his work on the very best sources (Who can oppose the authority of Caesar when he reports a military event?), and the best historians stand beside him as compurgators. Nevertheless, this whole account is fantasy. From the very start of my studies of military history, I had the conviction, on the basis of objective analysis, that offensive maneuvering with wagon forts was impossible, but in order to reject these accounts with source material, it was necessary to find a scholar with knowledge of the Czech language. Each semester I asked in my seminar whether there was not a student of Slavic in the group. Finally, I found a Baltic gentleman, Max von Wulf, who, knowing the Russian language, was also confident of mastering Czech, tackled the job, and, as I may well say, solved the problem masterfully, although, since I was at that time not yet a member of the faculty myself, it cost me no small amount of trouble to manage the acceptance of his dissertation by his professor.[3]

The reference to Caesar had shown itself to be invalid from the start, since the cited passages do not say at all what Jähns believed he could understand from them. Wulf went on to prove that, even in the case of Enea Silvio, the passages cited by Jähns do not exist. The entire description of the skillful maneuvering and the forms of letters is first found in the work of Balbinus, a Jesuit of the seventeenth century. From his work, the historian Aschbach had taken a description in his *History of Emperor Sigismund (Geschichte Kaiser Sigismunds)*. This was taken verbatim from Aschbach by Meynert in his *Geschichte der Kriegskunst,* without naming the author and with the erroneous addition "reports Eneas Silvius." Jähns took his account, in turn, from Meynert, without checking to see whether that passage really did occur in Enea Silvio.

And just as the skillful maneuvering of the wagons does not go back to an original source, so too does the binding of the wagons together with chains while on the move have no basis in the source material. It is a simple fabrication by Palacky.

But the fact still remains that such a well-informed witness as Enea Silvio actually did write of the offensive action of the wagon stronghold and that his account is confirmed by a positive report of Andreas of Regensburg on the battle of Klattau (1426). But Wulf not only proved that these two bits of evidence, which are mutually supporting and seem unassailable, were based on misunderstandings, but he also discovered the origin of these misunderstandings. Fortunately, the report on the battle of Klattau by Captain Heinrich von Stoffel of Ulm to his city has been preserved, and it enables us to correct Andreas's account. As for the error in Enea Silvio, we shall discuss it more at length below.

I have gone into somewhat more detail concerning this chain of errors and their final solution for the sake of their methodological value and the multifold analogies to this that we find in military history. In most of these other cases, however, the clarification cannot be reached to this same extent from the sources, and therefore the scholarly world finds it very difficult to abandon the source account, no matter how clearly the error lies before the eyes of the expert. Livy's account (8. 8) of the Roman manipular tactics, which scholars copied for such a long time and which Mommsen refused to give up to the end, the formation of the legionaries in close combat with 6 feet of interval between them, which still hovers in the minds of some, the peasant armies of Charlemagne, the foot soldiers drawn up in a triangle—all these things, I believe, are complete counterparts to Jähns's account of the offensive wagon stronghold, the "rolling fortress." What happened to the "rolling fortress" when an enemy spear or arrow caused only a single horse to fall? Were the enemy armies content to let the Hussite drivers move through their ranks, forming the intricate figures indicated by their signal flags?

Just as Livy, through a misunderstanding, transformed a drill exercise into a battle account, so did Enea Silvio, according to Wulf's expression,[4] fail to distinguish between the march order of the lines of wagons and their battle formation. When he wrote out his account twenty-five years after the events, he blended the two together in a negligent and fantastic manner into the picture of a mobile attacking wagon stronghold. Thus we have here, as in the other case, an originally good source that has been distorted through misunderstandings in its documentary offspring into accounts that are monstrosities from an objective viewpoint. But those critics who do not have the courage to work through such situations but attempt through weak solutions and disguises to awaken a certain appearance of actual possibility necessarily miss their aim for true knowledge.

Before we go into the explanation itself, let us look briefly at the earlier precursor of the Hussites' characteristic combat method, the wagon.

War chariots occur principally in the most ancient period of history, before the point at which this work begins. Later, they appear a few times as scythed chariots of but little effectiveness.[5] The war chariots which the Britons used in the manner known to us from the *Iliad,* the "*essedi,*" are described by Caesar as very useful and effective. But since he himself did not copy them or take into his service Britons with chariots of this type, as he did in the case of the German horsemen, the use of such vehicles in military history remained too transitory to be drawn into our consideration. Let us only refer back to them now, at this point where wagons suddenly attained an unquestionably great historical significance.[6]

The wagons with which we are now dealing, however, have nothing to do with either the scythed chariot or the battle chariot that served in place of a saddle horse. Instead, they served exclusively to form a fortress, the wagon stronghold.

In the most ancient times the wagon stronghold was already recognized as a useful instrument of defense in warfare. In the *Phoenician Women* (v. 450), Euripides has one side protecting itself from the other by a wagon stronghold. Among the Germans, this use of wagons undoubtedly played a role during the migrations of the peoples with women and children, for example, at Adrianople.

In the Middle Ages, too, wagon strongholds are mentioned now and then. The idea of using the wagons that were taken along in any case as a light protection for the camp and a barricade in case of necessity was common enough. There is preserved from Bohemia a war decree of the year 1413 (consequently, before the Hussite wars) by Hajek of Hodjetin, a field commander of King Wenceslaus, in which battlewagons and the wagon stronghold were prescribed. Now, as a result of the Hussite movement, this traditional means of camp fortification suddenly takes on a new importance.

The Hussite movement was both religious and patriotic, a Czech national movement. A manifesto of the city of Prague at the beginning of the war proclaimed that the Germans "were the natural enemies of the Czech people,"[7] and Ziska said in a war proclamation that he was bearing arms not only for the liberation of the truth of God's laws, but also particularly for the liberation of the Bohemian and Slavic nation.[8] Some of the nobles, and the municipal council of Prague and of many other cities, also joined the movement. Those principally involved, however, were the aroused burghers and peasants.

We know how slight the military capabilities of burgher and peasant levies are. The knights scornfully tore apart such groups. Even the most powerful combination of religious and patriotic enthusiasm, no matter how high it raises personal courage, does not increase military usefulness enough to enable such groups to fight successfully against professional warriors—just as the consciousness of fighting for their property and their lives, their wives and children, did not enable the inhabitants of the Frankish and Anglo-Saxon kingdoms to defend themselves from the Vikings, or the Romans successfully to oppose the Germans.

And so the Bohemians, too, were not initially capable of opposing in the open field the German military forces that King Sigismund led against them in order to subdue once again his rebellious subjects. He moved up before Prague and tried to besiege it, but he was not successful. The crusading army which he led was paralyzed by inner discord, and the opposition of the country in its defense remained tough enough to force him finally to withdraw. He was opposed not simply by a disorderly mass but in no small part by those authorities holding estates of the realm, who led the movement. The numerous engagements that took place in this first period and in which the Germans were still victorious on many occasions give the same impression as other battles of the later Middle Ages, except that the Bohemian lords and knights were supported by numerous burghers and peasants, who had taken up arms for the religious-patriotic cause.

And so the war soon came to a certain stalemate, and the Hussites gained time to apply themselves in warfare and to create their own unique system through the war itself. The more conservative elements, who had initially cooperated, soon fell into discord with the radicals. In the resulting civil war, the radicals gained the upper hand and developed the new combat methods. But they were still not capable of conducting a large-scale offensive. The incursions into Germany did not begin until the eighth year of the war, 1427. This development is quite similar to that experienced later in the English and French revolutions. Religious or national zeal does not directly create a new, all-powerful army, but this zeal creates conditions from which such a military force can be formed. It was not until a number of years had passed that Cromwell's warriors and those of the French Revolution attained qualitative superiority. The successful opposition by the French Republic in 1792 against the Prussian-Austrian invasion was due much more to the remnants of the old royal army that had come over to the republic, and to the fortresses, than to the mobilized volunteers.[9]

The principal task of the Hussite leaders was to make their soldiers steadfast against charging knights. Their soldiers were armed with whatever weapons were at hand—spears, halberds, axes, spiked clubs, and flails—and had practically no armor such as helmets, body armor, and shields.

It was probably Ziska, a war-hardened nobleman, who conceived and carried out the idea of using the wagon stronghold for this purpose. At the start, it was no doubt the normal peasant carts that were pushed together, but later special wagons were constructed for this purpose. They were provided with strong protective planks; under the wagon, a long board was suspended between the wheels so that nobody could crawl through, and iron chains were taken along to bind the wagons to one another so that spaces could not be opened up by pulling out individual wagons. Each wagon had a team of four horses. Whenever they were in the vicinity of the enemy, the wagons moved, where possible, in several parallel columns so that they could be quickly drawn up into a rectangle. Shovels, axes, and picks were on hand to clear the way where necessary, an action that, of course, can refer only to the final moments of taking a position. Quite often a ditch was also dug in front of the wagons, and the earth was thrown against the wheels, so that they were covered. In both the front and rear a wide sallyport remained open, and it was probably covered at the start by special shields. Wherever possible, the wagon stronghold was drawn up on a ridge, and behind the wagons stood the defenders with missiles: spears, slings, stones, bows, and crossbows. Between the normal wagons, each of which had ten men assigned to it, stood the wagons on which were placed the firearms that had been in use for some time.[10] If the Germans wished to attack such a wagon fort, the knights had first of all to dismount and climb the slope in their heavy armor, where they were greeted with a hail of shots, especially from the firearms. Even if they succeeded in reaching the wagons, it was not easy to break through. They suffered losses without being able to do their enemies any serious harm. But as soon as any disorder or withdrawal became noticeable, the Hussites' reserve, held in readiness, stormed out the sallyport with close-combat weapons—a feat that is, of course, possible only when the masses, aroused by their religious fervor, have already been imbued militarily with strong self-confidence and trust in their leaders and the leaders have gained a sufficient sense of security through experience and training and have necessarily learned to control the troops. We must note and realize that not just any group of rebellious peasants would have been able at other periods to defeat knightly armies with an improvised wagon stronghold. The development of these Hussite tactics required the religious and national base on which good order, leadership, organization, reliability, and trust grew and thrived, as well as important men who knew how to form and employ such forces.

As a characteristic example of popular history writing, let us notice how Enea Silvio reported the circumstance that heavily armored men naturally fell down easily when they were attacking a wagon fort formed on a height.[11] He traces this back to a ruse of the Hussites, whose wives spread their robes on the ground in front of the wagons. If the dismounted knights walked on these garments, their spurs became entangled in them, and they fell over and were killed. This little story reminds us of the one told by the Romans, according to Polybius, concerning the naked Gauls and their soft swords, except that here the Gauls were the fools and the Romans were the crafty ones (see Vol. I, p. 305).

The great effect obtained by the Hussites with their artillery led to the belief that Ziska produced an advance in this arm through technical improvements. But nothing of this sort is demonstrable; rather, the decisive point is to be found elsewhere. The Hussites were not superior to their opponents either in numbers or in the type of their artillery. The muskets were placed uncovered on wagons especially made for that purpose, bound with iron bands to strong wooden platforms. Whenever the wagon barricade was formed, the muzzle was pointed outward, but in this position it could neither be elevated nor traversed.[12] The loading process was complicated and slow. During movement and in an attack, this kind of weapon could hardly be used at all. They were useful for the Hussites, however, because their tactics were, of course, based on awaiting the attack. As soon as the enemy was close enough, all the muskets were fired in salvo, and that naturally made a powerful impression, an impression that was probably considerably stronger than the actual effect. The supremacy of the Hussite firearm therefore lay principally not so much in the weapon itself as in the Hussites' tactics.

The battle of Horic, 1423, is described as follows in the ancient Bohemian annals:

> Ziska camped with them near the church of Saint Gotthard, so that he could take position with his firearms on the heights and so that those who came up on horseback would be obliged to dismount from their horses without having anything to which they could tie them, and with their armor they would be more heavily burdened than the foot troops. They moved up the slope and became tired as they stormed the wagons. Ziska awaited them with his guns and fresh men, and, before they could storm the wagons, he mowed them down at will, and when he had beaten them back, he turned his fresh soldiers loose against them.

They give a similar account of Ziska's battles in Hungary in 1423:

> But once they had started to attack him, as the horsemen dismounted and charged against him on foot, they were beaten down by him. For the skill of horsemen in battle is different from that of the foot soldiers, because it is something to which they are not accustomed.[13]

Ziska also gradually created a body of mounted troops by "picking out," in the expression of a chronicle, the best suited of the Taborites, "the knightly soldiers," and giving them the equipment of captured knights. While they never became important and could not stand up to the enemy on their own, they were still helpful in supporting the foot troops and exploiting success. They were normally formed inside the wagon stronghold, toward the rear, and they dashed out the rear gate when the foot troops broke out of the forward one. Riding around the sides of the wagon fort, they sought to attack the enemy in the flanks or to take up the pursuit.

It was of decisive importance in a Hussite battle that the right moment be chosen for the sortie. It happened a number of times that this took place too soon, and the enemy, who was not yet sufficiently shaken by his unsuccessful attack on the wagon stronghold, himself attacked the troops who sallied forth and overpowered them outside the fortification, where they were without their protection. Or it even happened that the Hussites were intentionally lured out by a feigned flight and were then attacked and defeated by troops held ready for that purpose.[14] That happened at Nachod in 1427 to a part of the Orphan Army and at Waidhofen in Austria in 1431 to the Taborites.

The account of a regular alternation between the Hussite home group and field group is incorrect, just as incorrect as was the account of the ancient Germans, of whom the Romans reported something similar. Rather, from the original overall popular movement, the truly warlike element gradually separated itself and was organized independently, so that it became a standing army. Those who were most strongly aroused by the spirit of the movement assembled in Southern Bohemia on the Luschnitz with their wives and children, and there, as God's army, they erected a camp they called Tabor, from the inspiration of the Old Testament. In addition to the Taborites, the city of Prague formed its own army.

While Ziska was still living, a point of discord once arose among the Taborites, and after his death in 1424 the dissent became constant. Those who were faithful to Ziska called themselves the "orphans," because in his death they had lost their father. Procopius the Priest, or the Bald, became the leader of the other faction, which was called the Taborites in the more narrow sense. The army of Prague always had the character of a people's levy, but the two Taborite armies took on the character of permanent large military fraternities and steadily developed into professional soldiers with all their virtues and soon also their vices. They represented the real Hussite military system and the Hussite art of war, which terrified the world and lived on in the legend. From time to time, each of these two armies strengthened itself through a special levy from the regions and towns dominated by their adherents. In contrast to the field army, which was then called the "great Tabor," the levy from their area was called the "house community" or the "old Tabor."[15] All in all, then, we must distinguish between five different armies, two of a standing type and three consisting of levies, but they were never all together in a battle. The individual army can probably be estimated at a strength between 5,000 and 6,000 men, hardly ever more than that, but occasionally probably considerably smaller. A few times three such armies were together, for example, in the battle of Aussig in 1426 and the battle of Glatz in 1428.[16] At the time of the invasion of Germany in 1430, all the Hussite armies, the entire Bohemian armed forces, were supposedly together; and in 1431 at Tauss it was the total Bohemian force that caused the crusading army to take flight. Whenever a large mass was assembled, they broke up on the march. The difficulty of moving with many thousands on a single road, with which we are familiar, must have been especially great here, where a particularly large train of women and children was following the movement, and there were also battlewagons in addition to the vehicles for rations and baggage.

Once the warlike character had gained the upper hand and had become completely dominant, the Hussites were preceded by a wave of fear so that the Germans dispersed before them whenever they simply heard their battle song from afar. Such a Hussite movement must have been very similar in both its interior and exterior aspects to the moves of the Cimbri and Teutones or to an army of the *Völkerwanderung*.

The weakness of the Hussite wagon-stronghold tactics is obvious. It is similar to that which was also inherent in the tactics developed by the English kings—that is, it could only be used defensively. Indeed, the wagon fort was much weaker than the English combination of marksmen and dismounted knights, because it was much more cumbersome and because it could not even be used offensively by way of exception. But despite this one-sided defensive applicability and despite its cumbersomeness, the wagon stronghold was still of great importance because, on the one hand, it made possible a strong effective use of missile weapons, including firearms, which had been invented a short time previously, and, on the other hand, it gave an independent and strong significance particularly to the common, unarmored foot troops with their close-combat weapons, including even spiked clubs and flails. The protection offered by the wagon fort, then the sortie, and then the victory—this sequence gave the Hussites a strength of morale that led still further—not to the creation of an organized infantry that would basically dare to face up to knights in the open field without the protection of the wagon fort, to be sure—but to occasional offensive actions under favorable circumstances. In light of the character of the opposing armies, such actions were sufficient to enable them to win the most decisive successes and to create at times for the heretics the reputation of being invincible.

Again, as we have found everywhere, a proper understanding of the Hussite wars has been made particularly difficult as a result of false army strengths. But these did not consist so much of exaggerations of the strength of the Hussites, as one might expect, for this occurred only occasionally. More remarkably, it was precisely the opposite, exaggerations in the German chronicles of the strength of the German armies which were defeated by the Hussites. It is no doubt not entirely unnatural that whenever the defeated side itself acknowledges having lost to a much smaller army, the immediate tendency is to consider that as credible. But there is no doubt at all that such is not the case; in their grief and their terror of the fearfulness of the Hussites, the German chroniclers took a masochistic joy in exaggerating their own defeats by giving the strength of their own armies as much too large.[17] The second Christian army, which invaded Bohemia in 1421 via Eger, moved to Saaz, and turned back without fighting when Ziska approached with the Bohemians, was said by a participant to consist of 100,000 horsemen and "the wagons and foot troops."[18] In general agreement with this report, another source estimates the army strength at 200,000 men and more.[19] But, by chance, a letter has been preserved in which it is reported that the heralds had estimated the army strength and found "that we have among the knights around 4,000 knights and serving men."[20] That was certainly a stately army, since we must also add the foot troops to that number. But when Saaz courageously withstood the siege for several weeks, individual contingents willfully moved away, and the remainder of the army finally did not feel strong enough to do battle with the approaching Bohemians but, instead, also took up the withdrawal.

In 1426 at the diet in Nuremberg, Sigismund called for an army of 6,000 *gleves*. The princes replied that such a large army could not be assembled in Germany and could not be fed in Bohemia.[21] They were willing to provide 3,000 or 4,000 *gleves*, of which 1,000 should be made available by the cities. The latter, however, were unwilling to provide even nearly that number.[22]

The largest pitched battle that the Germans lost against the Hussites was the battle of Aussig on 16 June 1426. The Germans moved up to relieve the Bohemian city of Aussig on the Elbe, which was loyal to them and was being besieged by the Hussites. The army was composed almost entirely of men from Meissen and Thuringia, with an additional force from Lausitz. We have authentic information that the main body was composed of 1,106 horses and a total of 8,000 men; with the additional contingents, the army could hardly have exceeded a total of 12,000 men. It was quite generally agreed that the Hussites had 25,000 men. That may well be too large a figure, even though both Taborite armies and the Prague levy were on hand. In any case, the Hussites were considerably stronger. The princess elector of Saxony had not been wrong when, in her speech to the departing warriors, she had requested that they not "become hesitant or fearful because of the mass of their enemies." The chroniclers, however, attribute 100,000 men to the Saxons, and Matthias Döring claims there were five Germans for each Bohemian.[23]

Despite their smaller numbers, the Saxons attempted to storm the

Hussite wagon fort and even succeeded in penetrating at one spot, but they were finally defeated with heavy losses (between 3,000 and 4,000 men) when Procopius led his men out for a sortie.

In 1427 an army said by a number of chronicles to be between 160,000 and 200,000 men strong, under the command of Elector Frederick I of Brandenburg, again invaded Bohemia.[24] Against this estimate, we have the statements by Windecke in his *Life of Sigismund* (*Leben Sigismunds*) and by a participant, the knight Heinrich von Stoffel, who reported to the city council in Ulm from the field camp that the army was "quite small." When the Hussites approached as this army was besieging the small town of Mies, the army took flight, despite the strong efforts of the elector and the cardinal of England to have it stand fast.

In 1431 the German diet decided to raise a levy of no fewer than 8,200 *gleves*. But from the start this number was illusory, for a part of the number was allocated to Burgundy, Savoy, and the Teutonic Knights, and it was known in advance that they would not send anybody. Almost more illusory than that was the further decision that, in addition to the mounted men, one out of twenty-five men from the closer regions and one out of fifty men from the more distant areas would move out as foot soldiers.[25] I have found no basis to determine how large the assembled army actually was. Applying the tests with which we have become familiar, we can place no credence in the numbers given in the chronicles (for example, 90,000 foot soldiers and 40,000 mounted men). Although the Palatinate, Hesse, and other parts of the empire also failed to send their contingents, and Austria and Saxony attacked in another area, the imperial army that Frederick of Brandenburg again led out may still have been considerably stronger than the one that had fled at Mies in 1427. But whether it was also stronger than the Hussite army that now confronted it at Tauss and before which it fled in exactly the same way as at Mies, without fighting, cannot be determined.[26]

We should not be surprised that the mighty German Empire did not assemble any larger armies if we remember in what condition the German imperial organization was at that time. With respect to many regions and cities, it was not certain whether or not they really belonged to the empire. The imperial body was completely dissolved and was without any definite and permanent institutions. While the diet was deciding on the war against the Hussites, the electors of Mainz and Cologne were declaring war on the landgrave of Hesse (1427). In 1428, when the taxes for the Hussite war were announced, the bishop of Augsburg, for example, collected 3,000 guilders from his clerics, but he did not turn this sum over, since he himself was threatened by the Appenzeller war. The small amount of money that was paid into the central treasury was used up for emissaries to warn the recalcitrants, for neither princes nor nobles nor free cities gave anything—"neither little nor much," as a contemporary expressed it.[27]

How is it possible for the chronicles to report at this same time on the gigantic armies that the Germans supposedly raised against the heretics?

The tendency of mankind to exaggerate is ineradicable. If a defeat has been so great that no bombast can eliminate it or cover it up, the distortion swings to the other side, and he who can no longer find satisfaction in boasting finds it in lamenting. The Hussites came only once to the Electoral March of Brandenburg; in 1432 they stood for a day before Bernau, attacked in vain the strongly walled city, and then withdrew, undefeated.[28] Likewise, in Saxony they appeared only once on the right bank and once on the left of the Elbe. They never moved as far as Naumburg.

Since the Hussites derived such great advantages from their wagon fort, the Germans decided to copy this practice, but with the Germans it never reached the point of the interesting drama of having two armies with wagon forts, each of which would therefore leave the attack to the other, maneuver against one another. At Aussig the Saxons attacked the Bohemians without delay, and the two crusading armies of 1429 and 1431 took to their heels without awaiting the arrival of the Bohemians. But when the Bohemians themselves invaded Germany, there were no armies on hand that could have opposed them, and only the fortified places were defended.

In this manner, offensive campaigns could be conducted with purely defensive tactics.

All the wild fantasizing into which the legends and the later descriptions fell—the encircling of the enemy with the wagons, the complicated figures, the chaining together of the wagons on the move, the rolling fortress—can be traced back to a single original error: that the wagon fort was employed offensively. It was nothing more—could not possibly be more—than a defensive protection for foot troops who did not yet dare to face knights in the open field. Precisely because a wagon stronghold is much too cumbersome ever to be used offensively, these tactics were not capable of further development, and in the history of the art of war the Hussite method of warfare forms not a phase of development, but only an episode. The erroneous belief that the wagon fort moved out offensively is actually already found, as we have seen, in the most important original source of the period, the works of Enea Silvio. But this author, who would have been in such a good position to assemble the best and most accurate reports, had too little appreciation for such realities to grasp and substantiate from a truly historical viewpoint the picture that his fantasy developed like a fairy story. In keeping with the general spirit of the times, to the effect that the brave man drove against his enemy and attacked him, Silvio assumed the same thing for the famous, so successful wagon fort and developed his account accordingly.

The Hussites remained undefeated; they did not, for example, cause the Germans to react by creating a still stronger method of warfare. But they were not capable of creating an organized political body as a religious counterpart to the entire surrounding world, and that fact evoked the reaction in their own body. The two armies that first overthrew the most moderate leaders in the civil war and that maintained their leadership for ten years finally became so intolerable for their own countrymen that the nobility and the cities, including Prague, joined together, raised an army, and at Lipany in 1434 conquered and destroyed the two opposing armies. Both sides stood facing each other in wagon forts. The army of the Ultraquists finally dared to attack, was thrown back or moved back intentionally in a kind of feigned flight, and thus lured the Taborites out of their wagon fort. Then the knights, after driving off the Taborite horsemen, fell on them, broke up their formation, and, together with their own foot troops, stormed the stronghold and cut down the Taborites inside.[29]

The remnants of the Taborites, "brother squads," as they called themselves, or "Zebracki," continued in existence for a long time as mercenary bands that entered the service now of one lord and then of another, throughout all of Germany and as far as Poland and Hungary, and they continued this existence throughout the entire century.

EXCURSUS

For purposes of illustration, Wulf has drawn up a numerical estimate for a Hussite army (Dissertation, p. 38). He assumes a rather large, independent army of 6,000 men, including 600 horsemen. According to later reports, one wagon is to be assumed for every fifteen to twenty men, ten of whom formed the wagon's actual garrison. Consequently, there were 300 wagons for the army of 6,000 men. If these wagons moved in four columns, with the outer columns half again as long as the inner ones, each of the outer columns had ninety wagons. If we estimate a four-horse team for each wagon and an interval of 40 feet, there results a march length of 90 times 40, or 3,600 feet, which is about 1 kilometer. The two exterior columns, some 180 wagons, formed the outer edge of the wagon fort; the wagon was about 10 feet long, and so the camp, with its two sallyports, had a circumference of about 2,000 feet and an area of some 250,000 square feet or 25,000 square meters.

In this estimate, however, no consideration was given to the mass of ration and baggage wagons. With the large size of this train, the camp for an army of 6,000 men seems to me considerably too small. The provision in later wagon fort regulations, to the effect that a portion of the combat wagons, the two inner columns, were to be used to form a second inner wagon fort, seems to me quite questionable from a practical viewpoint. It would be more logical for all the combat wagons to be used for the actual wagon fort, while on the interior the baggage and ration wagons drew up in a second ring.

From the fifteenth century we have numerous wagon fort regulations, of which Jähns has given a summary in *Handbuch,* pp. 897, 943, and *Geschichte der Kriegswissenschaften,* 1: 304. See Wulf, dissertation, p. 9. But these regulations are to be treated with caution, since we can never know to what extent the theory was carried out in practice. In Philip von Seldeneck's composition (about 1480) *Emergency Arrangement and Use of the Wagon Fort in a Field against the Enemy and by the Enemies,* it is recommended, for example, that a few squads of exposed soldiers should be assigned to the outer columns of the wagon fort to make much smoke with wet straw and hay in order to blind the enemy so that he may not recognize the maneuver undertaken by the wagon fort. It is recommended that a mountain range best be crossed during the night. In doing so, the men are to work and strike the ground with their picks so that it will sound as if they are fortifying the wagon fort, whereas they are really withdrawing across the heights.

In a *Book of Musketry* (*Büchsenbuch*), with illustrations, by Augustinus Dachssberg, "a miller and a musketeer" (1443), the wagon fort is shown in the shape of a wedge. The illustration has the accompanying description:

> A wise fighter should have his wagons in good order: in the front, one wagon; behind it, two side by side; after them, three; then four, and so on toward the rear according to the strength of the army. The mounted troops are also to participate, and so everything is arranged with a point. If this formation is broken, then you are thrown into confusion.

The two passages in which Enea Silvio reports on the Hussite combat methods read verbatim as follows:

HIST. BOH. CAP. XLVII.

Muro circumdatas urbes nisi necessariorum emendorum gratia perraro ingredi, cum liberis et uxoribus in castris vitam agere. Carros quam plurimos habere, his pro vallo uti. Procedentes ad pugnam duo ex his cornua facere, in medio peditatum claudere, alae equitum extra munitiones prope adesse. Ubi congredi tempus visum, aurigae, qui cornua ducerent, ad imperatoris signum comprehensa sensim, qua voluerunt, hostium parte, ordines quadrigarum contrahere; intercepti hostes, quibus sui subvenire non possent, partim gladio a peditatu par-

ON THE HISTORY OF THE BOHEMIANS.

They rarely entered walled cities except to buy provisions; they spent their life with children and wives in camps. They had as many wagons as possible and used them as a rampart. When they advanced to battle, two [columns of ?] wagons formed their flanks and enclosed the foot soldiers in the center. Troops of horsemen were nearby outside the fortifications. When the time seemed right to join battle after the part of the enemy which they wanted had gradually been enclosed, the wagon drivers who commanded the

tim missilibus ab his, qui erant in carris, viris ac mulieribus necari. Equitatus extra munimenta depugnare, quem si forte quis oppressisset, fugientem mox aperti currus excipere indeque velut ex civitate moenibus cincta defendi, eoque modo victorias quam plurimas consequi, cum eam pugnandi peritiam vicinae gentes ignorarent et ager ille Septentrionalis late patens ad explicandas bigarum quadrigarumve ordines peridoneus haberetur.

flanks drew together the ranks of the wagons at the signal of the commander. The enemy whom his own men could not aid were captured and killed, partly by the swords of the foot soldiers, partly by the missiles of the men and women in the wagons. The cavalry fought outside the fortifications, which, if anyone had perchance attacked, the wagons soon opened and received in retreat. Then they were defended like a walled city and in this way they gained as many victories as possible, since the neighboring nations were ignorant of this method of fighting and that northern area extensively exposed was considered very suitable for deploying ranks of two- and four-horse wagons.

The other passage, *Commentarii od Alphonsum regem lib.* IV, 44, (*Memoirs to King Alphonse,* Book IV, 44), reads as follows:

Bohemi, apud quos multa plana, raras fossas invenias, equitatum peditatumque omnem intra currus claudunt, in curribus vero quasi moenibus armatos collocant, qui missilibus hostem arceant. Cum praelium committitur ex curribus quasi duo cornua efficiunt eaque pro multitudine pugnatorum et loci necessitate explicant, retroque et a lateribus tecti in fronte pugnant, interea paulatim aurigae procedunt, hostiumque acies circumvenire atque includere conantur. Quo facto haud dubie victoriam parant, cum hostes undique feriantur. Est quoque plaustrorum compages ea arte composita, ut ad Imperatoris jussum, qua velit et quando velit aperiatur sive ad fugam sive ad insequendos hostes ratio postulaverit.

The Bohemians, among whom you would find much level ground and few ditches, enclose their cavalry and infantry within wagons. Indeed, they assemble their armed men in these wagons as if on walls to keep off the enemy with missiles. When they begin battle, they make two flanks of these wagons and deploy them in proportion to the number of fighters and the requirement of the locale. Covered in rear and on the flanks, they fight in front. Meanwhile, the wagon-drivers gradually advance, and they attempt to surround and enclose the battle line of the enemy. After this has been done, they certainly gain the victory, since they strike the enemy from all sides. Also, the joining of the wagons is arranged with this craft—to be opened at the order of the commander, where and when he desires, either for flight or for pursuing the enemy as the situation will have demanded.

The information on battlewagons was systematically assembled for the first time in the document *The Battlewagon: a Historical Study with Observations on the Unique Features and the Employment of the Battlewagon (Der Streitwagen. Eine Geschichtsstudie nebst Betrachtungen über die Eigenschaften und den Gebrauch des Streitwagens)*, dedicated to tacticians and horselovers, by Kammby, Lieutenant Colonel, retired, Berlin, 1864, under commission of the Springer Book Company. Frequently, the author did not go back to the original sources but took his information and references from some intermediate source. He also fails to give any true historical critique. Nevertheless, this little document is valuable and very interesting because of the practical purpose which is the author's real concern, that is, to indicate the possibility of a battlewagon for the future, which, as an arm between cavalry and infantry, could blend the numerous advantages of both those arms. It is easy to understand that transported infantry could be very useful in some circumstances, but it is astonishing to what extent the author, who as an old artilleryman is a competent driver, believes that wagons could compete with cavalry in accomplishing the truly cavalry mission. This document fails to be helpful in the matter of the Hussites' wagons, because the author, who is caught up in his pet idea, has read it to some extent into the sources and so, from the fantasy of Enea Silvio, has drawn still another fantasy, one that, to be sure, is not quite so impossible but has just as little historical background. He imagines that the Hussite wagons are battlewagons like cavalry, which bring shock action against the enemy and break up his closed formations.

NOTES FOR CHAPTER IV

1. *Handbuch,* p. 943.
2. *Geschichte Böhmens (History of Bohemia)*, 3: 2: 67.
3. "The Hussite Wagon Fort" ("Die hussitische Wagenburg") by Max von Wulf, Berlin dissertation, 1889. "Hussite Military System" ("Hussitisches Kriegswesen"), by Max von Wulf, *Preussische Jahrbücher,* 69: 673. May 1892.
4. *Preussische Jahrbücher,* 69: 674. Dissertation, p. 21.
5. See Vol. I, pp. 162, 211, 218, 241.
6. Jähns, *Kriegswissenschaften,* p. 943.
7. Loserth, p. 489.
8. Palacky, *Geschichte Böhmens,* 3: 2: 361.
9. That the Hussites had already won a great victory over the Germans on 14 June 1420 at the Witkoberg (Ziska Mountain), east of Prague, is but a fable. See Bezold, *King Sigismund and the Wars of the Empire against the Hussites (König Sigmund und die Reichskriege gegen die Hussiten)*, 1: 41 ff. Loserth, *History of the Later Middle Ages (Geschichte des späteren Mittelalters)*, p. 490. This battle may very well be compared with the engagement at Valmy in 1792. They only repulsed an attack by the enemy. But that very success was sufficient and aroused belief in the future. Likewise the victory at Wischerad on 1 November 1420 does not yet show anything of the special Hussite combat methods. Since the

German princes had returned home, Sigismund had only his own forces at hand, consisting principally of Moravians. He planned to relieve Wischerad, near Prague, and was definitely counting on a sortie by the garrison. But since the garrison had already agreed to an armistice, it could not act. We may therefore assume that the army of Prague, with its reinforcements from lords and other cities, had a large numerical superiority. Only a small mounted contingent of the Taborites was present.

10. The *Mitteilungen des Vereins für Geschichte der Deutschen in Böhmen*, 31 (1893): 297, contains the description of the illustration of a Hussite battlewagon in a Munich manuscript by A. Wiedemann. Despite the very definite caption "This is the Hussite wagon fort on which the Hussites fight. It is good and straight," the illustration does not seem to me to be very reliable.

The regulation that the wagons were to move in four columns and the two outer columns were somewhat longer than the inner ones, in order to form the forward and rear sides of the camp with the additional wagons, is, after all, only theory, or it refers only to the last formation before the deployment. Entire marches in the prescribed four columns could be carried out in only a very few places on this earth. See Wulf, pp. 27, 29. The two inner columns formed a small rectangle in the interior, with entry passages.

According to Wulf's dissertation, p. 43, in Hungary in 1423 Ziska made a bastion in front of the forward and rear gates of his wagon fort, surrounded them with a trench, and placed muskets in them.

11. *Historia Bohemorum,* Chap. 40, as cited in Wulf, Dissertation, p. 16.

12. Wulf, Dissertation, p. 43; according to Köhler, 3: 1: 303 ff.

13. As an example of how far an oral legend that is correct in itself can lead astray an author who no longer understands it, let us observe what Ludwig von Eyb has to say about the formation on a ridge. Eyb was a Brandenburg captain and wrote his *Kriegsbuch* around 1500. In the chapter on the wagon forts, he, too, points out the requirement that they were to deploy on a ridge, but as the reason for this he says that it was to prevent the possibility of their being placed under water.

14. Wulf, Dissertation, p. 53.

15. Wulf, *Preussische Jahrbücher,* p. 680.

16. A tabulation by von Wulf of the army strengths shown in the sources is to be found in the *Mitteilungen des Vereins für die Geschichte der Deutschen in Böhmen,* 31: 92. Prague, 1893.

17. We owe this knowledge to an excellent treatment by Ernst

Kroker, "Saxony and the Hussite Wars" ("Sachsen und die Hussiten-kriege"), in the *Neues Archiv für sächsische Geschichte,* 21 (1900): 1. The following citations are also taken from this article and the book by Fr. von Bezold, *König Sigmund und die Reichskriege gegen die Hussiten* (1872-1877).

18. *Acts of the German Imperial Diet (Deutsche Reichstagsakten),* VIII, No. 93.

19. Palacky, *Geschichte von Böhmen,* 3: 2: 250.

20. *Deutsche Reichstagsakten,* VIII, No. 94.

21. *Deutsche Reichstagsakten,* VIII, No. 390.

22. Bezold, 2: 78.

23. Riedel, *Codex Diplomaticus Brandenburgensis (Documentary Codex of Brandenburg),* 4: 1: 210.

24. Bezold, 2: 110.

25. It is interesting to see from the discussions how confused they were on the decisive numerical relationships. It was proposed that the tenth man, the twentieth, and the thirtieth should be taken, but the men from Ulm thought that even if only one man in 100 was outfitted, that would still result in a large army. In 1428, however, they had planned to outfit every fourth man. Erben, "The Levy of Albrecht V against the Hussites" ("Der Aufgebot Albrechts V. gegen die Hussiten"), *Mitteilungen des Oesterreichischen Instituts,* 23: 264.

26. Bezold, 3: 144, assumes a strength of 100,000 men for this army, but without sufficient basis. Kroker did not discuss this campaign.

27. According to Bezold, 2: 153.

28. Sello, *Zeitschrift für Preussische Geschichte,* 19 (1882): 614, "The Incursions of the Hussites into the March Brandenburg" ("Die Einfälle der Hussiten in die Mark Brandenburg"). An excellent article, which is also worth reading for all those who would like to know to what extent a patriotic attitude can lead to the exaggeration of historical events.

29. The actual course of the battle may have run about this way. Wulf, *Dissertation,* p. 55 ff. Köhler, *Kriegswesen,* 3: 3: 394.

Chapter V

Condottieri, *Compagnies d'Ordonnance*, and *Freischützen*

Of the three elements of warriorhood that we encounter in the Middle Ages, the people's levy, vassalage, and mercenaries, the third proved to be the strongest; it increased from generation to generation and came close to being the one dominant element. In this development, however, there were certain distinctions between the four countries which we are principally discussing: Germany, Italy, England, and France. The mercenary system gained the ascendancy first and most decisively in England, but the main area of employment for the English mercenaries was not the island kingdom itself but France, where the English kings fought out the Hundred Years' War with their Capetian primary vassals and rivals and in doing so also forced the latter to constant expansion of their mercenary forces.

Germany, too, had its fill of feuds and civil wars in the thirteenth, fourteenth, and fifteenth centuries, but still not to the same degree as France and Italy, particularly because the German cities did not develop into independent states to the same extent as the Italian cities but maintained a more economics-oriented, more peaceful character. The largest and most important of the German city alliances, the Hanseatic League, never fought a war in that capacity. The wars between cities, which were waged partially by individual communes and partially by the various leagues of cities, still fell far short of the intensity of the wars that the Italian communes fought, partly against princes and partly against each other. Consequently, the German soldiers who followed the wars as mercenaries found their employment for the most part outside of Germany, in the Anglo-French wars and especially in Italy.[1]

In Italy the warrior class had probably already shifted to a significant degree into mercenary forces during the Hohenstaufen wars. If the proud Otto von Freisingen scornfully speaks of the sons of artisans who are knighted in Italy, there is no other basis for his remark. The movements to arm the people that were made in the years of most intensive warring and were occasionally resumed had only temporary success. The fight against the Hohenstaufen Kingdom was on the one hand a conflict of competing communes with one another and on the other hand a conflict of the factions within the communes against one another. Hence, this confusion did not end with the fall of the Hohenstaufens but continued from generation to generation under the old faction names of the Guelphs and the Ghibellines. The natural result was that the citizenry tired of political matters, and the power was turned over to the mercenaries and mercenary leaders, who became stronger and stronger and continuously more independent, freeing themselves from the political powers in whose service they had moved up and become great. The mercenaries formed close groups, either fraternities that elected their commander and their subordinate leaders, or the retinue of a captain, a condottiere, who took individuals into his service. These bands and leaders of bands shifted over from one service to another and considered themselves independent forces. The conditions again became similar to those of the *Völkerwanderung,* where Germanic warrior kings or groups of clans moved through the countryside, burning and pillaging or subjecting them to their own domination. Like Odoacer as leader of the German mercenaries in Rome or the Lombard dukes in the sixth and seventh centuries, in the fourteenth century clan chieftains at the head of mercenary bands or simple condottieri made themselves lords in the cities in whose service they had once been. Thus it happened with the Visconti in Milan, the Scalas in Verona, the Bonacorsi and then the Gonzagas in Mantua, the Estes in Ferrara, the Malatestas in Rimini, and the Pepoli in Bologna.

Other mercenary leaders contented themselves with extortion, which a Swabian knight, Duke Werner von Urslingen, developed into a complete system. Werner, who was called Guarnerio by the Italians and who had the ducal title because his ancestors had once been dukes of Spoleto under the Hohenstaufens, was the leader of a warrior band that the Pisans had taken into their service when they were warring against the Florentines over Lucca. Upon the conclusion of peace, the Pisans were concerned as to how to get rid of their mercenaries. They arrived at the solution of not simply discharging them, which could have caused them to become dangerous for the city itself, but of paying them a discharge bonus, at the same time telling them to move into enemy territory and live at the expense of the people there. This proposal pleased the mercenaries, who decided to remain together as an organized, free army with constables and corporals as leaders and Werner as commander (September 1342). They named themselves "*la gran Compagna*," "the great company," and for half a year they moved from region to region, forcing the inhabitants to pay them to continue their march, or, when that did not succeed, plundering and burning the area and seeking by torture to force those inhabitants who fell into their hands to turn over their hidden treasures. Every attempt through complaints and pleas to persuade the commander to limit the fury of his men fell on deaf ears, for he called himself "the enemy of God, of pity, and of compassion." Everything that was taken in the form of money as well as valuable objects, weapons, and horses had to be turned in and was divided into shares and distributed according to a definite plan, so that in the end each of the robbers departed from the organization with a considerable amount of property.

France suffered almost more than Italy under the large mercenary bands that were formed by both sides in the Hundred Years' War and formed a focal point for all the bellicose and robbing riff-raff of the surrounding peoples.

From the start, not only pay but also a share of the booty, especially of the ransom money for prisoners, was promised the troops. The less regularly they were paid, the more they sought to find their own pay. They refused to turn over to the king again cities in which they had been assigned as garrisons.

Many of these bands were not in the service of the king at all but were formed in accordance with the medieval right of feudal lords. Then, once in existence, they had grown at will and lived off the regions through which they marched or which they dominated from the fortified places they captured. They treated as independent powers with the various estates of the realm and provincial authorities and forced the latter to pay them blackmail to spare their land. They promised to move on if their demands were met, or they plundered cities and countryside. If they were supposed to move against the enemy, often enough they refused to obey as long as they did not receive their pay. But after the war they became completely terrifying, moving through the country independently like Werner von Urslingen, robbing and placing themselves at the disposal of some lord or another against his enemies. After the peace of Bretigny (1360), when they were uncertain in France as to how to get rid of the "extortioners," Pope Urban V, who was living in Avignon and was likewise threatened by them, had the grotesque idea of uniting all good purposes by summoning the bands for a Crusade. He negotiated with Emperor Charles IV and King Louis of Hungary concerning passage through their lands. Nothing could have served Christianity better; the west would have been protected from the heathens and would at the same time have been liberated from its protectors. But the bands had no inclination to agree with this proposal. An attempt was then made to move them out of France by leading them into Alsace, Switzerland (1375), and Spain.[2] Even those bands that had originally fought under the English colors had no hesitation about entering the service of the French. Whether they were English, Flemish, German, or French, they had a completely international viewpoint.

Gradually, these later movements wore down the bands that the great war had created, as those individuals who finally decided to return to a peaceful trade at home also did so. But with the renewed outbreak of the war, there also immediately arose the situation where one's own country could not be protected from the troops that had been summoned for the war, and when peace returned, it was impossible to get rid of them.

In England they were spared the terrible plague of these bands, since, of course, the great war had been fought exclusively on French soil. Germany, too, had suffered only to the extent of having French bands spill over their border a number of times. In Italy, as we have seen, some of the commanders of the bands finally established those enduring positions of dominance. In France, necessity gave birth to the decision for a sweeping overall reform.

In order to get rid of the bands, the French kings created the standing army in the modern sense.

According to the sources, this development was carried out when Charles VII, after he had achieved the first great successes against the English with the help of the Maid of Orléans, moved by the growing French national sentiment, proposed the great reform for adoption at a general parliament at Orléans in 1439. The parliament approved the necessary taxes to maintain a standing army of fifteen companies of 100 lances of six men each, or 9,000 horsemen all together. A rich burgher and ingenious statesman, Jacques Coeur, advanced the first monies and was the motivating force of the project. The best elements of the former bands were taken into the new "compagnies d'ordonnance," and they helped to overcome the remainder of the robber groups, forcing them to disband.

While more recent research allows us to summarize this whole development in about that way, the details of these events were, nevertheless, much more complicated. It was only very gradually that they took the form described above and then continued their development.[3]

At the parliament in Orléans, initially approval was not given for continuing taxes, nor was it definitely agreed that a standing army should be created for peacetime also, nor was the number of fifteen companies of 100 lances of six men each established. The decisions of this parliament initially only went so far as to deny the feudal lords the right to maintain troops and to have them provided for by the region; thereafter, the lords were permitted to have garrisons only at their own castles. Beyond that, only the king was allowed to maintain troops, to appoint their officers, and to raise taxes for their maintenance. The captains were to be responsible for their men; the bands and marauders that were not taken into the service of the king were to be pursued by everybody and turned over to justice.

Through the moral force of these decisions, so many resources were gradually assembled in the provinces with the help of the provincial leaders as to be able to pay sufficiently the reliable bands that they had or that they organized and with their help gradually to overcome the resistance of the other bands. For both the feudal lords, who were supposed to lose their military retinues and who feared the concentration of power in the hands of the king, and the bands themselves, which did not wish to be dissolved, offered resistance. Resort was had to the old method of leading them over the border, and they were sent to Lorraine, into Alsace, and into Switzerland. In Switzerland there took place the bloody engagement of Saint Jacob near Basel, where the Armagnacs, as they were now called, although victorious, themselves suffered heavy losses (1444). In the following year they moved back and forth in South Germany and fought a number of battles. After some of them had been wiped out in these moves, Charles VII, with the help of his outstanding Constable Richemont, succeeded in subduing the remainder. A few of the most rebellious captains were executed, and with the announcement of an amnesty for all past acts, the men were forced to return to their homes and take up their civilian occupations. The ordinances covering the organization date only from the year 1445, six years after the parliament of Orléans. Curiously, the first and basic ordinance has not been preserved in its original text, so that we do not know exactly to what extent the initial organization already provided for the forms we find later in practice. For our purpose, this does not matter very much. The decisive point is that, despite all the complaints that were raised on all sides concerning the unbearable burden, finally a permanent and definite tax system was nevertheless introduced. Even the providing of goods and rations in kind, which initially were still given to a great extent by the authorities and the regions, were transposed into money taxes, and with the regular provision of pay that was thus made possible, everything else was also facilitated.

The actual Middle Ages did not know, or at least did not wish, permanent taxes but only occasional ones, as a supplementary measure, according to specific needs.

Lacking a tax system, the kings had no doubt resorted to the expedient of calling all Frenchmen to arms in accordance with the traditional right to do so, while at the same time permitting a payment as satisfying this obligation, so that the levy was transformed into a tax assessment.[4] The permanent tax, which now came into being in the fifteenth century, provided the basis for the permanent, standing, paid army, which pushed out and replaced the undisciplined mercenary bands that had been recruited only for war.

The usual stereotyped statement in historical works to the effect that the creation of these "compagnies d'ordonnance" marked the beginning of the standing army in France and in Europe in general is not entirely correct from a formal viewpoint. For we have seen that the Carolingians already had a type of standing military force in the *scara,* and in addition the later emperors and kings always had a small number of warriors as castle garrison or immediately available near them. But these older watches, guards, and garrisons were organized and maintained on the base of a barter economy and were therefore strictly limited. The formation of the French "compagnies d'ordonnance" on the basis of a permanent tax system and regular pay is of itself, both qualitatively and quantitatively, such a great step forward, and particularly of such capability for development, that we may still retain the expression that standing armies began with the "compagnies d'ordonnance." We leave aside the janissaries as belonging to a completely different world.

In France, under Saint Louis, certain officials and forms for the administration of the mercenary system had already been created in the thirteenth century. At the head of the entire military system and representing the king was the constable, who had under him the marshals, the master of the marksmen, and the military paymaster (*trésorier de guerre*).

The logical organization of the feudal army was in accordance with the banners of the lords, in which the various weapons were mixed. It was impossible to strive for uniformity, either in the number of knights or in the blend of arms, and nothing of this kind was necessary. Each banneret decided in accordance with his own interests and his own fortune how large a unit he should have and how it should be composed in order to perform best in combat. With the mercenaries, the banneret had been replaced by the captain.[5]

The mercenaries of Emperor Frederick II, as well as the mercenaries who were raised by the Lombard League,[6] were already organized into sections under a *capitaneus* or *comestabulus*,[7] and the mercenaries of Edward I of England were organized into groups of 100 with a *centenarius* at their head. From 1382 on, there also appears the group of 1,000 and the name *millenarius* for its leader (in 1296 for the first time).[8] In 1264, when Florence made a treaty with two counts of Hapsburg to provide 200 horsemen, it was specified that they were to be divided into eight banners of twenty-five men each,[9] and in the "great company" of Werner von Urslingen we have learned of constables and corporals. As Charles VII of France created the "compagnies d'ordonnance," this organization was tied in with that of the existing companies, the mercenary bands.

The word "company" is derived from *cum* and *panis* and therefore means "bread comrades." Originally, it had no military relationship but simply meant "society," "community," "fraternity," as it does today in commercial language. In the militia formation which Florence gave itself around the middle of the thirteenth century, the associations of burghers, on which levies and equipment were based, were called "companies," just as in the German cities, for example, in Bern, they were called "societies" ("*Gesellschaften*"). The first use of the word in a directly military sense seems to have occurred about the same time in the writings of the French chronicler Philip Mouskés.[10] A hundred years later, "company" had become the normal name for the mercenary units we have gotten to know.[11]

It also appears that a definite scheme for the strength and command hierarchy of the "compagnies d'ordonnance" was developed and established only gradually. In the oldest ordinances we find neither the fifteen companies, nor the 100 lances, nor the six men to each lance. Instead, we find something to the effect that the captain was to be a man of means, who "had something to lose" so that he could be depended on and be held responsible for his men. In time, there developed the situation that the company had a chief who was usually a very eminent lord, his lieutenant, who really exercised the regular leadership of the unit, two color bearers, the *enseigne* and the *guidon,* and the *maréchal des logis* (sergeant).

The most important point is that the company was composed, not of individual warriors, but of "lances" (*gleves*), according to the custom that had become a fixed concept in the fourteenth century (see p. 270, above). The number of soldiers belonging to a lance always remained fluid, varying with the periods, the countries, the lords, and the circumstances.[12] Their strengths in the "compagnies d' ordonnance" of Charles VII are also reported in varying numbers—on one occasion a knight, a *coutillier* (light horseman), a page, and three marksmen, and on another occasion only two marksmen and a serving man (*valet*).[13] They were all mounted, but the page, who was often only a boy, and the serving man were not combatants, and the marksmen used their horses only as a means of transportation, dismounting for combat.

As important as the formation of the "compagnies d'ordonnance" was not only for French military history but also for the consolidation of the French nation, this army was still much too small to fill the requirements of such a large country. In addition to these units, there still remained in existence the levy of the entire body of knights (the nobility) and of all fief-holders in case of war, and this institution was also used. But these groups of vassals were now likewise organized into regular companies and received various levels of compensation, depending on the equipment they brought with them.[14]

As great as the role of the marksmen might appear, it was still not sufficient, with the type of training which that arm had had in the English wars. Therefore, the king tried to create, in addition to his other forces, a large independent body of marksmen.[15]

Back in 1368 Charles V had already ordered that the entire nation should practice archery, and in 1394 that order was repeated. Both times the order was supposedly retracted, because the nobility feared and suppressed the arming of the people.[16] It is probably more likely that the order had no satisfactory success, since bows and arrows could not so easily be produced in large numbers, and the inclination to train oneself in the art of archery was probably very limited. Consequently, the nobility hardly had any reason for being concerned. Now the king issued no general regulation, but ordered in 1448 that for every fifty households one robust man was to be selected from the community and trained as a marksman. On each holiday this soldier was to practice his marksmanship, and he was to be obligated under oath to take to the field at the call of the king at any time. Initially, the man was supposed to provide his own equipment, but later it was added that men of insufficient means could also be taken, and the community had to provide their weapons for them. Like the knights, they were organized in companies and placed under captains who were to assemble them and occasionally have them participate together in drills. As compensation, the marksmen were excused from all taxes except the salt tax and special war taxes. As a result of this freedom they were given the name *francs archers.* If they were mobilized for war, they received pay of 4 pounds per month.

In practice this organization proved to be unusable. The drill in the use of the bow and the crossbow was not sufficient, and, more importantly, the warlike spirit of the citizen marksmen did not prove strong enough to stand up midst the dangers of the battlefield.

Louis XI, the son of Charles VII, even if he did not formally do away with the *francs archers,* did let them deteriorate. Therefore, it is a complete error to see in them the origin of the French infantry. On the contrary, they are an example of an unsuccessful creation in the military area and as such are just as interesting as the positive, successful examples.

We shall best explain what is to be learned from this example if we compare it with the opinion that the scholarly world has had up to now, to the effect that Charlemagne's army consisted of alternating peasant levies. It is clear that the *francs archers* of Charles VII had great advantages over such a levy in the eighth century: one man was to be provided only for every fifty peasant farms, and not one man for every three to six, and therefore it was much easier to select a strong and willing man. The chosen man did not simply receive a burden, but he was given something in return: freedom from taxation in peacetime and pay in war. He was trained and governed by captains. Nevertheless, the *francs archers* proved to be unusable warriors. It was said of them that they only killed chickens. How then would the levies have looked which were supposed at their own expense every few years to have been obligated for a campaign hundreds of miles away?

The type of soldier that replaced them, among whom the true fathers of the French infantry are to be found, we shall determine in the next volume.

Whereas the *francs archers* declined, the "compagnies d'ordonnance" constantly maintained their position and were brought to the peak of their development through the organizing genius of another French prince, Charles the Bold. Under the title of duke of Burgundy, he united under his control a group of French and German fiefs, Flanders, Brabant, Hainaut, Luxembourg, the Free County of Burgundy, and Burgundy.[17]

The military weaknesses of the traditional, recognized feudal levy—the lack of punctual obedience, the unreliability, the poor equipment, and the unsatisfactory training in arms of the nobles—were so great that this system no longer appeared tolerable.[18] Charles created remedies for this in two ways. He paid a small regular compensation to those nobles who obligated themselves to be ready at any time to mount up and who personally and in their equipment seemed capable at the assemblies. These were the "*soudoyers à gages ménagers*".[19] But that was still not sufficient.

If we hear how unsatisfactorily armed, untrained, and unreliable the feudal levies often were in the fifteenth century, it is also possible that the same situation occurred under Barbarossa or Charlemagne, but the system could not be changed on that account. The advances in the mercenary system not only enabled the feudal service to be improved by pay but also brought about its dissolution. Charles issued drastic orders on this subject and, with the means he thus won, and following the example of his cousins, the French kings, he formed his "compagnies d'ordonnance" in 1471.[20] He gave them definite subordinate units, initially ten units of ten lances each, later four *escadres*, which, in turn, were composed of four *chambres* of six lances each. The twenty-fifth lance was that of the *chef d'escadre*.

The banners of the various company commanders were to have different colors, and the subordinate units were distinguished by having one, two, three, or four large "C's" embroidered on their banneret and under these "C's" the number 1, 2, 3, or 4.

The lance was composed not only of horsemen and marksmen but also of foot soldiers. It included a knight, a *coustillier,* a page, three mounted archers and one crossbowman, one *couleuvrinier* (marksman armed with a culverin), and one dismounted spearman—a total of nine men, whose number was quite often increased by several volunteers.[21] Charles had regulations issued concerning rations, pay, leave, and discipline. In peacetime no more than five men-at-arms and fifteen marksmen from each *escadre* were to be granted leave, and in wartime two men-at-arms and six marksmen. No more than thirty women were to follow each company, and nobody was allowed to claim one of them as his own.

In addition to the organization in lances, Charles also carried out a division by weapons, something that was also quite often required in practical wartime situations. Finally, he even issued detailed regulations prescribing combat exercises. One of these regulations reads as follows:

> In order to be able to make the men all the more skillful in the use of their weapons while serving in war through training, the duke orders the leaders of the companies, *escadres*, and platoons, while in garrison or otherwise having free time, to lead their men-at-arms from time to time into the field, sometimes with only upper body armor and sometimes fully equipped. There they are to drill

them in a closed front to charge with lances couched, while always remaining near their colors at a full gallop, or also to spread out on command and then assemble again and give mutual support to one another in order to stop an enemy attack. The marksmen, too, with their horses, must be trained in the use of their weapons; they are to become accustomed to dismount and shoot with their bows. In doing so they are to be shown how to have their horses led behind them in line, with their bridles tied together, every three horses to be tied to the hook that is placed on the pommel of the saddle of the squire's horse. They are also to deploy quickly into line to shoot without falling into disorder, and finally to have the spearmen march in front of the marksmen in a closed line. At a given signal, however, the spearmen are to fall down on one knee with their spears extended forward at the height of a horse's chest, so that the marksmen will be able to shoot their arrows over them as over a wall. When the spearmen see that the enemy is falling into disorder, they are to be ready to charge him in the manner in which they are commanded to do so. And the spearmen are also to practice taking position back to back for the purpose of two-sided defense, as well as taking up a square or circular formation. They are always to be outside the marksmen and in close formation, in order to repulse an attack by enemy horsemen while they also encircle the pages and the horses of the marksmen. The officers can practice these exercises first in small groups, and when one of them can learn it, then another learns it also. And while doing this, the officers are watchful of all their men, who will not dare to move off or to sell their horses or equipment, because they will not know in advance on which day the officers intend to drill them. In this way, each man will be obliged to do his duty and to prepare for war.

As we read these drill regulations, we have the impression of leaving the Middle Ages far behind us; a number of the drills even give the impression of being quite modern. But this impression is deceiving. The transition from one period of world history into another does not take place so quickly and so easily. We have seen above how difficult it was for the kings in France to transform the mercenary bands into regular companies. In like manner, we shall also see how slowly and with what difficulty modern cavalry and infantry developed from the knights and foot soldiers of the Middle Ages. The drill rules of Charles the Bold were not even a step in this direction. They were the product of an energetic, ingenious, and forceful spirit, and they were also headed in the right direction. But they still did not create the transition into the new period, because the elements with which they were working were soon to be overpowered by a much stronger one. The military organization of this last duke of Burgundy was nothing of a modern nature, but, on the contrary, it was the last and finest—we might even say the most subtle—offshoot of the Middle Ages. The truly significant start toward continuing development in this system was the incipient division of the combat branches. The prescribed drills, however, are an illusion; at least, whatever was accomplished through those drills had nothing to do with what we understand today under drills. The latter require an application of force of a completely different type from these regulations promulgated from above, which are not much more than good advice. We shall also have a great deal more to say about this in the remainder of this work. While it is true that the "compagnies d'ordonnance," to the extent that they were formed of horsemen, were a change that led over from knights to cavalry, there was still a long way to go, and first of all, these men-at-arms were still full-fledged knights. But the foot soldiers and marksmen in the "compagnies" have absolutely no connection with the future infantry in Europe. That infantry grew from a completely different root. The decisive characteristic that held the "compagnies d'ordonnance" within the circle of medieval warriorhood was the basis of the organization, the formation built on the concept of the "lance." Inherent in the "lance" was the idea that the knight was the combatant, and all the others were only supporting arms. Indeed, the number of the supporting arms was so great that we might imagine that, in the small troop, the knight was the officer. When we remember that the knight, by dismounting and taking position in the line of common soldiers, did indeed provide the effective factor of lending moral force to the mass, that is also a point leading toward the modern concept of the officer. But here, too, we have only a suggestion of that concept; the knight within the "lance" is definitely not what we and military history call "officer," but he remains the principal combatant. Furthermore, Charles the Bold, by starting to separate the combat branches, created a factor that likewise pointed to the future but that again eliminated the transition from the knight to the "officer," since the knights and the foot soldiers were now no longer side by side. Consequently, the lance within the "compagnie d'ordonnance" was only a refinement of the normal medieval organization, that is, the effort to bring into the "mixed combat" support of the knights by the auxiliary arms and a certain measure of order and direction.

It was logical for the rising principalities to adopt this system at the end of the Middle Ages, but in the end the system had to remain fruitless. A completely different force will take over the leadership. It is therefore not necessary for us to penetrate as far into the details of the organizations of the fifteenth century as we did for the earlier centuries of this epoch. As soon as we recognize the new power that is to bring the end of knighthood, the efforts of the closing period toward improvement lose their interest.

NOTES FOR CHAPTER V

1. On the German knights in Italy, H. Niese has published a study with original documents in the "Sources and Studies from Italian Archives" ("Quellen und Forschungen aus italienischen Archiven"), published by the *Historisches Institut,* 8 (1905): 217.

2. R. Bott, "The Campaigns of the Anglo-French Mercenary Companies to Alsace and Switzerland" ("Die Kriegszüge der englisch-französischen Soldkompagnien nach dem Elsass und der Schweiz"), Halle dissertation, 1891.

Luce, *Histoire de Bertrand du Guesclin et de son époque,* Paris, 1876.

3. This reform in its entire context has been treated in an exemplary way by G. Roloff in an article "The French Army under Charles VII" ("Das französische Heer unter Karl VII."), *Historische Zeitschrift,* 93. 427. Of the more recent French writings on which this study is based, especially valuable is E. Cosneau, *Le Connétable de Richemont (Artur de Bretagne),* Paris, 1886.

4. Boutaric, p. 214. The *levées générales* under Philip IV were nothing but "a pretext to establish taxes." Likewise Luce, *Bertrand du Guesclin,* p. 155, concerning the levies under Philip VI.

5. When William of Tyre speaks of *centuriones* and *quinquagenarii* as early as the battle of Dorylaeum in the First Crusade, that has no other significance than when Widukind speaks of *legiones* at the battle on the Lechfeld. Barbarossa, of course, sought on his Crusade to organize his army on a regular numerical basis.

6. According to the treaty of alliance of 1252, the pay was to be handed out to the *milites* by the *capitanei.* Muratori, *Antiquitates Italicae Medii Aevi (Italian Antiquities of the Middle Ages),* 6. 491.

7. Rosenhagen, "History of the Imperial Army Move into Italy from Henry VI to Rudolf" ("Geschichte der Reichsheerfahrt von Heinrich VI. bis Rudolph"), Leipzig dissertation, 1885, p. 65.

8. Morris, *The Welsh Wars.*

9. *Archiv. storico Ital.,* 15. 53. According to Köhler, 3: 2: 167.

10. La Curne, *Dictionnaire de l'ancien langage français.*

11. As early as in the *lex Salica,* title 66, para. 2, the word is used twice referring to the fraternity of warriors. This singular case, however, no doubt lies outside the history of language development. In the Latin sources and chronicles of the Valois period, the word is still translated by *"societas"* or *"Comitiva."* Du Cange. Bott, p. 4.

A proclamation by King John of 30 April 1351 (cited by Guilhiermoz, *Origine de la noblesse,* p. 251, from *Ordonnances des Rois de France,* 4. 69) reads as follows:

> With respect to whatever *gens d'armes* come in small groups, without master or chief, we desire and order that a worthy knight be sought out and selected by our constable, marshals, masters of crossbowmen, or others to whom he may belong, who is approved by them, to whom a unit of twenty-five or thirty such men at arms will be given and assigned . . . and we desire that this knight who shall have such a company will have a pennon with his coat of arms and will receive the same pay as a banneret.

Froissart, ed. Kervyn de Lettenh., 7. 80: "At this time the companies were so large in France that one did not know what to do with them."

12. Köhler, 3: 2: 116, 118, considers that the basis for the formation of the *gleves* in 1364 was the fact that it was precisely at that time that the knights started the custom of fighting on foot. Consequently, he is surprised that the *gleves* were also adopted in Germany (1365), since the knights only seldom fought on foot there. His surprise is out of place, since there was no relationship at all between the dismounting of the knights and the formation of the gleves.

In 3: 2: 173, Köhler states that there were lances of two horses, three horses, four, five, six, eight, and ten horses.

Würdinger, *Miliary History of Bavaria (Kriegsgeschichte von Bayern),* 1: 102, states: "The number of men forming a *gleve* varied. In Swabia there were four horses (Jäger, *Ulm,* 1: 418), in Nuremberg two horses to one spear (Ulman Stromer, 45), in Strasbourg five horses to one *gleve* (Schaab, 2: 277), in Ratisbon one spear and one marksman with three saddle horses (*reg. boica,* 10. 303). It might almost seem that the spear first got the meaning of "lance" or *gleve* as a result of its combination with one marksman." Other examples are to be found in Arnold, *Constitutional History of the German Free Cities (Verfassungsgeschichte der deutschen*

Freistädte), 2: 239. Vischer, *Studies in German History* (*Forschungen zur deutschen Geschichte*), 2: 77. Fischer, note, p. 385. Köhler, 3: 2: 117, 173.

When the chronicles report, as, for example, Königshofen on Döffingen, that an army had 800 *gleves* and 2,000 foot soldiers, that gives the impression that the 800 *gleves* are nothing more than 800 heavy horsemen. But then we also find cases of counting by "helmets" and that there were three horsemen to each "helmet." Chr. F. Stälin, *Württembergische Geschichte,* 3: 321.

In 1381 the cities formed a league army of 1,400 spears and 500 foot soldiers. For this force Augsburg provided forty-eight *hastatos* (spearmen), thirty *sagittarios equites* (mounted archers), and 300 *pedites armatos* (armed foot soldiers). Würdinger, 1: 93. See also pp. 96 and 98 of the same work.

Fischer states in *Participation of the Free Cities in the Imperial Army March to Italy* (*Teilnahme der Reichsstädte an der Reichsheerfahrt*), p. 30, that in 1310 at the imperial diet in Speyer a roster was drawn up showing how many *gleves* each free city was to provide for the march to Rome, each *gleve* having three horses, that is, three horsemen. This would therefore indicate that the concept and name of the *gleve* already existed in Germany in 1310. Nevertheless, this conclusion is subject to question, since the numbers are from a much later period, and the decision of 1310 may have been worded differently.

Morris, *The Welsh Wars,* p. 80, claims that in England the combining of the various combat arms into units was first seen at the siege of Dunbar in 1337. Previously, to include the reign of Edward I, the various combat arms appeared as separate units.

Cosneau, p. 358, note, states that the English had three marksmen in each lance. He gives an example in which two men-at-arms and two marksmen formed all together a group of nine men and nine horses.

13. Cosneau, p. 357. The ordinance of Luppé-le-Chastel of 26 May 1445 is reproduced on p. 610. This shows the lance as consisting of one knight, one *coutillier,* one page, two marksmen, one serving man, and six horses.

14. We find used very often the formula " '*ban et arrière-ban*' ('vassals and subvassals') were levied."

According to Guilhiermoz, p. 294, the "*arrière-ban*" in France was originally the same thing as the *Landwehr* (militia) in Germany, that is, the general levy of all men capable of bearing arms. He says that the feudal service was later limited to the "*arrière-ban*" and the "*arrière-ban*" was limited to men holding fiefs.

Boutaric, p. 140 f., reports in detail on the conditions that were issued on the levy under Louis IX and were specified in numerous "*coutumes*" (customs). They limited the rights of the lord to an extreme degree. He was allowed to levy his men only for defense, or only in the region governed by the lord, or only so far as to allow the man to return home on the same evening.

Luce, *Bertrand du Guesclin*, p. 159, recounts that, according to an unpublished ordinance, on 17 May 1355 King John called up "the *ban et l'arrière-ban,* that is to say, all physically qualified men between the ages of eighteen and sixty." That can hardly have been the intention of the ordinance, and Luce himself believes that the French communes did not obey this order. When Luce adds that Edward III in England really gave the *arrière-ban* "a truly practical character" by having all his subjects carry out weapons training, that is also an error.

15. In addition to the references already cited, see Spont, "La Milice des francs-archers," *Revue des questions historiques,* Vol. 61.

16. Boutaric, *Institutions militaires de la France,* p. 218. Jähns, *Handbuch,* p. 759. According to Juvénal des Ursins and the Monk of Saint Denis. The latter author states that the people carried out the drills with great zeal.

17. The military system of Charles the Bold is treated excellently by M. Guillaume, "Histoire de l'organisation militaire sous les ducs de Bourgogne," in the *Mémoires couronnés et mémoires des savants étrangers publiés par l'Académie de Belgique,* Vol. 22, Brussels, 1848. Much valuable material is also to be found in La Chauvelays, *La Composition des armées de Charles le Téméraire,* 1879. In the *Mémoires de l'Académie de Dijon,* Tome VI. (also published in Paris as a separate edition). I have discussed it myself in my *Perser- und Burgunderkriege.*

18. In 1340 the count of Armagnac had only 300 fully equipped men-at-arms in a force of 800 (*Grande chronique de St. Denys,* 5: 393, ed. Paulin).

In 1429 the noblemen who reinforced Charles VII "did not have the means of arming themselves or providing themselves with mounts." (*Chronique de la Pucelle, Panthéon littéraire,* p. 442).

In 1467 Charles the Bold selected, from the vassals who had been levied, those who had full equipment; they numbered 400 of the total group of 1,400. But it happened that the nobles took their pay and rode back home (according to Guillaume, p. 89).

19. Lachauvelays, p. 170, estimates that the two Burgundies provided Charles the Bold with thirty-two companies of *soudoyers à gages ménagers.*

The thirty-two companies numbered 899 men-at-arms with three horses each (that is, 899 pages and 899 valets), 541 *gens de trait à cheval* (mounted marksmen), 178 *coutilliers à cheval* (light horsemen), and 177 *demi-lances*. (A *demi-lance* is an individual knight who receives the same pay as two marksmen.)

The totals were therefore as follows:

In the *lances*	2,697	men	
Individuals	541	"	
"	178	"	
"	177	"	
	3,593		
less	899	pages, noncombatants	
	2,694	men	

20. A regulation for Hainaut appeared in 1470 and, according to Guillaume, p. 113, stated the following: A fief-holder with more than 360 pounds of annual income had to provide one man-at-arms with a *coutillier,* a page, and six dismounted archers. A fief-holder with 240 pounds of income was to provide one man-at-arms. A fief-holder with 120 pounds was to provide three men on foot (dismounted archers, crossbowmen, or spearmen). The smaller and larger groups were combined in accordance with the corresponding mission. Fiefs under 64 sous had no obligation. Anyone who could not serve personally was to provide an appropriate substitute, and if he could not do so, the commanders took over that responsibility for him. Every four months the items of equipment were to be inspected.

A similar regulation appeared in 1475 for Flanders.

Let us note that a certain progression upward occurred, that the smallest fief-holders were completely free, and that possessions of quite a significant extent called for providing one man on foot or even on horseback, and that the men in service were paid. Let us compare with this situation the concept that in the Carolingian Empire ownership of a few hides was burdened with providing one man at his own expense.

According to Lachauvelays, p. 258, the largest number of fiefs had an income of less than 50 francs, often only 10 francs.

The wording of the levy that Charles' governor for Burgundy issued on 3 May 1471 is very remarkable: "All types of men, both nobles and others, regardless of their class or profession, who are accustomed to bearing and using arms, whether or not they have fiefs and whether or not they have provided somebody for the present army" (quoted in Lachauvelays, p. 187). We might use this regulation as a paraphrase of the "cuncta generalitas populi" ("the whole mass of the people") in the capitulary of Charlemagne (p. 42, above) or the *"universi"* ("all") in the levy of 817 (p. 36, above).

21. This is specified in this way by the regulation of 31 July 1471. Olivier de la Marche, who commanded a company himself, states in his memoirs that the lance was composed of two archers, two men armed with the culverin, and two spearmen (according to Guillaume, p. 121).

Chapter VI

The Battles of Tannenberg and Montl'héry, and a Few Other Engagements of the Period

BATTLE OF TANNENBERG
15 JULY 1410

As important as the battle of Tannenberg and its outcome were, and as extensively as the battle was described at that time, it has, nevertheless, come down to us only in very uncertain reports.[1]

The author who continued Detmar's *Lübeck Chronicle* gives the Polish-Lithuanian army a strength of 5.1 million men, thereby exceeding even the numbers given by the Father of History for Xerxes' army. Consistent with this number is the report in the Magdeburg *Schöppen-chronik* that the total number killed amounted to 630,000. The smallest number in the chronicles is 83,000 for the Germans and 163,000 for the Poles. Heveker estimates the strength of the Teutonic Order at some 11,000 men, including 3,850 heavily armed warriors, 3,000 squires, and 4,000 marksmen, who were also mounted but fought on foot. In addition, there were also a few foot soldiers, who did not go into the battle but remained in the wagon fort during the fight.

Heveker estimates the strength of the Poles and Lithuanians as 16,500 horsemen, that is, about half as many more as the German strength. Our principal source for the battle, the Pole Dlugoss, also states that they were considerably stronger. At the head of the army was King Ladislaus

Jagiello, but the real animating spirit was his cousin Witold, the grand duke of Lithuania.

The grand master, Ulrich von Jungingen, left the initiative to the Poles, and when they moved up on the right bank of the Vistula, he took up a position behind the Drewenz, a tributary of the Vistula. According to the sources, it appears as if the Germans had opposed the crossing of the Drewenz by the enemy near Kauernick. It is difficult to see why they did this, since there eventually had to be a battle in any case. Either the Prussians did not yet have their forces assembled, or their intention was to let the Poles cross the river and attack them during the crossing. But regardless of this, the Poles realized the difficulty of the situation, turned about, and moved around toward the east in order to bypass the Drewenz at its source.

The Germans marched along parallel to them, and, since the river makes a sharp bend toward the north, they crossed it themselves and deployed for battle in sight of the enemy camp near the village of Tannenberg. Our sources, both Polish and German, agree that the Teutonic army committed an error by remaining in place deployed instead of immediately attacking the Polish army, which was not yet drawn up. But this is obviously nothing more than the superior wisdom of hindsight. The Prussians' rear guard did not arrive until the battle was almost over, and the heavy artillery appeared completely too late and could be emplaced only for the defense of the camp. Consequently, this army, too, was not yet completely deployed at the start of the fight; the account of the long wait came from men who by chance were among the foremost units and did not understand the reason they remained so long in place. They had already started their march from the vicinity of Löbau in the night, during which it had rained heavily, and had made a march of no less than 25 kilometers, as the crow flies, in the hot July sun. It was therefore quite natural that the deployment went on for a very long time. As for the Poles, they had started out around six o'clock in the morning, had marched only about 7 miles, had already pitched camp, and only needed to form up in front of their camp. There could therefore be no thought of a sudden attack. Rather, the strategy of the grand master appears wisely consistent only if we assume that he intended to fight a defensive-offensive battle. He was quite strong in crossbowmen and even in cannon, whose effect could reach its maximum only in the defensive. If he planned to attack the enemy at Tannenberg, we cannot understand why he had not already done so five days earlier at Kauernick and why he had allowed the Poles to remain so long in Prussian territory, which they were plundering fearfully. But if he intended to force the enemy to attack, everything becomes clear: that he awaited his opponent in his own land, that he took position behind the Drewenz, and that he had his troops stand passively for so long at Tannenberg. There he had a position so close on the flank of the Polish direction of march that they could not move by it. On his right he could rest his flank advantageously on the Grünfeld Forest, on his left on the village of Tannenberg, and before his position he had a generally level terrain which, however, was somewhat rolling and cut by small ravines and therefore still presented the attacker with numerous difficulties.[2]

While the Poles at the first report of the proximity of the Teutonic army were saddling up and deploying as quickly as possible, two messengers came to King Ladislaus and on behalf of the grand master handed him two swords and challenged him to fight. If we may be allowed to view this ceremony as an attempt by the grand master to gain more time, this point would fit very well into our overall concept of the battle.

As the reader has probably already noticed, the battle position is very similar to that of Beyazid at Nikopol. While we do not hear that the German marksmen had erected a palisade barrier in front of themselves as the janissaries had done (incidentally, this point is specifically mentioned at Kauernick), instead they did have a number of cannon along their front.

The outcome, however, was the opposite of that at Nikopol. The cannon had only minimal effect, a situation aggravated by a thundershower just at the start of the battle which wet the powder. The crossbowmen and archers had good success, at least on the left flank opposite the lightly armed Lithuanians, who, when the knights then charged them, were thrown back and fled. In the center and on the right flank, however, the Germans, after a hard fight, were overcome by the great superiority of the Poles, who did not make the same error as the French at Crécy and at Nikopol, where they had attacked piecemeal, but they first had their army deploy completely and then had the entire mass move forward simultaneously. Against this mass, the effect of the Prussian crossbowmen and cannon was lost, and the bravery of the brothers of the order was also to no avail. Even those knights returning from the pursuit of the Lithuanians were no longer able to turn the tide. Among the members of the order, it was said later that treason had played a role, that the knights of Kulm, who were opposed to the administration of the order, had lowered their banner and fled.

We need not believe this. When we observe the different outcomes of Nikopol and Tannenberg, we can only assume that neither the marksmen nor the horsemen of the order who were levied from the territory were to be compared in warrior quality and devotion to their cause with the janissaries and *sipahi* of Beyazid. The teachings of Mohammed and the discipline flowing from them contain a very powerful warlike force. If we also consider that the numerical relationship was the opposite from that of Nikopol—that Beyazid was probably the stronger numerically, while Jungingen was in any case considerably weaker in numbers than his opponent and did not even have all his forces on hand—the different outcome under similar conditions of position and tactics is no longer a cause for wonder.

The wagon fort that the Teutonic army had drawn up behind its battle line and had provided with the heavy cannon was stormed by the pursuing Poles. The grand master himself and 205 members of the order fell on the battlefield.[3]

MONSTRELET ON TANNENBERG

As an example of how greatly things can become distorted at some distance in time, I wish to add here the account of the battle of Tannenberg in the French chronicle by Monstrelet, who continued the work of Froissart and was one of the most important and the most widely used source authors of the period. He reports:

On 16 June 1410 the grand master of Prussia, accompanied by a number of his knights, members of the order and others from various nations, amounting to a strength of 300,000 Christians, invaded Lithuania to lay waste the country. The king of this country, together with the king of the Sarmatians, with a total of perhaps 400,000 Saracens, immediately moved against him, and they fought a battle with each other. The Christians won the victory, and some 36,000 Saracens were left dead. Among them the most important were the admiral of Lithuania and the constable of the Sarmatians. The others who survived took to flight. Some 200 of the Christians were left dead on the field, but they also had many wounded.

Shortly thereafter the king of Poland, who was a great enemy of the grand master of Prussia and had just recently pretended to become a Christian in order to win the Polish crown, came with his Poles to the aid of the Saracens already mentioned and encouraged them to resume the war against the Prussians. Consequently, eight days after that defeat they assembled again facing one another, that is, the king of Poland and the two other kings named above on the one side, with some 600,000 warriors, against the grand master of Prussia and several other great Christian lords, who were beaten by the Saracens. And there were some 60,000 or more dead left on the field. Among them were the master of Prussia and a nobleman from Normandy, Sir Jean de Ferrière, son of the seigneur de Vieuville, and also from Picardy the son of the seigneur du Bois d'Annequin. It was generally said that their cause was lost through the fault of the constable of the king of Hungary, who was in the second echelon of the Christians and fled with all the Hungarians.[4]

But the Saracens in no way won their fame and victory without losses, for in addition to 10,000 Poles, 120,000 of their men were also killed, as all of this was reported by the heralds and also by the Bastard of Scotland, who was named count de Hembe.

THE BATTLE OF MONTL'HÉRY ACCORDING TO COMINES[5]
16 JULY 1465

The count of Charolais (Charles the Bold) reconciled himself with his father as best he could and without delay led the men-at-arms into the field, and accompanying him was the count of Saint Paul, the manager of his affairs and the most important leader of his army. He may well have had 300 men-at-arms and 4,000 archers under his command, and many good knights and noblemen (*écuyers*) from Artois, Hainaut, and Flanders were serving under the count in the command of the count of Charolais. Similar bodies of troops (*bandes*) of comparable size were present under seigneur de Ravastin, brother of the duke of Cleve, and Anton, the Bastard of Burgundy, both of whom had brave and respected knights under their commands. And there were other leaders there, whom, for purposes of brevity, I shall not all name here, including two knights who were held in high regard by the count of Charolais: the seigneur de Haubourdin, an old knight and bastard brother of the count of Saint Paul, who had become famous in the battles between France and England at the time when Henry V of England ruled in France and Duke Philip was allied with him; and the seigneur de Contay, who was of about the same age. Both men were brave and wise knights and were entrusted with the most important leadership positions of the army.

And there were also enough young knights, one of whom was a man of high reputation named Philip of Lalain, from a family in which there were but few men who were not bold and courageous and almost all of whom died in battle in the service of their lords. The army consisted of some 1,400 poorly armed and unskilled men-at-arms, for these men had lived in peace for a long time and since the treaty of Arras had seen but little warfare of any length. In my opinion, they had lived in peace for more than thirty-six years, except for a few small engagements of short duration against the forces of Ghent. The men-at-arms were very strong, well mounted, and well provided for, for but few of them would have been found who did not have five or six large horses. There may well have been 8,000 or 9,000 archers, and when the mobilization was completed and the best men selected, it was more difficult to send the excess number home than it had been to recruit them all.

At that time the subjects of the House of Burgundy were living very comfortably as a result of the long period of peace and the goodness of their prince, who imposed but little tax on them. It seems to me that their kingdom, more than any other on earth, could be called the promised land. They had an overabundance of richness and lived in great ease, something they no longer did later; and it has now been twenty-three years since that began. The luxurious life and the clothing of men and women were sumptuous and extravagant. The parties and revelry were bigger and more extravagant than in any other place that I have known, and the baths and other festivities with women were extensive, profligate, and shameless (I refer to women of lower standing). In sum, no prince seemed to satisfy the subjects of this house, and today I do not know in this world any country as sad as this one, and I think that the sins of this period of prosperity brought this fate on them. And they were especially unaware of the fact that all this grace came to them from God, who distributes it wherever it pleases Him.

So when the army was ready with everything I have already mentioned—and that came about very quickly—the count of Charolais moved out with the entire army, which was completely mounted except for those who were driving his artillery, which for that period was large and excellent, with numerous transport, which inclosed the largest part of the army; all of which was his own.

The count moved toward Noyon and besieged the small but well-garrisoned castle of Nesle, which he captured in a few days. Marshal Joachin, marshal of France, who had come from Péronne, continued to stay close by, but since he had only a few men, he could do him no harm, and when the count approached, he withdrew toward Paris.

The count covered the whole distance without any fighting, and since his men took nothing without paying, the cities on the Somme and all the others allowed him to enter with a number of troops and provided them what they needed, in return for their money. It appeared as if they were eager to find out who would be stronger, the king or the lords.

The count arrived at Saint Denis, near Paris, where the other lords intended to join forces with him, but they had not appeared. The duke of Brittany was represented there by his vice-chancellor, who had with him signed *cartes blanches* from his lord, which he filled out as needed. He was from Normandy and a very clever gentleman, a quality he sorely needed because of the slander directed against him.

The count engaged in large-scale skirmishing right up to the gates of Paris, to the detriment of the burghers. In the way of men-at-arms, the city had only Marshal Joachin with his company and the seigneur de Nantouillet, later grand master, who that year served the king as loyally as ever a subject has served a king of France and who finally was poorly rewarded for it, less by the fault of the king than as a result of the hounding of his enemies, none of whom had an excuse for it. At that time (as I was later told) there were many people in Paris who were in such great fear that they shouted: "They are in the city," but that was unfounded. Nevertheless, the seigneur de Haubourdin, of whom I have previously spoken and who had grown up there, believed that they should have attacked the city, which was then not nearly as strong as it is today. And the men-at-arms, too, would gladly have wanted to do so; they derided the population and skirmished up to the gates. But it is likely that the city could not have been taken. The count withdrew to Saint Denis.

On the following day they discussed whether they should move toward the duke of Berry and the duke of Brittany, who, according to the vice-chancellor of Brittany, were in the area. He showed letters from them which he himself, however, had written on his signed *cartes blanches*. Actually, he knew nothing about their situation. It was decided to cross the Seine, although many were in favor of withdrawing, since the other princes had not kept their promise, and since it might well be considered sufficient that they had crossed the Somme and the Marne. A number of them were uneasy because they had behind them no fortified places into which they could withdraw if it were necessary. The entire army grumbled very much about the count of Saint Paul and the vice-chancellor, but the count of Charolais crossed the Seine and pitched camp near the bridge of Saint Cloud. The day after his arrival there he received a letter from a lady of this kingdom telling him that the king of Bourbonnais (Louis XI) was starting out in order to move against him by forced marches.

Since the king saw that the count of Charolais was approaching Paris, and since he was concerned that the Parisians might open the gates to him as well as to his brother and the duke of Brittany, who were approaching from Brittany, because they were all supporting the League of Public Weal, and that the other cities would also do what Paris had done, he moved out by forced marches in order to enter Paris and to prevent the two large armies from joining forces. And, as he told me several times when he spoke of these matters, he did not come with the intention of fighting.

So now, as I have already reported, when the count of Charolais had learned that the king of Bourbonnais had moved out and was marching against him, he also decided to move against the king. He announced the content of the letters, without naming the lady who had written them, and he called on everybody to do his best, for he had decided to risk his chance. He established his camp at the village of Longjumeau near Paris, and the constable with his entire advance guard pitched his camp at Montl'héry, 14 miles farther upstream. Scouts were sent out to reconnoiter the approach of the king and his route. In the presence of the count of Saint Paul, the position by Longjumeau was then selected as the place where they intended to fight. It was agreed that the count of Saint Paul was to pull back to Longjumeau when the king approached. The seigneur de Haubourdin and the seigneur de Contay were also present when this decision was made.

While the count of Charolais was encamped near Longjumeau, with his advance guard near Montl'héry, he learned from a prisoner who was brought before him that the count de Maine had joined forces with the king and that all the troops of the kingdom were there, some 2,200 men-at-arms and also the levy from Dauphiné, as well as forty or fifty noblemen from Savoy, and that the king was taking counsel with the count de Maine, the grand seneschal of Normandy, Breszey, the admiral of France, of the House of

Montauban, and others. Finally, the king decided, regardless of opposing viewpoints, not to fight, but simply to move to Paris without approaching the camp of the Burgundians. In my opinion, his plan was a good one. Since he mistrusted the seneschal, he demanded from him information as to whether or not he had given his seal to the princes who were allied against him. To this the seneschal, laughing as was his custom, replied that he had indeed done so and that they were also to keep it, but that his body belonged to the king. The king was satisfied with this answer and assigned him command of the advance guard as well as responsibility for selecting the route, since the king, as we have said, wanted to avoid battle. Thereupon the grand seneschal, following his own desires, said to one of his confidants: "Today I will bring them so close to one another that anyone would have to be very clever in order to separate them." And that he did, but the first man to fall was the seneschal himself. These words were related to me by the king, for at that time I was with the count of Charolais.

On 16 July 1465 this advance guard arrived at Montl'héry, where the count of Saint Paul was encamped. The latter hastily sent a messenger to the count of Charolais, who was encamped 14 miles away at the place selected for the battle, requesting him to come to his aid as quickly as possible, for men-at-arms and archers had already dismounted from their horses and were close to his wagon fort. He said that it was impossible for him to withdraw as ordered, since that could look like flight and could be dangerous for the entire army. The count sent in great haste the Bastard Anton of Burgundy with many men. He himself hesitated as to whether or not he should go, but he finally moved out after the others and arrived toward seven o'clock in the morning. Five or six units of the king's force had already arrived there, along a large ditch that was between the two armies.

The count of Charolais found the count of Saint Paul on foot, and all the others fell into line as they arrived. The archers had dismounted, and each one had implanted a pole in front of himself. Several kegs of wine were tapped so that they could drink, and to judge from the brief view that I had, there could not have been any men more eager for battle, a point that made a very good impression on me. At first it was decided that everybody, without exception, should fight on foot, but later they changed this decision, and the men-at-arms mounted on horseback. But several brave knights were ordered to remain dismounted, including the seigneur de Cordes and his brother. Seigneur Philip of Lalain had also dismounted, for among the Burgundians those men were most highly honored who fought on foot with the archers, and there were many prominent lords in this group, in order that the foot soldiers might feel more secure and fight better. They had learned that from the English warriors with whom Duke Philip had previously fought against France in the war that lasted thirty-two years without an armistice. But at that time the principal battles were fought by those Englishmen who were rich and powerful, under a wise, handsome, and very courageous king, Henry, who also had wise and brave brothers and great army commanders, such as the count of Salisbury, Talbot, and others whom I shall not mention, since they were not of my time, even though I have seen so many reminders of them. For when God was tired of being favorable to them, this wise king died in the Forest of Vincennes, and his demented son was crowned in Paris as king of France and England. And thus the other outstanding dignitaries in England also changed, and there arose between them a division that has lasted until today, or almost to the present time. The members of the House of York usurped the monarchy or had it legally—I do not know by what right, for the apportionment of such things is decided in heaven.

The Burgundians lost a great deal of time and suffered losses because they first dismounted and then mounted their horses again. The brave young knight Philip of Lalain fell because he was poorly armored. The king's men moved in a column through the Forest of Tourfou. They were not yet 400 men strong when we arrived, and many believed that if we had attacked them at once, we would have found no resistance, for, as I have already said, those coming up from the rear could only move one behind the other. Nevertheless, their number kept increasing. When the noble knight of Contay saw this, he hastened to the count of Charolais and recommended to him that, if he wanted to win the battle, it was time to advance. He gave him his reasons and said that if they had attacked earlier, the enemy would already have been defeated, for he had found their number to be small, whereas now they were obviously increasing. And that was also correct.

Then all order and all discussion ended, for each one wanted to give his opinion. Furthermore, a large skirmish had already begun at the edge of the village of Montl'héry. Each side had only archers. Those of the king's army were led by Poncet de Rivière, and they were all archers of the "compagnie d'ordonnance," with uniforms trimmed in gold and in good order, while those of the Burgundians were without order or leadership, such men as easily start skirmishes. On foot with them were seigneur Philip of Lalain and Jacques du Mas, a man of high renown and later the senior master of the horse of Duke Charles of Burgundy. The Burgundians were stronger in number; they captured a house, took two or three doors, which they used as shields, and began to push into the street, setting fire to one house. The wind came to their assistance and blew the fire toward the king's troops, who began to withdraw, mount on horseback, and flee. On hearing this noise, the count of Charolais moved out and gave up all of the formation that had previously been decided on. They had planned to march in three phases because the distance between the two armies was so great. The king's unit was near the castle of Montl'héry and had a large hedge and a ditch in front of it. There was also grain standing in the fields, as well as beans and other thick crops, for the soil there is good. All the archers of the count were marching in front of him on foot and in disorder. In my opinion, the archers are the most important thing in the world for battle, but they must number in the thousands; in small numbers they are worthless. They should also be men who are poorly mounted, who do not regret losing their horses, or even men who have no horses at all. Best of all, however, some day those men will prove themselves in this branch who have never seen any other men but well-trained ones. This is also the opinion of the English, who are the flower of the world's marksmen.

As I have said, it had been decided that they would rest twice on the march because of the long distance and the thick crops, which were an obstacle to the movement of the men. But it was precisely the opposite that occurred, as if they had intentionally wanted to destroy themselves. In this matter God showed that He has the outcome of battles in His hand and gives victory as He pleases. It also seems impossible to me that the intellect of one man should be able to bring such a large number of men into an orderly formation and keep them there, or that everything should develop in the field as was previously planned in the council room. It also seems to me that whoever might believe those things would be sinning against God, if he were a man of sound understanding. Rather, each man must do what he can and what he must and recognize that this is a work controlled by God, often through small measures and incidents, and He gives the victory now to the one side and then to the other. This mystery is so great that kingdoms and great domains sometimes fall and are destroyed in its workings, and others begin to grow and become dominant.

To come back to our account, the count marched without interruption and without allowing the archers and foot troops to catch their breath. The king's troops moved out of the hedge on two sides, and when they were close enough to one another to couch their lances, the Burgundian men-at-arms broke through the archers without giving them time for a single shot, even though they were the flower and the hope of the army; for I do not believe that among the 1,200 men-at-arms there were even as many as fifty who would have understood how to couch their lances. Not even 400 of them had cuirasses or an armed servant. All of this resulted from the long period of peace and the fact that the dukes of Burgundy, in order not to burden the people with taxes, did not maintain a standing army. From that day up to the present hour, this region has never had peace, and now the situation is worse than ever.

And thus the Burgundians themselves destroyed the flower and hope of their army. But God, who leads in such a wonderful way, willed that the count, who was fighting on the right side, opposite the castle, without encountering opposition, should be victorious. On that day I was always close to him and had less fear than at any time afterwards, since I was so young and did not know fear. But I was astonished that nobody risked defending himself against this prince, whom I considered the most powerful of all. People who have little experience are like that, and thus it happens that they confuse their opinion with poor reasons and little understanding. Consequently, one should preferably hold to the opinion of the person who knows that a man never regrets having spoken but little, but very often regrets having spoken too much.

On the left side were the seigneur von Ravenstein, Jacques of Saint Paul, and a number of others, to whom it seemed that they did not have enough men-at-arms to be able to hold their own, but they were already too close to the enemy to think of taking up a new formation. And so they were indeed quickly defeated and driven back to their wagons; most of them fled to the forest, more than 2 miles from there. A few Burgundian foot troops reassembled near the wagons. Among the pursuers were the knights of the Dauphiné and of Savoy and many men-at-arms. They thought the battle was already won, for on this side of the Burgundians there was a great flight, including many prominent lords, who sought to reach the bridge of Sainte Maxence, which they believed was still in our hands. Many remained in the forest, and along with others, the count of Saint Paul had also withdrawn with a considerable escort (the wagon barricade was quite close to the forest). Afterwards he showed clearly that he did not yet consider that the day was lost.

For his part, the count of Charolais, with but few companions, pursued the enemy some 2 miles beyond Montl'héry, as no one of that large number defended himself, and he already believed he had won the victory. An old nobleman from Luxembourg named Anton le Breton tried to bring him back and told him that the French had assembled again and that he would be lost if he went any farther. And although he repeated this two or three times, the count did not stop. Then the seigneur de Contay, of whom I have spoken above, also came quickly to him and told him the same thing and in such a forceful manner that he listened to his words and turned about. I believe that he would have been captured, like a number of others, if he had advanced two arrow trajectories farther. When he came through the village, he met a troop of fleeing foot soldiers. He pursued them, even though he did not have 100 horses all together. But one of them turned around and pierced him in the belly with his spear, and in the evening I myself saw the wound. Most of the others escaped through the gardens, but that one man was killed. When the count passed close to the castle, he saw the archers of the king's guard standing before the gate. He was very surprised, for he had not thought that the royal troops were still defending themselves. He turned to the side in order to win the field, and there he was attacked by some fifteen or sixteen men-at-arms. (A number of his men had already separated themselves from him.) They killed his companion, Philip d'Orgnis, who was carrying a standard with his coat of arms. The count, too, was in great danger and was struck several times, once with a dagger at the neck, the scar from which he has carried his whole life long, as a result of the failure of his chin piece, which had fallen down in the morning and had been poorly fastened. I myself saw it fall down. One man placed a hand on him and cried: "Surrender, gracious lord! I know you well; do not have yourself killed!" But he continued to defend himself. But then there came up the son of a doctor from Paris, Johann Cadet, who himself was tall, heavy, and strong and was mounted on a horse of corresponding size, and he spread them all apart. The king's men withdrew again to the ditch along which they were formed in the morning, for they saw men from our side approaching. The count, who was bleeding profusely, moved out to them in about the middle of the field. The banner of the Bastard of Burgundy was so cut up that it was no more than a foot long, and around the banner of the count's archers there were all together no more than forty men; our group, which no longer numbered as many as thirty, joined forces with them under great pressure. The count unhesitatingly mounted another horse that was given him by his page, Simon de Quingy, who later became famous. The count moved through the field in order to assemble his men, but we who had remained there had no other thought than to flee if some 100 of the enemy had come. Ten men, twenty men on foot and on horseback joined us; the foot troops were wounded and exhausted from the exertions of the march and the battle. The count quickly returned but did not bring 100 men; nevertheless, gradually a few more came. The field, in which the grain had stood so high a half-hour earlier, was now bare and full of the most terrible dust. Fallen men and horses lay everywhere, but it was impossible to recognize the dead because of the dust.

Shortly afterward we saw the count of Saint Paul approaching from the wood; he had perhaps forty men-at-arms and his banner with him. He came straight toward us, and more men gathered around him, but they still seemed to be quite far away. Three or four times we sent messengers to him, saying that he should hurry, but he did not change his pace and came on at a walk. He had his men take up the lances that were lying on the trail and came in good order, a point that greatly encouraged our men. When he reached us, so many men had joined him that we numbered some 800 men-at-arms. He had few if any foot troops, and that prevented the count from winning the complete victory, for a ditch and a large hedge separated the two battle lines.

On the king's side, the count de Maine and a number of others, some 800 men-at-arms, fled. A number of men claimed that the count de Maine was in league with the Burgundians, but I do not believe that that was so. Never was there such a great flight on both sides, but the two leaders both remained on the battlefield. On the king's side, a man of high position fled as far as Lusignan without stopping to rest, and on the count's side a prominent lord fled to Quesnoy-le-Conte. Neither one of them was interested in fighting.

When the two armies were drawn up opposite each other, several cannon shots were fired, killing men on both sides. Nobody any longer had the desire to fight. Our troops were more numerous, but the presence of the king and the encouraging words that he directed to his men-at-arms were very effective. I really believe, judging from what I heard there, that without him they would all have fled. On our side, a few men wanted to start the fighting again, especially seigneur de Haubourdin, who said that he saw a column of the enemy fleeing and that if we could only have found 100 archers to shoot through the hedge, everybody on our side would have advanced.

While such proposals and ideas were being stated, night came on without there having been even a skirmish. The king moved back to Corbeil, while we believed that he was spending the night in the field. By chance, a powder keg was ignited at the spot where the king had been, and it spread to a few wagons and along the entire hedge. We believed that it was the enemies' campfires.

The count of Saint Paul, who appeared as the real leader of the war, and seigneur de Haubourdin even more strongly, ordered that the wagon fort be moved up to the position where we were and that it be drawn up to encircle us. And this was done. When we were again assembled there in battle formation, many of the king's men who had been in pursuit came up and believed that everything had been won for them. Now they were obliged to move by our position, and a few of them managed to escape, but most of them were killed. Of the king's famous men, there fell Lord Godfrey of Saint Bellin, the grand seneschal, and Flocquet, captain. On the side of the Burgundians, Lord Philip of Lalain was killed, and more foot troops and men of lesser importance fell than among the king's forces. But the royal troops lost more mounted men. The king's men had more important prisoners from those who had fled. On the two sides all together, at least 2,000 men were killed. Men fought well, and on both sides there were brave men and cowards. But, in my opinion, it was a great thing for the two armies to assemble again on the battlefield and to remain facing each other between three and four hours. The two leaders must have appreciated those men who stood there bravely with them, but in this matter they behaved like humans and not at all like angels. One man lost his positions and his dignities because he had fled, and they were given to others who had fled 45 miles farther. One of our men lost his position and was banned from the sight of his lord, but a month later he was more respected than previously.

Surrounded by our wagons, we camped as best we could. We had many wounded, and most of them were very discouraged and fearful that the Parisians and Marshal Joachin with the 200 men-at-arms who were in Paris would attack and that we would have to fight on two sides. Since the night was very dark, fifty lances were sent out to determine where the king was encamped; by chance, only twenty of them moved out. It may have been three arrow trajectories from our camp to the point where we supposed the king to be. In the meantime, the count of Charolais ate and drank a little, as did all the others, and the wound on his neck was bandaged. In order to make room for him, four or five dead men had to be moved away from the place where he ate. There were two small bundles of straw there, and he sat down on them. When they were moving away one of the poor fallen men, he began to ask for something to drink. They poured into him a little of the medicine from which the count had drunk, and he recovered and became known as a highly considered archer guard of the count by the name of Savorot. He was bandaged and healed.

Now they took counsel as to what was to be done. The count of Saint Paul spoke first; he believed that we were in danger and recommended that at daybreak we should start marching toward Burgundy, burning a part of the vehicles and saving only the cannon. Nobody should take along any vehicle unless he had more than ten lances. He said it was impossible without rations to remain between Paris and the king. Thereupon seigneur de Haubourdin said he thought they should first hear what information the scouts brought back. Three or four others demanded the same thing. Finally, seigneur de Contay said that if the rumor spread through the army, everybody would take flight and would be taken prisoner before moving 90 miles. He gave several good reasons and said that, in his opinion, everybody should rest as best he could that night, and then at daybreak they should attack the king and fight it out to the bitter end. He found this action more secure than taking flight. On hearing this opinion of seigneur de Contay, the count decided that everybody should rest for two hours but should be ready if the trumpet should sound. He then sent out several lords to encourage the soldiers.

Toward midnight the scouts returned (and one can imagine that they had not gone very far) and reported that the king was camped near the fires that had been seen. Without delay other scouts were sent out, and an hour later everybody prepared for battle; most of them would have preferred to flee. Toward morning the men who had been sent out from the camp met a wagon driver from our side who had been captured in the morning and was bringing a load of wine from the village, and he told them that everybody had left. They then sent this message back to the army and themselves proceeded to verify the report. They found the situation as the man had said, and they returned to report this. This caused great joy in the army, and many men who had been very subdued an hour earlier now said that they should go after them. I had an old, very tired horse which drank a bucketful of wine. He had happened to stick his muzzle into it and I let him go on drinking. I had never seen him so spirited and fresh as he was today.

When day had come, everybody mounted up, and the units were drawn up. In the meantime, many men returned who had been hiding in the woods. The count of Charolais called a Franciscan monk before him and ordered him to say that he came from the army of the Bretons and that they would arrive during the day. This encouraged the men very much, but not all of them believed it.

All day long the count of Charolais remained on the battlefield, very happy, since he gave himself credit for the situation, something that later cost him dearly, since from that time he never again took the advice of another person but only his own. Before that day he was no military commander and did not like anything that was associated with such a position; but after that he changed his mind, for he continued with this new attitude to the day of his death, and as a result he lost his life and destroyed his house, or if it was not completely destroyed, it was in any case very much devastated. Three great and wise princes, his predecessors, had raised it very high, and few kings, aside from the king of France, are more powerful than he was, and none of them has larger and more beautiful cities. He who has too high an estimate of himself, especially if he is a great prince, fails to recognize that grace and happiness come from God. Two more things I would like to say about him: first, I believe that there was never a person who could accomplish more work than he, wherever it might be; second, that I have never known a bolder person. I have never heard him say that he was tired and have never seen him appear to be afraid, and yet I was with him in war for seven consecutive years, at least through the summer, but also in winter. His thoughts and decisions were great ones, but no human could have carried them out if God had not helped with His might.

EXCURSUS

BATTLE OF MONS-EN-PÉVÈLE
18 AUGUST 1304

This battle has been thoroughly treated by Köhler, 2: 250; the result, however, is obviously a piece of pure fantasy. Perhaps a renewed special study will throw light on this subject. For the time being, I am inclined to think that there was no battle at all but that individual brawls were exaggerated into a battle.

BATTLE OF MÜHLDORF
28 SEPTEMBER 1322

In the eighth year of the civil war between the two counterkings, Louis the Bavarian and Frederick the Fair, the Hapsburger sought to bring on the decision by invading Bavaria with his united forces from the east, while his brother Leopold came from the west, from Swabia, in order to join forces in the territory of the enemy. Louis and his ally, King John of Bohemia, with their superior forces, attacked Frederick just after he had crossed the Inn. The battle has been thoroughly treated a number of times, especially by Pfannschmidt, *Studies in German History (Forschungen zur deutschen Geschichte)*, Vols. III and IV, by Weech, *Forschungen zur deutschen Geschichte,* Vol. IV, who gives an analytical survey of the sources, and Köhler, 2: 283. I am not convinced by any of these accounts.

It is impossible to tell from the sources why Frederick, instead of initially withdrawing and seeking to join forces with Leopold, who had already approached within 85 miles, accepted battle against superior forces. Presumably, he was advised to do this by his colleagues, but he is supposed to have said that the war had already made so many widows and orphans that he could no longer postpone the decision. Pfannschmidt, p. 58, believes the Bavarians had blocked the withdrawal of the Austrians across the Inn and had therefore forced them into the battle, but we cannot see just how impossible it had become for them to withdraw. On this point Köhler expresses himself somewhat unclearly and contradictorily.

The services of the Munich burghers on behalf of their lords in this battle are just as fictitious as Seyfried Schweppermann.

The outcome seems to have been brought on by a group of knights which the burgrave of Nuremberg belatedly led into the fight. It is impossible to say whether it was according to some plan or simply a matter of chance that Frederick entered the conflict so late. Since the numerical superiority lay with the Bavarians, we cannot see why this superiority could not have won the victory just as well if it was engaged from the start rather than in successive stages.

The claim of an Austrian source that 500 Bohemian knights who had already surrendered took up arms again in violation of their word when they saw the successes of the burgrave may be eliminated as a partisan legend. Where would these prisoners have obtained weapons again?

Also based on false concepts is the sentence in Pfannschmidt, p. 65: "The knights dismounted from their horses in order to prevent them from being shot down or cut down by the Hungarian archers, as had previously happened to them and the Bohemians; now they planned to fight fire with fire."

That would indeed have been a poor method for knights to fight with enemy marksmen if, instead of riding them down, they dismounted. After all, on foot they could certainly not have met them hand to hand.

(Added in the third [*sic.* second?] edition). In 1917 W. Erben published a carefully edited collection of all the sources on the battle of Mühldorf, on the basis of which, together with thorough investigation of the geographical conditions, Government Councilor Dr. Reiner in Munich studied the battle from every viewpoint. This study was available to me in manuscript form. It indicates that the battle took place close to Mühldorf (and not near Ampfing, which is situated 8 kilometers farther upstream). The battlefield is near the village of Erharting on the Isen, a tributary of the Inn, at the foot of the Dornberg, which is to be found between Erharting and Pleisskirchen. It was entirely a battle between knights. Frederick had some 1,400 helmets, while Louis, allied with John of Bohemia, had 1,800. Frederick also had between 500 and 600 mounted Hungarian archers. Foot troops played no role in the battle. According to Reiner's reconstruction, the Hungarian archers were sent out across the Isen in advance by Frederick in order to shoot at the enemy knights as they crossed the small river. This maneuver failed, since Louis had the Hungarians driven away before he crossed the river. Now he had unquestioned numerical superiority, and he defeated the Austrians and took all of them prisoner by having the burgrave of Nuremberg, who had at first driven away the Hungarians, move against the flank and the rear of the Austrians. The strategic concept remains unexplained—that is, in what way Frederick planned the junction with his brother Leopold, who would have given him the certain numerical superiority. How did it happen that this junction failed, while Louis and John of Bohemia succeeded in joining forces? The campaign must have been planned by both sides far in advance. From the tactical viewpoint, too, it remains unclear as to why the Hungarian marksmen allowed themselves to be separated from the main body.

BATTLE OF BAESWEILER
20 AUGUST 1371

Duke Wenzel of Brabant believed he had already defeated his opponent, William of Jülich, when, presumably because he did not cover his flanks securely enough, Count Edward of Geldern, whose forces were still at full strength, attacked him from the flank and reversed the situation. Count William, who was already withdrawing, faced about, and Wenzel himself was taken prisoner. The battle is recounted in this way by Ennen, *History of the City of Cologne* (*Geschichte der Stadt Köln*), 2: 654. It appears to be of note as an example of the so frequent reversal of the situation in knightly battles.

ENGAGEMENT AT NOGENT-SUR-SEINE
23 JUNE 1359

Auberchicourt was in position with archers on a hill and defended himself in the English way. But his flanks were not sufficiently secured, and he was finally enveloped by French spearmen and defeated.

BATTLE OF BARNET
14 APRIL 1471

Edward IV defeated Warwick, who was killed. We cannot tell from the two thorough accounts we have in the *Historie of the arrivall of Edward IV in England,*[6] which was composed by a contemporary follower and servant of Edward, and the *Chronicle of Warkworth,*[7] which has a Lancastrian bias, whether the battle was fought on horseback or on foot. But the *Historie* says that Edward found Warwick's troops drawn up "under a hedge side," and Warkworth reports that when Warwick saw that the battle was lost, he "lepte on a horse and flede." This would therefore indicate that even the commander had fought on foot. This point is confirmed by Comines (Book IV, Chap. 7), who reports that everybody on both sides was on foot. He states that Warwick himself on other occasions had the habit of mounting on horseback again after drawing up his units, so that, if things went badly, he could escape. This time, however, his brother reportedly induced him to fight on foot.

BATTLE OF TEWKSBURY
4 MAY 1471

It is also impossible to learn from the account of this battle in the *Historie* (p. 28) whether the knights fought on horseback or on foot.

Consequently, I consider it very questionable whether the statement in De La Chauvelay's *Cavalry Combat on Foot in the Middle Ages* (*Le Combat à pied de la cavallerie au moyen-âge*), p. 51, that Edward IV fought on foot the nine battles that he won, is correct.

BATTLE OF BOSWORTH

This battle has been treated by J. Cairdner. London, 1896.

NOTES FOR CHAPTER VI

1. While the special study by Karl Heveker, "The Battle of Tannenberg" ("Die Schlacht bei Tannenberg"), Berlin dissertation, 1906, published by Georg Nauck, has greatly advanced the understanding of the battle and has eliminated many false ideas, it still leaves important points in the dark. If I attempt to arrive at a clear picture from it, I must add that a number of points in my account are based only on supposition. Among more recent works, I cite an article by S. Kujot in *Die altpreussische Monatsschrift*, Vol. 48, Issue No. 1, and Krollmann, *Oberländische Geschichtsblätter*, Issue No. 13, 1911. Also worthy of note is the study "The Knights' Grave of Tannenberg" ("Das Rittergrab von Tannenberg"), by E. Schnippel in the *Oberländische Geschichtsblätter*, Issue No. 11, 1909.

2. The valuable description of the terrain is to be found in Köhler, *Warfare of the Knightly Period* (*Kriegswesen der Ritterzeit*), 2: 717.

3. Kujot and Krollmann arrived at other conclusions on a number of points. Nevertheless, I have in general stood by my earlier account.

4. There is probably injected into this description an account of French knights from the battle of Nikopol, which took place fourteen years earlier. There were no Hungarians at Tannenberg.

5. See p. 264, above. The translation is taken from the edition by Mandrot, *Mémoires de Philippe de Commynes,* Vol. I, Chap. 2, p. 13.

6. Edited by John Bruce, Camden Society, 1838, p. 19.

7. Edited by J. O. Halliwell, Camden Society, 1839, p. 16.

BOOK V

The Swiss

Chapter I

Introduction

When the Frankish counties turned from administrative districts into fiefs and from fiefs into hereditary domains, they were gradually dissolved. The kings first gave individual families, but especially bishops, convents, and monasteries, immunity from the count's authority and eventually turned over to them the count's authority itself. From the dissolved official authority which had become private property, many cities won for themselves political independence. In addition, a number of country communities, fairly large districts, and villages freed themselves from feudal domination and became directly subject to the empire.

In doing so, they were partly assisted by special circumstances, as ducal families died out, leaving them in the clear, so to speak, and in part they had attained a special status as royal domains, and in part there also survived in them the ancient right of the Hundred to choose its own leader, the *hunno* (*tunginus*). Whereas this official elsewhere descended to a subordinate administrator appointed by the count, there was maintained here and there a certain right of approval by the community and through it the nucleus for the possible development of a new independence.

Such peasant communities dependent directly on the emperor existed on the North Sea coast from Ditmarsh to Friesland, in Westphalia, on the Moselle, in the Wetterau, in Alsace, and in Swabia, both on the plain and in the Alpine valleys. Some of these developed into completely independent republics and held out as such for a long time, such as Ditmarsh. Others were forcibly overthrown, such as Stedingen on the lower Weser, which was defeated by the archbishop of Bremen with his mercenaries at Altenesch in 1234. Others maintained a certain degree of self-government until 1803. But the free communities in the high Alps attained lasting importance in world history.

When in the eighth and ninth centuries the distinction between the military class and the peasant class also developed in the Germanic parts of the Frankish Empire, the Alpine areas were not excluded from this development. There also arose in the mountain valleys of the Duchy of Alamannia or Swabia hereditary counties, families of counts with castles and warriors, knightly families and peasants in the most varied degrees of freedom and serfdom. But, whereas in the lowlands the original large marches were divided up among the newly established small villages with the spread of agriculture, in the mountain valleys the great common marches still held out, despite the growing populations and the establishment of new towns. For even if there was more farming there in the Middle Ages than there is today, the raising of livestock on the large, common *allmende* remained the principal economic activity. And with the common march there was also maintained the assemblage of all the inhabitants of the march, and this organization remained particularly strong in those places where it coincided with the political body, the old Hundred. This was the case in the district of Schwyz, where the great *allmende,* ten hours (48 kilometers) long and five hours (24 kilometers) wide, still exists today. Southeast of the town of Schwyz was the "free *Weidhub,* where court is often held," and where the territorial community, the people's assemblage of the Hundred, was held. It was a certain Konrad Hunn who in 1217 made a peace treaty for his community with the monastery of Einsiedeln, whether it be that he held the office of *hunno,*[1] or whether the title of the position had come down from an ancestor, having become a family name. From the thirteenth century on, the name "*ammann*" became customary for the *hunno.* It is assumed that this march of Schwyz—in the ancient Germanic sense we could also say "Hundred" or "district"—in the fourteenth century was almost as thickly populated as it is today. Therefore it numbered some 18,000 souls,[2] which would have meant more than 4,000 men, of whom 3,000 could always be called up by their *ammann* and assembled in orderly fashion within a few hours for the defense of the country. In Schwyz there were also a number of farms that were subject to foreign owners, the count of Lenzburg, or the monastery of Einsiedeln, but the great majority of the inhabitants consisted of free peasants, and the common march also held the socially displaced elements together with the whole.

The common march was such a strong tie that even Uri, where the inhabitants consisted of subjects, partly of the convent in Zurich and partly of nobles such as the baron of Attinghausen, remained in this form a compact community. The ownership by the distant convent was so mild from a practical viewpoint that it differed but little from freedom.

If the geographical and economic factor had formed the basis for maintaining the strong organization of a few territorial communities, it also contributed toward sustaining and nourishing a warlike spirit in them. The more aristocratic the knightly class had become in the twelfth and thirteenth centuries, as we know, the less numerous it became and the more it needed to fill out its ranks with selected private soldiers from the people. As in the British Isles, where the mountainous territory of Wales constantly remained a fruitful source of recruits for the English kings, so too did the Alpine areas play the same role for the German kings. The life of the shepherd and the hunter in the mountains was more appropriate for sustaining the warlike adventuresome spirit than were the agricultural lowlands, and the poverty existing in the mountains obliged men to look outward for profit or pay.

In the thirteenth century we find men from Schwyz and Uri mentioned in the sources as mercenaries,[3] and no fewer than 1,500 Schwyzers accompanied Rudolf of Hapsburg in 1289 on his campaign into Burgundy. This warrior element no doubt extends much further back than is apparent in the historical accounts and sources. We can recognize the belligerent warrior spirit of the Schwyzers in their repeated friction with their principal neighbor, the monastery of Einsiedeln. As early as 1114, under Emperor Henry V, they had a border dispute with the monastery, which reached back a hundred years earlier to the period of Henry II and which the Schwyzers constantly renewed.

In Uri and Unterwalden the suppression of the peasants into conditions of hereditary serfdom had already made further advances than in Schwyz, but under Emperor Frederick II, first Uri (1231) and then also Schwyz (1240) succeeded in obtaining letters of freedom, in which it was established that they were not subordinate to any count or other feudal authority but were directly under the empire. Since the empire fell into a position of complete weakness with the fall of the Hohenstaufens, the imperial letters of freedom would have been of little use to the cantons; they were symptoms and evidence of their striving and their will rather than means for reaching such a position. The decisive point is that these groups of peasants were able to oppose the knightly domination with weapons in hand. As early as the last years of the reign of Frederick II, Schwyz, Uri, Unterwalden, and also the city of Lucerne had allied themselves. Even if they were still far from becoming completely independent, we can still recognize that they were treated in a conciliatory and careful manner by their count, even when that lord himself became king. That was Rudolf of Hapsburg, whose family united a large part of Switzerland with Alsatian areas into a large holding through the inheritances of daughters, as the families of counts and lords gradually died out.

Rudolf's death encouraged the three peasant cantons to join in an "eternal alliance" (1 August 1291), in which they obligated themselves to accept no judge who was not one of their inhabitants or compatriots. They still did not bring up the demand for selecting native *ammanns* themselves, but King Albrecht, for his part, anticipated their wish and appointed only *ammanns* from the native, leading families of the people—Attinghausens, Stauffachers, and others.

The murder of Albrecht by his nephew in 1308 brought into motion these political relationships that were not clearly defined and were based on mutual understanding and restraint. There arose a situation which encouraged the peasant groups to consider the complete rejection of the Hapsburg domination. The Hapsburgs lost the kingship, which passed over to the count of Luxembourg, Henry VII, as a result of the choice of the Electors. In 1309 the allies obtained from him a declaration of their freedom from the Hapsburgs, and after Henry's death, when the selection of a king was divided between the Hapsburg Frederick and the Bavarian Louis, they spoke out in favor of the latter and took the offensive against their former ruler.

As we have already heard, Schwyz lived in a long-lasting state of enmity with the monastery of Einsiedeln, which was now under Hapsburg control. The Schwyzers had often plundered the Einsiedeln area without interference from the Hapsburg governors, who dared not intervene despite their power. Now the Schwyzers came under the command of their *ammann* Werner Stauffacher, completely plundered the monastery, and took a number of monks off with them as prisoners.[4] The younger brother of King Frederick, Duke Leopold, thereupon undertook to punish the peasants, who would necessarily be doubly dangerous as partisans of Louis the Bavarian in the dynastic civil war that was erupting.

EXCURSUS

Recent references: Karl Meyer, *The Influence of the Saint Gothard Pass on the Beginnings of the Confederation (Die Einwirkung des Gotthardpasses auf die Anfänge der Eidgenossenschaft), Geschichte Freud,* Vol. 74, 1919. *Jahrbücher für Schweizer Geschichte,* Vol. 45, 1920.

NOTES FOR CHAPTER I

1. That is the opinion of Oechsli, in *The Beginnings of the Swiss Confederation (Die Anfänge der Schweizerischen Eidgenossenschaft),* p. 121.

2. Oechsli, p. 230. Durrer, *The Unity of Unterwalden* (*Die Einheit Unterwaldens*) *Jahrbücher für Schweizerische Geschichte*, 1910, p. 96, confirms Oechsli's assumption.

3. In 1252 the abbot of Saint Gall took them into his service in a feud with the bishop of Constance. Oechsli, p. 229.

4. One of the captured monks composed a very interesting cultural-historical poem in Latin on this subject. An old German translation of this poem with explanatory remarks has been edited by Leo Wirth, *A Prelude to the Battle on the Morgarten* (*Ein Vorspiel der Morgartenschlacht*), Aarau, 1909. 114 pages.

Chapter II

Battle on the Morgarten 15 November 1315

The rubble-like mass of legends and accounts that buried the early history of Switzerland and first had to be removed with so much effort and struggle had also buried beneath it the battle on the Morgarten, as a result of the individual fables, such as that of the Austrian knight Hünenberg, who supposedly warned the Swiss "Be on your guard on the Morgarten" by means of a note shot over to them; or as the result of descriptions of the battle scene, which caused researchers to place the battle at the wrong spot. The battlefield was sought a half-hour too far to the south, on the Figlerfluh. Because the lake, which plays an important role in the accounts, did not extend that far, historians resorted to the expedient of assuming that the surface of the lake at that time was much higher. It fell to two dilettantes, a doctor, Christian Ithen, and a master tanner, Karl Bürkli, in opposition to all the military men and scholars, to discover the truth and fight through to its acceptance. As early as 1818, Ithen showed General Zurlauben that the level of the lake had not changed, a point that was verified both geologically and historically. Bürkli, by going back to the contemporary sources and interpreting them with understanding of the military aspects and study of the terrain, found the correct strategic and tactical relationships, so that today his concept is no doubt generally accepted. My attention was drawn to him by his work *The True Winkelried (Der wahre Winkelried)*, which appeared while my *Perser- und Burgunderkriege* was in press, and I looked him up when I was passing through Zurich in 1888. He was an unusual old gentleman; he explained to me that in his youth he had gone to Texas with Victor Considérant in order to found a communistic utopia there. When that failed, despite an adequate supply of money, he said he experienced numerous adventures in Mexican military service until he returned home, where, as a social democratic politician, he kept himself constantly in the public eye and also no doubt stirred things up so much that both because of that and his heretical views on questions of his country's military history, the Swiss scholarly world was not interested in hearing anything from him. But he was not only very well read, but he also had a natural instinct for historical criticism and an astonishing power of observation for past times, especially in military history matters. Now and then his lively fantasy had misled him into recounting more than could be deduced directly from the sources, but hardly anything that in itself was not possible and indeed not psychologically probable.

The point of departure is the fact that it was not a question of the desperate revolutionary rising of a peaceful peasantry but rather of a well-planned struggle of a warlike community with battle-hardened leaders under the command of their own top authority. In the case of men with such military experience, we are justified in filling in, in keeping with the concept of a well-planned, systematic action, the individual reports and indications of their acts that have been preserved for us.

From ancient times, people in mountainous areas have strengthened their natural protection against enemy attacks by blocking the entrances in the valleys through some kind of man-made works. In Switzerland such obstacles were called "*letzi*" or "*letzinen*," which is related to the word "*lass*," whose superlative form is "*letzt*"; there are still eighty-five of them that can be confirmed today.[1] The Röuschiben *letzi* is supposed to be from the pre-Roman period, the Serviezel *letzi* and also the foundation of the one at Näfels are supposed to be of Roman origin, and four others are thought to be from the fourth century. In Schwyz six *letzinen* can be confirmed; they covered not only the entrances to the country, but a few of them also consisted of palisades in Vierwaldstätter Lake and Zuger Lake in order also to prevent landings. Certainly some of these installations reached back into the thirteenth century and even earlier, long before the battle of Morgarten. When the great decisive battle for their liberation from the power of the count now approached, the Schwyzer had nothing to do that was more important than reinforcing their *letzinen*.[2] There is also in existence a document indicating that the community of the march, the people of Schwyz, in 1310 sold parcels of the land to two brothers, in order to apply the profit "an die Mur ze Altum mata," that is, the *letzi* at Rothenthurm bei Altmatt, of which one tower still exists today. Basically, however, we must assume that in 1315 they erected the mighty, 5-kilometer-long *letzi* which, extending from Rossberg (between Zuger Lake and Aegeri Lake) to Rigi, blocked the whole south end of Zuger Lake and the roads along its banks. While the report that this *letzi* had been erected at that specific time dates only from the year 1571, the fact that it existed is already confirmed in a document from the year 1354. Every logical probability points to the fact that its construction is related to the situation existing in the war for liberation. It cannot be older, for the real Schwyz does not reach that far but ended at Lowerzer Lake. But the march community of Arth, which formed a Hapsburg domain, joined the side of Schwyz at the outbreak of hostilities and then had to be protected. Important parts of the fortification still exist today, and a very large part stood until 1805, from which period we have an exact description of the work. It was a thick wall about 5 kilometers long, no less than 12 feet high, with gates at the entrances and three mighty towers.

Between the accesses at Altmatt and Arth there was also the road that led along the east bank of Aegeri Lake via Morgarten, Schorno, and Sattel to Schwyz.[3] One would be led to assume that this road was also blocked by a *letzi,* but once again surviving sources tell us it was not until 1322 that the people of Schwyz sold five pieces of property in order to build with the purchase price the *letzi* here near Schorno. If there already existed here in 1315 a *letzi,* which was repaired and strengthened in 1322, then Schwyz would already have been a kind of giant fortress at that time. But it is not at all impossible that in 1315 the Schwyzers intentionally neglected the *letzi* of Schorno and left open the access by Aegeri Lake.[4] No matter how strong each individual point of the defense might be either naturally or by construction, it is still very difficult to defend continuously a fortification stretching over such a wide area. An alert and tough enemy can only too easily find a spot that is unguarded, where he can penetrate and take the defenders from the rear. That was experienced by the Greeks at Thermopylae. In all probability, from the start the Schwyzers, under the command of their *ammann,* Werner Stauffacher, had a completely different plan, and to carry it out they intentionally left open the road from Schorno.

Duke Leopold assembled his knights, with reinforcements from the cities of Zurich, Zug, Winterthur, and Lucerne, near Zug and did not take the road along the right or the left of Zuger Lake via Arth, where the Schwyzers had erected their great wall, but along the east bank of the Aegeri Lake. This was either because along that route there was actually no fortification or because he believed that here he could more easily envelop any fortification or penetrate it by surprise. His army may have been between 2,000 and 3,000 strong, a size which at that time formed a considerable force and an unusually large levy against a mere group of peasants.[5]

The Schwyzers were joined by the men of Uri, but it is doubtful

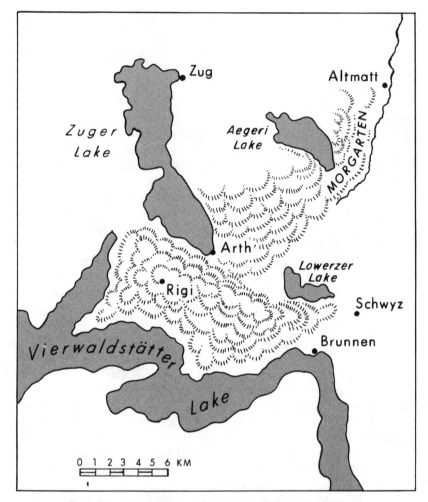

Fig. 6   BATTLE ON THE MORGARTEN

whether there was also a contingent from Unterwalden. Duke Leopold, as a matter of precaution, had their area attacked at the same time by one of his counts, who came over the Brünig Pass from Interlaken. Nevertheless, the army of the confederates, whose commander is assumed to have been Werner Stauffacher,[6] can be estimated at a strength between 3,000 and 4,000 men.[7]

Stauffacher, if he had not planned it from the start, had in any case foreseen that the duke would select the route via Morgarten. As soon as the scouts and observers whom the Schwyzers had out in the area brought the news that the Austrian army was marching up on that route, Stauffacher led his troops up to the Mattligütsch, a ridge above Aegeri Lake, where the Swiss could form in a concealed position and could only be discovered with difficulty, since the area on the right, toward the enemy, was protected against any direct reconnaissance by a deep cut, a wooded ravine, the Haselmattruse. From the Mattligütsch, more or less steep but generally passable, grassy slopes lead down to the lake. To the south, the mountain rises steeply close to the lake, so that the road could easily be blocked there with a single tree trunk.

Stauffacher sent a small unit, his advance guard, probably consisting mainly of crossbowmen, to this narrow spot near Buchwäldli.[8]

As well as Duke Leopold knew the military ability of the Schwyzers and was counting on a serious fight, still he hardly expected resistance at this early point, for the narrow spot near Buchwäldli is situated beyond the Schwyzer area. The confederates had been bold enough not to await the enemy in their own country but to move forward against him into his own territory, which belonged to the town of Zug. Stauffacher had undoubtedly examined the entire region for a long time and had selected this spot as a very suitable battlefield.

When the point of the Austrian army found the road blocked near Buchwäldli and was unable to drive off the enemy by shooting and skirmishing, a number of foot soldiers or dismounted knights probably climbed up the grassy slope on the left in order to envelop the improvised *letzi* from above and drive off the defenders. This required some time, and in the meantime the knightly column moved up closer, became congested in front of the obstacle, and was closely pressed together on the road and onto the flatter areas of the grassy slope. This was precisely what Stauffacher was waiting for. Suddenly stones and logs rolled down the steep slope under the horsemen, and the entire confederated force stormed down from the ridge in powerful, closely formed units. A hail of "handful" stones, thrown with great force, pelted down on knights and horses shortly before the impact, and then the far superior mass drove into the confused pack of knights and soldiers, cutting and thrusting. Their principal weapon was the halberd, which had been mentioned for the first time only a short time previously. The name means "*Halmbarte,*" that is, the axe with a very long handle, which also has an iron point, joining spear and axe in a single weapon. It was the reaction to the constantly increasing strength of the knight's armor, which could only be penetrated by the enormous weight of the long-shafted axe, and was therefore the weapon of the unarmored foot soldier against the heavy

horseman. In its later development it was also provided with a hook on
its rear side in order to pull the knight off his horse by his armor.
Sometimes it also had a pointed hammer.

What could the knights do against the wild onslaught of the peasant
units bearing such frightful arms? They could not press up the mountain
against them, and, with the lake behind them, they could not move to the
rear. In the melee they could hardly control their horses, stirred up as
they were by the rolling rocks and the hail of stones. A horseman who
can no longer move with his horse derives no further advantage from
him but only the disadvantage that part of his strength and attention must
be devoted to the horse, which, when it becomes wild, makes the rider
incapable of fighting, for all practical purposes.

The strength of the Schwyzers' battle plan, then, was based not only on
the sudden attack in a narrow pass but also very importantly on the jam
caused by the roadblock and the delay beside the Buchwäldli heights. If
the Schwyzers had simply launched a flank attack down on the marching
Austrian army from Morgarten Mountain, they would, to be sure, have
been victorious under these circumstances, but their success would only
have been a minor one; those troops not struck directly by the attack
would have withdrawn as fast as possible, and even most of those who
fled forward would no doubt have escaped via detours and trails. But the
congestion that preceded the attack had the effect of involving in the
battle a very large part of the Austrian army, even if not all of it, thus
preventing it from withdrawing while at the same time rendering it as
good as incapable of fighting in the jam-up in the narrow pass. Bürkli's
decisive achievement lay in having recognized these developments correctly. Associated with this analysis was not only military perspicacious-
ness but also complete inner liberation from the legend that pictured the
Schwyzers as peaceful shepherds and peasants. As long as one har-
bored this concept, it was naturally impossible to arrive at the idea
of finding among them an ingenious strategic concept, planned far in
advance. But the Schwyzers, who had been involved in numerous earlier
battles, had adopted as their special arm the weapon with which the
peasant could defeat the knight, the halberd. They also had the self-
confidence that makes it possible to attack, and in Stauffacher they had
the leader—we may say, the general—who inspired the blended forces to
the saving action, which was at the same time significant in world history.

The Austrian troops who were still moving up farther in the rear were
not capable of helping their comrades who were so closely pressed together. Soon they, too, were swept away by the retreating troops in the
general flight. Most of the knights and soldiers in the group that was

pressed together at the point were either slaughtered by the Swiss or pushed into the lake and drowned. Duke Leopold himself only barely managed to escape. The monk John of Winterthur (Vitoduran), to whom we are indebted for an account of the battle, recounts how he himself, as a boy, saw the duke ride into his home city with a crushed countenance; "He seemed to be half-dead from extreme sorrow."

The important point on which I have reached out beyond Bürkli's account is the emphasis on the strategic and tactical leadership of the Schwyzers. Bürkli is aroused over the later legend and false report, which gives credit for the victory to a knight of Hünenberg, who supposedly called the attention of the Schwyzers to the position on the Morgarten, and to another aristocrat, Itel Reding, who supposedly gave good advice. His anger is out of place in that the bias of these fables in no way takes from the people their achievement, but it is only a question of the psychological factor with which we are familiar, the substitution of something of a colorful personal nature for the hard-to-grasp practical historical facts. But Bürkli is completely wrong in believing that a battle like Morgarten is a direct deed of the people, so to speak, an expression of the popular instinct. He himself points out admirably how everything was well planned far in advance; but this is a function of leadership. No matter how much military experience these Schwyzer peasants already had, the community of many thousand souls can, in the final analysis, still not do what was done here. There must have been on hand a well-functioning observation and communication service; Zug, where the Hapsburg commander assembled his troops, is situated only three hours from the Schwyzer border. Vitoduran has the account that the Schwyzers had learned through the count of Toggenburg where Leopold would move up. This report is completely incredible; the count would have brought on his own death by such treason, for as a loyal knight of his lord he was killed at Morgarten. We also cannot believe that, in the course of attempts at mediation which he made, he unintentionally betrayed the duke's plan. Even if this were true, it would have no significance—for what prevented the duke, even at the moment of starting his march, from changing his direction and taking the road toward Arth or Altmatt? The Schwyzer command must also have been prepared for this possibility. The observers and messengers it had near Zug must also have been so alert and wise that they did not allow themselves to be deceived by possible deceptive movements. Vitoduran expressly reports that Leopold moved forward not only on the Morgarten road but also on other roads, and that the troops on these other routes turned around and escaped without losses on hearing the news of the defeat of the main

army. Why did Leopold send out such parallel columns and not keep his
forces together? He was certainly contemplating a very serious fight, and
if he was victorious in it, everything was decided and it was unimportant
as to which route they followed into the country. The secondary columns
cannot have been strong; certainly the entire body of knights was with
the duke. Leopold probably expected that if he encountered tough opposition, perhaps at the *letzi* near Schorno, the Schwyzers would be induced to withdraw on hearing that enemies were also appearing on the
right or the left. Or perhaps Leopold thought that his approach on various roads would mislead them from the start into dividing up their forces
between the various *letzinen*. On the other hand, it was decisive for the
Schwyzers to recognize early enough where the real attacking force was
moving up, so that they could oppose it with their maximum possible
strength. That cannot have been left to chance but was a matter of
well-planned, decisive leadership. At the moment when the report came
that the enemy was marching along the eastern bank of Aegeri Lake, the
commander must have been so sure of his messenger and his plan that he
immediately ordered his men to move out. Whether his forces had been
assembled at the *letzi* near Arth or near Schwyz, the march they had to
make was not much shorter than that of the duke. If they arrived an hour
too late, that is, if the *letzi* on the Buchwäldli had already been attacked
and the main body of the Austrians had passed it, the war plan was
destroyed and Schwyz was probably lost.

Consequently, the Schwyzers must have had a commander who not
only had an alert eye for judging the terrain and organizing his reconnaissance service, as well as good leadership, but who also had his troops
completely under control, so that they trusted his leadership and moved
out at the moment when he gave the command. Neither a general assembly of warriors nor a war captain chosen at will could have carried out
a war plan based so very much on immediate execution. We may be
allowed to make a comparison with the leadership of the Athenians by
Miltiades at Marathon. But Miltiades' social status was so high above the
mass of the Athenian burghers that, once he had been chosen as their
general, the mass also gave him a natural obedience. The authority with
which the peasant man, Stauffacher, led the Schwyzers at Morgarten was
of a different origin. We have already become acquainted with it in the
earliest Germanic history—the Schwyz *ammann,* who also governed the
community (association of the march) politically and economically and
drew the strength of his military commands from the unity of the entire
body at whose head he stood. The people in this case were able to defeat
the knights only because here in Schwyz the ancient German clan still
lived on in its original concept, because the military efficiency of the

individuals was blended into a mighty unit with a unified will, and because this democracy had a commander.

The principal source for the battle of Morgarten is a rather long account by the monk John of Winterthur (Vitoduran), written some twenty-five to thirty years after the event. The men of Winterthur were subjects of the Hapsburgs and had their contingent, from which only one man perished, in Leopold's army. Consequently, John had his information from eyewitnesses, principally from his own father, who was also present. But his account clearly shows that he also had information from Schwyzers.[9]

NOTES FOR CHAPTER II

1. A. Nüscheler, in "The *Letzinen* in Switzerland" ("Die Letzinen in der Schweiz"), *Mitteilungen der antiquarischen Gesellschaft in Zürich,* Vol. 18, Issue No. 1, Zurich, 1872. With respect to Näfels, see Dändliker, *Geschichte der Schweiz,* 1: 531, note.

2. This is expressly reported by Vitoduran.

3. Morgarten is the mountain east of the lake. Schorno is 1,100 meters south of the lake, and Sattel is somewhat farther south, where the road from Schorno meets the road from Altmatt.

4. One might ask why the Schwyzers later (1322) extended the *letzi* near Schorno, since its absence had, after all, done them the good service in 1315 of attracting the duke onto the dangerous route. The answer may be that they could in no case count on surprising the enemy a second time at the same place and therefore preferred to protect the land here also.

5. The fact that Vitoduran gives a strength of 20,000 men is, of course, meaningless.

6. Werner Stauffacher had led the Schwyzers in January 1314 in the raid on Einsiedeln and appears again in sources after the battle at the head of his country. Oechsli, p. 352.

7. As we have already seen above, Oechsli estimates the population of Schwyz at that time at some 18,000. Even if it should have been a few thousand smaller, we must still assume that in the most extreme danger even the last available man was called up. We surely cannot go below a figure of 3,000. In addition, there were also the men of Arth, those of Uri, and perhaps also men of Unterwalden. But we must make a small deduction for the garrison of the *letzi* of Arth and perhaps also of Brunnen, to defend against an attack by water.

The numerical superiority of the confederates in the actual battle was even greater because part of the Hapsburg troops, for example, the Winterthur contingent, were still on the way.

8. In later accounts, the advance guard is designated as the "banished ones" ("*Verbannten*"), and this has given rise to the most varied interpretations. Nevertheless, this is simply a question of a misunderstood word. The misunderstanding is clarified by H. Herzog in the *Schweizerische Monatshefte für Offiziere aller Waffen,* 1906.

9. All available accounts have been printed one after the other by Thomas von Liebenau in the *Mitteilungen des historischen Vereins des Kantons Schwyz,* Issue No. 3, 1884.

Of value in this analysis are the notes Dändliker added in the fourth edition of his *Geschichte der Schweiz,* after he changed his earlier account in favor of the Bürkli concept (p. 700).

Bürkli followed up his first work, *The Creation of the Swiss Confederation and the Battle on the Morgarten* (*Die Entstehung der Schweizer Eidgenossenschaft und die Schlacht am Morgarten*), 1891, with a second treatment under the title "A Monument on the Morgarten" ("Ein Denkmal am Morgarten"), in the *Zuger Neujahrsblatt für das Jahr 1895* (published by W. Anderwert). This article is also accompanied by a good special map.

Chapter III

Battle of Laupen
21 June 1339

When the great family of the Zähringens died out, in 1218, a portion of its domains reverted to the empire. Since precisely at that time the imperial power under the last Hohenstaufen, Frederick II, was breaking up, in these areas at the borders of the Duchy of Swabia and the Kingdom of Burgundy a group of small areas and cities (some of them extremely small) became direct dependencies of the empire and independent, including the city of Bern, which had been founded only a short time before by the last Zähringen. Constant feuding between neighbors was the result of the disappearance of that higher, supreme power in the mountainous area. In these feuds, in the course of the century, the city of Bern had won numerous successes, had made peasant communities dependent on it, and had forced noblemen to have themselves, together with their territory and their castles, absorbed into the political body of the city. The city had an organization that was particularly adapted to a policy of conquest: an aristocratic council that governed with the political instinct and sense of mastery of the aristocrats, but that was doubled by another council which, without giving free vent to a real democracy, still managed to maintain a government close enough to the people to bind the total citizenry to the politics of the government and to place all their powers in its service.

The bold and successful expansion of the city in all directions finally forced its principal rival, the city of Fribourg, only 18 miles away and also a creation of the Zähringens, to join forces with the surrounding small dynasties, the counts of Greyerz, Neuenburg, Valengin, Nidau, Waadt, Aarburg, and others, in order, first of all, to wrest away from Bern the little town of Laupen on the Sense, near the Saane.

Faced with this large coalition, the Bernese were somewhat discouraged; on their side stood the city of Solothurn alone, but with their

far-sighted political skill they were able to cope with the situation. The
Bernese policy of expansion had already moved forward in Oberland,
across the Lake of Brienze and into contact with Unterwalden and Uri.
Since their victory at Morgarten, the forest cantons enjoyed far and wide
the highest military fame, and Bern had initiated friendly relationships
with them. Now this city turned to them for help, and indeed for help in
return for pay; the forest cantons did not have any kind of political
interest in the feud over Laupen.[1] Consequently, the war over Laupen
was the first forerunner still within the borders of Switzerland itself of
the Swiss system of mercenary soldiers (*Reisläufer*), which later grew to
such great importance. A document that has by chance been preserved
indicates that Uri received 250 pounds of pennies after the victory. The
city of Bern, with its financial strength, which, even if it was certainly still
very small, was still strained to the utmost by its determined government,
took into its service the proven military strength of the peasants, who
were not capable of setting a political target for themselves. The feud had
a deeper political background, even if it was no doubt principally applied
only from a decorative viewpoint, in that Bern was not willing to recognize Louis the Bavarian as emperor and aligned itself with the papacy. A
secular priest, Diebold Baselwind, used this point to strengthen and
excite the combativeness of the people.

Concerning the sequence of the feud and the battle, we have, apparently from the circle of this priest, a detailed account, the *"Conflictus
Laupensis"* ("Battle of Laupen"), which is very animated and interesting
but is unjustifiably famed as an important achievement of military history
literature.[2] The decisive traits from the military viewpoint are to be
gleaned from it only rather uncertainly and indirectly. Since the later
account in Justinger's *Bernese Chronicle,* which was drawn up eighty years
after the event, is obviously strongly overgrown with legendary material,
and since any witness from the other side for control purposes is lacking,
we cannot speak with certainty of the battle of Laupen, which we would
like to do in view of its undoubtedly great importance in military history.

The allies besieged and attacked Laupen, which was garrisoned by 600
Bernese, when finally, on the twelfth day, the Bernese with their allies
moved up to the relief (21 June 1339). The *Conflictus* gives the strength
of the siege army as 16,000 dismounted and 1,000 mounted men; Justinger even gives a total strength of 30,000 men. Of course, these figures
do not have the slightest value. If the allied dynasties and the city of
Fribourg together put 4,000 men into the field, that would already have
been a considerable number. In the *Conflictus* the Bernese army is stated
to have had a total of 6,000 men, including 1,000 men from the forest

cantons. This figure appears to be quite credible.[3] In any case it can be assumed that Bern, with its large area and the reinforcements from the forest cantons, was able to field a larger army than the enemies, where only Fribourg could appear with a certain mass levy, whereas the counts allied with that city appeared only with their knights and soldiers, always only very small numbers.[4] This army's confidence in victory was naturally based not on numbers, but on its warrior and knightly abilities, in contrast with the popular mass of burghers and peasants.

When the Bernese marched out of the forest between their city and Laupen, on the heights of the Bramberg, they saw below them the allies, who had moved a short distance toward them. Although the battlefield is only 2 to 2½ kilometers from Laupen, the besieged garrison could still not observe the events from the city.

The Bernese did not proceed immediately to the attack but took up position on the heights, apparently with the hope of letting the enemies, especially the knights, take up the attack on their side, while the Bernese took advantage of some kinds of terrain obstacles. They could assume that the allies would either have to attack or give up the siege of Laupen, for if they continued the siege without first having driven away the relief army that was so near, they would be exposing themselves to a sudden attack. The situation was therefore similar to that at Nikopol.

The Bernese army was presumably drawn up in three squares, with the advance guard formed of the men from the forest cantons, 1,000 strong, some thirty men wide and thirty men deep. The main unit was 3,000 men strong, some fifty men wide and fifty men deep, and the rear guard was 2,000 men strong, forty men wide and forty men deep. In front of each unit a number of marksmen moved about,[5] with the knights and their mounted followers, who, even though only in small numbers, were present, between the marksmen and the units.[6]

The allies hesitated to attack the Bernese directly in their advantageous position and sent a detachment out to make an envelopment, while the knights paraded in front of the enemy position and young lords were dubbed knights. It was almost evening before the envelopment was completed, in the face of which the rear guard of the Bernese immediately fled. But the main body stood fast against the frontal attack that was now launched and that the Fribourgers carried out, meeting them with the bolts of the marksmen and a hail of stones. Going over to the offensive, they then charged out against the enemy. In the face of this shock action, the Fribourgers dispersed. The advance guard had also stormed forward simultaneously with the main body, but as soon as it descended from the ridge, it was attacked by the knights, was brought to a standstill, and was soon surrounded on all sides. Even if the knights were not able to penetrate into the tightly formed "porcupine," from which spears protruded against them on all sides, still the men of the forest cantons would have been lost as soon as the knights brought up their marksmen. But in the meantime the main body of the Bernese had already been victorious. The men of the forest cantons had done their part by drawing the knights to them, so that the Bernese had only the Fribourgers to contend with. As soon as they had finished with them, they turned about, moved against the knights, and fell on them from the rear. There was nothing the knights could do but save themselves by fleeing; a large number of them were killed. The contingent of the allies which, for its part, had defeated the unit of the Bernese rear guard did not enter the fight again. Presumably, the men were not under the control of their leaders or had no true leadership at all and were pursuing the fleeing enemy in order to take prisoners and to plunder.

The battle of Laupen shows so much strategic and tactical thought and leadership on the part of the Bernese that we may well ask who the general was who accomplished this feat. The assumption of a threatening defensive position and the shift from the defensive into the attack remind us again of Marathon, and, strangely enough, there exists on the Bernese general a source account quite similar to that on Miltiades. To be sure, the contemporary source, the *Conflictus,* makes no mention at all of a commander, but this account is completely defective from the military viewpoint. On the other hand, Justinger's account, in which, of course, legend and history can no longer be completely separated from one another, reports that the knight Rudolf von Erlach held the high command position. This man, very rich and respected, was at the same time the vassal of one of the allied enemies, the count of Nidau, and a burgher of Bern. When the war clouds formed, he freed himself from his feudal lord and placed himself at the disposition of the Bernese. His father had already once commanded the Bernese at the engagement on the Dornbühl in 1298, and he himself had "proven himself well in six battles." The Bernese believed they had found in him the right commander, "that he would show and teach them how they should start and end their affairs, since in war wisdom is better than strength." But Erlach at first hesitated to accept the high command because the burghers were too proud, and the commander who might wish to act with strictness had to be concerned about harm and shame later from their revenge. Finally, after lengthy requests, it was agreed that the entire community would swear to him to be obedient to him in all matters. If the leader should strike a disobedient man, even if he wounded him or even killed him, neither the city nor the friends of the victim might hold him responsible or take revenge on him for that act.

And so Erlach had the high command, which otherwise lay in the hand of the *Schultheiss* (burgomaster). At that time this office was held by Johann von Bubenberg, also a knight and of a very respected family; his son commanded the garrison of Laupen. As remarkable as it is that the contemporary account makes no mention of Erlach's command, nevertheless that account can hardly be pure legend. For Bern, everything was at stake in this war; consequently, they sought the most competent soldier for the high command. Again, much later, in the battle of Murten, the high command was turned over to a knight—for other reasons, to be sure—and this fact was later almost completely suppressed in the chronicles. I believe, therefore, that the account of the command by the knight Rudolf von Erlach at Laupen, as late and legendary as it is, may not be rejected as lacking in credibility. It is a real general that we can sense in this battle. If he had also been the burgomaster, this personality would have been emphasized quite differently in the history of Bern. It seems much more understandable that the author of the *Conflictus,* who saw everything from a clerical viewpoint and had neither interest nor understanding for the military aspects, simply forgot to name the leader. Consequently, I have no hesitation in identifying the ingenious warrior whom military history sees riding across the field of Laupen as Rudolf von Erlach. That he was the victor remained in the memory of following generations, even though he was not named by the contemporary chronicler.

The central point of his action is the special, formal obedience that he had the citizenry swear to him and to which he was able to give meaning by the strength of his personality. In the following year, when on one occasion he set up an ambush for the Fribourgers, and eight soldiers, who against orders had moved out in order to steal horses, were surrounded by the Fribourgers, he forbade that they be helped and allowed all of them to be stabbed to death by the enemies, "for they were perjured scoundrels who were more interested in their booty than in the honor of Bern."[7] Thus he kept his men under control and at Laupen was able to withdraw his main body after its victory over the Fribourgers and lead it against the rear of the knights. Without this leadership the battle would have been lost, since, after their defeat of the men of the forest cantons, the knights would undoubtedly also have overcome the Bernese, who in their broken formation could no longer have stood up to the knights.

EXCURSUS

I confess that the preceding account of the battle of Laupen is based largely only on supposition and cannot be proven directly from the sources. Indeed, in a few respects it is in contradiction to the source accounts. If I nevertheless risk giving this picture as a very probable one, that is based on the fact that the account in the *Conflictus* contains a few contradictions and unexplained points that seem to me capable of solution in hardly any other way than as I have done above.

The *Conflicuts* says: "Videntes Bernenses hostium multitudinem contra se esse validam omnes coadunati in unum quasi unus parvus cuneus, ad unum parvulum collem se congregantes stabant." ("All the men of Bern, seeing that the number of the enemy against them was strong, joined themselves into one body as a small wedge and stood in mass on a small hill.") These words seem to say clearly that the Bernese had formed only a single large battle square and not three of them, as I have assumed. But the fact that the men of the forest cantons formed a special unit, as the account goes on to show, cannot be reconciled with the single unit, unless one limits strictly the word "Bernese" and understands by it only the warriors from the city.

The *Conflictus* goes on to relate that, as the enemy attacked, 2,000 Bernese, overcome with terror, took flight, and that a few of these fugitives were unarmed, but there were also warriors among them. The account states, however, that 3,000 of the Bernese had not been able to see the flight of the others, had stood fast, and then went over to the attack and defeated the Fribourgers.

From this account we must conclude that, aside from the men from the forest cantons, the Bernese, together with the other reinforcements, formed two units of 3,000 and 2,000 men, respectively. For if that was not the case, how could it have happened that the 3,000 men did not see the flight of the 2,000?

This question seems to be answered in the later account by Justinger. It reads as follows:

And so they wanted to move up together, and each man had taken two or three stones; their captain ordered them to throw the stones at the enemy and then move back into the clear so as to be aligned on the hillside. Then the men in the rear thought that those in front intended to flee, and so a large number of them took flight. But when they saw that those in front were standing fast and none of them were inclined to flee, they turned back again into the fray and conducted themselves like brave and honest men and fought like heroes, except for a few who fled into the forest and did not return; and they were always called "foresters." Later, men wished to punish them corporally and by forfeiture of their possessions, since it had been ordered that nobody should do anything to benefit the enemy; and so, afterwards, they were never again esteemed and were shamed and considered as worthless. And as the men in the rear were fleeing, the captain and the men in front did not see them, but those in the middle, who saw them, said to the captain: "Sir, there in the rear quite a lot of our men are fleeing." Then the captain replied: "It is good that the bad ones not be with the brave men; the wheat is separated from the chaff."

This account seems to show that it was the rear ranks of the main body that did not understand the backward movement of the front ranks, those that were throwing the stones, and consequently they took flight. But in this case, how would it have been possible for the commander and the foremost ranks not to have noticed the flight? After all, the flight cannot have been delayed until just the moment when the foremost ranks had again reformed! These two facts can be reduced to one: either the rear ranks fled because the leading ranks made a backward movement—and in that case the men in front must have seen it—or the leading ranks did not see the flight of those in the rear, and in that case they cannot have made the movement backward themselves but must have held their front facing forward. But if we eliminate the factor of the misunderstood rearward move as a later invention to excuse the flight, then the question arises as to how it happened that it was specifically the rearmost ranks, those least threatened, who were so fearful and allowed themselves to be so terrified by the approach of the enemy?

Justinger's account contains an obvious contradiction, which is easily explained, however, by the contamination of two different sources. From the *Conflictus* he took the fact that the unit that was later victorious did not see the flight of the others, whereas in the oral tradition he found the excuse that they had thought the rearward movement of the stone-throwers to be a flight.

But the account does not become understandable until we assume that it was a question of two different units, one of which, the one that fled, was in position so far to the flank behind the other one that it was not seen by the latter.

There are two other factors to be considered. In the *Conflictus* it is recounted that the secular priest, Baselwind, who accompanied the army with the holy sacrament, fell into the hands of the enemies and was treated scornfully by them. How is that supposed to have happened? If the priest had been sent over as an intermediary and had been held there in violation of international law, the author would not have failed to mention that. The only possible explanation seems to be that he was among the "unarmed men" who fled, and therefore with the train; and that, consequently, enemies appeared at the train, that is, behind the main body. Since not only the train but also a large number of warriors took part in this flight, it must be a question of a special detachment, not the rear ranks of the main body, which of course itself, attacked in the flank or the rear, could not have gone over to the attack against the Fribourgers.

Not until we assume a separate unit do we have an explanation of the definite statement of our source that there were 2,000 men who fled. If the author had only estimated the number, he would certainly either not have stated it at all or would have made it smaller, for we see how he takes pains to make this unpleasant event appear in the mildest possible light through the excuse—we may call it outright fiction—that most of the men returned to the battle. Only the fact that an entire unit of definitely known strength was at fault can have made such an impression as to force an author who was far from telling a direct untruth, to make the positive statement as to the strength. In Justinger this number has already disappeared and instead the exculpatory reason has been added, that is, that they had thought the movement of the stone-throwers to be a flight. Justinger himself seems not even to have known any longer that it had been the entire rear guard that had been guilty of the shameful flight. He, too, already understood from the *Conflictus* that it was the rear ranks of the main unit. He attempted to offset the account in the *Conflictus,* that the main body had not noticed the flight, with the legendary account of the words of the commander, "It is good that the chaff was separated from the wheat," by the insertion of the men in the middle, who make the report.

The *Conflictus* reports, and Justinger developed the point further, that the Fribourger allies did not attack at once but "they carried on courtly activity, dubbed knights and conducted themselves in a hostile manner" before the front line of their enemies. He also says expressly that the battle was not fought until the evening, "after the hour for vespers." This fact requires an explanation. It does happen, of course, that two armies stand facing one another and each waits for the other to attack. But in this case it was entirely clear that the Fribourgers, if they did not withdraw, had to attack. If they hesitated to do so, that would depress the morale of their troops, who saw that their leaders were afraid of the good position of the Bernese. Furthermore, the garrison of Laupen could at all times notice what was going on in front of them and could make a sortie and appear in the rear of the allies.

Nevertheless, the hesitation apparently lasted for a rather long time. It is explained when we learn that in the meanwhile a detachment was making an envelopment, and the leaders were smart enough to fill the time during this pause with all kinds of play in the interest of the morale of their troops.

At the end of his account, Justinger again points out that the defeated knights fled in various directions, the Germans downstream from Laupen and across the Saane, and the men of Valais above Laupen across the Sense. Such a difference in the direction of flight leads to the conclusion that in the battle, too, various directions were followed; in other words, one detachment was the original enveloping corps.

But how can we now clarify the positive statement in the *Conflictus* that the Bernese had formed in a single unit? The author is lacking in his knowledge of Latin. The word "*unus*" therefore flowed from his pen only as a translation of the German indefinite article, just as he writes directly afterward "ad unum parvulum collem" ("on a small hill"), where he certainly does not intend to emphasize particularly that it was *one* hill on or beside which the Bernese were drawn up.[8] The enemy army was no doubt broadly extended; the author intends to emphasize the small, compact unit of the Bernese on the opposite side, and he neglects to mention that they were drawn up in three units, just as, in fact, he also fails to mention the special unit of the men of the forest cantons, which was undoubtedly present. The reporter, who was present himself and recounted the events to the author of the *Conflictus,* was naturally impressed principally with the victorious main body and spoke only of it. But the writer was a priest, who did not have an adequate concept of military-analytical matters to avoid misunderstandings, especially on points that did not interest him. We may accept from him as quite certain the fact that the 3,000 men did not notice the flight of the 2,000, but whether the Bernese formed one or two or three "small units" was undoubtedly not clear in his own eyes.

That the guilty corps was the rear guard I conclude from an account in Justinger to the effect that there was initially disagreement over the opening fight, which the Bernese had then finally turned over to the men of the forest cantons. There cannot have been such a dispute in the real sense of the word, since the Bernese, of course, did not intend to attack but to occupy a defensive position. The account is probably the legendary distortion of the fact that the advance guard was formed of the men of the forest cantons, on which, in keeping with the position assigned to the three units—but which we can no longer recognize in detail—necessarily would fall the prospect of the battle with the main part of the knights.

In his *Geschichte der Infanterie,* 1: 154, Rüstow, based on Justinger's account concerning the stone-throwing and the rearward movement, has concluded that this was a special maneuver. He believes that when the enemy foot troops were preparing to move forward to the attack, Erlach noticed that he "had forgotten" to assure himself the advantage of the superior heights and therefore had his "phalanx" turn about and move some 100 paces up the slope, in order to have the attack start from above. This interpretation seems to me to be impossible in every respect. While Justinger's words are very indefinite, in no case do they state that the *entire* force of foot soldiers was to make a rearward move. Such a movement in view of an attacking enemy is also no doubt feasible only for the very best disciplined troops. For a popular levy, it is just as incredible as is the fact that the commander is not supposed to have noticed until the army was already deployed that there was a better position 100 paces to the rear.

As proof of how quickly real historical tradition is erased and becomes fantastic, we may add the fact that Tschudi gives the Swiss at Morgarten javelins, which they never had, and at Laupen even a kind of scythed chariot, "for they had iron war carts made which violently broke up the formations of the enemy. These wagons were so made that they could not be attacked from the rear and they broke up the formation of the enemy and drove him to flight."[9]

NOTES FOR CHAPTER III

1. It is an unproven supposition that Austria stood behind the alliance against Bern. If the House of Hapsburg had really wanted to defeat Bern at that time, it would have acted very foolishly by keeping itself in reserve instead of immediately sending so many forces to join the allies that the victory would be assured. I mention this only so that it will not be concluded possibly from the presumed secret alliance of Austria with the enemies of Bern, that the forest cantons, too, because they were also enemies of Austria, would have had an interest in the war.

In 1383 Uri and Unterwalden received 4,445 pounds from Bern for military assistance given in the Kyburg war.

The letter of alliance of 1353 provided that the men of the forest cantons, when called by the Bernese for help, would move over the Brünig Pass to Unterseeen (Interlaken) without pay, but from there on they would receive one groschen *Tournois* for each man daily. Von Elgger, *Military System and Military Skill of the Swiss Confederation in the Fourteenth, Fifteenth, and Sixteenth Centuries (Kriegswesen und Kriegskunst der schweizerischen Eidgenossenschaft im 14., 15. und 16. Jahrhundert)*, Lucerne, 1873, p. 40.

Also, when the peasants of Appenzell, who certainly did not have much, called on the Schwyzers for help against their abbot (1403), they had to pay them. Dierauer, *Geschichte der Schweizerischen Eidgenossenschaft*, 1: 400, Note 2.

2. Köhler, *Ritterzeit*, 2: 605.

3. All the more so in that it is confirmed by the *Chronica de Berno*, a short contemporary account. Edited by Studer as a supplement to Justinger, p. 300.

4. Studer has also quite correctly pointed out in the *Archiv des historischen Vereins Bern*, Vol. IV, (1858–1860), Issue No. 3, that, according to

the contemporary report, Fribourg was the real enemy of Bern. Not until a later time, in keeping with the then existing animosities, was the war branded as a conflict against the nobility.

The bishop of Lausanne, too, had troops at Laupen as an ally of Fribourg, as is proven in the sources. Studer, p. 27.

5. Rüstow, *Geschichte der Infanterie,* 1: 152, believes that the Bernese did not have any missile weapons. That is extremely improbable, in fact impossible. In any event, it is not to be concluded from the fact that they do not happen to be mentioned in the accounts of this battle.

6. Solothurn had provided eighteen helmets, and the baron of Weissenburg fought on the side of the Bernese. In the battle of Hutwil (1340) there is mention of a mounted banner of Bernese that moved out in front of the main banner with the skirmishers. Justinger, pp. 97, 99. Later, the Bernese mounted troops enjoyed a particularly high respect. Elgger, p. 302.

7. Justinger, p. 99.

8. I have explained this interpretation to my colleague, Tangl, who believes it completely acceptable, saying that it was frequent in late medieval Latin for "*unus*" to be written for the simple indefinite article of the mother tongue.

9. Bürkli, p. 106. *Chronikon Helveticum,* ed. Iselin, 1: 359.

Chapter IV

Battle of Sempach
9 July 1386

As great as the victory of Morgarten had been, the stratagem and the surprise attack played too large a role in it for the final decision between the mighty House of Hapsburg and the independent peasant forces to have been achieved with this one blow. Just as the battle in the Teutoburger Forest became the battle for Germanic independence, not in and of itself, but only through its interplay with the internal relationships of the Roman Empire, the battle on the Morgarten reached its full importance only through the fact that it became a mesh in the fabric of the overall politics. If the forest cantons had already won the legal titles for their direct dependence on the empire in the context of the struggle of church and state under Frederick II and later of the rivalry of the different great princely houses for the monarchy, now the House of Hapsburg was prevented from avenging the defeat of Morgarten, because it was completely occupied with all its force by the conflict with Louis the Bavarian, who, for his part, confirmed the imperial freedom for all three cantons and issued letters accordingly. But in order to give up nothing for the future, the Hapsburgs did not make peace with the forest cantons but only an armistice. However, the armistice was extended from year to year, interrupted by feuds and then renewed, and it allowed the confederates to consolidate their independent position. The effective assistance they had given Bern at Laupen raised their reputation further, and even Zurich and Lucerne sought their friendship and alliance. (Alliance with Lucerne, 1332; alliance of Zurich with the four forest cantons, 1351.) Finally, fully conscious of their strength and also no doubt encouraged by the great success Bern had had in extending its hegemony, these allies went over to the attack. Lucerne, which up to that point was still an Austrian provincial town, wished to shake off that domination entirely, took the surrounding Austrian peasantry and the small town of Sempach under its protection, and thus took the territory away from its lord, Duke Leopold III. The Hapsburg castles in the region were attacked and destroyed, and the areas that remained loyal to the old administration were laid waste. The duke tried in vain to arrive at a cheap peace by being indulgent; the confederates moved forward from conquest to conquest.

And so Leopold finally decided to assemble all his forces in order to save the possessions and the honor of his house and also perhaps to win back the areas that had long been lost, if he was victorious. He pawned cities in Italy in order to obtain money, and he sought allies among the knightly lords on all sides, and mercenaries as well. He even received help from the Tyrol and Milan. We may assume that his army was considerably stronger than that of his uncle, Leopold I, had been at Morgarten, but the army of the four forest cantons was probably also twice as large as the army at Morgarten, since not only was Lucerne represented but also Schwyz had in the meantime significantly increased in size. We may estimate the strength of Leopold's army at Sempach at 3,000 or perhaps 4,000 men and that of the Confederation somewhere between 6,000 and 8,000 men. The sources vary in their figures for the strengths of the Swiss between 1,300 men (Justinger and Russ) and 33,000 men (Detmar).

At first the Swiss considered Zurich to be threatened, and so from the forest cantons they sent reinforcements, which made incursions into the closest parts of Austria. But initially Leopold wisely concentrated on neither of the two principal places, Zurich or Lucerne, but turned against the little town of Sempach some 9 to 10 miles north of Lucerne, which had defected from him and gone over to the Swiss. He said to himself that, no matter what place he attacked, the Swiss would move up to relieve it and would thereby bring on a battle. In front of Zurich or Lucerne, the conditions for such a battle would have been unfavorable for Austria, since security against one of these large places would absorb a part of his troops. But a small place like Sempach required only a small force to besiege it and left almost the entire army available for the open battle.

And so Leopold assembled his army at Sursee, only about 5 miles down from Sempach, at the exit from the lake, surrounded Sempach on the same day that he started his march (9 July), and immediately marched on farther toward the expected relief army. To accept battle at Sempach itself, directly beside the lake, would have been wrong both strategically and tactically; there the Austrians would have fallen into a similar situation to that of Morgarten. Nevertheless, the duke did not take the direct route to Lucerne, toward the south, but rather toward the east. He must, therefore, have known that the enemy army was approaching from that direction. This direction of approach is easily understandable. A part of the confederates' army came from Zurich, marching from the northeast, and would have had to make a long detour in order to move on Sempach from the south. There was all the less reason for that in view of the fact that an attack from the east was particularly dangerous for the duke, because in case of a defeat his troops would be pushed against the lake, and withdrawal would only be possible toward the flanks. We can assume that the bridge over the Reuss at Gislikon was the point where the men of the four cantons had assembled and from which they were moving up.

Thus, the two armies moved toward each other from the west and the east, with the Swiss presumably thinking they would catch the knightly army at Sempach itself, with its back to the lake,[1] and the Austrians having no clear idea as to whether the encounter would take place on this same day, in the evening, or perhaps not until the following day. "One enemy did not know the whereabouts of the other," said the Austrian poet Suchenwirt in his battle account. A short half-hour above Sempach, close to the village of Hildisrieden, the points of the two armies made contact toward noon. The battlefield is proven definitely by the old battle chapel.

The terrain rises from the lake quite steeply toward the east, forming terraces and cut by numerous ravines. In front of Hildisrieden is a small plateau, and the ground then rises again more steeply to the village. The opponents may at first have spotted one another on this plateau. The Swiss advance guard probably took position at the steepest spot, where a high point, a sunken road, and small streams on both sides favored the defense. Trees or cattle fences may also have made the approach more difficult. As the knights came up, they sprang from their horses and sought to storm the high ground which was of very difficult access to mounted men. Their marksmen took the Swiss under heavy fire. Duke Leopold, probably believing that he already had all the Swiss in front of him, was reckless enough to participate personally in the fight before the rear units of his army had moved up from the march column. The knights drove with such force into the enemy units that the Lucerne banner had already fallen and was perhaps captured by them. But it was only the confederates' advance guard with which they were fighting, and this advance guard probably accepted battle because it had occupied a position very favorable for the defense and had perhaps also quickly reinforced the position artificially. Each moment it awaited the arrival of the main body, which was perhaps somewhat longer delayed than had been

Fig. 7   BATTLE OF SEMPACH

expected. Finally, however, the main body had completed its deployment from the march column, formed up, and suddenly attacked the
knights from the flank with a great shout and throwing a hail of stones in
front of it. It is not clear from the reports whether a third unit, the rear
guard, was also deployed, but this can be assumed.

The attack was so powerful that the knights fighting on foot were
immediately overrun. Not only the soldiers, who were holding their
horses in the rear, and, overcome by panic, now took flight, but also that
part of the Hapsburg army which was still moving up on horseback,
instead of deploying and attacking, was carried away by the fugitives. The
duke himself and with him a large number of nobles and knights were
slain.

The excuse that treason had played a role in the panic we may relegate to the series of traitor stories that have been common since Marathon. To judge from the situation, the flight of those knights who were still on horseback, even though hardly praiseworthy, is only too understandable.

THE WINKELRIED LEGEND

A truly valuable fruit of Bürkli's impartial sense of scholarship is the discovery of the origin of the Winkelried legend. Arnold von Winkelried of Unterwalden was a famous Swiss mercenary leader at the beginning of the sixteenth century. He was killed in the battle of Bicocca, 1522, when he tried to penetrate into the spear-studded formation of the lansquenets, who had in the meantime adopted this Swiss method of combat. The battle of Bicocca was the first serious and complete defeat of the Swiss, in which they lost more men than in all their earlier victories together. Lansquenets' songs mocked them because of this shame. The Swiss replied with songs about their earlier victorious feats. In these songs, the various battles flowed into one another and blended together.

We can clearly follow the gradual growth of the legend. The older accounts, extending over ninety years, do not even mention a Winkelried deed, neither the name nor any kind of similar event. In fact, they could not contain anything of the sort, since, of course, the conditions offered no opportunity for this. The copy of an older Zurich chronicle, made in 1476, inserted for the first time an account that at Sempach, when things were going poorly and the lords with their spears were striking down the Swiss, who were armed with their shorter halberds, a loyal man seized many spears and pushed them down so that the confederates could strike them down with their halberds. At the same time the loyal man cried out that all in the rear were fleeing. In this account, the name of the hero is not given, and it is also not said that he died in the course of his feat. The Sempach battle song, which was widely known at this time (contained in the *Chronicle of Russ,* 1480), still contained nothing concerning this whole incident. It was not until fifty years later (1531) that the battle song, which had undergone numerous changes and had been reworked quite often, appeared again with the Winkelried verses. That was nine years after the battle of Bicocca. But here, too, it was at first "a Winkelried," who then became "a man of Unterwalden from the family of Winkelried," and finally, in the second edition of Tschudi (about 1570), "Arnold von Winkelried." By now, so much time had passed since the battle of Bicocca that the transposing of the hero who fell there over to the Sempach battle, from the bad defeat with its sad memories to the most famous victory, no longer caused any shock. With the hero of Bicocca, there was also soon carried over into the battle of Sempach, according to Tschudi, the entire battle formation of the lansquenets on whose spears he had died, and even their fortification. The intervening battle of Murten (1476) must also have contributed an impressive recollection toward increasing the vividness of the description. At Murten, the Burgundians' cannonballs tore down branches from the trees, which fell in front of the Swiss units. And this is recounted now in the battle song of Sempach, where there were no cannons at all. Even from the battle prayer we can recognize how late this song originated; there is no appeal in it to the Virgin Mary, a sure proof that it stems from the period of the Reformation. Such an omission would have been completely impossible at an earlier time.

The discovery of this sequence of events is just as important and interesting from the viewpoints of popular psychology, literary history, and history as from the methodological viewpoint. As in the *Nibelungenlied*, we see events blended together which were actually separated by many generations, from 1386 until after the spread of the Reformation. But what confusion the history of the military falls into if one trustingly accepts such accounts! The legend transfers the tactics of the lansquenets to the knights, who are the direct opposite of them. Furthermore, the tactics of the lansquenets are no other than those of the Swiss. Consequently, the Swiss legend itself attributes their own tactics to the enemy. And there is also the cannon fire and the form of the prayer, which is so very contradictory of the spirit of the Sempach period.

Since it was not the knights but the Swiss who fought in a tightly closed unit with protruding spears, so, too, were the Winkelried feats, which were more or less definitely confirmed by history, carried out by knights. The first one is recounted by Johann von Winterthur in 1271 about a Hapsburg knight who attempted to break up a Bernese unit and died in the attempt.[2] A similar story is told of the battle on the Schlosshalde in 1289, where a son of King Rudolf of Hapsburg surprised the Bernese and defeated them. On that occasion, Count Ludwig von Homberg-Rapperswyl is named as the hero. In 1332 the same heroic deed was carried out again by the Austrian knight Stülinger von Regensberg in a battle against the Bernese and the Solothurners, whose unit he broke up and himself perished in the fight but gave victory to his side.[3] In the battle of Grandson (1476), the same feat was undertaken by a Burgundian, the knight of Chateauguyon, who also penetrated with his horse into the main body but was killed without being able to break up the formation. He is named Tschättegü in the Swiss reports, which relate on several occasions the deed of the enemy, not without admiration. The only confederate to whom this feat is attributed, in addition to Arnold Winkelried of Bicocca, is a mercenary leader from Uri, Heini Wolleben, who, according to an account by Pirkheimer, in the battle of Frastenz (1499) pressed down the spears of the imperial formation by laying his own across the top of them, thus opening up an access for his men, but he himself was cut down at that moment by a musket shot.

Even though it is not directly proven, we can assume as certain that members of the Unterwalden knightly family of Winkelried also fought at Sempach. An attempt at least to rescue the name of Arnold Winkelried as one of those killed at Sempach, because that name presumably actually appears at the head of the list of those killed in the *Journal of Stans (Jahrzeitbuch von Stans)*, turns out to be invalid.[4] The list has been retained only in copies that were prepared around 1560—therefore at a time when the wonderful verses of the battle song of Winkelried's "bold deed" had already been common knowledge among the Swiss, and every copyist felt justified in adding the name to the list of the dead, on which he could have been omitted, of course, only by chance.

EXCURSUS

Bürkli created the basis for the correct military history treatment of the battle of Sempach, but his own reconstruction still suffered from a few such obvious errors that it not only could not be accepted, but even the correct portions of it were not recognized. The credit for having solved all aspects of the problem therefore goes to the study by Erich Stössel (Berlin dissertation, 1905, published by Georg Nauck), which Häne, to be sure, challenged in the *Deutsche Literaturzeitung,* 1906, Issue No. 17, Column 1063, but without being able to make convincing objections.

Bürkli found as the decisive point the fact that the battle must have been fought, not with the front facing southward, but with the front toward the east. But he explained the dismounting of the knights by saying that while they were setting up camp, they were suddenly attacked by the confederates, whose proximity they did not suspect. To explain this, he assumed that the confederate contingent at Zurich moved up in a forced march by night. None of this can be reconciled with the sources. From the departures of the confederates it was proven that the men of the forest cantons left Zurich at the latest on the seventh, and all the sources agree that the knights were not initially on foot but dismounted for the purpose of the battle. Suchenwirt says that the enemy was suddenly encountered unexpectedly; Hagen says "not formed in orderly fashion for the fight," and Königshofen says "disordered, careless." Then the sources expressly have the knights dismounting:

The knights (*"piderben"*) halted, they fell off
And moved toward the formation.

These are the words of Suchenwirt, and the expression "fell off" ("*abfallen*") in this context has no other meaning than "dismounted." The same is to be found in Hagen, Königshofen, and the so-called *Klingenberg Chronicle*.

Of the two versions, to the effect that Leopold himself dismounted in order to sell his life dearly (Hagen and Suchenwirt), and in order to support the battle against the Swiss advance guard (Königshofen), the latter deserves the preference. For if the first assumption had been well attested, it would also have come to the attention of Königshofen, who then would hardly have suppressed it, even though he was not amicably inclined toward Austria. It is also not impossible that the custom of dismounting in order to encourage the common soldiers, which at that time had just started in France, had an influence on the brave Hapsburg. Bürkli uses as his principal witness the *Constance Chronicle* of Gebhard Dacher, in which it was supposedly said that the horses of the knights were "ungezäumt" ("unbridled"). But it could be questioned as to whether the expression did not mean "untamed" ("ungezämt") in the sense of "unmanageable." On this point I turned to the archivist of the monastery of Saint Gall, Mr. Johann Müller, who was kind enough to copy for me with philological exactness the entire passage from the manuscript of the monastery. It reads as follows:

> And in the year in which one thousand three hundred and eighty-six years were counted from the birth of Christ Our Lord, on the ninth day of July in the twelfth hour of the said day, there took place the battle at Sempach between Duke Leopold and many noble men whom he had with him and also from his cities and from the countryside, and the men of Lucerne, Unterwalden, those of Uri and those of Schwyz, whom the duke accused and complained as to how the men of the forest cantons had taken twelve castles from him and had taken them for their own lands. But for that they were secretly responsible with the help of their confederates. But after many words and letters and ancient custom, it came to this conflict.
>
> And then they began fighting, and the men of Lucerne and the confederates lost some 300 men when the duke moved into the field with many men. And among them was a certain von Hennenberg with some 500 men under him whom they heard fleeing with his banner with a terrifying shout. And so the duke's men were seized with panic; and some knights ran to the horses, intending and wishing to come to the aid of the foot troops with their horses. Then the frightened and unmanageable ("*ungezämpten*") horses became wild, and they could do nothing with them but trample, overrun, and injure the foot troops. They became confused and lost their formation, and nobody knew which way to turn. In the meanwhile, the confederates attacked them in good order and with great force, cutting, thrusting, and shooting, and they suffered great losses from the men of the forest cantons, particularly the nobles who were still there, who would gladly have stood fast, did not want to yield, and wished that they had foot troops with them in the field; and they were struck down and killed.

Mr. Müller also added that the orthography of "*ungezämpten*" ("wild," "out of control") is completely clear. Furthermore, I found in a document of the Council of Bern to its captains dated October 1474 (*Zeitschrift für Geschichte des Oberrheins*, 49. 217) "lediglich etlich ungezämpt lut" ("only a few unmanageable people") had been responsible. Consequently, there can be no doubt that the meaning of the word is "unmanageable."

With this point, Bürkli's construction is rejected. There remains the account given above, which is supported primarily by the excellent, quite contemporary report on the battle in the chronicle of the reading master Detmar in Lübeck. The value of this report is not lessened by the fact that we find it so far from the location of the feat. On the battles of Grandson and Murten, direct written reports are to be found in numerous places in the country, including Lübeck. Even if we do not know whether Detmar had a first-hand written document for his Sempach report, it is still clear that we have before us not a matter of simple hearsay but the account of an eyewitness on the Austrian side without many intervening links. The only important error that he makes is that he estimates the strength of the Swiss much too high (33,000), but if we were in general to reject an author as a witness on account of excessively high strength figures, few authors in antiquity and the Middle Ages would remain. All the other reports, no matter how large the contradictions seem to be at first glance, are nevertheless in full agreement with Detmar's report, interpreted in accordance with the testimony which the battlefield itself offers. This agreement becomes clear as soon as we test each individual report as to its type and origin and eliminate the obvious inaccuracies and disturbing points. Stössel convincingly explains all of this, up to the most detailed point.

As a special point of interest with respect to the consistency of the sources, we must still mention the fact that the Zurich account has not the confederates but the knights throwing stones as they attack with a large shout. Consequently, this is a counterpart to Froissart's report on the council of war of Seclin before the battle of Rosebeke, in which the two sides are also confused. We have still a third example of the same kind of confusion in the battle of Murten. The fact that the Zurich chronicler misunderstood the account that reached his ears is incontrovertibly explained by Stössel.

One particular error in Bürkli is the fact that he believes Leopold planned to march on Lucerne and took the road via Hildisrieden because he could cross the Reuss only far downstream, at Gislikon. From the start, I have considered as impossible the assumption that Leopold planned to march on Lucerne, a point which is nowhere mentioned in the sources. Of course, we do not know what the fortification of Lucerne was like at that time, but, after all, it is completely out of the question that the burghers, while taking up the fight with powerful Austria, should not have secured themselves under all circumstances against a coup. In no case could Leopold count on a surprise attack. But if he laid siege to the city, he would have to be prepared for a battle with a relief force. For that he would have been forced to select between the lake, the city, and the Reuss such an unfavorable position that it would be hard to imagine a worse one. This point is already so clear that it is not at all necessary to enumerate all the other reasons that also speak against this concept. We may say on the contrary with complete certainty that when Leopold marched on Hildisrieden, he did *not* intend to move to Lucerne. But then there remains no other motive but that he intended to march against the army of the Confederation, which he had lured forward by the siege of Sempach.

From this point it follows that he fought the battle with his front toward Hildisrieden and not, as everyone except Bürkli generally accepts, with his front toward the south. If the confederate army had moved up from the south, from Lucerne, for the relief of Sempach, we cannot see why either the duke or the Swiss climbed onto the heights. Furthermore, we know from the sources that part of the Swiss army marched up from Zurich. The less the Swiss could know as to where the duke would direct his attack, all the more advisable it was for them to establish their own assembly point not at Lucerne, for example, but farther eastward in the direction of Zurich. The bridge over the Reuss at Gislikon was the ideal point. From there they could move quickly either to Zurich, or Lucerne, or Sempach, and there it was possible for the men of Lucerne to join forces the most quickly with the men of Unterwalden from one side, the Schwyzers to join with the men of Uri from the other, and the men of the forest cantons who were fighting at Zurich from the third side.

Fritz Jacobsohn, in his Berlin dissertation, 1914, "The Descriptive Style of the Historic Folk Songs of the Fourteenth and Fifteenth Centuries and the Songs of the Battle of Sempach" ("Der Darstellungsstil der historischen Volkslieder des 14. und 15. Jahrhunderts und die Lieder von der Schlacht bei Sempach"), comes to a different conclusion. While he also believes that the Winkelried verses are not based on historical fact, he nevertheless places their appearance in the years 1512-1516, and therefore *before* the battle of Bicocca, but still with respect to the same Winkelried who was later killed at Bicocca but was already a famous leader before that. Jacobsohn's testimony, however, is not conclusive, and the author also bases his work on false military assumptions. He assumes (p. 85) that at that time both armies attacked each other with their spears extended forward and that then it was basically always a single man who determined the outcome of the battle by creating at one point a break in the foremost closed ranks of the enemy. This is false as applied to the battle of Sempach, and everything depends on that point. The knights had no closed ranks in which a break had to be made or could be made.

NOTES FOR CHAPTER IV

1. The Swiss must have learned several days in advance that the duke's attack was imminent, for otherwise they could not have had their army on hand right on the day of his departure. The reinforcements from the original cantons, who were at Zurich, marched off from there on 7 July at the latest, as is to be concluded from a decision of the council of 7 July. *Eidgenössische Abschrifte,* 1. 72.

2. "Nam cum utraque pars in campo ante civitatem sito convenisset pars Bernensium stetit contra hostes conglobata in modum corone et compressa, cuspitibus suis pretensis. Quam dum de adversa parte nemo aggredi presumeret . . . quidam cordatus miles . . . in eos efferatus fuisset et in corum lanceas receptus, in frusta discerptus et concisus lamentabiliter periit." ("Now when each side had assembled in the field lying in front of the city, the Bernese stood massed against the enemy in a circle and in close order, with the tips of their spears extended before them. When no one from the enemy side dared to attack them . . . a courageous soldier . . . was infuriated with them and penetrated up to their spears; lamentably, he died in vain, torn apart and cut to pieces.")

3. Bürkli, p. 90. Lorenz, *Germany's Historical Sources (Deutschlands Geschichtsquellen),* p. 46. Stössel, p. 47.

4. Oechsli in the *Allgemeine Deutsche Biographie,* 44. 446.

Chapter V

Battle of Döffingen
23 August 1388

The battle of Döffingen is normally considered the counterpart to the battle of Sempach. If the count of Württemberg had been killed here, as was the count of Hapsburg in the other battle, it would have brought an end to the princely hegemony and the knighthood in the lower Duchy of Swabia just as happened in the upper duchy. It will therefore be correct to interrupt the sequence of Swiss military history at this point and to interject a study on Döffingen.[1]

The great alliance of cities had formed an army that was assembled in January and spent the entire year 1388 in the field, plundering and burning the villages of the enemy princes, especially those of the count of Württemberg. Everything was so destroyed in Swabia that, according to Königshofen's expression, outside of the cities and forts, not a village or house was left standing for a distance of 45 to 55 miles.

Württemberg peasants had taken refuge with their possessions in the fortified churchyard of Döffingen near Weil, and there they were besieged by the troops of the cities. Then there appeared Count Eberhard, who had been joined by the Count Palatine Ruprecht, Margrave Rudolf of Baden, Burgrave Frederick of Nuremberg, the bishop of Würzburg, and the counts of Oettingen, Helfenstein, and Katzenellenbogen, and he attacked the army of the cities. This army was stated in the chronicles to have a strength of 700 to 800 lances on horseback and between 1,100 and 2,000 men on foot,[2] and the princely army between 600 and 1,100 gleves and 2,000 peasants, or between 2,000 and 6,000 men on foot.[3] No serious credence can be given to these figures. Six hundred gleves seems to be quite a small number for a levy of so many princes. The large alliance of the cities, thirty-nine in number, including Nuremberg, Augsburg, Ratisbon, Ulm, Constance, and Basel, would, of course, have been able to assemble much larger numbers for a decisive battle. But since it was a question of a force that was constantly in the field, the number 2,000 to 3,000 men corresponds quite closely to the truth.

When the battle started, Count Ulrich, Eberhard's son, along with a majority of the knights, dismounted. We are not told for what reason.

Count Ulrich and a large number of nobles had already been killed when the seigneurs of Bitsch and Rosenfeld arrived with 100 fresh *gleves* and decided the battle in favor of the count of Württemberg. The mercenaries of Nuremberg and those from the Rhine were accused of having fled first of all, and the leader of the Nurembergers, a certain Count von Henneberg, is even blamed for fleeing intentionally in a treacherous manner.[4] It is not clear what role the peasants played in the battle, either those surrounded in the churchyard or those led by Eberhard, although Königshofen says specifically that many of them were also killed.

We may consider the report of the treachery of the Nuremberg commander as worthy of little credence. It belongs among the many stories of treason that were supposed to explain defeats[5]—all the more so in that the Count von Henneberg is also supposed to have been the leader of the Hapsburg knights who remained on horseback at Sempach and took flight.

Very noteworthy, however, is an account in the *Nuremberg Chronicle* by Ulman Stromer, which reads: "There was Count Eberhard of Württemberg on horseback and behind the units, and he beat and drove the foot soldiers so that they had to defend themselves and therefore the cities lost the battle." One might feel tempted to combine this report with the dismounting of Count Ulrich—that is, that he placed himself, together with a number of knights, at the head of a large, tightly formed unit composed of foot soldiers and peasants, whom his father held together from the rear with mighty shouts and threats. Stromer recounts nothing of the reinforcements for the Württembergers that suddenly arrived during the battle, but we could, of course, assume that both factors worked together. That is, the unit of foot troops held fast, and an attack by the reserve knights decided the outcome.[6] The driving by Eberhard cannot have referred to the knights. Consequently, the unusual aspect of Döffingen would be that the large unit of foot troops, reinforced by peasants and stiffened by knights, was formed with a comprehensive and foresighted perspicacity. This point becomes even more interesting if we realize that here we would have before us a piece of Swiss tactics but on the side of the nobility. The alliance of the cities represents nothing other than the usual medieval military organization: knights, partly patricians and partly mercenaries, and foot troops as mere auxiliaries, and likewise, according to their character, mercenaries, even if there were burghers and the sons of burghers among them. But the peasants, who were missing in the army of the cities, were fighting under and with their count. Did Eberhard perhaps intentionally copy the tactics of the Swiss at Sempach? How it happened that the knightly army there was so shamefully inferior must, after all, have been discussed at every princely court and knightly round table. The fact that the highest commander, instead of setting his men an example by fighting at their head, remained on horseback in the rear was unheard of throughout the Middle Ages and contradicted every knightly custom. If it happened, it was not incidental.

It immediately appears to us only natural that the large free cities were defeated at Döffingen, whereas the small cities, Bern and Lucerne, were victorious. The political character of the two alliances was completely different. The German free cities were primarily aristocratic formations and intended to fight their wars with mercenaries, or at least principally with mercenaries. Indeed, the Swiss cities were not absolute democracies either, especially Bern, but there was so much of the democratic blended in their aristocratic regime, and the membership of the large peasant communities gave the entire alliance such a democratic character, that the army represented a folk levy. Even if the alliance of the cities had won at Döffingen, it would never have been able to become a federation like that of the Swiss, because of the lack of this popular element. The battle of Döffingen was therefore not really a great decisive action, but only a witness as to how small, basically, the warlike strength of the free cities was. Even the German princes had a relationship to the peasant-democratic element, and with the help of this levy the "cantankerous one" defeated the proud burghers.

Whether Count Eberhard actually organized and employed his foot troops in such an ingenious manner as we have construed the situation above must remain a matter of speculation. The indications in the sources are too uncertain to serve as proof, and the seal that impresses the stamp of credibility on uncertain documents, the further development of the situation, is lacking here. Even if the Swabian nobles were supposed to have led their peasants to victory in the battle of Döffingen, that would still have been only an episode in the history of the military art, and that very point casts strong doubt on the entire hypothesis. Such a great success would have prompted the count of Württemberg to repeat the procedure, and we would hear of something similar in later battles. There is not a complete absence of traces of this, a point on which we shall see more later. But, of course, in that area where we would expect something of the sort first of all, in the Hussite wars, we find nothing.

NOTES FOR CHAPTER V

1. The sources are, of course, quite meager, and our principal source, Königshofen, is fable-like and unreliable. Christian Friedrich Stälin, *Württembergische Geschichte,* 3: 334. Paul Friedrich Stälin, *Geschichte Württembergs,* 1: 569. G. von der Au, *Zur Kritik Königshofen,* Tübingen, 1881. The *Annales Stuttgartenses,* copied in the *Württembergisches Jahrbuch,* 1849, contains nothing of importance.

2. According to Königshofen, 800 *gleves* and 2,000 foot soldiers; according to the *Constance Chronicle,* 700 lances on horseback and 1,100 on foot.

3. According to Königshofen (*Städtische Chronik,* 9. 839), 550 *gleves* and 2,000 peasants; according to the *Constance Chronicle,* 600 lances and 6,000 men on foot; according to Ulman Stromer, 1,100 lances and some 6,000 foot soldiers; according to Justinger, 800 lances and 2,000 mercenaries.

4. *Augsburg Chronicle,* 1. 87 (see also 2. 40).

5. Rupp, in the "Battle of Döffingen" ("Die Schlacht bei Döffingen"), *Forschungen zur deutschen Geschichte,* 14: 551, feels obliged to consider as correct the account of the treachery of von Henneberg, and he sees that as the reason for the defeat. Nevertheless, his reasons have not convinced me. Von der Au also rejects Rupp's arguments.

6. Königshofen says: "and the first attack of the battle was won over the lords"; now the fresh *gleves* arrived—"then the attack was successful against the cities, so that they were defeated."

Chapter VI

Military Organization of the Confederation[1]

The three battles that formed the basis of the greatness of the Swiss were fought by the peasantry of the original cantons: Morgarten by them alone, Laupen together with the Bernese, and Sempach together with the men of Lucerne. Other mountain communities of the surrounding area won similar victories on a smaller scale. Glarus broke loose from the Hapsburg domination, and two years after Sempach it threw back an invasion of Austrian units in a fight at the *letzi* of Näfels (9 April 1388), the details of which have come down in only legendary form.

The citizens of Appenzell rebelled against the domination of the Abbot of Saint Gall and called on the Schwyzers for help. The latter first of all sent them a commander (*ammann*) and marched up with auxiliaries when the abbot and his allies moved in to subdue the peasants once again. The engagement at Vögelinseck (15 May 1403) was quite similar to the battle of Morgarten in that the abbot's troops, when they attempted to break through a *letzi,* were attacked from the flank. They lost some 200 killed. At the Stoss (17 June 1405) the Appenzellers defeated an Austrian army in a battle similar to that at Vögelinseck, except that the sudden attack from the flank took place, not while the attacking enemy was fighting in front of a *letzi,* but when he was just working his way through the undefended *letzi* after breaking a small opening in it. Particular mention is made of the hail of stones with which the Appenzellers opened their attack.

The forces of Valais defeated a large Bernese army in 1419 at Ulrichen by attacking it on the march—once again a similar situation to that at Morgarten.

The military organization in all the cantons was the original Germanic one, the general levy throughout the region, the general military obligation. The concept and traces of this kind of levy were retained extensively in the purely Germanic peoples and even in the Romanic-Germanic races, but its actual application, usefulness, and finally great development can only be found in this section of the Alpine regions.

A decision by the cantonal administration of Schwyz in 1438 provided that each man was to possess his good weapon and equipment in accordance with his means.[2] Annually, at the regular general assembly, three men were to be chosen for each district. They were to inspect the armor and weapons in each house and to decide whether or not they were in keeping with the means of the occupant, and they were to assess punishment accordingly. In Uri a similar law was passed on All Saints' Day in 1362; such a law was a matter of course for the cities.

The military obligation originally started in the fourteenth year but was later deferred to the sixteenth year.

We may assume that at Morgarten practically all of the physically qualified men of Schwyz were present. Even if not all were on the battlefield, they were at the border, and for the two, three, or four days at the most that they were away from home, they brought their own rations. The farther one lived from the scene of operations and the longer a campaign lasted, the less possible was such a system of individual provisions. The cantonal authorities then decided how large the levy was to be, and this number was allocated among the individual communities,[3] which decided, at their discretion, which men were to be called up. In keeping with the most ancient edict of the Zähringen towns, anyone who failed to report would have his house destroyed. On some occasions it appears that those to be called were chosen by lot, but normally, because of the expectation of booty, more men were ready to move out than were called, and they then went along as "free groups." In 1494 a number of common soldiers brought home from the Naples campaign between 100 and 300 gold pieces, which by present standards had a value perhaps as high as 50,000 francs.[4]

The communities also had to provide rations for the levied men as well as the necessary pack animals. The "travel expense" (*Reiskost*) which was required as a tax for this purpose frequently caused friction.[5]

Even in the cities, the levy and responsibility for rations were decentralized. In Bern, seventeen chambers or companies gave their members rations and whatever equipment was needed to complete their armament, and especially pay in cash, "travel money" (*Reisgeld*), which is to be found in the sources after 1337. These chambers were responsible to the city for their men.[6]

In addition to the rations given to the soldiers and delivered to them, steps were also taken, depending on circumstances, to see that traders took foodstuffs to the camps for sale.[7]

In a description of Switzerland which was given to Louis XI of France by the dean of Einsiedeln, Albrecht von Bonstetten, at the time of the Burgundian wars, it was estimated that Bern alone could assemble 20,000 men, the confederation of the eight communities 54,000, and the entire alliance with its adherents and subjects, 70,000 men. It is assumed that approximately that many qualified men were actually on hand. At Murten, Bern, with its region, actually had some 8,000 men in the field; that is approximately 10 percent of the population, which can be estimated at 80,000.

The nature of the formation, to which we shall return later, is the simplest one imaginable, the tightly formed square, which has the same number of men in the front as on the flank and is equally strong on all sides. This was no new discovery, but the old Germanic wedge or boar's head, which we have already thoroughly discussed in the previous volume (p. 49 ff.), the formation prescribed by nature, in which foot troops can move and at the same time defend themselves when they are threatened by horsemen. On the defensive, the corners tend to round themselves off more or less. The Swiss, applying an analogy, named such a unit, with its spears protruding on all sides, a hedgehog. We have also found such formations elsewhere in the Middle Ages. If they do not occur more frequently, the reason is that foot soldiers, of course, appeared very seldom in an independent role. They were always considered an auxiliary arm for the mounted men, for which purpose the foot troops broke their formation, unless they served as a rallying point for the knights in precisely such a formation. That the Bernese, the men of Lucerne, and the men of Zurich adopted the custom of fighting in such formations is undoubtedly the result of their joining with the peasantry. Especially among the Bernese, we find indications that their original military organization was quite the same as that of other German cities: knights supported by foot troops armed with the spear and crossbow. Not until they were allied with the forest cantons and considered the latter's successes did the Bernese leaders learn what could be accomplished by these tactics—that one did not simply have the knights supported by the foot soldiers as individuals, but produced heavy impact by tightly formed masses of men, masses for which one drew not only from burghers but also from the subject peasantry. The peasants of the original cantons, we may well say, still having a certain relationship to the combat methods of the ancient Germans, were the fathers of this method of fighting.[8]

We hear nothing of any kind of common exercises, and it is certain that they did not take place.[9] Each individual practiced for himself the simple grips for the spear and halberd, as well as stone-throwing, and finally also the more difficult shooting with the crossbow, something that required much practice but that the owner of such a weapon did not easily neglect, especially if he also used it for hunting. Even the youth practiced with it, and the boys from Uri and Lucerne extended mutual invitations to one another in 1507 and 1509 for shooting tournaments.

If numerous levy documents prescribe that the officials who conduct the inspection of armor are to see to it that the troops "know how to handle the weapons they bring with them,"[10] that can probably only have referred to the fact that nobody should ever report as a marksman with a crossbow which he may have procured somehow but which he did not know how to use. The man with a close-combat weapon was trained to do one thing alone: to remain close to his banner and to march forward behind his preceding file, between his comrades on each side, from the place assigned him by his captain, and if he became separated by any kind of obstacle, to close in tightly once again.

Since they marched by the beat of the drum, there was also on the march a certain cadence and step, "justis passibus ad tympanorum pulsum" ("with regular steps to the beat of drums"),[11] something that, of course, we need not yet consider as the equivalent of the marching in step of modern, trained soldiers. Even the Germans of the earliest times had, of course, already known a certain cadence and step (Vol. II, p. 47).

Each locality had its banner. In battle, the banners were all assembled in the middle of the large square unit. At Murten in the largest unit, the main body, there were twenty-seven banners together. But they could no longer have had a practical significance there. On the march, however, and in camp, the individual was instructed to remain by his banner, and anyone who moved away from it without orders was held responsible.

The linking with the civil authorities gave the Swiss general levies the basis of military obedience. Despite the authority of the feudal lord or the mercenary leader, in the knightly armies the habit of obedience was still very weak. The reason was that this type of warriorhood was based completely on personal skill, bravery, and love of glory, and there was hardly any question of leadership in combat. Even though the Swiss might have been just as brutal on the march or in camp or while plundering as were the mercenary bands of the period, in battle in their closed units, they followed the command, and in dangerous situations their obligation to obey was stressed with special formality, as we have seen by Erlach at Laupen. The *Bernese Chronicle* by Justinger (about 1420) points out again and again how disaster in war results from disobedience and lack of good order. It cautions the leaders not to treat mildly the "perjurers" and dishonorable men who have abandoned their banner.[12] The men of Bern were praised (p. 73) because they "chose for their captains outstanding men who were listened to and obeyed and whose commands, calls, and orders were followed."

Anyone who fled or cried out for flight was subject to the judge for both his person and his property, or he could be struck down on the spot by his flanking comrade.[13] In accordance with a decision taken at the assembly in Lucerne at the beginning of 1475, before each battle the captains were to have their men swear that they would not plunder before the battle was over. A number of men were to be stationed in the rear guard to observe and to strike down on the spot anyone acting contrary to this oath.[14]

A revealing description of a Swiss army's move into the field is preserved in the report of a Milanese ambassador, Bernhardinus Imperialis, who observed the Zurich levy as it marched out in 1490. He wrote:[15]

And so today . . ., with . . . eighteen men with banners, all in orderly formation marched into a large square surrounded by walls; and there, in accordance with the custom, they all took the soldier's oath of loyalty and promised obedience to their captain. With such a ceremony they mutually forgive one another for wrongs and hate.

Thereupon they moved out in march order; and first there came twelve crossbowmen on horseback, nobles uniformly attired; and then came two horsemen and after them several pioneers with their axes, and then drummers and the company of long spears, more than 500. The captains were sons of knights; and they marched on foot and all formed three by three and well armed. They were followed by 200 musketeers, and after them came 200 men bearing halberds in the manner of our *"spedi."* After them came a large drummer and the pipers, followed by the banner, carried by a handsome man. All of these were on foot; one cannot carry those things on horseback. Accompanying the mentioned color bearer were two judicial servants of the country with staff in hand, an indication that they are the administrators of justice. Each of them, if he wishes, can place his hand on the chest of a man and lead him to prison; no one will oppose him. Then there followed—as I respectfully report—the executioner with three assistants, and after them six prostitutes selected to go into the field and paid by the city. After this group more than 400 additional halberdiers marched by in formation, chosen from the strongest men and best armed of all, because, as they say, they serve as the guard for the standards. Their weapons give the impression of a thick forest. There then followed 400 crossbowmen, and among them were many sons of nobles and men from all the classes of the country;

they all marched along with a bold tread. Many more spearmen followed them. All together, they were some 4,000 men, including the troops from a few surrounding areas, who are subordinate to this city. In the whole column there were more than twenty drums, and at the end came three trumpeters on horseback, bearing the colors of the city on their attire and on their trumpets. Directly behind them came the commander, Seigneur Konrad Schwend, knight, handsomely equipped and on horseback with many things bearing the golden crest, with a commander's baton and bearing a bouquet of flowers on his head. Behind him was his page with his lance, and his banner above, at the point, carried his gilded coat of arms, as did his shield. After them came six life-guards with their lances on their thighs and twelve crossbowmen, all well mounted, uniformly attired, and bearing similar lances, with their attendants. The entire army had put on white crosses, either on their armor or their hats or their stockings.

After the commander came another knight, who is responsible for order in the field, with more lances and crossbowmen on horseback, all in similar attire. There were also perhaps thirty vehicles with munitions and artillery, including four heavy pieces, 50- to 60- to 70-pounders.

Behind these men (from Zurich) the remainder of the alliance (Confederation) will march through. It is due to be a large and combat-ready army.

Medieval warriorhood was characterized by class distinctions; the leadership formed a nobility. But the Swiss military, both by its origin and its nature, was democratic. From the battle of Morgarten to the victories over Charles the Bold, the Swiss felt that their battles were struggles against the "lords," and nothing made the lords more unhappy than to be defeated by "coarse peasants." Nevertheless, we may well note the fact that even in the Swiss Confederation there was a very significant aristocratic element, just as, in the ultrademocratic Athens from Cleisthenes to Pericles, the hereditary aristocracy, even if deprived of its specific political rights, continued to be a very important, indeed leading, element. In Switzerland this aristocratic element was even stronger, in that, in the Swiss cantons and particularly in the one that was finally the most powerful of all, Bern, the organization constantly remained an aristocratic one, with a moderately strong democratic base. It was older and newer knightly families who here held the government and the leadership in their hands, and the city, for its part, treated the peasantry as underlings who had no influence on municipal politics and also demanded none. The families in Bern governed their rural peasantry like feudal lords. That such peasants nevertheless fought their lords' battles with such patriotic devotion is explained by the historical development and the form of the Swiss military system. Even peasant levies that from the start were motivated only by a moderate willingness for action could be placed in the large square units of these foot troops. But the repeated victories, the success, and the booty blended the peasantry and the city into an inseparable political-military unit. The counts of Kiburg, Nidau, Greyerz, the baron of Weissenberg, the Bubenbergs, Ringenbergs, Scharnachthals, Erlachs would by themselves have accomplished nothing with a levy of their peasants for a feudal conflict in the field. But within the overall Bernese levy, carried along by the mass and filled with its esprit, these very peasants accomplished unsurpassable military deeds without wanting to free themselves from the leadership of their lords. Indeed, even the purely peasant original cantons, the *"Länder"* as they were called in contrast to the cities, despite all their hate for the nobility, still had a very clear realization of how much they owed the nobles in their own ranks. Of course, these peasants had been able by themselves to win the prototype of all these victories, the battle of Morgarten, and we have seen what a stroke of genius this battle was. But it was only a victory on the defensive. The power of these peasant groups did not extend beyond the borders of their cantons, unless it be for plundering raids. The final political success, the complete expulsion of the House of Hapsburg from the Alpine area and with it the founding of the Swiss nation became possible only as a result of the participation of the cities with their broader political vision and their multifaceted economic and military means. On this point we have a very revealing bit of testimony in the story of the so-called Bernese *"Twingherrn"* conflict. The feudal demands by the Bernese knightly families in governing their peasants had given rise to a conflict there in 1470, shortly before the Burgundian wars. A democratically minded burgomaster named Kistler, a butcher by trade, wanted to reduce these rights and diminish the position of the families in general, including the demanding attitudes of their ladies. It was proposed that they seek the mediation of the confederated cantons, but the burgomaster (*"Schultheiss"*) declined this mediation, specifically because the confederated cantons were presumably too favorably inclined toward the great families. He said:[16]

They esteem no Bernese but the nobles. I have met with them some three or four times, just as they have been here. I have sought their company more eagerly than any Bernese. But there they ask about nobody, they care for nobody, they are grateful to nobody. Nobody has done anything favorable for them and helped them but the Bernese nobles. Indeed, they gladly acknowledge that in the Zurich War and against the emperor and the Austrians they would not have been able to prevail without the help of the mounted men and the Bernese nobility, and they say frankly they would not have needed your foot troops, for they have enough men of their own for that, but mounted troops and captains were needed, and those they received from them. They praise the manner in which the nobles provided rations for them, stopped the enemy, informed them of everything—great things which they acknowledge from them and deny having received from all the rest of us.

Kistler's opponent, Fränkli the Treasurer, could only confirm this account: the confederated cantons always talked about the old wars and could not give enough praise to the Bernese horsemen and the leadership of the captains, without whom they would often have been put to shame.[17]

MERCENARY SERVICE IN FOREIGN COUNTRIES (*DAS REISLAUFEN*)

Mercenary service, to which the inhabitants of the mountains had already resorted in the earliest times, gradually increased as warfare was practiced by them more and more. Finally, the authorities themselves took over the negotiations for such arrangements.[18] The first agreement of this kind was made in 1373, with Visconti, lord of Milan—a counterpart of those mercenary contracts by which German princes and knights placed their military forces in the service of a foreign king or a free city.

Whether Tschudi's report (2: 197) to the effect that in 1430 Zurich provided Ulm a force of 1,100 "well-equipped troops" against the Hussites is correct seems questionable to me.

Nevertheless, in 1388 100 spears—that is, undoubtedly knights—and 1,000 armored men from Bern helped the duke of Savoy against the bishop of Sitten. In 1443, 338 horsemen and 981 foot soldiers moved to his aid against the plundering French mercenary bands, the "*écorcheurs.*" In 1448–1449 many negotiations were carried out again with a view to having Bern provide the duke mercenaries against Sforza. But nothing came of these talks, since the duke did not have the necessary money.

His father, Pope Felix V, warned him that if he could not pay the Swiss afterward, he would have this people, up to then his best friends, as enemies.

About that same time, in 1449, in its war with Albrecht Achilles, the German League of Cities requested from Lucerne a corps of "800 knowledgeable, well-armed men, who also previously fought in your wars." We shall soon have occasion to speak of these Swiss reinforcements.

In 1453 Charles VII wanted to hire Swiss for his war with England, but the assembly rejected his offer, saying they were not accustomed to allowing their soldiers to fight for foreigners. But so many Swiss individually accepted French pay that the assembly decided in January 1455 that each locality was to forbid its men to travel, on penalty of death and forfeiture of property. Nevertheless, in the very next year, 1454 [*sic*], some 3,000 Bernese went to the aid of the duke of Savoy against the dauphin. But no combat action resulted.

In the battles between Louis XI and Charles the Bold (League of Public Weal, 1465), once more a decree forbidding foreign mercenary service was announced by the Confederation, and it is not correct that Swiss participated in the battle of Montl'héry. It was not until after that battle that a corps moved to join the duke of Burgundy. But when the men returned home, the councils of Bern decided that the disobedient mercenaries were each to forfeit 3 guilders from their pay for the construction of Saint Vincent's Church and spend eight days in the Tower. Any man who returned without 3 guilders was to remain in prison on bread and water until the council saw fit to release him.

Of course, the mercenary campaigns contributed in no small way toward nurturing the warlike spirit and military experience among the Swiss, even in those periods of peace at home. On the other hand, there are indications that the Swiss were already beginning to carry the special aspects of their military system to other countries. To be sure, what Olivier de la Marche recounts of the mercenaries (*Reisläufer*) previously mentioned in the service of Charles the Bold is more a testimonial to their versatility and their courage than to any specifically Swiss quality.[19] In skirmishing, he says, a pikeman, a crossbowman, and a man armed with a culverin always moved out together and gave each other mutual support, so that they did not fear the horsemen. The fact that Olivier made such a point of this is no doubt primarily an indication as to how little the individual crossbowman or musketeer could actually be counted on against a mounted man. Peculiarly Swiss characteristics do appear in the following passages.

IN THE SERVICE OF NUREMBERG

Reverting to the letter from the citizens of Ulm to Lucerne that we have already mentioned, we see that Nuremberg, while taking into its pay at the same time both German and Bohemian nobles, also hired Swiss soldiers in 1450 to serve against Albrecht Achilles. Instead of the 600 men that the recruiter Hans Müller was commissioned to hire, he soon had a thousand applicants. The contract he made with them has been preserved. The monthly pay amounted to 5 Rhine guilders, and the bounty to 2 guilders. In addition, they received rations and a share of the booty, and wounded men also received their pay and rations. Before the start of the campaign the soldiers had to swear to certain articles of war in which, among other things, they promised to spare the countryside and the inhabitants to a certain degree and to get on well with one another. The leaders had the right to punish quarrels with fines, but there is no other mention of their disciplinary power.

The campaign for which the engagement of Pillenreuth formed the introduction (p. 275, above) no doubt deserves closer examination. We have important information on the campaign from the poem by Hans Rosenplüt in his "Nuremberg Campaign" ("Nürnberger Rais"), Lilienkron, *Historische Volkslieder,* 1: 428). Rosenplüt speaks repeatedly of the "Swiss with the long spears," but how this contingent, which formed a very significant part of the army with its 800 to 1,000 men, was combined with the other troops is not clear. According to Rosenplüt, the margrave, when he attacked the Nurembergers, is supposed to have said: "The Swiss with the long spears, they are the ones we want to separate first." That sounds as if they had formed a tightly closed unit.

The captain of the Swiss, Heinrich von Malters, had been appointed leader of all the Nuremberg foot troops and had inspected them before moving out, including both burghers and peasants in addition to the mercenaries (*"Trabanten"*). According to the report concerning this inspection, he required that each man have a good crossbow, musket, or halberd. He forbade "small, bad spears," which is probably to be understood as meaning that he wanted to have either halberds or long spears. He attempted, then, to have the native Nuremberg foot soldiers adopt the Swiss armament. In addition to his principal weapon, each man was also to have a close-combat short weapon—knife, sword, or axe—hanging at his side.

But with these foot troops Malters did not advance freely into the plain, but at the same time he also had a wagon fort.

The Nurembergers moved out with 2,800 men on foot and 600

horsemen, took booty, and on their return march, when they wished to cross the Rednitz at Hembach, they were attacked by Albrecht. There was a great deal of shooting from both sides, but the engagement was undecisive.

BATTLE OF SECKENHEIM
30 JUNE 1462

Elector Frederick of the Palatinate had 1,100 horsemen and 2,000 foot soldiers, and with them he attacked by surprise the margrave of Baden, the count of Württemberg, and the bishops of Metz and Speier, who were laying waste his country, in the angle between the Neckar and the Rhine. He had also levied the peasants of the region and had a considerable superiority. At the first clash of the horsemen, the elector himself fell, and his men withdrew somewhat. But the foot troops, of whom it was expressly reported that they were formed in square units and had long spears, and among whom were a number of Swiss mercenaries commanded by Hans Waldmann of Zurich, stood fast against the attack of the enemy knights.[20] The intervention of other knights of the Palatinate, who had not previously entered the fight, decided the outcome of the battle.

On the side of the Palatinate only eight men were killed, while the enemy lost forty-five. The margrave, the count of Württemberg, and the bishop of Metz were captured; both the margrave and his brother, the bishop, were seriously wounded. Because the allies were in position with their rear toward the angle of the Rhine and the Neckar, their flight was almost completely cut off.

NOTES FOR CHAPTER VI

1. Em. von Rodt, *History of the Bernese Military System* (*Geschichte des Bernerischen Kriegswesens*), 1831.

J. J. Blumer, *Political and Legal History of the Swiss Democracies* (*Staats- und Rechtsgeschichte der schweizerischen Demokratien*), 1848.

K. von Elgger, *Military System and Military Art of the Swiss Confederation in the Fourteenth, Fifteenth, and Sixteenth Centuries* (*Kriegswesen und Kriegskunst der schweizerischen Eidgenossen im 14., 15., und 16. Jahrhundert*), 1873.

Johann Häne, *On the Defensive and Military Systems in the High Period of the Ancient Confederation (Zum Wehr- und Kriegswesen in der Blütezeit der alten Eidgenossenschaft)*, Zurich, Schulthess and Co., 1900.

Hermann Escher, "The Swiss Infantry in the Fifteenth Century and at the Beginning of the Sixteenth Century" ("Das schweizerische Fussvolk im 15. und im Anfang des 16. Jahrhunderts"), Part I. *Neujahrsblatt der Züricher Feuerwerksgesellschaft*, 1905.

2. Blumer, 1: 373.

3. For example, in 1444 Bern demanded that Thun send fifty up-right, capable soldiers, whose oath and honor could be trusted, with-out . . ., who bring along spear and armor. This according to Elgger, p. 118, as taken from the *Schweizer Geschichtsforscher*, 6: 354. I prefer to read "rations" (*Speise*) instead of "spears" (*Spiesse*).

In 1389 the Entlebuchers promised that in case Lucerne had to take to the field, they would come to its aid with 600 armed men. Elgger, *Kriegswesen*, p. 38. In noticeable contradiction is the report that in 1513 Lucerne on one occasion had to provide 1,300 men, including 150 from Entlebuch, 300 from Willisau, and only 100 from Lucerne itself. Elgger, p. 68.

Quite often there were quarrels over these allocations; for example, in 1448 the small community of Krattigen complained that, of the seven men to be provided by the region, it was to furnish two, since, after all, the community did not have more than twenty or twenty-one farms. For that reason, in 1499 and 1512 a census of all households was ordered. We cannot help wondering that this was not done until then, when we remember at what an early period Ancient Rome had similar statistics. Rodt, p. 27.

4. According to Häne, p. 23.

5. Häne, p. 24.

6. Rodt, 1: 6.

7. Minutes of the Council of Bern, 22 June 1476:

> To Fribourg, Solothurn, and Biel, that, with respect to the proper conduct of the war, they allow goods for sale in the way of wine, grain, and other goods and necessities to go to the army.
>
> The same applies to Nidau and Aarberg.
>
> To my lords in the field, that they see to it that there be no kind of forceful haggling with those who provide you with goods for sale, and that they receive their just payment.

The decisive action is called for quickly, "for my lords cannot provide supplies for such an army over a long period."

Ochsenbein, *Documents on the Battle of Murten* (*Urkunden zur Schlacht von Murten*), p. 301.

8. Escher, p. 26, states that in the Zurich archives there is an explanation of the formation of the battle unit, indicating that it was fifty-six men wide and twenty men deep. Consequently, that would be a phalanx rather than a wedge. In a later period, where a unit formed a true square in space rather than a rectangle with an equal number of men in its width and depth, these approximate figures were to be found quite often. But at the time of the old Zurich war, the period to which Escher attributes his explanation, I can hardly imagine that it was applied from a practical viewpoint.

9. Häne, p. 8, concludes from the military games of boys and other indications that maneuvers had actually taken place. I am not convinced of this. In particular, the fact that a knight once threatened that he would *teach* the soldiers (lansquenets) in such a way that one of them would be worth more than two men of the Confederation is no proof that he had Swiss drills in mind.

10. Elgger, p. 253.

11. Paulus Jovius, in 1494.

12. The passages have been assembled by Studer in the *Archiv des Historischen Vereins Bern*, IV, Book 4, p. 36.

13. Sempach letter of 1394. Blumer, p. 374. *Kriegsordnung* of 1468 and 1490. Rodt, *Berner Kriegswesen*, 1: 250, 253. Elgger, p. 215.

14. Rodt, *Campaigns of Charles the Bold* (*Feldzüge Karls des Kühnen*), 1: 331.

15. According to the extract in Häne, p. 29.

16. According to Thüring Frickhart's *Twingherrenstreit,* edited by Studer, *Quellen zur Schweizer Geschichte,* 1 (1877): 137.

17. Studer, *Quellen zur Schweizer Geschichte,* 1 (1877): 145.

18. W. F. von Mülinen, *History of the Swiss Mercenaries up to the Formation of the First Permanent Guard in 1497* (*Geschichte der Schweizer Söldner bis zur Errichtung der ersten stehenden Garde, 1497*), Bern, 1887.

19. *Collection Petitot,* 10: 245.

20. "Et jam Palatini cessurus equitatus fuerat, nisi prodeuntes a latebris pedites longis hastis Badensium equos confodere cepissent." ("And the Palatine cavalry had already been about to yield, if the foot soldiers advancing from their hideouts had not undertaken to strike the horses of the Badensians with their long spears.") Gobellinus, cited by Roder in *Die Schlacht bei Seckenheim,* Billingen, 1877. The principal source is a poetic work by Michael Beheim.

Chapter VII

The Burgundian Wars

ORIGIN

Despite their victories at Sempach and Näfels, the Confederation did not shift to a policy of large-scale conquest and domination, as the Greeks had done after their victories over the Persian king. As early as 1389 they made peace with the Hapsburgs, first for seven years, then for twenty (1394), and finally for fifty years (1412). In these treaties the ancient ruling line no doubt temporarily gave up its claim to certain areas and rights, but it continued to hold very large parts of present-day Switzerland. When we compare this peace with the victories of the Confederation, we could momentarily be puzzled as to whether their military superiority was really so great, since, in the end, they were content with quite modest results. But we may still accept the fact that this new military power was in fact far superior to a knightly levy of the old type,[1] for the reason why this new power did not assert itself more strongly politically is to be sought in politics and not in the military. The loose form of a league of eight members with equal rights (Schwyz, Uri, Unterwalden, Lucerne, Zug, Zurich, Bern, Glarus) was not suitable for great conquests. It was only under and thanks to the leadership of the ruling community of Athens that the Greeks were able to capitalize on the victories of Salamis and Plataeae to drive the Persians completely from Greek territory and even to enlarge the areas of the cities in Asia Minor. If the Swiss Confederation had had a policy of conquest in the grand style, the confederated cantons would very soon have become engaged in disputes among themselves, since they established not only a common policy for mutual gain, but each canton also had its own policy. In view of the danger of internal quarrels that could arise from this situation, and that did in fact occasionally occur, they had to limit their conquests within narrow bounds and proceed very carefully. Instead of resorting to the power of the sword, the city cantons, especially, sought to extend their territories by peaceful means. It has been estimated that in the period from 1358 to 1408 Zurich used a capital fund of 2 million francs by present value for the purchase and leasing of neighboring knightly and princely domains.[2] Not until the youngest son of Leopold III, Duke Frederick of the Empty Pocket, was so careless as to fall into conflict with the Council of Constance and, outlawed, was fallen on from all sides, did the Swiss also take arms again and seize the Aargau (1415). It was not until more than a generation later (1460) that they took the Thurgau and followed that up by soon crossing the Rhine and attacking the Austrian possessions in the southern part of the Black Forest and in Alsace.

Sigismund, duke of Austria, was unable to cope with this conquering people that was constantly reaching out farther. He finally sought help from the dukes of Burgundy, who, as a branch of the French royal house, had united under their control a large number of French and German fiefs and at that time formed the most powerful dynasty in Central Europe. Sigismund mortgaged to Charles the Bold his remaining possessions in Alsace and the Black Forest bordering on Switzerland, hoping that Charles would be strong enough to defend them, and further, that from such action conflicts would arise in which the powerful Burgundian would defeat the Swiss and help the House of Hapsburg regain its former possessions (1469). But the result of this diplomacy was quite different. Charles the Bold was an old friend of the Confederation and not at all inclined to let himself be drawn into conflict with its members. His expansionist plans lay in a completely opposite direction, looking toward the lower Rhine and Lorraine, which was situated between his two territories, the Netherlands in the north, and the two Burgundies in the south. Duke Sigismund therefore soon realized that the result of his diplomacy would be no other than that he had once and for all relinquished the former possessions of his line to the House of Burgundy in return for the pledged sum of 50,000 guilders. In order to regain those possessions, he decided to go over to the opposite side; if the Burgundians would not help him fight the Swiss, then the Swiss should help him fight the Burgundians. King Louis XI of France, the deadly enemy of Charles the Bold, mediated the agreement between the Austrian and the Confederation. Whereas, in the preceding century and a half, peace treaties had been concluded for only specific periods of time and were, consequently, mere armistices, Duke Sigismund was now ready to renounce finally, in a "constant and eternal policy" (1474), his right to the Swiss areas. In return for this concession, the Swiss obligated themselves to provide him mercenaries under certain circumstances and to help him in case he was attacked.

From this defensive treaty, the Confederation gradually allowed itself to be drawn into a general alliance for attack against the duke of Burgundy. There has been much disagreement as to the final reason for this war. Just as in the older conflicts against the Hapsburgs, the Swiss still like to present the matter as if they themselves, if not actually the ones that were attacked, were the ones who were somehow threatened by Burgundy, even if only indirectly, by the Burgundians' occupation of Alsace. There can be no question of this. If at the first uprising of the original cantons against the Hapsburgs it was in no way a peaceful population of shepherds and peasants that moved into the fight, but rather a battle-hardened and militarily skillful community, now the military power of the Confederation was all the more respected and feared by their neighbors on all sides. They themselves were so conscious of their own strength that any idea of a threat by Burgundy, or even of a feeling on the part of the Swiss of being threatened, is out of the question. Nowhere is this even suggested in the many documents or negotiations. Rather, the question can only be as to the extent to which the Swiss began the war against Charles the Bold and carried it through until the duke was finally defeated, from their own political motives—motives for their own expansion, booty, and conquest—or simply as mercenaries of a foreign power, namely, the king of France. The opinion that the Swiss fought the war only as mercenaries arose very early in Switzerland itself and, as I have become convinced from repeated investigation, is essentially correct, even if not entirely so. While the Confederation had a certain interest in not having the duke of Burgundy establish himself in Alsace and the Black Forest and felt themselves obliged to help the cities of the "Lower Union"—Strasbourg, Colmar, Schlettstadt, and Basel— which wanted to drive off the Burgundian domination from before their gates, this interest by the Swiss was satisfied by a defensive treaty that was concluded, and the seven eastern cantons also declined to move further because conquests in a war with Burgundy would have benefited only Bern, which was pushing forward. Consequently, the policy of the Confederation presented the same obstacle we have already seen: the military power and warlike zeal, as well as the idea of conquest, were present but did not come into full activity because they were restrained by the mutual envy of the cantons. The original cantons found that the way to fame and booty led over the Saint Gotthard Pass, toward Italy. But in Bern they had the idea of directing their offensive toward the west, in order to conquer the Jura and the Waadt, which belonged to

Burgundy's ally, Savoy. But Bern would never have been able to force acceptance of its plans of conquest by the other cantons if it had not been aided by the gold of Louis XI. Even the leading statesmen of Bern themselves were in the French pay, but the French money and Bern's political concept coincided, so that we cannot simply say that Bern sold out to the king of France. Of the seven other cantons, however, there is no doubt that they only followed the leadership of Bern and French money when they turned their weapons against Burgundy.

It is therefore not a matter in some sense or other of a war of liberation or even only a defensive war that the Swiss undertook, but an offensive war, regardless of whether one might wish to place the principal emphasis on Bern's concept of conquest, or on the theoretical opposition to the growing Burgundian power in the area, or on the money of Louis XI, who took into his pay both the leading statesmen personally and the entire cantons. This political character of the war is also of great importance for the strategy in it and therefore needed to be explained at some length.

But now the war developed quite differently from what the Swiss had imagined. Whereas, as they specifically emphasized in their declaration of war, they thought they were waging a profitable secondary war with but little danger, not as the "principal actors" but simply as allies of the German Empire, the House of Hapsburg, the "Lower Union," and the king of France, they soon learned that both the Emperor Frederick III and the king of France made peace with the Burgundian, and that the latter was now turning against them, hungry for revenge.

The war that originated in this way became of the greatest importance, not only politically and militarily but also from the historical-methodological viewpoint and that of folk psychology. In addition to the contemporary sources on the war, there is an account written two to three generations later from the pen of the reformer, Bullinger, which repeats the popular legend. In my *Perser- und Burgunderkriege* I published this passage from Bullinger's historical work, which had never previously been published, not because something concerning the course of events was to be derived from it, something we did not already know from other sources, but because the account forms such a completely instructive counterpart to Herodotus's account of the Persian wars—nowhere so much similarity as to suggest imitation, but trait by trait the same work of fantasy. Even the conversations of the exiled king, Demarat of Sparta, with the Persian king before Thermopylae are not missing. Charles the Bold had taken prisoner a Swiss colonel, Brandolf von Stein, who had to explain the methods of the Swiss to the duke, to the duke's astonishment and dismay. From this account by Bullinger we learn how folk tradition in the manner of Herodotus is to be appraised from the viewpoint of source analysis.

EXCURSUS

REFERENCES

Shortly before I treated for the first time in my *Perser- und Burgunderkriege* (1887) the political relationships of Switzerland with Charles the Bold, there was published a study by Heinrich Witte, "On the History of the Origin of the Burgundian Wars" ("Zur Geschichte der Entstehung der Burgunderkriege"), Program of Hagenau, 1885, which reached me too late to be taken into consideration. The same scholar then published in the *Zeitschrift für die Geschichte des Oberrheins,* Vols. 45, 47, 49 (1891, 1893, 1895), a series of further studies on this subject which are extremely valuable as a result of careful selection and comparison of sources, both printed and archival. Despite the scrupulous exactitude of the study, however, it is not without a certain bias for the Swiss as the "Germans" against the duke as the "Valencian," and I have not been able to derive from this work any reasons for changing my concept as I presented it in the *Perser- und Burgunderkriege.* If, for example, it is said on p. 8 of the *Program* that Sigismund could have had peace with the Confederation even without the Burgundian alliance if he had sincerely wished it—"As warlike as the Confederation was in general, as much as the consciousness of their superiority in the field and their hate for the knightly class drove them onward, they would nevertheless still have been ready to make peace at any time if Sigismund went seriously about restraining his knights and if he gave up what he had, after all, already lost"—I consider this concept as incorrect. In the Confederation there existed a drive toward conquest which, although it was restrained by internal obstacles, would still finally have broken out again, no matter how much the Hapsburgs would have wanted to keep the peace. It was only by diverting the warlike urge toward mercenary service that conquest by the Swiss came to an end starting with the next generation. Witte himself adds the following remark: "Sigismund might perhaps have feared the ambitious plans of Bern, but the Waldshut war had shown that the Confederation was not at all so inclined to support such plans with its means. And furthermore, even Bern was not so warlike as is usually believed." Against this viewpoint we may say that if Bern had not been warlike and thirsty for conquest to the highest degree, there would remain no political reason for the rebuff to the duke of Burgundy on 25 October 1474, but then we would simply have to accept the old concept that this war had been absolutely nothing other than mercenary service in the pay of the king of France.

In the *Zeitschrift für die Geschichte des Oberrheins,* Vol. 45, p. 16, Witte states that the peace between the Confederation and Austria would have come about even without the intervention of King Louis. "The common danger, which cannot be denied and which was becoming greater and greater, even without Hagenbach's intervention, the more definitely Charles planned to found a Kingdom of Burgundy, necessarily brought Duke Sigismund and the Confederation together." This statement is partially correct in that the Confederation did not desire the establishment of the major power of Burgundy on its borders and that in this situation there was a political reason for them to join forces with the Hapsburgs and to provide these ancient enemies a certain measure of support for their recovery of their pawned territories on the upper Rhine. But it is too much to declare that the Kingdom of Burgundy signified for the Confederation a "danger which cannot be denied." Quite to the contrary, this danger must be absolutely denied. Not even the great-grandson and heir of Charles the Bold, Emperor Charles V, who had at his disposal a completely different degree of power than his ancestor, became a danger for the Swiss. On p. 74, Witte himself says very correctly, on the basis of a dispatch from the Milanese ambassador Cerrati to his lord: "Bern had the highest concept of its military power and that of the Confederation; within its mountains it felt strong enough to be able to take on Burgundy, Savoy, and Milan together, and King Louis knew what he was doing when he foisted on the Confederation the fight against his Burgundian opponent."

There is no doubt a basic contradiction with this statement when Witte speaks on p. 72 of a "condition of self-defense" in which the Confederation, according to Witte, found itself with respect to conquest-hungry Burgundy, and when he states on p. 367 that Bern would presumably have left untouched the possessions of the count of Romont if the count had not acted against the interests of Bern. I believe, on the contrary, that no matter what attitude the count of Romont might have taken, the Bernese would always have found an excuse on the occasion of this war to take possession of at least part of his territories, Murten at the very least.

A real correction of the situation has been provided by Vischer in an excursus to his edition of Knebel's journal, *Basel Chronicles*, 3: 369, where it is shown that the representatives sent by the duke of Burgundy to the Confederation, who found a very friendly attitude there and to which I referred on p. 175 of *Geschichte der Perser- und Burgunderkriege*, did not travel into the cantons in the spring of 1474 but carried out their mission in 1469. Nevertheless, no conclusions on the whole political situation result from this, as, for example, Dändliker states in his *Geschichte der Schweiz*, 2: 841 (3d ed.), for even Bern sent the following word to the duke as late as 15 March 1474: "The city of Bern has not forgotten how much good will existed between the duke's ancestors, and especially the duke's father, and the city, from which there grew the mutual understanding which Bern has traditionally maintained." The message went on to say that the city even now intended so to live vis-à-vis everyone as befitted its honor and its reputation. (Witte, *Zeitschrift für die Geschichte des Oberrheins*, New Series, 6: 23, note). We see quite clearly from these affected words how Bern was preparing to shift over to hostility from the good relationship that existed up to this moment.

With outstanding impartiality, Dierauer judges these relationships in his *History of the Swiss Confederation* (*Geschichte der Schweizerischen Eidgenossenschaft*), Vol. II, 1892, a very valuable book in all respects.

Dändliker, *Geschichte der Schweiz*, Vol. II, seeks, like Witte, to show the Swiss as threatened and the war as a defensive one. On p. 200 he speaks of the "worried concern" of the Confederation, and on p. 201 he states that the people were filled with "fear of the cruel, erratic duke." All of these sensations were certainly quite foreign to the Confederation and give a very false picture of it. On p. 841 Dändliker draws from my *Perser- und Burgunderkriege* the conclusion that I, too, consider that French money played only a secondary role, but he neglects to mention the factors that are decisive for me—first, the opposition between Bern and the seven other cantons, and second, that the political motives for Bern were based on conquest and not defense. In the case of the seven eastern cantons, I in no way attributed merely a secondary role to French money.

The authoritative work for the Burgundian wars, based on the sources, still remains that of Em. von Rodt, *The Campaigns of Charles the Bold, Duke of Burgundy, and his Heirs. With Special Reference to the Participation of the Swiss* (*Die Feldzüge Karls des Kühnen, Herzogs von Burgund, und seiner Erben. Mit besonderem Bezug auf die Teilnahme der Schweizer an denselben*), 2 volumes, Schaffhausen, 1843. Also of value is the comprehensive biography by the

American J. Foster Kirk, *History of Charles the Bold, Duke of Burgundy,* 3 volumes, London, 1863–1868.

C. Toutey, *Charles the Bold and the League of Constance* (*Charles le Téméraire et la Ligue de Constance*), Paris, 1902, is a very thorough study but does not provide anything for our purposes.

ENGAGEMENT AT HÉRICOURT
13 NOVEMBER 1474

Immediately after the declaration of war, while Duke Charles was on the lower Rhine with his main army, the Swiss, Alsatians, and Austrians had moved out with an army of 18,000 men to besiege Héricourt. A Burgundian relief army approached from the north, but since it was in any case much weaker than the besieging army (it could hardly have been as strong as 10,000 men, the figure that was reported),[3] it is difficult to see what it really intended to do—perhaps only to make an attempt at a demonstration. The allies moved out to meet it, and the Burgundians took flight without any serious fighting. The report that the Burgundian horsemen are supposed to have been astonished at the unaccustomed boldness with which they were so unhesitatingly attacked by mere foot soldiers is merely a figment of the Swiss imagination.[4]

Of interest from the viewpoint of source analysis are the casualty figures.

The captains from Solothurn reported back home that 600 of the enemy were killed. The captains from Biel reported back home that "some 1,000 men of the enemy were killed."

The Bernese reported to the king of France that 1,617 enemy corpses had been counted on the battlefield,[5] in addition to the large number that had died in a village as a result of fire, so that the enemy himself supposedly estimated his losses as 3,000 men.

Another official report states 2,000 killed.

The Bernese chronicler Schilling gives a figure of 2,000 dead on the battlefield and 1,000 burned to death.

At first, one is no doubt inclined to regard as authentic the 1,617 enemy bodies claimed to have been counted by the Bernese, in addition to those who were burned to death. Modern scholars have attempted to reconcile the estimate of the Solothurners, which was written to the home city on the very night after the battle, with this number by assuming that on the following day the victory turned out to be much greater than it had seemed at first. Of course, this has occurred frequently enough, but it is not consistent with the nature of the battle and the losses of the allies.

The city scribe of Basel, Nicholas Rüsch,[6] and the Bernese chronicler Diebold Schilling both state that the Confederation did not have a single man killed, only a few wounded, who recovered. Other reports list up to three men killed;[7] the captains from Biel reported two deaths to their town. Rodt claims to have read the figure 70 in a source he does not name.[8]

Even if the Swiss lost seventy men, we can hardly believe a figure of 2,000 and more on the other side, since the Burgundians were attacked neither from the flank nor from the rear and encountered no obstacles in their flight. This is all the less believable, since the false figures for the Swiss losses are given directly beside those for the enemy. But if we in some way decide to accept the statement that the Confederation had no losses at all, or two to three at the most, then the thousands of Burgundians killed really becomes incredible. Consequently, the figure of 1,617 enemy dead, seemingly so carefully counted, is in no way to be considered as authentic.

Of the prisoners, eighteen Lombard mercenaries, accused of having profaned churches and committed other sacrileges during an incursion into Alsace, were tortured and burned alive. But for the future it was established in a resolution by the assembly that, as had already been the case earlier in the Confederation, no prisoners would be taken at all, but all were to be killed.

BATTLE OF GRANDSON
2 MARCH 1476

It was a full year and a half until the duke, occupied on the lower Rhine and in Lorraine, was able to appear on the border of Switzerland in order to defend his territory. In the meantime, the Swiss had carried out one campaign after another and had bled dry the neighboring areas, Burgundy and Waadt. The small town of Stäffis, a peaceful locality on Neuenburg Lake, which had offered resistance, was completely wiped out. The garrison of the castle, which was stormed at the end, had been thrown alive from the top of the tower. Even the men who were later found hiding here and there were bound together with a rope and thrown into the lake to drown. Then the men of Fribourg came with 100 wagons to haul away the cloths that were made in the little town and were the basis of its wealth. Not the slightest belonging was left for the women and children who had survived. Even the plunderers are said to have been taken with pity over the dreadful laments, and the Council of Bern sent a mild reproach to its captains because of the "inhuman hardness."[9]

The Bernese had taken advantage of these common plundering expeditions by taking for themselves possession of the fortified places, especially at the Jura passes. But when the duke now appeared with a powerful army, they gave those castles up, for it was apparent that the eastern cantons were no more inclined now than previously to fight battles for Bern's conquests. The most advanced post that the Bernese risked holding was Grandson. They placed a garrison of 500 men there, estimating that they could hold out, and if their situation became more critical, the Confederation would finally not refuse to move out to relieve them.

We are very well informed on this campaign, not only by thorough accounts in Swiss and Burgundian chronicles, but especially through the reports which Panigarola, ambassador of the duke of Milan, who was in Charles's entourage, sent in great detail to his master every few days and which are available to us in printed form.[10]

The closest route by which the duke of Burgundy could enter the territory of the Swiss would have led over the Jura, probably to Neuchâtel or to Biel. Nevertheless, Charles did not take this route. The goal he set for himself was, first of all, not yet the invasion of Swiss territory, but the liberation of Waadt, the Savoy territory that had been conquered by the Swiss. Charles therefore turned in this direction and made the Waadt his base of operations, so that during the actual campaign his front faced northeastward.

The first strategic objective that the duke planned was the reconquest of Grandson. That place is not situated on the route that would have led him directly toward his archenemy, the city of Bern. But it was precisely for this reason, no doubt, that Charles chose this maneuver. His estimates were probably quite parallel to those of the Council of Bern, but in the opposite direction. He knew that not all the cantons were by any means in agreement with Bern's policy. If he had now moved directly on Bern, it could be assumed that, despite all their differences, the Confederation would not leave Bern in the lurch. But Charles, by attacking Grandson, only placed the cantons first of all face to face with the question as to whether they had reason to support Bern in the defense of that conquest. It was possible that with this feeling they would appear with only half their strength, or negligently, or would not aid at all. Whether Bern then wanted to risk a relief battle with its own forces only and those of its nearest allies, or to leave the town and its garrison to their own resources, the chances for this undertaking seemed in either case to be especially favorable.

Events turned out just as the duke had calculated. All the reports of the Burgundian approach and all the daily pleas for help from Bern did not succeed in persuading the easterly cantons to take immediate action. It was not until more than three weeks later, after the Burgundians had started to cross the mountain, that the army of the Confederation, even though not yet at full strength, was ready for action. In the meantime, the garrison of Grandson had been obliged to surrender unconditionally and had been executed by the angered duke as a well-deserved punishment for its misdeeds.

It would undoubtedly have been safest for the duke if he had awaited the attack of the Swiss in his well-equipped camp, protected by artillery, on the plain near Grandson. His army was some 14,000 men strong, with 2,000 to 3,000 heavy horsemen, 7,000 to 8,000 marksmen, and the remainder dismounted spearmen. The Swiss, with a strength of about 19,000, were a few thousand men stronger to be sure, but it was doubtful whether they would risk an attack on the camp, and Charles therefore decided to move out to meet them. With his professional warriors and his artillery, he felt certain of success against the people's levy. The road leads along the Neuenburg Lake. Along a certain stretch of this route the mountains, approaching close to the lake, form a narrow pass. In order to secure his march through this pass, Charles first captured the Vaumarcus castle at the opposite (northern) exit and installed a garrison there (1 March).[11]

This movement also determined the advance of the Swiss. They had indeed been hesitant about attacking the Burgundians' fortified camp. Now they decided to turn at once against Vaumarcus. It could be assumed with certainty that Charles would hasten up to the relief of the garrison and would thus offer the opportunity for a battle in a place that was not prepared in advance, especially one not occupied by artillery. On the morning of 2 March the two armies moved toward each other, the Swiss toward the northern exit of the pass, against Vaumarcus, and the Burgundians toward the southern exit. Charles intended to move his army forward only to that point, about 5 miles from Grandson. Consequently, the ridge of the mountain, about 2½ miles wide, would still have been situated between the two opponents. But then the battle developed, unexpectedly for both sides.

Part of the Swiss, principally Schwyzers, Bernese, and Fribourgers, entered into combat with a Burgundian outpost which was in position on

Fig. 8   BATTLE OF GRANDSON

the road leading over the ridge. The fight drew one unit after another onto this road, and when they arrived at the other side of the mountain in pursuit of the enemy, they saw on the plain before them the enemy's entire army. The advance guard had already arrived and had begun to pitch camp; the main body was still on the march.

The duke himself was with his advance guard and took up the fight with the Swiss who were welling out of the pass, primarily with his marksmen.

From a theoretical viewpoint, the situation was as favorable as possible for the Burgundian army. Both armies were still in the approach march, but the Burgundians were crossing a plain, while the Swiss were passing through a difficult pass. We must therefore assume that the Burgundian army could be assembled and deployed faster than the Swiss. It could then attack the Swiss, who were still involved in their development, and if it succeeded in throwing them back, they would necessarily have been pressed together and held up at the entrance of the defile, suffering heavy losses.

But the characteristic composition and tactics of the two armies made this maneuver, quite logical in itself, impossible for the Burgundians. The road along which the Swiss were moving up did not emerge directly from the wooded mountain onto the plain, but gradually sloped downward across hills planted with vineyards. On this terrain it was hardly possible for Charles to bring into action the two arms on which he relied the most, his knights and his artillery. If he had had only the powerful mass of his marksmen move forward in the attack, they would perhaps have obliged the Swiss to move back into the pass, but alone they could not inflict a real defeat on them, since they could not trust themselves to move up very close to the enemy or to allow a hand-to-hand fight to develop. Charles therefore decided to deploy his army on the plain and let it be attacked there by the Swiss. One would think that in doing so he gave up the principal advantage which the situation offered him, that is, the possibility of joining battle before the full force of the enemy was at hand. But he still succeeded in arranging even that. He had the fight continued by a few units of marksmen, which, superior to the Swiss marksmen, presumably harassed strongly the Swiss square that was forming on the hills. Consequently, the Swiss unit, composed of some 8,000 men and not yet comprising half of the Swiss army, moved into the attack without awaiting the arrival of the others.

The small number of horsemen,[12] and the few marksmen which the Bernese had with them, accompanied this attack. We can hardly imagine a more favorable situation for the Burgundian army if, for its part, it had now already been completely deployed. But that was not yet the case. We may assume that the Burgundian army was completely in the area but partially still involved in the rear in moving out from the train and forming up, as the Swiss approached. Perhaps the Swiss were drawn into this piecemeal attack precisely in the realization that the Burgundians, too, were not yet completely ready.

Regardless of the reasons for the attack, the duke still believed he had all the advantages on his side. If the Swiss square came onto the plain, he would be able to attack it in the flanks with his men-at-arms, while having it fired on in the front by the artillery and marksmen. The few Swiss horsemen and marksmen who were accompanying the square would not have been able to protect it from flank attacks, to say nothing of possible attacks from the rear that might develop. The Swiss square, in order to defend itself, would have had to halt and would finally have succumbed to the attacks from all sides.

Charles therefore ordered a few detachments of his men-at-arms to attack the enemy flank from the direction of the mountain and had others withdraw from the front to unmask the artillery. The cannonballs drove into the Swiss main body. The attack by the men-at-arms was carried out with great élan. The skirmishers of the Confederation fled back into the square, and the men-at-arms moved right up to the spear points, but they were unable to penetrate into the massive square from which the long spears were extended against them. The seigneur de Châteauguyon, who forced his horse into the line, was cut down, and the others turned about. The attack was repulsed, having shattered itself against the firm stand of the Swiss square and the long, extended spears.

Thus the fate of the day was already decided. Panic had broken out among the Burgundian units that were still farther to the rear—that is, probably those that were still forming up—as well as in the train, and this panic continued to spread. With the cry "Sauve qui peut," one unit after another took flight. As the reason for this panic, Panigarola states that the rearward units had interpreted as flight the movement to the rear that was made in order to open up the field of fire for the artillery. The Swiss assumed that the arrival of their other units, which poured forward in a steady stream from both passes (over the mountain and along the lake shore), had filled the Burgundians with fear. It is possible that both these points and also the repelling of the attack of the men-at-arms under Châteauguyon combined for the final effect.[13] At any rate, a general battle never developed. Of course, the main body of the Burgundian army was composed of marksmen, who could not stand up to close combat with spearmen and halberds, and the firm steadfastness of a tactical body that protects individuals from becoming infected by panic was missing. The Burgundian army rushed from the scene. Charles sought in vain to stop his men and turn them back into the fight here and there. The Swiss pursued the fugitives, but since only a few of their horsemen were on hand and they did not dare move forward individually, they could cause the enemy no further harm. The loss of 1,000 men, a figure given by some, is in any case too high. Panigarola says, apparently in keeping with the nature of the fight, that only very few were killed, and the captain of the men from Saint Gall, Baron Peter von Hewen, reported to his abbot on the day after the battle that only 200 Burgundians were left on the field.[14]

On the side of the Swiss, a not completely insignificant number were

killed and wounded by the cannon and the arrows of the Burgundians,
even in the contingents that were not in the advance guard but in the
main square. The men of Lucerne, for example, had fifty-two wounded.
Most of these were presumably hit during the pursuit by arrows fired
back at them. A number of individuals from all the contingents supposedly attached themselves to the advance unit, and some of them may
have been wounded in the battle itself.[15]

EXCURSUS

Dierauer, 2: 207, has taken exception to my estimate of the strength of the Burgundian
army as 13,000 to 14,000 men, since, in addition to the 11,000 which Charles led up (plus
400 lances sent out in advance), there were also reinforcements from Savoy and Milan. But
it is very doubtful whether reinforcements came from Milan and whether Savoyards were
present at Grandson, whereas, on the other hand, it is very possible that individual parts of
Charles' army had been detached. (See *Perser- und Burgunderkriege*, p. 150.)

Feldmann, *Die Schlacht bei Granson* (Freienfeld, 1902), arrives at a higher figure, because, according to him, I did not include the artillery crews, the men-at-arms, and the
Savoyards. But the artillery crews were composed mainly of noncombatants; a *"gensdar-
merie"* which I had not included is not shown in the sources, and we have already spoken
about the Savoyards.

Feldmann also considers as important the shout from Charles, "20,000 men fled," and he
believes that the duke did not, after all, wish to show the victory of the Swiss as greater than
it actually was. My reply is: It is quite clear that the duke, angry over the cowardice of his
men, exaggerated to put them in a more unfavorable light.

In his dispatch of 31 December 1475, Panigarola states that the duke claimed he already
had 2,300 lances and 10,000 archers. I have assumed (*Perser- und Burgunderkriege*, p. 149)
that the 10,000 archers were at the same time parts of the lances. Feldmann rejects this
interpretation, and he may possibly be correct: The duke actually meant to say 2,300 lances
(equals 13,800 men) and 10,000 marksmen. But for the strength estimate at Grandson,
nothing is gained from this. For this purpose, only Panigarola's report of 16 January is
authoritative, and it shows that that earlier statement by the duke was a strong exaggeration.

BATTLE OF MURTEN
22 JUNE 1476

No matter how strongly the Bernese requested it, the Swiss still did
not turn their victory into the base for a broad strategic offensive. They
did not even follow it up far beyond the camp of Grandson but immediately returned with their booty to their home cantons.[16] And so
Charles was able to reorganize his army in the Waadt itself, some 50
miles from Bern. His headquarters was at Lausanne. In two months he

had completed his preparations there, had assembled an army considerably stronger than that at Grandson, probably between 18,000 and 20,000 men, and he again began his campaign.[17]

This time the Bernese had not risked retaining outposts as far forward as that of Grandson had been. The only place in Savoy territory which they held was Murten. This place, situated 14 miles from Bern, blocked the more northerly of the two roads linking Lausanne and Bern, just as Fribourg blocked the more southerly road. Consequently, Charles was obliged first to attack one of these two places. There would have been no advantage for him to bypass them and move directly on Bern. The Bernese alone would hardly have offered battle in the open field. The duke would have been obliged to besiege the city and would then have been attacked by the relief army in the same manner but under very much more unfavorable circumstances in comparison with what he might expect at Murten or Fribourg. The duke, therefore, had first of all to turn against one of these two cities. Foreseeing this, the Council of Bern had strengthened the Fribourg citizenry with a "supplement" of 1,000 men. The city of Murten, situated on foreign territory and uncertain as to the attitude of its inhabitants, was provided a garrison of 1,580 men under the command of an especially experienced warrior, Adrian von Bubenberg.

The duke of Burgundy decided to turn against Murten. Whatever specific military reasons may have been considered in reaching this decision—as, for example, the better route of retreat or the terrain—the decisive point was the same consideration that had caused him to direct his first campaign against Grandson. The opposition of the eastern cantons to this war was just as strong after Grandson as before.[18] As a result, despite all of Bern's remonstrances and despite the most obvious military advantages that could be won, the forces of the cantons had returned home immediately after the victory and had allowed the Burgundians to establish their assembly area directly before their door. They did not even wish to help defend Murten, but simply to limit themselves to defense of the actual territory of the Confederation. An attack against Fribourg would have brought them immediately to arms with their maximum strength. In the case of Murten, there could easily be a repetition of the same game as at Grandson in the spring.

It is difficult to say what the duke further intended to do if he succeeded in capturing Murten before the arrival of the relieving army. Although he spoke to Panigarola about moving directly against Bern, we can imagine just as well that he might have awaited an attack by the Swiss in a fortified position. Holding the 1,500 men of the garrison of Murten

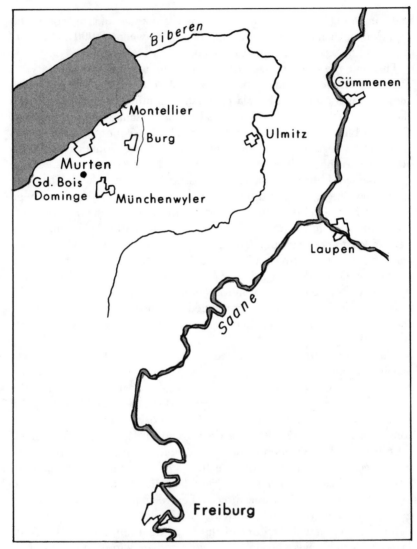

Fig. 9   BATTLE OF MURTEN

would perhaps even have sufficed to accomplish the purpose of the war if he held them prisoner as a pawn. And if he had them executed, like the garrison of Grandson, he would not have needed to go to Bern in order to see the Swiss come storming up for the desired battle in the open field.

Charles therefore moved up to Murten in a deliberate manner, began the siege on 9 June, and at the same time erected fortifications facing outward to defend against the possible approach of a relief army. He did not directly inclose his camp near the city with this fortification, since in that place it would have been overlooked by the rising terrain, but moved it forward onto the next ridge, 1½ to 2 kilometers from the city, in front of which a relatively flat area, the Wyler Field, extended eastward from Burg and Münchenwyler. It provided an excellent field of battle for receiving the approaching enemy from afar with cannon and then with the balls, bolts, and arrows of the marksmen and finally, moving out with knights and foot soldiers, going over into the attack.[19]

At another place, probably near Montellier, Charles dammed a stream in order to block the approach. The fortification was composed of a "*Grünhag*," as the Swiss chroniclers called it, partly intermeshed fence, partly palisade, which was occupied, on the rises in the ground, by cannon. To provide for sorties, breaches were left in this "*Grünhag*." It is not reported how far it extended eastward around the camp, but no doubt far enough so that at most the south side was open, and perhaps even completely around. Possibly on that side the forest south of Münchenwyler served as a point of support, having been made impassable by the felling of trees. The Swiss, whose natural assembly point lay in the northeast, could probably not move any further around.

In view of the strength of his position, the duke was convinced that the Swiss would not even risk moving up to it. It would depend on him alone as to whether battle would be joined; that is, whether he moved out of his fortified camp or remained in it.[20]

The movement of supplies to his fortified camp was protected by troops that were stationed at intervals at appropriate strongpoints.

The duke would have protected himself best against a surprise attack by a relief army if he had occupied the crossings of the Saane, which flows from south to north about halfway between Murten and Bern, especially the crossings at Laupen and Gümmenen. And he did indeed at the very start, on 12 June, make an attempt to take possession of these places, but when these moves were repulsed, he did not try again. He probably did not want to have outlying posts exposed to the danger of being captured or to be obliged because of them to move out to a relief battle.

The Swiss were now able to assemble their army directly behind the Saane and, when the main body was assembled, to move across the river to Ulmitz (12 June), no farther than 5 or 6 kilometers from the Burgundian palisade. In addition to the Swiss themselves, on hand were Duke René of Lorraine with several hundred horsemen, Austrian horsemen, troops from Strasbourg, and other contingents from Alsace. But it was not until 22 June, the thirteenth day after the start of the siege, that the army was more or less at full strength. The cantons had called up their troops, not at the news of the advance of the Burgundians and not even at the report of the siege of Murten, but when the ancient Bern area was really violated—which occurred on the occasion of the outpost fight on the Saane on 12 June.

Despite strong efforts, the Burgundians had not succeeded in overpowering Murten during this time. They had shot breaches in the walls and assaulted but had been repulsed. Bubenberg, the commander, conducted the defense with the greatest energy and vigilance. He kept the citizenry's hostile emotions under control, and he stirred up the decreasing courage of his troops with exhortations and strictness. Reinforcements, which were sent to him across the lake, came to his aid. The Burgundian captains therefore advised the duke to renounce any repetition of the attack, limit the action to continued firing at the town, and to apply all their strength to the coming battle, which would also determine the fate of the town.

When it was reported to the duke how close the Swiss were, he himself with a few of his captains made a reconnaissance on 21 June, the day before the battle. They came so close that the Swiss began to fire, and they discussed whether they should not suspend the siege and preferably move first against this enemy in the open field.[21] But the duke decided against that. The terrain near Ulmitz, which the Swiss had selected as their assembly area, was unusable for an attack by the knights, broken by ravines and surrounded by woods, so that it was also impossible to see the forces of the enemy and estimate their strength. The duke believed that not many of them had yet assembled. And he was all the less willing to interrupt the siege, which necessarily had to lead finally to success. He does not appear to have considered the possibility of dividing his army in order to continue the siege and at the same time attack the relief army near Ulmitz (as Frederick, for example, did when he moved from Prague to Kolin against Daun). Such a move was also not advisable, since they were not certain how strong the enemy near Ulmitz was, and he was so very well covered by the terrain. And so the duke continued with his plan to carry on the siege and await the attack of the relief army. Panigarola warned him that there was a treacherous stratagem in the conduct of the Swiss and that from one hour to the next they could suddenly appear. But after the Burgundian army had already deployed several times in the preceding days behind the palisades in order to receive the enemy attack, and day after day had passed without their coming, the duke no longer believed they would attack at all. He could, in the worst eventuality, protect himself against a surprise attack by garrisoning his position along the front facing Ulmitz, even for the night-time, with 2,000 foot troops and 300 lances. The main body of the army, which had already been formed in battle order for the entire afternoon, he allowed to return to camp.

During the night it began to rain hard and it rained the whole next morning. In the morning the Swiss made a reconnaissance, but then they immediately withdrew and nothing further was seen or heard of them. Now the duke believed he could be completely sure they would not risk an attack.

The Swiss, however, had actually intended to attack on the preceding days and were only awaiting the arrival of the Zurich forces, which by forced marches and at the end even with a night march from Bern, arrived at Ulmitz on Saturday morning. The Council of Zurich, which wanted to impress forcibly on the Bernese its opinion concerning the conquest of the Waadt, had not had its troops start the march until 18 June, more than three weeks after the Burgundians had taken up their advance from Lausanne and on the tenth day after the duke had begun the siege of Murten. Furthermore, the levy was very small for the situation, only about 1,450, or at the very most, 2,000 men.

The assembled army of the Confederation, however, still outnumbered the Burgundians by a larger margin than at Grandson. It can be estimated at some 26,000 men, and if we add the garrison of Murten, which, after all, was also an important consideration, since it tied down a part of the Burgundians and finally made a sortie, the overall strength approached 28,000. The Burgundian army, to repeat, had a strength of 18,000 to 20,000 men, from which a certain number must be subtracted for the chain of supply route garrisons.

The Swiss source, which had already attributed a strength of 100,000 men to the Burgundian army at Grandson, gave the duke's strength at Murten as up to three times that figure.

The duke, with a considerably smaller force, was also at a disadvantage strategically because of the beleaguered city with its strong garrison in his rear. But his forces were endangered most of all through the fact that his fortifications, in order to take advantage of the terrain, were pushed out more than a half-kilometer in advance of his camp and had therefore had to assume a very large circumference. In case of attack, everything depended on having the Burgundians in position at the palisades at the right time, and that had to be at the place being attacked by the Swiss, something that could not be known in advance.

A general must combine with the boldness of risks and the courage of decision the constantly alert watchfulness that notices the smallest clues and foresees the stratagems and deceptions of the enemy. When the Austrians planned to make a sudden attack on the Prussians at Chotusitz on 17 May 1742, the Prussians escaped defeat only because their commanding general, Crown Prince Leopold of Anhalt, was already on horseback at sunrise and at the report of the enemy's approach was able to take measures to alert his troops and have them deploy. When the Austrians thought they would surprise Frederick at Soor on 30 September 1745, the Prussian counterattack was made possible only because the king rose at four o'clock each morning and already had the general of the day with him when he received word of the enemy action. But even Frederick was taken by surprise at Hochkirch, and Gneisenau would presumably already have won the victory of Belle Alliance at Ligny if he had noticed Napoleon's approach march a few hours earlier. It would seem that the approach march of an entire army would be so massive that it could not go unnoticed. In reality, however, the phenomenon of entire armies remaining unnoticed in close proximity to the enemy has occurred very often in the history of warfare. Because this point can be made convincing only by citing repeated experiences, I would like to recall a few additional cases. On 16 October 1813, the French were awaiting the Silesian army in a well-prepared position at Wahren, but they abandoned the position when they thought no attack was imminent from that direction. Immediately thereafter the enemy was reported. He was already so close that the French could not return to that position but took up a position at Möckern, a little over a mile to the rear, where they had just arrived. Even crasser is the example of the battle of Königgrätz, where the Austrians on the right flank did not notice the approach march of the crown prince's troops until they were right in their midst. On 4 August 1870, the entire Third Army was in the approach march on Weissenburg without being observed by the French patrols. Based on the patrols' reports, General Douay had his troops cook their meal, when firing suddenly began on the outposts. The battles of Trautenau in 1866, where the Prussians were unaware of the arrival of the main body of Austrians, and of Beaumont in 1870, where the French were taken by surprise by the Prussians, also belong in this category to the extent that the error lay in the fact that the enemy was not observed because he was not expected. We may also cite the fact that it took the seventeenth and the entire morning of the eighteenth of August 1870 for the Germans to detect the right flank of the French position at Saint Privat, which was only about 5 miles from them.

Consequently, if the prompt observation of an enemy approach march, which in this case was also covered by woods, is in itself not so easy and is not to be taken for granted, the duke of Burgundy was completely lacking in the qualities of generalship that would have enabled him to cope with such a situation. Instead of observing most carefully the Swiss, whose camp he was, of course, familiar with, himself directing his entire attention to it or assigning it as a vital mission to his most reliable captain, he remained obstinately convinced that they would not risk an attack. Even at midday, when he received reports that they were approaching, he remained incredulous for a rather long time and took no measures.

The Swiss leaders had carefully considered where they should make their attack. The council of war had decided to direct the attack, not against the besieging corps on the north of the town, by the lake, but against the center of the Burgundian position on the Wyler Field. If they succeeded in penetrating there, a large part of the enemy army would necessarily be pushed back from the road to the rear and be cut off. It is worthwhile to repeat the words of the Bernese chronicler on this fateful decision:

> All the captains, ensigns, and councils from cities and territories, and also other allies and associates, were there together day after day considering and discussing how they might honorably attack and act on these matters, for they were constantly concerned lest the duke and his criminal leaders might escape them, as had happened previously at Grandson, and they counseled with one another that in the name of God and with His Godly help they would attack the right lord first and that they would hold him back so that he could not escape them, for they believed if they first attacked and defeated the count of Remond, who had erected his camp in a strong position here on this side of Murten, the duke and the other criminal leaders would be forced to flee.

The attack, then, moved from Ulmitz straight across the small plateau between the villages of Burg and Salvenach (about a mile south of Burg) against the Burgundian fortification, which probably extended about from the village of Münchenwyler northward in the direction of Burg or onto the Adera Hill. Between the three units of spears and halberds were the knights, no fewer than 1,800, and the marksmen.[22]

Characteristic enough of the internal tension in the Confederation was the fact that the high command was held, not by a Swiss, but by a vassal of the dynasty with which they had stood in deathly enmity until three years previously, the Austrian knight Wilhelm Herter. The Bernese chronicler was not able to bring himself to record this fact. He makes no mention at all of the commander and does not even name the captain of the main body, who was from Zurich, Hans Waldmann. Instead, he holds up for praise only the person of the leader of the advance guard, the Bernese Hans von Halwil, and the only other person he mentions is the leader of the rear guard, Kaspar Hartenstein.[23]

Curiously enough, this army of peasants and burghers made a rather long halt in the forest during their march forward, while the count of Thierstein dubbed as knights a rather large number of persons, including the burgomaster of Zurich, Waldmann. The ceremony lasted so long that the mass of men finally became impatient.

But despite this delay, the Burgundians were still not alerted when the masses of horsemen, marksmen, and finally the powerful squares with their flying banners moved out of the forest onto the Wyler Field. And the "Grünhag" was no more strongly occupied than during the night, with 2,000 foot soldiers and 300 lances.

As weak as the garrison was, the first attack was still repulsed. The reports on both sides agree on this point. Judging from the account of the Bernese Schilling, we would have to assume that the units moved right up to the Burgundian palisades, did not penetrate them, and turned about. It is probably more likely that the effect of the Burgundian cannon and the appearance of the fortification occupied by marksmen brought the attacking column to a halt farther away. The account of another eyewitness, the native of Lucerne, Etterlin, reads:

> The enemy had strengthened his position there, and large, heavy cannon, shooting with accurate and deadly effect against the troops of the Confederation in their formation, as well as against the knights who were then beside the formation in a small field, in the end caused great damage, for I, Peterman Etterlin, author of this chronicle, and many pious men who were there saw a few horsemen and knights who were shot in two in the middle so that their upper part was completely separated and their lower part remained in the saddle, and a few also had their heads shot off, but by the grace of God, not many of them.

If the Swiss had come all the way up to the palisades and had been forced back beyond the range of the enemy cannon, their losses would no doubt have been quite heavy. And so it was more the morale impression of the fearful wounds caused by the cannonballs than it was the number of those killed which brought the columns to a halt.

Panigarola reports that Captain Jacob Galioto and all the other captains had told him that, if the Burgundian army had been in position when the

Swiss turned about and withdrew toward the woods, it would undoubtedly have defeated them.[24] We may doubt whether the Swiss squares were really so badly shaken, but it is true that this would have been the right moment for the Burgundians to go over to the offensive.

A few knights were courageous enough to dash out against the Swiss,[25] but with their small number they could not accomplish anything, and the Burgundian army was not in position. Duke Charles in the camp below had only just given the word for the trumpets to blow the command to put on equipment, saddle up, and mount. Panigarola had gone onto the ridge himself, had seen the Swiss with his own eyes—the horsemen, the forest of bristling spears, the waving banners. He had rushed down to the duke and had helped him put on his armor. But even at this moment the duke was still in doubt. When he finally mounted his horse, the battle was already decided.

It could not have been difficult for the Swiss, in the rolling terrain, to find a slope where they were protected against the cannonballs. Furthermore, the cannon could not quickly be reloaded and pointed in another direction. An account from Basel reports that the *ammann* from Schwyz advised this movement and with halberd in hand placed himself at the point.[26]

When the Burgundian warriors—knights, archers, and spearmen—taken by surprise, were rushing from the camp in individual units, the *"Grünhag"* was already stormed and broken, the fleeing troops were already streaming back toward them, and they, in turn, were followed by the Swiss in masses, even if already in extended order.[27] The duke had great trouble saving himself and made no further effort to halt his men in a new position. The strongly superior force and the aggressive attack of the Swiss, and the confusion and breakup of units among the Burgundians, doomed all efforts to failure. Only a part of the mounted men escaped; the foot troops, including the famous English archers, were overtaken by the enemy horsemen, who were, of course, very numerous and were for the most part cut down. But all the units that were in position around the town of Murten were cut off before they learned what had happened. They were all slaughtered or drowned in the lake. Only Count Romont's detachment, which was encamped north of the town, escaped, by fleeing in a wide circle around the enemy army and along the Saane.

Let us mention here as examples of the unreliability of source reports, which, by their origin, should provide very acceptable evidence, the fact that the Lorraine chronicle reports that Duke René commanded the Swiss; Molinet, the Burgundian court historian, reported that the Swiss had fortified themselves with a *"Grünhag"* which the Burgundians tried in vain to storm; and Heuterus reported that Charles had his foot troops formed in a large square with the horsemen on the flanks and the marksmen in the rear.

On one occasion (8 July), Panigarola estimated the total losses at 8,000 to 10,000 men, including the train. Later, he stated (13 July) that of his 1,600 lances, the duke had saved 1,000 lances and 200 nobles, which is probably to be understood as meaning that the 1,000 lances were regarded as complete lances, that of 200 others, only those nobles with the best mounts escaped, while the privates and especially the marksmen fell, and finally, the 400 other lances were completely destroyed. According to this report, then, about one-third of the army, 6,000 to 7,000 men, perished, a figure that would agree approximately with the preceding figure (from which, of course, the train is to be subtracted). In a third dispatch (27 July), Panigarola reports on a review Charles held of the survivors. In it eleven companies assembled, which should have had 1,100 lances, but were hardly more than half that strong. That would make the losses appear very much greater than the preceding reports, but Panigarola adds that not all the missing men had been killed, but rather, many Italians and Burgundians had gone home. We may therefore assume that, of the total approaching 20,000 warriors in Charles's army, with the exception of the 2,000 to 3,000 Savoyards, some 8,000 to 10,000 were saved, while 6,000 to 8,000 and a large number of train servants and camp followers were killed.

We have no authentic report concerning the losses of the Swiss.[28] Panigarola himself during the flight had seen how Burgundian warriors, overcome by despair, had fallen down, crossed their hands, and allowed themselves to be slain without offering any defense. He reports later at length that he had heard from ransomed prisoners and rescued women how the Burgundians who were cut off had sold their lives dearly.

This is confirmed by the letters of Molbinger,[29] who claims to have learned that the German private soldiers, among whom there were even many Swiss deserters, "had stood fast" and "defended themselves in knightly fashion," before they were killed. Nevertheless, the loss of 3,000 men, which, according to Panigarola, was suffered by the Swiss army, is certainly too high.

EXCURSUS

REFERENCES AND CRITIQUE

Since I first treated the battle of Murten in the *Perser- und Burgunderkriege*, the source material has been significantly increased and modified, so that I have had to rework my account completely. Although the basic idea, the theoretical phenomenon in the history of the art of war, has remained the same as I already conceived of it at that time, the details have had to be rearranged. New critical editions of Knebel's *Tagebuch (Baseler Chroniken,* Vol. 3, 1887) and of Diebold Schilling's *Berner Chronik,* 2 volumes, 1897 and 1901, have appeared. Most important of all, however, Panigarola's report on the battle, dated Saint Claude, 25 June 1476, which was believed to have been lost, has been found and published in the *Archivo storico lombardo,* anno XIX, Milan, 1892. It has been translated with explanatory notes by Dierauer in the *Schweizerische Monatsschrift für Offiziere aller Waffen,* 4th year, 1892, No. 10, Frauenfeld, J. Huber Press. As important as this report is for the reconstruction of the battle, of still greater importance is a study by Doctor Hans Wattelet, *The Battle of Murten. A Historical-Critical Study (Die Schlacht bei Murten. Historisch-kritische Studie), Freiburger Geschichtsblätter,* published by the *Deutscher geschichtsforschende Verein des Kantons Freiburg,* 1st year, Freiburg, 1894, University Press, in which the author convincingly proves through source analysis and the archives that the Saint-Urbaine Chapel at Coussiberle, which was previously considered by all to be a battle chapel, is not. This concept did not arise until many generations later, as a result of all kinds of coincidences. As early as 1888, when I visited the battlefield with Mr. Ochsenbein, the editor of the source book for the quadricentennial observance of the battle, I had reservations as to whether the Swiss attack could really have extended so far around the position and the *Grünhag* could have been in this location. But there was nothing to do against the apparently unassailable fact that the battle chapel was located there. Now that this error has been removed from the source material as a result of Wattelet's discerning and careful research, and at the same time the true line of march and place of attack by the Swiss has been determined, all the other details have also been changed, but the entire sequence has become much more understandable. Charles did not draw up an extremely long defense line, which was nevertheless open on the Fribourg side, but he fortified his camp in a ring that was intentionally pushed out onto the rising terrain but was still so close to the camp areas that it could be quickly occupied, if the alarm was given promptly. I imagine that the main line of defense ran along on about contour line 540 on the far side (south) of the Forest of Craux by the Pierre Bessy and the Ermelsburg in the direction of Burg. There it was practically impossible to approach it because of the moat of the town of Burg. It was then probably curved around between Burg and Combettes and extended down to the lake near Montellier. It is possible that on the other side Charles was satisfied with resting his flank on the forest and its felled trees, but it is also possible that he protected himself against an attack from Fribourg. In that case, the fortified line would have extended somewhat farther from the Forest of Craux north of the burned-out village of Münchenwyler to the Petit Bois Dominge and from there northwesterly down the sunken road in the direction of the lake. Charles's command tent (a wooden hut) was situated on the Grand Bois Dominge, at a height of 531 meters, from which one has a very good view over the countryside. The circumference of this fortification was indeed very great. But as soon as it was known that the enemy was assembling at Gümmenen, and later that he was in position near Ulmitz, of course only the line on this side came into consideration.

I call attention to the following details in which Wattelet's otherwise outstanding study needs to be corrected.

On p. 25 it is said that the defenders of Murten had obliged Duke Charles "to lose the most valuable time for the attack against the still unassembled Swiss." The "still unassembled Swiss" would hardly have opposed such an attack. If Charles had taken Murten in the very first days and had then moved on, the Swiss would have moved back temporarily and left it up to the duke as to whether he should then besiege Bern or Fribourg.

On p. 68 it is stated that the position on the Wyler Field was covered on the left flank by the moat of Burg and Romont's camp on the north of the town; "in the rear the fortified camp stood as a fallback position." Romont's camp cannot very well be shown as "cover," since it was itself a part of the position and could be attacked. But I consider as objectively incorrect the idea that behind the line on the Wyler Field there stood a second direct fortified line for the camp. Nowhere is anything said about this, not even in the battle accounts, where an attempt to hold this position would necessarily have been mentioned in some manner, even if only negatively. The defensive line for the camp was precisely the line on the Wyler Field. Panigarola, in his report of 12 June (Gingins, 2: 248) states expressly: The duke "was so situated as to consider all these surrounding hills as strengthening this camp."

On p. 74 it is stated that on the twenty-second there could no longer have been a question of an attack on Romont, since the duke had taken up position on the Wyler Field. But it is impossible to see why the troops at the *Grünhag* on the Wyler Field were to prevent the Swiss from attacking Romont's corps near Montellier (via Büchslen-Löwenberg).

BATTLE OF NANCY[30]
5 JANUARY 1477

As a result of the victory of Murten, Duke René of Lorraine, with the help of the Lower Union, had repossessed his duchy and had also reconquered his capital after a short siege. Initially, Duke Charles had remained in Burgundy, still occupied with plans for the continuation of his struggle against the Swiss, when the news from Lorraine moved him to turn his attention first of all in that direction. This territory, which separated him from the Netherlands, the larger part of his possessions, was more important for him than any other area. He consolidated the remnants of his army from Murten, brought up reinforcements, and besieged Nancy. Again Duke René immediately had to fall back before him, since his unpaid mercenaries and allies of the Lower Union mutinied and refused to fight. But their concern that Charles would once again become master of Lorraine and would move from there into Alsace persuaded the cities to support Duke René with money. When he offered the Swiss, first 4, and then 4½ guilders of pay per man per month, the Swiss gave him permission to recruit among them under their official direction. And so René assembled an army approaching 20,000 men, composed of soldiers from Lorraine, Alsace, Austria, France, and Switzerland, against whom Charles could send at the most 10,000 men.

Charles could not make up his mind to abandon Nancy, which was already close to being captured through hunger. Instead, he continued the siege and drew up the main body of his troops facing the relief army close to the southern edge of the city. Thus he was obliged to leave behind still another part of his troops to protect his camp against a possible sortie, and he had behind him the enemy city, which blocked his natural line of retreat.[31]

Did he have no idea of the vastly superior forces that were approaching?[32] Or was he obstinately trying to prove the statement that he had angrily made to the Milanese ambassador after the battle of Murten concerning the poor conduct of his troops, to the effect that the next time he would form them in such a way that they would either have to fight or die?[33]

He had also told that same ambassador that the next time he fought against the Swiss he would have half of his lances dismount and fight on foot in one large unit. In arriving at this decision, he was estimating his army at a strength of 2,000 lances and 10,000 men in the infantry square. In this formation, some have claimed to detect a belated—and excessively late—imitation of the Swiss,[34] and in his *Geschichte der Infanterie* (1: 186) Rüstow has again remarked that one can see from this point that Charles had understood nothing at all of the true nature of the Swiss infantry tactics. For the Swiss main body was a column of close-combat weapons, which in its assault ran down the enemy and was accompanied only by a few marksmen firing from scattered points. Charles's lance supposedly consisted of three crossbowmen, three musketeers, three pikemen, and the knight.[35] Consequently, it was made up mainly of marksmen, who could not possibly withstand the assault of a strong, closed unit of halberd-bearers and spearmen. But the reproach that Charles had still not understood the Swiss tactics is unjustified. He definitely did not say that he intended to imitate the Swiss completely, but only that he would draw his infantry into a single powerful unit, because the Swiss also did that.[36] The change from his earlier instructions, therefore, consists only of the fact that, instead of fighting in nothing but individual lances, which allowed the various combat branches to support each other mutually, one-half of the army was now drawn together more closely and the knights dismounted, thus blending in more closely with the marksmen and pikemen. That forms a picture that was already known for a long time; in doing this, Charles did not create something that was new in theory, nor did he intend to. If the battles of Grandson and Murten had developed fully, instead of being thrown off from the start as a result of panic and the sudden attack, in those cases, too, something quite similar would have resulted. The difference is only that, as a result of the dismounting of the knights and the emphasis on the drawing together of the lances, from the start the structure of the formation was made firmer.

Charles now drew up his infantry that was constituted in this way and was numerically weak, in a position between the Meurthe on the left and a forest on the right, with his front facing south, to which there was only a moderately wide approach; the horsemen were formed on the right and left of the infantry. He was therefore estimating, just as he did previously, that the enemy in its approach would be strongly affected by the fire of the marksmen and especially that of the artillery, and would perhaps be brought to a halt and would then be thrown back by the attack of his knights. The infantry front was also protected by a small stream and partially by thick hedges.

The allies, however, hesitated to attack this strong position from the front. Charles must have deceived himself concerning his flank cover. The allies formed three masses, one of which, the rear guard, only made a demonstration on the road in the center,[37] while the main body on the left and the advance guard on the right simultaneously enveloped both flanks of the Burgundian army. The march was carried out in a thick snowstorm, which made it difficult but also concealed it. The crossing of the forest and a half-frozen stream on the right of the Burgundians was very difficult and fatiguing for the main body, but this led it, with its accompanying horsemen and marksmen, into the enemy's flank. A bold attack by the Burgundian knights against the Lotharingians initially had some success, but it was eventually broken up by the fire of the marksmen and the unit of spearmen. The Burgundian cannon, which they sought to turn quickly in this direction, had little effect. And so the main body, pushing quickly forward, rolled up the Burgundians.

From the other side the unit of the advance guard, which was approximately of the same strength, moved up in the same manner. By moving forward in tight formation quite close to the river, it had remained outside the effective range of the Burgundian cannon. For this unit, the snowstorm was probably even more important as cover than for the main body.

As soon as the two units with their greatly superior numbers had arrived at the Burgundian position, they had, of course, already won and were able to destroy a large part of the enemy army. Duke Charles himself was killed.

EXCURSUS

The envelopment and attack by the Swiss main body are described in the following manner in the *Chronique scandaleuse* by Jean de Troyes, in the *Collection Petitot*, 14: 50:

And as soon as the said Swiss found themselves above and beside the said duke of Burgundy, they suddenly turned to face him and his army, and without stopping they marched more impetuously and proudly than ever men had done. And on approaching the enemy line, they discharged their culverins, and at the said discharge, which was not one from the finance generals, all the foot soldiers of the said duke of Burgundy took flight.

We see that the author has a correct concept in general of the sequence of events, but if we had nothing further than his report, we would undoubtedly ascribe much too great a share in the outcome to the effect of the culverins. Perhaps Jean de Troyes only chose this exaggerated expression in order to be able to introduce his joke to the effect that the discharge by the marksmen was not a discharge (receipt) from the tax collectors.

Furthermore, Comines, too, exaggerates the role of the Swiss marksmen.

NOTES FOR CHAPTER VII

1. To be sure, the Swiss, too, suffered defeats a few times, when they moved out of their mountains, as, for example, the Appenzellers in 1405 at Altstetten, and in 1408 at Bregenz, and the troops of Uri in 1422 at Arbedo. But those were not very important engagements. "Ueber Arbedo," by Fr. Knorreck, Berlin dissertation, 1910.

2. Dändliker, *Geschichte der Schweiz*, p. 609.

3. Nicolaus Rüsch, the city scribe of Basel, even states that the Burgundians were 10,000 strong on horseback and 8,000 on foot. *Basler Chroniken*, Vol. III, p. 304, 1887.

4. Rodt, 1: 304.

5. According to the note in Tobler's *Schilling*, 1: 163, the Solothurners reported to their home town in 1635.

6. *Basler Chroniken*, 3: 305.

7. Witte, *Zeitschrift für Geschichte des Oberrheins*, 45: 394.

8. Vol. I, p. 326. Dierauer, 1: 197, also accepts the number 70.

9. Witte, *Zeitschrift für Geschichte des Oberrheins*, 49 (1895): 217.

10. F. de Gingins-la-Sarra, *Dispatches from the Milanese Ambassadors on the Campaigns of Charles the Bold, from 1474 to 1477* (*Dépêches des ambassadeurs Milanais sur les campagnes de Charles le Hardi, de 1474 à 1477*), Paris, 1858.

11. Olivier de la Marche, who, as a confidant of the duke, was able to know his intentions, states in his memoirs (which, unfortunately, are very brief with respect to this war) that Vaumarcus was occupied as a lure in order to entice the troops of the Confederation to move forward. This reason is not very clear, since on the far side of the narrow pass the duke would never be able to find a battlefield as favorable as the one offered

him by his fortified position at Grandson. In any case he could keep his army assembled and wait for a few weeks more easily than the Swiss. This point serves as factual confirmation of the impatience and underestimation of the enemy, outstanding characteristics attributed to the duke by many sources.

12. Principally the Baselers, whose strength is given as sixty men. But since the leader of the Austrian knights, Hermann von Eptingen, was also present (Meltinger's letter, cited by Knebel), at least a part of these Austrians must also have been present.

13. This point is stressed by the Burgundian court historian, Molinet.

14. Reported in *Saint Gall's Part in the Burgundian Wars* (*St. Gallens Anteil an den Burgunderkriegen*), published by the *Historischer Verein in St. Gallen,* Saint Gall, 1876.

15. In the minutes of the meeting of 15 May (*Eidgenössische Abschrifte,* 2: 593) there is stated only "and fifty men dead." The same minutes, however, state that 1,500 or 1,600 slain Burgundians were found, and that the duke had 60,000 actual mounted men and still more of the other troops. Consequently, it is not very trustworthy. The men of Schwyz had seventy wounded and seven killed (Knebel states that they lost eighty men all together). On the basis of the accounts for the care of the wounded, the total of wounded can be assumed to be about 700, and the figure for those killed may then be something between fifty and seventy.

Bernoulli, *Baseler Neujahrsblatt,* 1899, p. 23, and Feldmann, *Schlacht bei Granson,* p. 56, assume the losses to be only fifty dead and between 300 and 400 wounded.

16. Dändliker, in his *Geschichte der Schweiz,* 2: 224, explains the failure to exploit the victory at Grandson as completely due to the lack of military understanding on the part of the Confederation. He writes: "In their joy over the uplifting success at Grandson, the men of the Confederation were initially no longer concerned about Duke Charles. They considered their mission as accomplished. When Bern, which was not inclined to such a carefree and self-deceptive attitude and took the situation seriously, wanted to continue the war, the majority of the Confederation decided for the return home." Such experienced warriors as the troops of Zurich, with their burgomaster Waldmann, and the other members of the Confederation are not supposed to have been capable of understanding the situation when Bern explained to them that they could best protect themselves against a renewed attack by a pursuit of the defeated army? We see here to what point a false basic concept finally leads. Dändliker is not willing to concede that the Swiss were the aggressors in this war, but he would like to explain the war as a kind of

emergency defense, because the Swiss felt themselves threatened by the duke of Burgundy. If it were not absolutely clear from the original sources, then the conduct of the Swiss after the victory of Grandson would show how extremely far from the minds of the Swiss was the thought of feeling threatened by the Burgundian force.

17. My estimate of the strength of the Burgundians at Murten (20,000 men at most) has, of course, been disputed widely by the Swiss, but nothing tangible has been brought up to oppose my viewpoint. Dierauer, p. 211, would like to go up to a number between 23,000 and 25,000 men, but only on the basis of reported reinforcements in the last days before the battle, reinforcements that have not been proven. In my estimate, the only correction to be made is the note in *Perser- und Burgunderkriege,* p. 153, where, according to the latest critical edition of Comines by Mandrot, 1: 363, the number "18,000" means, after all, "18,000 dead," that is, all together, whereas, according to him, of those "prenant gages"—that is, warriors—8,000 are supposed to have fallen.

18. Panigarola, 10 June. Gingins, 2: 242.

19. Panigarola, 13 June. Gingins, 2: 258. Panigarola's statements that Charles had his camp fortified are confirmed and clarified by the illustrations in Schilling's *Chronik* (one of which is reproduced in Ochsenbein's *Urkundenbuch* and in the treatment by Colonel Meister) and by the battle song by Zoller (printed in Ochsenbein, p. 494). There it reads as follows:

> He inclosed his army all around
> As he desired, from lake to higher ground.
> A stream he dammed to make it swell.
> The work continued night and day,
> And soon Count Romont's camp completed lay.
> Great trees he caused his men to fell.
> Who has ever seen works so fine
> Accomplished in but two weeks' time?

20. Panigarola, 12 June, 13 June.

21. On 16 June the duke had the following report written to the municipal council of Dijon:

> Last night we were awake and on foot with the intention of marching with our whole army out toward our enemies, who are at a distance from us of two short leagues and who, as had been reported to us, had joined forces and assembled in order to move

closer to us and fight, and we await them from hour to hour.
(Ochsenbein, p. 280).

Wattelet, p. 29 ff. and notes 88 and 89, relates that to an idea of moving
out against the Swiss. But it is apparent that only the idea of accepting
battle on the *Grünhag* is meant. Wattelet has inadvertently interpreted
the same report twice, on the sixteenth and the nineteenth. And his
interpretation in Note 85, of Panigarola's report of the eighteenth, to the
effect that Charles intended to attack the Swiss near Gümmenen on the
nineteenth, I consider to be incorrect. The words "dar la bataglia" (to
give battle) refer to a planned attack on Murten, as Gingins has already
interpreted it in his translation.

22. A number of scholars, especially Wattelet (see below), have disputed the fact that the Swiss formed the usual three units of foot soldiers
at Murten. Schilling's positive statement on the point, however, cannot
possibly be invalidated by the fact that a few sources speak only of two
units, and least of all because Panigarola saw only two units or because
only two units are mentioned in Schilling's later account of the battle.
The third unit did not enter the fight itself but simply stormed into the
camp on the heels of the other two, and there the formations broke up.
Even if we did not have Schilling's testimony, it would be completely
incomprehensible that the Swiss should have abandoned the normal
formation in three units precisely here, with such a large army. They
could not know in advance whether the entire Burgundian army was not
in position at the palisade and whether there would develop a flanking
counterattack from one side or another, defending against which would
then have been the mission of the rear guard.

23. Herter's command position is definitely proven by the two mutually independent statements of Knebel and Etterlin. Schilling's silence on
this point, as it occurred, may not be considered as counterproof. Of
itself, it is not particularly important, since the top commander in such an
army was not necessarily the general charged with the mission and the
responsibility of strategic direction. In this case, the entire war council
was the final authority; Herter had only to take care of the technical
execution. This situation needs to be noted only because of the analogy
to the mutual relationships of the Greek cantons in the Persian wars: in
both cases, the great work succeeds only through constant surmounting
of the strongest internal tensions, the reflection of which can also be
detected throughout the sources.

Along with Dändliker, 3d ed., p. 842, I, too, prefer to accept as certain
that Waldmann was the leader of the main body.

24. Report of 8 July. Gingins, 2: 345.

25. Edlibach, p. 157.

26. *Baseler Chroniken, 3*: 26.

27. Schilling wrote that, after the *Grünhag* was taken, "and all the formations were broken from that moment on." The editors believe that this statement is unlikely, "or is it supposed to be the same maneuver that is indicated in the *Lurlebatlied* (one of the songs composed about this battle and recorded by Schilling) as 'the point which spread out' "? Such is no doubt the case, except that it is not a question of a "maneuver," but of the natural breaking up of a closed formation in the course of and following such an assault.

28. The reports in the *Jahrzeitbuch von Schwyz* in the *Anzeiger für Schweizerische Geschichte,* 1895, p. 160, are probably worthless.

29. In Ochsenbein, *Urkunden,* pp. 339, 341.

30. Two special studies have been devoted to the battle of Nancy: one by Robert Schoeber (Erlangen dissertation, 1891) and one by Max Laux (Rostock dissertation, 1895, Süssenguth Press, Berlin). Laux's work has a useful plan of the battle, a comprehensive basis in the sources, and corrects a number of the errors of his predecessors, but it is not without its own errors and oversights.

31. Laux, p. 20, estimates Charles's strength at the end of July as 4,000 to 5,000 men, which he believes was not increased by significant reinforcements. Consequently, he believes that, for the battle, the scouting report that was made to the Confederation to the effect that the duke had only a small column, some 6,000 men, is the figure closest to the truth. But there were probably more than that; for when Laux bases his estimate on the fact that Panigarola reports nothing about reinforcements, it can be said in rebuttal that Panigarola had already left the duke when they marched into Lorraine, and his last report was dated 19 October. From then until January, the duke could have drawn many reinforcements from the Netherlands. Schoeber estimates a strength between 7,000 and 8,000, but without any real computation.

The sources with a Burgundian bias go as low as 2,000 or even 1,200 (Rodt, 2: 392). Rodt has assumed 14,000, of whom 4,000 guarded the camp against a possible sortie from Nancy, while 10,000 participated in the battle. But his estimate is based on statements by the duke himself, which can be proven to have been intentionally exaggerated. See Laux, p. 20. *Mémoires de Comines,* ed. Mandrot, 1: 386.

Let us mention here Olivier de la Marche as an example of how little credence can be given to the figures of authors, even those who appear to have had the most reliable information at their disposal. He was majordomo of the duke of Burgundy and was taken prisoner at Nancy by the duke of Lorraine, buying his freedom for a high ransom. He was thus able to learn of the situation on both sides. His memoirs are printed in the *Collection Petitot*, Vols. IX and X. He states: "a good 12,000 combatants" (instead of almost 20,000), "and the duke of Burgundy went before them; and I swear that he did not have 2,000 combatants" (instead of 8,000 to 10,000).

32. According to Comines's account (cited by Mandrot, p. 386), he was, of course, supposedly directly informed of René's great numerical superiority, but such later accounts have but little credibility.

33. *Dispatches of the Milanese Ambassadors* (*Dépêches des ambassadeurs Milanais*), ed. by Gingins, 2: 349.

34. von Rodt, *Wars of Charles the Bold* (*Kriege Karls des Kühnen*), 2: 315.

35. There is nothing of importance in the small variations in the interpretation of this passage. See Schoeber, p. 33, note; Jähns, *Manual of Military History* (*Handbuch der Geschichte des Kriegswesens*), p. 1009. See also pp. 511 and 514, above.

36. The passage reads verbatim:

intendendo di questi 2 m (2000) lanze mettere mille a piedi quando si trovara con Svicerj, li quali habiano 14 (10?) combatenti per uno, cive tri archieri, tri fanti con lanze longhe e tri schiopeteri e balestrieri, che venirano ad essere 10 m (10,000) combatenti in uno squadrone, poiche Sviceri li fanno cosi grossi. Li altri mille lanze a cavallo, con loro cinque millia archieri a cavallo, e lo resto, dil campo, in modo dice havera circa 30 m (30,000) combatenti.
Gingins La Sarra, 2: 361.

intending, when he encountered the Swiss, to put on foot 1,000 of these 2,000 lances, each of which would have 14 (10?) combatants, that is, three archers, three infantrymen with long lances and three musketeers and crossbowmen, which will amount to 10,000 combatants in a squadron, since the Swiss make them that large. The other 1,000 lances on horseback, with their 5,000 mounted archers, and the rest from the camp so that there will be about 30,000 combatants.

37. In the "true declaration" ("vraye déclaration"), Comines, Lenglet, 3: 492, it is said that the rear guard consisted only of 8,000 musketeers, who marched along "one cannonball-ball range" behind the main body, to protect it from the rear. I cannot visualize this. What was such a large num-

ber of marksmen supposed to do behind the close-combat weapons during the march through the forest? They could not have repelled a real attack from this direction, in case such an attack was somehow to be suspected. The *Lorraine Chronicle* (*Lothringer Chronik*), p. 293, speaks of a unit, but one apparently consisting of only 100 men, which was to skirmish along the meadows and keep the enemy occupied. Those 800 [8,000?] marksmen would have been so very appropriately employed there that we are perhaps justified in assuming an oversight or a lacuna in the "vraye déclaration."

Chapter VIII

Military Theory in the Middle Ages

According to my plan, Book V, which brings to an end the medieval period of military history with the movement of the Swiss infantry out into the surrounding lowlands, was to be followed by a sixth book in which I intended to assemble a variety of materials of a general nature that did not fit well into the continuing historical account, or that resulted from it. But this volume has already become so full that I have changed my arrangement. The points I still intended to make concerning the history of weapons and the construction of strongholds can be completely dispensed with in the context of this work. With respect to the question touched on in note no. 19 on p. 254, above, as to whether around 1400 the knight's armor temporarily became lighter again (Boutaric states this also, p. 286), I have still not come to a completely definite conclusion. The most important point, the origin of firearms, I am postponing to the next volume. From the chronological viewpoint, of course, this study belongs in the Middle Ages. But, as we have seen, this weapon, although it had already been in use for a century and a half, had not yet assumed real significance by 1477. Knighthood was not only not overpowered by this invention, a claim that continues to be repeated, but on the contrary, it was overpowered by foot soldiers with cold steel, even though at the end it sought to strengthen itself by adopting firearms.[1] Consequently, we shall be justified in discussing the origin and the nature of the firearm at that place in our account where the new instrument begins to have a decisive significance in the conduct of war, and not simply, as has been the case until now, as a weapon of different construction employed in addition to bow and crossbow and *blide* and trebuchet but having a similar effect. Other small studies, like a listing of the reported and actual army strengths, of those legends that keep reappearing, and similar matters I shall also omit and simply proceed to what can be said concerning military theory in the Middle Ages.

THEORY

Even in classical antiquity, as we have seen, with the exception of a few reflections by Xenophon, military theory remained very rare. And all the less are we able to require something from the Middle Ages, where the class of warriors remained basically separated from that of the supporters of culture, the clerical class.

Rabanus Maurus, abbot of Fulda and archbishop of Mainz (died in 856), dedicated to King Lothair II, a grandson of Louis the Pious, a document concerning the soul with a supplement on the exemplary value of the Roman military system. The sufferings which the separate kingdoms of the Carolingian Empire had to endure from the Normans no doubt provided the incentive for seeking means of relief even in literature. And since the learned archbishop belonged to a Frankish—and therefore warrior—family, there were blended in him the necessary characteristics and knowledge for such an undertaking. What he was able to do was, of course, nothing other than prepare an extract from Vegetius, whose work, indeed, had owed its composition to quite the same motive. To the extent that Rabanus simply repeats Vegetius, he tells us nothing new. But his little work becomes interesting when we compare what Rabanus extracted, what he eliminated, and what he added.[2] Of what Vegetius said concerning Roman drills—which is, to be sure, not very much—only one sentence is repeated, to the effect that the Romans maintained their formations and guarded their colors in the melee ("ordines seruare scirent et uexilla sua in permixtione bellica custodirent" [Chap. 13]: "They knew how to keep their ranks and guarded their flags of war in battle"). For the most part, Vegetius's remarks concerning the physical ability of the recruits and the various combat exercises are reproduced. Concerning the drills of the horsemen, the archbishop expressly adds that this skill blossomed among the Franks (Chap. 12). But most interesting of all is the remark (Chap. 3) that the young men destined for military service had to be trained and hardened for their profession at an early age, and that such was also still the case at the time of the writer, that is, at the courts of the princes. ("Legebantur autem et assignabantur apud antiquos milites incipiente pubertate: quod et hodie seruatur, ut uidelicet pueri et adholescentes in domibus principum nutriantur, quatinus dura et aduersa tollerare discant, famesque et frigora caloresque solis sufferre": "Moreover, they were selected and assigned to the houses of old soldiers at the beginning of puberty. Even today this is observed: namely, that boys and youths are raised in the houses of princes so that they may learn to bear harsh and adverse conditions and to suffer hunger, cold, and the heat of the sun.")

The next medieval theoretician whom we meet, not until 450 years later, is once again a cleric, Aegidius Romanus, or Columnus, or "a Columnis" (born 1247, died 1316), an Italian by origin, Augustinian-general, professor in Paris, archbishop of Bourges, and cardinal. He wrote for King Philip the Fair as crown prince a book, *de regimine principum* (*On the Rule of Princes*), in which the military system was also discussed.[3] Aegidius, too, reproduced Vegetius for the most part and was not capable of eliminating those things that did not correspond to the conditions of his time or of making logical substitutions for them. In keeping with his Roman example (I, Chap. 26), he describes for us (Chap. XII) drills for foot soldiers and horsemen: they are to become accustomed to form in lines, to double, to form a square, a triangle, a circle, and so forth—some of which things never existed either in Vegetius's time nor at any other, and least of all in the Middle Ages.[4] But Aegidius multiplies and improves the gray theory by adding the pretty statement that the triangle is not difficult to form; one only needs to cut through the square by the diagonal and put the sides of the square together. Even for the most famous drillmaster of the Old Prussian Army of 1806, General von Saldern, the execution of this rule might have offered difficulties.

Of course, Aegidius also repeats the seven famous battle formations of Vegetius (3. 20), the circle, the wedge, the horseshoe. He omits only the oblique battle formation, and the "quadrangularis forma" ("quadrangular shape") he considers to be "magis inutilis" ("more useless"), apparently because it did not produce such nice pictures as the tongs or the horseshoe.

Our author encounters a certain extent of embarrassment (Chap. V), since his authority, Vegetius, says that the *"rustica plebs"* ("country people") are the men best suited for war. Aegidius opposes this with the *urbani* (city-dwellers) and the *nobiles,* and finally finds it good that, for fighting, not only a calloused hand but also "velle honorari ex pugna et erubescere turpem fugam" ("to want to be honored from battle and to be ashamed of disgraceful flight"), as well as "industria et prudencia, sagacitas et versutia" ("diligence and prudence, sagacity and cunning") were needed. These things the *nobiles* have, and for that reason, despite Vegetius, they are to be preferred to the *rusticis,* especially when on horseback, which helps them bear the physical efforts. This medieval scholar does not arrive at a distinction between the type of fighting of the knight and that of the Romans; precisely for this reason, his hesitation and his reflection may serve us as a welcome witness.

Finally, let us examine the twelve things Aegidius believes are to be observed in a battle, in doing which we shall find something of the medieval outlook showing through here and there. He requires above all (Chap. IX) that the general be *"sobrius, prudens, vigilans, industrius"* ("temperate, prudent, watchful, diligent") and that he be attentive to:

1. The number of combatants.
2. Drill (*exercitatio*): "nam habentes bracchia inassueta ad percuciendum et membra inexercitata ad bellandum" ("in fact, having arms unaccustomed to striking and limbs untrained for fighting") would accomplish nothing. In this he considers only individual practice, and not drill in common, as we mean by that word.
3. Toughening to endure hardship.
4. Courage and *"duricies corporis"* ("hardness of body").
5. "Versutia et industria" ("cunning and diligence").
6. "Virilitas et audacia mentis" ("manliness and boldness of mind").

Also the following factors:

1. Whoever has the most and best horses.
2. The best *sagitarii* (archers).
3. The most rations.
4. The battlefield "qui sunt in altiori situ, vel meliori ad pugnandum" ("which is in a higher position and better for fighting").
5. Sun and wind.
6. Whoever *expects* more auxiliaries.

Neither here nor in a later chapter (XIV), where the author returns again to the execution of battle, does he introduce anything of a tactical nature except the remark that one can fight better in an orderly formation than in disorder. On those points on which we would most like to hear something—on the interplay of the branches, of heavy and light horsemen, dismounted spearmen and marksmen—we find nothing in Aegidius, even though Vegetius says a good deal about them, except for the remark that arrows and slings are good for harming the enemy, even before the battle lines make contact.

About the same time, King Alfonso the Wise of Castile had a law book drawn up (1260) which also contains tactical regulations,[5] once again borrowings from Vegetius. How little they have to do with the actual warfare of the time is shown even more by the addition that is made concerning the form of the hollow square than by the material copied from the ancient author. The square is formed, says the wise ruler, so that the king may withdraw within it from his enemies and find protection there—thus far, it reminds us of the mission that was actually assigned to the medieval foot soldiers—but we now hear that the men's feet are tied together so that they cannot flee. Of course, King Alfonso goes on to say that in this way one cannot pursue when one is victorious, but, by one's lack of motion, one then shows that he disdains the enemy. Is this supposed to be a joke? Not at all. It is related in a tone of complete seriousness, and the most serious aspect of this is that two practical military men of our time, General Köhler (3: 2: 264) and Lieutenant Colonel Jähns,[6] have repeated in their accounts, without any question, this matter of the warriors with their feet tied together. Jähns expressly agrees with Delpech on this point, to the effect that it is a question "not at all simply of scholarly imitation," but of the description of combat forms that were actually normal in the thirteenth century. It was not only that the Latin expressions were everywhere replaced by Castilian; "also the threatened punishments which backed up the law obliged the leaders to follow the tactical regulations just as much as the disciplinary ones, and this could only happen under the prerequisite that the troops were capable of obeying them." Since not only in the thirteenth century, but at all times, an important factor for victory lies in the fact that the soldiers do not run, perhaps even today we could once again try tying the feet together, and to prevent the fellows from possibly cutting the cord, let us preferably also take their weapons away from them. Then the enemy would see right away how much we disdained him.

Moral: Let us think gently of the learned professors who have Xerxes' hundreds of thousands moving through the narrow Greek passes and who come to somewhat unlikely results in estimating the interval between members of the Macedonian phalanx or Roman legionaries.

I have no doubt that the man who was well acquainted with Vegetius and composed the military regulations of King Alfonso was no warrior, but, like Rabanus and Aegidius, a cleric who was misled into introducing those reflections into the book of laws precisely because of his knowledge of the classical author.

The next military author of the Middle Ages who can be considered with the clerics is, once again, no warrior but a woman, Christine de Pisan.[7] Born in 1364, she was the daughter of an Italian doctor and astrologer who was called to the French court. Consequently, Christine lived in an aristocratic ambiance, having relationships with the English and Burgundian courts as well as the French, and she was highly respected as a scholar, author, and poet. Shortly before her death, she celebrated and welcomed in a poem the appearance of the Maid of Orléans. Among her numerous works is a military history treatment under the title *Faits d'armes et de chevalerie* (*Feats of Arms and of Chivalry*), written between 1404 and 1407.[8] This work, too, is based principally on the reworking of ancient authors, especially Frontinus, in addition to Vegetius. Christine had somewhat more insight into the differences between the periods than Aegidius and Alfonso, but she was still capable of writing (Book I, Chap. 24) that the ancients had seen to it that the *hommes d'armes* were not frightened during their deployment for battle by the shouting that was sometimes done by the *gens de commune* or by those who were afraid. Consequently, the ancients had controlled the situation with trumpet signals.

She is in favor of military training for youths, but she makes a distinction between the nobility and the common people. The nobles were to be trained in all the knightly skills from childhood on, whereas the young men of the people were to be trained only in slinging and archery.

When she wants to speak about battle formation (Chap. 23), she begins with the perceptive remark that her time differed from that of Vegetius in that now there was more mounted combat than dismounted. But instead of informing us about her time, unfortunately she continues by saying that she will be very brief on that subject, since it is well known to those familiar with the profession of arms.

A generation younger than Christine was Jean de Bueil (died 1477), who was a respected captain under Charles VII. As an older man (between 1461 and 1466), he partly wrote and partly inspired a book in the form of a novel, comparable to the *Cyropaedia,* which was intended to serve as a guide in the military education of the young nobleman. The book is entitled *Le Jouvencel* (*The Stripling*) and can be considered as both historical and theoretical literature,[9] since it presents Bueil's war memoirs under fictitious names (Amidas is King Charles VII). The actual authors seem to have been three of the captain's retainers, who no doubt also added the scholarly embellishment from ancient authors. *Le Jouvencel* is supposed to teach the young nobleman "to obey, to fight, and finally to command," and it thus awakens in us high expectations. I have also found in it a number of interesting points. For example, a prince is supposed to use one-third of his expenses for intelligence service (*en espie*), and there is a very urgent warning, supported by many examples, that one should not attack on foot but should allow oneself to be attacked.[10]

It would be a suitable subject for a special study to work up systematically the theoretical ideas of the fifteenth century concerning tactics and strategy as contained in *Le Jouvencel* and Christine and a few shorter writings, and to compare them with reality. For the reasons given on p. 429, I have felt that I could omit doing so in the present work. The gain from such an effort would also not be very great.

At about the same time as Christine de Pisan, a Frankish nobleman from Eichstädt, Konrad Kyeser, wrote in Bohemia a military book which he called *Bellifortis* and which has an entirely different character. It is of a completely technical nature and consists of a large number of illustrations with corresponding Latin explanations, mostly in hexameters. The basis for these illustrations is much older and perhaps goes back partially to a Byzantine example. Throughout the entire fifteenth century these illustrated military books thrived, were extended, and were newly fabricated in Germany as well as Italy. The momentum for this kind of literature was provided by the new art of pyrotechnics, but it corresponds even more deeply to the spirit of the times and is admirably characterized by Jähns as follows:[11]

> The technical illustrations of ancient codices, particularly as they are frequently found in the Byzantine military encyclopedias, were uniquely compatible with the tendencies of the dying Middle Ages. That was, after all, the period in which it was hoped that every possible secret could be revealed "with levers and screws." A period in which men fancied they could lift the bolt that locked the entrance to supernatural power, if the bit of the key was only "curly" enough. That which was not understood was not rejected, but, the less one was capable of grasping it, all the more carefully was it passed down. Ancient traditions and modern discoveries were amalgamated in a peculiar manner with astrological, mystical, and alchemical elements, and pyrotechnics especially formed the bridge between this mysterious knowledge and practical experience, all the more since the largest part of that period was applied to that partially necromantic technique in warfare. At the end of the fourteenth century and the beginning of the fifteenth, a peculiar nimbus still surrounded pyrotechnics and the manufacture of muskets. This nimbus was not entirely lacking in weird secondary lights, and it made those who were knowledgeable in pyrotechnics appear to be one of the most outstanding classes of

the initiated in general and especially as chosen instruments of
secret military skills.

Of decisive significance in this characterization is the statement that
one did not reject that which was not understood but passed it on all the
more carefully. That which was added by contemporaries was of a similar
nature—as Jähns again says very appropriately in another passage (p.
291), a mixture of experience and imagination, often in unsophisticated
innocence. For the history of the art of war, consequently, there is practically nothing to be learned from these numerous books, not only because
they treat of technical matters, which we do not consider in their own
right in this work, but also because the chance statements on other
subjects do not deserve any credence. We have already established in our
treatment of antiquity how little is to be derived from theoretical writings, because they stand in such incomprehensible contradiction to reality instead of being a reflection of it. If even antiquity, which was, after
all, so much better trained for rational thinking, is to be appraised in this
way, then this judgment applies all the more sternly to the Middle Ages,
which were not at all educated for the exercise of critical analysis. These
technical writings of the fifteenth century are full of strange occurrences.
For this reason we may not even believe those aspects which at first
glance do not appear so impossible until we are able to adduce some kind
of basis for such confidence. We find in Kyeser sickle chariots, swim
boots, horses loaded with burning pieces of wood who terrify the enemy,
a cannon that is supposed to shoot a stone ball 1½ feet in diameter but
that is of such weak construction that it obviously cannot withstand any
shot. To this school there also belongs Dachssberg, the "miller and musketeer" already mentioned above, who plans to attack the enemy with a
wagon fort formed in wedge shape and recommends that in naval warfare
one should hurl at the enemy barrels of powdered chalk to blind his eyes
or barrels of thin soap to make the ship's deck slippery. There is also to
be found a cannon that shoots around a corner and is rightfully named
"*machina mirabilis*" ("wonderful machine").

Tactical rules are to be found mainly in an anonymous document of
about 1450,[12] and in unpublished writings of one Philip of Seldeneck,
around 1480.[13] But the spirit is quite the same as in the illustrated
manuscripts: impractical theorizing from which it is difficult to learn
anything. We must give Seldeneck credit for at least not working like the
anonymous author with the triangular formation of the foot troops which
is supposed to split the enemy apart with its point.

The most important of these works was written by the Italian Roberto

Valturio in about 1460 and was printed in 1472, perhaps the first book to be printed in Italy. In Jähns's *Geschichte der Kriegswissenschaften* we find careful references to all these writings, which save us the trouble of giving further details here.

EXCURSUS

SUPPLEMENT CONCERNING THE WORK OF GENERAL KÖHLER

The book with which I have had to take exception the most frequently in this volume is the large work of General Köhler.[14] It is therefore appropriate that I now finally give a cohesive explanation of my judgment of it.

After the author had spent forty-one years as an artilleryman in active service, he took up the study of the military history of the Middle Ages and with extreme energy mastered the huge amount of material in the original sources in the most varied languages, as well as the modern writings on that subject. He knows what the historical method requires, and in his foreword (as well as in his third volume, p. xiv) he develops completely correct bases and viewpoints on the significance and treatment of military history. He emphasizes not only that the historian needs special preparatory training for the treatment of military history events, but also that the military man is still in no way qualified, as a result of his knowledge of modern warfare, to treat and judge correctly past periods of warfare. In this connection, he cites a list of quite respectable names of military men who set out on such tasks without the proper historical viewpoint and in doing so, in Köhler's undoubtedly correct judgment, failed. He also does not fall—and we should give him particular credit for this—into the obvious error of overestimating the value of military history for the soldier. In fact, he says specifically (Vol. I, p. xxxi) that it does not contribute anything to the practical education of the young officer.

But as felicitous as his combination of military experience, serious scholarship, and energetic striving for intellectual mastery seems to be, he did not arrive at the unity of characteristics that is the prerequisite for scholarly fruitfulness. In discussing the battle of Cortenuova (1: 212), it happens that he translates "cum ad rem ventum est, neutrum eligerunt" ("When it came to a decision, they selected neither") as: "that the battle should take place under similar circumstances, even with respect to the wind," so that we might doubt whether he understands Latin at all. But, after all, this is a question of a momentary slip; only very seldom do we find other small translation errors, which are easily counterbalanced by the fact that the same author was able to correct the text of a Latin source, the *Weissenburg Service Laws*, in a clear manner (see p. 294, above). He was actually not wanting, then, in practical equipment, but neither his critical powers nor his perceptiveness were sufficient. Waitz did not have the power of perception either, but he still accomplished much by his energetic analysis. Jähns basically had but little of either analytical ability or perceptiveness—or, I might say, had them only in spots—but through his untiring energy, broad sense of order, and outstanding talent for description, both in his *Handbuch einer Geschichte des Kriegswesens von der Urzeit bis zur Renaissance* and in his *Geschichte der Kriegswissenschaften*, he created works that were both enjoyable and useful. Köhler set a higher goal for himself, but since his abilities were not sufficient, he failed in his main purpose. He no doubt understood correctly a number of details, something that could not be otherwise. His remarks concerning archery (2: 367; 3: foreword) are excellent; his description of the Tannenberg terrain is exemplary; his views concerning the armed retinue of the knights have the value of a discovery; his sharp rejection of the work of Delpech was justified;[15] and we could thus cite a number of other points. But, unfortunately, the praiseworthy and meritorious aspects of his books do not extend beyond such details. The very basis of the work is distorted.

Köhler says (1: 33) that the beginning of his work was determined "by the complete change in the military system that occurred as a result of the introduction of the feudal system, which around the middle of the eleventh century, when that system had taken on a certain definite form, assumed a distinct difference from the earlier period." But around the middle of the eleventh century nothing at all took on a definite form. The creation of a military organization by means of feudalism became definite in the ninth century, and the specific change of the warriorhood that was thus formed into an hereditary class was completed in the twelfth century, after it had flourished widely in the eleventh.

The false point of departure formed the basis for the most outrageous combinations. Weapons and military systems of the Germanic-Romanic peoples are supposed to have originated in Byzantium. "The Ripuarian Law recognizes as weapons only the sword, the spear, and the shield. Those are the usual Byzantine weapons of that period" (3: 1: 4; 3: 1: 8). "The Occident owes the basis on which its military skills stood in the thirteenth century only to the 800-year contact with Byzantium" (3: 1). "Not only that the Middle Ages took over the bases of conduct of combat of the Roman legions, as they had been carried over in Byzantium to mounted combat, but they continued to develop them further and created essentially the combat methods that are still the governing ones today" (3: 3: 1).

The lack of historical instinct which is evident in these remarks also appears constantly in individual details, in amazing contradiction to the critical method which the author theoretically recognizes with good perceptiveness.

In 1302, because it is thus recounted in the source, he has the Flemish deployed in the form of a shield, with the point forward and the individuals tied to one another, so that the enemy could not break through (3: 2: 261). And at Falkirk also he has the Scots tied to one another (3: 2: 264). At Nikopol the brave French knights are so terrified by the Turkish main body that they are unable even to draw their swords (2: 650). And at Agincourt, too, the French knights allow themselves to be cut down while offering hardly any opposition (2: 771).

In 3: 2: 266, Köhler has Richard the Lion-Hearted, with eighty knights and 400 crossbowmen, hold off an army of 20,000 horsemen under Saladin's personal command. The fight lasted from morning until three o'clock in the afternoon, when Richard himself went over to the attack.

Köhler regards the wagon fort as a protection during the march (3: 3: 384).

"The Freedom," we hear in 3: 3: 382, "are the predecessors of the lansquenets, but they could not form any organization at that time because they were destroyed after the war." We may ask why the strong men who eliminated the "Freedom" after the war did not prefer to wage the war without them. The answer to this question is not helped by the recognition that: "Duke Ruprecht the Younger in 1386 had sixty of these 'mischievous men of the Bloody Unit (Blutharst)' thrown into a brick kiln and burned to death" (Königshoven, 845). "After the Bishop's wars of Strasbourg in 1393, they were formally hunted down" (Königshoven, 691).

The genesis of all these contradictions is clear and instructive. Köhler makes the same error that our philologists make so often in their treatment of ancient history; that is, he is too dependent on the individual source accounts, accounts that have come down to us by chance and that are colored in one way or another. If the situation remained like that, his book could still present a well-ordered and very useful register. But since at the same time he interprets and fills out the sources in what he believes to be an objective analytical method but which in reality is highly arbitrary and fanciful, the result is of the type we have seen again and again.

His battle accounts and analyses, on which every history of the art of war must be based, we have been obliged to reject in all cases after thorough examination of the sources. They have often proven to be pure fantasies; it is not necessary to repeat that point here. He has caused the most damage in that, based on his authority and that of Jähns, against the opinions of Rüstow and Bürkli, the more modern Swiss scholars have again accepted the nonsensical concept of the battle formation in a triangle. W. Oechsli, particularly, has sought in an article in the *Schweizerische Monatsschrift für Offiziere aller Waffen* (1902) to defend the "point" as a triangle, basing his arguments on the sources. Consequently, I briefly repeat here what is to be said on that subject. First of all, we must distinguish between foot troops and horsemen. It is impossible for horsemen to have any kind of deep combat formation. The "points" that are reported of them are not combat formations but approach march formations, and as such they are a contrived refinement without practical value, which was the fashion for a while (see p. 278, above). It is different with foot troops. With them the formation in depth allows the rearmost ranks to push the leading ones forward, something that does not occur with mounted men. If a unit is very deep (and even the square of men is much deeper than wide because of the larger distance between ranks than the interval between files), it happens very easily that either the two forward corners hold back somewhat or the rear corners in their enthusiasm surge out and forward, or both things happen at the same time, so that the square unit at the moment of contact actually takes on a form similar to a triangle. That can even happen in a linear formation, of which Frederick the Great recounts an example in the battle of Fontenay, 1745 (*Histoire de mon temps,* 2: 355). This is also reported of English squares in the battle of Belle Alliance. From time to time, even if very seldom, this deformation appears in medieval battle reports as if it was intended,[16] and those theoreticians whose sense of reality we have become acquainted with, from Vegetius on, come forward again and again with the idea that one can "break apart" the enemy with such a point. But that is impossible, for, in order to break open the enemy unit, the man at the point of the triangle would first have to overcome the man with whom he clashes. But he cannot do that, even if he should be very superior to him personally, because during the fight he will also be attacked by the two flanking men of his opponent, who do not have anybody directly against them, and even the strongest man cannot hold out against three. Even if not one man but several stand in the first rank of the triangle, it would not be any different; the outer men would always be enveloped. Not until the point of the wedge has a certain width, that is, when it forms not a triangle but a rectangle, does this disadvantage become so minor that it disappears. (See Vol. II, pp. 49 and 374.)

The words "point" and "*cuneus*" (wedge) prove nothing at all in the way of a triangular formation. "Point" is translated simply by *acies* (line) in cases where we have reports in two languages. As early as in the writings of Livy, *cuneus* was an expression for the phalanx and was translated in Old High German glosses by "*folch*" or "*heriganoscaf*" (like "*multitudo*"); it was translated in the German version of Vegetius by Ludwig Hohenwang (printed about 1475) as "an assembled crowd of knights," and battle songs use the expression "drew up their army in point and formation like a wall."[17]

On the same plane with the triangular formation is Köhler's concept of the three echelons of knights. Just imagine: each of these echelons consists in turn of "wedges," that is, columns with a depth of twenty to thirty horses, and those are supposed to be, not march formations, but battle formations! The only warriors in such a combat formation who are in a position to make use of their weapons are those of the first rank of the first echelon. Consequently, that would be one-sixtieth or one-ninetieth of the army, and this with horsemen, where the rear ranks are not even able to press the leading ranks forward and the natural weakness of the flanks is much greater than with foot troops! It is no wonder, then, that an author with such concepts believes in the formation of the Spaniards in which the soldiers have their feet tied together.

The closing point of these citations may be provided by the "round" phalanxes of the Germans reported by Caesar and in which the Alamanni are supposed to have fought at Strasbourg (3: 2: 233, 235; 3: 3: 136).

The Saxons, too, in the battle on the Unstrut in 1075, are supposed to have formed a tight circle, "which, however, after a courageous defense, was overcome by the repeated attacks of the imperial army" (3: 2: 257). The passage that is cited as authority for this reads as follows in Lambert, p. 184 (*M. G.* SS., 5. 227): "vix tandem ex illa trepidatione resumpto spiritu cum in globum densissimum tumultuaria se statione stipassent, non expectato signo, ut consuetudo est pugnaturis" ("Finally, after scarcely catching their breath from that alarm, when they had packed themselves together from a disordered state into the thickest mass, at an unexpected signal, as the custom is for those about to fight"); that is the extent of Köhler's quotation. But Lambert continues: "equis subdant calcaria ut summo nisu praecipites feruntur in adversarios" ("they plunged their spurs into their horses with the greatest possible effort and were carried headlong against the enemy").

After all this, Köhler does not have a claim to be recognized as an authority in the field of the history of warfare, and he did not have the right to treat arrogantly, in a coarse tone, scholars like Rüstow, Oman, Bürkli, and Baltzer.

NOTES FOR CHAPTER VIII

1. On the theoretical aspect of this question, see the article "On the Importance of Discoveries in History" ("Ueber die Bedeutung der Erfindungen in der Geschichte") in my *Historische und politische Aufsätze* (1887).

2. Edited by Dümmler in the *Zeitschrift für Deutsches Altertum,* 15 (1872): 433.

3. This part is also reprinted in Hahn, *Collectio monumentorum,* Vol. I, Braunschweig, 1724.

4. Alwin Schultz, *Courtly Life at the Time of the Minnesingers* (*Höfisches Leben zur Zeit der Minnesänger*), 2: 160, believes on the basis of this statement that drill exercises took place in the Middle Ages. How that is supposed to have been possible seems unclear to the author himself, of course (p. 162), since the peasants were forbidden to bear arms.

5. These regulations are copied in the original Spanish text and translated in Köhler, 3: 2: 230. Some translation errors have been corrected

by H. Escher, *Neujahrsblatt der Züricher Feuerwerker-Gesellschaft auf das Jahr 1905,* p. 44.

6. *Geschichte der Kriegswissenschaften,* 1: 212.

7. "Life and Works of Christine de Pisan" ("Leben und Werke der Christine de Pizan"), by Friedrich Koch. Leipzig dissertation, 1885. Ludwig Koch Press, Goslar.

8. Printed under the title *L'art de chevalerie selon Végèce,* 1488.

9. Jähns passed over this in his *Geschichte der Kriegswissenschaften.* It was edited by C. Favre and L. Lecestre, 2 volumes, Paris, 1887, 1889.

10. *Le Jouvencel,* Book I, Chap. 17, Vol. II, 63: "A combat unit on foot should not march at all but is always to await its enemies in place. For when they march, they are not all of the same strength and they cannot hold their formation. It takes no more than a bush to break them up."

11. *Geschichte der Kriegswissenschaften,* 1: 248.

12. Published by Köhler in the *Anzeiger für die Kunde der deutschen Vorzeit,* 1870.

13. Cited in Jähns, 1: 323.

14. *The Development of the Military System and of the Conduct of War in the Knightly Period from the Middle of the Eleventh Century to the Hussite Wars* (*Die Entwickelung des Kriegswesens und der Kriegführung in der Ritterzeit von Mitte des 11. Jahrhunderts bis zu den Hussitenkriegen*). Three parts in five volumes. By G. Köhler, Major General, Retired. 1886 to 1889.

15. Henri Delpech, *La Tactique au XIIIme siècle.* Paris, 1886. A. Molinier, too, in a detailed discussion in *Revue historique,* 36 (1888): 185, explains that the most fundamental principles of historical criticism are unknown to Delpech.

16. The battle of Visp, on which Oechsli bases his concept, is known to us only from a source written eighty years later, and it is methodologically false to accept as evidence this obviously completely legendary account, even only to the extent that a member of the Confederation of the fifteenth century conceived of the same thing under the word "point." A chronicler who recounts events so far in the past often has no hesitation at all in weaving in the most miraculous fairy stories. There is just as little evidence for a triangular formation in the report that the knight Baron von Stein from Swabia rode "in the most forward position" at the point in the battle of Ragaz in 1446, tried to penetrate into the unit of the Confederation forces, and was killed. The knight may have been ahead of his comrades and may have tried to open up a passage for his men, "for horse and rider were covered with armor," but it would most certainly

have been to his liking if the others had done the same thing beside him, instead of remaining a horse's length behind because of the triangular formation. An enemy battle formation is not best divided and broken up if at first it is penetrated by only one man or a few, but, on the contrary, when the largest possible number drive in simultaneously.

17. Lilienkron, 2: 310.

Chapter IX

Conclusion

In the Middle Ages, the disciplined legions of antiquity had been replaced by a warriorhood based entirely on the bravery and skill of the individual. At the same time that the tactical bodies of antiquity were breaking up, the specialized combat branches with their opposite characteristics disappeared, as they blended into one another. The elite individual warrior fought on horseback or on foot, and used spear, sword, and bow alternately and as circumstances required. The combat branches, which gradually became distinct again in the Middle Ages, sprang from a process of differentiation. As the summit of individual warriorhood there developed on the one side the very heavily armored knight mounted on an armored horse, and on the other side, as a result of the one-sided and inflexible nature of that arm, all kinds of secondary arms on horseback and on foot, which did not rise above the role of simple support troops and did not develop independence.

The dismounted spearmen, in particular, could not hold their own against knights in the open field; they would be broken up by the attack of knights, who were supported where necessary by marksmen, and they were without offensive power. Marksmen, too, alone in the open field, were no match for attacking knights.

These knights and foot soldiers were not what we call cavalry and infantry. Despite the great similarity of their armament, they were basically different in spirit, actions, and concept.

Let us look first at the foot soldiers armed with close-combat weapons. The difference between a group of medieval spearmen and a phalanx, legion, or cohort is that it formed no tactical body, that is, a formation in which a mass of warriors is joined into a force with a unified will. Only foot troops organized in this way can be designated as infantry. The test is combat against mounted men in the open field.

With the help of the wagon fort, the Hussites succeeded with their foot troops in standing up to knightly armies. But this was only an episode. The wagon fort was much too cumbersome to fill the overall needs of the conduct of war. The Hussite method of warfare did not have any kind of lasting effect.

A true infantry was not formed again until the period of the Swiss dominance. With the battles of Laupen and Sempach, Grandson, Murten, and Nancy we once again have foot troops comparable to the phalanx and the legions.

A series of factors coincided to create the new skill and power in this part of the German Alpine areas. Mountainous terrain is inherently favorable for maintaining pristine warrior strength. The dissolution of the Duchy of Swabia with the fall of its ducal family, the Hohenstaufens, and the extinction of the great House of Zähringen caused the appearance in that region of the innumerable small areas directly subordinate to the empire, which, like the small Greek cantons centuries earlier, developed and exercised their military strength in continuing combat with one another. The nature of the mountainous terrain also gave communities of peasants and burghers the possibility from the start, through ingenious exploitation of the terrain, to meet and defeat knightly armies.

In these battles, they developed the appropriate weapons and formations—first the throwing of stones and the halberd, and then the long spear, which several successive ranks could extend forward and thus prevent knights from penetrating into the formation. Scholars have differed as to when the long spear was introduced and have even disputed its invention by the Swiss, claiming it was not a peasant weapon but one appropriate for city-dwellers. This question cannot be answered so directly, and it is also not so very important. Long spears were already mentioned among the weapons of the early Germans (Tacitus, *Annals*, 2. 14. See Vol. II, p. 48), then again among the Quadi and Sarmatians (Ammianus, 17. 12), among the Saxons (Widukind, 1. 9; Cosmas, 4. 27), and in Italy (*Annales Januenses* [*Annals of Genoa*] for the year 1240).[1] Individual soldiers in all periods may have chosen longer spears in order to hold the enemy farther away from them, while others may have preferred shorter spears in order to be able to handle them better. The very long spear, more than 20 feet, is very uncomfortable to carry (see Vol. I, p. 405) and can be used for nothing else than for combat in close formation, particularly not even for hunting. The attacks of heavy knights could also be repelled with spears 10 and 12 feet long if the mass only remained tightly closed. It is therefore not necessary to assume that the Swiss peasantry was already using long spears at Morgarten or even earlier. It was not until battles of this kind were fought repeatedly and it was realized how decisively important it was to be able to repel horsemen that the transition could have been made to placing men with the longest possible spears in the exterior ranks of the square. The experience at Laupen was well suited to give birth to the idea that in the future they would hold their own better with lengthened spears. But whether these spears were used at Sempach is not clear either from the events of the battle or the sources. Recently, the presumption has been advanced that the very long spears were not adopted until after the Burgundian wars (Vol. IV, Book I, Chap. 1).

The use of the shield is not compatible with either the halberd or the long spear, since each of those weapons is manipulated with both hands. And the men armed with halberds do not wear any armor. They are protected through the fact that they form the interior ranks and files of the square. It was not until the closed mass had "gained the pressure advantage," thrown the enemy back, broken its own close formation, and started pursuing that the work of the halberdiers started, and they then needed no significant protective armor, since the enemy's real strength was already broken. But the spearmen, who formed the exterior ranks of the square in order to repulse the knights and drive forward to push them back, were also provided with armor and helmet in order to be protected not only against the lances and swords of the knights but also against the arrows, bolts, and bullets of the enemy marksmen. Spear and armor go together so naturally that no special mention was made of the spear together with the harness, but it was taken for granted.[2]

The marksmen moved along beside the square, skirmishing out and then pushing back into the square when pressed.

The larger a closed square is, the less easily it can be broken up by horsemen and the more strongly it can push forward. But it is still not advisable to place all the troops in one square, because such a mass can quite easily be stopped by an attack from two directions, as happened to the troops of the forest cantons at Laupen, and then the unit becomes helpless. And so the Swiss developed their method of always forming in three large squares, regardless of the size of their army, so that they could mutually support one another. These three squares were formed neither in a straight column nor directly side by side, but in staggered echelons, so that they did not interfere with one another. The one to the rear, entering the fight somewhat later than the one in front of it, maintained a certain freedom of maneuver up to the last moment. Even a very large square, of say 10,000 men, has great flexibility of movement because of the narrowness of its front, only 100 men. It is not until the fifteenth century that this formation in three squares can be definitely proven. At Morgarten and Sempach only two squares specifically appear in the battle, one maintaining a defensive stance and the other making the flanking attack. But it is not impossible that there was also a third square present, and since this unit actually did appear at Laupen, we may assume that this division into three units probably was already normal in the fourteenth century.

Possessing appropriate weapons, the most suitable battle formations, and experienced leaders who understood how to exploit the advantages of the mountain terrain, the peasants and burghers developed a sense of confidence that turned the entire people into a warriorhood.

Even today, Swiss patriotism has difficulty tearing itself away, not only from the William Tell and Winkelried legends, but also from the idea that their ancestors were an innocent people of pious shepherds who only became warlike as they defended their freedom against foreign tyrants, first the Hapsburgs and then the duke of Burgundy, both of whom were seen as leading huge masses against the small nation. Every bit of historical consistency is eliminated by these concepts and every possibility of understanding is suppressed. Of course, the popular concept can hardly work in any other way than with such pictures. We have already seen this point among the Greeks, who did not know how to express the fame of their Persian wars in any other way than by the victory of a small minority over a superior force of countless numbers. In both cases, scholarship must correct those kinds of ideas, and in doing so it takes nothing from the fame of the heroic deeds of the peoples but simply transposes that fame into another sphere.

The warriorhood of the Swiss had the same plundering and forcefully cruel trait as the Germans of early times. The Swiss communities, as soon as their success had injected self-confidence into the masses, and in their immediate area, where there was no problem of obtaining provisions, were able to put into the field superior numbers, even against the strongest medieval army. For knightly armies, even with their serving men and mercenaries, were by their very nature always small. From Morgarten to Nancy the armies of the Confederation were always considerably larger than those of their enemies, at times as high as double their strength. It was only as a result of this that they were able to develop their gigantic power. The individual elements of their strength increased to the utmost. Whereas everywhere else in Europe only a small part of the population entered the warriorhood, in the Swabian Alpine areas the closeness to nature, success, and the training of the entire body of men lent the character and the readiness of professional warriorhood, and the masses that could now be called into service redoubled their confidence and their certainty of being victorious. The national leadership intentionally saw to it that they were preceded by a reputation that struck terror into their enemies. Whereas in European professional warriorhood, among knights as well as mercenaries, a certain tendency toward mutual mercy had taken hold, and men were satisfied with the taking of prisoners in cases where killing did not seem absolutely necessary, the Swiss, for their part, from the very start struck down every man they could reach. They were expressly forbidden to take prisoners, and any prisoners taken were killed later. Even when in a civil war between the members of the Confederation themselves, the old Zurich war, troops of the forest cantons, along with the Bernese and other cantons, captured the castle of Greifensee, they had the garrison of Zurich troops, who had had to surrender "at the mercilessness of their enemy," executed (1444). The savage bloodthirstiness with which all the burghers in the peaceful town of Stäffi were killed presumably evoked some reproach within the Confederation itself, but it was, after all, only the usual application of the principle that in battle no man might be spared. It is reported as a mitigating factor when "young boys" were spared. In the first general military regulations of the Confederation, the Sempach letter of 1393, it had to be expressly prescribed that, since "the well-being of all men was renewed and expanded by the concept of woman," wives and daughters were not to be struck, stabbed, or mistreated. The strongest reason for this severity in the conduct of war was the danger that plundering and the taking of prisoners created for the military action itself. The Sempach letter was drawn up in consideration of the fact that in the battle many more of the enemy could have been killed if the victors had not been so very anxious to seize booty immediately. But by going to such an extreme as absolutely forbidding the taking of prisoners, they increased the fear in the enemy camp. The panic that broke out in the Austrian rear guard at Sempach, and in the Burgundian army at Grandson and Murten, as soon as there was an unfavorable turn in the battle or even the appearance of such a turn, may also be considered to have been an after-effect of the well-known custom of the Swiss to grant no mercy.

Charles the Bold, as his troops were marching out of Nancy against the Swiss, made a speech to his captains,[3] saying that the enemies, according to their custom, would immediately form for battle at the border. If they were defeated, he went on to say, and suffered even only a small reverse, they would be broken and lost from that point on. Somewhat exaggerated in its form, this statement was still correct in its concept. That is, the bravery of the Swiss arose from their success, while their success gave them confidence in their unstoppable assault, before which the loosely knit squares of the enemy armies disintegrated, no matter how much personal bravery still existed in the individual knights or mercenaries.

We can compare the Swiss of this period with the Athenians of the Age of Pericles, just as we have compared them with the early Germans. The inhabitants of the peninsula of Attica were not by their nature braver or more skilled in naval matters than the other Greeks. The march of historical development and politics, however, had formed the entire population into a warriorhood on land and on sea, and this gave them in their civic life important characteristics of professional soldiery. That was held up to them by their general Nicias, when he addressed them before the battle against the Syracusans. The latter, he said, were a simple people's levy, whereas his own troops were selected men who understood war.[4] There is also between the Swiss and the other Germans not a distinction of race but of historical development and political training. Most of the Hapsburg warriors were just as good Swiss as the men of the forest cantons. The victors of Grandson and Murten were in great part the defeated of Morgarten, Laupen, and Sempach. These defeated men, by entering partly voluntarily and partly through force, into the circle of victors, also assumed their characteristics.

The squares of the Swiss risked moving forward offensively as foot troops against knightly armies and even storming fortified positions. That was something completely new since the decline of antiquity and the rise of the feudal military organization. As late as 1475, at the beginning of the Burgundian war, on the occasion of a withdrawal out of Franche-Comté, the foot troops of the Confederation protected themselves against Burgundian knights by forming a wagon fort. Never again do we hear of this kind of action.

Once again there was a body of foot troops that was not simply a supporting arm for the knights and that risked fighting against knights, not simply when supported by entrenchments, but with complete confidence in its own power accepted any kind of battle with any enemy. The formation—the tactical body of the square, the weapons—the long spear and the halberd, the mass of men resulting from the people's levy, and the warlike spirit nurtured and developed in continuing battles, all worked effectively together. When the French mercenaries, the Armagnacs, threatened to make their incursion into Switzerland in 1444, a body of 1,500 men with rash courage took up the fight with them at Saint Jacob on the Birs in the vicinity of Basel (26 August). Although the battle ended with their complete destruction, they had fought it through with such courage that even their enemies were filled with admiration.

Swiss mercenaries were highly esteemed and recruited by the peoples on all sides.

The victories over Charles the Bold, even though, of course, chance and the errors of the Burgundian leaders had played a large role in them, gave the final and highest boost to the belief in Swiss competence and to the self-confidence of the Confederation. No longer considered as simple soldiers of fortune among other mercenaries, but as a unique, completely new military power, the men of the Confederation marched out of their mountains and won the victory of Nancy. This victory was not to remain an isolated episode, such as the victory of the Flemish at Courtrai. It opened access to a new epoch in the history of the art of war. The Middle Ages in military history already came to a close on the day of Murten, where, in the person of the duke of Burgundy and his army, medieval methods of war were theoretically overcome—not by chance, not in a moment of weakness, not in a condition of decay, but on the contrary, at the highest imaginable degree of their perfection and even especially supported by the new discovery of firearms. It can be assumed that a better general than Duke Charles would have made the victory much more difficult for the Swiss, but we may also conclude as a certainty that the Swiss would still have been victorious in the end. For no marksmen with bows, crossbows, and culverins were sufficient to hold up the attack of these huge aggressive squares with spears and halberds, which their captains skillfully led through the favorable areas of the terrain, and no body of knights was capable of breaking them up or of halting all three at the same time by flank attacks. Marksmen alone cannot stand fast against close-combat weapons, and knights alone do not have any tactical leadership to enable them to paralyze the squares with coordinated maneuvers. The Swiss infantry formed tactical bodies, while the knights, marksmen, and spearmen of the Middle Ages did not have them. The Swiss had not only defensive and offensive power, but also leadership. With the Flemish, too, 100 years earlier, a start was made in this direction, but as Rosebeke showed, this strength was not yet sufficient. The Confederation of the mountain cantons had for 150 years developed and confirmed its strength in a gradual progression. This force had now definitely conquered, and, moving out of the mountains, it was to transform methods of warfare in all of Europe. We are now at a point of departure for new developments similar to that at the battle of Marathon. As in the Persian wars, the foot troops with close-combat weapons had been victorious in the Burgundian wars over the army of knights and marksmen. This victory necessarily had to transform everything. For the methods of warfare of a period form a unity, and a significant change in one spot reacts on all the other parts. We have recognized as a natural complement of knighthood the fact that the period had no infantry but only soldiers on foot. Now these foot soldiers have become infantry, and soon that would be the case everywhere. Then knighthood would also necessarily become cavalry.

NOTES FOR CHAPTER IX

1. *M. G. SS.*, 18. 192. H. Escher, *The Swiss Foot Troops* (*Das schweizerische Fussvolk*), p. 19, also states (without citing a source) that in 1202 a distinction was made in Italy between *"lanceae longae"* ("long spears") and *"lanceae de milite"* ("soldiers' spears"), and that in 1327 the burghers of Turin were ordered to carry "spears of 18 feet." Köhler, 3: 1: 50, states that the knight's lance was originally no longer than 10 feet, and that in the fourteenth century it was lengthened to 14 feet and became so heavy that a man on foot could no longer manipulate it (3: 1: 85).

2. Bürkli believes that this is the meaning of the expression *"Stangharnisch."* G. Escher, p. 44, note to p. 19, disputes this point, but he concedes that no other explanation of the word *"Stangharnisch"* has yet been found. Of course, Bürkli is in error when he says that by this word *"Stange"* we must necessarily understand the later, long spear. Escher, *Feuerwerksblatt*, 102 (1907): 34, arrives at the solution that any kind of weapon with a staff, both the spear and the halberd, is meant to accompany the harness.

3. *Report of the Milanese Ambassador Panigarola of 16 January 1476.* Gingins, *Dépêches Milanaises*, 1: 266. "There is no doubt that, in keeping with their custom, they will offer battle; at the first penetration they will necessarily be broken, because every little defeat throws them off; from the start they will definitely be disheartened and lost."

4. Volume I, p. 145. Thucydides, 6. 68.

Appendix 1

Chronological Listing of the Battles Referred to in This Volume

Date		*Battle*	*Page*
11 August	1086	Bleichfeld	144
1 July	1097	Dorylaeum	403
9 February	1098	On the Lake of Antioch	404
Early March	1098	At the Bridge Gate of Antioch	404
28 June	1098	Decisive Battle of Antioch	404
12 August	1099	Ascalon	406
7 September	1101	Ramleh	408
May	1102	Ramleh	408
27 August	1105	Ramleh	408
28 September	1106	Tinchebrai	399
14 September	1115	Sarmin	408
28 June	1119	Athareb (Belath)	409
13 August	1119	Hab	409
20 August	1119	Brémule	400
	1123	Ashdod	219
26 March	1124	Bourgthéroulde	400
	1125	Hazarth	409
	1126	Merdj-Sefer	409
22 August	1138	Northallerton	400
2 February	1141	Lincoln	402
	1146	With the Hungarians	282
9 August	1160	Carcano	334
29 May	1167	Tusculum	337
16 March	1176	Carseoli	342
29 May	1176	Legnano	342
4 July	1187	Hittin	410
4 October	1189	Acre	410
7 September	1191	Arsuf	410
5 August	1192	Jaffa	410
27 July	1206	Wasserberg	344
12 September	1213	Muret	413
13 October	1213	Steppes	414
27 July	1214	Bouvines	415
22 July	1227	Bornhöved	419
27 November	1237	Cortenuova	346
	1247-1248	Parma (Siege)	348
23 November	1249	Krücken	379
	1257	Frechen	367
13 July	1260	Durban	380
4 September	1260	Monte Aperto	420
8 March	1262	Hausbergen	368
13 July	1263	Löbau	380

Date		Battle	Page
	1426	Klattau	487
	1427	Nachod	493
	1428	Glatz	493
	1431	Bullegneville	469
	1431	Waidhofen	493
	1431	Tauss	493
	1433	Hiltersried	307
16 June	1434	Lipany	498
26 August	1444	Saint Jacob	654
	1446	Ragaz	647
11 March	1450	Pillenreuth	275
30 June	1462	Seckenheim	595
16 July	1465	Montl'héry	527
14 April	1471	Barnet	541
4 May	1471	Tewksbury	542
13 November	1474	Héricourt	605
2 March	1476	Grandson	606
22 June	1476	Murten	612
5 January	1477	Nancy	624
	1499	Frastenz	577
	1522	Bicocca	575

Appendix 2

Latin Text of the Oath in the *Capitulare missorum* (M. G., 1. 66) (Note 24, p. 57)

Quomodo illum sacramentum juratum esse debeat ab episcopis et abbatis, sive comitibus vel bassis regalibus, necon vicedominis, archidiaconibus adque canonicis.

3. Clerici, qui monachorum nomine non pleniter conversare videntur; et ubi regula s. Benedicti secundum ordinem tenent, ipsi in verbum tantum et in veritate prommittant, de quibus specialiter abbates adducant domno nostro.

4. Deinde advocatis et vicariis, centenariis, sive fore censiti presbiteri, atque cunctas generalitas populi, tam puerilitate annorum XII quamque de senili, qui ad placita venissent et jussionem adimplere seniorum et conservare possunt, sive pagenses sive episcoporum et abbatissuarum vel comitum homines et reliquorum homines, fiscilini quoque et coloni et ecclesiasticis adque servi, qui honorati beneficia et ministeria tenent vel in bassallatico honorati sunt cum domini sui et caballos, arma et scuto et lancea, spata et senespasio habere possunt, omnes jurent. Et nomina vel numerum de ipsi missi in brebem secum adportent, et comites similiter de singulis centinis semoti, tam de illos qui infra pago nati sunt et pagensales fuerint quamque et de illos qui infra pago nati sunt et pagensales fuerint quamque et de illis qui aliunde in basallitico commendati sunt.

Appendix 3

Latin Texts of the Carolingian and Other Capitularies on Military Service (Pages 31 to 51)

EXTRACT FROM THE GENERAL *CAPITULARE MISSORUM* (CAPITULARY OF LEGATES) OF 802. *M. G.*, 1. 93 (PAGE 31)

7. Ut ostile bannum domni imperatori nemo pretermittere presumat nullusque comis tam presumtiosum sit, ut ullum de his qui hostem facere debiti sunt exinde vel aliqua propinquitatis defensionem vel cuius muneris adolationem dimitere audeant.

* * *

EXTRACT FROM A CAPITULARY FOR THE REGIONS WEST OF THE SEINE. 807. *M. G.*, 1. 134 (Page 31)

Memoratorium qualiter ordinavimus propter famis inopiam, ut de ultra Sequane omnes exercitare debeant.

In primis quicunque beneficia habere videntur omnes in hostem veniant.

Quicumque liber mansos quinque de proprietate habere videtur, similiter in hostem veniat, et qui quattuor mansos habeat similiter faciat. Qui tres habere videtur similiter agat. Ubicumque autem inventi fuerint duo, quorum unusquisque duos mansos habere videtur, unus alium praeparare faciat; et qui melius ex ipsis potuerit, in hostem veniat. Et ubi inventi fuerint duo, quorum unus habeat duos mansos, et alter habeat unum mansum, similiter se sociare faciant et unus alterum praeparet; et qui melius potuerit in hostem veniat. Ubicumque autem tres fuerint inventi, quorum unusquisque mansum unum habeat, duo tercium praeparare faciant; ex quibus qui melius potest in hostem veniat. Illi vero qui dimidium mansum habent, quinque sextum praeparare faciant. Et qui sic pauper inventus fuerit, qui nec mancipia nec propriam possessionem terrarum habeat, tamen in praecio valente [? quinque libras?], quinque sextum praeparent. [Et ubi duo tercium de illis qui parvulas possessiones de terra habere videntur;]³⁴ Et unicuique ex ipsis qui in hoste pergunt, fiant conjectati solidi quinque a suprascriptis pauperioribus qui nullam possession habere videntur in terra. Et pro hac consideratione nullus suum seniorem dimittat.

* * *

CAPITULARE MISSORUM (CAPITULARY OF LEGATES) OF 808. *M. G.*, 1. 137 (PAGE 32)

1. Ut omnis liber homo qui quattuor mansos vestitos de proprio suo sive de alicuius beneficio habet, ipse se praeparet et per se in hostem pergat, sive cum seniore suo si senior eius perrexerit, sive cum comite suo. Qui vero tres mansos de proprio habuerit, huic adiungatur qui unum mansum habeat et det illi adjutorium ut ille pro ambobus possit. Qui autem duos habet de proprio tantum, iungatur illi alter qui similiter duos mansos habeat, et unus ex eis altero illum adjuvante, pergat in hostem. Qui etiam tantum unum mansum de proprio habet, adjungatur ei tres qui similiter habeant et dent ei adjutorium et ille pergat tantum; tres vero qui ille adjutorium dederunt, domi remaneant.

* * *

CAPITULARY OF UNCERTAIN DATE, PROBABLY 807 OR 808. *M. G.*, 1. 136 (PAGE 32)

2. Si partibus Hispaniae sive Avariae solatium ferre fuerit necesse praebendi, tunc de Saxonibus quinque sextum praeparare faciant. Et si partibus Beheim fuerit necesse solatium ferre, duo tercium praeparent. Si vero circa Surabis patria defendenda necessitas fuerit, tunc omnes generaliter veniant.

3. De Frisionibus volumus, ut comites et vasalli nostri, qui beneficia habere videntur, et caballarii, omnes generaliter ad placitum nostrum veniant bene praeparati. Reliqui vero pauperiores; sex septimum praeparare faciant, et sic ad condictum placitum bene praeparati hostiliter veniant.

* * *

FOUR VERSIONS OF THE REGULATIONS FOR THE BASIC ROSTERS OF 829. *M. G.*, II: P. 7, CHAP. 7; P. 10, CHAP. 5; P. 19, CHAP. 7 (PAGE 33)

Volumus atque jubemus, ut missi nostri diligenter inquirant, quanti homines liberi in singulis comitatibus maneant, qui possint expeditionem per se facere vel quanti de his, quibus unus alium adiuvet, quanti etiam de his, qui a duobus tertius adiuvetur et praeparetur, necnon de his, qui a tribus quartus adiuvetur et praeparetur sive de his, qui a quattuor quintus adiuvetur et praeparetur eandem expeditionem exercitalem facere possint, et eorum summam ad nostram notitiam deferant.

* * *

Volumus atque jubemus, ut missi nostri diligenter inquirant, quanti homines liberi in singulis comitatibus maneant, qui possint expeditionem exercitalem per se facere vel quanti de his qui a duobus tertius adiutus et praeparatus, et de his qui a tribus quartus adiutus et praeparatus, et de his qui a quattuor quintus vel sextus adiutus et praeparatus ad expeditionem exercitalem facere, nobisque brevem eorum summam deferant.

* * *

Volumus atque jubemus, ut missi nostri diligenter inquirant, quanti liberi homines in singulis comitatibus maneant. Hinc vero ea diligentia et haec ratio examinetur per singulas centenas, ut veraciter sciant illos atque describant, qui in exercitalem ire possunt expeditionem; ac deinde videlicet secundum ordinem de his qui per se ire non possunt ut duo tertio adiutorium praeparent. Et qui necdum nobis fidelitatem promiserunt cum sacramento nobis fidelitatem promittere faciant.

* * *

Volumus atque iubemus, ut missi nostri diligenter inquirant, quanti liberi homines in singulis comitatibus maneant, qui possint expeditionem exercitalem facere nobisque per brevem eorum summam deferant. Et qui nondum fidelitatem promiserunt cum sacramento nobis fidelitatem promittere faciant.

* * *

REPORT IN THE *ANNAL. BERTINIANI* OF THE YEAR 869 (PAGE 35)

Et antequam ad Conadam pergeret, per omne regnum suum litteras misit, ut episcopi, abbates et abbatissae breves de honoribus suis, quanta mansa quisque haberet, ad futuras Kalendas Mai deferre curarent, vassalli autem dominici comitum beneficia et comites vassallorum beneficia inbreviarent et praedicto placito aedium breves inde deferrent, et de centum mansis unum haistaldum et de mille mansis unum carrum cum duobus bobus praedicto placito cum aliis exeniis, quae regnum illius admodum gravant, ad Pistas mitti praecepit, quatenus ipsi haistaldi castellum, quod ibidem ex ligno et lapide fieri praecepit, excolerent et custodirent.

* * *

LETTER OF 817 FROM ARCHBISHOP OF TRIER TO BISHOP OF TOUL (PAGE 36)

Quatinus universi se praeparent, qualiter proficisci valeant ad bellum in Italiam .... ut solerti sagacitate studeas cum summa festinatione omnibus abbatibus, abbatissis, comitibus, vassis dominicis vel cuncto populo parrochiae tuae, quibus convenit militiam regiae potestati exhibere, indicare, quatenus omnes praeparati sint, ut si vespere eis adnuntiatum fuerit, mane, et si mane, vesperi absque ulla tarditate proficiscantur in partes Italiae.

*   *   *

MEMORIAL OF 811. *M. G.*, 1. 165 (PAGE 36)

3. Dicunt etiam, quod quicumque proprium suum episcopo, abbati vel comiti aut iudici vel centenario dare noluerit, occasiones quaerunt super illum pauperem, quomodo eum condempnare possint et illum semper in hostem faciant ire, usque dum pauper factus volens nolens suum proprium tradat aut vendat; alii vero qui traditum habent absque ullius inquietudine domi resideant.

5. Dicunt etiam alii, quod illos pauperiores constringant et in hostem ire faciant, et illos qui habent quod dare possint ad propria dimittunt.

*   *   *

REGULATIONS CONCERNING PUNISHMENTS

CAPITULARY OF 802. *M. G.*, 1. 96 (PAGE 37)

.29. De pauperinis vero qui [quibus] in sua elymosyna domnus imperator concedit qui [quod] pro banno suo solvere debent, ut eos judices, comites vel missi nostri pro concesso non habeant constringere parte sua.

. . . .

34. Ut omnes pleniter bene parati sint, quandocunque iussio nostra vel annuntiatio advenerit. Si quis autem tunc se inparatum esse dixerit et praeterierit mandatum, ad palatium perducatur; et non solum ille, sed etiam omnes qui bannum vel praeceptum nostrum transgredere praesumunt.

*   *   *

CAPITULARY OF 805. *M. G.*, 1. 125 (PAGE 37)

19. De heribanno volumus ut missi nostri hoc anno fideliter exactare debeant absque ullius personae gratia, blanditia seu terrore secundum iussionem nostram; id est ut de homine habente libras sex in auro, in argento, bruneis, aeramento, pannis integris, caballis, boves, vaccis vel alio peculio (et uxores vel infantes non fiant dispoliati pro hac re de eorum vestimentis) accipiant legitimum heribannum, id est libras tres. Qui vero non habuerint amplius in suprascripto praecio valente nisi libras tres, solidi triginta ab eo exigantur (id est libra et dimidia). Qui autem non habuerit amplius nisi duas libras, solidi decem. Si vero una habuerit, solidi quinque, ita ut iterum se valeat praeparare ad Dei servitium et nostram utilitatem. Et nostri missi caveant et diligenter inquirant, ne per aliquod malum ingenium subtrahant nostram iustitiam, alteri tradendo aut commendando.

*   *   *

CAPITULARY OF 808. *M. G.*, 1. 137 (PAGE 37)

2. Volumus atque jubemus, ut idem missi nostri diligenter inquirant, qui anno praeterito de hoste bannito remansissent super illam ordinationem quam modo superius comprehenso de liberis et pauperioribus hominibus fieri iussimus; et quicumque fuerit inventus qui nec parem suum ad hostem suum faciendum secundum nostram iussionem adjuvit neque perrexit, haribannum nostrum pleniter rewadiet et de solvendo illo secundum legem fidem faciat.

3. Quod si forte talis homo inventus fuerit qui dicat, quod iussione comitis vel vicarii aut centenarii sui hoc quo ipse semetipsum praeparare debeat eidem comiti vel vicario aut centenario vel quibuslibet hominibus eorum dedisset et propter hoc illud demisisset iter et missi nostri hoc ita verum esse investigare potuerint, is per cuius iussionem ille remansit bannum nostrum rewadiet atque persolvat, sive sit comes sive vicarius sive advocatus episcopi atque abbatis.

*   *   *

CAPITULARY OF 810. *M. G.*, 1. 153 (PAGE 38)

12. De heribanno, ut diligenter inquirant missi. Qui hostem facere potuit et non fecit, ipsum bannum componat si habet unde componere possit; et si non habuerit unde componere valeat, rewadiatum fiat et inbreviatum et nihil pro hoc exhactatum fiat usque dum ad notitiam domni imperatoris veniat.

*   *   *

CAPITULARY OF BOULOGNE. 811. *M. G.*, 1. 166 (PAGE 38)

1. Quicunque liber homo in hostem bannitus fuerit et venire contempserit, plenum heribannum id est solidos sexaginta persolvat aut si non habuerit unde illam summam persolvat semetipsum pro wadio in servitium principis tradat donec per tempora ipse bannus ab eo fiat persolutus; et tunc iterum ad statum libertatis suae revertatur. Et si ille homo qui se propter heribannum in servitium tradidit in illo servitio defunctus fuerit, heredes eius hereditatem quae ad eos pertenet non perdant nec libertatem nec de ipso heribanno obnoxii fiant.

2. Ut non per aliquam occasionem nec de wacta nec de scara nec de warda nec pro heribergare neque pro alio banno heribannum comis exactare praesumat, nisi missus noster prius heribannum ad partem nostram recipiat et ei suam tertiam partem exinde per iussionem nostram donet. Ipse vero heribannus non exactetur neque in terris neque in mancipiis, sed in auro et argento, pannis atque armis et animalibus atque pecoribus sive talibus speciebus quae ad utilitatem pertinent.

*   *   *

MEMORIAL OF 811. *M. G.*, 1. 165 (PAGE 38)

6. Dicunt ipsi comites, quod alii eorum pagenses non illis obediant nec bannum domni imperatoris adimplere volunt, dicentes quod contra missos domni

imperatoris pro heribanno debeant rationem reddere, nam non contra comitem; etiam etsi comes suam domum illi in bannum miserit, nullam exinde habeat reverentiam, nisi intret in domum suam et faciat quaecumque ei libitum fuerit.

*   *   *

CAPITULARY OF BOULOGNE. 811. *M. G.*, 1. 166 (PAGE 40)

3. Quincumque homo nostros honores habens in ostem bannitus fuerit et ad condictum placitum non venerit, quot diebus post placitum condictum venisse conprobatus fuerit, tot diebus abstineat a carne et vino.

*   *   *

DISPENSATIONS

CAPITULARY OF 808. *M. G.*, 1. 137 (PAGE 41)

4. De hominibus comitum casatis isti sunt excipiendi et bannum rewadiare non iubeantur: duo qui dimissi fuerunt cum uxore illius et alii duo qui propter ministerium eius custodiendum et servitium nostrum faciendum remanere iussi sunt. In qua causa modo praecipimus, ut quanta ministeria unusquisque comes habuerit, totiens duos homines ad ea custodienda domi dimittat praeter illos duos quos cum uxore sua. Ceteros vero omnes secum pleniter habeat vel si ipsi domi remanserit cum illo qui pro eo in hostem proficiscitur dirigat. Episcopus vero vel abbas duo tantum de casatis et laicis hominibus suis domi dimittant.

*   *   *

CAPITULARY OF BOULOGNE. 811. *M. G.*, 1. 167 (PAGE 41)

9. Quicumque liber homo inventus fuerit anno praesente cum seniore suo in hoste non fuisse, plenum heribannum persolvere cogatur. Et si senior vel comis illius eum domi dimiserit, ipse pro eo eundum bannum persolvat; et tot heribanni ab eo exigantur quot homines domi dimisit. Et quia nos anno praesente unicuique seniori duo homines quos domi dimitteret concessimus, illos volumus ut missis nostris ostendant, quia hisque tantummodo heribannum concedimus.

*   *   *

CAPITULARY OF LEGATES OF 819. *M. G.*, 1. 291, CHAP. 27 (PAGE 41)

Ut vassi nostri et vassi episcoporum, abbatum abbatissarum et comitum qui anno praesente in hoste non fuerunt heribannum rewadient; exceptis his qui propter necessarias causas et a domno ac genitore nostro Karolo constitutas domi dimissi fuerunt, id est qui a comite propter pacem conservandam et propter conjugem ac domum eius custodiendam et ab episcopo vel abbate vel abbatissa similiter propter pacem conservandam et propter fruges colligendas et familiam constringendam et missos recipiendos dimissi fuerunt.

*   *   *

EQUIPMENT

CAPITULARY OF ESTATES OF THE YEAR 800 OR EARLIER. *M. G.,* 1. 82 (PAGE 42)

64. Ut carra nostra quae in hostem pergunt basternae bene factae sint, et operculi bene sint cum coriis cooperti, et ita sint consuti, ut, si necessitas evenerit aquas ad natandum, cum ipsa expensa quae intus fuerit transire flumina possint, ut nequaquam aqua intus intrare valeat et bene salva causa nostra, sicut diximus, transire possit. Et hoc volumus, ut farina in unoquoque carro ad spensam nostram missa fiat, hoc est duodecim modia de farina: et in quibus vinum ducunt, modia XII ad nostrum modium mittant; et ad unumquodque carrum scutum et lanceam, cucurum et arcum habeant.

*   *   *

CAPITULARY OF AIX-LA-CHAPELLE. 801–813. *M. G.,* 1. 170 (PAGE 43)

10. Ut regis spensa in carra ducatur, simul episcoporum, comitum, abbatum et optimatum regis: farinam, vinum, baccones et victum abundanter, molas dolatorias, secures, taretros, fundibulas, et illos homines qui exinde bene sciant iactare. Et marscalci regis adducant eis petras, in saumas viginti, si opus est. Et unusquisque hostiliter sit paratus, et omnia utensilia sufficienter habeant. Et unusquisque comis duas partes de herba in suo comitatu defendat ad opus illius hostis, et habeat pontes bonos, naves bonas.

*   *   *

CAPITULARY OF LEGATES FOR THE REGIONS WEST OF THE SEINE. 807. *M. G.,* 1. 134 (PAGE 43)

3. Omnes itaque fideles nostri capitanei cum eorum hominibus et carra sive dona, quantum melius praeparare potuerint, ad condictum placitum veniant. Et unusquisque missorum nostrorum per singula ministeria considerare faciat unum de vasallis nostris et praecipiat de verbo nostro, ut cum illa minore manu et carra de singulis comitatibus veniat et eos post nos pacifice adducat ita, ut nihil exinde remaneat et mediante mense Augusto ad Renum sint.

*   *   *

EDICT OF LIUTPRAND OF THE YEAR 726. *M. G.*, 4. 140 (PAGE 46)

cap. 83. De omnibus iudicibus, quando in exercito ambolare necessitas fuerit, non dimittant alios homenis nisi tantummodo, qui unum cavallo habent, hoc est homines sex et tollant ad saumas suas ipsos cavallos sex; et de minimis hominibus qui nec casas nec terras suas habent, dimittant homenis decem, et ipsi homenis ad ipsum iudicem faciant per ebdomata una operas tres usque dum ipse iudex de exercito revertitur. Sculdahis vero dimittat homenis tres, qui cavallus habent, ut tollant ad saumas suas cavallos tres; et de minoribus hominibus dimittant homenis quinque qui faciant ei operas, dum ipse reversus fuerit, sicut ad iudicem discemus, per ebdomata una operas tres. Saltarius quidem tollat cavallo uno et de minoribus qui ei operas faciat tollat homine uno et faciat si operas, sicut supra legitur. Et si amplius iudex vel sculdahis aut saltarius dimittere presumpserit homines sine regis permisso aut iussione, qui in exercito ambolare devit, conponat wirgild suo in sagro palatio.

*   *   *

CAPITULARY OF AISTULF OF 750. *M. G.*, 4. 196 (PAGE 47)

cap. 2. De illos homines qui possunt loricam habere et minime habent, vel minores homines qui possunt habere cavallum et scutum et lanceam et minime habent, vel illi homines qui non possunt habere nec habent unde congregare, debeant habere scutum et coccura. Et stetit ut ille homo qui habet septem casas massarias habeat loricam suam cum reliqua conciatura sua, debeat habere et cavallos; et si super habuerit per isto numero debeat habere caballos et reliqua armatura. Item placuit, ut illi homines, qui non habent casas massarias et habent quadraginta jugis terrae, habeant cavallum et scutum et lanceam, item de minoribus hominibus principi placuit, ut si possunt habere scutum, habeant coccora cum sagittas et arcum, item di illis hominibus qui negotiantes sunt et pecunias non habent. Qui sunt majores et potentes, habeant loricam et cavallos, scutum et lanceam; qui sunt sequentes, habeant caballos, scutum et lanceam; et qui sunt minores, habeant coccoras cum sagittas et arcum.

cap. 7. De iudicis es sculdahis vel aactores, qui homines potentes dimittunt ad casa seu de exercitu; qui hoc faciunt conponant sicut edictus continet pagina.

*   *   *

EXTRACT FROM AN ITALIAN CAPITULARY OF LEGATES OF CHARLEMAGNE. *M. G.*, 1. 206 (PAGE 48)

7. De liberorum hominum possibilitate: ut iuxta qualitatem proprietatis exercitare debeant.

13. Ut haribannum aut aliquod conjectum pro exercitali causa comites de liberis hominibus recipere aut requirere non persumant, excepto si de palacio nostro aut filii nostri missus veniat qui illum haribannum requirat.

*   *   *

LOTHAIR'S LEVY FOR A CAMPAIGN AGAINST CORSICA. FEBRUARY 825. *M. G.*, 1. 324 (PAGE 48)

Volumus ut singuli comites hanc districtionem teneant inter eos qui cum eis introeant in Corsica vel remanere debeant.

1. Ut domnici vassalli qui austaldi sunt et in nostro palatio frequenter serviunt, volumus ut remaneant; eorum homines quos antea habuerunt, qui propter hanc occassionem eis se commendaverunt cum eorem senioribus remaneant. Qui autem in eorum proprietate manent, volumus scire qui sint et adhuc considerare volumus, quis eant aut quis remaneant. Illi vero qui beneficia nostra habent et foris manent, volumus ut eant.

2. Homines vero episcoporum seu abbatum qui foris manent, volumus ut cum comitibus eorum vadant, exceptis duobus quos ipse elegerit; et eorum austaldi liberi, exceptis quattour, volumus ut pleniter distringantur.

3. Ceteri vero liberi homines quos vocant bharigildi, volumus ut singuli comites hunc modum teneant: videlicet ut qui tantam substantiae facultatem habent qui per se ire possint et ad hoc sanitas et viris utiles adprobaverit, vadant; illi vero qui substantiam habent et tamen ipsi ire non valent, adiuvet valentem et minus habentem. Secundi vero ordinis liberis, quis pro paupertate sua per se ire non possunt et tamen ex parte possunt, coniungantur duo vel tres aut quattuor (alii vero si necesse fuerit) qui iuxta considerationem comitis eunti adiutorium faciant quomodo ire possit; et in hunc modum ordo iste servetur usque ad alios qui pro nimia paupertate neque ipsi ire valent neque adiutorium eunti praestare. A comitibus habeatur excusatus post antiqua consuetudo eis fidelium comitibus observanda.

*   *   *

EXTRACT FROM LOTHAIR'S CAPITULARY OF MAY 825. *M. G.*, 1. 319 (PAGE 49)

1. Statuimus ut liberi homines qui tantum proprietatis habent unde hostem bene facere possunt et iussi facere nolunt, ut prima vice secundum legem illorum statuto damno subiaceant; si vero secundo inventus fuerit neglegens, bannum nostrum id est LX solidos persolvat; si vero tertio quis in eadem culpa fuerit implicatus, sciat se omnem substantiam suam amissurum aut in exilio esse mittendum. De mediocribus quippe liberis qui non possunt per se hostem facere comitum fidelitati committimus, ut inter duos aut tres seu quattuor vel si necesse fuerit amplius uni qui melior esse videtur adiutorium praebeant ad nostrum servicium faciendum. De his quoque qui propter nimiam paupertatem neque per se hostem facere neque adiutorium prestare possunt, conserventur quousque valeant recuperare.

*   *   *

CAPITULARY OF LOUIS II OF THE YEAR 866. *M. G.*, 2. 94 (PAGE 49)

1. Quicumque de mobilibus widrigild suum habere potest, pergat in hoste; qui vero medium widrigild habet, duos iuncti in unum utiliorem instruant, ut bene ire possit. Pauperes vero personae ad custodiam maritimam vel patriae pergant, ita videlicet, ut qui plus, quam decem solidos habet de mobilibus, ad eandem custodiam vadant. Qui vero non plus, quam decem solidos habet de mobilibus, nil ei requiratur. Si pater quoque unum filium habuerit et ipse filius utilior patre est, instructus a patre pergat; nam si patre utilior est, ipse pergat. Si vero duos filios habuerit, quicumque ex eis utilior fuerit, ipse pergat; alius autem cum patre remaneat; quodsi plures filios habuerit, utiliores omnes pergant; tantum unus remaneat, qui inutilior fuerit. De fratribus indivisis, iuxta capitularem domini et genitoris nostri volumus, ut, si duos fuerint, ambo pergant; si tres fuerint, unus, qui inutilior apparuerit, remaneat, ceteri pergant; si quoque plures omnes utiliores apparuerint, pergant, unus inutilior remaneat. De qua condicione volumus, ut neque per praeceptum neque per advocationem aut quamcumque occasionem excusatus sit, aut comes aut gastaldus vel ministri eorum ullum excusatum habeant, praeter quod comes in unoquoque comitatu unum relinquat, qui eundem locum custodiat et duos cum uxore sua; episcopi ergo nullum laicum relinquant.

2. Quicumque enim contra hanc institutionem remanere presumpserit, proprium eius a missis, quos subter ordinatum habemus praesentaliter ad nostrum opus recipere iussimus et illum foras eicere. Omnibus enim notum esse volumus, quia iam a prioribus nostris iuxta hanc institutionem tultae fuerunt, sed pro misericordia recuperare meruerunt. Nunc autem certissime scitote, cuiuscumque proprietas tulta fuerit, vix a nobis promerebitur recuperatione.

3. ... Hi volumus, ut populum eiciant et custodiam praevideant et populum in castella residere faciant etiam et cum pace. Nam si missus aliquis ausus fuerit pretermittere, quin omnibus, [qui] remanserint, presentaliter proprium tollat et eum foris eiciat, et si inventus fuerit ipse missus, proprium suum perdat. Et si comes aliquem excusatum aut bassallum suum, preter quod superius diximus, dimiserit, honorem suum perdat; similiter eorum ministri, si aliquem dimiserint, et proprium et ministerium perdant.

4. Quodsi comes aut bassi nostri aliqua infirmitate [non] detenti remanserint, aut abbates vel abbatissae si plenissime homines suos non direxerint, ipsi suos honores perdant, et eorum bassalli et proprium et beneficium amittant. De episcopis autem cuiuscumque bassallus remanserit, et proprium et beneficium perdant. Si quoque episcopus absque manifesta infirmitate remanserit, pro tali neglegentia ita emendet, ut in ipsa marcha resideat, quousque alia vice exercitus illuc pergat, in quantum Dominus largire dignatus fuerit.

5. Et ut certissime sciatis, quia hanc expeditionem plenissime explere volumus, constituimus, ut episcopus, comes aut bassus noster, si in infirmitate incerta detentus fuerit, episcopus quippe per suum missum, quem meliorem habet, comes vero et bassi nostri per se ipsos hoc sub sacramentum affirment, quod pro

nulla occasione remansissent, nisi quod pro certissima infirmitate hoc agere non potuissent.

6. Omnes enim volumus, ut omni hostili apparatu secum deferant, ut, cum nos hoc prospexerimus et inbreviare fecerimus, non neglegentes appareant, sed gratiam quoque nostram habere mereantur. Vestimenta autem habeant ad annum unum, victualia vero quousque novum fructum ipsa patria habere poterit.

*   *   *

ADALHARD'S COURT REGULATIONS OF 826. *M. G., reg. Franc,* 2. 517 (PAGE 51)

27. Et ut illa multitudo quae in palatio semper esse debet, indeficienter persistere posset, his tribus ordinibus fovebatur. Uno videlicet, ut absque ministeriis expediti milites, anteposita dominorum benignitate et sollicitudine, qua nunc victu, nunc vestitu, nunc auro, nunc argento, modo equis vel caeteris ornamentis interdum specialiter, aliquando prout tempus, ratio et ordo condignam potestatem administrabat, saepius porrectis, in eo tamen indeficientem consolationem necnon ad regale obsequium inflammatum animum ardentius semper habebant: quod illos praefati capitanei ministeriales certatim de die in diem, nunc istos, nunc illos ad mansiones suas vocabant et non tam gulae voracitate, quam verae familiaritatis seu dilectionis amore, prout cuique possibile erat, impendere studebant; sicque fiebat, ut rarus quisque infra hebdomadam remaneret, qui non ab aliquo huiusmodi studio convocaretur.

28. Alter ordo per singula ministeria discipulis congruebat, qui magistro suo singuli adhaerentes et honorificabant et honorificabantur locisque singuli suis, prout opportunitas occurrebat, ut a domino videndo vel alloquendo consolarentur. Tertius ordo item erat tam maiorum quam minorum in pueris vel vasallis, quos unusquisque, prout gubernare et sustentare absque peccato, rapina videlicet vel furto, poterat, studiose habere procurabant. In quibus scilicet denominatis ordinibus absque his, qui semper eundo et redeundo palatium frequentabant, erat delectabile, quod interdum et necessitati, si repente ingrueret, semper sufficerent; et tamen semper, ut dictum est, major pars illius propter superius commemoratas benignitates cum jucunditate et hilaritate prompta et alacri mente persisterent.

Appendix 4

Latin Texts of the Assizes of Arms (Pages 174-177)

ASSISA DE ARMIS HABENDIS IN ANGLIA (P. 174)

1. Quicunque habet feodum unius militis habeat loricam et cassidem, clypeum et lanceam; et omnis miles habeat tot loricas et cassides, et clypeos et lanceas quot habuerit feoda militum in dominico suo.

2. Quicunque vero liber laicus habuerit in catallo vel in redditu ad valentiam de XVI. marcis, habeat loricam et cassidem et clypeum et lanceam; quicunque vero liber laicus habuerit in catallo vel redditu X. marcas habeat aubergel, et capellet ferri et lanceam.

3. Item omnes burgenses et tota communa liberorum hominum habeant wambais et capellet ferri et lanceam.

4. Unusquisque autem illorum juret, quod infra festum Sancti Hilarii haec arma habebit et domino regi Henrico scilicet filio Matildis imperatricis fidem portabit, et haec arma in suo servitio tenebit secundum praeceptum suum et ad fidem domini regis et regni sui. Et nullus ex quo arma haec habuerit, ea vendat, nec invadiet nec praestet, nec aliquo alio modo a se alienet; nec dominus suus ea aliquo modo ab homine suo alienet, nec per forisfactum, nec per donum, nec per vadium, nec aliquo alio modo.

5. Si quis haec arma habens obierit, arma sua remaneant haeredi suo. Si vero haeres de tali aetate non sit, quod armis uti possit, si opus fuerit, ille qui eum habebit in custodia habeat similiter custodiam armorum, et hominem inveniat qui armis uti possit in servitio domini regis, donec haeres de tali aetate sit quod arma portare possit, et tunc habeat.

6. Quicunque burgensis plura arma habuerit, quam habere oportuerit secundum hac assisam, ea vendat vel sic a se alienet tali homini qui ea servitio domini regis Angliae retineat. Et nullus eorum plura arma retineat quam eum secundum hanc assisam habere oportuerit.

7. Item nullus Judaeus loricam vel aubergellum penes se retineat, sed ea vendat, vel det, vel alio modo a se removeat, ita quod remaneant in servitio regis.

8. Item nullus portet arma extra Angliam nisi per praeceptum domini regis; nec aliquis vendat arma alicui, qui ea portet ab Anglia.

9. Item Justitiae faciant jurare per legales milites vel alios liberos et legales homines de hundredis et de burgis, quot viderint expedire, qui habebunt valentiam catalli secundum quod eum habere oportuerit loricam et galeam et lanceam et clypeum secundum quod dictum est; scilicet quod separatim nominabunt eis omnes de hundredis suis et de visnetis et de burgis, qui habebunt XVI. marcas vel in catallo vel in redditu, similiter et qui habebit X marcas. Et Justitiae postea omnes illos juratores et alios faciant inbreviari, qui quantum catalli vel redditus habuerint, et qui secundum valentiam catalli vel redditus, quae arma habere debuerint; et postea coram eis in communi audientia illorum faciant legere hanc assisam de armis habendis, et eos jurare quod ea arma habebunt secundum valentiam praedictam catallorum vel redditus, et ea tenebunt in servitio domini regis secundum hanc praedictam assisam in praecepto et fide domini regis Henrici et regni sui. Si vero contigerit quod aliquis illorum qui habere debuerint haec arma, non sint in comitatu ad terminum quando Justitiae in comitatu illo erunt, Justitiae ponant ei terminum in alio comitatu coram eis. Et si in nullo comitatu per quos iturae sunt, ad eos venerit, et non fuerit in terra ista, ponatur ei terminus apud Westmuster ad octavas Sancti Michaelis, quod sit ibi ad faciendum sacramentum suum, sicut se et omnia sua diliget. Et ei praecipiatur quod infra festum praedictum Sancti Hilarii habeat arma secundum quod ad eum pertinet habendum.

10. Item Justitiae faciant dici per omnes comitatus per quos iturae sunt, quod qui haec arma non habuerint secundum quod praedictum est, dominus rex capiet se ad eorum membra et nullo modo capiet ab eis terram vel catallum.

11. Item nullus juret super legales et liberos homines, qui non habeat XVI. marcas, vel X. marcas in castallo.

12. Item Justitiae praecipiant per omnes comitatus, quod nullus sicut se ipsum et omnia sua diligit, emat vel vendat aliquam navem ad ducendum ab Anglia, nec aliquis deferat vel deferre faciat maironiam extra Angliam. Et praecepit rex quod nullus reciperetur ad sacramentum armorum nisi liber homo.

*　　*　　*

WRIT FOR THE LEVYING OF A FORCE. 1205.

Rex etc. Vicecomiti Rotelandae, etc. Scias quod provisum est cum assensu archiepiscoporum, episcoporum, comitum, baronum et omnium fidelium nostrorum Angliae, quod novem milites per totam Angliam invenient decimum militem bene paratum equis et armis ad defensionem regni nostri; et quod illi novem milites inveniant decimo militi qualibet die II. solidos ad liberationem suam. Et ideo tibi praecipimus quod, sicut te ipsum et omnia tua diligis, provideas quod decimi milites de ballia tua sint apud Londonias a die Paschae in tres septimanas, bene parati equis et armis, cum liberationibus suis sicut praedictum est, parati ire in servitium nostrum quo praeceperimus et existere in servitio nostro ad defensionem regni nostri quantum opus fuerit. Provisum est etiam quod si alienigenae in terram nostram venerint, omnes unanimiter eis occurrant cum forcia et armis sine aliqua occasione et dilatione, auditis rumoribus de eorum adventu. Et si quis miles vel serviens vel alius terram tenens inventus fuerit, qui se inde retraxerit, dummodo tanta non fuerit gravatus infirmitate quod illuc venire non possit, ipse et haeredes sui in perpetuum exhaeredabuntur, et feodum suum remanebit domino fundi ad faciendum inde voluntatem suam; ita quod exhaeredatus vel haeredes sui nunquam inde aliquam habeant recuperationem. Si qui vero milites, servientes, vel alii qui terram non habent, inventi fuerint qui se similiter retraxerint, ipsi et haeredes sui servi fient in perpetuum reddendo singulis annis IV. denarios de capitibus suis, nec pro paupertate omittant ad praedictum negotium venire cum illud audierint, quia ex quo ad exercitum venerint, providebitur unde sufficienter in servitio nostro poterunt sustentari. Si vero vicecomes vel ballivus praepositus illos qui se retraxerint nobis per breve vel per scriptum vel viva voce non ostenderint, dicti vicecomes vel ballivus vel praepositus remanebit in misericordia nostra de vita et membris. Et ideo tibi praecipimus quod sub festinatione haec omnia proclamari facias in foris per totam balliam tuam, et in mercatis et nundinis et alibi, et ita te de negotio illo faciendo intromittas quod ad te pro defectu tui capere non debeamus. Et tu ipse sis apud Londonias ad praefatum terminum, vel aliquem discretum ex parte tua mittas, et facias tunc nobis scire nomina decimorum militum, et habeas ibi hoc breve. Teste me ipso apud Wintoniam III die Aprilis.

* * *

ASSIZE OF ARMS. 1252

Provisum est etiam quod singuli vicecomites una cum duobus militibus ad hoc specialiter assignatis, circumeant comitatus suos de hundredo in hundredum, et civitates et burgos, et convenire faciant coram eis in singulis hundredis, civitatibus et burgos, cives, burgenses libere tenentes, villanos et alios aetatis quindecim annorum usque ad aetatem sexaginta annorum, et eosdem faciant omnes jurare ad arma, secundum quantitatem terrarum et catallorum suorum; scilicet, ad quindecim libratas terrae, unam loricam, capellum ferreum, gladium, cultellum et equum; ad decem libratas terrae unum habergetum, capellum ferreum, gladium et cultellum; ad centum solidatas terrae unum purpunctum, capellum ferreum, gladium, lanceam et cultellum; ad quadraginta solidatas terrae, et eo amplius ad centum solidatas terrae, gladium, arcum, sagittas et cultellum. Qui minus habent quam quadraginta solidatas terrae, jurati sint ad falces, gisarmas, cultellos et alia arma minuta. Ad catalla sexaginta marcarum, unam loricam, capellum ferreum, gladium, cultellum et equum: ad catalla quadraginta marcarum, unum haubercum, capellum ferreum, gladium et cultellum: ad catalla viginti marcarum, unum purpunctum, capellum ferreum, gladium et cultellum; ad catalla novem marcarum, gladium, cultellum, arcum et sagittas; ad catalla quadraginta solidorum et eo amplius usque ad decem marcas, falces, gisarmas et alia arma minuta. Omnes etiam illi qui possunt habere arcus et sagittas extra forestam, habeant; qui vero in foresta, habeant arcus et pilatos.

In singulis civitatibus et burgis jurati ad arma sint coram majoribus civitatis et praepositis et ballivis burgorum, ubi non sunt majores, in singulis vero villatis aliis constituatur unus constabularius vel duo secundum numerum inhabitantium et provisionem praedictorum; in singulis vero hundredis constituatur unus capitalis constabulerius, ad cujus mandatum omnes jurati ad arma de hundredis suis conveniant, et ei sint intendentes ad faciendum ea quae spectant ad conservationem pacis nostrae.

Index

applied between Christians and
Moslems, 211; based on division of
powers into echelons, 99; basis of new
kingdoms following collapse of Carolingian Empire, 94; difference of in
England and on Continent, 167; in England, based on combination of money
and barter economy, 169; importance
of in Frankish Kingdom, 13; responsible for nation's dissolution after Charlemagne, 80
Feuds, 79, 366; in Alpine area, 561; in
German Empire, 496–97; in Germany,
France, Italy, 505; increased military
strength in Middle Ages, 95; between
Otto II and Lothair, 323
Fiefs: of counts, 79; as economic base of
knightly class, 227, 315; in England,
granted by crown, 169–70; imperial,
not to be converted to private property,
28; multiple, 109; necessity for in maintaining Frankish warriors, 14; of Ottoman Turks, 473–74; redemption of, by
fine, 169; under William the Conqueror, 164–65
Firearms: not truly significant in Middle
Ages, 635; use of by Hussites, 490–91,
494
"First contact," 281, 409; in battle of
Nikopol, 478
First Crusade, battles and engagements of,
402–12; Acre, 410; Antioch, 404–6;
Arsuf, 410; Ascalon, 406–7; Athareb
(Belath), 409; Dorylaeum, 403; Hab,
409; Hazarth, 409; Hittin, 410; Jaffa,
410–12; Lake of Antioch, 404; Merdj-
Sefer, 409–10; Ramleh (1101), 408;
Ramleh (1102), 408; Ramleh (1105),
408; Sarmin, 408
Fischer, H., on strength and starting date
of the *gleve*, 519n.12
Five classes, in England, 173; compared
with Roman organization, 174
Five-hide rule, 160
Flanders (count of), at Rosebeke, 442
Flanders, county of, 431, 444; burgher
levies in, 448; levy of fief-holders in,
521n.20; rebellion of against French,
431

Flarchheim, battle of, 135–36
Flavus, 68
Flemish: in battle of Courtrai, 432–38; in
battle of Rosebeke, 442–47; relation-
ship of with England, 453
Flintlock, 391
Florentines, 422–23, 511
Florentius Vigorniensis (Florence of
Worcester), 156
Floto: on battle on the Elster, 142; on
failure of Henry IV to pursue Saxons,
135
Fodrum, 99
Folk psychology, appraisal of, 602–3
Foot troops, 255n.24, 255n.26, 264; at
Acre, 410; at Ascalon, 407; in battle of
Antioch, 406; in battle of Courtrai,
431–38; in battle of Döffingen, 582; in
battle of Homburg on the Unstrut, 132;
on both sides at Lincoln, 402; at
Bouvines, 418–19; at Bridge Gate of
Antioch, 404; in Crusades, 234,
403–13; at Dorylaeum, 412–13; gained
final superiority over knights, 635; of
Italian cities, 357; at Jaffa, 411; against
knights, 265; loss of prestige of, 290; at
Merdj-Sefer, 409–10; of Milanese at
Legnano, 343; offensive action of, 266;
to remain on defensive, 647n.10; reportedly tied together, 639; steadfastness of Scottish at Falkirk, 393; in
support of knights, 270–71, 273, 403
Forest cantons: alliance of with Lucerne
and Zurich, 571; armistice of with
Hapsburgs, 571; in battle of Sempach,
572–74; freedom of confirmed, 571; in
league with Bern, 562; military fame of,
562
Formations. *See* Battle formations
Fortifications, 324, 326, 345; escape from,
380–81; of Teutonic Knights, 378–80
France: development of strong hereditary
monarchy in, 104; lack of royal authority in, 97; new kingdom of from ruins of
Carolingian Empire, 94; relationship of
with Scots, 453; suffering of at hands of
mercenaries, 507
Franconia, formation of duchy of, 94
Francs archers, 513–15